D1624971

GOING TO WAR

GOING TO WAR

HOW MISINFORMATION, DISINFORMATION, AND ARROGANCE LED AMERICA INTO IRAQ

RUSS HOYLE

THOMAS DUNNE BOOKS

ST. MARTIN'S PRESS   NEW YORK

THOMAS DUNNE BOOKS.
An imprint of St. Martin's Press.

www.thomasdunnebooks.com
www.stmartins.com

ISBN-13: 978-0-312-36035-1
ISBN-10: 0-312-36035-5

First Edition: March 2008

10 9 8 7 6 5 4 3 2 1

To my parents,
Alice Virginia Hulbert Hoyle
Royce Augustine Hoyle, Jr.

While it is perfectly legitimate to criticize my decision or the conduct of the war, it is deeply irresponsible to rewrite the history of how that war began.

—George W. Bush

CONTENTS

BUSH'S FOLLY

Just after the Vietnam War, Pulitzer Prize–winning historian Barbara Tuchman took a hard look at why political leaders and nations persisted in pursuing policies contrary to their own best interests. Tuchman identified four kinds of rampant misgovernment, often in combination, that seemed to qualify for this dubious honor. The first was the natural spawn of tyrannical and oppressive regimes, such as Stalin's Soviet Union or Saddam Hussein's Iraq. Another was caused by leaders with excessive ambition for themselves or their nations, such as Hitler in Germany or Mao Tse-tung in China. Still another kind of state inclined to act against its own best interests consisted of those crippled by outright incompetence or decadence. But what intrigued Tuchman were governments that acted contrary to their self-interest out of sheer misguided folly and perversity. Had she not died in 1989 at the age of seventy-seven, Tuchman plainly would have been fascinated by President George W. Bush, whose war policies since the terrorist attacks on the United States in September 2001 seem to fit with uncanny exactitude the template she created in her 1984 book, *The March of Folly*.

True folly, Tuchman found, is generally recognized as counterproductive in its own time, and not merely in hindsight. From its inception, President Bush's Iraq war policy fit the mold. It was rejected by tens of millions of people in allied countries around the world, and since has been summarily rejected by a majority of Americans. True folly, she continued, only ensues when a clear alternative path of action was available and ruled out. Again, the shoe fits. Bush and his senior advisers chose to abandon the fight against al-Qaeda in Afghanistan in 2002 and instead invaded Iraq to depose Saddam Hussein. Tuchman also stipulated that real folly was separate from the quirks or obsessions of individual leaders—tyrants or oligarchs, for example—and most often was the product of a group within an organized government. Bingo. Bush's war policy was dominated by the most powerful vice president in American history, who presided over a network of like-minded ideologues throughout the key policymaking and intelligence agencies.

Tuchman went further. Although impatient with the Platonic ideal of grooming philosopher-kings, she believed that governing is a special art that cannot be acquired except by disciplined study and experience. That would make President Bush at best a marginal practitioner. His primary qualifications for governing as a war president and commander-in-chief were his pedigree as the son of President George H. W. Bush, six years as governor of Texas, and co-ownership of the Texas Rangers baseball team.

In the absence of lengthy political seasoning and discipline, Tuchman alighted on a root cause of folly that, again, seemed tailor-made to describe the man and his presidency. She called this quality "wooden-headedness." To the historian seeking out the context of historical folly, the term connoted distinctive failings of character. Wooden-headedness, Tuchman wrote, could be defined in part as "assessing a situation in terms of preconceived fixed notions while ignoring or rejecting contrary information." She also saw wooden-headedness as a certain proclivity for "acting according to wish while not allowing oneself to be deflected by facts." Wooden-headedness, said Tuchman, was finally "the refusal to benefit from experience." After five years, the Bush White House still presides over a war that has morphed from a strongly supported U.S.-led retaliatory attack on al-Qaeda terrorists into a bloody and brutal civil war in Iraq that has killed tens of thousands, perhaps more. More than 140,000 U.S. troops are now entrapped and endangered in the military and political morass that Iraq has become, and that our own intelligence agencies believe has only nurtured the growth of anti-U.S., anti-Western terrorists in the Middle East, Europe, and Southeast Asia.

This is the plainest definition imaginable of a wooden-headed policy contrary to the best interests of the United States. In *Going to War*, I have set myself the modest task of sharpening the historical record of Bush's folly by constructing a detailed, readable narrative of how America went to war in Iraq—from the terrorist attacks in 2001 to the invasion of Iraq in 2003 through the conviction of I. Lewis "Scooter" Libby in 2007. My aim was to capture as fully as possible what we now know about the period leading up to the war. My strategy was simply to expose the unrecognized resonances and revelations that always emerge when a story is told in full.

In September 2001, I was the deputy Sunday editor at New York's *Daily News,* on Manhattan's West Side within sight of the Hudson River, a few short miles north of Ground Zero. Like many of my talented former colleagues at the *News,* for the next several years I was absorbed by coverage of the attacks and their aftermath. With our noses pressed up against the glass during the terrible experience of 9/11 and its consequences, I suppose the instinct to want to write about the nation's experience in its aftermath was inevitable. My generation of editors and reporters cut their teeth on the long-running Watergate controversy. The Watergate crisis and the terrorist attacks seemed to neatly bracket my three decades as a reporter and editor.

This book is an effort to move past the limitations of journalism and into the history of that charged and disturbing period after 9/11. A massive amount of material—what the intelligence types call open-source information—was available, and beginning to master it was a full-time occupation. Indeed, the available information increased almost daily as articles, books, and studies on the Iraq war, its beginnings, and its mismanagement proliferated, adding salient details to the story. Many of the important accounts, however, moved quickly past the run-up to the war to cover the more immediate misadventures during the occupation of Iraq, the U.S. military involvement there, and even the CIA leak case and the indictment of Scooter Libby. In addition, congressional oversight committees, even newly under Democratic control after 2006, tended to focus on the latest Bush mismanagement crisis, whether it was Hurricane Katrina, the Abramoff scandal, CIA interrogation policies, NSA surveillance activities, or the Justice Department's dismissal of U.S. attorneys. The consequence was that much of the administration's prewar decision-making was left officially unexamined. Even after the 2006 midterm elections, the Senate Intelligence Committee has not published the promised phase two of its 2004 report examining the political manipulation of intelligence by the Bush administration.

Going to War steps directly into this vacuum. The book focuses on the ebb and flow of flawed intelligence, carefully managed misinformation, and outright disinformation about Saddam's alleged weapons of mass destruction before the war and well afterward. Given the tightly controlled flow of information from the White House and other key national security agencies, there are necessarily holes in this account of the Bush administration's actions during that period. However comprehensive, *Going to War*, in this sense, is incomplete, primarily because of the secrecy and lack of accountability that shrouded so many of the administration's political decisions—as a result, too many details are still obscured or only partially visible. I have therefore swept up every account or fact that shed any light at all on events as they unfolded, and have not shied away from speculating about motivations or drawing conclusions based on what is now on the record. I have not hestitated to stray into this realm of informed speculation—always acknowledged as such—in the hope of prodding future researchers to examine areas of public concern and uncertainty that administration insiders eventually will have to answer for. If, here and there, this puts present or former Bush administration officials or their sympathizers in the uncomfortable position of having to prove a negative—to demonstrate decisively what they claim they did *not* do—they are free to set the record straight at any time.

Inevitably, fresh perspectives and new information on the origins of the war emerged in the course of researching and writing this book. *Going to War* will challenge some widely accepted notions about the run-up to the war. President Bush and the White House knew they were lying to the American people about weapons of mass destruction to further their war aims. Many readers will be surprised to learn that senior officials at both the White House and the Pentagon did not believe for a moment that Saddam possessed nuclear weapons programs, much less nuclear weapons that threatened the United States, Europe, or even the Middle East, as the administration claimed. The book presents a strong case that the strategy to focus on Saddam's WMD and go to the United Nations for approval of the war, generally attributed to the influence of Colin Powell and the flexibility of the president, was much more likely forced on a divided White House by British Prime Minister Tony Blair. *Going to War* also paints a picture of the Bush neoconservative clique that runs against the grain of conventional wisdom. Far from being a powerful influence on the president during the prewar period, more often than not they were divisive figures within the administration, heroes in their own minds who were at odds with President Bush and much of the White House on everything from the importance of seeking Britain as an ally and renewed UN arms inspections in Iraq during the fall of 2002 to a new war resolution from the United Nations.

What influence the neoconservatives enjoyed was limited mostly to the considerable impact of trumped-up intelligence that was channeled through Vice President Cheney's office to policymakers and the intelligence community. *Going to War* presents detailed accounts of the influence wielded by Cheney over the intelligence network that he and Lewis "Scooter" Libby tapped, from the Pentagon's Counter Terrorism Evaluation Group, to the Office of Special Plans, to the CIA. Many readers will learn for the first time that Vice President Cheney personally resurrected an eighteen-month-old CIA report on aluminum tubes intelligence in 2002—after it had been discredited by the Energy Department. These revived CIA assessments became a central justification for the administration's argument that Iraq was reconstituting its nuclear weapons program. Meanwhile, CIA director George Tenet, caught between pressures from Cheney and the White House on one side and congressional critics on the other, brushed off secret testimony and internal agency reports confirming that Baghdad had no biological weapons programs—incidents Tenet failed to mention in his 2007 memoir.

On the road to war, the White House knowingly distorted intelligence, seduced a compliant media, and deceived Congress to steamroll the nation into the politically self-serving folly of invading and occupying Iraq. Three major themes emerge from the narrative that unfolds in *Going to War* that will be of increasing importance to the United States' effectiveness as a superpower in the years ahead. The first is the real nature of the intelligence fiasco. This book traces the manipulation of the intelligence community in general—and the CIA in particular—by the White House and the Office of the Vice President, a process that distorted the traditional function of the strategic intelligence services that once served the interests of the president and the president alone. Unfortunately, the Bush intelligence reforms, which centralized power in a national director of intelligence, are a half measure that will not produce the quality of information critical to waging an effective defense against terrorism until clandestine operatives and intelligence analysts can provide reports to the president without fear of political interference or retribution.

The second motif in *Going to War* is the peril to the democratic process that followed efforts to concentrate war powers in the White House and shut Congress out of the war-making process. Even allowing for the terrorist threat, the Bush version of one-party rule after November 2002 exposed serious flaws in our democracy, among them, the failure of rigorous congressional oversight, especially concerning intelligence and the armed forces. *Going to War* demonstrates that White House efforts to consolidate power and end-run the democratic process invariably proved a formula for official corruption, incompetence, and a dysfunctional federal government unable to make coherent policy or to correct its own excesses. The misconceived and mismanaged Iraq war is only the worst and most costly example, and one that will take at least a generation and perhaps longer to correct before the damage it has wrought is undone.

Third, *Going to War* documents the dangers to democracy when checks and balances on the abuse of political power are shunted aside or weakened. Despite the inequities and excesses of the lapsed 1978 Independent Counsel Act, the trial and criminal conviction of Lewis Libby may in the end have delivered too little at too high a price. There is little question that Libby was guilty of the charges, despite President Bush's commutation of his sentence or the rhetoric of his partisan backers. Lying to a grand jury and federal investigators is a serious crime and a fundamental assault on our legal system. Libby is not the first convicted felon convinced that he served a higher cause, nor will he be the last. The grand jury inquiry into the CIA leak case and his subsequent indictment and conviction shed unprecedented light on one of the most secretive White House operations in U.S. history. Yet it did not tell the whole story. This historic task, critical to a functioning democracy, was limited by an investigation and trial that were not legally empowered to probe beyond the relevant facts of the criminal case.

Political corruption or unethical behavior that came up short of breaking the law was beyond the scope of the Justice Department investigation. Simultaneously, the investigative powers of Congress to root out official corruption and abuse of power were effectively short-circuited by one-party control of the White House and a compliant Republican leadership. Because the press was so central to Libby's case, his trial and conviction had a chilling effect on the ability of reporters to hold high public officials accountable for their misdeeds—a burden the Fourth Estate in any case should not bear alone. More legal challenges to the press in the future are a virtual certainty. Americans must face the limitations of a government-appointed special counsel to conduct investigations of officeholders and senior officials who, unlike Libby, may *not* have broken the law, but nonetheless have abused the power of their offices. Raising the bar of what is acceptable just shy of criminal behavior, as President Bush has done, is a perilous standard in a democracy that must depend not only on the freely given consent of the governed, but also on the character and sound judgment of those who govern.

The Libby case and the political narrative underlying it, the Bush administration's determined and deceitful march to war, are powerful evidence that effective new counterweights are needed in this new era of terrorist threats to deter runaway executive power, stiffen the backbone of submissive or corrupt congressional leaders, and provide a balance for the burdens of accountability placed on a newly vulnerable national press and media.

—Russ Hoyle
Farmington, Connecticut
September 2007

LAST MISSION TO AL MUHAWISH

M onday, April 7, 2003. MET Alpha seemed to be going nowhere.

As American troops pushed into Baghdad aboard M1 Abrams tanks, Bradley armored personnel carriers, and Humvees bristling with automatic weapons, Judith Miller of *The New York Times* was hunkered down with the U.S. Army's Mobile Exploitation Team Alpha at a remote desert camp in Kuwait, hundreds of miles to the south. Part of a special task force attached to the 101st Airborne Division, MET Alpha was one of four units assigned to search the rubble of war for evidence of Saddam's hotly discussed weapons of mass destruction. Miller, then fifty-five, a self-confident and seasoned *Times* veteran, was frustrated. She had managed to parlay what friends described as an obsession with chemical, biological, and nuclear weaponry into an impressive journalistic niche—and a plum wartime assignment with the U.S. Army. But things were not working out at all as she expected.

With a practiced eye for dysfunctional detail, Miller began to see that the Pentagon had botched planning for the postwar hunt for Saddam's unconventional weapons facilities, a critical venture since Saddam's alleged WMD arsenal was the Bush White House's justification for the war. The Pentagon-led teams, she reported in mid-April, had been "hampered by a lack of resources and by geography" from the start. Two transportable U.S. laboratories for on-the-spot analysis of chemical or biological agents had been left at a rear area in Kuwait to

1

keep them out of harm's way. The fleet of helicopters, Humvees, and secure communications promised to the weapons hunters before the war failed to materialize.

With most army vehicles assigned to forward combat and supply units, the weapons hunters could only hope for an occasional helicopter to fly into suspected weapons sites in and around Baghdad, where the Pentagon believed it had pinpointed the most important of Iraq's 578 suspected weapons labs and facilities. Miller lamented that many of the one hundred or so soldiers, scientists, intelligence specialists, and Pentagon weapons experts that made up the MET units "had done almost no weapons hunting until the fighting had largely concluded."[1]

Possible weapons dumps or potential WMD lab facilities they inspected had been cleaned out by looters or insurgents long before the weapons hunters made it to the scene. The Al-Qadisiyah State Establishment, for example, a Baghdad munitions factory that would become headquarters for the army's weapons-hunting group, a former artillery unit formally known as the 75th Exploitation Task Force, was looted and burned before its commander, Col. Richard L. McPhee, could move in.[2]

Miller, a Pulitzer Prize–winning reporter (for her part in a 2001 *Times* series on Osama bin Laden and Islamic terrorists), had parlayed a half-dozen major stories on Iraqi unconventional weapons since 9/11 into a special embedding arrangement with MET Alpha. Her book on biological warfare, *Germs,* written with two fellow *Times* staffers, William Broad and Stephen Engelberg, published just after the 9/11 attacks, burnished her reputation as an expert on what can happen if WMD fall into the hands of terrorists. During the previous eighteen months, she had reported highly influential stories on the front page of *The Times* revealing that the Iraqis had restarted programs to produce nuclear, biological, and chemical weapons of mass destruction, despite sanctions established over a decade before at the end of the 1991 Gulf War.

Miller's reporting had given her a stake in the outcome of the hunt. She was not the only U.S. journalist inside Iraq keenly focused on the Bush administration's quest for evidence of Saddam's prohibited weapons. But she was the only reporter embedded with MET Alpha, a privilege she protected aggressively. This special access to the unit assured her exclusive coverage for *The Times* from the moment the team discovered the Iraqi dictator's weapons of mass destruction, an eventuality that both Miller and the brass in Washington considered only a matter of time. Her arrangement with MET Alpha was the result of a painstakingly negotiated arrangement with the

Defense Department, reportedly approved by Secretary of Defense Donald Rumsfeld himself.[3]

The *Times* correspondent made her presence felt within the unit. She took to wearing military fatigues, a detail noted by the troops that had the effect to some of camouflaging her role as a reporter. When *Washington Post* correspondent Barton Gellman joined the unit for a day, Miller reportedly ordered MET Alpha soldiers not to cooperate with him. Yet her frustration with MET Alpha's lack of progress was all too obvious. In mid-April, the unit's commander ordered his troops to suspend a search mission and pull back to the nearby southern Iraqi town of Tallil. Miller hit the ceiling.

"I see no reason for me to waste time (or MET Alpha, for that matter) in Tallil," she wrote her army handlers from Baghdad. "Request permission to stay on here with colleagues at the Palestine Hotel til MET Alpha returns or order to return is rescinded. I intend to write about this decision in the *NY Times* to send a successful team back home just as progress on WMD is being made." Several officers interpreted Miller's note as a threat. They were not surprised. "Judith was always issuing threats of either going to *The New York Times* or to the secretary of defense," said one. "There was nothing veiled about the threat."[4]

To the astonishment of MET Alpha members, the pullback order was abruptly withdrawn. Miller had taken her complaint directly to Maj. Gen. David H. Petraeus, the highly respected commander of the 101st Airborne Division who would take a lead role in the training of Iraqi troops later in the occupation. The incident was one of several over the next several months that gave Miller a reputation for throwing her weight around to get what she wanted. "It's impossible to exaggerate the impact she had on the mission of this unit, and not for the better," said one MET Alpha senior officer. Another, skeptical of Miller's vaunted pull with the brass back in Washington, confirmed a deep uneasiness about her in the unit. "The sense I got was that she wasn't their problem anymore now that she was in Iraq," said Eugene Pomeroy, then public affairs officer for MET Alpha. "Maybe they were hoping she'd step on a mine. I know I was."[5]

In one sense, Miller's highhanded outburst at Tallil was understandable. It came only days after MET Alpha finally seemed to have achieved its first major breakthrough. Miller was fed up with the military's bureaucratic cautiousness and delays, and ready to get on with the hunt.

The break came a few days before the Tallil episode, when a small group from MET Alpha was ordered to inspect barrels filled with chemicals buried near the village of Al Muhawish, just south of Baghdad.

Members of the unit had heard from an officer with the 101st Airborne that a note in Arabic had come into his possession weeks before from an Iraqi who passed it to a U.S. ambulance driver during the fighting. Using a pseudonym, the Iraqi message-writer asked for a meeting with a "qualified" U.S. scientist and said he had seen Iraqi officials destroy hidden stores of chemical weapons and equipment before the war. He also wrote that Iraqi researchers had tested the chemical agents on animals. The note wound up at brigade headquarters, where it languished in the files. When MET Alpha's commander, Chief Warrant Officer Richard L. Gonzales, heard the story, he ran it down.[6]

Serendipitously, the note contained the Iraqi informant's address—in a town near Al Muhawish. A small MET Alpha force, with Miller in tow, found the Iraqi man at home. Identifying himself as a scientist, he told the soldiers that Iraqi officials had set fire to a chemical weapons research and development facility in the days before the war started. Members of the MET Alpha team who had debriefed the "scientist" then relayed his story to Miller, who was not allowed to interview the Iraqi herself or to pinpoint the location of the weapons facility. They told her, she wrote, that the "Iraqis buried chemical precursors and other sensitive material to conceal and preserve them for future use." The soldiers also said they had found buried material that "proved to be precursors for a toxic agent that is banned by chemical weapons treaties."

By the terms of her embedding agreement, Miller was not allowed to identify the prohibited chemicals that were uncovered. She was only permitted to observe the scientist from a distance—and wrote her story knowing full well it would be scrubbed by army censors of any detail that even suggested his identity or whereabouts. "Clad in nondescript clothes and a baseball cap," she reported in a classic passage of bland observation and artful suggestiveness, "he pointed to several spots in the sand where he said chemical precursors and other weapons material were buried."

Miller wrote that military officials believed the scientist's account was "the most important discovery to date in the hunt for illegal weapons" and "provided an explanation for why United States forces had not yet turned up banned weapons in Iraq." Petraeus chimed in that MET Alpha's potential breakthrough was "enormous." He went on: "What they've discovered could prove to be of incalculable value. Though much work must still be done to validate the information MET Alpha has uncovered, if it proves out it will clearly be one of the major discoveries of this operation, and it may be a major discovery."[7]

The Times ran Miller's story on the front page, despite the painful limitations imposed on her reporting. Its revelations galvanized Washington. "I think they found something more than a 'smoking gun,'" Miller told Ray Suarez of PBS's *NewsHour with Jim Lehrer* that night by satellite feed. "What they found is a silver bullet in the form of a person . . . who really worked on the programs, who knows them firsthand, and who has led MET Team Alpha people to some pretty startling conclusions . . . ," Miller said. "Those stockpiles that we've heard about, well, those have either been destroyed by Saddam Hussein, according to the scientists, or they have been shipped to Syria for safekeeping."[8]

The MET Alpha people, she told Suarez, "believe that Saddam Hussein wanted to destroy the evidence of his unconventional weapons programs, and that's what he has done—not only since 1995, but also in the weeks and months that led up to the war itself." Miller's on-air commentary went considerably beyond her reporting. Two days later President Bush, apparently swayed by the view that Saddam had destroyed or spirited away his weapons just before the war, admitted publicly for the first time that U.S. forces in Iraq might not find stockpiles of WMD. Said Colonel McPhee, the commander of the weapons-hunting task force: "It was a turning point."[9]

By the end of April, the MET teams had inspected more than half of the 150 Iraqi weapons sites considered the most likely hiding places for Saddam's hidden weapons. But they found no stockpiles of chemical or biological weapons or agents, or even much "dual use" equipment for civilian or military applications. Largely on the strength of their experience debriefing the anonymous Iraqi scientist in the baseball hat—whose credibility later came into question when he was identified as a former Iraqi intelligence official—the emphasis of MET commanders shifted from examining suspected weapons sites, which was proving consistently unproductive, to collecting documents and trying to locate key Iraqis who had knowledge about specific weapons programs.

Part of the problem was that the MET outfits' intelligence on the weapons sites was often hopeless. "The teams would be given a packet, with pictures and a tentative grid," an officer told Miller, using oblique language to avoid revealing classified information. "They would be told: 'Go to this place. You will find a McDonald's there. Look in the fridge. You will find French fries, cheeseburger, and Cokes.' And they would go there, and not only was there no fridge and no McDonald's, there was never even a thought of ever putting a McDonald's there. Day after day it was like that."[10]

The unit's new focus on human intelligence, Miller knew, was closer to the original spirit of the Defense Department's planning for the postwar WMD search in Iraq. "Former Iraqi scientists, military officers and contractors have provided American intelligence agencies with a portrait of Saddam Hussein's secret programs to develop and conceal chemical, biological and nuclear weapons that is starkly at odds with the findings so far of the United Nations weapons inspectors," she had written in January 2003, two months before the war began.

Two days before reporting the tactical shift by the weapons hunters, Miller accompanied a MET Alpha team on April 20 to meet with Ahmed Chalabi, the anti-Saddam Iraqi exile financier and dissident leader of the Iraqi National Congress (INC), a longtime favorite of Pentagon conservatives, at his headquarters in Baghdad "to explore the possibility of exchanging information." Miller knew Chalabi well. She had exchanged information with him about Saddam's Iraq for years. She was also well aware that senior Bush administration officials at the White House and the Pentagon strongly favored fresh intelligence from human sources, especially the Iraqi defectors Chalabi managed to turn up who provided new information about Saddam's alledgedly resurgent weapons programs.

Chalabi had been a fixture in U.S-Iraqi relations since soon after the Gulf War ended in 1991. Reporters who used Chalabi and the Iraqi National Congress to gain access to Iraqi defectors knew about his ties to the conservative wing of the U.S. defense establishment and his on-again, off-again history with the CIA. After a decade of expensive and duplicitous experience, agency operatives and journalists alike deeply distrusted the brilliant but erratic Iraqi opposition leader. "I thought he was unreliable and corrupt," said former veteran *Times* correspondent Chris Hedges. "But just because someone is a sleazebag doesn't mean he might not know something or that everything he says is wrong."[11]

Since 1992 Chalabi and the Iraqi National Congress had received in excess of $100 million from the U.S. government, at first funneled through the CIA, then through the State Department, and after the summer of 2002, through the Pentagon. Of that sum, an estimated $33 million came from the Bush administration between 2001 and May 2004, when Chalabi's funding from Washington was finally cut off after U.S. forces raided his offices in Baghdad. Exactly what those princely sums bought has caused bouts of head-scratching by successive administrations on the banks of the Potomac.

By September 11, 2001, Chalabi had so ingratiated himself with the

Bush administration's new defense establishment—including Vice President Cheney, Richard Perle, and Deputy Defense Secretary Paul Wolfowitz, among others—that he was invited to address a meeting of Perle's Defense Policy Board, a civilian advisory panel set up by Secretary of Defense Donald Rumsfeld. Chalabi counseled the Americans to forget about Afghanistan and go straight for Iraq. The Bush administration wisely chose not to heed his advice, but the specter of regime change in Iraq was never far in the background—and it had less to do with terrorism than Chalabi's personal ambitions. There had been a half-dozen Judith Miller stories in *The Times* since 9/11 with Chalabi's fingerprints all over them.

Chalabi, who hoped to return to Baghdad as a top official in the new U.S.-installed government, all but admitted to Jane Mayer of *The New Yorker* magazine in a 2004 interview that his anti-Saddam WMD campaign was the brainchild of the Bush administration. "Look, our focus was on Saddam's crimes, moral crimes, genocide," he told Mayer. "We were not focused on WMD. The U.S. *asked* us. We didn't bring these people up; they asked us! They requested help from us."[12] Chalabi did not name the official or officials who made the request, or exactly when it was made. Nor did he reveal whether the INC was asked to mount a campaign on Saddam's weapons aimed at the press and the intelligence community. But that is what Chalabi set about doing, long before he agreed to meet with Miller and MET Alpha officers in war-ravaged Baghdad.

The April 20 meeting between Chalabi and MET Alpha team members, with Miller present, was a red flag for the U.S. press in Iraq—including other staffers at *The Times*. The officers that Miller accompanied to Chalabi's headquarters in a former Baghdad sports club insisted that Miller initiated the visit. The information-gathering mission was complicated by the fact that Chalabi's organization was holding a son-in-law of Saddam's in protective custody and needed to find a safe way to hand him over to the Americans. Chalabi had no contacts with the weapons-hunting outfit until MET Alpha visited his Baghdad compound. The trip, said one officer bluntly, was undertaken "at Judy's direction." Another declared, "This woman had a plan. She was leading them . . . She ended up almost hijacking the mission."[13]

A top aide to Chalabi who was present at the meeting did not attempt to hide Miller's special relationship with Chalabi. The aide, Zaab Sethna, later said he didn't know whether Miller was there "because she's old friends with Dr. Chalabi or because she wanted to introduce that team she was working with to the INC." Whether the whereabouts of Saddam's WMD stockpiles was discussed at the meeting is unknown. But it was in a conversation with Miller, Sethna said, that Chalabi and his aides proposed the idea of turning over the son-in-law, Jamal Sultan al-Tikriti, whose face was on one of the cards in the Pentagon's famous "deck" identifying the fifty-five most wanted Iraqis from Saddam's regime, directly to MET Alpha. "We told Judy we thought it was a good story," Sethna said. "We needed some way to get the guy to the Americans."[14]

Miller wrote a brief story in *The Times* on April twenty-first reporting Sultan's handover without mentioning Chalabi's role, and the next day briefly mentioned the visit to Chalabi's headquarters without mentioning the transfer in her story about the weapons unit's new emphasis on human intelligence. An army spokesman supported MET Alpha's—and Miller's—role in the Chalabi meeting. "Commanders make decisions based on developing situations," said Col. Joe Curtin, noting that leads developed by reporters are fair game for military officers making decisions in the field. Such leads are an "open source, and we're going to use it." Curtin added, pointedly, that prisoner handoffs are usually "left to military intelligence people," not weapons-hunting units.[15]

Miller managed to postpone the inevitable fallout from the Chalabi visit by setting off another press firestorm on May 1, when she wrote a story without clearing it first with her superiors that detailed Chalabi's concerns about former Baathist party members participating in the U.S.-backed postwar Coalition Provisional Authority. Miller already had a reputation for disregarding editors in the *Times* chain of command when it suited her purposes. This time she neglected to inform then *Times* Baghdad bureau chief John Burns about the Chalabi piece—and Burns was furious. He fired off an angry e-mail to Miller that quickly found its way into a story by the *Washington Post*'s media critic, Howard Kurtz.

"I am deeply chagrined at your reporting and filing on Chalabi after I had told you on Monday night that we were planning a major piece on him—and without so much as telling me what you were doing," wrote Burns. "We have a bureau here; I am in charge of that bureau until I leave; I make assignments after considerable thought and discussion, and it was plain to all of us to whom the Chalabi story belonged. If you do this, what is to stop you doing it on any other story of your choosing?

And what of the distress it causes the correspondent who is usurped? It is not professional, and not collegial."[16]

Miller's impatience and proprietary stake in the WMD story was evident in her e-mailed response. "I've been covering Chalabi for about 10 years," she shot back, "and have done most of the stories about him for our paper, including the long takeout we recently did on him. He has provided most of the front page exclusives on WMD to our paper." Miller weakly apologized for creating any confusion. But she justified her actions by telling Burns that since MET Alpha was "using Chalabi's intelligence" and "since I'm there every day talking to him" she had a right to be consulted on stories about Chalabi.

The Times protested the publication of the internal e-mails and defended Miller's actions. "Of course we talk to Chalabi," Andrew Rosenthal, the Times' foreign editor, told The Post. "If you were in Iraq and weren't talking to Chalabi, I'd wonder if you were doing your job." Nonetheless, Kurtz had a question about Judith Miller and the Times' past WMD coverage that hung uncomfortably in the air. "Could Chalabi have been using The Times to build a drumbeat that Iraq was hiding weapons of mass destruction?" he asked.[17]

Finally, two months after the fact, Kurtz took aim at Miller and The Times by raising questions about her role in the Chalabi visit. After talking to a half-dozen officers, he reported in the June 25 Washington Post that "Miller acted as a middleman between the Army unit with which she was embedded and Iraqi National Congress Leader Ahmed Chalabi, on one occasion accompanying Army officers to Chalabi's headquarters . . ." One MET Alpha officer called the unit the "Judith Miller team." Her note protesting the unit's orders to withdraw at Tallil was mentioned high in the story.

Kurtz conceded only that "viewed from one perspective," Miller's actions during the visit to Chalabi were consistent with "acting as an aggressive journalist." Miller's refusal to comment for the story did not strengthen her case. Kurtz quoted the Times' Rosenthal again, who dismissed the idea Miller had somehow exerted undue influence over the outfit as "a baseless accusation. She doesn't direct MET Alpha, she's a civilian." Rosenthal added that Times editors thought "she did really good work there. We think she broke some important stories."[18]

After the excitement generated by the revelations of the Iraqi "scientist" in the baseball cap, who later turned out to be a former Iraqi intelligence officer, Miller's frustration and her proclivity for injecting herself into the story mounted as MET Alpha's mission steadily deteriorated. There was a flurry of activity in mid-May over two trailers the weapons hunters had found that they thought might be mobile labs for producing biological weapons material, a find that would have borne out earlier reports from a defector—code-named Curveball—that Saddam's scientists possessed movable "germ" labs.

Miller cowrote a story with science writer William Broad in early June that strongly suggested that speculation by U.S. intelligence agencies about the purpose of the supposed Iraqi mobile units might amount to "a rush to judgment." A U.S. official went so far as to suggest that the desire of the weapons hunters to find weapons might have resulted in seeing WMD where none existed. "Everyone has wanted to find the 'smoking gun' so much that they may have wanted to have reached this conclusion. I am very upset with the process," said one expert.[19] By the end of June, the *Times'* Washington-based intelligence specialist, Douglas Jehl, reported that the State Department's intelligence arm, the Bureau of Intelligence and Research (INR), openly disputed the CIA's conclusions about the mobile bioweapons labs. Dissenting scientists believed they were used for making hydrogen gas for weather balloons or for manufacturing pesticides.[20]

By then the hunt by the 75th Exploitation Task Force was practically out of business. Most of the MET units had disbanded or been reassigned. MET Alpha lost its chemical and biological experts. It was tasked with searching for evidence of covert Iraqi operations abroad and looking for stolen Jewish antiquities. Its last mission was to probe suspicious equipment stored in Basra, the strategic southern city on the Shatt-al-Arab waterway between Iraq and Iran, that weapons experts believed might be part of a nuclear weapons program. Instead the unit found crates of Russian-marked oil production equipment and industrial-size vegetable steamers.

The term "smoking gun," noted Barton Gellman in a May 11 story in *The Washington Post,* came to be used derisively by weapons hunters. When Colonel McPhee was asked about the whereabouts of a coalition mobile bio lab that had departed the airbase at Tallil, he joked: "I haven't got a clue where the WMD is, but we can find this lab . . ." The teams inspected more than 75 percent of the targeted potential weapons sites in Iraq. They interviewed thirteen scientists, out of about two hundred people on the Pentagon's "black list" of high-value targets and thousands of mid-level Iraqis on the so-called gray list. They had come up with virtually nothing.[21]

The weapons hunters, Miller wrote in a long, wrap-up story on the front page of the Sunday *Times* in mid-July, had been beset from the beginning by "chaos, disorganization, interagency feuds, disputes within and among various military units, and shortages of everything." They found no weapons or evidence of active WMD production. But Miller herself wasn't about to throw in the towel. "To this day, whether Saddam Hussein possessed such weapons when the war began remains unknown. It is the biggest mystery of the war . . ." she wrote. In the end, the MET teams had inspected more than 350 sites "without getting a single soldier killed," McPhee told her proudly. But the real puzzle to Miller seemed to be the Pentagon's lack of urgency about the weapons-hunting mission. In a July story about the confusion surrounding the weapons hunt, she quoted Fred C. Iklé, a Reagan defense official, who confirmed that he didn't "sense that this was much of a priority."[22]

How could that be? In fact, there may have been good reason for the brass's flagging interest in the work of the MET teams. A month earlier, Gellman had reported in *The Post* that Task Force 20, the elite army special operations team that would make headlines by capturing Saddam the following December, had entered Iraq before the invasion in a covert effort to locate, "seize, destroy, render safe, capture, or recover" Saddam's hidden chemical, biological, or nuclear weapons—and came up empty. "Its role in the search for illicit arms," wrote Gellman, citing military and intelligence sources, "turned out to be far more important than that of the search teams operating out in the open."[23]

Task Force 20, unlike the MET teams, was equipped with advanced DNA detection technology, collapsible biological and chemical labs that could fit on the back of a Humvee, and twenty-four-hour access to MH-60 Pave Hawk helicopters, MH-47 Special Operations Aircraft, and AH/MH-6 Little Bird gunships. They specialized in high-risk prisoner rescues. They could move out at an hour's notice, capture or kill high-ranking Iraqis, and engage in firefights or sabotage when necessary. Armed with lists of weapons sites, they were able to reach target locations and inspect them before they were stripped by looters. But, like the MET teams, they were unable to turn up any evidence Saddam had squirreled away WMD. Military and intelligence sources told Gellman they were unable to find any unconventional munitions, long-range missiles or missile parts, stores of chemical or biological agents, or enrichment technology for nuclear weapons.[24]

The failure of both Task Force 20 and the 75th Exploitation Task Force teams to unearth any weapons of mass destruction also put tremendous pressure on President Bush and the White House, with the presidential election less than a year off. Miller knew by this time that Bush administration officials had worked out a plan, under way since early May, to replace the army teams with a larger, more agile task force organized and assembled by the CIA. The Iraq Survey Group, under the leadership of U.S. arms inspector David Kay, would put some 1,500 weapons experts and intelligence specialists in the field and was expected to become operational by August. Its task: to come up with definitive conclusions about what happened to Saddam's WMD arsenal, or whether it even existed.

But for Judith Miller, the controversy over the Iraqi weapons wasn't over yet. Although she heard plenty of skepticism about the existence of Iraqi WMD when she returned to the United States in June, she continued to believe, along with senior members of the Bush administration, that the weapons would eventually be found by the CIA's Iraqi Survey Group team, or that Saddam's forces had destroyed them or spirited them across the Syrian border before the U.S. invasion. She refused to apologize for her reporting. "I think I was given information by people who believed the information they were giving the president," she said. She later added, "I accurately described the contents of the [2002] National Intelligence Estimate. I had no way of knowing that the underlying information on which the estimates were based was wrong. Much of that information was provided to the White House in the classified and unclassified versions of the NIE."[25]

Miller's nightmare was just beginning. Only weeks after she returned to the *Times*' Washington bureau, where she was preoccupied with putting together her two-thousand-word *Times* story on the failure of the U.S. Army weapons hunters that would appear on July 20, 2003, she met with I. Lewis "Scooter" Libby, the vice president's chief of staff, a well-known hawk on the Iraq war and critic of the CIA, and possibly several other administration officials. The second of three meetings with Libby took place in Washington on July 8.

The substance of their full conversation is not known, though Libby reportedly told federal investigators that he and Miller had discussed Valerie Plame Wilson, the CIA agent whose covert status may have been leaked illegally to the press by unnamed senior administration officials as retaliation against Valerie Wilson's husband, former ambassador to Niger Joseph C. Wilson IV. The meeting took place two days after Wilson's bombshell op-ed piece, titled "What I Didn't Find in Africa," appeared in

The Times, sharply questioning the president's use of intelligence about Iraq's interest in African uranium ore in the State of the Union speech the previous January. Miller and Libby met just six days before Robert Novak revealed in his syndicated column that Plame was an undercover CIA agent. The convenient timing later prompted blogger Arianna Huffington to print an unfounded rumor that perhaps Miller had passed this inside dope about Plame's covert status to Libby, who anonymously passed it to Novak.

Two years after the Miller-Libby meeting, special prosecutor Patrick Fitzgerald subpoenaed Miller to appear before the grand jury and to provide notes, e-mails, or documents "relating to any conversations" with "a government official whom she met in Washington on July 8, 2003, concerning Valerie Plame Wilson." Miller refused, setting the stage for her prison term for contempt of court in the summer of 2005.

Miller had a tremendous professional stake in the nuclear weapons story. She had coauthored an exclusive story ten months before her meeting with Libby, in September 2002, with *Times* military correspondent Michael Gordon. The report, citing unnamed "administration officials" as sources, revealed Iraq had imported aluminum tubes from China for centrifuges capable of refining yellowcake ore into weapons-grade uranium. The Niger uranium story and Miller's aluminum tubes story were the twin pillars of the administration's case that Saddam had restarted Iraq's nuclear weapons program.

In her affidavit responding to Fitzgerald's subpoena, Miller denied having any documents "responsive" to any discussions about Plame, and reminded Fitzgerald that "I have never written an article about Valerie Plame or Joe Wilson." She said she "did, however, contemplate writing one or more articles in July 2003 about issues related to Ambassador Wilson's op-ed piece. In preparation for those articles,"[26] she said, she spoke and/or met with several potential sources, and that at least one of them insisted on confidentiality. Was the July 8 conversation with Libby primarily for this series of stories Miller was planning to write about "issues" related to Ambassador Wilson's op-ed piece, not about Wilson or his wife? And was one of the "issues" the disappearance of Iraq's nuclear program? The timing of Miller's meetings with Libby and her statements in court documents strongly suggest that, though the two may have discussed Wilson and his wife, Miller was at the time intent on wrapping up her upcoming report on the army's unsuccessful search for weapons in Iraq—and for possible follow-up stories on Saddam's vanished nuclear weapons program.

If she and Libby did discuss the fate of the Iraqi nuclear program on July 8—and the evidence is that Libby went into some detail to persuade Miller that the intelligence on the Niger uranium deal was sound—that naturally raises another question: Was Libby also one of the anonymous "White House officials" behind the September 2002 leak of classified information about Iraq's purchase of aluminum tubes? Was Miller interested in meeting with Libby after returning from Iraq simply to find out if the Bush administration had any intelligence on why army teams found no WMD? As Vice President Cheney's chief national security advisor, Libby was well known to have been deeply involved in preparing elaborate intelligence reports on Saddam's WMD arsenal, virtually all of them later discredited. Miller and Gordon have never identified their sources for the 2002 *Times* story. The possibility that Libby had been a source for Miller before on the White House WMD claims casts her dramatic decision to go to jail in the summer of 2005 as something less than heroic. Miller may have been more concerned about concealing earlier conversations with Libby on classified subjects, like the status of Iraq's nuclear weapons program, than in the role Valerie Plame may or may not have played in her husband's trip to Niger.

That, of course, like so much else concerning White House representations of Iraq's fearsome WMD arsenal, is pure speculation. Still, it is well known and widely accepted that the ambiguous intelligence about the aluminum tubes, one of two foundations of the Bush White House's insistent and ultimately discredited arguments that Saddam would soon possess nuclear weapons, came from unidentified sources at the White House. But it is not known precisely whether the leak came from Libby and the secretive and increasingly manipulative Office of the Vice President, or from one of its network of allies in, say, the Defense Department, or from the president's senior staff or even the National Security Council. All were, at one time or another, to a greater or lesser degree, preoccupied during the eighteen months between September 11, 2001, and the invasion of Iraq on March 19, 2003, with a concerted, multifaceted, and brazenly deceptive campaign to persuade Americans and the world that Saddam possessed a dangerous arsenal of WMD and that a preemptive war with Iraq was both lawful and justified.

This gulf between our broad understanding of events that shaped the WMD controversy and our incomplete knowledge of the details that would explain how and why it happened still bedevils the entire fiasco.

But what could no longer be disputed by July 2003 was that Saddam's vaunted weapons of mass destruction had not been located, as Judith Miller and others began to report from Iraq. The gravest responsibility of American leadership was to send its sons and daughters to war—yet this White House seemed to have made some terrible mistake. The absence of chemical, biological, and nuclear weapons, or even credible evidence of operational Iraqi weapons-manufacturing facilities, was a severe blow to the prestige and credibility of the Bush White House, however deftly senior Republicans managed for a time to deflect it. Ultimately the U.S. military's failure to find WMD stores in Iraq badly compromised the legitimacy of the Iraq War itself. It was the moment the hemorrhaging began for the Bush presidency that inexorably sapped Washington's influence and leverage around the world, leaving U.S. credibility in tatters from North Korea to Iran and Israel, from Gaza and Lebanon to the ongoing sectarian strife in Baghdad.

Had the president and top officials of the most powerful nation in the world, with access to the most sophisticated intelligence networks on the planet, so seriously miscalculated the potential strength and capabilities of a second-rate Arab power that they took the country to war under false pretenses? To begin to answer that question, it is illuminating to go back to Tuesday, September 11, 2001, and the initial reactions of Secretary of Defense Donald Rumsfeld and other senior Bush officials in the hours after nineteen well-trained al-Qaeda terrorists hijacked three U.S. airliners and coldly murdered some three thousand unsuspecting American citizens and a handful of foreign nationals.

PART I

TARGET BAGHDAD

ANOTHER SHOT AT SADDAM

Best info fast. Judge whether good enough to hit S.H. @ same time—not only UBL. Go massive. Sweep it all up. Things related and not."

At 2:40 P.M. on September 11, 2001, Secretary of Defense Donald Rumsfeld dictated that brief memo about possible retaliation against Iraq to his Pentagon lieutenants. Earlier that morning, only minutes after hijacked U.S. passenger planes had crashed into the World Trade Center and the Pentagon, he learned that U.S. intelligence had intercepted a call from an al-Qaeda operative in Afghanistan who had "heard good news" and inquired about a fourth hijacked jet. Just after noon, CIA director George Tenet had informed Rumsfeld that passenger manifests indicated that three of the hijackers were Saudi members of al-Qaeda. "One," he was told, "is associate of a *Cole* bomber," a reference to the bombing of the destroyer USS *Cole* in the port of Aden in October 2000. Rumsfeld quickly put the bits of evidence together. In the makeshift shorthand of the memo "S.H." stood for Saddam Hussein, unmentioned in the intelligence, and "UBL" for Usama bin Laden. Rumsfeld thus became the first administration official on the record to blame both the Iraqi dictator and al-Qaeda for planning and carrying out the surprise terrorist attacks on the United States—a link that was utterly without merit, but would have a tremendous impact on public opinion in the eighteen months ahead.

Shuttling between the secure National Military Command Center and his cavernous office two hundred feet away, Rumsfeld was situated on the eastern side of the Pentagon, opposite the crash site. From his vantage he could not directly see the black smoke still curling into the sky from the flames that blackened the shattered western façade of the sprawling complex. But he could smell it in the corridors. Fewer than five hours had passed since terrorists boarded American Flight 77 at Dulles and slammed it at more than 400 mph into the nerve center of the U.S. military establishment. That morning the sixty-seven-year-old secretary of defense had witnessed emergency workers treating the charred and twisted bodies of his own employees outside on the grass and carrying them off on stretchers and in body bags.[1] He was not the first senior official in the administration of George W. Bush to contemplate targeting Baghdad, nor was it the first time since the end of hostilities in the 1991 Gulf War that such a scenario had been considered. Well before the pristine late summer day when terrorist attacks in Washington, New York, and over a Pennsylvania field killed 2,973 people and left twenty-four missing, there was little question that sooner or later the Bush administration was going to strike Saddam's regime, and strike hard.

The previous January 30, only ten days after President George W. Bush's inauguration, the fate of the Baghdad regime was the main agenda item for the first meeting of Bush's National Security Council (NSC), the elite inner sanctum of the new administration's foreign policy operations. Condoleezza Rice, the president's private foreign policy tutor during the election campaign and now his national security advisor, presided. The president spoke briefly about disengaging from the Israeli-Palestinian peace process and tilting toward support of Israel and Prime Minister Ariel Sharon. Then Rice opened the session by declaring the administration's view that Saddam was a destabilizing force in the Middle East whose well-documented efforts to develop nuclear, biological, and chemical weapons of mass destruction were only surpassed by his ruthless willingness to deploy them.

Rice did not have to provide chapter and verse to those present. Saddam had used his deadly chemical arsenal against neighboring Iran during the Iran-Iraq War, and against his own people in 1988, when Iraqi forces killed more than 3,200 Kurds with poison gas in the northern town of Halabja. There were reports that Baghdad provided cash rewards to the families of Palestinian suicide bombers after successful missions in Israel. Seated around the mahogany table in the White House Situation Room were the NSC "principals": Besides the president and Rice, they included Vice President Dick Cheney, Secretary of Defense Donald Rumsfeld, Secretary of

State Colin Powell, Secretary of the Treasury Paul O'Neill, and the president's chief of staff, Andrew Card. Also seated at the table as NSC "advisers" were CIA director George Tenet and Joint Chiefs of Staff Chairman Gen. Hugh Shelton. Arrayed in chairs around the periphery of the room behind them were the "backbenchers"—deputies, undersecretaries, key staffers who attended at the president's discretion—including Cheney's chief of staff, I. Lewis "Scooter" Libby, Deputy Secretary of Defense Paul Wolfowitz, Deputy Secretary of State Richard Armitage, and Karl Rove, the president's political wizard, among others.

The message couldn't have been clearer: The new Bush administration was going to shift the focus of U.S. policy in the Mideast from the Palestinian peace process to Iraq, with particular emphasis on what the president called Saddam's "destructive weapons." Rice then turned the meeting over to CIA director George Tenet, who unrolled a tablecloth-size photographic blowup of an Iraqi plant believed by the CIA to produce chemical or biological material for weapons. Former treasury secretary Paul O'Neill and others remembered Cheney poring over the photograph with "uncharacteristic excitement, waving his arm" at staff members lining the room and urging them to come up to the table and "take a look at this." O'Neill, a former corporate chief executive officer who had seen plenty of similar industrial plants around the world, was dubious about Tenet's dog-and-pony show. When he questioned Tenet, the CIA chief admitted that the agency had "no confirming intelligence" about what the plant actually produced. Each of the key cabinet members was tasked with fleshing out elements of the various options on the table. Powell, for example, was to focus on bringing more effective diplomatic pressure to bear on Baghdad and tightening sanctions. President Bush abruptly ended the meeting by ordering Rumsfeld and the Pentagon to "examine our military options" to take down Iraq.

After a second NSC meeting on February 1, Secretary of the Treasury O'Neill was struck by the tacit assumption among an inner circle of the NSC principals—namely, Rice, Rumsfeld, Cheney, and Tenet—that going after Saddam one way or other was a foregone conclusion. Before the meeting Rumsfeld had circulated a six-page memo laying out the costs of defending the United States against "asymmetrical threats," principally by rogue regimes or state-sponsored terror groups that might possess weapons of mass destruction. The secretary of defense's memo, thought O'Neill, could have been drafted by the neoconservatives whose views he had heard in many speeches at the American Enterprise Institute, an ultraconservative think tank in Washington. They argued, in essence, that the end of the Cold War had left a vacuum of power in the Middle East and elsewhere that was being filled by tinhorn dictators and regional powers intent on building powerful weapons to gain hegemony and threaten U.S. interests—and possibly hamper Washington's ability to project military power.[2]

A number of the participants in the Bush NSC meetings had attended lengthy meetings or written extensively about Iraq before signing on with the administration. Since many also had been architects of the 1991 Gulf War with the president's father, their ideas about Iraq's strategic importance and the threat posed by Saddam were already well formed. Even so, there were sharp differences around the table over the wisdom of targeting Iraq, most obviously between Rumsfeld and Powell. Rumsfeld's deputy at the Pentagon, Paul Wolfowitz, was already pushing hard for a plan he had written about in *The New Republic* two years before that called for inserting U.S. ground forces in southern Iraq to provide a safe sanctuary for Iraqi opposition groups planning to depose Saddam.[3] Powell bluntly called Wolfowitz's plan "lunacy." Powell argued that the United States should strengthen economic sanctions against Baghdad that had been in place since the end of the Gulf War and had in fact wreaked havoc on Saddam's ability to rearm.

During the February 1 NSC meeting, Rumsfeld held forth on Iraq, openly speculating about the sort of incident that might trigger an intentionally disproportionate American military response against Saddam—for example, if the Iraqis shot down a U.S. fighter in the no-fly zone over northern Iraq. Although official U.S. policy since 1998 called for regime change in Iraq, Rumsfeld insisted that was not the point. "It's not my specific objective to get rid of Saddam Hussein," he told the meeting. "I'm after the weapons of mass destruction. Regime change isn't my prime concern." Rather, Iraq would be an example for the rest of the world of how the United States would respond if it could be demonstrated that Saddam possessed or was trying to build powerful unconventional weapons prohibited by multiple UN resolutions since the 1991 Gulf War.

Despite the obvious policy differences on the table, it seemed to O'Neill that there was little inclination among the inner circle for much vigorous debate and no discernible process for a coherent assessment of policy toward Iraq. Powell appeared to be out of the loop from the start, causing O'Neill to wonder with some consternation, "Was there already an *in* group and an *out* group?"[4] The secretary of the treasury also noticed that the Pentagon's Defense Intelligence Agency, the military's version of the CIA, had prepared documents for Rumsfeld assaying Iraqi oil fields, the second-largest known petroleum reserves in the world, and designated areas still open for exploration and development that could be divvied up by foreign powers—a convenient complement to a preemptive attack on Saddam, he wryly noted. "There was never any rigorous talk about this sweeping idea that seemed to be driving all the specific actions," O'Neill recalled. "From the start, we were building the case against Hussein and looking at how we could take him out and change Iraq into a new country. And, if we did that, it would solve everything. It was all about finding a way to do it. That was the tone of it. The president saying, 'Fine. Go find me a way to do this.' "[5]

By June 2001, four policy alternatives for Iraq were on the table, but the direction the administration would take was far from clear. In an NSC principals meeting on Iraq that month, Condoleezza Rice laid out the options for the United States. First, Washington could continue to keep Saddam "in the box" through containment, essentially continuing to rely on tightening economic sanctions, combined with constant U.S. military pressure in the northern no-fly zone to eventually topple the Baghdad regime. It was well known that Rice favored this route. Second, the new administration might also continue to focus on containment, but in addition actively provide support and funding for Saddam's domestic opponents, the Shiite majority concentrated in the south and the independent-minded Kurds in the north. Proposals had been floated since the end of the Gulf War, reportedly by the Saudis, to carve out a safe haven for Iraqi insurgents in the southern part of the country dominated by Shiites. The idea had gained some traction over the years and now represented a third option. The fourth possibility was to invade Iraq and forcibly remove Saddam.

None of the members of the Bush National Security Council, including Rumsfeld, could have imagined the deadly and shattering provocation—far graver than a U.S. warplane shot down by Iraqi antiaircraft batteries in the no-fly zone—that came to pass seven months later on September 11, 2001. Within forty-eight hours, Rumsfeld formally raised the possibility of extending the war on terror beyond Afghanistan, arguing that any broad U.S. initiative against state-sponsored terrorism had to target Baghdad. "Do we focus on bin Laden and al Qaeda or terrorism more broadly?" he asked during an NSC meeting the morning of September 12. But the president, along with Secretary of State Powell and others, opposed moving against Saddam, preferring instead to go directly after bin Laden, al-Qaeda, and their Taliban sponsors in Afghanistan. Bush, who only that morning had spoken with British prime minister Tony Blair about possible U.S. responses, believed that the American people expected Washington to hunt down bin Laden, and wanted to avoid a response defined "too broadly for the average man to understand." The president sought a swift and effective U.S. strike. Rumsfeld had to concede that the military could do "very little, effectively"[6] on short notice. Richard Clarke, the Bush White House counterterrorism director, was incredulous that Rumsfeld would even bring up the idea of Iraq. "For us now to go bombing Iraq would be like our invading Mexico after the Japanese attack on Pearl Harbor," he said.

But Clarke got much the same message, this time directly from the president himself, when he ran into Bush that evening outside the White House Situation Room. Bush herded Clarke and several colleagues into the videoconferencing room. "Look, I know you have a lot to do and all," said the president. "But I want you, as soon as you can, to go back over everything, everything. See if Saddam did this. See if he's linked in any way . . ."

"Absolutely, we will look," Clarke promised. "But you know, we have looked several times for state sponsorship of al Qaeda and not found any real linkages to Iraq."

"Look into Iraq, Saddam," Bush repeated, a little irritably, Clarke thought.[7]

Within days, Clarke's staff produced a memo for the president advising him that all national security departments and agencies agreed that there was no evidence of cooperation between Iraq and al-Qaeda. The report, entitled "Survey of Intelligence Information on Any Iraq Involvement in the September 11 Attacks," was vetted by the NSC staffer responsible for Afghanistan, Zalmay Khalilzad, who four years later would become the Bush administration's U.S. ambassador to Iraq during the American occupation and later ambassador to the United Nations. The September 18 memo noted an unconfirmed Czech intelligence report that hijacker Mohamed Atta had met with an Iraqi intelligence agent in Prague in April 2001. There was also unconfirmed Polish information that Iraqi intelligence may have had forewarning of the attacks. Nonetheless Clarke's survey concluded that there was no "compelling case" that Iraq had played a role in planning or supporting the al-Qaeda attacks. Khalilzad agreed with Clarke's assessment. Bin Laden, a devout Islamist, was known to hold Saddam's secular Baathist regime in contempt. Perhaps most important, there was no credible evidence that Baghdad had any interest in aiding al-Qaeda in its quest for weapons of mass destruction.[8] President Bush apparently never saw the report.[9]

The following weekend the president and first lady slipped away to Camp David, the rustic presidential retreat in Maryland's Catoctin mountains, with Bush's war cabinet—an expanded version of the NSC team that now included Attorney General John Ashcroft and FBI director Robert S. Mueller III. Rumsfeld's deputy, Paul Wolfowitz, tried again to stir up interest in a retaliatory strike against Iraq during the marathon weekend meetings. The Defense Department prepared briefing papers for the senior officials laying out options for the war on terror that included three primary targets, al-Qaeda, the Taliban, and Iraq. Both al-Qaeda and Iraq were presented as strategic threats to the United States. Rice later explained that the president and his advisers were concerned that Saddam might take advantage of the chaos caused by 9/11. This time, Rumsfeld let his deputy do the talking. Wolfowitz expressed his concern that American troops would get bogged down in Afghanistan, and declared that there was a 10 percent to 50 percent chance that Iraq had been involved in the 9/11 attacks. He felt that Iraq was the source of the terrorist problem, though he could not prove it, and pressed for including Baghdad in the first wave of attacks. He was waved off by the president's chief of staff, Andy Card. Despite Cheney's hawkish posture and his previously stated preference for widening the war on terror, the vice president also opposed Wolfowitz and Rumsfeld. "If we go after Saddam, we lose our rightful place as a good guy," said Cheney. But he pointedly refused to rule out an attack on Saddam at some later date.[10]

Later that evening, President Bush told a small group sitting around the fire—including Wolfowitz and Cheney's chief of staff, Scooter Libby—that he wasn't impressed with the military plans he'd seen for attacking Iraq. Wolfowitz saw an opening to advance his own position. The U.S. military, he said, could invade a small enclave in southern Iraq near the Kuwait border that was rich in oil and populated by friendly Shiites who hated Saddam. Not only would the U.S. troop presence choke off Iraq's southern oil fields, but troops could actively support anti-Saddam insurgents and prepare them to march on Baghdad. Bush took it all in, and as the weekend wound down, the president took Gen. Hugh Shelton aside and asked him if focusing on al-Qaeda and not on Iraq was a mistake. Shelton told him no. The joint chiefs chairman, who was due to give up his job in a month, felt that attacking Iraq without provocation would needlessly complicate the process of building a coalition and result in increased tensions in the region. "We won't do Iraq now," the president told Condoleezza Rice on Sunday the sixteenth. "We're putting Iraq off. But eventually we'll have to return to that question."[11] The next day he signed the order to send U.S. troops into Afghanistan.

Within a week of the 9/11 attacks, the twin themes that drove the Bush administration's eighteen-month march to war in Iraq had the status of received wisdom in the highest councils of U.S. government. The first was the presumption that Saddam possessed weapons of mass destruction and therefore presented a threat to the United States. The second—which perhaps began as little more than a presidential suspicion, or a fig leaf for regime change—was that Saddam Hussein had somehow been involved with al-Qaeda in mounting the terror attacks on the United States that caught the new Bush administration so badly off guard. The president's professional experience as an owner and president of the Texas Rangers baseball team and his late-starting political career as two-term governor of Texas had hardly prepared him for the day-by-day operations of United States foreign policy, much less for commanding a war in the volatile and politically complex Middle East. Bush, however, was conscious of his shortcomings. While he was still governor, three years before taking up residence in the White House, he set about correcting his ignorance of international affairs by meeting for the first time with Republican policymakers, on whom he would come to depend as his inner circle of advisers during the prewar period. Some of them would later play critical roles in keeping alive fears about Saddam's arsenal of unconventional weapons and his links with Osama bin Laden and al-Qaeda.

As Bush had prepared to run for reelection as governor of Texas in the spring of 1998, George P. Shultz, President Ronald Reagan's former secretary of state, invited the fifty-five-year-old governor to his home in Palo Alto near the Stanford University campus to meet with a gathering of foreign policy scholars from the conservative Hoover Institution. Shultz had organized a similar gathering for Gov. Ronald Reagan two decades before. This time the relaxed Texas governor, who was making a swing through California on a fund-raising trip, seemed intent on wooing the old Reagan hands, though he was closemouthed about his presidential aspirations. Among those gathered to meet Bush was Stanford's youthful provost, Condoleezza Rice, a Soviet expert who had served on the NSC staff during the presidency of Bush's father. The following July, Governor Bush invited Rice and some of the Hoover people to Austin for another foreign policy session, along with former defense secretary Dick Cheney, then the top executive at Halliburton, the Houston-based energy services and construction firm, and Cheney's former deputy Paul Wolfowitz, who was then dean of the Johns Hopkins School of Advanced Studies. This time Bush was quite candid about seeking the presidency—and their support.

The pace of the meetings soon quickened. In August, Rice traveled to the senior Bushes' Kennebunkport, Maine, compound at the invitation of the former president. His son was also there, on vacation from his duties in Austin, and busy planning his presidential campaign. It was not the first time Rice had been to the Bushes' residence on the Maine coast, nor the first time she had met George W. Bush. As an NSC staffer she had been called on several times to accompany her boss, Gen. Brent Scowcroft, the elder President Bush's national security advisor, to Kennebunkport to brief the president on the Soviet Union, which was then in the throes of terminal political upheaval, and to review the administration's policies for the book Scowcroft and the former president were coauthoring, *A World Transformed*. Scowcroft was a close personal friend of the first president Bush—he would become a reluctant critic of the future president Bush over the Iraq War—and had made a generous effort to smooth the way for Rice with the Bushes.

The interlude in Kennebunkport was a formative one for both Bush and Rice, who was a talented pianist and figure skater, among her other achievements. The two spent hours talking together, working out on treadmills and rowing machines, fishing in the ocean, and discussing their mutual passion for sports.[12] Along the way, they explored the United States' relations with the rest of the world and found enough common ground between them to establish a relationship. Soon afterward, Bush decided to make Rice his chief foreign policy adviser for the presidential campaign. The tumult of presidential politicking and the crisis atmosphere following the 9/11 attacks would only strengthen the personal bond between the two that was forged at Kennebunkport and increase Bush's reliance on Rice.

Taking the advice of Cheney and Schultz, Bush asked Paul Wolfowitz to join Rice on his foreign policy team for his presidential campaign. Together the pair organized campaign events, drew up policy papers and advised the governor on international affairs, often on conference calls with the candidate. They put together a team of advisers in early 1999—a full two years before taking office—that included Richard Armitage, a former Defense Department official in the first Bush administration who was close to Colin Powell; Richard Perle, a conservative defense intellectual and adviser to the

Reagan administration; Stephen Hadley, a Pentagon aide to Wolfowitz who would become Rice's deputy at the NSC; and several others. In addition, this core group of veteran policymakers met and talked regularly with two powerful senior Republicans who over the years influenced their thinking and often guided their careers—and who would put their indelible marks for better or worse on the new president's war policy.

The first was Dick Cheney. Cheney had been onboard the Bush campaign since the Austin meeting in the summer of 1998 and from the outset took an active role supporting a second Bush administration. Although he had been out of government since 1992, Cheney had been secretary of defense under President George H. W. Bush during the Gulf War. His political career stretched back to the Nixon administration. In 1969, Cheney was hired to run the Office of Economic Opportunity by Donald Rumsfeld, then a former congressman from Illinois who had just been appointed a presidential assistant at the Nixon White House. After spending most of seven years as Rumsfeld's top aide at OEO and the White House, with a brief stint at a consulting firm while Rumsfeld was NATO ambassador in 1973 and 1974, Cheney was bumped up to President Gerald Ford's chief of staff. When Jimmy Carter was elected in 1976, Cheney returned to Wyoming and ran for Congress, where he built a reputation as an effective conservative legislator with a reputation for integrity and discretion, a penchant for behind-the-scenes dealing, and a special interest in intelligence affairs.

Cheney was in line to become House speaker when he was selected by Scowcroft and Bush in 1988 to run the Pentagon. As secretary of defense, Cheney became a household name during the Gulf War. At least in public, he worked seamlessly with Joint Chiefs of Staff Chairman Colin Powell during the planning and execution of Desert Storm, the 1991 campaign by U.S. and coalition forces to drive Iraqi occupation forces out of Kuwait. Cheney left government after Bill Clinton was elected president in 1992, and went into the private sector as chief executive officer of Halliburton, in Houston, where he reportedly earned $40 million during his five-year stay.

In the early months of George W. Bush's presidential campaign, Cheney oversaw Condi Rice's team as it prepared the candidate for a critical speech on defense policy in September 1999 at The Citadel, where Bush promised a smaller, more mobile, and deadlier U.S. military designed for war-fighting, not peacekeeping or nation-building. He pledged to appoint a strong defense secretary who would make missile defenses and high-tech weapons systems U.S. priorities. By early 2000, Bush was so smitten by Cheney's expertise and low-key style that he put the older man in charge of the vice presidential selection process. Cheney, for reasons he's never fully explained, reversed an earlier decision to count himself out of the VP sweepstakes, and announced that he would accept the vice presidency after all. Bush quickly offered him the job. "Gradually I realized that the person who was best qualified to be my vice presidential nominee was working by my side," Bush explained later.[13]

Cheney's old mentor, Donald H. Rumsfeld, was the other Republican *éminence grise* in the Bush camp. By the time the campaign got under way, Rumsfeld had been out of government for a quarter century, an absence that earned him the sobriquet "a modern-day Rip Van Winkle" from one skeptical political observer. But he remained sharply focused on defense issues. Rumsfeld headed a congressional commission on U.S. missile defenses in 1999 and 2000, with a membership that included Rice, Wolfowitz, Hadley, and Perle, an effort to revive Ronald Reagan's old Strategic Defense Initiative. Rumsfeld was well prepared for the task, having just served as chairman of the bipartisan Rumsfeld Commission, set up by Congress to examine existing U.S. intelligence on the ballistic missile threat to the United States. The nine-member commission, which included Wolfowitz, declared in 1998 that the danger of a foreign missile attack was greater than U.S. intelligence agencies had reported. The commission named North Korea, Iran, and Iraq as three countries capable of mounting such threats against the United States—foreshadowing Bush's famous "axis of evil" comments in his 2002 State of the Union Address.

Rumsfeld, too, brought impressive credentials to the table—and a reputation as a fierce and canny bureaucratic infighter. After a three-term congressional career, a stint in the Nixon White House in the early 1970s, and a meteoric rise to chief of staff for President Gerald R. Ford, he was appointed secretary of defense by Ford in 1975, making him the youngest person ever to hold the job. His tenure was cut short by Jimmy Carter's inauguration on January 20, 1977. Rumsfeld used his brief time at the Pentagon to lay down a marker in conservative circles by opposing détente with the Soviet Union and the arms control policies of then secretary of state Henry Kissinger. Rumsfeld was never far from government or Republican politics. He testified before the Senate against the Carter administration's revised Strategic Arms Limitation Treaty in 1979 and called for an increase in defense spending.

A year later he was stung when Ronald Reagan passed over him and chose George H. W. Bush as his vice presidential running mate, a choice that marked the beginning of the Bush dynasty. Rumsfeld mounted an unsuccessful presidential campaign in 1988, after years spent honing an

image in the private sector as a relentless top manager by turning around
G.D. Searle & Company, the prominent pharmaceutical multinational,
where he made his name in a determined and highly profitable campaign
to win federal regulatory approval of the controversial sweetener and
food supplement aspartame. In 1990 he became CEO of the General In-
strument Corporation, a cable and communications company. Rumsfeld's
business acumen netted him an estimated personal fortune of between
$50 million and $200 million.[14]

The third Republican national security heavyweight on the Bush team,
Colin Powell, whose prominence during the Gulf War persuaded many
Americans that he had the right stuff for the presidency, was nowhere to
be seen in the early days of the campaign. That began to change at the August Republican convention in Philadelphia, when Powell delivered an influential speech addressing Bush's appeal to minorities as a Republican.
Powell's name came up came up repeatedly on short lists as Bush's possible secretary of state. During the fall campaign, the former joint chiefs
chairman and Reagan national security advisor stumped for Bush among
veterans, minorities, and moderates of both parties. But Powell's name
was not on the list of senior Republican conservatives invited to join the
Congressional Policy Advisory Board, a group convened in the late 1990s
as a kind of shadow cabinet and meeting ground for former Republican
officials with aspirations for senior positions in the next GOP administration. Its top-level strategy sessions were a must for Republican foreign
policy luminaries like Cheney, Rumsfeld, Wolfowitz, and Rice.

Powell's absence was a sign of the insularity of the Republican foreign
policy establishment—and of underlying strains with senior GOP colleagues that dated back to the Gulf War. Even so, he had gained a broad-
based popularity, political independence, and military stature that the
others could only dream about. But he was distrusted by conservative policymakers and intellectuals, primarily for his moderation and his cautious
instincts during the 1991 campaign to drive Saddam's troops out of
Kuwait. Powell probably would not have joined the Congressional Policy
Board if he had been asked. He appeared to actively avoid foreign policy
study groups, and favored spending his time on minority youth organizations like the Boy and Girl Clubs of America and the United Negro College Fund.

For all its seasoned intellectual firepower and the candidate's late-
blooming passion for freedom and democracy in the Middle East, the

Bush campaign in the summer and fall of 2000 had very little to say about either terrorism or Iraq. Like his Democratic opponent, then vice president Al Gore, Bush vaguely called for retaliation against those responsible for the bombing of the destroyer USS *Cole* in Yemen in October 2000. He favored a "swift, sure and a clear signal to terrorists around the world that we are not going to tolerate terrorism," familiar rhetoric that dated back to the Carter and Reagan years. There was no hint that terrorism was on the agenda for Bush policymakers, or that Washington should take special measures to protect Americans at home from terrorist attacks, or even any pointed criticism of the Clinton administration's approach to terrorism. In fact, Republican foreign policy priorities in 2000 were substantially unchanged since Donald Rumsfeld served as campaign chairman for Robert Dole's unsuccessful Republican presidential bid in 1996. Bush wanted to resurrect Reagan's antimissile defense program, walk a fine line between Taiwan and Beijing out of deference to U.S. business interests (he would soon pledge to defend Taiwan from mainland Chinese incursions), strengthen traditional alliances like NATO, and refocus American policy on powerful states like post-Soviet Russia and an economically aggressive China.

Even after the Florida ballot recount and the Supreme Court decision that gave Bush the White House, the stars of the Bush foreign policy team had not hammered out a coherent position on Saddam Hussein's Iraq. While neoconservatives like William Kristol, the editor of *The Weekly Standard,* backed the Clinton administration's intervention in Kosovo and supported U.S. military action to overthrow Saddam's regime in Baghdad, the Bush campaign vowed to avoid such adventures and end Clinton-era policies of using U.S. forces for nonmilitary purposes. Back in 1998, prominent members of Bush's foreign policy team had signed an open letter to President Clinton from the neoconservative Project for the New American Century calling for a U.S. policy to remove Saddam from power. The signatories included Rumsfeld, Wolfowitz, and Armitage, among others who later joined the Bush administration.

But two years later, Condoleezza Rice wrote an article for *Foreign Affairs* that argued Saddam could be dealt with by strategies of deterrence similar to the containment doctrine that was used for two generations against the Soviets. "Rogue regimes," Rice wrote, referring to North Korea and Iraq, "are living on borrowed time, so there need be no sense of panic about them. Rather, the first line of defense should be a clear and classical statement of deterrence—if they do acquire weapons of mass destruction, that weapon will be unusable because any attempt to use them will bring national obliteration."[15] Rice no doubt knew that ever since Speaker Gingrich and Senate Majority Leader Lott, with the support of prominent conservatives like Cheney, Wolfowitz, and Perle, had pushed through the Iraq Liberation Act of 1998, regime change in Iraq had become official U.S. policy. Although the Republican Congress earmarked $97 million to support Iraqi opposition groups' efforts to bring about Saddam's collapse, how to actually depose the Iraqi dictator was another matter. Like Rice, most Clinton-era policymakers stopped well short of envisioning direct U.S. military intervention.

One member of the Bush team, Paul Wolfowitz, had become a strong proponent of forcing Saddam out of Baghdad militarily. But Wolfowitz arrived at his position via a circuitous route. He had been directly involved in Gulf War operations as undersecretary of defense with Cheney at the Pentagon, and underwent an evolution on the question of deposing Saddam. For several years after the 1991 war, Wolfowitz had little interest in regime change in Iraq. During the Iraqi retreat from Kuwait and the U.S. declaration of a ceasefire after one hundred hours of combat, there is no evidence that Wolfowitz or any other U.S. senior Pentagon officials, including Secretary of Defense Cheney, objected to President Bush's decision, backed by Powell and Gen. H. Norman Schwarzkopf, not to march on Baghdad to clean out the Iraqi Republican Guard and crush Saddam Hussein's government. Wolfowitz may have opposed the timing that ended combat operations during the Iraqi retreat from Kuwait, which allowed Saddam's best troops to escape with their weaponry and tanks, but he clearly understood at the time that marching on Baghdad involved prohibitive liabilities for the United States.

"A new regime would have become the United States' responsibility," Wolfowitz wrote in a 1997 essay. "Conceivably, this could have led the United States into a more or less permanent occupation of a country that could not govern itself, but where the rule of a foreign occupier would be increasingly resented."[16] Wolfowitz could have been describing the U.S. dilemma before invading Iraq six years later. Yet at the end of the Gulf War, many Bush officials, Wolfowitz among them, believed that as soon as U.S. forces left, Saddam would be overthrown by an Iraqi rebellion. The fact that he wasn't deposed left the Iraqi dictatorship intact as a strategic counterweight to Iran. But the brutal suppression of both the Kurds in the north and the Shiite uprising in the south, using Iraqi helicopters allowed by a loophole in the peace treaty, brought Wolfowitz around to the belief that regime change in Iraq was the only coherent U.S. policy toward Baghdad. The alternative, he thought, was that as the economic sanctions imposed on Iraq after the Gulf War eventually collapsed, Saddam would seek weapons of mass destruction and use terrorism to destabilize the region and choke off the oil supply of the industrial world.

That, at least, was Wolfowitz's vision. His conversion began to take shape in 1996, when he joined Rumsfeld as a foreign policy adviser to the Dole campaign, and began to criticize Democrats for their failure to contain Saddam or stand up for UN weapons inspectors against the bullying tactics of the Baghdad regime. Wolfowitz, an instinctively cautious and deliberate academic by nature, began to take an increasingly strident tone, writing in *The Wall Street Journal* in September 1996 that "the United States has virtually abandoned its commitment to protect a besieged people from a bloodthirsty dictator." By the end of 1997, he coauthored an article with his old Pentagon aide, Zalmay Khalilzad, arguing for the forcible overthrow of Saddam by Iraqi opposition leaders, with American military backing, who would form a government in exile in a liberated zone in southern Iraq and indict Saddam as a war criminal.

The concept was the brainchild of Gen. Wayne Downing, a former army special operations chief who drafted a plan after meeting with Iraqi exiles to liberate an area of southern Iraq, protect it with U.S. airpower, and incubate an Iraq liberation army that he believed would become ten thousand strong within a year. Wolfowitz and Khalilzad adapted Downing's strategy foreseeing that the old Gulf War coalition, with economic interests in Iraq, was unlikely to support such an aggressive U.S. initiative to back an opposition force, although they believed that allies like Russia and China would eventually fall in behind such a determined U.S. unilateral effort.[17]

Wolfowitz's assessment of the 1991 coalition partners underestimated the opposition to a U.S.-led military campaign against Saddam after 9/11—and seriously overestimated the strength of the Iraqi opposition. Once serious war planning began for Iraq in early 2002, the CIA advised the U.S. Army Central Command to dismiss any notion of military action against Saddam led by Iraqi dissidents. Despite their flawed military plan, the idea of regime change nonetheless gripped neoconservative intellectuals as an unambiguous, principled blueprint for action backed by overwhelming military force that would reassert the moral primacy and unchallenged political power of the United States as the world's lone superpower. Wolfowitz produced innumerable articles and testified before Congress, pressing for regime change in Iraq. His efforts were instrumental in formulating the positions spelled out in the Project for the New American Century document and the 1998 Iraq Liberation Act—and gaining the early support of senior Republicans who would dominate the Bush foreign policy team and take the war on terror from Afghanistan to Iraq.

In the days after 9/11, the spirit, if not the letter, of Wolfowitz's thinking, with its emphasis on neutralizing the threat Saddam posed to the region and his links to terrorism, clearly had been absorbed by his boss, Secretary of Defense Rumsfeld. But it is doubtful that Wolfowitz's idea alone would have carried the weight of policy without Rumsfeld's massaging. The secretary of defense had said he was not primarily interested in regime change, and in the sense that this involved not only deposing Saddam, but also finding a new Iraqi leader, Rumsfeld no doubt meant what he said.

The secretary of defense was at some pains to gather members of his Pentagon team after the terrorist attacks, sending an aircraft to Frankfurt, West Germany, on September 12 to pick up Undersecretary of Defense for Policy Douglas Feith, William Luti, then head of the Pentagon's Near Eastern and South Asian desk, and five other members of Feith's new Counter Terrorism Evaluation Group, who had been "on unrelated missions in Europe and the Middle East." On the long flight back to Washington, they rehashed the stunning events of the previous day and tried to foresee the implications of the Bush administration's foreign policy. "Right there on the plane, we took out our laptops and sketched out for Secretary Rumsfeld where we thought we had to go, what it meant to get things on a war footing," Luti later said. "Obviously we had Afghanistan on our minds straightaway. That was our immediate concern. But we also thought we had to learn about the terrorist networks, how they connected to the states."[18]

Over the next few days, Rumsfeld huddled frequently with his advisers, including Feith, a former aide to Wolfowitz and ardent neoconservative, and Luti, a navy captain who had come to Defense from the vice president's office. All strongly agreed that the United States had to take the war against terrorism beyond al-Qaeda and the Taliban in Afghanistan to demonstrate Washington's will. Feith drafted a memorandum on September 20 that suggested hitting a non–al-Qaeda target like Iraq as part of the initial U.S. response—perhaps even as far afield as Southeast Asia or South America—but otherwise seemed to capture the thrust of Rumsfeld's thinking on the subject. "Rumsfeld understood that the problem is not dealing with one problem in one place," Feith said later. "It would not be solved by fighting al-Qaeda inside Afghanistan. It was a bigger problem. His mind ran immediately to the extra danger of the nexus of terrorism and WMD. We were not going to solve this problem by focusing narrowly on the perpetrators of 9/11. Rumsfeld wanted some way to organize the military action so that it signaled that the global conflict would not be over if we struck one good blow in Afghanistan."[19]

Once more, at the core of Rumsfeld's strategic analysis was the fear that rogue nations like Iraq had or were building these weapons and were capable of making the technology of mass destruction available to terrorists like Osama bin Laden and al-Qaeda. The volatile mix of weapons of mass destruction and terrorism, in Rumsfeld's view, could only serve to destabilize the weaker nations of the Middle East, complicate the bloody, terror-strewn Israeli–Palestinian conflict, and threaten the world's oil supplies. In this view, Saddam's surprise invasion of Kuwait in 1990 presented a vital threat to Kuwaiti and Saudi oil fields and was only a harbinger of the chaos an unrestrained Saddam could loose upon the region.

The 9/11 attacks changed Rumsfeld's thinking about targeting Iraq. There was a new factor in play in the post-9/11 world, and Rumsfeld, who had been close to power for many years but never quite close enough to grab the brass ring, may have been tough-minded and opportunistic enough to understand what lay before him for the taking. As author Mark Danner observed, "The attacks had, after all, created a window during which the frightened and angry American public could be persuaded to support a 'war of choice.'" Such a war, he wrote, "would eliminate a threat that had now become intolerable."[20] Rumsfeld wanted a historic show of American military might that would deter terrorists everywhere. He recognized that he was in a position to deliver it and that, if the new administration moved quickly, the American public would support it. Iraq was a ready-made target. It wasn't that Iraq had changed—or somehow that Saddam had become a greater threat to the United States. It was that the circumstances around which the West had tolerated Saddam's presence in the region were altered radically by the terrorist attacks on the United States.

Much the same point was made by the political director of the British Foreign Office, Sir Peter Ricketts, in a background memo to Foreign Secretary Jack Straw on the eve of Prime Minister Tony Blair's visit to Crawford, Texas, in the spring of 2002. "The truth is," wrote Ricketts, "that what has changed is not the pace of Saddam Hussein's WMD programmes, but our tolerance of them post-11 September. . . . But even the best survey of Iraq's WMD programmes will not show much advance in recent years on the nuclear, missile or CW/BW [chemical weapons/biological weapons] fronts: the programmes are extremely worrying but have not, as far as we know, been stepped up."

That blunt and accurate assessment plainly indicated that high-level British officials knew a year before the invasion of Iraq that Saddam's WMD arsenal didn't amount to much. They also thought, as Ricketts wrote to Straw, that "U.S. scrambling to establish a link between Iraq and Al Qaida is so far frankly unconvincing."[21] In a subsequent memo to Blair, Straw instead sharply focussed the Iraq issue in terms of its psychological and strategic impact of 9/11 on the Bush administration. "If 11 September had not happened, it is doubtful the U.S. would now be considering military action against Iraq," Straw wrote. "In addition, there has been no credible evidence to link Iraq with UBL and Al Qaida. Objectively, the threat from Iraq has not worsened as a result of 11 September. What has however changed is the tolerance of the international community (especially that of the U.S.), the world having witnessed on September 11 just what determined evil people can these days perpetrate."[22]

Strategically speaking, the current state of Saddam's WMD arsenal was immaterial, since what Rumsfeld had in mind was in essence an overwhelming show of American military power against states that might even consider supporting terrorists. Yet, practically speaking, as subsequent events would show, the actual status of Iraqi weapons programs had devastating repercussions for U.S. war policy and the Bush administration.

2

CHENEY GOES OVER TO THE DARK SIDE

Shortly after President Bush's inauguration, Vice President Cheney was assigned by the new president to act as the White House's point man on intelligence. With that unusual order, Cheney set about remaking the Office of the Vice President, once a largely ceremonial stepping stone for ambitious politicians, into a powerful and secretive nerve center of Bush admistration policymaking, staffed by an unprecedented number of political aides, communications experts, and policy advisers. Al Gore had paved the way for a proactive vice presidency in the 1990s. But Gore's clout as vice president—advising President Clinton on science and environmental issues, foreign and military affairs, and efficiency in government—paled next to the power over war and peace Cheney amassed with the president's blessing and concentrated in the White House.

In the months after the attacks, Washington insiders began to compare the vice president's behind-the-scenes role as something more akin to that of a prime minister or copresident, and recognized that he was fast becoming the driving force behind national security policy. "The real president of the United States is Dick Cheney," declared Lawrence Wilkerson, former secretary of state Colin Powell's chief of staff and an outspoken critic of the Bush administration. Others came to similar conclusions. Vice President Cheney, "if he has not actually assumed the role of the presidency," observed author and White House policy scholar David J. Rothkopf, "has become much like a prime minister and... has certainly usurped many of the prerogatives that have traditionally accrued to national security advisor."[1] Cheney's fiercely loyal chief counsel, David Addington, a longtime aide and an expert in intelligence and national security law (and Cheney's chief of staff after Libby's resignation in October 2005), told a friend at the time that he and Cheney were "merging"[2] the vice president's office with the president's into one "executive office." He saw to it that important national security documents, from intelligence reports to policy papers and even internal NSC staff memos, were routed directly to Cheney's office in the West Wing. Cheney received an intelligence briefing as early as 6:30 each morning and sat in on the president's daily briefing an hour later, often by secure video link when he was traveling. "He's a voracious consumer of intelligence," said an aide. "Sometimes he asks for raw intelligence to make his own judgment. He wants it all." As the VP's legal counsel, Addington sat in all White House meetings with the CIA and National Security Council.[3]

Cheney's calling card with President Bush was, of course, that he did not harbor any presidential ambitions—if only for reasons of health. He had suffered multiple heart attacks, did not exercise, and still struggled to control his weight. Cheney let his staff know that he was only interested in advising the president. He was not bent on glory or getting credit. The press was strictly out of bounds. "He also made it clear to us," said Eric Edelman, Cheney's respected deputy chief of staff, a career foreign service officer who had worked in the Clinton State Department, "that he did not want us talking to anybody about what his advice to the president was. He was going to give private advice, and he was not going to talk about it in the press."[4]

The vice president surrounded himself for the most part with a group of partisan conservatives, led by Edelman's boss and chief of staff, Lewis Libby, a disciplined and discreet lawyer who had worked for Cheney at the Pentagon and understood his penchant for operating behind the scenes without leaving footprints. "Like Cheney, Scooter's a tomb," said one former press aide. "Information can go in, but most of the time it doesn't come out."[5] The OVP staff got the message. With the exception of Libby, they were to steer clear of reporters. The obsession with secrecy extended throughout the expanded executive offices of the Bush White House. This preference for operating out of public view, so reflective of Cheney's own personal modus vivendi—aided by the fact that the vice president's office was and is not subject to federal freedom of information laws—guaranteed well into the president's second term that accounts of its inner workings and influence on other government agencies remained murky and fragmentary. It wasn't until Libby was indicted in October 2005 by a Washington grand jury on charges of perjury and obstruction of justice that the façade of executive secrecy and the aura of *omerta* around the vice president's office began to dissipate.

Libby doubled as Cheney's principal national security advisor. A graduate of Columbia Law School, he was a veteran of the foreign policy wars in several Republican administrations going back two decades. He wielded considerable power atop the OVP organizational chart. Libby reportedly handpicked the vice president's staff, which metamorphosed overnight from the Gore foreign policy staff of three, whose offices were in the nearby Old Executive Office Building, to a mini–National Security Council that numbered at any given time between fifteen and thirty-five people. After the 2004 elections, the entire vice presidential staff was estimated at fifty to sixty people, including a small phalanx of public relations advisers and special consultants.[6] Besides presiding over the vice president's expanded domain, Libby also carried a third title, assistant to the president, that gave him unprecedented access to White House meetings and sensitive internal communications, providing the leverage that enabled him to be an energetic advocate for Cheney in internecine battles with the CIA, the State Department, and the National Security Council on questions involving Iraq and its weapons arsenal. Like Cheney, Libby was a savvy operator, an impassioned proponent of regime change in Iraq, and a determined critic of the CIA.

From the outset, the vice presidential operation began laying the groundwork for taking the war on terror to Baghdad, paying special attention to intelligence about Saddam's arsenal of weaponry with the help of a network of ideological allies and loyalists dispersed in key positions throughout Washington. The vice president, Libby, and OVP staff quickly became notorious for elbowing aside normally powerful players in Washington's foreign policy community to get their way on the emerging Iraqi war policy. Among the vice president's earliest challenges was assessing how to respond to terrorist attacks against the United States,[7] a task that was immediately overwhelmed by Iraq and other vice presidential priorities until it was too late.

Shifting responsibility for oversight of the intelligence community to Cheney seemed a deft move by the president. Bush's inability to name the president of Pakistan, Gen. Pervez Musharraf, during a videotaped campaign stop the previous fall had become an embarrassing political liability. Bush had been sharply criticized during the presidential campaign for his lack of experience in foreign affairs, so entrusting the intelligence portfolio to the vice president was a candid and honest acknowledgment of his lack of expertise in that sensitive area. Musharraf, of course, would become a household name to both Bush and the country barely a year later when the Pakistani leader, a next-door neighbor to Afghanistan, became a critical U.S. ally in the war on terror.

By contrast to the president, the vice president's background in the arcane thickets of national security and intelligence was truly impressive. Cheney began his career in presidential politics as President Gerald Ford's deputy chief of staff and then chief of staff in the mid-1970s, when the U.S. spy community was turned upside down by the Church Committee investigations into CIA assassination attempts abroad and shaken up by the subsequent intelligence reforms. He had served as a member of the House Intelligence Committee during the 1980s as a young congressman from Wyoming. After working his way up to become the second-ranking Republican in the House of Representatives, he served as a wartime secretary of defense under President George H. W. Bush, presiding over the operational planning and execution of the 1991 Gulf War with Joints Chiefs of Staff Chairman Colin Powell and Gen. H. Norman Schwarzkopf. His long experience in intelligence oversight instilled in him a deep distrust of the CIA, which as far as he was concerned was only confirmed by the agency's failure to anticipate both Saddam Hussein's incursion into Kuwait in 1990 and the collapse of the Soviet Union a year later.

Cheney's long experience in intelligence and military affairs had a deeply conservative cast. The secretive, hard-edged style of the intelligence world seemed to get under his skin. While he was still Ford's deputy chief of staff under Rumsfeld (1974–75), Cheney earned a reputation as a behind-the-scenes operator with a taste for cloak-and-dagger intrigue and keeping his mouth shut. His anonymous manner and disregard for publicity was so marked that the Secret Service code-named him "Backseat." In May 1975, the thirty-four-year-old Cheney was asked by the White House to examine the fallout from a *New York Times* article by Seymour Hersh about secret U.S. efforts to raise a sunken Soviet submarine in the Pacific. His brief was to decide whether the story compromised national security and, if it did, whether the Ford administration should retaliate against *The Times*. Ford's young deputy chief of staff recommended that the government indict Hersh and obtain a warrant to search the reporter's apartment. That would "discourage the NYT and other publications from similar action," wrote Cheney in handwritten notes.[8] In the end, the issue was moot. Intelligence officials decided the *Times* story had not compromised U.S. security after all.

After he was elected to Congress in November 1978, Cheney's reputation for integrity and quiet discretion landed him a seat on the House Intelligence Committee, where he observed the secretive world of surveillance and spycraft up close for the next decade. During a heated 1988 debate, he strongly opposed legislation that would have required the White House to notify Congress of undercover intelligence operations within forty-eight hours of approving them. "On the scale of risks, there is more reason to be concerned about depriving the president of his ability to act than about Congress's alleged ability to respond," Cheney wrote in an op-ed piece at the time. The bill did not pass.[9]

Then, as now, Cheney argued against any limitations on the power of the president, especially in the realms of war-making, foreign policy, and intelligence, a cause he had championed since witnessing the humiliation of Richard Nixon during the Watergate scandal and the ridicule Ford endured afterward for being an intellectual lightweight. Cheney believed he had seen the crippling effects of the loss of power and respect for the office of the presidency in the Ford White House. Later as chief executive of Halliburton, he had also come to understand that it was far easier to conduct business behind closed doors than in the glare of publicity. "I believe in a strong, robust executive authority, and I think that the world we live in demands it," he told *U.S. News & World Report*. The president "needs to have his constitutional powers unimpaired."[10]

But the vice president's most unusual brush with top-secret government operations came during his years in Congress, when Cheney participated in highly classified "continuity of government" exercises conducted in the 1980s by the Reagan administration. The purpose of the multimillion-dollar annual program was to prepare for the aftermath of a Soviet nuclear attack that left top elected American leaders dead and the U.S. government "decapitated." Without warning, some thirty to forty government officials and ex-officials (including Rumsfeld, then a Chicago business executive) would be spirited away in the middle of the night to secret destinations around the country without a word to their families or professional colleagues. The exercises were conducted in strict secrecy. Participants were forbidden to tell even their spouses what they were doing.

With his background at the Ford White House and immersion in intelligence, Cheney concentrated on the chief of staff's role for the "new president," often a stand-in cabinet member. A specially fitted-out Boeing 747 was deployed that allowed the acting president to stay in the air for three days at a time with midair refuelings.[11] Cheney was tasked with the ultimate in reality games: sorting out exactly how to proceed if both the president and vice president were killed. His job was to get a legitimate government up and running as quickly and efficiently as possible, right down to how the new civilian leader would issue commands to the military and how the military would be able to recognize his legitimacy. Cheney's regular participation in the Armageddon-like exercises ended when he was appointed secretary of defense in 1989.

What may have seemed to some like an exercise in Cold War paranoia was a dry run for Cheney. During the 9/11 terrorist attacks, the vice president smoothly and presciently insisted that President Bush stay aloft aboard Air Force One and away from Washington. He unflinchingly ordered U.S. fighters to shoot down United Flight 93 when it seemed headed toward Washington, moments before it crashed in a Pennsylvania field. Watching the vice president review the options on a secure line with President Bush in Florida that morning, Lewis Libby was reminded of Winston Churchill's famous remark about taking office in World War II: "I felt as if I were walking with destiny, and that all my past life had been but a preparation for this hour and for this trial." Cheney, too, thought Libby, had been born for this moment and was playing out his destiny.[12]

For the first time in U.S. history, the Bush White House activated the rusty continuity-of-government plans on the day of the attacks, ferrying mid-level managers from cabinet departments and key government agencies to two undisclosed hardened locations on the East Coast. Again, Cheney played a key role. As fears mounted during the fall that the terrorists might detonate a nuclear device in the capital, the vice president himself stayed away from Washington, presumably at one of two hardened sites on the East Coast, to assure constitutional succession if anything happened to the president, and to oversee an emergency command structure that could manage civil disorder or disruptions of the nation's communications and transportation networks.[13]

Cheney was primed for the real thing by political inclination and extensive training. It was no wonder that after 9/11 Colin Powell and others described the vice president as a changed man whose behavior seemed "fevered"—he had lived with the idea of just such a potential national catastrophe for two decades. When Cheney had accepted the intelligence portfolio six months earlier, the vice president, the veteran war-gamer steeped in Reagan-era preparation for unspeakable national disasters, promptly appointed himself the "examiner of worst-case scenarios." He would look, he said, at "the darker side, the truly bad and terrifying scenarios" posed by terrorists who might possess biological, chemical, and even nuclear weapons. "He felt they had to be prepared to think the unthinkable," Bob Woodward wrote of the vice president.[14]

In the spring of 2001, the new vice president made the rounds of the major U.S. intelligence agencies—the CIA, the National Security Agency, the Defense Intelligence Agency—in an effort to catch up with developments he had missed during the eight years he had been out of government. In May 2001 the president announced publicly that Cheney would direct a government-wide review about how to manage the consequences of a terrorist attack in the United States. Instead, in the months that followed, Cheney was busy supporting Rumsfeld's campaign to build a missile defense system, helping the president negotiate new tax cuts, and working with oil and power company executives to forge a new Bush energy policy. Despite warnings about the coming terrorist threat from former Clinton administration officials and intelligence reports warning of attacks that summer, the vice president had not gotten around to the review when the American Airlines Flight 11 struck the North Tower of the World Trade Center.[15]

The events of September 11, 2001, and their possible connection with Iraq focused the vice president's mind on the shortcomings of the U.S. intelligence community. The Bush administration's primary intelligence problem was that Saddam had expelled UN arms inspectors in 1998—and with them, the CIA's primary sources on Iraq's WMD arsenal. In the intervening years, despite the fact that Iraq's early nuclear weapons program had been destroyed after its existence was revealed in hidden documents found in 1995, rumors swirled that the Baghdad regime had restarted WMD production and that the weapons could easily wind up in the hands of terrorists. Given the limited and outdated nature of what they knew, most CIA analysts were nonetheless skeptical about the rumored Iraqi nuclear, biological, and chemical programs. The CIA had been unable to detect Saddam's carefully hidden WMD programs a decade before, and Cheney and others firmly believed that Langley was still inclined to underestimate Saddam's weapons arsenal.

Cheney had seen weapons controversies before—and he knew how they had been surmounted. During his tenure as President Ford's chief of staff in 1976, the White House had approved a request by CIA director George H. W. Bush to establish a Team B panel to look into charges made by a group of conservatives, led by Albert Wohlstetter at the University of Chicago, that the CIA had systematically underestimated Soviet military strength, leaving the United States behind in the arms race. Team B, an assemblage of well-known conservatives, concluded that the Soviets had developed new superweapons and outstripped the United States in military superiority. The findings ultimately proved false, but not before Team B's widely publicized conclusions triggered a multi-billion-dollar U.S. arms buildup during the Reagan administration that many conservatives believed led to the collapse of the Soviet Union.[16]

Cheney knew there was a better way to get a fix on Iraq's weapons. Along with others in the Bush defense establishment, the vice president had met with Ahmed Chalabi years before. He knew that the clever and sophisticated Iraqi opposition leader was able and willing to provide intelligence from Iraqi defectors on Saddam's weapons programs and his links to Middle East terror groups. Chalabi's Iraqi National Congress was already under contract with the U.S. government to work inside Iraq to prepare the political opposition for Saddam's downfall. Chalabi even reportedly received a firm request by unnamed American officials to concentrate on hard "humint," or human intelligence, on Saddam's allegedly resurgent WMD programs.[17]

Cheney's disdain for the CIA, oddly enough, seemed to create a blind spot in his vision about the spy agency's special relationship with the White House. Ever since the CIA was founded in 1947, American presidents have enjoyed virtually absolute power over the priorities of the sixteen agencies that make up the U.S. intelligence community. A president's relationship with the director of central intelligence, or DCI, was critical. Whatever secret directives or covert programs were approved by the president or under discussion with the DCI—now the DNI, or director of national intelligence, under the 2004 Bush reforms—fell into a gray zone of presidential discretion that was not subject to normal checks or balances and was inaccessible to Congress and the public. In this zone, the exercise of presidential power was personal and secrecy was absolute. It was therefore axiomatic in the intelligence world that the director of U.S. intelligence served at the pleasure of the president alone, and in critical matters answered to him alone—not to the Congress, the vice president, or anyone else. Practically speaking, that assured that presidential secrets stayed secret.

Most important, it also meant that nothing of consequence happened in the world of U.S. intelligence without the president's knowledge and approval.[18] Under President Bush's intelligence arrangement with Cheney, that was no longer guaranteed. By sweeping away the old system, the inexperienced president may have gained "plausible deniability" politically—subordinates like the vice president could protect him by dropping him out of the intelligence loop when expedient—but he also needlessly complicated his own special relationship with the CIA and Director of Central Intelligence George Tenet. Worse, the president, by making Cheney responsible for intelligence, created two masters for government analysts and their bosses at the spy agencies, whose job was to provide the president and other policymakers with coldly objective, let-the-chips-fall-where-they-may intelligence products.

Despite President Bush's easygoing, collegial relationship with the CIA director, his decision put Tenet on a collision course with Cheney. The vice president believed that the Clinton national security team—including Tenet, a holdover who already had served as Bill Clinton's intelligence chief for three years—had badly mishandled successive terrorist attacks on U.S. civilian, military, and diplomatic targets. The Clinton White House, it was true, had failed to retaliate against a series of terror bombings in the 1990s, including the 1993 World Trade Center bombing, the 1996 firebombing of U.S. troop quarters at Khobar Towers in Saudi Arabia, the coordinated U.S. embassy bombings in Dar es Salaam and Nairobi in 1998, and the suicide bombing of the USS. *Cole* in Yemen in 2000. Led by Tenet, the CIA had mounted an unsuccessful Predator strike on Osama bin Laden at al-Qaeda training camps in Afghanistan in June 1999. But that was seen by many Americans as little more than a wag-the-dog distraction from Clinton's impeachment trial in Washington. The vice president's facts were correct: Washington had failed to respond with a show of military strength to the increasing threat posed by bin Laden and al-Qaeda on Tenet's watch.

Cheney also wanted other fundamental changes at the CIA that would sooner or later put the White House and Tenet at loggerheads. After 9/11 the vice president wanted changes in how the CIA and other agencies gathered and analyzed intelligence. He felt "the standard of proof would have to be lowered" for evidence of gathering terrorist threats. The United States, he said, could no longer wait for irrefutable "smoking gun" intelligence to defend itself from terrorist attacks. Cheney declared that "the most serious threat now facing the United States was a nuclear weapon or a biological or chemical agent in the hands of a terrorist"—and the Bush administration had to go on the offensive to stop it.[19] There would be times, Cheney said in a November 2001 meeting with Tenet about unconfirmed reports that al-Qaeda might be acquiring nuclear weapons, that

U.S. decisions would not be "about our analysis, or finding a preponderance of evidence. It's about our response."[20]

In other words, if the stakes were high enough, evidence wouldn't matter—the United States would act anyway. Cheney's prescriptions not only posed direct and even subversive challenges to business-as-usual at the CIA; they also undermined Tenet's ability to operate effectively as an honest broker of intelligence for the president. By then, Tenet had figured out that Cheney was running U.S. foreign policy from the White House—and would call future shots on Saddam's WMD. President Bush's delegation of authority to Cheney had set in motion forces that would mercilessly whipsaw the CIA and other intelligence agencies during the run-up to the war and long afterward.

Bush completed his transfer of presidential powers to Cheney by quietly issuing Executive Order 13292 in March 2003, just as the war in Iraq began—and just before the White House was publicly accused for the first time of exaggerating intelligence on Iraq's weapons arsenal. Bush's directive gave the vice president the legal right to classify and declassify top-secret intelligence at his own discretion, a power until then wielded solely by the president and the DCI. In so doing, President Bush gave Cheney's operation unprecedented influence over national security policy[21]—and a potent tool for fending off unwanted public queries by refusing to answer questions or produce evidence about classified information.

Lewis Libby first caught Cheney's eye during the first Bush presidency in the early 1990s, when Libby presided over the drafting of a key defense planning document at the Pentagon that dramatically redefined the U.S. role as the world's sole superpower after the fall of the Soviet Union. At once a coolly restrained, impeccably tailored Washington lawyer and a spirited intellectual with an exotic novel about turn-of-the-century Japan under his belt, Libby was never far from the wholesale rethinking of American foreign policy undertaken by successive Republican administrations over two decades that finally crystallized in the Bush administration after the terrorist attacks. A militant neoconservative ideologue, Libby was described as "Cheney's Cheney," by a former aide, prepared by temperament and training to work far from the Washington limelight to implement the vice president's agenda. "What animates him is security," said Mary Matalin, a former OVP communications consultant. "On 9/12, there were but a handful of people who had the strategic grasp of terrorism that he did." Said Libby's former deputy, Dean

McGrath, "Scooter considered it to be part of his job to think about dire possibilities.[22]

Few were as instrumental as Libby in getting the vice president's war policies enacted. Unlike Cheney, he was often seen at social gatherings and could be a charming and impassioned dinner companion and conversationalist. Libby aggressively courted selected members of the Washington media—but rarely gave up anything beyond the administration's talking points. Along with Karl Rove, the president's chief political strategist, Libby quickly gained a reputation as one of the most powerful senior aides in Washington. He often met the vice president first thing in the morning at Cheney's official residence at the U.S. Naval Observatory and rode with him in the vice president's limousine to the White House. The two men were so close that Libby often anticipated the vice president's thoughts and took the initiative before Cheney gave the order. The relationship gave Libby not only extraordinary power over the vice president's office, but also a place in the inner circles of White House decision-making.

Born Irve Lewis Libby in New Haven in 1950, he was nicknamed "Scooter" by his father, an investment banker, who noticed that his infant son crawled, or scooted, with uncommon speed. Libby later changed this story, claiming that he was compared as a child to star New York Yankees shortshop Phil "Scooter" Rizzuto, and the nickname stuck. "I had the range but not the arm," he quipped.[23]

His family moved to Florida, where Libby reportedly spent his boyhood years before returning to New England to attend the Eaglebrook School, a private middle school in Deerfield, Massachusetts. Eaglebrook is perched on a hillside overlooking the Deerfield River valley and boasts its own ski area, which must have pleased the physically small but athletic youth who would become an avid downhill skier. From Eaglebrook, Libby entered the elite Phillips Academy Andover, where he graduated in 1968 after gaining admittance to Yale University. Like many young idealists who later became neoconservatives, Libby was a Democrat as an undergraduate who opposed the war in Vietnam and rose to become vice president of the campus Democrats.[24] Friends remember him with shoulder-length blond hair helping to silkscreen T-shirts proclaiming solidarity between Yale students and the Black Panthers. He knew all the *Star Trek* episodes by heart. "I think he always liked fantasy," recalled a friend.[25]

While at Yale, Libby came under the wing of Paul Wolfowitz, then a young professor of political science, who later went to work for the Reagan State Department as a policy planner. After graduating from Yale and receiving his law degree at Columbia, Libby was hired away from private practice in Philadelphia to work for the Reagan administration as a member of Wolfowitz's staff in 1981. Much of Libby's subsequent hands-on political education was spent as a protégé of Wolfowitz. The young lawyer seemed to relish sharpening his verbal skills in internal government policy debates. In 1982, Libby followed Wolfowitz to the Bureau of East Asian and Pacific Affairs, where he gained an expertise in that tumultuous region. When Wolfowitz was made undersecretary of defense for policy by President George H. W. Bush in 1989, he again hired the thirty-nine-year old Libby, this time as his senior aide, and assigned him to review U.S. defense policy toward the Soviet Union and its reform-minded leader, Mikhail Gorbachev—an assignment that would lead two years later to a prominent role in the wholesale reassessment of U.S. defense policy.

Early in the first year of President George H. W. Bush's administration, Libby and a colleague recommended a cautious approach to Moscow, since real political change in the Kremlin was still uncertain. But by the fall, the signals of change from the Gorbachev regime were loud and clear. Wolfowitz ordered his policy planners to review U.S. policy in the Persian Gulf, not so much to defend against Soviet incursions, but to protect the region and its oil from an aggressive regional power, such as Saddam Hussein's Iraq. Libby's boss had special reason for focusing on Iraq. A decade earlier, while working for the Carter administration, Wolfowitz had authored a prescient contingency study for the Pentagon that concluded Iraq might use military force against Kuwait or Saudi Arabia to secure their oil fields—and recommended for the first time that U.S. military force in the region might be necessary to deter such an Iraqi move.

Wolfowitz's review took on a new urgency when Iraq invaded Kuwait in July 1990. President Bush quickly made his famous declaration that the Iraqi invasion "will not stand." As Wolfowitz's top aide, Libby was quickly caught up in the extraordinary maneuvering at the Pentagon that accompanied the declaration of war. Despite the outward signs of amity between Powell, then chairman of the joints chiefs of staff, and Secretary of Defense Cheney, a fault line developed between the two men almost immediately, which would resurface again between the two in councils of war before the 2003 invasion of Iraq. Powell had apparently put off the secretary of defense by arguing that Iraq might be contained without going to war, which suggested to Cheney that the joint chiefs chairman was approaching a U.S. military effort against Saddam with undue caution.

While Powell and Gen. Norman Schwarzkopf cast about for a war plan, Cheney quietly ordered Wolfowitz and Libby to form a secret group to explore the idea of an invasion of Iraq from the western desert regions. Dubbed Operation Scorpion, the plan was the work of a conservative scholar on leave from the Stanford Business School, Henry Rowen, who was then consulting for Wolfowitz at the Defense Department, and was designed in part to protect Israel from Iraqi Scud missile attacks launched from hidden desert bases. Cheney presented Operation Scorpion to the White House while the two top U.S. generals were away in Saudi Arabia.[26]

Schwarzkopf hit the roof when he found out about Cheney's gambit, and angrily dismissed the invasion plan as a classic case of Pentagon civilian wannabes playacting as the brass, noting pointedly that it would have been impossible to resupply U.S. forces hundreds of miles across the desert from the nearest friendly bases. President Bush, to his credit, was unmoved by Powell's containment arguments and dismissed Cheney's plan as too risky. The White House was worried that Operation Scorpion would have raised the possibility of a U.S. attack on Baghdad and would have alarmed two principal coalition partners, Saudi Arabia and Turkey.

During the planning for the 1991 conflict, Libby steeped himself in the nuances of biological warfare and what was known about Iraq's arsenal of biological weapons, which Saddam had deployed in the Iran-Iraq War to devastating effect. In attempting to organize U.S. defenses against germ warfare, he was struck by the ambiguity and uncertainty of U.S. intelligence reports on the subject, and dispatched his senior aides to talk to scientists who had worked on U.S. biological weapons. He quickly discovered that Baghdad had just purchased forty Italian aerosol generators that could be mounted on trucks, boats, or small aircraft and, under favorable conditions, could deliver enough anthrax to kill thousands of soldiers. Libby's conclusion was that a well-mounted biological attack could be every bit as lethal as a nuclear attack. He also reported up the chain of command that a biological agent like weaponized anthrax could be even deadlier in the hands of terrorists intent on wreaking havoc in the United States. In the end, the Iraqi army was easily overrun and never deployed any biological or chemical weapons. But Libby absorbed a lesson about the dangers of Saddam's WMD capability that he would not soon forget.

After the Gulf War, the collapse of the Soviet Union and the Soviet Communist party in late 1991 forced a shift of priorities in Wolfowitz's policy shop at the Pentagon. In Congress there was suddenly excited talk of a so-called peace dividend—federal funds that Congress could divert from the military budget to domestic programs. The idea rattled defense-minded conservatives, who quickly recognized the implicit challenge to

American military superiority—and the Pentagon budget. Powell himself declared that since Moscow no longer presented a military threat, U.S. policymakers had to assume that the United States was now the lone superpower in the world. "We are the major player on the world stage with responsibilities around the world, with interests around the world," he told *The Washington Post*. Wolfowitz now ordered Libby, his top aide, to oversee the 1992 biennial *Defense Planning Guidance* report, the first since the fall of the Soviet empire. Libby in turn assigned Zalmay Khalilzad, a trusted staff member, to research and write the document.

Khalilzad invited prominent Defense Department officials and conservative intellectuals, including Richard Perle, to contribute ideas. By March he had finished the draft of the document and asked Libby for permission to circulate it internally at the Pentagon. Within days it leaked to *The New York Times*. Khalilzad had written a neoconservative tract calling for the United States to be "the predominant outside power" in the Middle East and Southwest Asia in order to "preserve U.S. and Western access to the region's oil." The United States should be prepared, wrote Khalilzad, to "prevent any hostile power" from amassing enough strength and resources to "generate global power." The United States, the draft document declared in a much-noted passage, should make it its business to block the emergence of any potential rival by economic and diplomatic means, but primarily by maintaining unassailable military superiority. A firestorm of criticism ensued, charging that Pentagon officials were looking for an "excuse" for undiminished military budgets. The prospect of a newly aggressive Washington holding its economic and military partners hostage to the new policy of operating as an unrivaled superpower did not play well in Japan, West Germany, or other foreign capitals. Cheney loved it. "You've discovered a new rationale for our role in the world," he gushed to Khalilzad.

The Bush White House backed away from the report. Libby, who said he hadn't read the draft before it leaked, felt Khalilzad at once had been too provocative and hadn't gone far enough.[27] He took it upon himself to rewrite the document. Libby's final version was not as confrontational as Khalilzad's, but it still warned that the United States should be aware of the emergence of regional powers in areas where Washington had strategic interests. Libby did not trumpet the importance of maintaining U.S. military superiority, but emphasized preserving what he termed the nation's "strategic depth" and its ability to shape "the future security environment," presumably by preventing threats from emerging powers. Libby was careful to reassure America's allies that it would continue to rely on diplomacy and collective security agreements. But when allied action was complicated by "sluggish or inadequate" international responses, the United States, he said, should reserve the right to respond to military threats unilaterally.

Libby's finished *Defense Planning Guidance* document provided a philosophical template for the U.S.-led invasion of Iraq eleven years later. But it was more than that. As secretary of defense, Cheney threw his weight behind the revised document and took credit for the historic reassessment of U.S. defense policy that Libby had engineered on his watch. Cheney also made sure that the general reassessment section of the *Defense Planning Guidance* report was declassified and made public by the time Bush left office in January 1993.[28] Even the incoming Clinton administration followed its principal tenets in the course of military actions over the next eight years in Somalia, Bosnia, and Kosovo, projecting overwhelming U.S. military power, on occasion without allied or UN support, in missions intended to stabilize critical regions to protect U.S. interests. The Democratic version of the new U.S. role in the world as the lone superpower probably relied more on economic components like globalization and open markets than the Republican variant, with its greater emphasis on military force alone. But the concept developed by Libby and Khalilzad in 1992 proved an influential and lasting redefinition of post–Cold War American power that received broad bipartisan support in Congress.

When President George H. W. Bush was defeated by Clinton in 1992, Libby returned to his lucrative law practice at the Washington office of Dechert, Price & Rhoads, specializing in litigation for major corporate clients such as Fiat, NBC, and UPS. Leonard Garment, Richard Nixon's lawyer and an influential Washington lawyer, was a close friend. Earning fees in excess of five hundred dollars an hour, for years Libby represented Marc Rich, the wealthy fugitive commodities trader who was eventually granted a controversial pardon by President Clinton. The Rich account alone was reportedly worth $2 million in fees, but Libby claimed no credit for securing the pardon.

Libby published his novel, *The Apprentice*, in 1996, more than twenty years after he had started it as a student. He said he once threw out three hundred pages of manuscript after deciding to change the setting of the story from Vermont to rural Japan, circa 1903. Libby himself described the novel—the story of a young innkeeper named Setsuo, who finds himself with a house full of guests, including a beautiful musician, during a blizzard while war with Russia threatens and a smallpox epidemic is raging—as "part mystery, part love story, part coming-of-age story." Some critics, noting the explicit and homoerotic sex scenes, dismissed it as pornography. But *The Washington Post* called it "strikingly original. A small triumph of meticulous craftsmanship," and *The Boston Globe* praised it as "an alluring novel of intrigue." In a brief interview with Larry King to talk about the book, which had just been reissued in paperback, King remarked to Libby that it sounded like a movie. Libby shot back, "Well, you know, say it louder."[29]

Libby the novelist was part of a less conventional, more enigmatic persona that friends say Libby cultivated. He told King that to write the book, he just "went out to Colorado, drank tequila and wrote"—a devil-may-care characterization that was a far cry from the "excruciatingly careful" Washington lawyer with a reputation for courtliness and prudence. The *Times'* Judith Miller, who had known Libby well before 2001, saw this side of Libby when she was once approached by a person she took to be a stranger in Jackson Hole, Wyoming, after a conference. "At a rodeo one afternoon, a man in jeans, a cowboy hat and sunglasses approached me," she later wrote. "He asked me how the Aspen conference had gone. I had no idea who he was." The cowboy turned out to be Libby.[30] Even at home in McLean, Virginia, where he lives with his two children and wife Harriet Grant, a former lawyer on the Democratic staff of the Senate Judiciary Committee, the buttoned-down and graying Libby reveled in weekly touch football games and his reputation as a daredevil skier.

Libby's appointment as chief of staff to the vice president in 2000 was part of an intricate series of chesslike moves orchestrated by Cheney that strategically placed seasoned policymakers with strong ties to the vice president, Rumsfeld, and Wolfowitz in key positions throughout the government. Khalilzad, who was close to Wolfowitz and Libby, was dispatched to the National Security Council, where he was placed in charge of Afghan and Iraq policy. Stephen J. Hadley, another former Wolfowitz aide, became Condoleezza Rice's deputy at the National Security Council. Wolfowitz himself, who lobbied to be appointed deputy secretary of state, was instead made deputy secretary of defense at the Pentagon under Rumsfeld, leaving the deputy secretary's slot at State open.

There were other lesser players in the network, all of whom would play key roles in the protracted run-up to war. Douglas Feith, a former Wolfowitz protégé at the Pentagon and hardline neoconservative intellectual, was appointed deputy assistant secretary of defense for policy under

Wolfowitz. Feith set up the Pentagon's Counterterrorism Evaluation Group, charged with establishing links between Saddam and al-Qaeda, and later the Office of Special Plans, which became a conduit for intelligence from Chalabi's Iraqi National Congress and eventually the center of post-combat occupation planning for Iraq. John Hannah, another staunch neoconservative, came to the OVP from the Washington Institute for Near East Policy, a think tank associated with the powerful pro-Israeli lobbying group the American-Israel Public Affairs Committee, or AIPAC. Hannah took a strong hand in tailoring U.S. Mideast policy to the hardline policies of former Israeli prime minister Ariel Sharon and his successor, Ehud Olmert. Hannah also served as Cheney's liaison with Chalabi, brokering intelligence reports on Saddam's weapons programs supplied by the Iraqi National Congress.

Robert Joseph was the pro-war head of Rice's nonproliferation office at the NSC, and Elliot Abrams, a sharp-elbowed veteran of the Reagan administration, ran the NSC Middle East desk. John Bolton, the undersecretary for arms control at the State Department, strongly backed the war in Iraq and later became the controversial U.S. ambassador to the United Nations (2005–6). Former navy captain William Luti, a top Cheney White House aide in 2001, moved over to the Pentagon in the summer of 2002 to run the Middle Eastern desk associated with the Office of Special Plans. Luti reportedly was in the habit of motivating his Pentagon staff by telling them he had to "get back to Scooter" at the White House. David Wurmser, an unabashedly pro-Israeli, virulently anti-Iranian veteran of the Washington Institute, was an analyst for Feith's Counter Terrorism Evaluation Group, who worked with Libby, Hannah, and a Pentagon official named Harold Rhode looking out after Chalabi and investigating Saddam's alleged links with al-Qaeda and 9/11. Wurmser later joined Vice President Cheney's staff.

Cheney's intricate maneuvering achieved another important, if littlenoticed, objective. Richard Armitage, the beefy former special operations commando in Vietnam who was a close personal friend of Colin Powell, had angled for a high-level appointment at the Pentagon—he had served in the first Bush administration as deputy secretary of defense under Cheney. But the vice president was reluctant to provide the immensely popular Powell with an ally high in the Pentagon, and recommended Powell's old comrade-in-arms Armitage for deputy secretary of state. On the surface, it was an inspired move, forging a new diplomatic team at State with deep military experience. But Armitage's appointment denied Powell a listening post and an influential ally at the Defense Department. Secretary of State

Powell was effectively isolated with his closest friend and aide at Foggy Bottom. His clout in future administration battles over foreign policy would be checked by Rumsfeld's influence at the Pentagon. Cheney saw to it that Powell would not have the reach within the government to dominate foreign policy, or emerge as a rival to the president. Rumsfeld's legendary skills as a bureaucratic infighter would take care of the rest.

3

MASTERS OF THE UNIVERSE

Libby had taken a rarified, intellectual path to the upper echelons of power. He and his staff in the Office of the Vice President were seasoned policy wonks, well placed to represent the powerful currents of neoconservative thought within the administration that favored military action in Iraq and animated Libby's national security and intelligence operations. Libby was the counterpart on the policy side of the president's senior political adviser, Karl Rove, who would be thrown together with the vice president's chief of staff in coming controversies over Saddam's elusive WMD and President Bush's war policies. Like Rove, Libby enjoyed a reputation for a razor-sharp intelligence, a canny instinct for bureaucratic maneuvering, and an impassioned sense of ideological certainty. Libby and the OVP quickly became notorious within the foreign policy community for their cocksure, ruthless tactics in policy meetings—running roughshod over career bureaucrats at the State Department, the CIA, and the National Security Council who did not share their war planning agenda—and for their close alliance with Rumsfeld's Pentagon.

In sharp contrast to Libby, Rove came up through the rough-and-tumble of Texas oil-patch politics. While Libby and others hammered out the intellectual framework of Bush's war policies, Rove worked the tougher political side of the street, channeling the war on terror into a formidable political juggernaut. With Libby, he was a member of the White House Iraq Group (WHIG), a collection of senior officials charged with selling the war to Congress and the public. Rove brought a swashbuckling legacy of down-home Texas political legerdemain and wizardry to the task, hatching a masterful plan to exploit the 9/11 terror attacks and the military campaign against the Taliban and al-Qaeda in Afghanistan to secure a Republican supermajority for the president's future antiterrorism initiatives. Those who knew Rove best were not surprised that he later wriggled out of a much-rumored indictment in the CIA leak case. He had eluded prosecution or even censure in similarly tight spots for years.

Rove was and is a meticulous political strategist with vast stores of political data packed in his head and a ruthless campaign operative who had never met an opposing candidate or political enemy he was not willing to savage personally. When things began to go sour for the White House after the Iraq invasion and former ambassador Joseph Wilson publicly questioned President Bush's statements on Saddam's nuclear weapons program, it was no surprise that Rove and Libby were in charge of finding a way to defuse the political crisis that followed. "No one would have dared to leak information on a CIA agent without getting Karl Rove to check the 'yes' box on the plan," wrote two Texas newsmen and veteran Rove-watchers, James Moore and Wayne Slater. "To believe that Rove was oblivious to what happened requires complete abandonment of any knowledge of his past behavior."[1]

The neoconservative push for the Iraq war, with its philosophical underpinnings of American exceptionalism and unrivaled U.S. military might, combined with bare-knuckle Texas power politics, made for a heady brew. The volatile alchemy seemed to imbue senior White House officials with an arrogance that rivaled, and perhaps fed on, the born-again president's messianic belief that he was destined by "a higher father" to avenge the trauma of 9/11 and spread the gospel of U.S. democracy to the Islamic world. Both Libby and Rove had gained the upper reaches of power and become masters of the political universe. Each was also in his own way deeply engaged in crafting the White House's public deceptions about Iraq's WMD. Libby and Rove would be forever linked as the two primary suspects in the two-year criminal investigation of senior officials at the White House for leaking the name of covert CIA agent Valerie Plame Wilson to discredit her husband, former U.S. ambassador Joseph Wilson.

Libby's indictment on five counts of perjury and obstruction of justice in late October 2005 would be a devastating blow to Vice President Cheney and the public stature of the Bush administration. Until the summer of 2006, when Rove was finally informed that he had escaped criminal indictment, the president's distracted deputy chief of staff was forced to make five separate appearances before the grand jury to explain his actions and endured constant speculation about his guilt in the press. In the process, the president's popularity polls bottomed out at levels not seen since the administration of Warren G. Harding.

The standard OVP operating procedure under Libby began to reveal itself in the weeks after 9/11 with complaints about the strong-arm tactics employed by the vice president's staff, which one writer compared to "disciplined Bolsheviks slicing through a fractious opposition." It was Libby's habit to sit quietly in meetings, his eyes locked on whoever was speaking, his fingers pressed against his lips. "He sits there in the background with this little half-smile," said former senator Alan Simpson of Wyoming, a close friend of Cheney. "He's a dissector. He is the ultimate, clinical professional."[2] Libby's staff followed his lead. With their goals generally well articulated in advance, the disciplined vice presidential staff enjoyed a great advantage over the sprawling government departments and agencies that depended upon internal debate to hammer out policy. They "didn't key anything up that wasn't what the vice president wanted," observed Lawrence Wilkerson, Colin Powell's top aide at the State Department. "Their style was simply to sit and listen, and take notes. And if things looked like they were going to go speedily to a decision that they knew that the vice president wasn't going to like, generally they would, at the end of the meeting, in great bureaucratic style, they'd say: 'We totally disagree. Meeting's over.'"[3]

Dean McGrath, whom Libby had known from the 1998 Cox Committee investigation and hired as his deputy chief of staff, knew the importance of hand-to-hand combat with the bureaucracy—and the value of strategically invoking the vice president with political opponents. "I tried to convey at meetings where he would come down on issues," said McGrath. "Often you'd have the permanent bureaucracy that was not on board, especially on all of the issues where you're trying to change things."[4]

The Office of the Vice President was obsessed with secrecy. It was equipped with oversize Mosler safes to protect office paperwork and is believed to have coined the term "Treated As: Top Secret/SCI"—for "sensitive compartmented information," usually a reference to the most closely held state secrets—as a security designation for such standard items as talking points for reporters. The OVP, which Cheney declared was not part of the executive or judicial branches of government and not bound by the rules of either, does not publish a public calendar and has ordered the Service Service to destroy Cheney's visitor logs. Since the OVP outranked other offices, senior staffers regularly deployed secrecy and deception to bypass other potentially troublesome government agencies and departments on important policy matters.[5] The vice president's staff didn't hesitate to press their advantage by monitoring the NSC's e-mail to eavesdrop on internal memos, which quickly forced NSC staff to find other means of communication to skirt unwanted OVP meddling. But in policy battles, the odds always seemed to favor the vice president's people. As former Bush State Department official Richard Haass put it, the OVP got at least "three bites of the apple."[6] If a proposal Cheney didn't like made it through committee meetings at the staff level, he or Libby could make a run at it in deputy-level meetings at the White House or the NSC. Failing that, Cheney could press his views directly in meetings with top officials like Rice, Tenet, or Powell. If the politically unpalatable proposal was still alive, Cheney simply walked into the Oval Office and made his case privately with the president. More often than not, he prevailed.

"There's no way in which he is not driving the train on this," said one Cheney adviser about the vice president's role in shaping Iraq war policy. "Analysis, advocacy—it's all done by Cheney or his protégés . . . It's about context. It's reflective not so much of Cheney's direct influence on the president as it is of his influence on—his dominance of—the decision-making process. It's about providing the facts and analysis to the decision maker that the decision maker needs. Bush is making the decision, but the Veep is directing the process toward the decision that he thinks is the right one."[7]

"There were several remarkable things about the vice president's staff," said Wilkerson. "One was how empowered they were, and one was how in sync they were. . . . They were going to win nine out of ten battles, because they are ruthless, because they have a strategy, and because they never, ever deviate from that strategy. . . . They make a decision, and they make it in secret, and they make in a different way than the rest of the bureaucracy makes it, and then suddenly foist it on the government."[8] The result was often confusion among out-of-the-loop government officials who would eventually have to implement White House policies, but who had little idea how those policies were arrived at, since they were left out of the decision-making process.

Next to Libby, David Addington and John Hannah, both militantly neoconservative and Cheney loyalists, were among the most influential

OVP officials. At age forty-six, Addington had worked with Cheney since the early 1980s, when he served in a succession of jobs as counsel for the CIA, the Iran-Contra committee, and the House Intelligence Committee. As a lawyer, he was widely considered an expert in intelligence and national security. When Cheney was defense secretary during the first Bush administration, he hired Addington as a special assistant and in short order promoted him to Defense Department general counsel. In the early 1990s, when Cheney was considering a run at the presidency, he brought in Addington to run his political action committee.

Addington's father was an army brigadier general who with his wife, Eleanore, raised his oldest son and two daughters in the suburbs of Washington. After high school, Addington attended the U.S. Naval Academy, but dropped out after a year. He quickly found his bearings and graduated from Georgetown and then Duke Law School. Like Cheney and Libby, he never joined the military.

Addington was behind the Bush White House's early efforts to expand the president's powers by chipping away at the prerogatives of Congress and the courts. With the aid of Justice Department lawyers and Attorney General John Ashcroft, he was instrumental in producing the Patriot Act, the controversial legislation rubber-stamped by Congress after 9/11 that streamlined the hunt for terrorists by curbing civil liberties and restructuring the FBI's traditional crime-fighting responsibilities. With lawyers from the White House counsel's office, he wrote counterterrorism policies creating military commissions that favored incarceration without due process and torturing captured terrorists. His handiwork fostered the legal climate for the Abu Ghraib and Guantánamo prison scandals, as well as laid the foundation for the warrantless surveillance of U.S. citizens that wouldn't become public knowledge for another three years. Addington, observed Jane Harman of California, at the time the ranking Democrat on the House Intelligence Committee, "believes that in time of war, there is total authority for the president to waive any rules to carry out his objectives. Those views have extremely dangerous implications."[9]

John Hannah was the vice president's top policy expert on the Middle East and handled intelligence reports on Iraqi weapons from Chalabi and the Iraqi National Congress sent directly to the OVP from Douglas Feith's office at the Pentagon. Using much of that intelligence, Hannah and Libby reportedly wrote many of the increasingly alarmist, inflammatory speeches given by both Cheney and the president in the second half of 2002 about Iraq's WMD and its reconstituted nuclear capabilities— virtually all of which later proved groundless. Hannah and Libby were deeply involved in developing and circulating intelligence, much of it contradicting the conclusions of the CIA and other government agencies—almost all later repudiated—that was designed to bolster efforts by the White House to sell the Iraq war to Congress, the UN Security Council, and the American people. After Libby's indictment and forced retirement in October 2005, Hannah took over as Cheney's national security adviser, while Addington stepped in as chief of staff.

Projects directed by top OVP officials like Libby, Hannah, and Addington were staffed by a group of smart and aggressive policy experts who represented a spectrum of experience. One young Asia specialist named Samantha Ravitch proved surprisingly effective, commanding the attention of both government bureaucratic rivals and Iraqi opposition leaders. Chalabi and his people "would run to Samantha when there were disagreements," reported David Phillips, a State Department consultant during the prewar period. "They would hold forth on their ties to the OVP as a form of threat over U.S. officials or other Iraqis. And U.S. officials felt that if there was a misstep, the Iraqis would go running to the OVP and they would have their chains yanked."[10]

"Vice President Cheney's role was kind of fundamentally shaped by 9/11 when a new enemy was upon us, and he went at it with a vengeance . . ." remarked Colin Powell later with considerable understatement.[11] The first casualty of the vice president's expanded responsibilities was National Security Advisor Condoleezza Rice, whose job was traditionally to mediate the conflicting views of cabinet officials like Powell and Rumsfeld. After 9/11 Bush turned away from the formality of the NSC and to his more exclusive "war cabinet" for guidance. The principals committee of the NSC continued to meet, with Vice President Cheney in attendance as "a really wonderfully wise voice," as Rice put it. Cheney was seen by others "as an 800-pound gorilla whose views carry much more weight than the others', and which skews discussions and quashes open dissent . . ."[12] Preoccupied with her own private role as President Bush's friend and personal foreign policy tutor, Rice was unable to mediate the mounting conflicts between the State Department and the Pentagon over the war on terror. "The guys in this administration are old hands, experienced players, and you can't leave them to their own devices, or they will eat your lunch," explained an administration official later.[13]

Rumsfeld wasted no time exploiting the NSC's weakness. Rice's staff at one point produced a memo on postwar troop strength in Iraq concluding that a force of some 500,000 would be needed to secure the country. The NSC estimate was based on the size of previous peacekeeping missions in relation to the size of the populations where they were deployed, and in line with other proposals from the State Department and the military, most notably the controversial suggestion by Gen. Eric Shinseki for "several hundred thousand" troops that brought about his early retirement. Rumsfeld ignored Rice and the NSC memo. "She's going to be crushed," said one Rumsfeld ally. "It's as simple as that."[14]

Cheney was prepared to step into the vacuum he had created by marginalizing Rice, but hardly to serve as a surrogate policy broker himself. The vice president had his own agenda, and Rumsfeld's views began to weigh more and more heavily on White House decisions. Rumsfeld's appointment as secretary of defense was perhaps the most important nomination Cheney had championed during the transition. The relationship between the two men was complicated. Like many senior Republican officials, Cheney admired the man that Henry Kissinger once called the most ruthless man in Washington. Rumsfeld worked very hard, was extremely intelligent and self-confident, and, like Cheney, was exceptionally skilled at manipulating both allies and enemies alike to get what he wanted.

Their professional relationship went back more than three decades, and although Cheney obviously outranked the secretary of defense—a job that the vice president himself once held—Rumsfeld had been Cheney's first boss in Washington during the Nixon years. There was evidence that the psychic imprint still lingered. On occasions the two were together, friends reported it was difficult to figure out who worked for whom. "When I look at Don Rumsfeld, I see a fine secretary of defense," Cheney would reportedly joke. "When Rumsfeld looks at me, he sees a former assistant to Don Rumsfeld."[15]

Rumsfeld made it clear early in his tenure at the Pentagon, correctly, that the chain of command above him ran directly to the president. But he seemed to make an exception for Cheney, accepting without complaint the deep involvement of the vice president's office in Pentagon affairs during the planning for the Iraq war. His newfound public popularity as administration spokesman during the war in Afghanistan—a grandfather of five, Rumsfeld was named one of the sexiest men alive in 2002 by *People* magazine—inevitably elicited speculation that the man the president called "Rumstud" was the most powerful secretary of defense since Robert McNamara.[16]

Yet things did not always go Rumsfeld's way, especially in Afghanistan. Days after 9/11, George Tenet produced a thick packet at Camp David, laying out the options for CIA-led covert operations in Afghanistan and around the world to bring the terrorists to heel. Drawing on years of CIA experience in Afghanistan, Tenet recommended inserting CIA paramilitary units to fund and strengthen the Northern Alliance to take on the Taliban, then bringing in the U.S. military and Special Forces to clean out al-Qaeda. He also asked that the CIA be allowed to use any means at its disposal to accomplish its aims. Tenet drove home the point by bringing in the theatrical Cofer Black, a veteran CIA agent who ran the agency's Counterterrorism Center. "When we're through with them," Black told Bush and other senior officials, "they will have flies walking across their eyeballs."

Rumsfeld recognized he was in a bind. "We had no plan," said Lt. Gen. Mike DeLong, Gen. Tommy Franks's deputy at Central Command. "There was none for Afghanistan."[17] Worse, the CIA was proposing a light mobile force of just the sort Rumsfeld hoped to field with his military transformation plans. Bush sent in the small CIA paramilitary force at the end of September. The Pentagon was suddenly playing second fiddle to Tenet and the CIA—and Rumsfeld and Cheney were not happy about it.

Rumsfeld was notorious for bypassing the interagency decision-making process, using a range of tactics to get his policies rubber-stamped by the White House without having to go to the service chiefs or other agencies. On numerous occasions, the secretary of defense bull-dozed his way through the bureaucracy, going directly to Cheney or Bush to get what he wanted, then giving orders to department or agency officials involved, who had no idea what he was talking about. This time, the CIA teams had completed the covert part of the Northern Alliance operation in short order—and then waited for the airlifts of U.S. troops. Nothing happened. The CIA units waited almost a month without support in the Panjshir Valley as the Afghan winter began to close in.

Finally, during an explosive NSC meeting in October, the CIA accused Rumsfeld of withholding the U.S. forces and refusing to follow the CIA's lead. "Rumsfeld went to the president and said, 'The CIA has to work for me, or this isn't going to work,' " DeLong said later.[18] The president put Rumsfeld in charge and U.S. forces began arriving in Afghanistan on October 19. Kabul fell a month later. Gary Schroen, the fifty-seven-year-old CIA veteran who led the CIA's stunning Afghan ground operation, reckoned the city would have fallen a month earlier if Rumsfeld had released U.S. troops as planned.

Repeated instances of such heavy-handed and counterproductive interference by the Office of the Secretary of Defense, or OSD, led to bitter criticism of Rumsfeld—and no doubt gave Cheney the upper hand in the relationship with his old friend. "You just can't run a system like that and expect it to work," said a former official. "I have never seen more high-level insubordination in the U.S. government in almost thirty years than I have seen in this administration," said another senior Bush official.[19] One former NSC official declared Defense "out of control, an endless nightmare."

Another put it more bluntly. The "OSD was nuts," this former official declared. "We would say they were out of their fucking minds . . . you had an OSD staff given the direction . . . not to play ball. Then you had a secretary of defense who was also a policy entrepreneur who liked to dabble . . . on issues that were totally out of his way . . . on the Middle East peace process . . . on how to deal with Syria. We would characterize Rumsfeld as Secretary Strangelove . . . one of the problems was that he didn't realize that when you are out of office for eight years the world has changed. The approach has changed [but] he had not." A foreign official concurred. "He was not of this century," he told friends after a meeting with Rumsfeld.[20]

By now, the sixty-seven-year-old secretary of defense had also gained a reputation for unpredictable behavior. Rumsfeld came to meetings without reading his briefing papers, but nonetheless was compelled to deliver extemporaneous speeches that caused eyeballs to roll. He sent his staff into meetings without knowing what his office wanted—or decided afterward that he had changed his mind. A fervent believer in civilian control over the sluggish Pentagon bureaucracy, he did not hesitate to undercut his military subordinates or "make them look like absolute fools," said one observer. He had "gone nuclear" on four-star generals and often dismissed the advice of other senior military officers out of hand, which quickly alienated them. A foreign service officer, who worked with the Pentagon during Bush's first term, believed that Rumsfeld's early successes in Washington had bred an arrogance that did not serve him well in his later years. "My assessment of Rumsfeld was that he was too self-confident, that he wasn't mastering his briefs, but he thought he knew everything," he said. "He thought he understood the world, [but] the world wasn't the way it was twenty years ago."[21]

As such views of Rumsfeld gained currency within the government, some officials believed that Cheney and the president were well aware of the problem, but were unwilling or unable to do anything about it. Firing Rumsfeld would have been a serious self-administered blow to the White House at a time the nation was under siege by an unprecedented terrorist threat, engaged in Afghanistan, and gearing up for war in Iraq. But what had become clear was that the combination of the hyper-aggressive OVP staff in the White House and Rumsfeld's arrogant and often irrational behavior at the Pentagon added up to a presidential decision-making process that was badly broken. Some, like Richard Armitage and others, placed the blame on Rice and the NSC, which he described as undisciplined and dysfunctional during preparations for the Iraq war.[22]

But Lawrence Wilkerson put the blame for the administration's dysfunctional behavior squarely on the "Oval office cabal" of Cheney and Rumsfeld. A retired army colonel and member of the faculty at the Naval War College who worked at Powell's side between 2001 and 2005, Wilkerson was intimately involved in preparations for the Iraq war and the Bush administration standoffs with Iran and North Korea.[23] "The case that I saw for four-plus years was a case that I have never seen in my studies of aberrations, bastardization, perturbations, changes to the national security decision-making process," Wilkerson said. "What I saw was a cabal between the vice president of the United States, Richard Cheney, and the secretary of defense, Donald Rumsfeld, on critical issues that made decisions that the bureaucracy did not know were being made. And then when the bureaucracy was presented with the decision to carry them out, it was presented in such a disjointed, incredible way that the bureaucracy did not know what it was doing as it moved to carry them out."

Wilkerson later wrote, "I believe that the decisions of this cabal were sometimes made with the full and witting support of the president and sometimes with something less. More often than not, then national security advisor Condoleezza Rice was simply steamrolled by this cabal. Its insular and secret workings were efficient and swift," he went on, "not unlike the decision-making one would associate more with a dictatorship than a democracy. This furtive process was camouflaged neatly by the dysfunction and inefficiency of the formal decision-making process . . . But the secret process was ultimately a failure. It produced a series of disastrous decisions and virtually ensured that the agencies charged with implementing them would not or could not execute them well."[24]

Foremost among those decisions was the administration's attempt to establish military commissions to try suspected terrorists—a foray into military law that was overturned by a 5–3 vote of the U.S. Supreme Court in 2006. The policy was the work of David Addington, who secretly put together a legal team in October 2001 to draft the order that included then White House counsel Alberto Gonzales, former Berkeley professor John Woo at the Justice Department, and White House deputy counsel Timothy Flanigan. The document declared a state of "extraordinary emergency" and that the rules governing the commissions would be decided by the secretary of defense, without congressional or judicial review. The commissions would try any foreigner who conspired to commit terrorism against the United States. No appeals would be allowed, except to the secretary or the president. Standard military rules of evidence would not apply. As later refined in Defense Department memos, defendants would have limited rights to examine the evidence against them, or even attend their own trials. Hearsay and evidence gained from coercion would be admissible; guilt would not have to be proved beyond a reasonable doubt. Under pressure from military lawyers, the coercion provisions were rescinded only weeks before the high court struck down the tribunals altogether.

President Bush signed the executive order on November 13, 2001, without fanfare. Secretary of State Powell, a former national security advisor under Reagan and head of the joint chiefs of staff, was not consulted. Neither was Rice, the president's personal foreign policy amanuensis and national security advisor. Addington and his small cadre of lawyers also bypassed Michael Chertoff, the head of the Justice Department's criminal division, and NSC lawyer and deputy White House counsel John Bellinger III, even as Addington pressed Bellinger's deputy into service. Bellinger fired off a letter to Rice warning that the new policy was in violation of international law and likely to alienate allied governments. Only belatedly he learned that all White House documents prepared for the national security advisor—including the letter—were also "routed outside the formal process" to Cheney's office. Once forewarned of Bellinger's opposition and knowing that former joint chiefs chairman Colin Powell would fight the new policy, Addington was taking no chances. He drafted a lengthy memo to Bush designed to undercut Powell's arguments in a scheduled meeting with the president. The memo archly dismissed the Geneva Conventions as "quaint" and warned that Powell could be expected to advocate their "obsolete" rules that no longer applied to "a new kind of war" on terrorism. Flanigan then reportedly passed the Addington memo to Gonzales, the White House counsel, who signed it and directed it to President Bush as "my judgment."[25]

The Addington memo, over Gonzales's signature, caused widespread consternation in the government, especially among military lawyers. Rear Adm. Donald Guter, then the navy's top judge advocate general, told Pentagon general counsel William J. Haynes he needed more information on the military commissions decision. Haynes, who had worked for Addington in the Pentagon counsel's office in the early 1990s and was still close to him, rebuffed Guter's request with a curt, "No, you don't." Said Guter later, "We were marginalized."[26]

While Cheney, Rumsfeld, and Libby concentrated on Bush's war policies, Rove sealed his reputation as Bush's "boy genius" with his high-risk plan for the 2002 elections that gave the Republicans dominant majorities in both the House and Senate, providing the president with a virtually unassailable supermajority—that lasted until the 2006 midterms. In the summer and fall, the White House was pressing hard for approval of its Iraq war plans in Congress and at the United Nations, which dominated the news as the campaign season approached. It fell to Rove as President Bush's political adviser to tease out Republican advantages and strengthen the hand of GOP candidates across the country. For Rove, the war on terror and Bush's stature as a war president presented a serendipitous confluence of events, and he lost no time exploiting it. He told a meeting of the Republican National Committee in January 2002 that the party could use the war against terror to good advantage at the polls.

"Americans trust the Republicans to do a better job of keeping our communities and our families safe," Rove said. "We can also go to the country on this issue because they trust the Republican Party to do a better job of protecting and strengthening America's military might and thereby protecting America."[27] The theme became a Rove mantra through the 2004 presidential election and beyond.

With his trademark thoroughness, Rove directed the nuts-and-bolts of the nationwide campaign, organizing specific Senate races and local Republican get-out-the-vote efforts in key states, even handpicking candidates like John Thune in South Dakota, Jim Talent in Missouri, and Norm Coleman in Minnesota because his internal polling told him they could beat weak Democratic opponents.

In June, documentation of Rove's preelection strategy fell into opposition hands when a CD-ROM diskette was found by a Democratic Senate aide in Lafayette Park across the street from the White House. (A more complete version, consisting of a more sophisticated PowerPoint version of the Republican plan, was leaked to Democratic campaign strategists after the election.) The computer-projected presentation, authored by Rove and his assistant, then White House political director Ken Mehlman, elaborated on Rove's theme, how overwhelming public support for the war on terror and the popularity of the wartime president could be used to advance the GOP's political agenda in the midterm congressional races.

The revelation caused a minor uproar in the press, and triggered charges that the administration was cynically exploiting the terrorist attacks and the deaths of the 9/11 victims for political gain. Rove himself may have been a bit defensive about the ruthless pragmatism of the strategy. Normally he tried to avoid the appearance of exploiting policy issues for crass political gain, at least in public. But this time may have been different. Bruce Buchanan, a University of Texas presidential historian, was stunned by Rove's brash willingness to mix politics and policy. "I think the way . . . Rove would rationalize it," said Buchanan, "is to explain to the President the . . . political consequences of each of the choices he is considering, and that so long as the policy is not disturbed by doing something that helps us politically, we should feel free to do something that helps us politically."[28]

The midterm strategy was all the more remarkable for its bold coup de grâce. Rove's plan called for the wartime president himself to go out on the hustings to campaign on behalf of Republican Senate candidates, a high-risk tactic that is almost unheard of in off-year elections. But the stakes were high, and Rove might not have had to do much persuading. "As far as Bush was concerned, the real risk would have been to sit on his hands when he had the opportunity to make the difference in some very close races. He and Karl were completely in synch," wrote *Time* correspondents James Carney and John Dickerson in a postelection wrap-up. "George W. Bush sees politics and government as seamless; his whole vision of the presidency intertwines the two."

Bush hit the campaign trial with a vengeance, parachuting into states with key Senate races to bolster the Republican candidate. The president traveled to Georgia no fewer than six times in two months to help assure Saxby Chambliss's upset of incumbent senator Max Cleland, a triple-amputee, decorated war veteran, and conservative Democrat who had voted for Bush's $1.3 billion tax cut. The victory was emblematic of the brutal efficiency of the fifteen-year-old Bush-Rove political partnership. The astonishing success of the campaign made it difficult to tell where the president left off and Rove began.

Karl Rove first set eyes on George W. Bush during a visit to Washington at Thanksgiving in 1973, when Rove was dispatched by a Texan client—George Bush senior—to meet the younger Bush at the train to hand off the family car keys. Rove never forgot the moment. Bush was wearing an Air National Guard flight jacket, cowboy boots, and blue jeans. "He was exuding more charisma than any one individual should be allowed to have," Rove recalled years later. Five years later, when the younger Bush ran for Congress from Texas's nineteenth district, a rural constituency in the western part of the state made up mainly of small-town shopkeepers, farmers, and oil-field workers, Rove was asked by Bush's father to advise his son's campaign. George W., then thirty-two, won the primary, but lost the election to a hardboiled rancher and conservative Democrat named Kent Hance.[29]

That was the last time George W. Bush lost an election, and the last time every detail of a George W. Bush political campaign wasn't orchestrated by Karl Rove. Rove was instrumental in George Bush's meteoric, late-blooming rise to national prominence. His nickname, "Bush's brain," suggested to many that, like the Scarecrow in *The Wizard of Oz*, George W. was seriously lacking gray matter between the ears. But Bush's lazy, almost simple-minded speaking style, his lack of intellectual fire or curiosity, and his inexperience on the national stage masked a pragmatic intelligence, a gift of natural charm, and shrewdness in dealing with people. Bush was a doer, not a thinker—and that was where Rove fit in, as Dick Cheney would years later. "Rove has carried into their collaboration a rigorous intellect, superior political expertise, and capacity for detail," wrote James Moore and Wayne Slater in their 2003 book on Rove, *Bush's Brain*. "The end result is obvious: Karl Rove thinks it, and George W. Bush does it."[30]

Rove was hardly a silver-spoon Republican like Bush. The son of a mineral geologist, he was one of five children—three brothers and two sisters—who moved from Nevada to Salt Lake City with their mother in the mid-1960s after his parents, Louis and Reba Rove, separated. As a teenager in Salt Lake, Karl threw himself into life at Olympus High School, where he quickly developed a taste for trouncing all comers on the debate team and in student politics. A skinny kid with outsize glasses, he won a school election by having a Volkswagen driven into the school gym as he and two pretty girls sat in the backseat waving to the crowd. On the debate team, he discovered early on that the size of his index card file, in which debaters kept notes on the arguments they would have to defend or attack, could intimidate his opponents. Most rival debaters lugged around a shoe box full of three-by-five cards. So Rove, the classic high school nerd, and his teammates regularly trundled three or four boxes into debates. "It was all psychological, to pyche out your opponent," explained a Rove classmate.[31]

Rove's life was not all teenage hijinks. On Christmas Eve 1969, his father moved away from Salt Lake, and Karl soon learned for the first time that the man he had grown up with was not his father. For years afterward, Rove never met his biological father or even learned his identity. He told an interviewer that he eventually tracked him down, but described his father's demeanor as chilly. After her divorce, Reba Wood Rove moved to Reno. Eleven years later she committed suicide.[32]

As the nation split into warring cultural and political camps over the Vietnam War, Rove was a freshman at the University of Utah. Ignoring the siren song of dissent that suffused the Provo campus, he resolutely chose the side of stolid, establishment Republican conservatism. The sharper, more emotional and divisive politics became, the more Rove seemed to gravitate to the respectability, order, and strength he saw in the Republican party. "The Democrats were the party of giveaways and lassitude," wrote Moore and Slater. "All around him was division. Salt Lake City was divided between those who were Mormon and those who were not. The nation was divided over Vietnam. His home was coming apart. His father was away much of the time and even on the occasions he came home, his parents always argued. In a city where the prevalent influences were political and religious, his family was neither. He grew up in an apolitical household, without religious mooring."[33]

Within a few years, politics had replaced the classroom, and though he later attended both the University of Utah and Rice University and taught classes at the University of Texas, he never earned a degree. Rove threw himself into college Republican politics. He first drew the attention of George H. W. Bush, then the chairman of the Republican National Committee, with a sophomoric stunt in 1970. Rove had disrupted the campaign kickoff gala for a Democratic candidate for state treasurer in Illinois by secretly inviting hundreds of hippies, homeless people, and drunks to the opening. Rove distributed hundreds of phony invitations, printed up on stationery stolen from Democrat Alan Dixon, promising "free food, free beers, girls and a good time for nothing." Hundreds of unwanted guests reportedly made a mess of the gathering.

Dixon eventually won the election and the stunt won the twenty-year-old Rove a rebuke from the senior Bush, who ordered him to apologize.[34] Whether Rove did as he was told is not known. But the fledgling operative soon landed a job at RNC headquarters in Washington, and began to travel the country addressing Young Republicans on the art of electing candidates, expounding occasionally on political pranks, dirty tricks, and espionage tactics, such as rifling through the garbage of opposing candidates in search of revealing documents.

Rove, it seemed, was attuned to the times. In June 1972, a team of burglars working for the Committee to Re-elect the President broke into Democratic campaign offices at Washington's Watergate Hotel. Rove's traveling tours, with their impromptu seminars on dirty tricks, came to Bush's attention when a rival GOP youth faction, battling for the Republican leadership with Rove and another rising GOP star, Lee Atwater, leaked the story to *The Washington Post*. With the Watergate break-in fresh on everyone's minds, Bush was forced to publicly distance himself from Rove. Privately he was infuriated, not at Rove, but at his opponents. The RNC chief felt that the leak violated the GOP's eleventh commandment that Republicans should never publicly speak ill of fellow Republicans. After a standoff with their rivals, Bush awarded the Young Republican leadership to Rove and Atwater. Within months, Rove became Bush's special assistant at the RNC.

Atwater went on to engineer the senior Bush's presidential victory in 1988 and died of an inoperable brain tumor in 1991. He made an enormous impression on Rove. The bookish young Texan was awed by Atwater's outsize self-confidence and style. He instinctively understood Atwater's special strengths, his grasp of how to draw socially conservative voters into the GOP political orbit with wedge issues like gun control, prisoner furloughs, and flag-burning protests to peel them away from the Democratic party. Rove learned from Atwater that politics was warfare, including Atwater's specialty, smashmouth negative campaigning. "We're not alike," Rove said of Atwater. "He had an incredible gut instinct for how ordinary people would react. I guess I'm more cerebral." Rove had found a mentor.

Back in Texas, Rove set about engineering what would become a Republican renaissance in a state long dominated by conservative southern Democrats. A remarkable memo he wrote after Republican governor Bill Clements was thrown out of office in 1982 laid out a detailed blueprint for Clements's reelection as governor in 1986—and foreshadowed Rove's future modus operandi as a political strategist. Rove outlined how the rough-hewn Texas oilman would have to soften and polish his public image, making himself over as a candidate who had learned from his failures. The campaign would emphasize reform: welfare reform, tort reform, public-school reform. Clements would have to adjust his hard-driving, oil-field style to appeal to women—not to appeal to the feminist vote, but to attract voters among big city independents and moderate Republicans. He would support an increase in teachers' salaries—not to curry favor with teachers unions, but to reassure young suburban parents that their children would get a quality public education.

Likening politics to war, much like his hero Lee Atwater, Rove quoted Napoléon: " 'The whole art of war consists in a well-reasoned and extremely circumspect defensive, followed by rapid and audacious attack.' " Rove set forth in minute details how to depict Clements's opponent, Democratic incumbent Mark White, as an incompetent loser. Concluded Rove: "Attack. Attack. Attack."[35]

Rove's planning for Clements's campaign had all the characteristics of later Rove political operations—and could well have served as the model for the campaign of the White House Iraq Group waged to sell the Iraq war in 2002. The master plan covered every imaginable detail. Imagery was all important. Political reality was practically defined by the imagery Rove wanted to project. Policy was virtually indistinguishable from politics, and was arrived at only after meticulous political analysis of social and economic demographics. Above all, policy was designed to serve hardball political ends tailored to major Republican interests: big money, small government, upward mobility, the sanctity of hearth and home, physical security, a strong military—and reelection. Above all, it was essential to stick to the plan. Once defenses were built around that fortress, the trick was to roll out the heavy artillery in a show of character and strength—and then simultaneously deploy guerrilla forces in the shadows to execute the deceptions of political warfare that would assure the opponent's defeat.

Rove was—and is—a formidable data-cruncher, constructing multiple, layered spreadsheets showing the electoral history of a particular office, district, or issue, gathering data on where votes originated and which groups supported which candidates. His extensive experience in direct mail provided him with complex breakdowns on which issues motivated which voters. But what really set Rove above other national political consultants, besides his preternatural thoroughness and attentiveness to detail, was the exceptional guile and ruthlessness he brought to the arts of political deception. Rove exceeded even Lee Atwater's most storied campaign efforts, such as the famous Willie Horton TV ad that helped destroy the 1988 campaign of Democratic presidential contender Michael Dukakis. Rove's tactics were often more cerebral and better camouflaged than Atwater's visceral jabs.

Among the legends of no-holds-barred mendaciousness that trail behind Rove, few have caused as much controversy as the charges made during the 1984 Clements race against Democratic incumbent Mark White that Rove bugged his own office, then manipulated investigators and the news media into blaming Democratic operatives for illegally planting the electronic surveillance device in *his* office. White angrily protested that his people were not involved. A lackluster FBI investigation of the installation of the bug in Rove's office—during the final weeks of the campaign, when polls showed Governor White closing on his Republican challenger—was inconclusive. No one ever proved that Rove was behind the bugging, and the uproar created enough doubt in voters' minds that White's surge in the polls stalled. Whether or not Rove was responsible, Clements got the boost he needed to win the election.

Rove was masterful at insulating himself from these tactics, but word of his dirty tricks and brutal whispering campaigns trailed even his greatest successes. When George W. Bush ran for governor in 1994 against the charismatic and sharp-witted incumbent, Ann Richards, Rove put her on the defensive with a media strategy that drummed home the message that Richards was soft on crime. In fact, crime had dropped in Texas while she was governor. But she was a woman and a Democrat, and Rove's data told him that was enough to raise questions in the minds of Texas voters. Richards had also hired a record number of women and minorities in Texas government. Out of that fact, a whispering campaign began that the unmarried Democratic governor was filling the government with lesbians and minorities.

Rove reportedly encouraged conservative business and religious groups to question the professional qualifications of her appointments. This was done with some subtlety, and candidate Bush was a witting participant in the lie. Bush would set the stage by innocently suggesting that Richards's appointments were "people who have had agendas that may have been personal in nature." In the meantime, Rove insisted that his candidate would run an aboveboard campaign and would not stoop to personal attacks. He didn't have to. There was no ambiguity among conservative Texans about the meaning of "personal in nature." Rove was a master of creating illusions in the air—with devastating effect.

Presidential politics only sharpened Rove's no-holds-barred tactics. Going into the March 2000 South Carolina presidential primary, Republican rival John McCain enjoyed a healthy lead in the polls after thrashing Bush in New Hampshire. Shaken by McCain's win in the trendsetting New Hampshire primary, Rove and Bush responded by executing a sharp turn to the right, while trying to co-opt McCain's image as a reformer. They went into full attack mode, launching a fusillade of TV ads and direct mail accusing McCain of wanting to pull the pro-life plank from the Republican platform, which was an outright lie. The campaign pressed Ralph Reed's Christian Coalition into service, recruiting religious conservatives as surrogates. An e-mail message was widely circulated declaring that McCain was the father of illegitimate children. South Carolina Republicans began receiving telephone calls informing them that McCain's wife Cindy had a drug habit and he had an illegitimate black child. The word was also passed that McCain had broken under torture in Vietnam and given up national secrets.

McCain was furious. During a break in their debate in Columbia, South Carolina, Bush privately suggested the two declare a truce and extended his hand. "Don't give me that shit," McCain said. "And take your hands off me."[36] McCain, the navy veteran who had been tortured as a prisoner of war in Vietnam, got the Rove treatment in South Carolina. He lost to Bush by eleven points.

Rove's "seamless" linkage of the Republican war policy with his political strategy for the fall 2002 midterm congressional elections coincided with another major political task, working with the White House Iraq Group to persuade the American people and Congress—and ultimately, the UN Security Council—to support a preemptive war against Iraq to depose Saddam Hussein. The WHIG group reportedly began meeting weekly in the White House Situation Room during the summer of 2002, at about the same time Feith's Office of Special Plans was set up in the Pentagon. In attendance were Rove, Rice and her deputy Stephen Hadley, Libby, communication consultants Karen Hughes and Mary Matalin from the White House and the OVP respectively, and Nicholas Calio, the White House congressional liaison. The blitzkrieg of information justifying a U.S. decision to invade Iraq was scheduled to coincide with both the fall election season and White House initiatives to bring Congress and the United Nations into the fold. "From a marketing point of view," presidential chief of staff Andy Card explained famously at the time, "you don't introduce new products in August."

Vice President Cheney, however, softened up the ground in August with dramatic speeches on Saddam's nuclear weapons reportedly written by Libby and Hannah. There has been speculation that the disinformation blitz that began in September—notably, the infamous White House leak to *The New York Times* about Iraq's purchase of aluminum tubes, followed within hours by Cheney, Rice, and ultimately the president himself warning that "the smoking gun could come in the form of a mushroom cloud"—was the work of Rove and the WHIG. Throughout the fall, the handling of Joe Wilson and the Niger yellowcake deal, decisions about how to deploy WMD intelligence gleaned from Chalabi and the Iraqi National Congress, and, finally, the spectacle of Colin Powell before the UN Security Council presenting the evidence supporting a war against Iraq—a pared-back list again authored by Libby and Hannah—all bore earmarks of orchestration by WHIG, and by association, Rove.

These events, wrote national security expert James Bamford, produced "exactly the sort of propaganda . . . that the White House Iraq Group had been set up to stage-manage. First OSP supplies false or exaggerated intelligence; then members of the WHIG leak it to friendly reporters, complete with prepackaged vivid imagery; finally, when the story breaks, senior officials point to it as proof and parrot the unnamed quotes they or their colleagues previously supplied."[37] However credible this may sound to White House critics, it is at best knowledgeable speculation. No documentation has surfaced linking WHIG to any of these events, and no WHIG participants have stepped forward to explain how the group achieved its purposes.

Did Rove have an active hand in shaping or exploiting Bush's war policies to meet the administration's multiple political goals during the summer and fall of 2002—namely, securing congressional approval for the war and UN resolutions supporting U.S. military action? Rove may have been unprepared by training and experience to advise Bush on matters of war and peace, but he was known to be deeply involved in discussions of foreign policy issues during senior staff meetings with the president. Formally, his job description as political adviser to the president encompassed national security affairs. He enjoyed the highest level of top-secret clearance at the White House, or TS/SCI—Top-Secret/Sensitive Compartmentalized Information—and had regular access to sensitive classified intelligence about WMD and war planning.[38]

The strategies adopted by the president and vice president to sell their war policy to Congress and the American people have Rove's fingerprints all over them—the layering and insulation of anonymous sources of information, made to order for manipulating intelligence, the use of the press to confirm or confuse explanations of conflicting information, the tendency to discredit or spread lies about critics, the disciplined secrecy and projection of illusory political imagery. And, as his 2002 midterm election triumph vividly illustrated, Rove had a special relationship with George W. Bush. "Karl has the absolute, utter trust of the President of the United States," said Bill Paxon, a prominent GOP operative and former congressman. "That's really what makes him so good."[39]

Rove, like Libby on the policy side, had a tremendous personal and professional stake in Iraq and the war on terror. But the political ground on which the war was being fought shifted after the midterm elections from the realm of theory, political imagery, and hardball politics to the harder-to-control exigencies of battlefields in the real world. Despite the president's tough talk that bin Laden would be caught "dead or alive," the U.S. military would let him slip out of Afghanistan and allow him to hole up in the mountainous provinces on the Afghan and Pakistani border. The threat of Saddam's WMD was now at the heart of the Bush White House's war imagery. The worst-case scenario for Rove and the WHIG team, even as the political constraints against going to war in Iraq began to fall away, was that the threat of Iraqi weapons of mass destruction would prove to be groundless.

4

WAR FEVER ON THE POTOMAC

For most Americans, fear, confusion and anger were unnervingly close to the surface as they absorbed the shock of the 9/11 terrorist attacks. There was good reason for the roiling surge of emotions. The cluster of deadly, well-organized attacks was fully intended to inflict the horror it did. That awareness alone struck a cold, penetrating, unfamiliar fear into tens of millions of Americans who had not been alive on December 7, 1941, and could not remember the Japanese attack at Pearl Harbor. For older generations, heading into their retirement years after living a lifetime of relative progress and prosperity, the terror attacks brought back a sharp, brutal reality they thought had ended with World War II and had hoped never to experience again. It was precisely this uncomprehending and panicky collective fear that opened a window of opportunity for those determined to take the country to war, not just against the attackers, but also against a well-established and comprehensible enemy.

The words, photographs, and video footage transmitted to all corners of America from Ground Zero, the Pentagon crash site, and the wreckage of Flight 93 in a rural Pennsylvania meadow created indelible images of war, death, and unimaginable devastation. The smoldering ruins of the World Trade Center, with jagged, broken steel support beams rising haphazardly into the eerie, fire-illuminated haze, and the surrounding buildings sagging under the weight of collapsing floors and debris, were a twenty-first-century vision of hell. "It was hallucinogenic," wrote

William Langewiesche in his vivid account of the aftermath, "quasi-druggy, with flares shooting up and death in the air. There was a sense of crazed panic, people fighting to save lives, fire hoses cascading all over the place."[1] As rescuers walked through the wreckage where the towers had been they saw shoes, literally hundreds of empty shoes, ripped only hours before from the feet of the dead. But, Langewiesche reported, there were few whole bodies visible among the shoes on the littered killing ground.

Although the search for human remains would go on for months, the last survivor of the attack, a Jamaican woman, Genelle Guzman, then thirty-one, a clerk at the Port Authority, was found on the afternoon of September 12. Guzman had made it down the stairwell with a coworker from the sixty-fourth floor to the thirteenth floor of the South Tower before she heard a booming sound and felt the building break apart around her. Her friend disappeared. Guzman found herself wedged into a cocoon in the rubble, her legs pinned and crushed in the darkness. For twenty-seven hours, until the next afternoon, she lay trapped next to two dead firemen, praying for a miracle. She heard a search party and yelled. A voice answered, Langewiesche recounted. "The voice said, 'Do you see the light?' She did not. She took a piece of concrete and banged it against a broken stairway overhead—presumably the same structure that had saved her life. The searchers homed in on the noise. Guzman wedged her hand through a crack in the wall, and felt someone take it. A voice said, 'I've got you,' and Guzman said, 'Thank God.'"[2]

Another victim was not so lucky. Discovered by a heavy machine operator in December beneath a tangle of steel beams, he was sitting upright and perfectly intact in his suit and tie, his wallet firmly in his pocket, after falling from the offices of Cantor Fitzgerald, a financial services firm on the hundredth floor of the North Tower. Though somewhat shrunken, he was fully intact, Langewiesche reported. He "had not been entombed in the pumicelike Trade Center powder that helped to preserve others." By then, workers at Ground Zero had learned that the great piles of steel, which hid pockets and crevices of space beneath and within them, were the most likely places they would find intact bodies. Areas of tightly compacted burned debris, whatever the dimensions, were ignored by searchers. Many of the dead, and even most body parts of those who were identified, had simply been atomized by the superheated fires or pulverized by the enormous chaotic forces set loose as the buildings imploded.

The devastation wrought by the attacks was not the only source of fear. The enemy itself was simply unknown to most Americans, despite the 1993 attack on the World Trade Center, and was seemingly unburdened by the usual constraints of legitimate nations. Worst, the band of terrorist hijackers had seemed all but invisible to U.S. officials. This, too, had a dramatically corrosive effect on public confidence. After a halting start in the days after the attack, President Bush began to find his voice in a speech delivered at Washington's National Cathedral on September 13, evoking the frightening ruthlessness of the event and summoning the anger and resolve of a "peaceful" nation to strike back. "We are here in the middle hour of our grief," the president began. "So many have suffered so great a loss, and today we express our nation's sorrow. We come before God to pray for the missing and the dead, and for those who love them. On Tuesday, our country was attacked with deliberate and massive cruelty. We have seen the images of fire and ashes, and bent steel." But even as Americans grieved, he declared, the way ahead was clear. "War has been waged against us by stealth and deceit and murder. This nation is peaceful, but fierce when stirred to anger. This conflict was begun on the timing and terms of others. It will end in a way, and at an hour, of our choosing."

They were memorable, speechwriter's words. But the next morning, as George W. Bush was touring Ground Zero, his tone of measured piety gave way to something at once more casual and bracing. As the president, wearing a windbreaker against the chilly drizzle, climbed atop a pile of rubble to address the crowd, several voices called out that they couldn't hear him. Without missing a beat, Bush declared, "I can hear you! The rest of the world hears you! And the people who knocked these buildings down will hear all of us soon." By the time he was addressing a joint session of Congress six days later, the president's transformation was complete. "Tonight we are a country awakened to danger and called to defend freedom," he intoned, taking on the mantle of commander-in-chief. "Our grief has turned to anger, and anger to resolution. Whether we bring our enemies to justice, or bring justice to our enemies, justice will be done." For the first time, Bush publicly held al-Qaeda responsible for initiating the attacks.

Then he described the task ahead:

Our response involves far more than instant retaliation and isolated strikes. Americans should not expect one battle, but a lengthy campaign, unlike any other we have ever seen. It may include dramatic strikes, visible on TV, and covert operations, secret even in success. We will starve terrorists of funding, turn them one against another, drive them from place to place, until there is no refuge or no rest. And we will pursue nations that provide aid or safe haven to terrorism. Every nation, in every region, now has a decision to make. Either you are with us, or you are with the terrorists.

The speech was stirring, and had the desired effect of rallying Congress and prodding the American people into a patriotic fervor. Yet it was not a comforting speech. The president noted sweepingly that "fear and freedom are at war," yet seemed not to grasp how true that was within Americans themselves. The fear—even paranoia—that underlay the bright patriotism of the president's call to arms did not dissipate in the weeks and months that followed. Perhaps its most disturbing manifestation was the anthrax scare that began in October. Four people around the country, beginning with a tabloid photo editor in Florida, died in separate anthrax attacks and thirteen more showed symptoms of poisoning by deadly anthrax spores that were believed to be spread in a powderlike substance that could be fatal if inhaled or touched. Letters tainted with the deadly biological agent were discovered in the mail of then Senate majority leader Tom Daschle, a South Dakota Democrat, of Tom Brokaw, the NBC news anchor at the time, and of *The New York Post*. U.S. biological weapons programs had experimented with weaponizing anthrax and were believed by some to have shared the technology with Iraqi scientists during the Iran–Iraq war. The Soviet Union, too, had purportedly also experimented with anthrax as a biological weapon. Authorities were unable to pin down the sources of anthrax, although a disgruntled U.S. biological weapons expert was a suspect for a time.

The uproar created tremendous pressure on the federal government to stockpile an anthrax antidote in sufficient quantity to offset further incidents. Thanks to the discovery of documents about nuclear "dirty bombs" found on the hard drive of an al-Qaeda computer captured by U.S. forces in Afghanistan, the threat of weapons-grade nuclear fuel falling into the hands of terrorists intent on making such a device, in addition to anthrax and other biological and chemical agents, took on a new life. News reports reminded the public that sarin gas, which had been used in a 1995 Tokyo subway attack, killed twelve and incapacitated thousands. Sarin too, was linked to the Iraqis. Credible evidence from the Gulf War suggested that Iraqi rockets blown up in weapons dumps by U.S. forces after the 1991 conflict may have contained the gas. Some researchers even thought that the inadvertent releases of sarin contributed to the mysterious Gulf War Syndrome that afflicted many American soldiers after the war.

The fear of another terror attack became an uneasy fact of life. While going about their daily business, many New Yorkers made a habit of avoiding the subway system and crowded places like Grand Central Terminal that might become targets for terrorist bombings. Those who were able fled to weekend houses outside the city, while others moved away altogether, despite soaring property values in New York's suburbs. The great majority of New Yorkers, of course, had no such escape routes. For months after 9/11, theater attendance on Broadway came to a virtual standstill as the tourist business in New York reached record lows. When President Bush threw out the first ball for the opener of the 2002 season at Yankee Stadium without incident, many New Yorkers breathed more easily.

Washington, also a traditional destination for vacationing Americans, became in the popular mind another potential Ground Zero for future terrorist attacks. James Fallows, a Washington-based columnist for *The Atlantic Monthly,* thought that the "eeriest reminder" the capital was in uncharted territory in the weeks after the attacks was "the silence," literally "the absence of *sound,* while National Airport remained closed for three full weeks." Fallows explained that "until the weeks passed without traffic at National, it was hard to appreciate that the rumble of a low-altitude approach along the Potomac, every minute or so from seven in the morning until ten at night, is the characteristic sound of the capital." He added: "But through September my ears rang with the quiet—except when military helicopters flew past or fighter jets screeched through on patrol, often just before dawn."[3]

The transformation of everyday life was unsettling for many Washingtonians. Ever since he was a second lieutenant in the army assigned to the Pentagon in the 1970s, Thomas DeFrank, the Washington bureau chief of New York's *Daily News,* had driven over to the PX at Fort Myers, Virginia, to buy cut-rate gas. Making the trip several days after 9/11, he flashed his military ID as usual at the gate. Instead of being waved through, however, he was brusquely ordered by a young guard to pull over. His car was thoroughly searched. The gravity of the situation was not driven home until the guard began inspecting the underbody of his car with a mirror, presumably for hidden explosives. DeFrank had not witnessed that for thirty-one years, since East German authorities stopped his train before dawn in Soviet-controlled East Berlin to conduct a similar search. He remembered watching from the platform as the *Volkspolizei* had methodically inspected the undercarriage of the train with a mirrored device. After all these years, did they suspect he was a suicide bomber, smuggling explosives onto the base? What's happened to my country? he thought. "I haven't seen an inspection with an undercarriage mirror since I was in East Berlin as a soldier," DeFrank remarked to the young American guard. "Times have changed since then, sir," the soldier promptly replied.[4]

Beefed-up security at military bases was the least of it. Both New York and Washington were patrolled for months by U.S. Air Force F-14 and F-16 fighters and AWACS surveillance planes, providing a psychological boost for those on the ground as well as monitoring the heavily traveled East Coast air corridors for suspicious aircraft. For tourists from the heartland, this level of vigilance was disconcerting. So was draconian-sounding legislation rushed through Congress by the Justice Department, with the blessing of the Bush White House and the Democratic leadership, which ordered the roundup of thousands of immigrants with visa problems, especially those from Arab countries. In short order, the U.S. government declared that suspected terrorists would be considered combatants without due process or recourse to the American justice system. And a new system of color-coded terror alerts brought little comfort or clarity, but signaled the dead seriousness with which Attorney General John Ashcroft and President Bush were taking the terrorist threat against America.

The nation's capital came to seem so dangerous to everyday Americans that one-quarter of the country's school districts banned student field trips to Washington. Before 2001, an estimated one million students a year traveled to Washington with school groups. "I'm sure I'll go to Washington someday, but never with my senior class," said Anna Berkowitz, a senior at Central High School in St. Joseph, Missouri, a town of 74,000 best known for the Pony Express and the untimely end of legendary outlaw Jesse James. "President Bush said the best thing to do is go on with life, but I guess this is one experience the terrorists stopped us from having."[5]

By February 2002, those who made the trip to Washington had plenty to see and think about. Near the Capitol, American flags hung in the windows of a Senate office building where there had been a recent anthrax scare. The burnt-out hole in one façade of the Pentagon where Flight 77 crashed, killing a total of 184 people, not including the five hijackers, had been cleared of debris and covered with plywood. At 1600 Pennsylvania Avenue, the public had not been allowed inside the White House for four and a half months. The Capitol building and the Library of Congress were shuttered for almost as long, and the FBI was still closed to groups of children. Attendance at Washington's great cultural institutions, from the Smithsonian National Air and Space Museum to the elegant Hirshhorn Gallery on the Mall, was down forty-five percent.[6]

Inevitably, across the country Arab-Americans became targets of attacks and harassment, a variant of the racial profiling adopted by airline security officials that often ran afoul of hard-won civil rights laws. An armed Secret Service agent of Arab descent on President Bush's security detail was thrown off a flight after being challenged by the pilot. A Fresno, California, hairstylist threw a Pakistani neurologist out of his barbershop for declining to discuss Osama bin Laden. In Washington, D.C., high school senior Muhammed El-Nasleh at first shrugged off coworkers at McDonald's when they started asking him why his "cousins" bombed the World Trade Center. But when his boss cracked, "Hey, Muhammed, we're going to have to check you for bombs," he felt he was being unfairly singled out. "I felt like I was being targeted," said El-Nasleh. "It was humiliating. Some things just aren't funny."[7]

As cleanup crews swarmed over the smoldering wreckage of the World Trade Center, the first of a drumbeat of articles appeared that began to play on Americans' fears, anger, and paranoia over the attacks. On September 13, *The New Republic*, the venerated liberal Washington journal with a strong neoconservative tilt on defense issues, published an article by former Clinton CIA director R. James Woolsey exhorting U.S. intelligence and law enforcement authorities to look into the possibility that the attacks "were sponsored, supported, and perhaps even ordered by Saddam Hussein."

Woolsey argued against the commonly held assumption that Ramzi Yousef, the mastermind of the 1993 World Trade Center bombing, was in all probability a twenty-seven-year-old Pakistan student named Abdul Basit, as U.S. prosecutors believed. Instead, Woolsey believed he was an Iraqi agent who had traveled under a fictitious passport stolen from a Kuwaiti of the same name who died during the Iraqi occupation of Kuwait. This scenario, first advanced by the senior FBI agent on the 1993 case, the late James Fox, and a conservative academic named Laurie Mylroie, suggested not only that Iraq had been involved in the first Trade Center bombing but also that Baghdad had been behind the 9/11 attacks as well. Mylroie got her start in the 1980s as an assistant professor of political science at Harvard with a special interest in Iraq. After the 1991

Gulf War, she coauthored a book with *New York Times* reporter Judith Miller on the Iraqi dictator. After the 1993 World Trade Center bombing, Mylroie attracted attention by publishing a book advancing the theory that Ramzi Yousef was an alias for a shadowy Iraqi agent who had taken Basit's name. Her book, *Study of Revenge: Saddam Hussein's Unfinished War Against America*, which appeared in 2000, included a foreword by Woolsey and was warmly endorsed by Paul Wolfowitz. FBI and CIA officials reportedly met with Mylroie in the mid-1990s and discounted her evidence.

Nonetheless, Woolsey persisted.[8] To nail the theory down, the former CIA director proposed that American authorities examine forensic evidence the real Abdul Basit handled during a stay in London in 1998 and 1999, including photocopied pages of old passports, among other things, then in the keeping of Scotland Yard. If the fingerprints on them did not match Yousef's (who had been sentenced by U.S. authorities to life to 240 years in Florence, Colorado's high-security Supermax prison), authorities could conclude Yousef had expropriated Basit's identity and might well be an Iraqi agent. If Ramzi Yousef's fingerprints matched Basit's, Woolsey conceded, there was probably nothing to the Iraqi angle.

What *The New Republic* and the rest of Washington did not know until mid-October was that senior Pentagon officials, including Paul Wolfowitz and his deputy Douglas Feith, had already sent Woolsey off to London twice, once in February and again in September right after 9/11, presumably to examine the evidence at Scotland Yard and at the Swansea Institute, a technical school in South Wales where Basit had studied.[9] Woolsey was not the only former official sympathetic to neoconservatives who suspected Saddam was involved in 9/11. "I would be surprised if Saddam Hussein's fingerprints were not in some ways on this," said former secretary of state George P. Shultz. "An Iraq ruled by Saddam Hussein is basically a Kmart for terrorist weapons."

If Woolsey returned to the United States with any incriminating evidence against Saddam, neither he nor the Pentagon ever said anything about it. Speculation that Yousef was an Iraqi agent seemed to dry up. Unnamed sources who knew about Woolsey's travels told reporters he failed to produce any new evidence. Nonetheless, Woolsey remained tightlipped about what he had found, and continued to add his voice to those who believed Saddam was involved in the U.S. terror attacks. "We ought to seriously consider removing Saddam's regime if he has been involved in any terror in recent years against us," he told a London paper. "I think some day—hopefully soon—they will come to the same conclusion that Admiral Yamamoto did after Pearl Harbor, which was to remark that Japan had awakened a sleeping giant."[10]

Interestingly, Woolsey's formulation about Saddam's involvement—that if the Iraqi dictator had supported or conducted terrorist acts against the United States, he should be forcibly removed from power—had been the subject of a spirited dispute between Wolfowitz and White House counterterrorism adviser Richard Clarke during a meeting of the NSC deputies the previous April. Clarke recalled that when he said the focus should be bin Laden and al-Qaeda, Wolfowitz countered that the real issue was Iraqi terrorism. "I said, that's interesting, because there hasn't been any Iraqi terrorism against the United States," Clarke later told a reporter. He continued:

There hasn't been any for 8 years. And [Wolfowitz] said something derisive about how I shouldn't believe the CIA and FBI, that they've been wrong. And I said if you know more than I know, tell me what it is, because I've been doing this for 8 years and I don't know about any Iraqi-sponsored terrorism against the U.S. since 1993. . . . He said bin Laden couldn't possibly have attacked the World Trade Center in '93. One little terrorist group like that couldn't possibly have staged that operation. It must have been Iraq.[11]

The Iraqi terrorist operation in 1993 alluded to by Clarke was, of course, the assassination attempt on President Bush's father during the former president's visit to Kuwait in 1993. Although the Iraqi plan was disrupted in the early stages, observers have cited the assassination attempt as a powerful personal motivation for his son to take out the Iraqi leader. The opportunity to assassinate the elder Bush arose in April 1993, when the former president and a family entourage flew to Kuwait for a three-day tribute to the U.S. commander-in-chief who liberated the tiny desert monarchy from Saddam's occupying forces during the Gulf War. The high point of the celebrations was the awarding of an honorary degree to Bush at Kuwait University. Days before, the CIA reportedly learned that an Iraqi named Wali al-Ghazali had been ordered by Saddam to detonate two hundred pounds of plastic explosives hidden in the side panels of a Toyota Land Cruiser near the president's motorcade, intended to kill both Bush and the emir of Kuwait.[12]

Although the details are vague, Wali al-Ghazali and thirteen other plotters were reportedly caught before the Kuwait University event. Afterward, the circumstances surrounding their capture were questioned as disinformation supplied by the Kuwaitis.[13] There were also charges that Iraqi involvement in the plot was drummed up by the Kuwaitis. Al-Ghazali, however, confessed to taking part in the assassination conspiracy and told Kuwaiti prosecutors he was dispatched by the Mukhabarat, Saddam's intelligence service. If the plot had succeeded, the president's father, mother, wife, brothers Marvin and Neil, and Neil's wife, Sharon, would probably have been killed, possibly along with family friends and colleagues who were in Kuwait to fete their old boss, including former secretary of state James A. Baker III, former treasury secretary Nicholas F. Brady, and former chief of staff John Sununu.

Bush was reportedly privy to U.S. intelligence reports about the Iraqi assassination attempt on his father. His public comments on the subject were by turns oddly casual and overheated. "After all, this is the guy who tried to kill my dad," he remarked of Saddam during a Houston fundraiser. On another occasion, he lashed out, "The SOB tried to kill my dad." Whether the new and unseasoned president's views of Iraqi complicity in 9/11 were colored by the attempted assassination is not known. Whatever his predilections, the president knew within days of the attacks that the U.S. intelligence community did not believe there was any significant connection between Saddam and al-Qaeda—or that the Iraqis had been involved at all in 9/11. There was simply no credible evidence of recent Iraq-related terrorist activity. Richard Clarke and Zalmay Khalilzad already had presented the president with a report asserting there were no significant ties between Saddam and al-Qaeda.

The message was reinforced on September 21, 2001, when George Tenet told Bush during his morning intelligence briefing that there was no evidence of Iraqi involvement in the attacks ten days before, nor any links between Iraq and al-Qaeda. Bush had expressed his interest to Clarke in finding anything that would tie Saddam to al-Qaeda, and he reportedly also requested the Tenet briefing. The U.S. intelligence community believed that the few credible reports of any contact between the two may have involved either Saddam's attempts to monitor al-Qaeda or his interest in infiltrating the group with Iraqi agents to learn more about a terrorist group he considered a threat to his secular regime.

"What the President was told on September 21 was consistent with everything he has been told since—that the evidence was just not there," a former administration official later said. The Bush administration later acknowledged the existence of the September 21 President's Daily Briefing, or PDB, but refused to release the text, even on a classified basis to congressional oversight committees.[14]

5

A PREEMPTIVE FOG OF WAR

For the majority of Americans, Iraq was not yet on the radar screen. Most were still rattled by the horror of the terror attacks and preoccupied by cable news accounts of the first U.S. reprisals under way in Afghanistan, which began October 7, 2001. Hundreds of tons of American ordnance pounded positions of troops loyal to the Taliban, the ultra-fundamentalist Islamic group that governed the country and provided support and cover for Osama bin Laden's terrorist activities. With the military campaign gearing up in Afghanistan, few newspapers around the country had mentioned Iraq's possible role as a sponsor of terror. But Washington insiders, aware that the president's top advisers had been privately debating the subject of regime change in Iraq for months, knew it was only a matter of time before the subject of targeting Iraq would come up.

Early in October an op-ed appeared in *The Washington Post* that strongly echoed Woolsey's views about Saddam's likely support for terrorism. On October 12, Edward Hoagland, a respected columnist for *The Post* and the paper's former foreign editor, raised the possibility that Saddam Hussein had colluded with al-Qaeda in the attacks in an article entitled "What About Iraq?" The question set a critical theme in play for the White House's march to war against Iraq that would be amplified many times over through 2002 and early 2003. Like Woolsey, Hoagland was worried that U.S. law enforcement officials had been lax in their treatment

of terrorists and their associates. The FBI, he pointed out, had allowed another al-Qaeda member involved in the 1993 World Trade Center bombing, Abdul Rahman Yasin, to leave the United States for safe haven in
Baghdad after his release. If the Bush administration was serious about isolating state sponsors of terrorism, Hoagland wrote, Washington should
initiate "a thorough examination of the accumulating evidence of Iraq's
role in sponsoring the development on its soil of weapons and techniques
for international terrorism."

Like the Ramzi Yousef story, the allegation that Abdul Rahman Yasin
may have been an Iraqi agent sent by Baghdad in 1993 to bomb the
World Trade Center fizzled before it could get any serious traction. After
the 1993 Manhattan bombing, U.S. authorities questioned Yasin and released him after concluding he was a bit player in the attack. An FBI agent
actually drove Yasin from the interrogation back to his home in New Jer-
sey, but within days Yasin saw his opportunity and fled to Iraq. The Justice Department appeared to take his escape and asylum in Baghdad in
stride. It was only eight years later, in the weeks after 9/11, that the FBI
suddenly slapped a $5 million price tag on Yasin's head for his role in the
1993 bombing. He was in fact an American citizen, born in Bloomington,
Indiana, while his father was studying for his Ph.D. at the University of Indiana, but had later grown up in Baghdad. When Yasin returned in 1993,
Iraqi authorities at first allowed him his freedom. After a year, they detained the star-crossed bomber and threw him in jail, apparently to avoid
possible reprisals from the United States.

On May 23, 2002, Lesley Stahl of CBS located Yasin in a Baghdad
prison and was granted permission to interview him. He had been in jail
for eight years. Yasin talked openly with Stahl about his relationship with
Ramzi Yousef and the third 1993 conspirator, Mohamed Salameh, freely
incriminating himself for his role in the bombing. He recounted his own
naïveté at the time and his gradual recognition that Yousef was a trained
terrorist who had learned bomb-making in Peshawar, Pakistan, and had
come to New York to blow up Jews in Brooklyn before switching his target to the World Trade Center. He expressed remorse for the six deaths
and injuries they had caused. Stahl confirmed that in 1994 Baghdad had
sent an emissary to Washington to negotiate Yasin's return, but the Clinton administration did not respond, apparently unaware he was officially
in Iraqi custody. The final twist came in October 2001, when the Baghdad regime tried for a second time to return Yasin, whose photo now
graced an FBI wanted poster, to U.S. authorities. Washington spurned the
offer. U.S. officials reportedly refused to sign documents that would have

acknowledged Baghdad's role in voluntarily extraditing him to the United States.[1] Yasin is the only one of the 1993 bombers who has not stood trial in the United States for his crimes.

The sequence of events scotched any credible charge that Yasin had acted as an Iraqi agent—or that the United States, which had twice refused to extradite him, cared. Yet in the Bush White House, he still had propaganda value. Appearing on *Meet the Press* in September 2003, after the White House had come under heavy fire for the CIA leak case, Vice President Cheney tried again to use Yasin as a link between Saddam and terrorism. "We know . . . that one of the bombers was Iraqi, [and] returned to Iraq after the attack of '93," Cheney told Tim Russert. "And we've learned subsequent to that, since we went into Baghdad and got into the intelligence files, that this individual probably also received financing from the Iraqi government as well as safe haven."[2] The vice president did not explain why Yasin wasn't arrested by U.S. troops in Baghdad and brought back to the United States to stand trial.

But the centerpiece of Hoagland's "What About Iraq?" column was an alleged Iraqi training camp for foreign terrorists near Salman Pak, a town just south of Baghdad. It was described to Hoagland by a forty-seven-year old former Iraqi military officer named Sabah Khalifa Khodada al-Lami. The story told by al-Lami and others about collusion between Saddam and foreign Arab terrorists would have a considerably longer shelf life. From 1994 until 1998 Alami was a military instructor in the elite militia known as the Fedayeen Saddam, or Saddam's Fighters. He had immigrated to the United States in 2000 and settled in Fort Worth, Texas. The Iraqi National Congress, which brought him to Washington for a meeting with the FBI, set up the interview with Hoagland. Besides showering Hoagland with tales of U.S. immigration and intelligence officials who were unreceptive to his evidence of Iraqi links to 9/11, al-Lami "guardedly outlined to me here Wednesday details of the training given for airliner hijacking and assassinations in the Salman Pak area of Baghdad while he was there."

Hoagland's second source for the story was identified only as "an Iraqi ex–intelligence officer," who reportedly "told the Iraqi National Congress" about "sightings of 'Islamicists'" training on a Boeing 707 parked in Salman Pak as recently as September 2000. The unidentified former Iraqi intelligence officer, Hoagland reported, told INC agents that he, too, had met with agents of the CIA in Ankara, Turkey, just that week and was "treated dismissively." He was later identified as Abu Zeinab al-Qurairy.

Revelations about the alleged terrorist training camp at Salman Pak—which would be discredited by U.S. intelligence long after the U.S. occupation of Iraq began—did not end there. *The Washington Post* had injected a provocative allegation into the national debate—which, if true, strongly suggested that Saddam Hussein's regime could have trained al-Qaeda terrorists to hijack a commercial aircraft. Hoagland's report was based on the sketchy outline of one source, supported by secondhand hearsay from a highly motivated dissident lobbying group that was attributed to an anonymous source. But before the story was finally put to rest, it would be elaborated upon in some detail elsewhere in the media—and by U.S. officials in support of war against Iraq.

Additional detail on the alleged Salman Pak terrorist training camp was not long in coming. A November 8, 2001, *New York Times* article by Chris Hedges, a veteran correspondent in *The Times*' Paris bureau, relied heavily on two defectors identified as former officers of Iraq's intelligence service, the Mukhabarat. The first said he was a lieutenant general and a top dog in Saddam's spy service. He asserted that "these Islamic radicals" were from countries including Saudi Arabia, Yemen, Algeria, Egypt, and Morocco. "We were training these people to attack installations important to the United States," he said. "The gulf war never ended for Saddam Hussein. He is at war with the United States." The second Iraqi was identified as a former "sergeant" in the intelligence service who had spent five years at the camp.

The stories of the two former Iraqi officials, Hedges wrote, provided "the first look at the workings of the camp from those who took part in its administration." They told him the Mukhabarat ran the camp, which was divided into two physically separate areas, one for training Iraqi fighters, the Fedayeen Saddam, in espionage, assassination attempts, and sabotage. The other, "separated by a small lake, trees and barbed wire," was equipped with the fuselage of a Boeing 707 and dedicated to training the foreign fighters. The detail reported was vivid. "There were rarely more than 40 or 50 Islamic radicals in the camp at one time," Hedges reported. They trained in groups of four or five. "We could see them train around the fuselage . . . We could see them practice taking over the plane," the former sergeant told Hedges. His sources told him that there was a heavily guarded biological weapons compound within the camp, where Iraqi scientists were overseen by "a German." But they claimed the installation was wiped out by coalition bombing in the Gulf War.

Although Hedges did not name his informants, he was straightforward about identifying them as Iraqi defectors with an interest in overthrowing

Saddam. Once again, Chalabi's Iraqi National Congress helped set up interviews with the two men for Hedges in London. Hedges made clear from the outset that his sources did not really know whether the foreign fighters, referred to as "Islamic terrorists" or "Islamic militants," were linked to Osama bin Laden and al-Qaeda or not—a classic formulation of news reporting that suggested that they *might be* linked. In the same cautiously crafted prose, Hedges quoted an unnamed UN weapons inspector who asserted that although he had no evidence for saying so, he always suspected Salman Pak might be used by Saddam to train terrorists. The inspectors, he said, had been told by the Iraqis that Salman Pak was an anti-terror training camp for Iraqi special forces. Only in the thirteenth paragraph of the story did Hedges mention that American intelligence officials, still grappling with the devastating political fallout of the historic terrorist attacks on the United States, nonetheless believed "it was unlikely" that there was any link between the Iraqi camp and the 9/11 hijackings.

The news of the terror training camp at Salman Pak spread like a bad rash. For the next six weeks, news organizations as far flung as the *Birmingham Post*, *The Vancouver Sun*, *The Times* of London, and Agence France-Presse picked up on the INC-sourced stories spreading the allegations about Saddam's terrorist training camps and his links with al-Qaeda and involvement in the 9/11 attacks.

More promising evidence that Iraq had provided al-Qaeda with training in biological and chemical weapons emerged after the November 11 capture in Afghanistan of a ranking bin Laden lieutenant named Ibn al-Shaykh al-Libi, a Libyan militant who ran al-Qaeda's Khaldan paramilitary training camp. Al-Libi was captured by Pakistani forces, who turned him over to the CIA in January. After some uncertainty in Washington about what to do with such a big fish, the CIA got clearance to secretly transfer, or "render," al-Libi to a prison in Cairo, where Egyptian intelligence would take over his questioning. His CIA handlers, according to one witness, "duct-taped his mouth, cinched him up and sent him to Cairo. At the airport the CIA case officer goes up to him and says, 'You're going to Cairo, you know. Before you get there I'm going to find your mother and I'm going to fuck her.' "[3]

In Cairo, under some duress at the hands of his Arabic-speaking hosts, al-Libi provided the Egyptians with information that later led to the capture of senior al-Qaeda leader Abu Zubaydah, one of the plotters behind 9/11. He also told his interrogators that al-Qaeda leaders, frustrated at their inability to make chemical or biological weapons, had asked Baghdad for help. At Iraq's invitation, al-Libi claimed, al-Qaeda officials had sent an envoy named Abu Adula al-Iraqi several times beginning in 1997 to seek help in acquiring poisons and gases, and that Iraq as recently as 2000 had offered "chemical or biological weapons training for two Al Qaeda associates," as Colin Powell would later phrase it before the UN Security Council. Bush, Cheney, Powell, and other administration officials repeatedly trumpeted his testimony as proof positive of cooperation between the Iraqi regime and al-Qaeda. Al-Libi was returned to the Americans in early 2003 and sent to the U.S. detention camp at Guantánamo Bay, Cuba.[4]

The White House, however, did not know, or did not acknowledge, that as early as February 2002, months before senior officials began using the al-Libi intelligence in their fall information blitz, the Defense Intelligence Agency issued a report skeptical of his credibility and expressed the suspicion he was "intentionally misleading the debriefers" and might have fabricated the claims to avoid harsh treatment in prison. In January 2004, long after U.S. troops were bogged down trying to secure Baghdad, al-Libi recanted his testimony after he was confronted with information from two other senior al-Qaeda captives, Khalid Sheikh Mohammed and Abu Zubaydah, that the terrorist organization had no substantial relations with Baghdad.[5] Al-Libi said he told the story to avoid being tortured by his Egyptian interrogators. The CIA reported al-Libi's reversal to senior U.S. officials in a January 2004 intelligence document.

It was a foreign intelligence report, however, leaked by the Bush administration fall of 2001, that seemed to provide, if not confirmation, strong additional evidence that Iraq may have played a pivotal role with al-Qaeda in planning the attacks on the United States. The story began circulating several months before 9/11, when an Iraqi diplomat who had been under surveillance for two years on suspicion of plotting to blow up Radio Free Europe's headquarters in Prague was spotted meeting with an unidentified Arab man in his twenties in a restaurant outside the city. The Czech government promptly ordered the Iraqi diplomat, Ahmed Khalil Ibrahim Samir al-Ani, to leave the country, apparently fearing that he was recruiting the young Arab for the Radio Free Europe job. There the matter seemed to rest.

But soon after the terrorist attacks in the United States, the informant who reported al-Ani's meeting on April 8, himself recruited from Prague's Arab community, told his Czech counterintelligence handlers that he believed the young Arab he saw with al-Ani was Mohamed Atta, the Egyptian-born terrorist and alleged ringleader of the hijacking plot who learned to fly jumbo jets in Florida. Atta was believed to be at the controls of United Flight 11 when it disintegrated in a fireball after slamming into the North Tower of the Trade Center at 8:46 A.M.

The Czech Security Information Service, known by its Czech acronym, BIS,[6] was skeptical of the new report. Atta's photo had been displayed prominently in the news, along with sketchy reports that the terrorist had once traveled to Prague. Three days after 9/11, BIS passed the information to the CIA, which disseminated the classified report to other intelligence agencies and government officials. The FBI promptly flew a team of investigators to Prague to review the Czech intelligence. Four days later, the Associated Press reported that an unidentified U.S. official "speaking on condition of anonymity, said the United States has received information from a foreign intelligence service that Mohamed Atta, a hijacker aboard one of the planes that slammed into the World Trade Center, met earlier this year in Europe with an Iraqi intelligence agent."[7] The information, stripped of nuance and cautionary phrasing, was transformed into a statement of fact. The identity of the Bush administration official who leaked the Atta story to AP is not known.

It wasn't until late October that senior Czech officials began to confirm parts of a story that would be thoroughly discredited by Czech president Václav Havel less than a year later. It is hard to say whether these Czech senior officials were victims of gullibility, confusion, or their own political agendas. In mid-October, Czech foreign minister Jan Kavan traveled to Washington and told Secretary of State Colin Powell that the Czech counterintelligence service believed that Atta may have met with al-Ani outside Prague. Several days later, Stanislav Gross, the Czech interior minister, told reporters he could "only confirm one visit in the summer" made by Atta to Prague. Atta had reportedly been in the Prague airport briefly and had transferred from a plane from Hamburg, Germany, to his Newark flight. But the layover was apparently in June 2000, not April 2001. At about the same time, Peter Necas, a defense expert in the Czech parliament, declared bluntly, "I haven't seen any direct evidence that Mr. Atta met any Iraqi agent."

Finally, on October 27, Czech government officials confirmed, mistakenly, that Iraqi diplomat al-Ani had met with Atta near Prague on April 8, 2001. Though the timing of the meeting still aroused suspicion, since Atta was known to be in Virginia Beach several days before the alleged meeting and in Florida just afterward, the details were intriguing. Reporting from Washington, then national political correspondent Patrick Tyler and reporter John Tagliabue of *The Times* wrote that "a senior Bush administration official" volunteered that it was a "Czech decision" to go public with information that "we have known about for some time." The story speculated helpfully that the administration "had put pressure on the Czechs to keep quiet."[8]

But in Prague, the Czech officials, who had said only weeks earlier that they knew Atta was in the country but had no evidence he had met with an Iraqi agent, could not or would not say why they had changed their minds. "Speaking at a news conference in Prague," Tyler and Tagliabue wrote, "the Czech interior minister, Stanislav Gross, said that Mr. Atta met Mr. Ani, an Iraqi diplomat identified by Czech authorities as an intelligence officer, in early April." Gross, the minister to whom BIS officials reported, was backed up by Prime Minister Milos Zeman, who also confirmed that the meeting with Atta had taken place. The Czech Republic's president, Václav Havel, was apparently not apprised of the decision to go public with the shaky intelligence. Across the Atlantic, the news came as no surprise to some. "The Czech confirmation seems to me very important," said former CIA chief James Woolsey. "It is yet another lead that points toward Iraqi involvement in some sort of terrorism against the United States that ought to be followed up rigorously."[9]

Over the course of the next year, the story came unraveled. Federal investigators could find no records indicating that Atta had left or reentered the United States during April 2001. In December, Czech police official Jiri Kolar declared that there was no evidence that Atta met with al-Ani on April 8, or for that matter proof that Atta was in the Czech Republic at that time. A Czech newspaper, citing an unnamed intelligence official, reported that al-Ani had not met with Atta at all, but with an older man from Nuremberg who resembled Atta and had a similar name.

As evidence mounted that Atta had spent early April 2001 in the United States at Virginia Beach and in Coral Springs, Florida, both U.S. and Czech officials began backing away from the story. CIA and FBI investigations found no record that Atta visited Prague during that time. BIS, however, stuck by its initial report, and so did the determined Czech interior minister, Stanislav Gross. "I do not have the slightest information that anything is wrong with the details I obtained from BIS counterintelligence," he said. "I trust the BIS more than journalists."[10]

In the late spring of 2002, Czech president Václav Havel, who had assigned trusted aides to investigate the reports of the Atta meeting

through government back channels in Prague, was told that Czech counterintelligence officials had no evidence such a meeting had taken place on
April 8. In an apparent effort not to embarrass ministers in his government who initially stood behind the intelligence reports, Havel quietly
and directly informed the White House that no meeting had taken place
between the al-Qaeda terrorist and the Iraqi diplomat-spy. "Quite simply,
we think the source for this story may have invented the meeting that he
reported," a high-ranking source close to BIS said later. "We can find no
corroborative evidence for the meeting and the source has real credibility
problems."[11] CIA director George Tenet told Congress his agency could
not confirm that a meeting took place, and the *9/11 Commission Report*
later confirmed that there was no evidence Mohamed Atta had traveled to
Prague in April 2001.

Havel's message to the White House seriously undermined widespread
speculation that an Iraqi agent had met with Atta about the 9/11 attacks
on America, as well as the Bush administration's contention that the
Baghdad regime had colluded with al-Qaeda in planning them. But far
from correcting the misinformation about Atta, the White House kept
silent, while others in the administration pursued measures aimed at
showing that the discredited meeting had taken place after all.

In early August, Deputy Defense Secretary Paul Wolfowitz led a delegation of defense officials to meet with the FBI's assistant director of
counterterrorism to discuss the alleged Atta meeting in Prague. Weeks after Czech officials dismissed it as a mistake, Wolfowitz pressed the FBI to
concede the possibility that the Atta meeting had happened as reported,
according to people present at the meeting.[12] At about the same time, Undersecretary of Defense for Policy Douglas Feith sent a team from the Pentagon's new Office of Special Plans to meet with George Tenet about the
final draft of a CIA report, entitled *Iraq and al Qaeda: A Murky Relationship*, which took a skeptical view of Iraq's alleged operational links
with terrorists. The particular target of the OSP analysis was the CIA's
conclusion that the Czech report of the al-Ani–Atta meeting was not
credible. At one point, a Pentagon official waved a photo, allegedly of a
Praque meeting between al-Ani and Atta, that was later shown to be
phony. Tenet reportedly did not think much of the Feith team's briefing. On
September 16, 2002, shortly after the president first addressed the United
Nations seeking a resolution against Iraq and the early reports appeared
about's Saddam's nuclear weapons program, Feith sent the OSP team directly to the White House, where they briefed vice presidential chief of staff
Lewis Libby and Deputy National Security Advisor Stephen Hadley about

the flaws of CIA intelligence-gathering methods and the details of the April 8 Prague meeting. Libby proved more receptive than Tenet, and ordered up a chronology of Atta's travels.[13]

Havel's message to the White House remained secret for another four or five months, effectively extending the shelf life of the Atta-in-Prague story throughout the fall of 2002, when White House saber-rattling over Iraq had reached a crescendo. It was not officially discredited until the 9/11 Commission and the Senate Intelligence Committee published their reports eighteen months later. No one disputed that there had been occasional contacts between the Iraqi regime and al-Qaeda, but there was no evidence whatsoever of any alliance or collaboration between Saddam's secular Baathist regime and Osama's Islamic militants, as the White House obsessively claimed. Indeed, there were reports in 1990 that the terrorist leader was so incensed at Saddam's treatment of his coreligionists, both inside and outside and Iraq, that he had proposed leading a war against Saddam himself to keep U.S. troops out of the region.

"Our report found that the intelligence community's judgments were right on Iraq's ties to terrorists," said Senator Jay Rockefeller of West Virginia, the Democratic cochairman of the Senate Intelligence Committee. "There was no evidence of the formal relationship, however you want to describe it, between Iraq and al-Qa'eda, and no evidence that existed of Iraq's complicity or assistance in al-Qa'eda's terrorist attacks." CIA director Tenet told the Senate Armed Services Committee that the Atta meeting probably hadn't taken place. "Although we cannot rule it out, we are increasingly skeptical that such a meeting occurred," he said. "In the absence of any credible information that the April 2001 meeting occurred, we assess that Atta would have been unlikely to undertake the substantial risk of contacting any Iraqi official as late as April 2001, with the plot already well along toward execution."[14]

The misinformation that had originated in the Czech Republic, which the White House and Pentagon repeatedly attempted to capitalize on, had a powerful effect on public opinion during the run-up to war. That the story had been given such credence by members of the Prague government and released to the press embarrassed both the Czech intelligence service and Havel's office. In the end, Czech border police records showed that Atta had been in Prague in June 2000. But beyond that, there was "no hard evidence" that his alleged contact, Samir al-Ani, the Iraqi diplomat-cum-spy, was involved in terrorist activities or had held a meeting with Atta almost a year later. And no reason was given for precisely why a member of Iraqi intelligence masquerading as a diplomat, a common enough practice, was forced to leave Czechoslovakia.

But the story was not quite dead. Since Atta lived for a time in Hamburg and apparently had gotten travel documents in Frankfurt, the German federal police got into the act. In August 2004, three years after reports of the Atta meeting surfaced and some eighteen months after the invasion of Iraq, German and Czech intelligence determined that the whole business had been a case of mistaken identity. True, a man named Mohammed Atta had arrived on a flight from Germany on May 31, 2000, but he was sent back to Frankfurt because he didn't have a Czech visa, and returned to Prague June 2 with legitimate papers. But this *Mohammed* Atta was a Pakistani businessman. *Mohamed* Atta, the hijacker, entered Prague June 2 by bus and boarded a plane for the United States the next day.[15] There is no evidence at all that the hijacker was in Prague in 2001, when the famous meeting allegedly took place. Czech and German intelligence officials chalk up the confusion to the ethnic Arab Czech agent tailing al-Ani who thought he recognized Atta.

The whole elaborate story that had begun in the days after 9/11 had been based on confusion wrapped in conjecture. But by the time it was cleared up, the damage had been done. A meeting between the 9/11 terrorist and an Iraqi agent in Prague had become part of the popular lore of the war on terror. A *USA Today* survey taken in October 2002 revealed that 86 percent of Americans surveyed thought that Iraq would be behind any future terrorist attacks on the United States. In another poll taken at about the same time by the Pew Research Center for the People and the Press, 66 percent of respondents believed Saddam Hussein was involved in the 9/11 attacks.

By November 2001, at about the time news was spreading that Saddam had trained Islamic hijackers at Salman Pak, U.S. soldiers in Afghanistan along with anti-Taliban fighters from the Northern Alliance overran the northern city of Mazar-e Sharif, a Taliban stronghold, and liberated Kabul from its fundamentalist rulers. In so doing, they rooted out a treasure trove of intelligence in captured al-Qaeda documents, including plans for acquiring crude nuclear "dirty bombs." As American and allied forces set about closing the noose on Osama bin Laden in the rugged northeastern Tora Bora region, in Washington Secretary of Defense Donald Rumsfeld, at the request of the president, ordered Gen. Tommy Franks, the commander of the U.S. Central Command, to conduct a formal review of standing Iraq war plans. On December 1, almost sixteen months before the invasion of Iraq, Rumsfeld, again with the president's backing, issued a top-secret planning order for regime change in Baghdad to the joints chiefs of staff.

One hundred days after 9/11, on December 20, as still-shaken New Yorkers and Washingtonians prepared for the Christmas holidays, *The New York Times* published a front-page story that turned the glare of the media spotlight directly on Iraq and Saddam's WMD arsenal. The reporter, Judith Miller, quoted an Iraqi defector who said he had worked at some twenty hidden biological, chemical, and nuclear weapons sites that were undergoing renovations on Saddam's orders. The self-described Iraqi civil engineer, identified as Adnan Ihsan Saeed al-Haideri, told Miller he had worked upgrading the sites and discussed the projects in some detail during a lengthy interview. Miller, who had been in touch with Chalabi, traveled to Bangkok, Thailand, for the meeting with al-Haideri, which was arranged by the Iraqi National Congress, a fact she reported high in the story. If his account checked out, Miller wrote, "Mr. Saeed's allegations would provide ammunition to officials within the Bush administration who have been arguing that Mr. Hussein should be driven from power partly because of his unwillingness to stop making weapons of mass destruction, despite his pledges to do so."

Al-Haideri's story, she continued, "gives new clues about the types and possible locations of illegal laboratories, facilities and storage sites that American officials and international inspectors have long suspected Iraq of trying to hide. It also suggests that Baghdad continued renovating and repairing such illegal facilities after barring international inspectors from the country three years ago." Charles Duelfer, the former UN weapons inspector who would later conduct the final unsuccessful search for such weapons during the U.S. occupation, commented that al-Haideri's "account was consistent with other reports that continue to emerge from Iraq about prohibited weapons activities," wrote Miller. " 'The evidence shows that Iraq has not given up its desire for weapons of mass destruction,' said Mr. Duelfer."

Despite the voluminous detail offered by her source, Miller wrote that "there was no means to independently verify Mr. Saeed's allegations." The lengthy story was larded with caveats about the skepticism U.S. officials exercised toward defectors and the "ongoing debate" within the administration about expanding the war on terror to Iraq. Stephen Engelberg, a former *Times* editor and Miller's *Germs* coauthor who shepherded the story into print, realized it had to be treated with skepticism. "I guess the question you get to is whether you should run such pieces at all," said Engelberg. "We decided to qualify it and let the readers decide."[16]

Despite multiple efforts to locate the "refurbished" weapons sites in Iraq, none was found by teams of inspectors—including one with al-Haideri in tow to guide them. More than two years later, the Defense Intelligence Agency, the Pentagon's main intelligence arm, dismissed al-Haideri's accounts as unreliable. Still, within hours of its publication, Miller's details about Saddam's reconstituted weapons facilities—especially al-Haideri's revelations that some of the production facilities were hidden under a hospital in Baghdad or behind government buildings and in private villas—were picked up by news outlets around the world, amplifying the reach of *The Times* hundreds of times over. These nonexistent WMD sites too, became part of the anti-Saddam lore. As late as January 2003, weeks before the U.S. invasion, al-Haideri was considered by "administration intelligence analysts" one of the three or four most credible defectors among a "growing number" whose information was suspect and driven by personal motives. The White House, wrote Miller, sought to use information from these defectors "as part of a 'bill of particulars' that the administration hopes will convince skeptical allies and the American public that Iraq's behavior warrants military action." Miller went so far as to report that the administration might incorporate them into President Bush's 2002 State of the Union Address on January 28.

The timing was noteworthy. The *Times* report was published eight days before Gen. Tommy Franks, the commander of U.S. forces in Afghanistan, secretly flew to President Bush's Crawford, Texas, ranch to brief the commander-in-chief for the first time on the Pentagon's recently completed secret war plans for Iraq.

PART II

THE INVESTIGATION THAT
WON'T GO AWAY

6

THE VICE PRESIDENT AND
THE NIGER DEAL

On February 12, 2002, a briefing paper from the Pentagon's Defense Intelligence Agency landed on Vice President Cheney's desk in the West Wing of the White House. The "finished intelligence product," as it was referred to in the bureaucratic vernacular, was entitled "Niamey Signed an Agreement to Sell 500 Tons of Yellowcake a Year to Baghdad." Niamey is the dusty capital of Niger, a tiny former French colony in northwest Africa on the edge of the Sahara. "Yellowcake" is mining jargon for processed uranium oxide ore, a yellowish substance the consistency of grainy powder that is the raw ingredient of weapons-grade uranium. The Pentagon report was based on the second wave of reports about a Niger-Iraqi yellowcake deal that had reached U.S. intelligence agencies. There had been a sketchier first report the previous October, barely a month after the terrorist attacks on New York and Washington. Both were sent by the Italian military intelligence service, or SISMI.[1]

The second document provided more detail than the first, and apparently gave DIA analysts enough information to conclude that "Iraq probably is searching abroad for natural uranium to assist in its nuclear weapons programs." The DIA could not vouch for the credibility of the second Italian report, but the reference to Saddam's "nuclear weapons program" caught the attention of the vice president, whose staff may have already briefed him about the earlier October document. After reading the

DIA intelligence, Vice President Cheney asked his morning intelligence briefer for the CIA's analysis of the Niger question.[2]

The vice president's request directly set in motion a sequence of events that embroiled the White House war effort in a near-crippling political battle over alleged events in a small former French African colony (10.3 million people, 500,000 sq. mi.) halfway around the world. Within days, retired U.S. ambassador Joseph C. Wilson IV was dispatched by the CIA to Niger, where he had been posted a decade before, on an unsuccessful wild-goose chase seeking evidence that an Iraqi-Nigerien uranium deal had taken place. (Wilson had been ambassador to several African nations and was acting ambassador to Iraq after Saddam's 1990 invasion of Kuwait.) His trip was tinder for the political firestorm that engulfed the White House eighteen months later when Wilson publicly questioned the president's use of the discredited Niger intelligence in his State of the Union Address, less than two months before the U.S.-led invasion of Iraq. Wilson's revelations—along with a secret White House effort to retaliate against the former diplomat by revealing his wife's identity as an undercover CIA agent—in turn set in motion a criminal investigation of the White House by a Washington grand jury that lasted more than two years and helped send the president's popularity skidding, as a *Time* magazine writer put it, into "Warren Harding territory."

The Niger affair—the subject of multiple probes by the FBI, the CIA, the Defense Intelligence Agency, the State Department, the Senate Intelligence Committee, the Robb-Silberman Commission, and a half-dozen major newspaper and magazines—is the investigation that won't go away. Exactly what happened—or appeared to happen—in Niger in 1999 and 2000 was at the heart of the intrigue and scandal that consumed Washington in the late spring of 2003. It turned the CIA against the White House and vividly demonstrated to the American press and public, really for the first time, the lengths the Bush White House had gone to manipulate intelligence in building its case for war against Iraq. And it was also at the heart of a concentrated campaign by senior officials of the Bush administration to convince Americans that Saddam Hussein possessed or soon would possess a lethal arsenal of nuclear weapons that threatened the United States.

The first post-9/11 report of the Niger uranium deal reached the CIA on October 15, 2001, just as the massive cleanup operations at the Pentagon and Ground Zero in New York City were getting into full swing. Analysts at the CIA's Directorate of Operations had initially looked skeptically on the SISMI report, which revealed that since 1999 Iraq had been negotiating to buy a shipment of yellowcake uranium from Niger. The Italian intelligence said that an agreement had been approved by the State Court of Niger in 2000 and that Niger planned to ship "several tons" of uranium to Iraq. The cable indicated that Nigerien president Mamadou Tandja had personally okayed the deal. There was no documentary evidence of the sale, however, nor any evidence that any uranium had been shipped. Intelligence analysts warily regarded the report as "very limited" and "lacking needed detail." State Department analysts at the in-house Bureau of Intelligence and Research considered the intelligence "highly suspect."[3]

The CIA, however, keenly aware of the sensitivity of a possible uranium sale to Iraq, decided to distribute the Italian information to other U.S. intelligence agencies, standard practice in the intelligence community. Since the 1991 Gulf War, Iraq's indigenous sources of uranium oxide and the enrichment facilities to refine it into weapons-grade uranium had been destroyed by coalition forces. Iraq had bought processed uranium ore in the 1970s and 1980s from Niger, Brazil, and elsewhere for its nuclear programs—and there was no reason to believe Baghdad wouldn't try again. After the Gulf War, both British and American intelligence estimated that Iraq could speed up nuclear weapons production as much as two or three years by purchasing uranium ore or yellowcake on world markets. In December 2000, British intelligence, noting Iraq's past uranium purchases, reported that Iraqi officials had visited several African countries including Niger in early 1999. British analysts "judged that Iraqi purchase of uranium ore could have been the subject of discussions . . ."

Six months later, in the summer of 2001, when U.S. and European spy agencies were picking up increased chatter about terrorist attacks, the CIA was reportedly offered documents from an Italian source detailing an Iraqi purchase of uranium from Niger. Agency analysts quickly rejected them as forgeries. But the CIA took the precaution of asking French intelligence to look into the security of uranium production in Niger,[4] an ally that would jeopardize its badly needed U.S. aid if it violated post–Gulf War sanctions against sales of uranium.

It was thin stuff. The October CIA report conceded that there was "no corroboration from other sources that such an agreement was reached or that uranium was transferred" and noted that "Iraq has no known facilities for processing or enriching the material." Even so, CIA analysts demurred,

"The quantity of yellowcake to be transferred could support the enrichment of enough uranium for at least one nuclear weapon." In November, the U.S. embassy in Niger also poured cold water on the uranium intelligence. In a cable to Washington, the embassy reported that the top official of the French-government-led uranium-mining consortium in Niger had told U.S. ambassador Barbro Owens-Kirkpatrick "there was no possibility" Niger had diverted any of the "3,000 tons of yellowcake produced in its two uranium mines."

The CIA received the second installment of intelligence on the Niger deal on February 5, 2002, from the same "foreign service," as declassified documents later euphemistically referred to the Italian military intelligence agency. This time there was more convincing detail and what purported to be "verbatim text" of the Niger-Iraq agreement. The report identified the Iraqi official who had traveled to Niger in February 1999 as Wissam al-Zahawi, Baghdad's ambassador to the Vatican in Rome. The details were consistent with the 2000 British report. The new report also put the amount of yellowcake at five hundred tons. It was unclear whether actual documents accompanied the "verbatim text" of the uranium accord. But the second report clearly inferred the existence of such a document, though no documents supporting the story would surface for another eight or nine months.

In early February, the Pentagon's Defense Intelligence Agency wrote and distributed its "intelligence product," based on the new information about Niger's "agreement to sell 500 tons of uranium a year to Baghdad," that found its way to Cheney's desk. The sheer volume of the purported sale raised eyebrows—and serious doubts—among analysts. That was sufficient to make fuel for fifty nuclear bombs, by a later CIA estimate. One analyst at the State Department had even suggested that the source for the Italian report should submit to a lie detector test. The DIA, however, blandly concluded that "Iraq probably is searching abroad for natural uranium to assist in its nuclear weapons program" and once more offered no opinion about the overall credibility of the Italian information.

That was apparently good enough for Cheney, who expressed interest in the Niger information for the first time on February 12. "After reading the DIA report, the Vice President asked his morning briefer for the CIA's analysis of the issue," said the 2004 report of the Senate Select Committee on Intelligence. In response, Tenet's Center for Weapons Intelligence, Nonproliferation, and Arms Control, known as WINPAC, which coordinated overall intelligence for the DCI on weapons of mass destruction, issued its assessment that the "information on the alleged uranium contract between Iraq and Niger . . . lacks crucial details," and stated that "we are working to clarify the information and to determine whether it can be corroborated." The agency was casting about for a knowledgeable envoy to send on a fact-finding trip to Niger. WINPAC acknowledged that the intelligence was flatly contradicted by the U.S. embassy in Niamey. A separate version of the WINPAC assessment was sent directly to Cheney's office, naming the "foreign government service" as Italy's SISMI.

By late February, Cheney's interest in the Niger intelligence was well enough known in the intelligence community that it was foremost on the mind of a State Department intelligence analyst who drafted a March 1 assessment for the Bureau of Intelligence and Research, "Niger: Sale of Uranium to Iraq Is Unlikely." The analyst told the Senate Intelligence Committee that his report "was in response to interest from the Vice President's office in the alleged Iraq-Niger uranium deal." At this time Joe Wilson was still in Niger, and had not yet been debriefed by the CIA. The INR analyst's report was highly skeptical. France, he reminded policymakers, controlled the Niger uranium industry and "would take action to block a sale of the kind alleged in a CIA report of questionable credibility from a foreign government service." He said that "some officials may have conspired for individual gain to arrange a uranium sale," but that President Tandja's government was unlikely to risk loss of aid from the United States and other donors. Cheney reportedly never saw the State Department assessment.

Within the next few days, "the vice president asked his morning briefer for an update on the Niger uranium issue."[5] His query was his second to the CIA about the Niger intelligence in three weeks, certainly a signal of vice presidential interest. In their March 5 response, WINPAC analysts stalled, informing Cheney's briefer that Niger was making every effort to make sure its uranium would be used for peaceful purposes, and that Italian intelligence "was unable to provide new information." Cheney's briefer was also informed that the CIA would "be debriefing a source who may have information related to the alleged sale" that very day.

That would be Joe Wilson, who was arriving that afternoon in Washington. An hour after his plane touched down at Dulles International Airport, the former ambassador and his wife, Valerie Plame Wilson, hosted the two Directorate of Operations debriefers that evening at their modern, multilevel home in the Palisades Heights section west of Georgetown. Wilson's wife excused herself while her husband gave his account of what he had learned in Niger and the CIA reports officer asked questions and took copious notes.

Three days later, on March 8, the CIA distributed its report on Wilson. Directorate of Operations officials alerted their WINPAC colleagues because of the "high priority of the issue." Cheney had asked about it at least twice. Intelligence analysts in the trenches were aware of his avid interest. Yet Senate Intelligence Committee staff, who bent over backward to suggest that Cheney had not seen the highly skeptical March 1 State Department assessment because it not been sent "directly to the vice president in a special delivery," now blandly suggested that Cheney did not see the CIA report either. The CIA's account of Wilson's trip, they declared, "was widely distributed in routine channels," but Cheney's "CIA briefer did not brief the vice president on the report, despite the vice president's previous questions about the issue."[6] The frankly incredible suggestion that Cheney had not been briefed about the CIA report was consistent with a steady stream of denials that the vice president knew about Wilson's trips that later came from the Office of the Vice President. The denials did not square with the trouble counsel David Addington had taken to make certain intelligence documents were routed through the OVP, assuring that even if Cheney had not seen the report himself, Libby would have and was likely to have told the boss about it.

A year before the Senate intelligence report was published, Cheney aides not only claimed that the vice president had never read the CIA report on Wilson's trip—suggesting that he had no idea the intelligence was hotly disputed before the war—they also told the CIA he was not aware that his request for an analysis of the uranium deal had triggered Wilson's Niger trip. "They were very uptight about the vice president being tagged that way," a former senior CIA official said later.[7] Libby and other senior White House officials would work overtime to insulate the vice president from an embarrassing controversy by telling reporters again and again that it was Wilson's wife, not the vice president, who had sent her husband on a fact-finding mission to Niger.

7

HOW JOSEPH WILSON GOT TO AFRICA AND WHAT HE FOUND THERE

With the demise of Africa as a major theater of East-West rivalries after the fall of the Soviet Union, the United States withdrew its intelligence assets from many countries like Niger, leaving American embassies in backwater capitals like Niamey to fend for themselves when it came to information gathering. When the CIA suddenly needed up-to-date information about the Nigerien uranium industry in 2002, Langley had no agents in the field to turn to for real-time intelligence, and was forced to look for sources with relevant experience and expertise in the region. In the case of Niger, there were additional circumstances that made it difficult to get a fix on Iraq's rumored yellowcake purchase. Business was bad. Revenues from Niger's sales of uranium had plummeted since the 1980s, when a Canadian mine began producing uranium ore at lower cost, although uranium mining still made up 72 percent of the country's exports. The country's two mines, Somair and Cominak, were both located deep in the Sahara Desert, making transport to ports or other transit points expensive and difficult. Niger owned the industry in a consortium with four other countries—France, Germany, Japan, and Spain—under the management of a French company named COGEMA, as it had for the past quarter century. Niger had not exported uranium on its own since the 1980s.

There also had been crippling political troubles. In 1996 Niger's coalition government was overthrown in a military coup. Previously warm relations between Washington and Niamey went into the deep freeze. The

Clinton administration promptly shut off badly needed U.S. aid to Niger and distanced itself from the new regime of Col. Ibrahim Baré Mainassara. Two years later, Mainassara was gunned down by his own security detail and succeeded by another military leader, Maj. Daouda Malam Wanké. At the time the Iraqi trade delegation visited Niamey in 1999, Wanke was in the process of turning the government back over to a civilian leadership and leaving for exile in neighboring Nigeria. The elected government was still unsettled and in the process of staking its claim to power.

Under the circumstances, Joseph Wilson was a logical person to send to Niger on a fact-finding mission. As a junior diplomat in Niger during the 1970s, he and embassy colleagues closely monitored the burgeoning uranium industry. Between 1992 and 1995, Wilson was ambassador to Gabon, where following the nation's uranium production was a major part of his duties. His interest and familiarity with the African uranium business carried over into his appointment as senior director of the Africa desk for the Clinton National Security Council in 1997. Even after he retired from government, Wilson had traveled to Niamey three times, once in 1998 at the invitation of President Mainassara for unofficial discussions about holding elections, and again in 1999 after Mainassara's assassination, when he was asked by Prime Minister Ibrahim Mayaki to advise the new military dictator, Major Wanké, on the protocol of ceding power to a democratically elected government. The third time was in 2000, just as Wanke was preparing to hand over power. The CIA had dealt with Wilson before. "During my 23 year career as a diplomat," Wilson wrote in his memoir, *The Politics of Truth* (2004), "I had often met with members of the intelligence community to share my knowledge of the countries I worked in." He continued: "While we policy types rely on the analysts to provide necessary underpinning for decisions the U.S. government makes, so too do the analysts want to hear what we have to say. It gives them a chance to test their working hypotheses and also to get closer to the nitty-gritty."[1] Aside from his long professional experience, Wilson also had another personal connection to the intelligence world—by marriage. Unbeknownst even to Wilson's former colleagues at the State Department, his wife, Valerie Plame Wilson, whom he had married four years before, was a veteran CIA officer.

The CIA, of course, was well aware of the connection. Since leaving the government, Joe Wilson had worked with the CIA at least once before, during his 1999 trip to Niger after General Mainassara's assassination. That time, Valerie Wilson had suggested her husband for the assignment. "The former ambassador was selected for the 1999 trip after his wife mentioned to her supervisors that her husband was planning a business trip to Niger in the near future and might be willing to use his contacts in the region . . ."[2] A week before CIA officials invited Wilson to their Langley headquarters for a preliminary meeting about returning to Niger in February 2002, the deputy chief of the Counterproliferation Division asked Valerie Wilson to draft a memorandum outlining her husband's qualifications to look into the Nigerien uranium question. "My husband has good relations with both the PM and the former minister of mines (not to mention lots of French contacts), both of whom could shed light on this sort of activity," she wrote in her February 12 internal memorandum.[3]

The memo was one of several documents later used as proof by the Republican chairman of the Senate Intelligence Committee, Senator Pat Roberts of Kansas, that the "plan to send the former ambassador to Niger was suggested by the former ambassador's wife, a CIA employee." But there was no evidence that Valerie Wilson's memo went beyond citing her husband's qualifications, as her boss had requested, or that she even mentioned a trip to Niger.[4] The CIA, for its part, maintained from the beginning that officials of the Counterproliferation Division selected the former ambassador as a candidate for the Niger trip, and explicitly denied that any nepotistic maneuvering was behind Wilson's selection. A senior intelligence official not only confirmed to the Long Island newspaper *Newsday* that Valerie Plame Wilson worked undercover " 'alongside' the operations officers who asked her husband to travel to Niger," but said she "did not recommend her husband to undertake the Niger assignment."[5]

All parties to the February 19 meeting at Langley agreed, however, that Valerie Wilson briefly introduced her husband to the gathering and, within minutes, left the basement room where it took place. Beyond that she acted only as an occasional "conduit" between the agency and her husband. The intelligence analysts in attendance were for the most part uranium experts or Africa specialists at the State Department or the CIA. Wilson's CIA hosts told him, according to his account, that "a report purporting to be a memorandum of sale of uranium from Niger to Iraq had aroused the interest of Vice President Dick Cheney." Wilson said he was told the document "was not very detailed." It was unclear to him, Wilson later wrote, whether the "reporting officer"—presumably the DIA analyst who wrote the assessment of the uranium deal, who was not present—"had actually laid eyes on the document or was simply relaying information provided by a third party." Wilson also had the impression that the amount of yellowcake involved "was estimated to have been up to five hundred tons, but could also have been fifty," an indication to him that the source of the information may have been relying on memory, and perhaps a faulty one at that.

Wilson was skeptical. He was acutely aware that he had been away from Africa for two years, and at best could only provide the analysts with background information on the uranium business. But he knew it might be useful background. He personally knew Ibrahim Mayaki, who would have been prime minister at the time the government allegedly signed the uranium agreement with the Iraqis, as well as the former minister for energy and mines, Mai Manga, and other Nigerien officials who might have been involved. As a deputy U.S. ambassador at the Baghdad embassy in the lead-up to the first Gulf War, he had a better grasp than most of the stakes if it turned out that Saddam was breaking "out of the box" of UN sanctions and seeking uranium from Niger to restart his nuclear weapons program.

After Wilson had briefed the assembled analysts on the logistics of possible yellowcake shipments, from security precautions to transportation routes, he was asked if he would travel to Niamey, as he later put it, "to check out the report in question." According to notes and e-mails later made available to the Senate Intelligence Committee staff, State Department analysts at the Bureau of Intelligence and Research once more expressed doubt that Niger could pull off such a large shipment of yellowcake under the noses of the French, who "appear to have control of the uranium mining" and "would seem to have little interest in selling uranium to the Iraqis." The State Department analysts doubted that a Wilson mission would add much to what the U.S. embassy in Niamey already knew. Others felt that "the Nigeriens would be unlikely to admit to a uranium sales agreement with Iraq, even if one was negotiated." One CIA analyst, who worked at WINPAC, concluded that "the results from this source [Wilson] will be suspect at best, and not believable under most scenarios."

Wilson made it clear that he was a professional diplomat, not a spy, and that he was too well known in Niger to operate clandestinely. He would have to travel openly as a representative of the U.S. government, he said, and would not accept a fee, but only reimbursement of his expenses from the CIA. In return, he agreed to give the CIA an oral report of his findings. The next day, February 20, 2002, Counterproliferation Division officials provided Wilson with general talking points "for his use with contacts in Niger." Other analysts present confirmed Wilson's account that "specific details of the classified report on the Iraq-Niger uranium deal were discussed at the meeting." The Senate report noted that the CIA gave Wilson "operational clearance" for classified material up to the secret level, without giving him formal security clearance.[6]

Wilson arrived in Niamey on February 26. He checked into the Gaweye, a modern concrete-and-glass downtown hotel that stood on the site of what had been a dusty refugee camp for Tuareg tribesmen—who had fled the countryside during one of Niger's periodic droughts—when Wilson lived there in the 1970s. After attempting to get messages to former acquaintances via messengers and the ancient telephone system, he met with Ambassador Barbro Owens-Kirkpatrick at the U.S. embassy. Wilson was impressed by the connections she had made in the capital, despite the fact that Niamey was her first post in Africa. But he was a bit taken aback when she described her own efforts to investigate the same uranium allegations he was sent by the CIA to look into. Owens-Kirkpatrick admitted that she, too, had been surprised when she heard Wilson was making the trip, since she felt she had officially discredited the Niger-Iraq yellowcake deal as unfounded.[7]

Owens-Kirkpatrick had gone to considerable lengths to investigate the rumors. She had known that Gen. Carlton Fulford, then deputy U.S. commander in Europe and responsible for military-to-military relations with African forces, was scheduled to make a refueling stop in Niamey in mid-February. So when Washington first cabled her about about the uranium question early in the month, she asked Fulford to put the yellowcake issue on his agenda with Nigerien officials. With the assistance of the CIA, she then prepared talking points for meetings with President Mamadou Tandja and Foreign Minister Aichatou Mindaoudou. Her CIA instructions directed Owens-Kirkpatrick and Fulford to ask officials in general whether "Niger had been approached, conducted discussions, or entered into any agreements concerning uranium transfers with any 'countries of concern,' " without referring to the specific intelligence report on the Iraq-Niger deal.[8]

The ambassador told Wilson that they had discussed the yellowcake rumors with the president and other members of his government, and that she and Fulford were satisfied with his "denial" that any transaction had occurred and his "explanation of why such a uranium deal could not possibly have taken place."[9] Tandja assured the U.S. ambassador and the general that Niger's goal was to keep its uranium "in safe hands." Owens-Kirkpatrick told Wilson that Fulford was also persuaded that the uranium sales story wasn't true. The ambassador and the general filed separate reports outlining their findings to the State Department and the Defense Department. Both received wide circulation in the intelligence community. At the end of their initial meeting, Owens-Fitzpatrick and Wilson agreed that he could still make himself useful by getting in touch with officials in the former government who were no longer among the embassy's principal contacts.

As his eight-day stay progressed, Wilson began to get a picture from his discussions with former government officials of what it would take to sell five hundred tons of yellowcake to Iraq. To begin with, a shipment of five hundred tons would mean a production increase of 40 percent, in any given year. Normally the first priority of the Niger mines was to supply uranium ore to the four outside consortium members for their nuclear programs. That would mean adding more workers, more barrels for shipping, beefed-up production schedules, and more complicated transportation and security arrangements. Such an undertaking could not happen without the knowledge of the French managing partner, COGEMA, which would find itself in violation of international law and risk sanctions if it tried to sell prohibited material for nuclear fuel to Iraq.

The newly elected Niger government would risk another painful cutoff of critical American aid if it sold Iraq uranium. And a deal with Iraq would require the knowledge and approval not only of the minister of mines, but of the foreign ministry, since the transaction would be with a country outside the consortium. A final decision would have to be made by Niger's top leadership in the Council of Ministers. Wilson noted that without the valid signatures of top officials in each of those government agencies, there would be no deal. He knew who they were. Moreover, once completed, the sale would throw off a huge amount of money in additional government tax revenues. After questioning current and former officials, Wilson felt there was virtually no way such an agreement could be kept secret in the insular, gossipy world of Niamey politics.

Among the former government officials Wilson met with was former prime minister Mayaki, who had served in the governments of Colonel Wanké between 1997 and 1999 and General Mainassara before that. Mayaki told Wilson he "was unaware of any contracts that had been signed between Niger and any rogue states for the sale of yellowcake." He added, however, that he had been approached at a ministerial meeting of the Organization of African Unity[10] in June 1999 and asked if he would meet with an Iraqi delegation to discuss "expanding commercial relations." Mayaki said it had occurred to him that perhaps the Iraqis wanted to discuss yellowcake sales. The former prime minister told Wilson that a meeting with the Iraqis had taken place, but there had been no discussion of uranium. He said he "let the matter drop due to the UN sanctions on Iraq."[11]

Mayaki explained to Wilson that he "was wary of discussing any trade issue with a country under United Nations sanctions" and "made a successful effort to steer the conversation away from a discussion of trade with the Iraqi delegation." In another conversation two years later, Mayaki told Wilson that just before the U.S. invasion of Iraq in the spring of 2003, he had been watching an Iraqi press conference on television and recognized one of the Iraqis in the 1999 delegation. Only then did he realize that the man who had approached him at the OAU conference was Mohammed Saeed al-Sahaf, the well-known spokesman for Saddam's regime nicknamed "Baghdad Bob" by news correspondents.[12]

Wilson also met with Niger's former minister of mines, Mai Manga. The former minister told Wilson that there had been no uranium sales outside the prescribed oversight channels established by the International Atomic Energy Agency since the 1980s and he knew of no illegal sales to rogue states. Manga recalled that a visiting Iranian delegation in 1998 had been interested in buying four hundred tons of yellowcake from Niger, but no contract was ever signed. Manga said he believed it would be almost impossible to pull off such a "special shipment of uranium to a pariah state" because the French-run consortium watched every step, from extraction at the Niger mines to loading ships docked in Benin for transport overseas.[13]

The full report of Wilson's debriefing by the CIA circulated to the intelligence community and policymakers on October 8 was classified, although a declassified version was produced for public consumption two years later in the Senate Intelligence Committee report; it is not known how the two versions differed. The weight of evidence that Wilson presented to the CIA—and, before him, that Ambassador Owens-Kirkpatrick and General Fulford had reported—strongly suggested that the Iraqi yellowcake deal had never happened, indeed had never been considered, much less approved, by Niger government officials, and would have been nearly impossible to arrange secretly, even if it had been approved. Even if the Iraqi trade delegation was intent on such a deal, there was no evidence that they had presented it to any Nigerien or French official. Yet the Senate report focused on the CIA's contention that Wilson "did not refute the possibility that Iraq had approached Niger to purchase uranium."

The declassified account accurately reflected the conclusion of CIA and DIA analysts that Wilson's trip had not "supplied much new information and [they] did not think that it clarified the story on the alleged Iraq-Niger scheme." Far from debunking the Niger sale, analysts found that "the former ambassador's report lent more credibility, not less, to the reported Niger-Iraq uranium deal."[14] Indeed, they reportedly found it "interesting" that Mayaki had mentioned that "an Iraqi delegation had visited Niger for what he believed was to discuss uranium sales." Mayaki, of course, neither believed nor said any such thing, as Wilson made clear to his CIA interlocutors. At best, Mayaki's account was idle speculation, which he sensibly chose not to act on. But the intelligence analysts seized on it. After the Italian documents purporting to show an Iraqi yellowcake purchase were discredited as forgeries in March 2003, more than a year later, this gossamer thread provided by Mayaki was the only evidence left to support the Bush administration's contention that Iraq was buying uranium for its allegedly resurgent nuclear weapons program, and therefore posed a deadly threat to the United States.

CIA analysts, who had been dismissive of the Niger intelligence before 9/11 and deeply skeptical afterward, were suddenly grasping at straws to support the possibility of an Iraqi uranium purchase. The inconsistency that surfaced in the assessment of the Niger intelligence after Wilson's trip did not surprise some agency veterans. It was an early sign that the analysts were beginning to tailor their work not only to the questions asked by senior policymakers, but to their perceived preferences as well. At the CIA, analysts and their managers had picked up clear signs that the Bush White House was heading for war in Iraq. No one had to look hard to find the source. Vice President Cheney repeatedly had expressed his personal interest in knowing more about Iraqi interest in Niger's uranium. The intelligence bureaucracy was responding, albeit with inconsistency and some discomfort, in kind. No one had to explain to CIA analysts, wrote Paul Pillar, the CIA's top analyst for the Middle East who witnessed the gradual deterioration of intelligence firsthand, that "reports that conform to policy preferences have an easier time making it through the gauntlet of coordination and approval than ones that do not."[15]

In truth, Wilson hadn't supplied the CIA analysts with enough substance to manage even that. Counterproliferation Division officials might have sent the right messenger, but Wilson brought back the wrong message. As a consequence, the much-anticipated CIA report on his trip was at once "widely distributed in routine channels," which presumably included the vice president's office, but was not highlighted for policymakers and "the CIA's briefer did not brief the Vice President on the report, despite the Vice President's previous questions about the issue."[16] That, of course, raised questions about whether Cheney had seen the CIA report at all. His office later insisted he hadn't. By marginalizing Wilson's findings and broadcasting that the CIA report was distributed only through routine channels, analysts handed Vice President Cheney that old executive branch plum, plausible deniability. No one would say it outright, but the CIA was feeling the heat from the White House—and displaying classic symptoms of a meltdown.

AN ONSLAUGHT OF
BAD INTELLIGENCE

The CIA's changing perspective on the Niger affair could not have been clearer. The public account of Wilson's mission to Niger provided a snapshot of a skeptical and cautious agency suddenly bent on dredging up dimly conceivable rumors, idle speculation, and outright gossip, ignoring contrary reporting from U.S. diplomats and intelligence analysts, while pushing forward selected "intelligence" that would build the case for war. The vice president was demonstrably the primary client for intelligence gathering on the Niger sale. Even official suggestions that the CIA report may not have reached Cheney, or that he had not read it and had not been briefed about it, only raised strong suspicions that just the opposite was true, given the vice president's distrustful and meticulous nature.

Despite the thinness of available information, there was no evidence that the intelligence community tried to steer clear of the Niger business after Wilson's trip. To the contrary, the volume of reporting on the issue was stepped up, another sign to insiders that dubious intelligence was getting a tail wind from insistent policymakers. Late in March 2002, the CIA received a third report from Italian intelligence about the Niger sale, contending that the deal was for five hundred tons *a year*,[1] although redactions obscured the duration of the alleged sales. In early May, Paul Pillar's shop in the Directorate of Intelligence prepared a briefing book for the cabinet-level members of the National Security Council, noting, accurately enough, that "a foreign government service says Iraq was trying to acquire 500 tons of uranium from Niger." Dismissing the continued skepticism of State Department analysts, the CIA now believed that "the intelligence showed both that Iraq may have been trying to procure uranium in Africa and that it was possible Niger could supply it."[2] This finding was bolstered in part by reports from "separate sources" that Iraqis had sought uranium sales in the Congo and Somalia in 1998 and 1999.

The U.S. embassy in Niger cabled at the end of June 2002 that the Tandja government had signed a comprehensive safeguards agreement with the IAEA covering sales of uranium, which was read as a sign of government resolve that Niger's uranium production was for "peaceful purposes" only. Nonetheless, in mid-July the intelligence arm of the Department of Energy published a daily intelligence brief entitled, "Nuclear Reconstitution Efforts Underway?" which for the first time raised the possibility that Saddam was rebuilding his nuclear weapons arsenal. The Niger deal, DOE analysts believed, was one of several indications that Iraq "might be reconstituting its nuclear program." They cautioned that there was no evidence that shipments had taken place, and noted the "amount of uranium specified far exceeds what Iraq would need even for a robust nuclear weapons program."

By midsummer, The New York Times and The Washington Post finally confirmed that the Bush White House was planning for war in Iraq, a process that the president had secretly put in motion six months before. The public acknowledgment had several repercussions. On the debit side, dubious Republican stalwarts from Brent Scowcroft to Henry Kissinger commandeered the op-ed pages to question the White House's emerging strategy for preemptive war. For his part, Vice President Cheney began to escalate his rhetoric on the Iraqi threat, telling gatherings of U.S. veterans and GOP faithful in San Antonio and Nashville in August that there was "no question" Saddam had restarted his nuclear weapons programs. Within weeks, some Democrats in Congress had grown uneasy with administration saber-rattling and increasingly skeptical about the pumped-up rhetoric on Iraq's WMD programs. They wanted to see proof. The rumblings of discontent from Capitol Hill and critical noises from former Republican colleagues seemed only to irritate Cheney, who was privately furious at news that the State Department had cut off funding to Ahmed Chalabi, the Iraqi dissident leader who was supplying the United States with new intelligence on Saddam's weapons programs.[3]

It took until the next month for intelligence to catch up with the vice president's pronouncements. The tentative question asked by DOE analysts about Iraq's nuclear activities in July became a confident assertion of fact in a new September DIA report called simply *Iraq's Reemerging Nuclear Program*. The DIA report tossed out the carefully circumscribed language of earlier reports and bluntly asserted that "Iraq has been vigorously trying to procure uranium ore and yellowcake." It bolstered the claim by citing the March reports of the four-year-old alleged Iraqi interest in uranium from the Congo and Somalia. There was no mention of any fresh intelligence to support the new tone of certainty for good reason; none existed.

In fact, the credibility of the Niger intelligence, which was increasingly critical to the vice president's case, took a severe blow in the summer of 2002—but the CIA never reported it. During the summer, CIA officials, who maintained close relations with their counterparts in French intelligence despite fraying diplomatic ties between their two countries, quietly but with some urgency asked Paris to investigate the Italian reports about the alleged Niger uranium deal.[4] The French intelligence agency, DGSE,[5] had examined and dismissed a similar claim a year before. But the urgency and new detail of the American request persuaded the French counterterrorism chief, Alain Chouet, to send a half-dozen agents to Niger to recheck reports of a sale or attempted purchase. The French had a proprietary interest in the uranium allegations. "We've always been very careful about both problems of uranium production in Niger and Iraqi attempts to get uranium from Africa," Chouet later explained. "After the first Gulf War, we were very cautious with that problem, as the French government didn't care to be accused of maintaining relations with Saddam in that field."[6]

The French team came back from Niger empty-handed, unable to find evidence of a deal. Chouet and his staff, however, noticed that the allegations were similar to those in documents an Italian informant named Rocco Martino had tried to sell the French in 2001. Within days, French analysts had dismissed them as forgeries. "We thought they [the Americans] were in possession of the documents. The words were very similar," Chouet told the *Los Angeles Times*. "We told the Americans, 'Bullshit, it doesn't make any sense.'" Formal cables, somewhat more delicately phrased, to that effect were sent to CIA headquarters in Langley and the CIA's Paris office. The CIA will not confirm whether it received the French messages.

As autumn approached, the administration ramped up its efforts to sell the war to the public. On Sunday September 8, days before President Bush was scheduled to address the UN General Assembly seeking a resolution to support U.S. military action in Iraq, *The New York Times* published a front-page blockbuster by Michael Gordon, the paper's military correspondent, and Pulitzer Prize–winning journalist Judith Miller reporting that Iraq recently attempted to procure special aluminum tubes for its nuclear weapons program.[7] "More than a decade after Saddam Hussein agreed to give up weapons of mass destruction," Gordon and Miller wrote, "Iraq has stepped up its quest for nuclear weapons and has embarked on a worldwide hunt for material to make an atomic bomb, Bush administration officials said today." For the moment, the Niger yellowcake was forgotten, though it would resurface again soon enough.

"In the last 14 months," the article went on, "Iraq has sought to buy thousands of specially designed aluminum tubes, which American officals believe were intended as components of centrifuges to enrich uranium." The *Times* story quoted an anonymous "senior administration official," who underscored the importance of Saddam's renewed nuclear weapons program. "The jewel in the crown is nuclear," the official declared. "The closer Saddam Hussein gets to a nuclear weapon, the harder he will be to deal with." The story was larded with phrases about "Hussein's dogged insistence on pursuing his nuclear ambitions" and how "acquiring nuclear arms is again a top Iraqi priority." The new details about Saddam's nuclear weapons programs rocketed around the world, as the Internet amplified many times over the already massive secondary dissemination of the *Times* story by television, wire services, and news agencies.

Who leaked the infamous aluminum tubes story to Gordon and Miller? Neither reporter has said, but there is little doubt senior Bush officials with access to top-secret classified intelligence funneled it to *The Times*.[8] An examination of intelligence available to the White House at the time strongly suggests that the story was the result of a highly selective reading of classified reports about Iraqi efforts "to procure 60,000 high-strength aluminum tubes" first received by the CIA in late March or early April 2001. The CIA then quickly assessed on April 10 that "the tubes were probably intended for an Iraqi uranium enrichment program," though it acknowledged that "using aluminum tubes in a centrifuge effort would be inefficient and a step backward from the specialty steel machines Iraq was poised to mass-produce at the onset of the Gulf War."[9] The very next day, intelligence analysts at the Department of Energy, citing technical specifications inconsistent with gas centrifuge use and a pattern of Iraqi procurement unlikely for a major clandestine weapons program, concluded that although "the gas centrifuge application cannot be ruled out," the tubes sought by the Iraqis were probably intended for use as "launch tubes for man-held anti-armor rockets or as tactical rocket casings." Within a month, DOE confirmed that Iraq had purchased similar aluminum tubes before to use as launch tubes "for a multiple rocket-launcher."

In short, hardly a month after it was first reported, the intelligence about the aluminum tubes was already mired in an intra-agency dispute about whether they were intended for uranium enrichment centrifuge rotors or rocket launchers. The CIA, with the later support of the Defense Intelligence Agency at the Pentagon, took the position that the tubes were intended for Zippe centrifuges, an outdated gas centrifuge design from the 1950s. The DOE stood by the strong evidence presented by its analysts that they were for rocket motor casings or rocket launchers, a view that was eventually vindicated by the CIA's own experts.[10] But between July 2001 and September 2002, when the classified intelligence was leaked to *The New York Times,* the CIA produced no fewer than nine additional assessments of the aluminum tubes—all without the benefit of any additional intelligence beyond the original report a year before. Not surprisingly, senior Bush policymakers chose to use the CIA assessment to make its point about the development of an Iraqi nuclear enrichment capability—and ignored the DOE's powerful dissent over the aluminum tubes.

Three days after the tubes story broke, the White House suddenly showed renewed interest in the purported Niger yellowcake deal. On September 11, 2002, members of the National Security Council staff asked the CIA to clear language about the aluminum tubes and the uranium deal for possible use by the president. The NSC submitted the following passage:

Iraq has made several attempts to buy high strength aluminum tubes used in centrifuges to enrich uranium for nuclear weapons. And we also know this: within the past few years, Iraq has resumed efforts to obtain large quantities of a type of uranium oxide known as yellowcake, which is an essential ingredient of the process. The regime was caught trying to purchase 500 metric tons of this material. It takes about 10 tons to produce enough enriched uranium for a single nuclear weapon.[11]

Curiously, the CIA—which thanks to the French now had reason to suspect that the Niger uranium deal was an outright fraud—okayed the NSC passage, which made no mention of Niger or Africa.

Then, on September 24, the British government for the first time since 9/11, published a "white paper"—in other words, a summary of its own intelligence for British public consumption—addressing Iraq's weapons of mass destruction. The British report came on the heels of a July war summit at the president's Texas ranch with Prime Minister Tony Blair and meetings between key British and American intelligence officials in Washington. Picking up on earlier British reports, it noted in part that "there is intelligence that Iraq has sought the supply of significant quantities of uranium from Africa." The British assessment was significant not only because it appeared to confirm the U.S. intelligence about Niger, but it also provided a separate, apparently corroborating source that the Iraqis were foraging looking for illicit uranium in Africa.

The same day the British white paper arrived in Washington, NSC staff went back to the CIA with a rephrased passage about the yellow-cake intelligence to clear for the president's public use. The new passage read, "We also have intelligence that Iraq has sought large amounts of uranium and uranium oxide, known as yellowcake, from Africa. Yellow-cake is an essential ingredient of the process to enrich uranium for nuclear weapons." The CIA approved the passage, as it had done two weeks before. Although the formulation conjoining the aluminum tubes and the African yellowcake was never used by Bush, the two NSC requests mark the first time the Bush White House attempted to make a case that Iraq had reconstituted its nuclear weapons program by linking purported Iraqi interest in building centrifuges for enriching uranium to the alleged attempt to buy raw African yellowcake for its enrichment program. In the emerging U.S. view, these were the two foundations of evidence that Saddam was intent on acquiring nuclear weapons, and they would be pressed into service soon enough—even though readily available intelligence showed that Saddam's nuclear program had been a shambles since the Gulf War. But at the time, no one, including members of Congress and editors of The New York Times and The Washington Post, was any the wiser.

The handling of the alleged Niger-Iraqi deal by U.S. intelligence agencies was off to a rocky start. Nonetheless, the official charade continued. The intelligence took on a life of its own in the pages of the critical 2002 National Intelligence Estimate, entitled Iraq's Continuing Programs for Weapons of Mass Destruction. The document was produced at the request of Democrat Bob Graham of Florida, then the chairman of the Senate

Intelligence Committee, and other skeptical members of Congress. Graham initially asked the CIA director Tenet in September for the NIE— periodic, authoritative assessments of the U.S. intelligence community's collective position on critical issues of national security—on Iraq's arsenal of prohibited weapons. Graham was stunned to find that none existed, despite the fact that the president, the vice president, and other cabinet officials had been publicly touting the dangers of Saddam's nuclear program for weeks. Tenet managed to rush a classified version of the NIE into print in just under a month, just in time for the October vote on congressional authorization of the president's plans to prepare for war against Iraq.

Tenet's NIE borrowed the pumped-up phrasing of the September DIA report *Iraq's Reemerging Nuclear Program* to describe the Niger sale. "Iraq also began vigorously trying to procure uranium ore and yellowcake; acquiring either would shorten the time Baghdad needs to produce nuclear weapons," the NIE stated. As of early 2001, it added, "Niger planned to send several tons of 'pure uranium' (probably yellowcake) to Iraq," noting that "Niger and Iraq reportedly were still working out arrangements for this deal, which could be for up to 500 tons of yellowcake."[12] Despite the confident, documentary tone, the NIE did concede that "we do not know the status of this arrangement." The account of the Niger deal was a case study in what senators Rockefeller, Levin, and Durbin later sharply criticized as "stale, fragmentary, speculative," and "unsupported" intelligence.[13]

It got worse. When State Department analysts balked at a draft version of the NIE's account, a statement was prepared for a sidebar indicating that "the claims of Iraqi pursuit of natural uranium in Africa are, in INR's assessment, highly dubious." The caveat, intended to show that the intelligence community did not unanimously support the Niger story, also undermined the administration position that Saddam had reconstituted his nuclear weapons program. Somehow the INR's dissenting text bloc on the Niger uranium was "inadvertently" separated by "some 60 pages" from the section on the Iraqi nuclear program in the final version the CIA sent to Congress on October 1. No one could say how the sidebar had been misplaced.[14]

Shortly afterward, Congress voted overwhelmingly to give President Bush the authority to use military force in Iraq in the Joint Resolution to Authorize the Use of United States Armed Forces Against Iraq. But the text bloc incident and continued queasiness about the Italian-supplied intelligence may have had the unanticipated effect of creating cold feet on the Niger case in some quarters at the CIA. In September, a CIA analyst reportedly suggested to an NSC staff member that any reference to Iraqi attempts to buy African uranium should be deleted from an upcoming speech, only to be told that this would leave the British "flapping in the wind," suggesting that the NSC believed that dropping the evidence from the British white paper would somehow embarrass the British and leave them exposed. The NSC staffer denied that he had used the phrase or been advised not to approve the African uranium intelligence.[15]

The CIA had a completely different take. Asked about the British report, the CIA's deputy director, John McLaughlin, told the Senate intelligence committee on October 2 that "the one thing where I think they stretched a little bit beyond where we would stretch is on the points about Iraq seeking uranium from various African locations. We've looked at those reports and we don't think they are very credible. It doesn't diminish our conviction that [Saddam's] going for nuclear weapons, but I think they reached a little bit on that one point."[16] The split over the British yellowcake intelligence between the CIA and the NSC came to a head early in October, when the NSC submitted a draft speech with a sentence about the African uranium deal that President Bush was to give in Cincinnati on October 7. The speech, which declared that "the regime has been caught attempting to purchase up to 500 metric tons of uranium oxide from Africa—an essential ingredient in the enrichment process," went through multiple drafts before the reference to African uranium was dropped altogether at the order of Deputy National Security Advisor Stephen Hadley.

On October 6, the CIA faxed a memo to the White House explaining why it recommended deleting the sentence:

(1) The evidence is weak. One of the two mines cited by the source as the location of the uranium oxide is flooded. The other mine cited by the source is under the control of the French authorities. (2) The procurement is not particularly significant to Iraq's nuclear ambitions because the Iraqis already have a large stock of uranium oxide in their inventory. And (3) we have shared points one and two with Congress, telling them that the Africa story is overblown and telling them this is one of the two issues where we differed with the British.[17]

The author of the CIA fax to the White House was not identified. But Hadley had received *his* orders to withdraw the sentence about Niger in the president's speech directly from DCI George Tenet. "The President should not be a fact witness on this," Tenet recalled telling Hadley in testimony before the Senate Intelligence Committee on July 16, 2003, nine months later. The "reporting was weak." Tenet's remarks came ten days after former ambassador Wilson's op-ed article appeared in *The New York Times* charging that the White House had "twisted" intelligence "to exaggerate the Iraqi threat"—and two days after columnist Bob Novak outed Wilson's wife as a CIA agent.

No changes were made in the declassified version of the NIE, which had been delivered to House and Senate members a week earlier. Nor was Congress made aware of the CIA's newly dismissive position on the Niger intelligence before it authorized President Bush to use military force in Iraq.

At about the time of the president's Cincinnati speech, the U.S. embassy in Rome received photocopies of twenty-two pages allegedly documenting the Niger deal. The papers were made available to the embassy on October 9 for authentication by Italian journalist Elisabetta Burba, a reporter for the weekly *Panorama,* which was owned by conservative Italian prime minister Silvio Berlusconi. Burba reportedly received the documents from Rocco Martino, an Italian businessman with financial and intelligence contacts whom she had dealt with before; he wanted ten thousand dollars for them. The Rome embassy cabled photocopies to Washington in mid-October. At least one set went to the State Department's Bureau of Intelligence and Research (INR). Another eventually wound up at the CIA's Counterproliferation Division. Like the French intelligence team before her, Burba traveled to Niger and concluded there wasn't anything to the story.

The reception the papers got at the CIA was muted, to say the least. They were widely distributed by State Department analysts to the various government intelligence agencies at a special meeting on October 16 attended by least four CIA representatives. None of the four CIA people could remember getting copies when they were later questioned about it.[18]

At the CIA, the Niger papers mysteriously dropped from sight—for three months. After an investigation months later by the CIA's inspector general, one copy was found in a vault at the Counterproliferation Division. The Center for Weapons Intelligence, Nonproliferation, and Arms

Control (WINPAC), which reported directly to Tenet on key questions of concern to the larger intelligence community, did not receive a copy until January 2003, when it requested the documents from the State Department.

As far as the CIA was concerned, the Niger documents seemed to be a nonissue. At the time, the agency was preoccupied with the immediate problem of getting UN approval for U.S. military force if Washington could show that Baghdad was in breach of UN resolutions outlawing weapons of mass destruction. One CIA analyst later explained that a "foreign government service" (Italian intelligence) had already provided "verbatim text," therefore the documents themselves wouldn't advance the case. Another said they were working on the reconstituted nuclear program and the uranium reporting wasn't important. The lack of interest strongly suggested that CIA analysts had already seen the actual documents that turned up at the U.S. embassy in Rome—and not just the paraphrased or "verbatim" text of documents—long before the set of photocopies from Rome came over the transom in October. It also suggested that French counterterror chief Alain Chouet may have been right—that the CIA had received the Niger documents in some form as early as October 2001 and already believed they were bogus.

It didn't take long for analysts outside the CIA to sniff out problems with the documents. At the State Department, an INR analyst was skeptical, noting in an e-mail that one of the documents "bears a funky Emb of Niger stamp (to make it look official, I guess)." The suspicious INR analyst noticed that a separate document included in the photocopies mentioned a military campaign by Iran and Iraq against world powers being orchestrated by the Nigerien embassy in Rome. "Completely implausible," he wrote.

After UN Resolution 1441, which called for Iraq to comply with stringent U.S. and British disarmament requirements, was negotiated by Colin Powell, the next hurdle was to develop a response to Iraq's 12,000-page disclosure, submitted on December 7, denying it had any WMD programs. On December 17, WINPAC produced an analysis of Baghdad's disclosure, pointing out that Iraq had breached its agreement by failing to explain its procurement of aluminum tubes to build centrifuges that could be used in a nuclear program. And Baghdad did "not acknowledge efforts to procure uranium from Niger, one of the points addressed in the U.K. dossier."

With this, the CIA had once more restored the Niger sale to respectability, even after Tenet himself had so carefully and thoroughly discredited it two months before by insisting on its deletion from the president's Cincinnati speech. On top of that, the CIA was attributing the intelligence to the British white paper that the CIA received in late September 2002 rather than to the original Italian reports. Once more the agency was distancing itself from the Italian intelligence. Why was that?

The formulation by the Weapons Intelligence group also sprung the trap Vice President Cheney had set for the Iraqis. If the Iraqis admitted to having any unconventional weapons, they were in material breach of UN Resolution 687 of 1991, which banned them from building or possessing weapons of mass destruction. If Saddam tried to hide his weapons programs, well, he was also in violation. "That would be sufficient cause to say he's lied again, he's not come clean and you'd find material breach and away you'd go," said the vice president.[19] The White House declared Baghdad in material breach for attempting to conceal its "procurement" of aluminum tubes for enriching uranium fuel and for its "effort" to procure supplies of yellowcake uranium to feed the centrifuges.

The CIA had once more also failed to include mention of the State Department's well-known doubts about the actual use of the tubes and the yellowcake deal in its report to the NSC. A December 23 exchange of e-mails, reported by Senate committee staff, between an analyst at the Department of Energy's intelligence section and a counterpart at INR made the obvious connection. "It is most disturbing that WINPAC is essentially directing foreign policy in this matter," wrote the DOE analyst. "There are some very strong points to be made about Iraq's non-compliance. However, when individuals attempt to convert those 'strong statements' into the 'knock out' punch, the Administration will ultimately look foolish—i.e., the tubes and Niger!"

On December 19, a State Department rebuttal to the Iraq disclosure mentioned Niger publicly for the first time, asking: "Why is the Iraqi regime hiding their Niger procurement?" The U.S. response to Iraq's disclosure by then UN ambassador John Negroponte, who was later appointed to the newly created post of director of national intelligence by President Bush, elicited prompt denials from Nigerien president Mamadou Tandja that Niger had sold uranium to Iraq or been approached to do since he took office in 2000.

By then, suspicions about the Niger documents from Rome were mounting. On January 13, the skeptical INR analyst spelled out in an e-mail to colleagues why he had concluded that "the uranium purchase agreement is probably a forgery." When an analyst at WINPAC read it and realized that the CIA did not have copies of the documents he requested them from the State Department. The CIA received the papers, said the

Senate report, on January 16, 2003.Two CIA analysts studied the copies and later reported that "it was not jumping out at us that the documents were forgeries."[20]

Jacques Baute, the director of the nuclear verification office for the International Atomic Energy Agency (IAEA), asked the U.S. government for its evidence about the Niger uranium deal in January after Negroponte's speech, and was met with silence. His interest was piqued again when Colin Powell addressed the World Economic Forum in Switzerland on January 26, conflating the twin pillars of Iraq's allegedly reconstituted nuclear program, the Niger yellowcake, and the aluminum tubes. "Why is Iraq still trying to procure uranium and the special equipment to turn it into material for nuclear weapons?" Powell asked. On January 28, President Bush declared in the State of the Union Address that Iraq "sought significant quantities of uranium from Africa," avoiding mention of Niger by attributing the information to the British government. CIA director Tenet testified that he never read the speech, but in the end took responsibility for the mention of the uranium deal, which it was later confirmed had been borrowed by White House speechwriters from the problematic 2002 National Intelligence Estimate and the September 2002 British white paper.

The IAEA's Baute flew from Vienna to New York and was finally given copies of the Niger documents on February 4. The next day, Colin Powell made his famous presentation to the UN Security Council stating the U.S. case for war. He did not mention the Niger uranium deal, an omission Baute noticed.

On February 3, the CIA headquarters at Langley sent off a message to Rome that may explain why Powell dropped the reference to an Iraqi uranium deal—and perhaps why the documents were turned over to Baute the very next day. Apparently in response to Powell's tough vetting of the uranium deal before his speech, the CIA message requested "information from the foreign government service"—presumably Italian military intelligence—about an earlier report on the 1999 Iraq-Niger uranium deal. "The issue of Iraqi uranium procurement continues to resonate with senior policymakers," the CIA cable read, "and may be part of SecState's speech to the UN Security Council of 5 Feb 2003 if [a foreign government service] is able to provide a contract for the 1999 uranium deal, confirm that the information was not from another foreign government service."[21]

"The same day," the Senate Intelligence Committee later reported in a heavily redacted passage, "CIA [redacted] responded that the foreign government service does not have a copy of the contract, the information was of 'national origin.' " Was CIA headquarters asking the CIA station chief in Rome whether Italian intelligence could provide a legitimate contract for the uranium deal? And could the Rome office assure Washington that the reporting on the 1999 deal did not originate with a third intelligence service, such as Britain's MI6 or France's DGSE? Was the answer, in fact, that SISMI could not provide Secretary Powell with a legitimate contract? And that the documents on the alleged 1999 uranium sale originated in Italy, with assistance from SISMI?

After Baute got the Niger papers in New York, he turned them over to IAEA investigators. A month later, on March 3, 2003, his office in Vienna informed the U.S. mission there that the documents were forgeries and, in the words of the Senate report, "did not substantiate any assessment that Iraq sought to buy uranium from Niger." Four days later, IAEA Director General Mohamed ElBaradei publicly declared that the documents were frauds.

Vice President Cheney responded on March 16 with an attack on El-Baradei. "I think Mr. ElBaradei frankly is wrong," he said. "And I think if you look at the track record of the International Atomic Energy Agency on this kind of issue, especially where Iraq's concerned, they have consistently underestimated or missed what it was Saddam Hussein was doing." Three days later, the U.S. "shock and awe" campaign against Iraq began. Two weeks later, the National Intelligence Council, the U.S. group responsible for national intelligence estimates, published a Sense of the Community Memorandum entitled "Niger: No Recent Uranium Sales to Iraq."

"We judge it highly unlikely that Niamey has sold uranium yellowcake to Baghdad in recent years," the memo read. "The Intelligence Community agrees with the IAEA assessment that key documents purportedly showing a recent Iraq-Niger sales accord are a fabrication. We judge that other reports from 2002—one alleging warehousing of yellowcake for shipment to Iraq, a second alleging a1999 visit by an Iraqi delegation to Niamey—do not constitute evidence of a recent or impending sale." It did not say whether it still believed that Iraq had been "vigorously trying to procure uranium ore and yellowcake" from Niger. In mid-June, CIA analysts forwarded a classified memo to CIA chief George Tenet in response to queries from Scooter Libby and the vice president's office, explicitly disavowing the Niger story. "Since learning that the Iraqi-Niger uranium deal was based on false documents earlier this spring," said the memo, "we no longer believe that there is sufficient other reporting to conclude that Iraq purchased uranium from abroad."[22]

The British, however, refused to recant the African intelligence in their September 2002 white paper. That allowed Cheney, either by design or delusion, to cling publicly to the possibility that Niger in fact had a yellowcake deal in the works with Saddam, despite repeated and forceful assessments to the contrary from the U.S. intelligence community. Discussing the subject with Tim Russert on *Meet the Press* in September 2003, the vice president seemed to attribute the widespread repudiation of the Niger intelligence to confusion between the British and the U.S. spy agencies. "[O]n the whole thing, the question of whether or not the Iraqis were trying to acquire uranium in Africa—In the British report, this week, the Committee of the British Parliament, which just spent 90 days investigating all of this, revalidated their claim that Saddam was, in fact, trying to acquire uranium in Africa. What was in the State of the Union speech and what was in the original British white papers. So there may be difference of opinion there. I don't know what the truth is on the ground with respect to that."[23]

9

THE MYSTERY OF THE FORGED DOCUMENTS

In the summer of 2004, the *Sunday Times* and the *Financial Times* of London identified a former Italian spy-turned-businessman named Rocco Martino as the go-between who provided the forged Niger documents to *Panorama*'s Elisabetta Burba. A former cop, Martino reportedly had ties to Italy's SISMI and other European intelligence agencies, and may have been linked to an employee at the Nigerien embassy in Rome, who apparently pilfered stationery for the fabricated documents. *Panorama* wasn't the only organization Martino approached with the phony Niger papers. As early as the fall of 2001, he also provided them to the French and to Britain's agency, MI6, for as much as $10,000. In Burba's case at least, Martino turned over the documents without collecting his fee, suggesting to investigators that money was not his primary objective. Martino was also believed to have been working for a second operative associated with SISMI who engineered the burglary at the Niger embassy and brought in Martino to pass the Niger documents on to his foreign intelligence connections.

In August, a team of investigative reporters for CBS's *60 Minutes* located the sixty-six-year-old Martino in Rome and persuaded him to fly back to New York to film an interview, since Italian law enforcement authorities reportedly had a warrant out for him. But bringing him back to New York created another set of problems. The CBS crew was afraid that if the FBI discovered that Martino was in the United States, agents might try to snatch him. Theoretically at least, the FBI had a keen interest in talking to Martino. After the IAEA had pronounced the Niger documents forgeries, the FBI had agreed to investigate their shadowy origins following a request from Senate Intelligence Committee minority cochairman Jay Rockefeller of West Virginia. "There is a possibility that the fabrication of these documents may be part of a larger deception campaign aimed at manipulating public opinion and foreign policy regarding Iraq," Rockefeller wrote to FBI director Robert S. Mueller III at the time.[1]

Fears that the FBI would pick up Martino in the United States proved unfounded—only confirming the reporters' suspicions that the FBI wasn't pressing its investigation too aggressively. *Newsweek* reported that the FBI wanted to speak to Martino, but had "not yet received permission to do so from the Italian government." That odd explanation fueled questions "about whether the right-wing government of Italian Prime Minister Silvio Berlusconi had helped manufacture evidence . . . to persuade Americans to support an invasion," according to the online magazine *Salon*. Martino was questioned by Italian authorities on his return in September about how the Niger documents came into his hands.

The CBS interview with Martino raised more questions than it answered, and was finally cut from the final thirty-minute piece on the Niger report, which was scheduled to air the week before the 2004 presidential election. Copies of the segment were distributed to reviewers. Hours before the Niger story was to air, CBS shelved it and instead ran its now-infamous investigative fiasco about President Bush's National Guard service, triggering an embarrassing internal CBS probe and multiple staff firings and ending the career of the network's veteran news anchor, Dan Rather. *60 Minutes* correspondent Ed Bradley was said by colleagues to be infuriated that the Niger report was spiked. CBS News president Andrew Heyward later claimed the Niger investigation was pulled off the air because it was "inappropriate" during the presidential campaign.

The precise origin of the forged Italian documents and who was behind their fabrication is still swathed in mystery. But the identification of Martino, with his shadowy connections to the world of Italian military intelligence, has lent credibility to suspicions by Rockefeller and others that the entire Niger affair may have been a fiction, cooked up by Western spy services, and subsequent investigations have supplied credible details about the involvement of the Italian military intelligence service SISMI—possibly in concert with an American with close ties to the Bush administration.

Early on, the British were high on the list of suspects, due in part to the close partnership between the United States and the United Kingdom before the invasion of Iraq. Both American and British agents reportedly had used forged documents and disinformation before in their dealings with Iraq. A member of the UN weapons monitoring team sympathetic to U.S. war aims reportedly provided unverifiable intelligence reports and tips to British MI6 agents who then passed them along to London newspapers,[2] a prewar tactic also used by Iraqi dissidents to plant disinformation in the Western press. A Senate Intelligence Committee staffer was on record stating that "the Niger documents were initially circulated by the British." London's most lasting contribution to U.S. prewar intelligence was the September 2002 white paper on Iraq's weapons of mass destruction, which purported that Saddam had approached an African country to purchase uranium. But the British intelligence assessment did not reach the CIA until almost a year after the initial Italian reports landed in Washington.

The French, too, were under suspicion after London's *Financial Times* reported that officials in Paris told the United States in November 2002 that France had also come by information on an Iraqi attempt to buy uranium from Niger—which turned out to be copies of the same forged documents the United States later turned over to the IAEA. It was a fine example of the Western intelligence echo chamber but not much else. French intelligence told the CIA on March 4, 2003, two weeks before the Iraq invasion, that their Niger information was based on the fraudulent documents.[3]

Investigators for the left-wing Italian daily *La Repubblica* confirmed in late 2005 that Martino was involved with a ragtag group of accomplices in actually creating the forged documents and circulated them to major European intelligence agencies as well as *Panorama*. But who put Martino and his gang up to the job is unclear, though all signs point to SISMI. Reporters Carlo Bonini and Giuseppe d'Avanzo published evidence that Martino, along with an SISMI official and a female accomplice inside the Niger embassy, conspired to fabricate the Niger documents using shreds of credible information and Nigerien embassy letterheads. Martino, a native of the Calabria region of southern Italy, was a former policeman with a background in intelligence. After he was fired from the police force, he then moonlighted as a small-time crook and double agent for SISMI until 1999. He had an arrest record in Italy and West Germany for extortion and possessing stolen checks. Martino was reportedly on retainer with French intelligence, and passed information on the Italians to Paris and, in his capacity as double agent, inside dope on the French to SISMI headquarters in Rome.

Martino's primary accomplice in the forgeries, according to *La Repubblica,* was an old acquaintance and former carabineer named Antonio Nucera, SISMI's deputy chief for technology transfers and counterproliferation for Africa and the Middle East. Nucera allegedly supplied Martino with an authentic "telex from Ambassador Adamou Chékou to the Niger Foreign Ministry informing Niamey that Wissam al-Zahawi, the Iraqi Ambassador to the Vatican, would be coming to Niger as a representative of Saddam Hussein,"[4] as well as other documents intended to lend plausibility to the phony dossier.[5] Nucera reportedly involved a third key player, an unnamed sixty-something female employee of Niger's Rome embassy who had worked as a mole for SISMI before. She was described as looking like a once pretty "old auntie" who spoke with a heavy French accent in a flutelike whisper. The involvement of both Nucera and "La Signora," as the embassy employee was nicknamed, was reportedly later confirmed by SISMI chief Nicolò Pollari. La Signora received "a few thousand lira" for her work. Nucera's motivation was also portrayed as financial.

On January 2, 2001, the three, along with a fourth accomplice, First Embassy Counselor Zakaria Yaou Maiga, staged a burglary at Niger's embassy in Rome. Little of value was reported missing besides a watch and two bottles of perfume, but official stationery, an official embassy stamp, and letterheads apparently disappeared as well. Old papers detailing Niger uranium sales from the 1980s, Nigerien codebooks, and other documents like Ambassador Chékou's telex that had been supplied by Nucera from SISMI archives were then copied and used with the official stationery and embassy stamps to fashion phony correspondence, contracts, and a memorandum of understanding between the government of Niger and Iraq "concerning the supply of uranium on 5 and 6 July in Niamey." Attached was a two-page "agreement" from the State Court of Niger approving the uranium sale "in compliance with Article 20 of Ordinance No. 74-13 of 5 July 2000." Martino then reportedly handed over the faked papers to the French intelligence arm, DGSE, in exchange for an undisclosed sum of money. DGSE officials quickly determined the documents were "a useless parcel of garbage."[6]

French intelligence had a vital interest in the Niger documents for the same reason SISMI closely monitored the Niger embassy in the 1980s: The tiny Francophone country was once a major supplier of uranium to world markets. But the French government and French mining interests were still responsible for oversight of Niger's uranium operations, and any irregularities or violations of international law directly concerned

Paris. "We know how they do things there," a French agent told *La Re-pubblica*. "But no one would have mistaken one minister for another in they way they did . . ." The phony package ginned up by Martino and company was badly flawed. He and his cohorts included a letter dated July 30, 1999, purportedly from Foreign Minister Nassirou Sabo to the ambassador in Rome, that referred to an agreement reached on June 29, 2000. The first problem was evident to a schoolchild: June 29, 2000, was still a year in the future. The second problem required basic knowledge of Niger politics. Unfortunately for the forgers, Nassirou Sabo wasn't appointed foreign minister until October 10, 2000.

Another letter dated July 27, 2000, to "Monsieur le Président" Saddam Hussein from President Mamidou Tandja, confirming the yellowcake purchase agreement, mistakenly referred to Niger's constitution of 1966. The constitution then in force was adopted in 1999—and was the fourth approved by successive governments in the troubled country since 1966. Yet a fourth letter, dated October 10, 2000, to the ambassador in Rome, with the memorandum of understanding attached, was from Foreign Minister Allele Dihadj Habibou—who hadn't been Niger's foreign minister since 1989.

It has never been clear whether SISMI based its early reporting to the CIA in October 2001 on the same twenty-two-page Niger documents that eventually were passed from Burba to the U.S. embassy in Rome and finally arrived in Washington in the fall of 2002. After all, if SISMI knew about the forged documents from the beginning and bore at least some responsibility for their fabrication, why did the Italians hold off until February 2002, when the second SISMI report arrived at Langley, before even mentioning that their hot intelligence about an Iraqi uranium purchase was based on "real" documents? And what kept them from producing the actual pages until the next October, when copies were finally sent to Washington via the State Department?

One answer is that although the Berlusconi government and SISMI quickly recognized the potential political value of the intelligence to the post-9/11 Bush administration, SISMI also knew the documents were phony and therefore had to distance itself from their dissemination. At first, the expedient course seems to have been to show the documents to the CIA station chief in Rome, Jeff Castelli, without allowing him to keep a copy. Castelli in fact was permitted to look over the papers and even take notes, but that was all. His subsequent report to Langley was probably the basis for the CIA's October 18, 2001, Senior Executive Intelligence Brief, which was routinely distributed to the other U.S. intelligence agencies. There is also some evidence that SISMI might have become aware of flaws in the Niger documents that led officials to change the most glaring mistakes in them, but leave others in—such as the reference to the 1966 constitution in the Tandja letter—as tolerable risks.

That would have made it necessary to build a firewall between SISMI and Martino, effectively pinning the blame on him for fabricating and distributing the documents, while ensuring that the forged papers were widely circulated among intelligence agencies. This is what appears to have happened. But Martino himself, hardly the most reliable of sources, told the *Financial Times* that the U.S. and Italian governments were behind the creation of the Niger dossier as part of a campaign of deception. Very little hard evidence has emerged, amid some provocative—and so far highly circumstantial—speculation, that suggests Rome and Washington conspired to forge a set of documents to support a casus belli against Iraq. The fact is, like so much disinformation, the limited but potent half-life of the Niger documents only required that SISMI ensure their injection into the intelligence stream. Strictly speaking, SISMI did not require U.S. collusion, though the Italian service may have used American help to get the Niger intelligence to the right policymakers in Washington.

Gen. Nicolò Pollari, the head of SISMI, has insisted that his agency had no role in creating the forgeries, although he readily confirmed to investigators that they came from Martino and La Signora and that Nucera was involved. If there was a U.S. connection to the forged documents, investigators pointed to Michael Ledeen, a well-known conservative hardliner with ties to the Bush White House who was in Rome at the time on contract with the Pentagon's Office of Special Plans. Ledeen has denied categorically that he had any role in the forgeries. Bonini and d'Avanzo make a persuasive case that Pollari and SISMI were aware of Martino's scam and the existence of the faked documents soon after the 9/11 terrorist attacks, when they began to take on a meaning beyond parochial French interests in Africa. The real question about the forged documents is whether Pollari and the Berlusconi government took it upon themselves, possibly using Ledeen as a middleman, to press their case with Washington.

Whoever was behind them, the Niger forgeries have all the makings of one of the most audacious—and sloppily executed—campaigns of deception in the history of modern intelligence. According to U.S. government records, Washington's first inkling of fresh allegations that the Iraqis were interested in buying raw uranium from Niger was the report from SISMI that arrived in Washington on October 15, 2001.[7] That same day, after spending weeks trying to get an audience with the new conservative American president, recently elected Italian prime minister Silvio Berlusconi, a wealthy conservative and publishing magnate, was finally ushered into the Oval Office for a meeting with Bush. General Pollari, who had been head of SISMI for only three weeks, was reportedly under pressure from Prime Minister Berlusconi to supply useful information for the Americans in the war on terror to give Italy a foothold in the effort. Pollari was well aware of the Bush administration's obsession with regime change in Iraq. The same day, the CIA received a report from "a foreign intelligence service," later identified as SISMI, indicating that Iraq had signed an agreement in 2000 to buy several tons of uranium from Niger. U.S. analysts judged the Italian report questionable enough to ask SISMI for a clarification. Pollari responded in a one-and-a-half-page letter to Langley assuring CIA officials that "the information comes from a creditable source, La Signora," who "in the past . . . has given SISMI the cryptographic codes and memorandum ledgers from the Niger Embassy. So those documents could be good."[8]

There was no indication that any documentary evidence of the uranium transaction existed until February 5, 2002, when the second report from SISMI arrived at the CIA, this time elaborating that the deal was for five hundred tons of yellowcake a year and providing "verbatim text" of the purported accord. The CIA declined to produce a formal report on the new Italian intelligence, and instead took a backseat to the Defense Intelligence Agency, which prepared an "executive highlight" brief for top administration officials. Investigators believe that after the initial lukewarm response to the Italian intelligence from the State Department and the CIA, Pollari began casting about for a way to approach the Iraq hardliners in the Bush administration about the Niger uranium sale.

At about this time Pollari was reportedly introduced by Italian defense minister Antonio Martino to Michael A. Ledeen, an ultraconservative, pro-Israel, Reagan-era veteran of the Iran-Contra scandal and fellow at the American Enterprise Institute who was then in Rome on contract with Douglas Feith's policy office at the Pentagon, which included the Counter Terrorism Evaluation Group, a small unit set up by Wolfowitz and Feith[9] to develop intelligence to back military intervention in Iraq. Ledeen, a confidant of Vice President Cheney with ready access to senior National Security Council officials Condoleezza Rice, Stephen Hadley, and others, was the perfect liaison between SISMI and the Bush hardliners. The possibility that Ledeen may have played a role in U.S.-Italian skullduggery was first mentioned by an anonymous SISMI official at Forte Braschi, SISMI's headquarters in Rome, who explained to *La Repubblica* that the SISMI chief "talks to Ledeen" because "Pollari is very shrewd. He understands that in order to push the uranium story he cannot rely on the CIA alone. He has to work, as he was advised by Palazzo Chigi [the Italian prime minister's residence in Rome] and the Defense Department, with the Pentagon and the National Security advisor, Rice. . . . In reality, we wanted to keep the CIA out of our work. So he keeps all his moves quiet . . . his more important meetings happen elsewhere."[10]

In December 2001, Defense Minister Martino asked Pollari to arrange clandestine meetings in Rome for Ledeen and two officials of Feith's Pentagon policy shop: Lawrence Franklin (later indicted for passing classified information to Israel) and Harold Rhode. They met at an SISMI safe house near Rome's Piazza di Spagna and possibly a second time, at the nearby Parco dei Principi Hotel. A group later described as Iranian dissidents, but whom Pollari identified as agents of Tehran, joined the gathering, along with representatives of the Shiite Supreme Council for Islamic Revolution in Iraq, known by its acronym, SCIRI, Iraq's largest and most powerful Shiite political organization. The secret back-channel meeting between Pentagon officials, Iranian government officials—the two countries have had no diplomatic relations since the 1979 hostage crisis—and the Iran-backed SCIRI was also attended by Ahmed Chalabi, the dissident Iraqi Shiite leader of the Iraqi National Congress, with two of his deputies, Aras Habib Karim and Francis Brooke, an American.[11]

The session was reportedly the brainchild of Manucher Ghorbanifar, an Iranian arms dealer who had been involved with Ledeen in the Iran-Contra arms deal during the Reagan administration. "Ghorbanifar called me, and at first I said, 'Are you insane?'" Ledeen told *The New York Times*.[12] "But he said he could arrange meetings with Iranians with current information about what Iran was doing. It wasn't information coming from him. He was just arranging the meetings." Ghorbanifar, who had arranged for Israel to deliver 508 TOW missiles to Iran, had been declared persona non grata by the CIA, which regarded him as "a fabricator and a nuisance." Pollari, who arranged the locations for the meetings, also attended the sessions with an SISMI deputy, he told *La Repubblica*, because "I wanted to know what was cooking." By his account, the Iranians were not only sent by Tehran, they weren't particularly interested in exposing Tehran's double-dealing with al-Qaeda in Afghanistan or garnering support for the Iranian anticlerical terrorist group Mujahedin-e Khalq that was seeking regime change in Tehran, a longtime goal of such hardcore neoconservatives as Ledeen, Franklin, and Rhode.

Pollari intimated that Ghorbanifar's presence and all the anti-Iranian rhetoric were pretexts designed to provide cover for the real purpose of the meetings. Were the twenty-five men gathered at a Rome safe house around a table spread with large maps of Iraq, Iran, and Syria really intent on sharing intelligence about the Iraqi regime with the Pentagon? All were in a position to do so and had significant interests in Iraq: SCIRI wanted to be the potential leader of a new majority government in Baghdad, with its own intelligence sources and its heavily armed, fifteen thousand–strong militia, the Badr Brigade; Iran had its strategic interest in developing an alliance with the majority Iraqi Shiites when the United States deposed Saddam; and Chalabi, whose organization was rumored to have had a hand in the Niger forgeries, was busy positioning himself for a high position in any post-Saddam government in Baghdad.

Whatever actually transpired in Rome, news of the secret, unauthorized meeting filtered back to the United States and caused an immediate furor inside the Bush administration. Both the CIA and the State Department protested that Pentagon officials had met secretly with Iranian dissidents to discuss destabilizing other countries in the region. Secretary of Defense Rumsfeld denied that the meeting was designed to circumvent official U.S. policy. "Oh, absolutely not," he said. "I mean, everyone in the interagency process, I'm told, was apprised of it, and it went nowhere."[13] Ledeen, for his part, refused to shed light on what was discussed. "I'm not going to comment on any private meetings with any private people," he said. "It's nobody's business."[14]

Pollari's favor for Ledeen in setting up the Rome meetings seems to have been returned quickly. By one account, Ledeen went back to Washington in early 2002, at about the same time the CIA received the second SISMI report on the Niger uranium purchase. At Ledeen's urging, Deputy Secretary of Defense Paul Wolfowitz reportedly soon thereafter prevailed upon Vice President Cheney to look into the second Italian account of the Iraqi uranium purchase[15] that was reported in the February 12 Defense Intelligence Agency executive briefing.

Ledeen, of course, denied that he had any involvement in the fabrication of the Niger documents. But in the weeks before Martino conveyed the forged papers to Burba at *Panorama*, Ledeen and Italy's ambassador to Washington, Gianni Castellaneta, reportedly helped Pollari set up meetings in Washington with Rice, Wolfowitz, and Feith. On September 9, the day after the aluminum tubes story broke in the United States, Pollari met with Rice's deputy, Stephen Hadley, at the White House. Next to nothing is known about meetings with Wolfowitz or Feith, or whether they happened. Little is known about the substance of the meeting with Hadley. ("What do you think they discussed in the summer of 2002?" exclaimed the Forte Braschi insider.) But Hadley insisted later that the Niger uranium deal did not come up. "Nobody participating in that meeting or asked about that meeting has any recollection of a discussion of natural uranium, or any recollection of any documents being passed," Hadley said. "And that's also my recollection."[16] After seeing Hadley, Pollari returned to Italy, and turned to promoting himself and SISMI before intelligence oversight committees of the Italian parliament, declaring in one session, with modest exaggeration, that "we do have documented proof that a central African nation has sold pure uranium to Baghdad."

A month later, in October, Pollari pumped up SISMI's intelligence coup, claiming that "we have documented proof of an Iraqi acquisition of pure uranium in a central African nation. We also know of an Iraqi attempt to purchase centrifuges, to be used to enrich uranium, from companies in Germany and possibly in Italy as well." By that time, the forged Niger documents were safely in the hands of Elisabetta Burba and the editors of *Panorama*.

Two years later, as the insurgency in Iraq strengthened and public security all but disintegrated, an Italian reporter, accompanied by an Italian intelligence officer, was shot and killed by nervous U.S. soldiers manning a checkpoint on the "highway of death" between Baghdad's airport and the city. With national elections approaching and Italian antiwar sentiment surging after the shooting, Berlusconi was forced to withdraw his small contingent of Italian troops from Iraq. General Pollari, appearing before a closed parliamentary oversight committee hearing in late October 2005, also changed his tune. Facing the senators, the SISMI chief produced a classified letter from FBI director Robert Mueller, dated July 20, that praised Italy's cooperation with the FBI investigation into the forgeries. The FBI, the letter said, found that the documents in question were produced and circulated by one or more people in a moneymaking scheme and had concluded that there was no evidence that the Italian military intelligence service had tried to influence U.S. policy toward Iraq. As a result, the letter concluded, the FBI was closing down its two-year probe.

The Italian spymaster also told the assembled senators that Rocco

Martino, whom he identified as a former SISMI informer who had been "kicked out of the agency," had circulated the forged documents, though he stopped short of accusing Martino of involvement in fabricating the papers. Pollari did not explain how transcripts or a "verbatim text" of the forged papers found their way into SISMI intelligence reports to the CIA in 2001 and 2002, or why no action had been taken against Martino. He emphasized to the lawmakers that Martino was "offering the documents not on behalf of SISMI but on behalf of the French," and said that Mr. Martino had told Italian authorities that he worked for French intelligence. A senior French intelligence official dismissed the charge as "scandalous." A member of the parliamentary committee present at the hearing reported that Italian intelligence had warned the United States in early 2003 that the Niger documents were false. "At about the same time as the State of the Union address," said Sen. Massimo Brutti, "they said that the dossier doesn't correspond to the truth."[17] Pollari apparently did not explain to the committee how SISMI reached that conclusion.

Pollari's revelation that the FBI had quietly shut down its investigation of the forged documents three months earlier had an immediate impact in Washington. Within a week, the FBI reversed itself, responding in part to news reports that its agents somehow had failed to interview Rocco Martino, and reopened the investigation. The decision to restart the FBI probe occurred amid the supercharged political atmosphere following the Libby indictment in October 2005, and a dramatic shutdown of the U.S. Senate by Democrats intent on forcing Republicans to get moving on a long-stalled investigation of the White House's handling of prewar intelligence.

Democrats welcomed the renewed probe. "I was surprised that [the FBI] ever closed it without coming to a conclusion as to the source," said former senator Bob Graham, who was chairman of the Senate Intelligence Committee when the CIA first heard about the Niger claims. "It looks as if it's a fairly straightforward investigation trail to who the source was. And I'm glad the FBI has resumed the hunt."[18]

Despite Senator Jay Rockefeller's original charge to FBI director Robert S. Mueller III to look into the possibility of a larger deception campaign behind the forgeries, the FBI investigation was limited to the involvement of foreign governments and found nothing. Federal officials hinted that the new inquiry might investigate whether the fabrications were the work of U.S. citizens who supported a war against Iraq, or possibly even of Iraqi defectors associated with Ahmed Chalabi and the Iraqi National Congress. But they downplayed the outcome of the new inquiry. "I don't expect the results to be any different," said one federal official.

"I think the answer is going to be that [Martino] wasn't acting in behalf of any government or intelligence agency. This guy was trying to peddle this to whoever he could."[19]

Senate Democrats, however, were not ready to give up. "This is such a high-profile issue for a lot of reasons, and we think it's important to make sure there aren't lingering questions," said an aide to Rockefeller, the vice chairman of the Senate committee. "There's always a chance that you do a little more investigating and you uncover something you hadn't seen before or you hadn't realized."[20]

PART III

ALL EYES ON SADDAM'S ARSENAL

10

PRIMED FOR DISINFORMATION

B y the winter of 2002, efforts to identify the extent of Iraq's arsenal of chemical, biological, and nuclear weapons had quietly become the highest priority to Bush's inner circle. Saddam's WMD had been a focus of American interest for more than a decade. In the seven years following the Gulf War, UN weapons hunters employed increasingly successful—and controversial—methods to uncover the extent of Saddam's lethal weaponry, eventually destroying huge stores of Iraq's unconventional arsenal and weapons-production facilities in the process. During that time, the arms inspectors of the UN Special Commission on Iraq (known as UNSCOM) effectively gutted Baghdad's potential threat as a regional nuclear power. They destroyed tons of chemical weapons stores and the missiles and warheads designed to deliver them. In the meantime, the United States and Britain, the leaders of the Gulf War coalition, effectively checked Saddam's martial ambitions with a combination of economic sanctions and military surveillance in the designated Iraqi "no-fly" zones.

But there were significant gaps in UNSCOM's knowledge of Iraq's WMD capabilities. The weapons inspections ended in late 1998, when UNSCOM personnel were forced out of Iraq on the eve of a four-day U.S.-British bombing campaign known as Operation Desert Fox. Due in large part to Iraqi duplicity and hostility, there was no way to confirm that Baghdad was sufficiently disarmed to enable the UN Security Council to lift the economic sanctions imposed on Iraq by Resolution 687 in

1991. Little was known, for example, about Saddam's germ warfare programs or his supersecret VX nerve gas research. By 2002 such lingering uncertainties, combined with a virtual intelligence blackout of Iraq's activities for the three years since UNSCOM left Baghdad, would provide the Bush administration with fertile ground for a lethal mix of paranoia, speculation, and dissembling about the state of Saddam's illegal weapons programs.

The early search for Saddam's WMD, conducted from the outset in the face of tireless obstruction and harassment by the Baghdad regime, began in earnest during a tense confrontation at an Iraqi military base outside of Baghdad in June 1991. Dr. David A. Kay, the American leader of the UNSCOM inspection team, who had done a brief stint at the International Atomic Energy Agency, had been chief UN weapons inspector for a matter of weeks. Kay had access to U.S. satellite photos that suggested the Iraqi military facility might be the site of secret activity related to Saddam's nuclear weapons program. Despite insistent Iraqi denials, Kay knew that such a program existed. Before the Gulf War, Baghdad had declared that it possessed a Soviet-made research reactor and a stockpile of highly enriched uranium purchased from France. He was now interested in finding out what other nuclear assets Saddam might have squirreled away. Kay and his convoy of weapons inspectors arrived unannounced at the base and demanded access.

"I have no orders to let you in," protested the Iraqi commander at the gate. Kay was unfazed by the rebuff. He had made a calculated decision not to give the Iraqis the usual advance notice of the visit, taking advantage of new ground rules for arms inspections in the April Security Council Resolution 687, which required Iraq to fully account for any proscribed WMD as part of the ceasefire accord between Iraq and the U.S.-led coalition. Kay asked if his team could stay just outside the gate to monitor any traffic exiting the base. Noting a water tower just inside the fence, he asked permission to allow several men to climb up the tower for a better view. "You can put up as many members of your team as you want," the Iraqi commander answered. It was a major mistake. What the agile UN inspectors saw in the distance in the next ninety seconds was astonishing. "I had four of my daring-do members climb this 50 meter water tower," Kay said later, "and literally—because we video-taped this—it looks like dinosaurs rolling around the back of the base, there's so much dust being stirred up. What had happened is they were—the calutrons were—stored on these very large tank transporters, which are about 90 feet long . . . And they were charging out the back of the base."[1]

Kay quickly dispatched his team in vehicles to catch up with the Iraqi transport trucks and photograph their cargo as the drivers raced out of the sprawling base through a rear gate, with dust swirling and hastily secured tarps flapping in the wind. Iraqi guards fired shots over the heads of the weapons hunters as they sped off in hot pursuit and drew up parallel to the trucks, snapping photographs all the way. The bulky, half-covered objects on the trucks were identified by nuclear experts as calutrons, which are essentially large soft iron magnets as large as fifty feet in diameter and used to enrich weapons-grade uranium, similar to those used to produce the first U.S. atomic bombs. Like much of the high-tech equipment purchased for Iraqi weapons programs in Western Europe, most of the calutrons were made by an Austrian company. The photographs were proof positive that Iraq, despite its strenuous denials, had an extensive uranium enrichment program that was previously unknown.

The June 1991 inspection was the first breakthrough for the weapons team. The UNSCOM group, comprised of several dozen specialists in everything from missile technology to the nuclear fuel cycle, was tasked with the arduous process of cataloguing Saddam's weapons programs and destroying them. Kay's water tower gambit not only suggested the previously unknown extent of Iraq's nuclear program; it also confirmed for the first time that Baghdad was bent on subverting UNSCOM's efforts through a variety of schemes, from moving weapons and weapons-making equipment around the country and hiding them in the desert to unilaterally destroying them without proof or documentation.

The discovery of the Iraqi campaign to hide its WMD programs from the weapons inspectors revealed basic details of how Iraqi obstruction worked. Senior Iraqi officials, mostly members of the supersecret Special Security Organization Directorate and Saddam's inner circle—dubbed the "Joint Committee" by UNSCOM—would make a great show of sacrificing their oldest and most basic chemical weapons, like sarin and mustard gas, and even destroying older missiles and their payloads. Iraqi nuclear research, they explained, was intended to produce nuclear energy, not weapons. But they were careful to remove any sensitive files that inspectors might request about their more sophisticated binary chemical weapons; or what would eventually be revealed as Saddam's full-blown, $10 billion prewar nuclear weapons program; or Iraq's advanced missile research, which would theoretically put Tehran and Tel Aviv in range of Baghdad's nuclear arsenal. The Joint Committee was also intent on keeping Iraq's biological weapons program away from the UN weapons inspectors.

The extent of the Iraqi deception, though hinted at in the June incident, did not become clear until September 1991. Armed with intelligence from a defector that the Iraqis were consolidating sensitive documents that described Saddam's nuclear weapons program, Kay's team descended on a government building in downtown Baghdad. The intelligence proved accurate, and UNSCOM inspectors quickly located the nuclear documents, rounded them up, and spirited them out of the building before the Iraqis could stop them. As it dawned on Iraqi officials what had happened, they forcibly ejected Kay's inspectors from the building and corralled them in the parking area outside, forbidding them to carry off the files on the nuclear program. "You can leave the parking lot, but you're not taking these documents," snapped an Iraqi official. The resulting standoff in the parking lot quickly escalated into a potentially deadly international incident. The UNSCOM team, which Iraqi officials began referring to euphemistically as "guests of the state," was equipped with satellite telephones and quickly made their predicament known to the Western media. After a tense, four-day siege, the Iraqis backed down under intense international pressure and the threat of a UN-backed U.S. military strike to rescue the weapons inspectors.

A second trove of nuclear documents, it turned out, had been safely smuggled out of the parking lot moments before the protracted hostage siege began. Among the Iraqi papers was a two-week-old official memo to the building's security chief ordering him to clear out all sensitive files and records before the UN weapons inspectors arrived. On the back of the memo, the security official had scribbled, "I can't do it in this time frame."[2] Kay's team collected thousands of documents detailing the full—and until then unknown—extent of Saddam's nuclear weapons program, including the names of Iraq's top nuclear scientists and the locations of well-hidden, widely dispersed facilities for enriching weapons-grade uranium and producing successful designs for nuclear weapons. After the crisis was defused, the United States quietly prepositioned a Delta Force hostage rescue team in the region in case UNSCOM inspectors found themselves in trouble again.[3] Kay believed that a rescue attempt, amid Baghdad's narrow streets and tall buildings, would have been a disaster.

But he now had more immediate problems. The more effectively the Iraqis used disinformation and deception to obscure the true dimensions of their WMD arsenal, the more Kay and his lieutenants went back to member states of the Security Council, especially the United States and

Britain, to request sophisticated high-technology surveillance that would help them penetrate the Iraqi wall of secrecy that had been thrown up around its weapons programs. At first they asked for helicopters to photograph sites from the air with high-powered telephoto lenses. It didn't take long for the Iraqis to figure out what they were doing and take measures to stop them. When U.S. intelligence agencies offered to set aside a U-2 spy plane to take high-altitude reconnaissance photographs for UNSCOM, Rolf Ekeus, the UN executive chairman of the weapons-hunting program, readily accepted.

The agreement with U.S. intelligence, Kay later declared, was from the beginning "a Faustian bargain." Mindful of the political chaos that would follow if the Security Council appeared to sanction one UN member nation spying on another, Ekeus insisted that any state intelligence assets aiding the weapons hunters would have to work solely under UNSCOM's direction, independently of their governments. Intelligence would flow in one direction only, to UNSCOM—not from UNSCOM back to governments in Washington or London or Paris. The early signs did not augur well. During Kay's parking lot crisis, the UN weapons chief listened at one point as U.S. joint chiefs chairman Colin Powell announced publicly that the UN weapons inspectors had just turned up the first evidence of an active Iraqi nuclear program. The U.S. government was obviously up to speed. Powell aside, Ekeus was gambling that member states of the UN Security Council would exercise the discretion to subordinate their national intelligence interests to UNSCOM.

Shortly after the parking lot standoff, Ekeus brought in Scott Ritter, a gung ho and sharp-witted former U.S. Marine intelligence officer who had served in the Gulf War, to help create a program he euphemistically called the Information Assessment Unit ("That's Ekeus-speak for an intelligence capability," said Ritter) to process material about Iraqi arms gathered with state-assisted intelligence. Ritter quickly grasped that ready access to U-2 photographs of possible Iraqi weapons would accomplish only half of UNSCOM's mission. He would also need experienced photo analysts to interpret the photographs. To do that, as Ritter put it, "you have to get people who do it for a living, and they come from governments. Now, who in governments look at photographs from U-2 aircraft for a living? People who work in intelligence organizations . . ."[4] Ritter bought into Ekeus's approach and got the chairman's approval to bring in intelligence analysts to help assess the intelligence gathered by the U-2 flights over Iraq. "But they worked for us, they worked for Rolf Ekeus," Ritter insisted. "They didn't take orders from anybody else."

In the end, that would prove wishful thinking. But the arrangement seemed to work well enough for several years. "I'm convinced that in the period of 1991, '92, '93 the intelligence community contributed a lot more to UNSCOM's success than they ever got out of it," Kay said later. "I think by 1994 and '95, the balance inevitably started swaying . . ." He ascribed the change to a dawning realization that Saddam's drawn-out refusal to cooperate with UNSCOM—after all, Resolution 687 called for Baghdad to declare its WMD arsenal to UNSCOM during the first fifteen days of the process—meant that the only way to disarm Iraq was to depose Saddam by force, preferably through a domestic rebellion or coup. In any case, the CIA and other foreign spy services, anticipating possible military action aimed at Saddam's regime, began to understand that the only access they had to intelligence about the Baghdad government was through the UN inspection teams. "And my view is, that's the point where the relationship started to tilt," said Kay, who left UNSCOM in late 1992.[5] He was replaced by Charles Duelfer, a former CIA weapons expert who later directed the postwar search for Saddam's WMD by the Iraq Survey Group in 2003 and 2004.

Inevitable complications set in for UNSCOM. Trying to analyze single photos with distant U.S. analysts proved cumbersome. Ritter went back to Washington and asked if he could spend several weeks with photo analysts from the CIA and NSA going over all the film and pick their brains about how the Iraqis might be hiding their weapons. U.S. intelligence officials believed their efforts were adequate and rejected Ritter's request as too labor intensive and time consuming. In December 1994, Ritter approached the Israelis. He found that the Israeli government employed a highly qualified team of photo analysts who were willing to help interpret the Iraqi surveillance. The U.S. government formally signed off on the deal, which would mean showing classified U-2 film to Israeli intelligence analysts. But some U.S. officials balked at Israeli involvement—in Ritter's words "because they started losing control of the process . . . and in this case the United State had lost control of the flow to UNSCOM." But it was not only that. Under Ritter's arrangement, beginning in July 1995, Israeli analysts not only got a firsthand look at sophisticated U.S. aerial surveillance imaging of the region, they were also unconstrained from passing the information along to other Israeli officials to use as they saw fit.

Ekeus and Ritter had effectively interjected UNSCOM business into the work of U.S. and foreign spies and was in turn allowing itself to be infiltrated by them. Besides high-altitude surveillance of potential weapons sites, they had already asked for the help of European intelligence services for export records of German, French, and British manufacturers who had supplied equipment and technical expertise to Iraq. One thing led to another, and the sharing of resources became quite elaborate. UNSCOM inspectors, for example, had come across evidence that the Iraqis were manufacturing their own Scud missiles, based on an outdated Soviet design, and theorized that the Iraqis might be hiding countless missile components by burying them in underground vaults in the desert. In a time of potential conflict, the theory went, they would excavate the disassembled missile components, restore them to operational condition, and use them as offensive weapons against regional foes like Israel or Iran. In discussions with U.S. intelligence, the UNSCOM inspectors lit upon the idea of using American ground-penetrating radar technology to scour the desert for buried Iraqi-made missiles.

Ritter and his colleagues devised an elaborate secret plan called Operation Cabbage Patch, named after a Soviet missile manufacturing facility, where the Soviets had trained the Iraqis in techniques to camouflage or hide missiles. The idea was to ask Moscow exactly how they had instructed the Iraqis to bury the Scuds and to determine what the missiles or components would look like on ground-penetrating radar. This was to be accomplished by flying over the Russian missile installation to get radar images of buried missile hardware. Although the Soviet Union was a key player in the Security Council, the approach was never made.[6] UNSCOM did secure the ground-penetrating radar from other sources and Operation Cabbage Patch went forward in Iraq to search the desert for Scuds, though none was found. The mission was deemed successful, since the weapons inspectors had managed to use the highly sophisticated technology to rule out the possibility that Saddam was hiding elements of Iraq's missile arsenal in buried desert locations, a conclusion that freed up UNSCOM resources and allowed the weapons hunters to turn to more pressing matters.

There was, however, a telling coda. A French inspector on the UNSCOM team learned about the Scud operation, though under Ekeus's "information assessment" policy he was bound by strict confidentiality not to reveal it to anyone. Ritter, however, told Barton Gellman of The Washington Post that he later spotted a letter in French in Ekeus's out basket describing "Le Cabbage Patch" to the French defense ministry. "This kind of thing happened all the time," said Gellman, ". . . you had a French representative on UNSCOM reporting back to his own government . . ."[7]

Ritter was one of the few UNSCOM officials, besides Rolf Ekeus and

Richard Butler, an Australian arms control specialist who replaced Ekeus as executive director when he became Swedish ambassador to the United States in 1997, who was aware of an extensive secret UNSCOM eavesdropping program conducted against the Iraqi military. In addition to the UNSCOM cameras that were trained on three hundred sites across Iraq to monitor illicit weapons activity, the eavesdropping network, comprised of fixed and portable radio scanners, allowed the weapons hunters to tap into Iraqi radio transmissions as inspections were under way, giving them critical knowledge of whether certain equipment was being moved between sites or hidden from inspectors. UNSCOM monitors were able to call on American, British, and Israeli resources to break Iraqi military communication codes or simply provide translations of the Arabic messages. The eavesdropping program gave inspectors an instrumental tool for maintaining a real-time picture of what the Iraqis were up to at any given time and devising strategies to defeat Iraqi deceptions.

The UNSCOM visual monitoring program had a major technical liability, which was soon exploited by the CIA to devise a more sophisticated eavesdropping system of its own. The fixed-site monitoring cameras ran continuously on batteries and recorded images on tape. That meant an UNSCOM technician periodically had to change hundreds of batteries and install new tapes and collect old ones on a regular basis at hundreds of sites across Iraq. The United States offered to build UNSCOM a new monitoring system of radio relay towers that would transmit signals from distant cameras and other sensors continuously by remote control back to UNSCOM weapons monitors. The U.S. government failed to mention that the new verification and monitoring system would be installed by operatives working covertly for a joint CIA and National Security Agency team, called the Special Collection Service, with its own secret agenda: to eavesdrop on official Iraqi military and governmental microwave communications.

If UNSCOM and the government spy services had been walking a very fine line before, the new U.S. microwave-interception system trampled it with impunity. After the Gulf War, the CIA and other spy agencies had a high-priority mission to collect information about Saddam's command structure, his inner circle, troop movements, the availability of conventional weapons and military materiel. UNSCOM, said *The Washington Post*'s Gellman, was "readily available cover for human agents. There's an international trade embargo on Iraq, so there's no businessmen coming in and out, and no flights in and out. They don't have academic exchanges and so on. They don't have all the usual covers that they use. Here they're given the opportunity, on a periodic basis, to include Americans on UN-SCOM inspection teams, and to carry large amounts of equipment and to build things and leave them in Iraq. The temptation was simply too great."[8]

The weapons hunters knew the score, too, in spite of their efforts to maintain UNSCOM's independence. Ritter, like Kay, readily acknowledged the role American and Israeli intelligence agencies played for UNSCOM. Israel, especially, had been crucial. "We needed Israeli help, and I'll be frank with you," he said. "If it weren't for the government of Israel and the assistance it provided the special commission, the information fuel that feeds the inspection process would have run dry by the end of 1995. It was Israel and Israel alone that kept us going, through some very difficult times . . ."[9] But Ritter was also keenly aware that relations between the Tel Aviv government and UNSCOM required maintaining a fiction that amounted to duplicity. "You don't want to advertise the fact that you have this intelligence relationship with the Israelis," Ritter said. "We insisted, with the Americans, that they respect our need for security on this and that the Americans don't leak the fact that we have this Israeli connection."

Covert U.S. activities were another matter. Ritter later said he reported a scheme strikingly similar to the microwave interceptions to the American deputy UNSCOM chief Charles Duelfer. According to Ritter, Duelfer waved him off the case, saying it involved espionage and law enforcement, and warned him that any further digging could result in an FBI investigation. In late 1996, he found himself under investigation by the FBI for his Israeli connections and, it was rumored, his Russian wife's past connections to the Soviet government.[10] Within months, as his personal credibility was undercut by what he considered trumped-up U.S. probes, Ritter began to feel that his efforts to step up inspections were blocked by Butler's overattentiveness to Clinton administration wishes and shifts in American policy. Ritter viewed Secretary of State Madeleine Albright's March 1997 declaration that the United States had no intention of lifting economic sanctions against Iraq as a betrayal of UNSCOM's mission. Albright, he felt, effectively removed Saddam's motivation to cooperate with the arms inspectors. Butler and others began to view Ritter as a hothead who "had a thousand ideas and 800 of them were bad" and needed to be controlled.[11] Ritter, who had once worked closely with CIA counterparts, complained bitterly about American interference in UNSCOM's mission and blew the whistle on CIA infiltration.

In August 1998, after Saddam declared that U.S. weapons inspectors were no longer welcome in Iraq, Ritter submitted his resignation to Butler. In no time top UN officials like Secretary General Kofi Annan began backing away from the weapons inspectors, calling them "a group of wild cowboys." By then, Iraqi foreign minister Tariq Aziz had been charging for some time that UNSCOM was a nest of American spies and could not be trusted to monitor Iraqi weapons.

Yet before UNSCOM began to self-destruct, beset by forces set in motion by Iraq's recalcitrance, the heavy-handedness of the Clinton administration, and a growing distrust of Washington that splintered the once-unified Security Council, UNSCOM seemed to have accomplished much of what it set out to do in Iraq. By early 1995, the weapons hunters had made no more major strides in locating Saddam's proscribed weapons or production facilities and had turned from the discovery phase of their work to concentrate on monitoring and verification. Then in August, Saddam's son-in-law, minister of industry and minerals Lt. Gen. Hussein Kamel, a trusted member of Saddam's inner circle who was directly involved in developing Iraq's weapons programs, defected to Jordan with his family. After a long-simmering feud with Uday Hussein, Saddam's bloody-minded son, Kamel apparently feared for his continued status in the government and his family's safety.

Kamel's defection was a windfall for U.S. and other foreign intelligence agencies. But it was a mixed blessing for the UNSCOM inspectors. Kamel's revelations forced them to recognize the dimensions of Saddam's weapons programs that they had failed to uncover in four years, yet also provided them with a road map to the rest of the hidden arsenal. In other words, it was back to aggressive, tension-filled inspection missions. Once more, UNSCOM officials were under intense pressure to step up their inspections—and confronted by new evidence of how badly they had been hoodwinked by the Iraqis. Kamel revealed new details about the Iraqis' biological weapons program and provided fresh information about Saddam's nuclear programs and elaborate new descriptions of Baghdad's deceptions.

Besides turning to U.S. intelligence to facilitate their renewed search for weapons, UNSCOM was inundated with literally millions of pages of new documentation about Iraqi weapons programs. Confronted by Kamel's evidence, Iraqi officials claimed blandly that they had no idea that Kamel had been hiding weapons and documentation. To show the regime's good faith, the Iraqis released a large cache of material they claimed Kamel had hidden away in hundreds of crates at a chicken farm he owned outside Baghdad. The newly declared documents revealed the existence of biological weapons research programs, chemical weapons activity, and new detail on the nuclear weapons and missile programs. As before, the weapons inspectors discovered interesting gaps even in this mother lode of Iraqi documentation. There was little to nothing on weaponization, whether it involved a biological agent like anthrax, or a nuclear warhead designed for an offensive missile system. Kamel, for his part, was persuaded to return to Iraq. He was summarily executed by Saddam's henchmen.

The Kamel chicken farm documents, combined with the knowledge of Iraq's WMD programs that the IAEA and UNSCOM had pieced together in hundreds of inspections before 1995, left little doubt about the extent of Saddam's ambitions for developing weapons of mass destruction. But by the end of UNSCOM's seven-year mission, despite the gaps in knowledge about some weapons systems, a remarkably complete picture of Saddam's unconventional weapons arsenal emerged, one that had been largely neutralized and no longer presented a threat to the outside world. Still, it was practically impossible to guarantee that Iraq was 100 percent weapons-free, mostly because Baghdad could not or would not document the weapons it claimed to have destroyed unilaterally and stonewalled the inspectors on details of its weapons programs.

Despite the remaining uncertainty, most assessments of Iraq's WMD capabilities before 9/11 acknowledged that with ongoing verification monitoring and the destruction of Iraqi weapons systems and production facilities, Saddam was effectively disarmed by 1998—a conclusion that was confirmed by the CIA's Iraq Survey Group after the war six years later. "The means of verification and the work of UNSCOM has been very successful," declared UNSCOM executive chairman Richard Butler in 1999, "but it won't hit 100 percent," without the political commitment of Iraq to disarm and the political will of the "enforcers"—i.e., the Security Council—"to enforce the law."[12] Butler blamed the shortfall "from the beginning" on "a decision by the central government of Iraq not to comply with the resolutions" and hinted that the early post–Gulf War resolve of the Security Council had dissipated.

In testimony before a joint session of the Senate Armed Services and Foreign Relations committees in September 1998, former chief UNSCOM inspector Scott Ritter testified that "Iraq had not been fully disarmed," but estimated that UNSCOM "could account for 90 percent to 95 percent of Iraq's proscribed weaponry." He identified critical gaps in the inspectors' knowledge: namely, details of Iraq's VX nerve agent program, its disposition of biological weapons, and its development of ballistic missiles with a range of more than one hundred and fifty kilometers.[13] Ritter, who had become a strident critic of U.S meddling in the weapons-inspection program, underscored the importance of sending UN inspectors back to Iraq to offset the possibility that Saddam would try to reconstitute his weapons programs. "If a substantiated case can be made that Iraq possesses actual weapons of mass destruction, then the debate is over—the justification for war is clear," he wrote in mid-2002. "But, to date the Bush administration has been unable—or unwilling—to back up its rhetoric concerning the Iraqi threat with any substantive facts."[14] Ritter's increasingly outspoken views earned him the enmity of conservatives, Bush administration officials, and most of the press in the months before the war began.

But he was hardly alone in his assessment of the state of Baghdad's WMD programs. Butler's January 1999 report on Iraqi disarmament to the Security Council discussed in detail the progress UNSCOM had made, down to the precise number of weapons and weapons facilities destroyed. *The Amorim Report* (named for its chairman, Brazilian ambassador to the United Nations Celso Amorim), which was published two months later in March 1999, described the progress made in Iraq by the IAEA and UN weapons inspections since 1991, using Butler's report as its source, and proposed a new regime for a disarmament and ongoing monitoring and verification regime in Iraq. *The Amorim Report* concluded that "in spite of well-known difficult circumstances, UNSCOM and IAEA have been effective in uncovering and destroying many elements of Iraq's proscribed weapons programmes.... Although important elements still have to be resolved, the bulk of Iraq's proscribed weapons programmes has been eliminated."[15]

UNSCOM, the report declared, "was able to destroy or otherwise account for" the great bulk of "imported operational missiles of proscribed range" (817 out of 819) that comprised Iraq's missile force, as well as most of its missile launchers, biological, chemical, and conventional warheads, both imported and produced in Iraq. The weapons hunters had also "obtained a broad understanding of Iraq's efforts to develop a missile delivery system for nuclear weapons and a detailed picture of Iraq's procurement effort for its proscribed missile programmes." The report noted that the Iraqis had failed to account for 50 conventional warheads (out of 210), proscribed propellants, seven Iraqi-made missiles, and "combustion chamber/nozzle assemblies" that they claimed to have destroyed.[16]

Similarly, UNSCOM confirmed that much of Iraq's chemical weapons development and production capacity was destroyed or rendered harmless, including 88,000 chemical munitions, such as artillery shells, 600 tons of weaponized or bulk chemical weapons agents, and 4,000 tons of precursor chemicals. UNSCOM also dismantled and closed down Iraq's prime chemical development and production complex and placed other chemical facilities under monitoring. The inspectors uncovered the Iraqi VX project, its chemical weapons research and development programs, and its procurement system. Even so, *The Amorim Report* noted that UNSCOM was unsatisfied with Iraqi declarations about the production and weaponization of the VX program and military use of VX gas, a deadly neurotoxin that kills within hours after absorption through the eyes and skin. The inspectors also noted that the Iraqis could not account for the chemical weapons they were believed to have deployed in the 1980s, or for some 550 artillery shells filled with mustard gas that they claimed had disappeared after the Gulf War.[17]

Despite the fact that Iraq's biological weapons program had been kept secret by Saddam's government until Kamel's defection in 1995, UNSCOM inspectors managed to "obtain significant insights" into Saddam's biowarfare capabilities. They had managed to acquire "a broad understanding" of its main delivery systems and a full, if incomplete, picture of procurement. UNSCOM oversaw the destruction of Al Hakam, Iraq's main bioweapons production and development facility, along with biological warfare production components, which included sixty pieces of equipment from three other facilities and twenty-two tons of growth media for bioweapons production from another four facilities. That comprised most of Iraq's declared biological warfare program, all rendered harmless. Nonetheless, UNSCOM inspectors were concerned that the Baghdad regime had not fully disclosed their biological weapons capabilities. They awaited a fuller picture, especially because large volumes of biological agent could be produced quickly, required simple, low-tech equipment that was readily adaptable for either commercial or military use, and involved sophisticated technical know-how that Iraqi scientists clearly possessed.[18]

On the critical subject of nuclear weapons, the 1999 Amorim report stated unambiguously that "there is no indication that Iraq possesses nuclear weapons or any meaningful amounts of weapon-usable nuclear material or that Iraq has retained any practical capability (facilities or hardware) for the production of such material."[19] The report also noted that questions remained about lack of technical documentation, external support of the clandestine program, and whether Saddam had entirely abandoned it. But, despite the failure of U.S. intelligence to grasp the ambitiousness and size of Saddam's pre–Gulf War nuclear weapons program, it was the one area of proscribed weaponry that in the end the IAEA and UNSCOM, for all their aggressive and controversial tactics, were most successful in penetrating and neutralizing—at least for the time being.[19]

As Rolf Ekeus and others have explained, in August 1990 Iraq began a crash program to build a complete nuclear weapon comprised of a warhead designed for a missile with a target range of six hundred kilometers, or about four hundred miles. This was far more than an explosive nuclear device. An operational nuclear ballistic missile would have given Baghdad the ability to project the threat of a nuclear attack. UNSCOM knew there had been disagreement among the top Iraqi project managers on whether they could build such a system within the designated time period. The Iraqis already had a "good grasp" of warhead design and some experience with the enrichment of uranium by centrifuge technology. But stringent export controls on enrichment technology made such a path prohibitive, and the plan for the crash program called for using fissile material in Iraq that was safeguarded by the IAEA. Unfortunately for the Iraqis, the UNSCOM inspectors intervened soon after the Gulf conflict, discovered the calutrons and other nuclear production infrastructure, and between 1993 and 1994 forced the shipment of Iraq's supply of highly enriched uranium to Russia. The lack of feedstock to produce weapons-grade uranium, together with the technical difficulties of miniaturizing a nuclear warhead for a missile delivery system, were serious obstacles for the Iraqi program. "The present nuclear threat from Iraq," said Ekeus in 1997, "is, in my judgment, linked to the possible import by Baghdad of highly enriched uranium (HEU)."[20]

Khidhir Hamza, an Iraqi physicist who had been a prominent figure in Saddam's nuclear program until his defection to the United States in 1994, and David Albright, a former nuclear arms inspector who heads the Institute for Science and International Security in Washington, concurred in 1998 that "Iraq has had an extremely difficult time making any progress in building nuclear weapons." They also emphasized Iraq's problems building a nuclear warhead missile delivery system and a centrifuge enrichment program to produce weapons-grade uranium. A combination of the allied bombing campaign during the Gulf War and the intrusive inspections by UNSCOM and the IAEA, as well as economic sanctions that disrupted imports vital to Saddam's $10 billion program, devastated Iraq's nuclear facilities, equipment, and materials. "Currently," Hamza and Albright wrote in 1998, "essentially all of Iraq's pre-Gulf War nuclear facilities and equipment have been eliminated or converted to nonproscribed purposes . . ."[21]

Like many others at the time, Hamza (whose many warnings about Saddam's renewed nuclear program were later discredited) and Albright were deeply concerned Iraq would be able to reconstitute its nuclear program as the UN inspection regime weakened and economic sanctions ended. Despite their assumption that Iraqi nuclear scientists had continued low-level research efforts since the Gulf War, they concluded that the Iraqis would still "still face formidable challenges" building a centrifuge to enrich weapons-grade uranium. Nor had they been able to purchase plutonium or highly enriched uranium on the international black market since the war. Others were more pessimistic. "Iraq knows the secrets of how to make nuclear weapons," said David Kay in 1999. "What they lack today is not scientific talent. They don't lack the secrets and technology. They've solved all those problems. What they lack is time and access to nuclear materials. If the Iraqis were able to import, for example, from a Soviet program—that has now fallen apart—nuclear material, plutonium or high-enriched uranium, it would take them only a matter of months to fabricate a crude weapon."[22]

That, of course, would obviate the need for the one-thousand-centrifuge cascade uranium enrichment facility called for in the Iraqi crash program—and would fall well short of providing the Baghdad regime with the threat of a nuclear-tipped ballistic missile. Hans Blix, the former head of the IAEA who was appointed to head the new UN Monitoring, Verification and Inspection Commission (UNMOVIC) that would replace UNSCOM, dismissed the idea that Saddam could have reconstituted his nuclear program in the eighteen months since the UN inspectors left Baghdad. "I do not have any preconceived notions as to what Iraq could have done," Blix told an interviewer in 2000. "But if I take the nuclear area, which I know best, there is no way that they could have built up an enrichment capacity in that period. Of course, it is possible that they could try to buy a nuclear weapon, but the Iraqi path in the past was one of going after enrichment, and that

...es a considerable infrastructure that would be seen from satellites. We ...e no indications of that happening."[23]

To the weapons hunters, the effective disarmament of a hostile, recalcitrant regime was a zero-sum game. Without hard evidence and documentation of absolute compliance in every category of weaponry, no professional arms inspector would be comfortable even suggesting that a country like Iraq was 100 percent disarmed. Indeed, as *The Amorim Report* carefully noted, "some uncertainty is inevitable in any country-wide technical verification process which aims to prove the absence of readily concealable objects or activities." For this reason, both UNSCOM and the IAEA explicitly adopted a pragmatic policy that assumed absolute certainty was unattainable and left it up to the Security Council to determine whether full disarmament had been achieved.

In that sense, Iraq was not in full compliance with Resolution 687. Even so, there was a vast difference between the arms inspectors' technical conclusion that Iraq was not fully disarmed and a military planner's judgment about just how much of a strategic threat was presented by the slim margin of uncertainty that remained in late 1998 about Iraq's WMD arsenal and production facilities. Even on the charge that Saddam later had secretly reconstituted weapons programs, there was plentiful evidence that such initiatives would have been very difficult after the arms inspectors had been forced out of the country.

The Iraqis had not yet built even a simple nuclear explosive device, for which they would have had to smuggle weapons-grade uranium or plutonium into the country under the noses of UNSCOM and IAEA inspectors, despite international economic sanctions. To build a deliverable nuclear weapon, Iraqi scientists would have had to miniaturize a 120-centimeter nuclear warhead design—which they had never built—to 70 to 80 centimeters for the long-range al-Hussein missile, a daunting technical challenge that Hamza and Albright believed would have taken "significant" time. Building a secret system of a thousand linked gas centrifuges to develop an indigenous supply of weapons-grade enriched uranium—an assumption implicit in the Niger uranium controversy—was similarly fraught. In reality, Iraqi scientists would have to illicitly import manufacturing equipment to fabricate centrifuge components, build a plant, conduct testing of a design, produce uranium hexafluoride, and manufacture as many as twice the centrifuges they needed. It was apparent in 1998 that Saddam would have needed between three and seven years to produce a clandestine gas centrifuge plant to make ten kilograms of weapons-grade uranium, the amount that would be needed for a single nuclear weapon.[24]

None of this ever happened. Evidence readily available at the time left little doubt that Saddam's ability to project a lethal unconventional military threat was in serious disarray by 1998—precisely the unsurprising conclusion reached in December 2005 by the CIA-backed Iraq Survey Group. Baghdad had other worries at the time. The Iraqis were under the constant threat of air attacks by U.S. and British patrols in the northern and southern no-fly zones. Although it has never been confirmed, U.S. espionage activities associated with UNSCOM may have covertly supported Iraqi officers in at least one unsuccessful coup attempt against Saddam, which infected the Baghdad regime with paranoia and uncertainty. Coalition military and political pressure was also felt by the low-profile infrastructure of Iraqi manufacturers and weapons scientists on the ground. Operation Desert Fox hit several Iraqi missile installations, according to the U.S. Central Command, setting back that critical part of Saddam's weapons program by as much as two years.

Still, distrust of the UN arms inspection process and uncertainty about Saddam's WMD remained strong in conservative Republican political circles in Washington who were busy positioning themselves for the 2000 presidential election, and who fervently suspected that Saddam was busy rebuilding his arsenal of proscribed weapons, at a time when much of the nation had all but forgotten Iraq. They had plenty of ammunition for their views, fed to them by insiders in the UNSCOM disarmament fraternity.

UNSCOM executive chairman Richard Butler conceded in June 1999 that he could not say what the Iraqis had "done in these last five months because we've not been there to see." But, he added, "in all honesty, if you look at their track record, there's every reason to assume that they are taking advantage of this time to make new chemical warfare agent, new biological warfare agent, and that's a matter of grave concern." Butler declared that since the weapons inspectors left, the Iraqis had probably "worked hard on increasing their missile capability, the range of those missiles and probably the number of them. I'm sure they've asked their nuclear team to start meeting again, and I feel certain, too, that they have commenced work again on making chemical and biological warfare agents."[25] David Kay, who had been out of UNSCOM for eight years, warned in 1999 that "Iraq knows the secrets of nuclear weapons. We do not know how to erase knowledge from the hands of scientists once they've solved a problem. All they lack is opportunity and will. That's why I'm personally convinced that as long as Saddam is in power, you've got a problem there."[26]

11

WHO IS AHMED CHALABI?

Gen. Khidhir Hamza, the defector and MIT-trained Iraqi nuclear physicist, was not a general or even a military man. He received the title when he was promoted to the upper ranks of Iraq's nuclear weapons program in 1987, and it signified little more than Hamza's new insider status in Saddam's secret intelligence group, the Special Security Organization. The honorary title was oddly appropriate. By the time Hamza was ready to defect, his career in the Iraqi nuclear organization, building Iraq's secret nuclear facilities and surreptitiously buying up internationally proscribed nuclear components, had steeped him in a world of commercial spies and double agents. So, one night in August 1994, when he finally abandoned Baghdad under cover of darkness and headed for the mountainous Kurdish region of northern Iraq, his most pressing priority was to establish his nuclear bona fides with the CIA and arrange for asylum in the United States. His contact with American intelligence was a brilliant but erratic Iraqi dissident from a wealthy Baghdad family whom he knew slightly from his years at MIT. His name was Ahmed Chalabi.

Hamza found Chalabi in his office at the antenna-studded headquarters of the Iraqi National Congress in Salahuddin, a town near Arbil in Kurdistan. Although there was some uncertainty at first whether Chalabi remembered him from their student days, the portly Iraqi dissident quickly sized up Hamza as someone who might supply the CIA with valuable information about Saddam's nuclear program. Chalabi told Hamza that he was responsible for screening defectors for the CIA and invited him to his residence for dinner, where he suggested that his visitor should withhold information from the Americans as a bargaining chip for relocating him. Chalabi explained that if Hamza allowed the U.S. agents to bleed him dry right away, they would quickly lose interest. He should try to get the best deal possible for himself and his family. Chalabi contacted his CIA connection on a secure satellite telephone.

Within hours an American returned the call. To Hamza's consternation, the agent at the other end of the line did not seem to know who he was, and apparently had not even bothered to run a background check on him. Nor did the CIA man have the slightest familiarity with Iraq's nuclear program, despite three years of high-profile IAEA and UNSCOM inspections. When the CIA caller put a nuclear specialist on the line, Hamza refused to offer more than tidbits unless he was offered asylum in the United States first. The conversation did not go well. After he hung up, without providing his debriefer with information or making a deal, Hamza was gently urged by Chalabi not to give up so easily.

Several days later, a suddenly brusque and unsympathetic Chalabi sent for Hamza and put through a second call to the CIA. This time, Chalabi coldly informed Hamza he would have to tell the CIA everything up front. During the call, his CIA interlocutor told him outright there would be no asylum, but they could give him plenty of money. Hamza, who had been alarmed at Chalabi's 180-degree reversal, wasn't interested. He instantly sensed his reliance on Chalabi had somehow backfired and the CIA had no interest in protecting him. By sunset the same day, Hamza slipped across the border into Turkey and into exile.[1]

Hamza's brief interlude at the INC's mountain outpost in Kurdistan offered a rare glimpse of Chalabi's role as a recruiter of well-placed Iraqi defectors and promising intelligence sources, a routine he would refine over the next decade into a controversial and lethally effective art. Although Chalabi did not succeed with Hamza or assist in his escape from Iraq, it was not the last time their paths would cross. Like many of the other defectors Chalabi and the INC cultivated, and whose stories they fed to the media and Western intelligence agencies, Hamza's widely read 2000 book, *Saddam's Bombmaker,* would later play a significant role in persuading Americans that the Iraqi dictator was aggressively rebuilding his nuclear weapons programs. And, as with many of Chalabi's defectors, whose stories of Saddam's burgeoning WMD arsenal fueled the Bush

White House's war machine, Hamza's account was also later discredited and dismissed as exaggerated.

The roster of voluble defectors that Chalabi and the INC rounded up to make the case for a U.S.-led invasion of Iraq represented a monumentally impressive edifice of propaganda and disinformation. They ranged from Iraqi engineer Adnan Ihsan Saeed al-Haideri, who shortly after 9/11 provided eyewitness accounts of Saddam's rebuilt weapons facilities to Judith Miller of *The New York Times* and the CIA; to Abu Zeinab al-Qurairy, a former Mukhabarat official who told the tale of Arab terrorists honing their murderous skills at Salman Pak; and the infamous "Curveball," the booze-addled alleged brother-in-law of a Chalabi INC lieutenant, who was allowed to speak exclusively with West German intelligence and supplied chapter and verse on the long-rumored—and ultimately nonexistent—Iraqi mobile bioweapons labs. Chalabi was also personally involved in other shadowy adventures. He reportedly attended the December 2001 Rome meeting set up by Iranian arms dealer Manucher Ghorbanifar for Michael Ledeen and Pentagon officials to meet a mysterious Iranian delegation. Chalabi had also tried to peddle the long-running story of the alleged meeting in Prague between 9/11 hijacker Mohamed Atta and an Iraqi diplomat to U.S. newspapers.

Chalabi spent years of political maneuvering, millions of dollars, and tireless calculation to position himself to feed the Pentagon and the White House a credible casus belli against Iraq. The WMD rationale for war that Chalabi served up, however unreliable and inaccurate, not only went down easily with a shocked and fearful American public, but was also palatable to the UN Security Council and Washington's only coalition partner that mattered, the government of British prime minister Tony Blair. Chalabi did not conceive this strategy on his own. He cultivated friends in high places—and, for the better part of a decade, commanded resources from successive administrations in Washington to get the job done.

Chalabi first attracted Washington's attention in the early 1990s as a U.S.-educated, London-based Iraqi exile and banker with a reputation for financial guile and administrative talent. Within a year he was established in northern Iraq as the leader of a CIA-funded dissident group charged with covertly undermining the regime of Saddam Hussein, an effort that led to a quixotic bid to foment an armed revolution against Baghdad in 1995. Chalabi's military misadventures ended a year later, when hundreds of his followers in the Iraqi National Congress were captured and executed by Iraqi forces. The debacle precipitated a sharp break with U.S. intelligence and the Clinton administration. But by the late 1990s, the resilient Chalabi had repositioned the organization as an anti-CIA, pro-Israeli ally of American neoconservatives and the conservative U.S. defense establishment.

The 9/11 attacks provided the long-awaited catalyst that transformed Chalabi into a political force whose private agenda would help set the Bush administration on a course to war. Chalabi's sole interest was removing the Baghdad government from power. It was no secret at the White House and the Pentagon—and among a handful of top American journalists—that Chalabi was personally obsessed with using U.S. troops to depose Saddam. His agenda was enthusiastically embraced in influential quarters in Washington—Bush officials would go so far as to put forward Chalabi's name for a high post in Iraq's postwar government. Less well known is that the Bush administration actively asked Chalabi to produce damning intelligence about Baghdad's prohibited weapons programs and then used a restructured U.S. national security apparatus to bypass the usual intelligence agencies to legitimize the claims of INC defectors. Along the way, Chalabi was privy to inside information from UNSCOM inspectors, and knew the critical gaps in their knowledge of Saddam's proscribed weapons programs. That meant Chalabi also knew precisely what important questions remained, and which new details U.S. arms experts and intelligence officials would find credible and troubling, but hadn't been able to nail down themselves. When no WMD were found months after the initial combat operations wound down in April 2003, Chalabi was unfazed and unapologetic. "We are heroes in error," he proclaimed. "What was said before is not important."[2] His mission was accomplished. The Americans had forcibly removed Saddam from office. "There's a smear campaign that says I am responsible for the liberation of Iraq," Chalabi told reporter Jane Mayer of *The New Yorker* after the initial combat ended. "But how bad is that?"[3]

Chalabi had been well known to U.S. officials and journalists in Washington since the Gulf War ended in 1991. *The Washington Post*'s Jim Hoagland and *The New York Times*' Judith Miller had been cultivating him as a source on Iraqi affairs for years. Chris Hedges, then a veteran *Times* correspondent, traveled from Paris to Lebanon to interview INC sources for the Salman Pak story. As with many reporters who knew Chalabi and used him to gain access to Iraqi defectors, Hedges instinctively distrusted the Iraqi opposition leader. "I thought he was unreliable and corrupt," he said. "But just because he is a sleazebag doesn't mean he might not know something or that everything he says is wrong." Chalabi had attempted earlier to interest Hedges in the story about Mohamed Atta's meeting with Iraqi intelligence agents in Prague. "Chalabi pushed really hard but I just didn't buy it," Hedges said.[4]

Chalabi's decade-long, hot-and-cold relationship with Washington certainly should have raised red flags about him among U.S. officials and journalists alike. In the end, the Bush administration spent an estimated $39 million on his services and those of the INC between 2001 and May 2004, when his funding from Washington was finally cut off. Chalabi's Baghdad offices were raided by Iraqi police, backed by U.S. security forces, on suspicion that INC operatives had engaged in espionage, embezzlement, fraud, and kidnapping. Chalabi and one of his top lieutenants were suspected of informing Tehran that the United States had broken secret Iranian intelligence codes. By then, Chalabi had become openly critical of the U.S. occupation and provisional government for retaining Baathist officials who had once served Saddam. As he had done many times before, Chalabi protested that the charges against him were merely politically motivated. "It's customary when great events happen that the U.S. punishes its friends and rewards its enemies," Chalabi later scoffed.[5] With White House approval, the Department of Defense stopped its payment of $342,000 per month to the INC.

Washington's financial support for Chalabi began with a covert finding signed in May 1991 by President George H. W. Bush that authorized the CIA to earmark $100 million to undermine Saddam's regime after the Gulf War. Through the London-based Rendon Group, a public relations firm founded by John Rendon, a former executive director of the Democratic National Committee, the CIA secretly funneled cash to the newly formed INC and Chalabi. The company specialized in shaping public opinion by a variety of means, including a traveling program documenting Saddam's human rights atrocities that was peddled to interested groups in Britain. Unlike other PR firms at the time, Rendon's staff had mastered the twenty-four-hour news cycle and was adept at tailoring media campaigns to new international outlets like CNN. Much of the early opposition campaign consisted of getting anti-Saddam propaganda published in the British press and electronic media—to the tune of some $40 million a year.

Rendon's secret CIA contract also reportedly called for supporting internal Iraqi opposition groups. The agency soon picked out Chalabi, age forty-seven, a secular Shiite and successful banker who spoke flawless English, dressed well, and had a knack for backroom wheeling and dealing, to manage the Iraqi exile forces. His wealthy Shiite banking family owned property in central Baghdad, thanks in part to the prominence of Chalabi's grandfather, who served in multiple cabinet posts under a succession of British-installed Iraqi governments. Chalabi's father was a finance minister for King Faisal II, the Iraqi monarch who was deposed in a 1958 military coup. Then thirteen, Chalabi with his brothers was forced to leave the Jesuit academy he had attended in Baghdad as a schoolboy and packed off to Jordan.

The elder Chalabi lost a fortune in real estate in the aftermath of the revolution. He sent his son to a boarding school in England, then to the Massachusetts Institute of Technology, where Chalabi spent his university years studying math. He ultimately earned his Ph.D. at the University of Chicago in an obscure branch of geometry known as knot theory. While in Chicago, he met Albert Wohlstetter, the mathematician and Cold War theorist who many years later would introduce him to top Washington neoconservatives. After graduate school, he returned to Lebanon, where he landed a job teaching mathematics at the University of Beirut. In 1977, Jordan's crown prince Hassan, impressed by Chalabi's academic credentials and his pedigree, invited him to start a bank in Jordan. Within a few years, his Petra Bank, profiting from modern banking innovations (Petra brought Visa cards to the Mideast and established branches on the Israeli-occupied West Bank) and international commercial transactions that moved large sums in and out of Amman, was the second largest bank in Jordan. Chalabi became wealthy and influential. He designed and built an opulent residence in the suburbs of Amman, where he lived with his wife and four children, surrounded by a collection of modern art. He reportedly lent some $30 million to Prince Hassan, which, like much of Chalabi's largesse, was apparently not repaid.

In 1989 Chalabi was charged under Jordanian martial law on multiple counts of embezzlement, theft, forgery, and other violations of banking liquidity regulations. He was spirited out of Jordan just ahead of an arrest warrant, according to one account, in the trunk of a Mercedes driven by his indebted friend Prince Hassan, along with $70 million in bank notes. He fled to London, where he relocated his wife and children to a house owned by his family financial empire in the ritzy Park Lane section. But ever since Baathist thugs had seized power in Baghdad and Saddam had become Iraq's president the decade before, the exiled banker's thoughts never strayed too far from Baghdad. "Ahmed wanted to avenge his father's ouster and the deprivation of his lands," said a childhood friend of Chalabi later. "Now he's trying to fit in his father's shoes . . ."[6]

The U.S.-led Desert Storm campaign in the winter of 1991, which drove Saddam's troops out of Kuwait, only whetted Chalabi's appetite for reclaiming his presumptive birthright in Baghdad. In June 1992, he plunged headlong into the first organizational meeting of the Iraqi National Congress in Vienna. His overbearing, privileged manner irritated other exiles and anti-Saddam dissidents, especially the Kurds. But Chalabi nonetheless managed eventually to consolidate his role as INC chief, despite his in absentia April conviction in Jordan on thirty-one counts of defrauding the Jordanian banking system of an amount variously reported at $200 to $300 million. He was sentenced to twenty-two years of hard labor by a Jordanian military court. Chalabi countered that he was set up by Jordanian officials, who were angry at his exposure of secret Iraqi-Jordanian trade deals and were under pressure from Baghdad to clamp down on Chalabi's open financial support of Iraqi opposition groups. Others, like James Akins, a former U.S. ambassador to Saudi Arabia, thought Chalabi was simply a crook. Akins dismissed Chalabi as "a criminal banker" and "a swindler . . . interested in getting money . . . into his bank accounts and those of his friends."[7]

Shortly after Desert Storm and Chalabi's coronation by the CIA as an opposition leader, Jordan's King Hussein offered him a royal pardon for the Petra Bank conviction, which Chalabi turned down on grounds that he had done nothing wrong. Although Hussein's son and successor King Abdullah II refused to lift the charges against Chalabi, citing the damage the collapse of Petra Bank had done to the Jordanian economy, the case against Chalabi fizzled out and was quickly subsumed by regional politics.

Chalabi's legal and political problems in Jordan barely slowed him down. By 1994 Chalabi and the INC had set up opposition outposts in Kurdistan, which had become an autonomous area under the protection of the U.S. military after the refugee crisis. "He was like the American Ambassador to Iraq," recalled Robert Baer, a former CIA agent stationed in the region. "He could get to the White House and the C.I.A. He would move around Iraq with five or six Land Cruisers."[8] But much of Chalabi's Kurdistan operation seemed to Baer to be for show. Intelligence that was rounded up by INC operatives about Iraqi troop movements or Baathist intrigue in Baghdad was not taken seriously by the CIA, and even when it was, it often lacked detail or credible sourcing.

Chalabi's operation in Kurdistan demonstrated an amateurish taste for

spycraft and deception. In 1994 Baer was taken on a tour of an INC forgery shop set up inside an old school building in Salahuddin where INC
specialists cranked out phony documents, including an exact replica of an
Iraqi newspaper with stories of Saddam's human rights abuses. "It was a
room where people were scanning Iraqi intelligence documents into computers, and doing disinformation," recalled Baer. "There was a whole
wing of it that he did forgeries in." In one ambitious ploy, INC craftsmen
forged a letter from President Clinton on U.S. National Security Council
stationery requesting Chalabi's aid in a U.S. plot to assassinate Saddam,
an apparent effort to trick Iranians into joining forces against the Baghdad regime. Baer denied that any such plot existed, but a young American
Rendon employee named Francis Brooke, a born-again Christian who
later became Chalabi's top aide in Washington, confirmed the existence of
the INC forgery operation.[9] The phony assassination letter found its way
back to Washington and briefly raised questions about CIA participation
in the scheme, which would have violated federal laws against forging
U.S. government documents and using federal funds for propaganda purposes to subvert American interests.

The Iraq operations triggered questions about Chalabi's spending
habits with his CIA bankroll. Kurdish members began questioning
how Chalabi spent the organization's money, since most of the transactions were in untraceable cash and Chalabi and his lieutenants were
closemouthed about finances. They refused to allow the INC's books to
be audited on the grounds that the organization's secrecy might be compromised. A secret team of auditors eventually stole into INC headquarters and, despite evidence of wasteful spending, found the accounts in
order.

Although Chalabi had no military experience, he was soon using his
CIA funding to launch a one-thousand-man INC militia, which he hoped
to use along with much larger Kurdish *peshmerga* forces to attack and
overrun elements of Iraq's down-at-the-heels 38th Infantry Division, then
deployed south of Arbil. The operation was supposed to spearhead a
drive of opposition forces and Iraqi army defectors from the 38th to
Baghdad with U.S. military support. There were considerable problems
with this scheme. Besides the fact that there were not enough American
troops nearby to ensure the plan's success, nobody in the Clinton White
House seemed to know anything about it. Word of the attack on Iraqi
troops reached Washington through intelligence reports that Iraqi spies
already knew about a key element of the plan to encourage the badly
equipped and ill-provisioned Iraqi soldiers of the 38th to defect. Anthony

several hours. That night the Iraqi army captured and executed more than two hundred INC personnel before pulling back to their lines outside the city the next morning. Once more, the United States did not have enough troops stationed in the region to retaliate for the devastating slaughter of its clients. When Clinton defense officials went to the Turks and Saudis for permission to mount air attacks in southern Iraq, for the first time a U.S. military request was rebuffed. The United States responded by expanding the southern no-fly zone to the 33rd parallel just south of Baghdad and hammered Iraqi military targets with forty-four cruise missiles on September 3 and 4. In the following days, some six hundred INC opposition members and another six thousand of their Iraqi allies were airlifted out of Kurdistan on U.S. aircraft and flown to Guam.[11]

After Saddam's devastating attack on Arbil, the CIA and the INC lost their base of operations in northern Iraq. Even Jordan's King Hussein declared that he could no longer guarantee the safety of anti-Saddam Iraqi exiles in Amman. The INC was finished as an umbrella organization for opposition groups inside Iraq. The Kurds splintered along old political lines, al-Wifaq was crippled, and the Shiites in the south had their own battles to fight. Besides being decimated by Saddam's forces, Chalabi's own INC personnel were widely disliked by other opposition groups and proved to be no match for Saddam's security forces. Francis Brooke, who had expedited correspondence between Chalabi and Vice President Al Gore—the vice president had promised U.S. protection for opposition forces in Kurdistan—was stunned at the news of the Arbil carnage. "I was sick for a week, just throwing up," Brooke recalled later. "I couldn't believe it. I'm not interested in getting a whole lot of people killed and being morally wrong. I was stunned." He called Chalabi, who had fled to London. "What are we going to do?" he asked.[12]

The CIA was fed up with Chalabi's feckless leadership. But the exiled remnants of the INC, including Chalabi, were angry that the CIA and the Clinton administration had failed to press harder for troops for the 1995 coup attempt, and despite promises to protect the opposition forces in the northern no-fly zone sanctuary, had failed for a second time to rescue opposition forces from Iraqi troops (the first failure was immediately after the Gulf War in early 1991). Chalabi responded by exploiting the intensely emotional reaction to Arbil of Brooke and other supporters and his newly developed skills manipulating the media to help ABC News produce a TV documentary highly critical of the CIA's meddling in northern

Lake, the president's national security advisor, and Secretary of
Warren Christopher saw a disaster in the making. The White H
promptly signaled opposition leaders in Kurdistan that Iraqi intellig
was onto their plans and that American forces would not be availab
back up the operation.[10]

The United States washed its hands of the military plan. Even so,
March 6, 1995, several hundred INC militiamen and thousands of *pe
merga* fighters mounted a full-fledged attack on two brigades of the 3
Division near Arbil, successfully routing them and triggering a mass
Iraqi surrender. After the initial success, however, Saddam's intelliger
forces quickly arrested the opposition agents and charged them with co
spiring to persuade Iraqi troops to defect. Worse, U.S. intelligence report(
that several well-equipped Republican Guard divisions and army uni
were rushing toward Arbil to reinforce the 38th and warned the Kurc
immediately to retreat to defensive positions. The opposition forces heede
the warning just in time. The INC's grand coup attempt against Saddan
sputtered and died. Although both the INC militia and the Kurdish force:
emerged relatively unscathed from what would likely have been a bloodbath, Chalabi and other opposition leaders blamed Washington for undercutting a campaign that could have toppled Saddam.

Although it was a near disaster for Chalabi's forces, Arbil was a humiliation for Saddam, highlighting the damage that could be done by a
determined opposition group inside Iraq. The anti-Saddam insurgency
was not so lucky the next time around. In early 1996, the CIA, working
with a group of dissident former army officers that called themselves al-
Wifaq ("the accord"), recruited officers from Saddam's military and security forces, including the Hammurabi division of the Special Republican
Guard that protected Saddam, to stage a coup against the Baghdad
regime. The CIA agents involved may have been operating under cover as
advisers to the UNSCOM arms inspection team. In any case, Saddam's
intelligence organization, the Mukhabarat, got wind of the coup plans.
After monitoring the operation for several months, Iraqi troops moved in
and arrested hundreds of the plotters, forced the CIA operatives to flee the
country, and left al-Wifaq in tatters.

The unraveling of the second CIA-sponsored coup plot was the beginning of the end for Chalabi and his INC opposition forces in Iraq. Later
that summer, exploiting a split between the two main Kurdish political
groups over smuggling routes, Saddam quietly moved two Republican
Guard divisions and three army divisions into position around Arbil. In a
nighttime attack on August 31, 1996, the Iraqi forces overran the city in

Iraq. The CIA was infuriated by Chalabi's show of ingratitude and promptly retaliated by cutting off funding for the INC.

His break with the CIA set the stage for a series of Machiavellian maneuvers by Chalabi that eventually resulted in the restoration of U.S. funding and an entrée to Washington's conservative defense establishment. In 1996, with the help of Brooke, Chalabi set up headquarters in a multimillion-dollar Georgetown town house owned by his family's Luxembourg-based Levantine Holdings. A careful reader of history, Chalabi studied how in South Africa the African National Congress had portrayed apartheid as a form of slavery to undermine the white government in Pretoria. He analyzed how Jewish groups in the United States set themselves up as an electoral force at the polls to support Israel, and hit upon the idea of using the American Israel Public Affairs Committee (AIPAC) as a model for a reinvigorated INC. Chalabi spearheaded his new campaign in June 1997 with a speech before the Jewish Institute for National Security Affairs (JINSA) in Washington. His message: Saddam could be overthrown and replaced with a government friendly to Israel. The speech was well received, and Chalabi later told *The Jerusalem Post* that a post-Saddam Baghdad government might restore an oil pipeline from Kirkuk to Haifa that had not been used in fifty years.[13]

Chalabi's subsequent anti-Saddam lobbying efforts created a stir among prominent conservatives like Trent Lott, Newt Gingrich, and Dick Cheney, who was then at Halliburton. Cheney, for one, was enthusiastic about toppling Saddam. "From the beginning, Cheney was in philosophical agreement with this plan," Francis Brooke said. "Cheney has said, 'Very seldom in life do you get a chance to fix something that went wrong.'"[14] Chalabi was also introduced to Richard Perle, Paul Wolfowitz, and other leading neoconservatives and pro-Israel defense intellectuals who would play key roles in the Bush administration's march to war in Iraq seven years later.

His turn to the right for support set up the next move, an astonishing coup de grâce against the Clinton administration. He and Brooke maneuvered with their new Republican friends to hold congressional hearings in 1998 on the CIA's misdeeds and botched operations in Iraq—which, of course, Chalabi had not only profited from, but was responsible for. The well-publicized hearings were an acute embarrassment to the Clinton administration, then preoccupied with the Monica Lewinsky scandal. Meantime, Chalabi was hard at work with his new Republican allies drafting the Iraq Liberation Act, which passed on October 7, 1998. The much-quoted Clinton-era legislation declared "regime change" in Iraq official U.S. policy. Chalabi had been intrigued by how President Franklin D. Roosevelt had used the lend-lease program with the British to commit the United States to World War II despite surging isolationist public opinion in America. "I studied it with a great deal of respect; we learned a lot from it," said Chalabi. "The Lend-Lease program committed Roosevelt to enter on Britain's side—so we had the Iraq Liberation Act, which committed the American people for the liberation against Saddam."[15]

Despite the insurgents' fiascos and the bloody military disasters at Arbil, Chalabi proposed that regime change would be an Iraqi-led affair, carried out by a homegrown force of rebel insurgents backed by U.S. military muscle. As Chalabi envisioned it, drawing heavily on Gen. Wayne Downing's enclave strategy, as many as ten thousand INC-sponsored forces, eventually renamed the Free Iraqi Forces, would be trained in a liberated zone of Iraq protected by U.S. airpower, where they would establish a provisional government and conduct intelligence missions and commando raids into the rest of the country, recruiting thousands of anti-Saddam converts along the way. Chalabi insisted that it would take less than three months to train the insurgent forces and supply them with antitank weapons and biological- and chemical-protection gear. "The United States will help us to train and equip light anti-tank battalions, well-trained and highly mobile," Chalabi declared later. "Those people, once on the ground, will be able to defeat Saddam's forces."[16] At the time, the Iraqi army numbered some 400,000 troops.

However far-fetched militarily, Chalabi's pitch shrewdly inoculated the Iraqi Liberation Act against political controversy on Capitol Hill—after all, no one was suggesting an expensive, full-scale U.S. military operation or putting American troops in harm's way. It also put Chalabi's organization first in line for a share of the supplementary funding that Congress passed along with the Iraq legislation "to support efforts to remove the regime headed by Saddam Hussein from power in Iraq and to promote the emergence of a democratic government to replace that regime." The act earmarked $97 million in military equipment and training, plus another $43 million for public relations and information-collection activities for Iraqi opposition groups that would shoulder the main burden of bringing about Saddam's downfall.

U.S. military leaders, especially those familiar with the brief, bloody history of Arbil, were openly contemptuous of an insurgent force under Chalabi. Gen. Anthony Zinni, then commander of U.S. forces in the Middle East, ridiculed Chalabi and INC officials as "silk-suited, Rolex-wearing guys in London," and called the plan for bringing down Saddam with Iraqi exile forces "pie in the sky, a fairy tale." Zinni, with a fresher memory than most of the bloodshed at Arbil and of aggressive Iraqi gunners in the no-fly zones, was worried in part that a small opposition force would be decimated by Iraqi troops. "I said, 'This is ridiculous, won't happen,' " recalled Zinni. " 'This is going to generate another one of our defeats there where we get a bunch of people slaughtered.' " He also sensed that the enclave scheme was a formula for dragging the United States into a war. "The second issue is, they lead us into a mess, they piecemeal us into a fight," Zinni said. "Okay, it's Special Forces, it's small units, create an enclave, it's air support. But what do they drag us into?"[17]

A 1999 article in *Foreign Affairs* dismissed the Iraqi insurgent operation as "militarily ludicrous" and declared that it "would almost certainly end in either direct American intervention or a massive bloodbath." The authors foresaw at best an Iraqi version of the Bay of Pigs, the disastrous 1961 invasion of Cuba staged by CIA-backed anti-Castro exiles.[18] Zinni and others contemptuously dubbed the prospective Iraqi replay "the Bay of Goats." Eventually, some seven hundred volunteers for the Free Iraqi Forces (FIF) received training at Hungary's Taszar military base, where the United States had set up a logistical center for multinational peacekeeping forces in Bosnia. By then, the administration and even the Pentagon itself were deeply divided over the efficacy of supporting any Iraqi insurgent force. FIF was variously envisioned in Washington as the military wing of the INC, the core of the new Iraqi army, a transitional police force to keep civil order, and a liaison between coalition forces and the Iraqi people after major combat ended.

Chalabi's bid for power—and a political base—seemed to hinge on these anti-Saddam insurgents. The FIF, however, fell far short of fulfilling any of the roles Chalabi envisioned for it. By the time the combat phase of Operation Iraqi Freedom ended, Chalabi's ragtag troops had accomplished very little. During the U.S. invasion four years later, he and his men were flown to Iraq on U.S. military transports and deposited in the northern no-fly zone, safely out of Saddam's reach. Despite warnings from U.S. Army brass to stay out of the war zone, the Pentagon arranged to airlift Chalabi and a contingent of FIF troops aboard a U.S. Air Force C-130 Hercules transport to an airbase near Nasiriyah in southern Iraq. Decked out in a black shirt and a bush hat with his entourage in tow, Chalabi seemed to observers to think he was Gen. Douglas MacArthur returning to the Philippines.[19] The exiled leader shortly made his way to Baghdad, where he set up headquarters in a former hunting club in the city's affluent Mansour district and was joined by Harold Rhode from

Doug Feith's Pentagon operation to await a post in the provisional government.[20]

Almost immediately, the U.S. Iraq command began hearing reports that Chalabi's people were engaged in reprisals against former Baathists. Training the opposition was "a waste of time and energy," said U.S. marine lieutenant general Michael DeLong, a top aide of Gen. Tommy Franks. "While some of them were helpful in small battles, we received many reports of their looting and thievery in Baghdad."[21]

While Chalabi was busy currying favor with his new conservative Republican allies and laying the groundwork for the Iraq Liberation Act in Washington, the UNSCOM inspectors in Baghdad were still sifting through the Kemal chicken farm documents and getting bogged down in an increasingly hostile impasse with Saddam's regime over access to Iraqi weapons sites and rumors of U.S. spying. Although he was spending most of his time in Washington and London, Chalabi and the INC were attuned to defectors and intelligence coming out of Iraq. Like many others, he was interested in new information on Saddam's prohibited weapons, which had become a preoccupation among his new American neoconservative friends. In early 1998, Chalabi arranged for a meeting with Scott Ritter, the ex-marine intelligence officer and weapons inspector who had grown increasingly frustrated by the Clinton administration's policy toward Iraq, which he felt was undermining the UNSCOM weapons inspection program.

The two met in baronial splendor at an apartment in London's Mayfair section on Conduit Street. Chalabi reportedly began by offering to help Ritter through his opposition contacts in Baghdad, whom he claimed had access to Saddam's inner circle. Ritter recalled that tea was served by a half-dozen Arab servants. Rather than take Chalabi up on his offer, however, Ritter let Chalabi steer him into an extended account of those parts of Saddam's WMD arsenal or production capacities that the UNSCOM inspectors had failed to account for or destroy. Over the course of several hours, with Chalabi sitting on a couch taking notes, Ritter unspooled a list that would have included more than a half-dozen proscribed Iraqi-built missiles, fifty conventional warheads, hundreds of artillery shells packed with chemical weapons, thousands of liters of missing anthrax, uncertainty about dual-use biological agents, and missing technical documentation about centrifuges for refining weapons-grade uranium.

Ritter also told Chalabi how UNSCOM inspectors went about their business using high-tech methods like U-2 spy planes to spot weapons facilities and ground-penetrating radar to search underground bunkers. He revealed the inspectors' theories about Saddam's weapons capabilities they hadn't been able to pin down, including a suspicion that the Iraqis might possess mobile laboratories mounted in tractor-trailer trucks for manufacturing chemical or biological weapons. Only belatedly did Ritter realize he had given away the store to Chalabi, providing him with invaluable information that he could use to indict Saddam in the public mind for harboring a frighteningly lethal WMD arsenal.

"I should have asked him what he could give me," Ritter said. "Instead, I let him ask me, 'What do you need?'" The result, he said, was that "we made the biggest mistake in the intelligence business: we identified all of our gaps." Ritter later came to believe that Chalabi passed the information about the holes in UNSCOM's knowledge to INC operatives who then found defectors to fabricate detailed intelligence to order about Saddam's WMD programs. The mobile weapons labs were a telling case in point. "We told Chalabi and, lo and behold, he's fabricated a source for the mobile labs," said Ritter. "It was all crap."[22]

Six months later, just before he resigned from the UN weapons-inspection team, Ritter met with Chalabi a second time at the INC town house in Georgetown. They discussed new details that had emerged about Saddam's VX nerve gas program. Chalabi took the opportunity to show the former marine a copy of the enclave plan for an Iraqi rebel force authored by his friend Gen. Wayne Downing. Ritter was unimpressed by the document, *An Alternative Strategy for Iraq*. Ritter suspected it was a ploy to get the U.S. military involved in deposing Saddam. "So how come the fact that you'd need more American assistance is not in the plan?" Ritter asked.

"Because it's too sensitive," answered Chalabi.[23]

Armed with such insider information, Chalabi had so ingratiated himself with the Bush administration's new defense establishment—Cheney, Rumsfeld, Wolfowitz, and Perle, among others—that on September 18, 2001, he was invited to address a special meeting of the Defense Policy Board, a civilian advisory panel set up by Rumsfeld that was headed by Perle. Chalabi was one of thirty people whisked in minibuses from a downtown Washington hotel, as one participant recalled, in "a full-blown police escort, motorcycle outriders, the works, and at the peak of the morning rush hour . . . across the 14th Street Bridge" to the Pentagon, where they convened in Secretary Rumsfeld's conference room. The first speaker was former Princeton professor Bernard Lewis, a respected Middle East expert. Lewis emphasized that the United States should respond strongly to the terror attacks, while supporting democratic reformers in the region "such as my friend here, Dr. Chalabi."[24] For his part, Chalabi counseled the Americans to forget about Afghanistan and go straight for Saddam's jugular in Iraq. The Bush administration chose not to heed his advice, but the specter of regime change that Chalabi had helped plant was never far in the background, even if it had less to do with anti-American terrorism than with his own personal ambitions.

Chalabi's meticulous networking and swashbuckling tactics began to pay off. At some point after the terrorist attacks, Chalabi and the INC were recruited by the Bush administration to gather intelligence from Iraqi defectors about Saddam Hussein's weapons of mass destruction. Chalabi has not revealed the identities of the Bush officials who made the request, or exactly when and where it was made. Nor has he revealed whether the INC was instructed to mount a sophisticated public information campaign about Saddam's weapons arsenal directed at the press, the intelligence community, and the American public. But that is precisely what Chalabi, his lieutenant Francis Brooke, and INC operatives set about doing. "Look, our focus was on Saddam's crimes, moral crimes, genocide," Chalabi said, speaking of the INC organization in general. "We were not focused on WMD. The U.S. *asked* us. We didn't bring these people up; they asked us! They requested help from us."[25] Brooke confirmed his boss's contention, admitting to a reporter that he told INC operatives to get the goods on Saddam's arsenal for the American war effort. "I told them, as their campaign manager, 'Go get me a terrorist and some W.M.D., because that's what the Bush administration is interested in.'"[26]

Within months, Chalabi's people were hard at work supplying information on Saddam's WMD to both journalists and intelligence agents in the United States, Europe, and elsewhere. It was a diabolically effective scheme, feeding hot information to competing news organizations and national spy services, thereby creating an echo chamber of cross-confirmation that made independent judgment about credibility of the information offered at best difficult, and at worst impossible. If the CIA and Czech intelligence assessed that Mohamed Atta probably met with an Iraqi agent in Prague, it was as good as confirmed, wasn't it? It was the same with Saddam's puported WMD. But the energy expended to forge dubious links between Saddam and 9/11 was a sideshow compared to the INC's efforts to make the case that Iraq had reconstituted its chemical, biological, and nuclear weapons programs.

Less than a year after 9/11, by the time INC agents and their defectors had erected an edifice of disinformation that would take years to deconstruct, Chalabi and the INC seemed to have their WMD voodoo down cold. In the summer of 2002, Chalabi, almost certainly elaborating on his Georgetown conversations with Scott Ritter, but "citing informants within the Iraqi intelligence community," told *The Washington Post* that "Hussein's VX stockpile is far larger than the 3.9 tons Iraq reported— something UNSCOM inspectors have long suspected . . ." Reporter Joby Warrick probed further and helpfully added, "UNSCOM officials said the account seemed credible, given what was learned about Iraq's VX program in the final months of weapons inspections."[27] There were no legitimate intelligence reports of "far larger" Iraqi VX stores. But while the fact-checkers were putting their boots on, the disinformation spread quickly around the world.

12

CHALABI'S ROGUE INTELLIGENCE OPERATION

On February 11, 2002, Deputy Assistant Defense Secretary Linton Wells received a telephone call from former CIA director R. James Woolsey passing along word that INC agents were in touch with a former Iraqi intelligence official, Maj. Mohammad Harith, whom Pentagon intelligence officials might want to interview. That Woolsey would serve as an intermediary for Chalabi was not surprising: Months before, he had served in much the same capacity for the INC, alerting the Pentagon about Khodada al-Lami and his story of the terrorist training camp at Salman Pak. A member of Defense Secretary Rumsfeld's Defense Advisory Board, Woolsey was a fervent believer that there had been collusion between Iraq and al-Qaeda. He served as a corporate officer of the Washington-based Iraqi National Congress Support Foundation, an organization set up to expedite the U.S. government funding of the INC.

Wells promptly issued an "executive referral" informing the Defense Intelligence Agency at the Pentagon how to contact Harith through the INC's London office. "I discussed the issue of an individual with information on Iraq weapons of mass destruction with intelligence community members. They said they would follow up," Wells said later, adding that he did not meet with INC officials himself or have any reason to question the defector's reliability. "I was aware that sources always need to be vetted and this instance would be no different. This was not a big deal. It was simply a tip that needed to get to folks working the issue."[1] But the former

CIA director's call to Wells had a secondary purpose. It effectively by-passed the CIA and the State Department, which regarded Chalabi and the INC with distrust bordering on disdain, and gave Pentagon policy-makers direct access to Harith's intelligence on Iraqi WMD.

Two DIA agents spoke with Chalabi the same day. They arranged to meet with Harith at an undisclosed location, most likely in the London area, where the defector reportedly passed a lie detector test without diffi-culty.[2] His story "seemed accurate" to DIA officials, although "much of it appeared embellished." Following more meetings and assessments in April, May, and as late as July 2002, however, intelligence analysts had second thoughts. They detected inconsistencies in Harith's story and be-gan to suspect he "had been coached on what information to provide."[3] The DIA concluded that Harith, who claimed he was a Mukhabarat offi-cer responsible for concealing Iraq's WMD, had fabricated his elaborate stories of Saddam's mobile bioweapons labs. In May 2002, nine months before coalition forces invaded Iraq, the DIA issued a "fabricator," or "burn," notice on Harith, putting the U.S. intelligence community on alert that he had been discredited and was an unreliable source.

Unfortunately, no one got the message. Due to an unexplained glitch, the DIA warning about Harith's credibility was never electronically cross-linked in Defense Department computers with assessments of his version of events that were distributed to the intelligence community. CBS's 60 Minutes, Vanity Fair magazine, and dozens of newspapers ran stories based on interviews with Harith in the next six months, oblivious to the fact that he had been discredited by U.S. intelligence. Bush administration officials claimed they did not know that Harith had been declared unreli-able until almost two years later, on February 13, 2004, when The New York Times first reported the DIA "burn" notice.

By then, the damage had been done. The intelligence Harith and several other INC defectors supplied about Saddam's sophisticated—and fictitious—mobile bioweapons labs was included as evidence of Saddam's WMD programs in both the National Intelligence Estimate of 2002 and the president's 2003 State of the Union Address, when Bush also declared that Iraq had tried to buy yellowcake uranium from Africa. A short time later, satellite photos purportedly showing the mobile labs provided a dramatic visual backdrop for Secretary of State Colin Powell's impressive-sounding but error-riddled February 5 presentation of U.S. intelligence on Iraqi WMD before the UN Security Council, with CIA director George Tenet sitting directly behind him. The effect was to create a powerful wave of misinformation in the media that resonated all the more with the public when it surfaced later in declassified government documents and authoritative public pronouncements by senior Bush administration officials.

Chalabi and the INC had mounted a classic disinformation campaign. General Hamza and Saeed al-Haideri, the Iraqi engineer whose accounts of Saddam's reconstructed weapons facilities surfaced in December 2002, were not the only Iraqi defectors with tales of reconstituted WMD programs to tell, thanks to timely help from Chalabi and his INC lieutenants. By luck or calculation, INC officials also had chosen to focus on Harith and the mobile bioweapons labs that Ritter had identified as one of the "gaps" in UNSCOM's knowledge of Iraq's weapons arsenal. But providing classified intelligence through the Pentagon to Washington decision-makers took place well out of public view—and therefore had its limitations. From the first, the INC game plan included a well-plotted campaign to bombard the public with information provided by defectors and to disseminate it as widely as possible through the media. The INC's funding agreement with the State Department barred the INC from "attempting to influence the policies of the United States government or Congress, or propagandizing the American people." So did U.S. law. But that is exactly what Chalabi set about doing.

Less than a month after Woolsey introduced Harith to the Defense Intelligence Agency, *60 Minutes* aired a segment reported by Lesley Stahl about the INC's efforts to "to win the backing of the Bush administration, which is divided over whether or not to give the INC the money and the military training they want" to wage an insurgency against Saddam. "Don't say that you—we want to drag the United States into a war with Iraq," Chalabi instructed Stahl, as the video cut from footage of Chalabi to President Bush's January 2002 "axis of evil" State of the Union Address and back again. "Say that we want to stop the United States' war on Iraq by removing Saddam."

Noting that the INC had hired the public relations firm Burson-Marsteller to help get out its message, Stahl reported near the top of the segment that the INC "runs a high-profile Iraqi defector program as an answer to their critics who say they don't have much of a following inside Iraq." The exile organization, Stahl said, had indeed "attracted a string of high-level Iraqi defectors." As proof, she showed footage of an INC official interviewing an unnamed defector in an undisclosed Middle Eastern country whom she identified as a former officer "in Iraq's ruthless intelligence service, the Mukhabarat."

Chalabi and the INC were well positioned to assist the American war-promotion effort. Since October 2000 the Clinton State Department had uneasily granted the INC a monthly stipend of $150,000 authorized by the 1998 Iraqi Liberation Act to subvert the Baghdad regime by supplying the media with tales of Saddam's deadly misdeeds. Soon after the Bush administration took office in January 2001, Vice President Cheney pushed for and received a reauthorization of Chalabi's funding. The secret funding agreement between the State Department and the INC authorized Chalabi to "implement a public information campaign to communicate with Iraqis inside and outside Iraq and also to promulgate its message to the international community at large."[4] The terms of the State Department deal strictly banned activities that even appeared to attempt to influence Americans about U.S. policy by using taxpayers' dollars. Until mid-2002, however, the ban was ignored.

In a misguided attempt to demonstrate their usefulness to the Bush administration, INC officials later provided Congress with documentation showing that for eight months after 9/11, through May 2002, its agents had placed more than one hundred anti-Saddam stories in the international media. Of those, fifty were placed with U.S. news organizations and published or broadcast in the United States. Some stories were skeptical of the INC or Chalabi. But about three-quarters of the stories, wrote Douglas McCollum in the *Columbia Journalism Review,* "advanced almost every claim that would eventually become the backbone of the Bush administration's case for war, including Saddam Hussein's contacts with al Qaeda, his attempts to develop nuclear weapons, and his extensive chemical and bioweapons facilities."[5] All such information supplied by Chalabi and the INC was eventually repudiated in a still-classified 2003 DIA intelligence report.[6]

The defector in Stahl's interview was not named during the *60 Minutes* segment, but CBS later identified him as Mohammad Harith. His INC handler, Nabeel Musawi, told Stahl on tape that the most important thing their unidentified source revealed was "probably the mobile bio-units." In a voice-over, Stahl paraphrased Harith's story: "The defector is telling Musawi that in order to evade the UN inspectors, Saddam Hussein put his biological weapons laboratories in trucks that the defector told us he personally bought from Renault. Refrigerator trucks . . ."

She then asked Harith directly, "How many?"

"Seven," he responded.

She repeated, "Seven Renault trucks."

Harith answered, "Yes. Seven."

Cutting away to Musawi, Stahl asked what the INC intended to do with such information. "Once we establish that a certain piece of information is credible," he said, "then we do share the information with others, for example, the US government." When Stahl pushed him on where in the government the INC sent the information, Musawi answered, "The Pentagon." Virtually everything else in the sequence was pure propaganda. Apart from Musawi's blunt (and self-aggrandizing) comment on passing intelligence to the Pentagon, nothing was accurate or truthful. There were no seven trucks. INC officials did not vouch for the credibility of the defectors it brought forward. (INC spokesman Entifadh Qanbar later explained, "We did not provide information. We provided defectors. We take no position on them. It's up to you reporters to decide if they are credible or not.") And Major Harith had been handed off to the Pentagon a month before without vetting.

News organizations snapped up the *60 Minutes* report like popcorn, quoting the anonymous former Iraqi intelligence officer as evidence that Saddam's biological weapons program was alive and well. The *Sunday Times* of London also interviewed Harith and added colorfully that the mobile labs were disguised as yogurt and milk trucks. But far and away the most gripping account of Harith's fictitious experiences was British journalist David Rose's special report in the May 2002 issue of *Vanity Fair*. Rose's admiring story, "Inside Saddam's Deadly Arsenal," filled in Harith's background and elaborated on his instrumental role in building the mobile bioweapons labs, all the while marshaling details that must have reflected the DIA's intelligence reports. He described Harith—whom he called "the defector" throughout—as a tall and slender man in his late thirties who was educated at the School of National Security in Baghdad and spoke serviceable English, but preferred Arabic. *Vanity Fair* too, later confirmed that the defector was indeed Harith.

After his graduation from Baghdad School of National Security in 1986, Rose wrote, Harith joined the Mukhabarat division that kept government ministers under surveillance for any deviations from Saddam's autocratic leadership. By 1992 he was transferred to a commercial division of "the Directorate for Secret Organizations and Relations," which, among its duties, said Harith, organized training for foreign terrorists at the by then notorious Salman Pak camp outside Baghdad. Harith revealed to Rose that among the Mukhabarat's clients were fighters from the Palestinian terrorist group Hamas. "Many weapons were being supplied to

Hamas," he told Rose. "Guns, ammunition both heavy and light, detonators, and explosives. It was Iraq which trained Hamas in how to make bombs."[7] Harith's assignment, Rose wrote, was to work with secret Iraqi front companies responsible for procuring weapons materials and parts from abroad for Saddam's WMD programs.

Harith claimed he had the idea for the mobile labs in the summer of 1996. Despite his youth and "his relatively junior rank—the equivalent of a major," Rose wrote, Harith "found himself at a meeting with Dr. Rihab Taha, also known as 'Dr. Germ,'" the female mastermind behind Iraq's biological weapons. In their discussion of how to hide the bioweapons programs from UNSCOM inspectors, Harith told Rose that he made a simple suggestion to Dr. Taha regarding the labs where biological weapons were manufactured. "They had the same problem as any stationary facility," he explained. "I suggested we go for mobile unit." Rose describes what happened next:

> He says he and Dr. Taha wrote a report for Saddam, who rapidly approved it. He organized the purchase of eight heavy Renault trucks from France—a perfectly legal deal carried out through Iraq's Ministry of Commerce. At the secret al-Iskandariyya facility in the Hilla Province, engineers converted them into factories of mass destruction. "They look like meat cars, yogurt cars," he says. "And inside is a laboratory, with incubators for bacteria, microscopes, air-conditioning."[8]

Milk had given way to meat, the yogurt ruse had become accepted wisdom, and seven Renault trucks had become eight. There were new, credible-sounding details about the locations where the mobile lab trucks were built.

But the mobile truck labs were not Harith's only revelations. He also told Rose about an earlier trip with other Iraqi agents and five Eastern Europeans to Africa to purchase nuclear material for an Iraqi dirty bomb. In Dar es Salaam, Tanzania, he claimed, the Iraqis exchanged a briefcase full of hundred-dollar bills for "pieces of black rock, glittery . . . the size and shape of fingers"—a description that Rose reported was consistent with "spent reactor fuel rods cut into sections, which could be used to build a 'dirty,' radiological bomb." In 1996 Harith said he was promoted to the late Hussein Kamel's Military Industrial Commission. After enduring six months of prison and torture on phony charges of conspiracy against Saddam, Rose wrote, Harith was rehabilitated by the Mukhabarat in 1997 and "found himself indoctrinated into Iraq's deepest secrets: its attempts to renew its arsenal of weapons of mass destruction, and build a new long-range-missile system with which to deliver them."

Harith claimed that Iraq's new Tammuz missile, which would have a range of six hundred to seven hundred miles and was therefore outlawed by the 1991 ceasefire agreement, was easily capable of reaching Cairo, Tehran, Riyadh, Saudi Arabia, and Ankara. "By the summer of 2000, the defector tells me, the Tammooz project was about halfway complete," wrote Rose. "The first and second stages of the rocket had been built and tested, using steel and carbon fiber imported illegally through the Mukhabarat's front-company web." Harith claimed that the Tammuz missile would have been ready in 2001 if components could have been purchased from China. He reeled off, with some accuracy, a list of manufacturing sites around Iraq that had been used for making various components of Saddam's old missile programs. Charles Duelfer, the former deputy chief weapons inspector for UNSCOM, told Rose the list was "highly credible."

Did Rose believe everything Harith told him? Rose readily acknowledged the INC's role in setting up two daylong interviews with Harith in March, and conceded that much of his information was impossible to verify independently. But he also noted that the DIA already had debriefed Harith at length, which he took as a measure of the defector's importance and credibility. Rose praised the INC operations, which, he wrote, "resemble nothing so much as the Underground Railroad, the clandestine network which rescued slaves from the American South before the Civil War." He also uncritically reported the INC's assurances that Harith's story largely corroborated that of Saeed al-Haideri, the Baghdad construction engineer. "Neither man knows what the other has told us," Nabeel Musawi explained to Rose. "But they're saying the same thing about weapons types and where they're being made." That was, generously, a half-truth. As U.S. intelligence later discredited information from INC's defectors, INC spokesmen quietly dropped their claims that the organization took responsibility for the credibility of its sources.

Rose went back to Duelfer repeatedly to check Harith's stories. Duelfer seemed to give Harith real credibility, but stopped well short of confirming or corroborating the information he provided, which Duelfer was in no position to know about, but merely suspected might be accurate. Such carefully parsed responses from otherwise knowledgeable sources explained a great deal about how Chalabi and the INC managed to pull off their deceptions. Duelfer told Rose, for example, that Harith's list of the missile manufacturing sites "tallies with other information in his database," but offered nothing on the question of how far the Tammuz system had progressed. In fact, an advanced Iraqi missile system was almost certainly discussed by Saddam's scientists and engineers before the 1991 Gulf War, but no evidence ever surfaced that any components were engineered or assembled in Iraq other than those for shorter-range missiles, allowable under UN Resolution 687. Harith's list was consistent with known manufacturing sites for these short-range missiles. Duelfer, then a Middle East expert at the Center for Strategic and International Studies, a Washington think tank, left the opposite impression without actually saying so. When Rose asked Duelfer to review all of Harith's "testimony" to *Vanity Fair,* Duelfer generally deemed it credible:

> I haven't found anything to make me disbelieve him. What he describes is consistent with what we know about how Iraq operates, both in terms of building weapons of mass destruction, and in terms of its efforts to procure the necessary equipment and materials. His evidence tells us that Iraq's weapons-of-mass-destruction program has only accelerated since UNSCOM was expelled from the country in 1998.[9]

Nothing of the sort had occurred and Duelfer had no knowledge that it had. But his answer fed the pro-war, anti-Saddam frenzy in Washington and sharply undermined those who would declare before the war that there was no evidence Baghdad had restarted its major WMD programs—and that Iraq's official corruption and deteriorating industrial infrastructure had rendered it incapable of supporting an arms buildup.

There was another reason that Harith's claims, particularly about the mobile bioweapons labs, were taken seriously by intelligence agencies and the press. His story seemed to confirm intelligence that BND, Germany's federal intelligence service, had first gathered in 1999 while vetting a young Iraqi engineer trying to defect to Germany, later code-named "Curveball." The Iraqi, who had flown into Munich seeking a German visa, told BND officials that he had been hired by Iraq's Military Industrial

Commission right out of Baghdad University in 1994 to work at the Chemical Engineering and Design Center. Like Harith, he claimed he was assigned to work with the infamous "Dr. Germ"—aka Rihab Taha— planning a secret program to build mobile biological weapons labs in trucks. The idea was to brew deadly germs while avoiding detection by determined UN weapons inspectors. There was, of course, no evidence that the Iraqis possessed such mobile labs. But in 1992 a member of the UNSCOM team had speculated in a report that the Iraqis might have deployed mobile germ labs to hide their biological warfare program, and the young Iraqi's information seemed to fit the profile.

BND agents pulled the Iraqi out of the queue in Zirndorf, near Nuremberg, where scores of Iraqis awaited German visas.[10] The Germans set him up with a new identity and home for his wife and young daughter, and in early 2000 they began serious interrogations, which would last on and off until 2001. Analysts were intrigued that the Iraqi, whom they code-named Curveball ("ball" was the BND cryptonym for "weapons," and "curve" apparently designated the young defector's volatile personality), was able to name six specific sites where the trucks were built, though he claimed he had only worked at one. His description of helping to assemble a truck-mounted bioweapons lab at the Djerf al Nadaf facility, in a run-down industrial slum southeast of Baghdad, impressed the Germans. Curveball showed a detailed familiarity with the place, indicating how the trucks were hidden inside the two-story warehouse with garage doors at each end, and even assisting BND analysts to build a scale model of the place. He claimed he was an eyewitness during a 1998 industrial accident at Djerf al Nadaf in which twelve workers were killed. His account of the tragedy raised his credibility in the eyes of the Germans.

Curveball told BND interrogators that he designed laboratory equipment for the mobile biological weapons units and provided details, such as dimensions, temperature settings, and diagrams of how the mobile labs worked. This time, however, they were struck by his vagueness. He couldn't say what biological agents or microbes the truck-mounted labs produced, and appeared to have no idea whether anthrax was involved—a critical subject for Western intelligence agencies since Iraq first admitted in 1995 to possessing weaponized anthrax and other bio-poisons before the Gulf War, some of it reportedly from the United States. The BND kept the local DIA office in Munich apprised of its progress interrogating Curveball, and first provided summaries of its debriefings to the United States in early 2000.

But the Germans steadfastly refused to allow the DIA or CIA to interview Curveball, since he was said to hate Americans.

Curveball's cooperation with his German interrogators abruptly ceased in 2001 when he was granted asylum. At about the same time, intelligence officials began to question his credibility. He had seemed very emotional, smelled of liquor, and seemed hungover to a CIA doctor who was allowed to examine him in May 2000. The British intelligence service, MI6, informed the CIA in early 2001 that Curveball did not seem "a wholly reliable source," adding that "elements of [his] behavior strike us as typical of . . . fabricators." The British reported that in 1997 reconnaissance satellite photos of the Djerf al Nadaf facility showed that a wall surrounded the central warehouse where Curveball had said the mobile weapons labs were hidden. That meant that, contrary to Curveball's testimony, trucks could not be moved easily in or out of the building.

After September 11, 2001, despite his deteriorating story and their lack of access to him, the CIA reassessed the information Curveball had given the Germans and dramatically upgraded the dangers presented by Iraq's bioweapons program. Although there was no new intelligence on Curveball or Iraq's bio-warfare program, in October 2001 the CIA's Center for Weapons Intelligence, Proliferation, and Arms Control (WINPAC) flatly asserted that Iraq "continues to produce at least . . . three BW agents" and its mobile bioweapons labs provide production "capabilities surpassing the pre–Gulf War era,"[11] estimated at 30,000 liters. WINPAC analysts had arrived at this stunning conclusion by estimating the production of seven mobile weapons fuel labs operating at full capacity for six months—at best an imaginative fiction.[12]

But U.S. and German intelligence officials had another worry. After Curveball told the Germans that his brother had served as Ahmed Chalabi's personal bodyguard in Iraq, they began to fear that Curveball might have been coached by the exile leader or INC operatives, who were on the lookout for useful Iraqi defectors. The Germans, however, couldn't prove anything, and were only somewhat mollified when they learned that Curveball and his brother did not have a close relationship. Of the three defectors whose testimony seemed to corroborate Curveball's account of the mobile labs, two had connections with Chalabi. The most important was Mohammad Harith. Since Harith's tale seemed to dovetail so effortlessly with Curveball's "eyewitness account," the disinformation about Iraqi mobile bioweapons labs gained unusually strong staying power. Secretary of State

Colin Powell would later describe Curveball's account as "one of the most worrisome things that emerge from the thick intelligence file."

On January 3, 2002, Cheney and his chief of staff, I. Lewis "Scooter" Libby, had received a special briefing at the vice president's office by CIA director George Tenet, a top agency analyst in the Near East Division, and two operatives explaining why the CIA had concluded that covert action to support an insurgency or stage a coup would fail to topple Saddam's regime. If Saddam had any impenetrable defenses, the CIA believed, it was the formidable ability of his Republican Guard and Special Security Organization to sniff out a plot against the Iraqi leader. Langley also had little confidence it could sustain covert operations inside Iraq without being discovered, and it was going to take time to persuade reluctant allies in the region to join such a campaign against Saddam. Tenet's team had concluded that a full-blown military invasion was the most certain route to regime change in Iraq, and declared that the CIA was prepared to mount intensive undercover preinvasion support operations.

Six weeks later, on February 16, 2002, shortly after the president's "axis of evil" State of the Union speech, which the conservative pundit Charles Krauthammer considered "just short of a declaration of war," Bush signed a top-secret intelligence order for regime change in Iraq that authorized $400 million over two years for the CIA to prepare the ground inside Iraq for war. Besides granting Tenet the authority to conduct an array of counterintelligence measures inside Iraq, including deception and sabotage operations to distract and mislead the Iraqis, the president gave CIA paramilitary groups inside the country the authority to "support opposition groups and individuals that want Saddam out." The secret presidential directive meant working with the opposition to gather intelligence and even conduct paramilitary operations against the Baghdad regime— and that included Chalabi and the Iraqi National Congress, as well as Kurdish forces in the north and Shiite political parties and militias in the south.

By the time the vice president set off on a tour of Arab capitals in March 2002 to discuss U.S. plans for regime change in Baghdad and lay the groundwork for war, influential publications on both sides of the Atlantic and in the Middle East were busily gearing up for stories about Saddam's military strength and the scope of his WMD arsenal, thanks to sources provided by Chalabi and the INC. Among their authors were some of the most senior reporters in Washington, including Judith Miller of *The New York Times*, Christopher Hitchens of London's *The Guardian*, Evan Thomas of *Newsweek*, and Mark Bowden of *The Atlantic Monthly*. Besides Lesley Stahl's *60 Minutes* segment and David Rose's two lengthy *Vanity Fair* features (he had written another story in January based on defector accounts), major stories about the Iraqi crisis that used Chalabi or INC-supplied defectors as sources appeared in *The Observer*, *Newsweek*, *Time*, *The New Yorker*, CNN International, and *The Wall Street Journal*, among others.

It was hardly coincidental that Chalabi suddenly began popping up everywhere in the media, given the secret funding agreement between the Bush administration and the INC.

But for leading news organizations, relying on INC information was at best a dicey business. More than one top journalist came away red-faced from the encounter with the INC. Although the U.S. newsmagazines produced plenty of strong reporting prior to the Iraq war, *Newsweek* ran a story in late March that took the INC's bait. The idea was to review the list of Iraqi generals who had defected, were willing to lead an insurrection against Saddam—and might have the toughness and skill to replace him. Authors Evan Thomas and Roy Gutman reported that King Abdullah II of Jordan told Cheney during his stopover in Amman that he would support a U.S. military effort against Baghdad, but he scornfully opposed Chalabi as a replacement for Saddam, especially after the Petra Bank scandal. Even so, *Newsweek* used the INC to contact former Iraqi general Mahdi al-Duleimi, among others. In an interview with General al-Duleimi in Germany, he outlined a plan strikingly similar to Gen. Wayne Downing's enclave plan for establishing a rebel force in Kurdistan supported by U.S. airpower—and assured the authors that the plan had "won high marks in Washington." There was no hint that Chalabi, along with al-Duleimi, might have had a mutual interest in staging an Iraqi rebellion.[13]

Time was also tripped up by the INC. In a carefully written assessment of Saddam's weapons arsenal in May, writer Josh Tyrangiel offered a mix of speculation from Duelfer with information provided by the INC to strongly suggest that Baghdad was busy rejuvenating its WMD programs. Citing an internal INC document, *Time* reported that Saddam had rolled out "new missiles, including ones that appeared to violate the UN ban on long-range missiles that is meant to prevent Iraq from threatening Europe," echoing Harith's phony account of the long-range Tammuz missile.[14]

If mainstream U.S. journalists fell hard for stories from INC defectors, conservative publications and writers like British columnist Christopher Hitchens treated them like manna from heaven. Hitchens was an avid supporter of the INC. His abrupt flip-flop after 9/11 from political progressive to militant conservative on Iraq was well known to readers of *The Guardian, Vanity Fair,* and the online magazine *Slate.* Writing in the March 20 edition of *The Guardian,* Hitchens cited INC client Khidhir Hamza's already discredited declarations that "the date by which Saddam will have [nuclear] bombs—'clean' or 'dirty'—is not much more than a year or so away" and that there was "no doubt that Saddam wants them in order to use them."[15] On Iraq's relations with al-Qaeda, Hitchens wrote, "one would still like to know why Mohamed Atta, chief pilot of the September 11 death squads, met an Iraqi diplomat in Prague last year." He cited the INC as his source for the apocryphal story. Even so, Hitchens later insisted to an interviewer that his work did not belong on the list of stories planted by the INC since he "rarely used INC-supplied defectors as sources, and never for WMD stories."[16]

Hitchens was not the only high-profile writer who had a hard time admitting that he had been caught in Chalabi's web. Mark Bowden, a former *Philadelphia Inquirer* reporter who had written the brilliant and disturbing account of the 1994 U.S. military disaster in Mogadishu, Somalia, *Blackhawk Down,* was similarly entrapped in his lengthy profile of Saddam's Iraq for the June 2002 issue of *The Atlantic Monthly.* In reporting "Tales of the Tyrant," Bowden conceded that he had used INC-supplied defectors as sources, but insisted that it was obvious they "were selling something, and I wasn't particularly interested in what they were selling." He said he turned away INC attempts to steer him toward issues such as WMD and terrorist training camps.

Yet in one of his most vivid passages, Bowden told the story of a secret meeting Saddam called to speak with Iraqi agents who "had been selected to meet with him, and to work at the terrorist camps where warriors were being trained to strike back at America." The scene was narrated through the eyes of the ubiquitous Khodada al-Lami, the former Mukhabarat official and Chalabi-supplied defector and source for the Salman Pak story. Bowden artfully kept the focus on Saddam:

The United States, he said, because of its reckless treatment of Arab nations and the Arab people, was a necessary target for revenge and destruction. American aggression must be stopped in order for Iraq to rebuild and to resume leadership of the Arab world. Saddam talked for almost two hours. Khodada could sense the great hatred in him, the anger over what America had done to his ambitions and to Iraq. Saddam blamed the United States for all the poverty, backwardness, and suffering in his country.[17]

Bowden absorbed al-Lami's perspective and presented details conjured up by the defector as fact. As unwitting anti-Saddam propaganda, it was powerful stuff. Saddam was gunning for America and training Arab terrorists for the task. As documentary reporting, it was pure fiction, supplied by an INC defector and brought to the *Atlantic Monthly*'s readers courtesy of a grant from the U.S. State Department. Bowden explained later that he had no reason to question such stories told to him by INC defectors. "To the extent it makes it appear I was duped in some way by the INC," he said, "I don't like being on that list and I don't think that's true."[18]

The Clinton State Department was uneasy with the INC information program from the start. Known formally as the Information Collection Program, or ICP, it resurrected the propaganda tactics and focus on intelligence gathering that the INC had deployed in Iraq during the 1990s. INC officials insisted they were collecting anti-Saddam information for their own broadcasts and publications. But it soon became evident that the exile group was feeding stories about Saddam's human rights abuses and his lethal arsenal of proscribed WMD to intelligence agencies and influential media outlets. Officials at the State Department's Division of Near Eastern Affairs, mindful of the INC's stormy past ties with the CIA, recognized that the covert information program was in essence a rogue intelligence and propaganda operation. "We agreed to it with a great deal of reluctance and put in as many safeguards as we could," said Allen Kieswetter, the deputy assistant secretary of the Near Eastern Division at the time. Kieswetter recommended that the INC program be transferred out of the State Department. "We aren't really in the intelligence business," he said.

At first, the State Department had a hard time pinning down exactly what the INC operation was up to. An INC memo described the information program this way: "Defectors, reports, and raw intelligence are cultivated and analyzed and the results are reported through the INC newspaper [*Al-Mutamar*], the Arabic and Western media, and to appropriate governmental, nongovernmental, and international agencies."[19] The information program was supposed to broadcast anti-Saddam news via INC's "Liberty Network" TV inside Iraq and publish it in its newspaper, which would be distributed to Iraqis. But it was not at all clear to State Department officials that the Liberty TV signal *could* even be received inside Iraq, and *Al-Mutamar* wasn't available in the country, except for the estimated 1 percent of Iraqis with access to the Internet.

When asked to account for $2.2 million of $4.3 million in expenditures doled out in part to the seven-member INC leadership council, INC brass, who regularly paid out available cash to Iraqi defectors, explained that there were "no receipts" in covert operations. State Department auditors found that almost a half million dollars that the INC had spent on the information program was either undocumented or badly documented. They promptly suspended further INC funding in late 2000. The INC fired back a two-hundred-page document that denied any wrongdoing, but agreed with "the need to strengthen internal [financial] controls." When Congress restored INC funding in early 2001, after the Bush administration took office, it no longer limited the Information Collection Program to operations inside Iraq.[20]

The State Department's effort to rid itself of the INC intelligence operation stalled after the September 11, 2001, terrorist attacks. INC officials were busily escorting defectors like Khodada al-Lami and Abu Zeinab al-Qurairy to editors and columnists to expose the terrorist training camps at Salman Pak, or parading Saeed al-Haideri, Mohammad Harith, and Khidhir Hamza before intelligence officers, reporters, and producers to warn of the dangers of Saddam's WMD programs. In May 2002, the month Rose's *Vanity Fair* story about Harith's revelations hit the newsstands, the State Department again cut off Chalabi's funding, which had by then reached $340,000 a month. The effort to dump the INC information program was reportedly led by Colin Powell's deputy, Richard Armitage. Patrick Leahy, then the Democratic head of the Senate Appropriations Committee, assigned the Foreign Operations Subcommittee to review the INC information program. Subcommittee members grilled Chalabi, spokesman Entifadh Qanbar, Francis Brooke, and other INC officials on the operation, focusing once more on the INC's use of government funding.

Qanbar responded on June 26 by signing off on a confidential INC memorandum to the Foreign Operations Subcommittee admitting that between October 2001 and May 2002 the INC had placed 108 stories in newspapers, magazines, and the electronic media on both sides of the Atlantic and in the Middle East. Attached was a complete list of the stories, their authors, dates, and news organization involved. Brooke admitted under questioning that the INC had spent State Department funds to support defectors, but he insisted there were no restrictions on the funding. "The INC paid some living and travel expenses of defectors with USG funds," said another Chalabi spokesman. "None of these expenses was related to meeting journalists." He claimed that INC "did not violate any U.S laws."[21]

Even so, senators Carl Levin of Michigan and John Kerry of Massachusetts requested that the Government Accountability Office investigate the INC's apparent violation of the State Department ban against attempting to influence U.S. policies with propaganda paid for by U.S. tax dollars. "This was clearly an ill-conceived, poorly managed program that received money largely because of its political connections," concluded a subcommittee clerk.[22] In its May 2004 findings, the GAO failed to address the legal questions raised by Levin and Kerry about the ICP operation. Instead, the report emphasized that Liberty TV remained dark after the cutoff of funds and dutifully observed that "through their inability to work together, State and [the INC] missed a chance to reach the Iraqi people at critical times prior to and during the March 2003 war in Iraq."[23]

Qanbar's June 2002 INC memorandum listing the 108 stories contained another bombshell. The INC's intelligence was being reported directly to the Office of the Vice President and Doug Feith's policy shop at the Pentagon, instead of to the CIA or other intelligence agencies. The INC memo identified a senior aide in Cheney's office, John Hannah, as "a principal point of contact" for ICP intelligence and one of several government officials who received reports from the INC program—and even included Hannah's White House telephone number.[24] Former navy captain William Luti, a former aide to Newt Gingrich who ran the Pentagon's Near East South Asia office, was another direct recipient of the INC information. Luti was a top Cheney aide at the Pentagon in the administration of George H. W. Bush and served as a top aide in the vice president's office in 2001 before moving across the Potomac to the Pentagon. Both Hannah and Luti refused to confirm that they served as conduits to top policymakers for the INC intelligence reports. But the State Department's Allen Kieswetter recalled both Hannah and Luti attending interdepartmental meetings about the INC and Chalabi. INC representative Francis Brooke admitted that he discussed Saddam's links with Arab terrorists and Iraq's WMD programs with Hannah, Luti, and Vice President Cheney's chief of staff Scooter Libby—but only, he insisted, after such information had been reported in the press.

Cheney, who had pushed the State Department to restore INC funding in early 2001, was furious when he learned that State was trying to shut down Chalabi's intelligence pipeline again. The vice president's strong support for Chalabi and his exile intelligence program was partly rooted in his well-known distrust of the CIA, an attitude that was broadly reflected by his staff. The agency, after all, had failed to anticipate the 9/11 attacks and had missed the full extent of Saddam's pre–Gulf War nuclear weapons program. Cheney also was keenly aware that U.S. intelligence had no human intelligence assets, or "humint" in the spy vernacular, inside Iraq since the UNSCOM inspectors left in 1998. He felt strongly that Chalabi and the INC were providing a critical service to U.S. antiterrorist efforts by producing firsthand human intelligence on the ground in Iraq. During a heated argument between State and Defense about refunding the INC during a National Security Council meeting, a former NSC staffer recalled that Cheney, who rarely aired his own views in such sessions, uncharacteristically "weighed in, in a really big way" in favor of releasing more money to Chalabi. "He said, 'We're getting ready to go to war, and we're nickel-and-diming the INC at a time when they're providing us with unique intelligence on Iraqi WMD,'" the staffer reported.[25]

The Defense Department finally took over funding responsibilities for the INC information program in September 2002. The DIA agreed with the State Department not to use political funds that were earmarked by the Iraqi Liberation Act, but to resume the $340,000 monthly payments to Chalabi out of a secret DIA intelligence account. By doing so, the Pentagon essentially formalized the arrangement between the INC and the DIA that had been going on for almost a year since former CIA director Woolsey began funneling the INC's Salman Pak sources to military intelligence. The new deal ensured that raw intelligence from the INC's defectors would bypass analysts at the CIA, the State Department, and other U.S. intelligence agencies. In October the INC and the DIA signed a four-page secrecy agreement that strictly prohibited the INC from releasing any information about its programs or findings without written permission from the DIA.[26] The terms of the INC's mission were unambiguous: Chalabi's agents were assigned to gather intelligence on "the location of Weapons of Mass Destruction (WMD) storage, development facilities and individuals associated with these facilities," information on "former Iraqi regime connections with Al Qaeda and other terrorist groups," and the physical whereabouts of Saddam Hussein.

The DIA attempted to rein in Chalabi's people by forcing them to agree that the "DIA and the INC will conduct initial joint debriefings of sources" and that the intelligence agency would "polygraph INC members who are involved in the debriefing of sources identified by the INC" as well as "polygraph sources surfaced by the INC." The agreements were designed in part to keep INC operatives from coaching their defector sources, as the DIA the suspected the INC had coached Harith. In order to ease the concerns of officials at the State Department and elsewhere that Chalabi was guilty of misusing U.S. funds for feeding prowar propaganda to Americans, the INC was forbidden to "publicize or communicate in any way with anyone any of its information collection operations . . . without prior written authorization from DIA."

That meant that any newspaper leak or magazine account of intelligence from INC sources to the media after October 2002 would either require the imprimatur of the Defense Intelligence Agency—or signal that Chalabi had ignored the DIA and gone off the reservation. The wording of the DIA-INC accord also barred the distribution of the INC raw intelligence to analysts at other U.S. intelligence agencies without formal DIA permission. Not only would the Pentagon serve as the exclusive conduit of Chalabi's intelligence, which was routed not only to the DIA but to selected policymakers in the vice president's office and the Office of Special Plans, but it would have exclusive control of Chalabi's entire operation.

But over the next two years—the INC's funding arrangement with the DIA lasted until May 2004, long after U.S. combat operations were over and the Baathist insurgency was in full swing—it did not always work out so neatly. Many U.S. officials doubted Chalabi could be relied upon to provide the United States with accurate intelligence. Others believed he would use the INC information program and the DIA money to build a political constituency inside Iraq. "He has no real political base," explained a former U.S. intelligence official. "Chalabi has always had to spend money to gain loyalty—to rent loyalty."[27] Yet a Chalabi lieutenant explained an even more basic reason INC agents would ignore DIA prohibitions with impunity. "Ahmed Chalabi," he said, "does not need permission from anyone."

13

BLAIR RAISES THE STAKES ON WMD

On March 12, 2002, Sir David Manning, British prime minister Tony Blair's senior foreign policy adviser, had a "frank" conversation about Iraq with Condoleezza Rice over dinner in Washington. Five months before, at a meeting with President Bush just after the 9/11 attacks, Blair had declared his support for the president's campaign against the Taliban and al-Qaeda in Afghanistan, and later deployed a small British force to back American troops. Now, with a summit between the two leaders planned for early April at the president's Texas ranch, Manning was intent on scouting out the mood of the White House. "Bush is grateful for your support and has registered that you are getting flak," he reported to Blair two days after meeting with Rice. Manning also gleaned that the president was still uncertain about how to persuade public opinion that military action against Baghdad was justified, and he still had unanswered questions about the value of the Iraqi opposition forces to a war effort. "Bush will want to pick your brains," Manning told Blair. "He will also want to hear whether he can expect coalition support."

As a potential U.S. coalition partner, 10 Downing Street had serious concerns about Iraq. Manning was prepared with talking points, and told Rice that Blair would not budge in his support for the president's war plans, but neither would he budge "in [his] insistence that . . . it must be very carefully done and produce the right result." Weapons inspectors would have to be redeployed "in a manner that would persuade European and wider opinion that the U.S. was conscious of the international framework, and the insistence of many countries on the need for a legal base" for the war. He also emphasized the "paramount importance" of "tackling" the Palestinian problem. "Unless we did," he told Rice, "we could find ourselves bombing Iraq and losing the Gulf."[1]

By the end of dinner, Manning was persuaded that the April meeting was a real opportunity for the prime minister. "Bush wants to hear your views on Iraq before taking decisions," Manning reported to Blair. "He also wants your support. . . . This gives you real influence: on the public relations strategy; on the UN and weapons inspections; and on US planning for any military campaign. This could be critically important." Manning had laid the groundwork with Rice for meeting Blair's legal and political conditions for signing on with the United States. But his advice to the prime minister also struck a pessimistic note. "I think there is a real risk that the Administration underestimates the difficulties," he summarized. "They may agree that failure isn't an option, but this does not mean that they will avoid it."

By late winter of 2002, intelligence about Saddam's WMD was already beginning to converge on Bush administration policymakers from a variety of quarters, accompanied by timely public amplification from Chalabi's defectors and the media. A month before, in February, Vice President Cheney had set in motion the CIA investigation of the alleged sale of Niger yellowcake uranium to Baghdad, a possibility British intelligence had speculated about several years before. Former ambassador Joseph Wilson had traveled to Niamey, the capital of Niger, to assess the likelihood of such a sale and had reported back to Langley that there was no evidence it had ever happened. The CIA, for its part, was in the midst of churning 2001 intelligence assessments of an Iraqi purchase of high-strength aluminum tubes from the Chinese, attempting to prove they were intended for Saddam's nuclear centrifuges—an end use sharply disputed by intelligence analysts at the Energy Department.

German intelligence reports from a defector who claimed to have helped build Iraqi mobile bioweapons labs created a new stir after 9/11 among U.S. analysts, who saw the claims as evidence that Saddam was reconstituting and upgrading his biological weapons program. Unfortunately, the Iraqi source code-named "Curveball" was no longer cooperating with the Germans, and the British intelligence service MI6 already had expressed serious doubts about his reliability. Lastly, fresh intelligence from Ahmed

Chalabi and the Iraqi National Congress seemed to corroborate the resurgence of Saddam's WMD programs to Pentagon and White House policymakers. This intelligence was also surfacing publicly in a wave of long and frighteningly detailed newspaper, magazine, and television stories.

Within six months, the British would add a critical dimension to this formidable-sounding but star-crossed torrent of intelligence. But, for now, London was feeling its way with deliberate caution on the question of joining an allied attack against Iraq. Blair's support for the president's war on terror was never in doubt. During dinner with Bush on September 20, 2001, nine days after the terrorist attacks, Blair made it clear he supported the U.S. incursion into Afghanistan to drive out al-Qaeda and the Taliban. But according to British ambassador to the United States, Sir Christopher Meyer, who was present at the meeting, Blair also advised Bush not to allow himself to be distracted from the war on al-Qaeda and securing Afghanistan from the Taliban. Bush agreed, but unhesitatingly let Blair know that the United States was headed toward a showdown with Saddam. "I agree with you, Tony," said the president, as Meyer recalled the conversation. "We must deal with this first. But when we have dealt with Afghanistan, we must come back to Iraq." Blair's response to the presidential revelation was guarded, but Meyer reported that outwardly at least the prime minister offered no objection. He knew that "regime change" was official U.S. policy and personally believed that if Saddam was going to go, it would take military force.[2]

Blair took the message about a U.S. attack on Baghdad to heart. By February 2002, 10 Downing Street was already gearing up for the Crawford summit with Bush. The top agenda item would be Iraq. The British had done their homework. The Overseas and Defence Secretariat of the Cabinet Office had put together a summary of British policy on Iraq and a review of military options that might lead to the overthrow of Saddam. A second document, prepared by the Foreign Office, led by Foreign Minister Jack Straw, explored how an attack on Iraq might be justified under international law. The briefing papers, which first surfaced when they were leaked with the famous Downing Street Memo to *The Times* of London and published in May 2005, painted a vivid picture of the conflicts that plagued the British-American partnership on critical issues concerning Iraq that were used to justify the U.S. attack on Saddam. Along with other British documents and parliamentary reports, the pre-Crawford memos also revealed the extent of the Blair government's own internal ambivalence about the legitimacy of a war against Iraq.[3] The British obsession with finding a legal rationale for the conflict forced a greater public emphasis by the White House on the importance of Saddam's illegal WMD arsenal. It also set in motion protracted negotiations during the fall of 2002 at the United Nations over successive resolutions seeking approval for the war effort. But, ultimately, it provided cover for White House deceptions and the highly politicized use of intelligence by the president and vice president that would later mislead Americans and Britons alike about Iraq's WMD programs.

The Bush-Blair partnership for going to war against Iraq followed a political agenda scripted in large part, not by Washington, but by London. From the outset, the British acknowledged that Saddam's WMD programs were not as well developed as those of Libya, Iran, or North Korea, and anticipated that this weakness would have to be addressed sooner or later to justify an attack on Iraq. Nor did British intelligence give much credence to the prevailing view within the Bush administration that Saddam Hussein had supported the al-Qaeda mission to destroy the World Trade Center, or had strong operational links to bin Laden and his band of fundamentalist Wahhabi-schooled jihadists. These concerns led 10 Downing Street to order the elite Joint Intelligence Committee, or JIC, made up of the chiefs of the major British spy services and other top national security agencies, to draw up a white paper, or formal assessment of the threat Saddam presented to the Western allies and Iraq's neighbors in the Middle East.

The white paper, which after multiple incarnations later came to be known in the British press as the "dodgy dossier," went through several drafts during the spring and summer of 2002 before Blair formally commissioned a final version in early September to sharpen the British case for Saddam's reconstituted WMD capabilities. The final product—the first time the British government had ever used classified intelligence to produce an unclassified document for public consumption, a radical departure from tradition—was finally approved by the Joint Intelligence Committee and 10 Downing Street and published on September 24.

The British dossier would later trigger a parliamentary investigation of charges that it had brazenly "sexed up" intelligence about Iraqi WMD, in the words of a controversial BBC report. However hyped or overheated the press reaction, the document was in fact instrumental in buttressing the phony U.S. case that Saddam was enriching yellowcake uranium for his nuclear program and possessed a formidable biological and chemical weapons arsenal, which the British dossier declared he could unleash on the battlefield "within 45 minutes." Blair's effort to beef up the U.S. case against Saddam dovetailed perfectly with his strategy to give the war a legal foundation. Any UN resolution to approve the use of force against Iraq had to be based on one of two contingencies, British policymakers reasoned: Passage was a virtual certainty if either Saddam refused to allow UN inspectors back into Baghdad or he did yield and was found in material breach of Resolution 687 for failing to account for Iraq's arsenal of weapons. The British dossier, by bolstering U.S. claims about Saddam's active WMD programs, would ultimately help ensure UN approval of a resolution to send weapons inspectors to Iraq and in turn confer legitimacy on the participation of the British Labour government.

If Blair calculated that his own political survival at 10 Downing Street depended on establishing a clear legal basis for going to war, President Bush was at first openly scornful of such mincing legal niceties. When Secretary Rumsfeld tried to brief the president about international law on the use of military force the day after the terror attacks, Bush cut him off cold. "I don't care what the international lawyers say," the president declared. "We are going to kick some ass."[4] Still, as Condoleezza Rice told David Manning during their March dinner, Bush recognized the domestic political pressure on Blair and seemed to take it seriously. In the end, the legal and political preoccupations of 10 Downing Street—and the dawning realization in Washington of the importance of Britain as a coalition partner—locked the White House into a political strategy that made Saddam's WMD the central justification of the war and UN approval the legal basis for invading Iraq.

From the beginning, it was a messy and uneven playing field. The Blair government, intent on making a legal case for committing British forces to Afghanistan, ran headlong into the White House disdain for legalities when it encouraged Washington to make the case that al-Qaeda was responsible for the 9/11 attacks. 10 Downing Street not only was concerned about British public opinion, but along with some U.S. officials at the State Department was also worried about the reaction of the Pakistani government, a critical ally whose powerful Inter-Services Intelligence (ISI) was known to have close ties to the Taliban. Blair wanted to see a public document that would leave no doubt that bin Laden and al-Qaeda had been behind the 9/11 attacks. He had an American ally in Secretary of State Powell, who told an MSNBC interviewer on Sunday, September 23, that the Bush administration would soon definitively link bin Laden to the attacks. "We are working at bringing all the information together, intelligence information, law enforcement information," declared Powell. "And

I think in the near future we will be able to put out a paper, a document that will describe quite clearly the evidence that we have linking him to this attack."[5]

The next day, it became evident that the White House had different ideas. Responding to a story in *The New York Times* that morning, presidential spokesman Ari Fleischer abruptly denied that a U.S. "white paper" on bin Laden was forthcoming—and left Powell and Blair hanging out to dry. "I think that there was just a misinterpretation of the exact words the secretary used on the Sunday shows . . ." said Fleischer. "I'm not aware of anybody who said white paper, and the secretary didn't say anything about a white paper yesterday."[6] Blair had little choice but to go to the press himself. Two weeks later in London, he publicly detailed the case again bin Laden in a seventy-point document, which drew on British intelligence reports and relied heavily on classified U.S. information. Blair's white paper presented compelling evidence of al-Qaeda's culpability and was quickly accepted by Pakistani officials.

The White House offered no explanation about why it had backed away from making the case itself. Bush administration officials tepidly concurred with Blair's findings—but seemed determined to keep the British effort at arm's length. "This is a British paper based on the information the British government has collected, and it offers their conclusions about the situation," said State Department spokesman Richard Boucher. "We coordinated with them, they coordinated with us, as we do on so many things. We saw it in advance. They put it out. Their paper, their conclusions."[7] The dustup over the bin Laden evidence was an eye-opener for the Blair government, revealing a growing penchant at the White House for abrupt, seat-of-the-pants course changes and mixed signals, and the British soon began to suspect the reason. "What we saw, more and more," a senior British official later said, "was that power in the government swirled around the vice president and the Department of Defense," not in the Oval Office or a disciplined interagency process.[8]

While there was no hard evidence that Cheney's office intervened to undercut Powell, officials in the Office of the Vice President held very clear views about the legality of U.S. war-making powers, particularly concerning a war against Iraq. In a word, they considered proof unnecessary. "Our position, Bush's position, was that Saddam was an outlaw," explained a senior Cheney official later. "We already had all the UN resolutions we needed to go to war. We didn't think we needed any more arguments to justify it, or its legality."[9] Like Blair, Cheney and his OVP lieutenants came to believe that Saddam would refuse the return of weapons inspectors and could be summarily declared in breach of UN ceasefire resolutions. But the presumption of legality by OVP officials, along with their certainty that Saddam commanded a bristling stockpile of deadly WMD, became a political liability for the British that short-circuited the orderly presentation of evidence and the sound formulation of policymaking.

As early as February 2002, British officials ordered up a white paper on the threat posed by Iraq and three other states—North Korea, Iran, and Libya—known to be developing WMD. If British forces were to join any U.S. operation against Iraq, Blair would have to convince skeptics in his own cabinet and the Labour Party, the House of Commons, and the British public that the Americans were on the right course. The British ambassador to the United States, Sir Christopher Meyer, said as much to U.S. deputy defense secretary Paul Wolfowitz during a luncheon on Sunday, March 17, 2002. "I said that the UK was giving serious thought to publishing a paper that would make the case against Saddam," Meyer wrote to David Manning, the British foreign policy adviser, in a memo the next day. "I said that I had been forcefully struck, when addressing university audiences in the US, how ready students were to gloss over Saddam's crimes and to blame the US and the UK for the suffering of the Iraqi people."[10]

The ambassador inadvertently teased out of Wolfowitz an unsettling split within the Bush administration. Wolfowitz agreed that the British white paper was a good idea, but unlike others in the administration who focused on Saddam's WMD, he said he "thought it indispensable to spell out in detail Saddam's barbarism." Like other prominent neoconservatives in the Pentagon and Cheney's office, Wolfowitz was primarily concerned about Saddam's ability to export terrorism in the region, especially to Israel. He told Meyer forthrightly that he felt "that it was absurd to deny the link between terrorism and Saddam"—and even asked whether the British had learned any more about the alleged meeting in Prague between an Iraqi agent and hijacker Mohamed Atta. Senior White House and Pentagon officials like Wolfowitz were deeply skeptical of the British push to seek Security Council approval for an invasion of Iraq. They felt in part that the burden of proof would be unacceptably high if Washington had to demonstrate Baghdad's capacity to launch weapons of mass death that would threaten the United States and its allies. And many of them—such as Vice President Cheney—simply didn't trust the United Nations to accept a pro-U.S. resolution.

"The imminence of the threat from Iraq's WMD was never the real issue for us," said the unnamed official in Cheney's office. "WMD were on our minds, but they weren't the key thing. What was really driving us was our overall view of terrorism, and the strategic conditions of the Middle East."[11] This powerful faction within the Bush administration, led by Wolfowitz and others, was attracted to the idea that Iraq could become a model democracy in the Middle East—a view that gained real prominence publicly, if not within the administration, only after U.S. and British occupation forces in Iraq failed to turn up evidence of active WMD programs.

The clash of views among senior Bush officials about how best to present Saddam's regime to the public only complicated matters for 10 Downing Street. In mid-March Blair decided to narrow the white paper to Iraq, then, apparently on the advice of Foreign Minister Jack Straw, decided to postpone the classified dossier on Saddam[12] altogether until after the meeting in Crawford scheduled for April.

Still, Blair's advisers continued to hammer home the importance of making President Bush understand the British emphasis on Iraqi WMD and the reintroduction of the weapons inspectors. The prime minister, noted Foreign Office political director Peter Ricketts in a March 22 memo to Straw, "can bring home to Bush some of the realities . . . by telling him things his own machine probably isn't." In Ricketts's judgment, it was not so much that Saddam's weapons programs had changed, but that Western tolerance of his behavior had decreased sharply after 9/11. He expressed relief that work on the dossier had been suspended and noted "that there is more work to do to ensure that the figures are accurate and consistent with those of the U.S."[13]

Ricketts bluntly outlined two major problems he felt Blair had to address with the president in Crawford. The first was the real nature of the threat Saddam posed. "Even the best survey of Iraq's WMD programmes," he wrote, "will not show much advance in recent years on the nuclear, missile or CW/BW [chemical and biological weapons] fronts: the programmes are extremely worrying but have not, as far as we know, been stepped up." In addition, Ricketts believed that "U.S. scrambling" to link Iraq and al-Qaeda was "so far frankly unconvincing." In short, the American claims about Saddam's WMD and his links to al-Qaeda were unlikely to hold up to scrutiny. Bringing public opinion around to understand "the imminence of a threat from Iraq," advised Ricketts, "is something the Prime Minister and President need to have a frank discussion about."

The second problem Ricketts addressed was even more fundamental. "Military operations need clear and compelling military objectives," wrote Ricketts. "For Iraq, 'regime change' does not stack up. It sounds like a grudge between Bush and Saddam."[14] Better, he thought, to persuade Bush to focus on "the threat to the international community from Iraqi WMD before Saddam uses it or gives it to terrorists" by emphasizing the elimination of proscribed weapons and the reintroduction of UN weapons inspectors, a possibility that Saddam would probably refuse, thereby handing both the United States and the U.K. coalition a legal casus belli.

In his own final briefing of Prime Minister Blair before his departure for Texas, Foreign Minister Straw painted a bleak picture of the political obstacles Blair's government faced if it joined forces with the United States. "The rewards from your visit to Crawford will be few," he wrote. "The risks are high, both for you and for the Government." There was no majority in the Labour Party clamoring for a war against Iraq. It would be difficult to make the case that Saddam was more of a threat now than before 9/11, or even that Iraq posed a greater threat than Iran or North Korea. Parliament and the British people would have to be convinced that the war was justified under international law and "that the consequence of military action would be a compliant, law-abiding replacement government" in Iraq. Finally, the entire exercise was complicated by the then acute state of Israeli-Palestinian tensions.

Straw's dour analysis did not shy away from the weakness of the U.S. position. Iraq "plainly poses a threat to its neighbors," he said, but there were no documents that distinguished the Iraqi threat significantly enough from that of Iran and Korea to justify military action. No credible evidence linked Iraq with bin Laden or al-Qaeda. Objectively, the threat from Iraq had not worsened since 9/11. Straw emphasized once again in the strongest terms that the core of an effective political strategy had to be based on international law. "If the argument is to be won," he advised, "the whole case against Iraq and in favour (if necessary) of military action needs to be narrated with reference to the international rule of law."[15]

Echoing Ricketts's March 22 memorandum, Straw warned Blair that "regime change per se is no justification for military action" and drove home the premise that the objective had to be "the elimination of Iraq's WMD capacity" through "the readmission of weapons inspectors." He wrote, "I believe that a demand for the unfettered readmission of weapons inspectors is essential, in terms of public explanation, and in terms of legal sanction for any subsequent military action." Straw had adopted language emphasizing that the inspectors must be allowed "to operate in a free and unfettered way" from public remarks made by Cheney, who hoped to trap Saddam into refusing such an arrangement. Straw judged, no doubt correctly, that the Bush White House was also likely to oppose seeking a new UN resolution that might authorize U.S.-led military action if Saddam refused. Still, he advised the prime minister that "the weight of legal advice here is that a fresh mandate may well be required." While recognizing the U.S. position made "a new mandate" unlikely, he warned Blair that a contrary Security Council draft resolution—against future U.S. military action—"could play very badly here."

With all his circumspect caution, however, Straw foresaw a fundamental problem with the American approach that suggested his own personal and professional ambivalence about the coming conflict. What would a military operation finally achieve? Straw noted that most assessments assumed regime change would also eliminate Iraq's WMD threat. "But none," he wrote, "has satisfactorily answered how that regime change is to be secured, and how there can be any certainty that the replacement regime will be better." Signing off on the memo, Straw made one final point to Blair: "Iraq has had NO history of democracy so no one has this habit or experience," he wrote.

Prime Minister Blair and his wife, Cherie, an attorney in London's progressive Matrix Chambers law firm, flew to the Crawford ranch on the weekend of April 6 for the summit and a low-key visit with the Bushes. Although no detailed record of the meeting between Bush and Blair has surfaced, Iraq was discussed at length and Blair committed the United Kingdom to "support military action to bring about regime change." According to a classified cabinet briefing paper circulated to British officials several months later,[16] Blair laid out his conditions for British involvement. They included undertaking efforts with the United States "to construct a coalition/shape public opinion," to ensure that "the Israel-Palestine crisis was quiescent," and to exhaust all "options to eliminate Iraq's WMD through the U.N. weapons inspectors."

At a press conference afterward at Crawford High School, attended mostly by the British press traveling with Blair, President Bush was obviously pleased with the outcome. Amid platitudes about fighting terrorism and the historic relationship between Britain and America, neither he nor

Blair mentioned Iraq in their opening remarks. Blair, however, revealed that he and Bush had agreed that "the issue of weapons of mass destruction cannot be ducked, it is a threat . . . and we must heed that threat and act to prevent it being realized." It wasn't until a reporter asked Blair halfway through the press conference if Bush had convinced him of "the need for a military action against Iraq" that Bush stepped in and acknowledged that they had discussed Iraq. "The Prime Minister and I, of course, talked about Iraq," said Bush. "We both recognize the danger of a man who's willing to kill his own people harboring and developing weapons of mass destruction . . . the Prime Minister and I both agree that he needs to prove that he isn't developing weapons of mass destruction."[17] Using diplomatic language to avoid directly answering the question about going to war, Bush added: "I explained to the Prime Minister that the policy of my government is the removal of Saddam and that all options are on the table."

That, of course, meant that military action was on the table. Blair jumped in quickly to offer assurances that no decision had been made, at once laying the groundwork for the British legal strategy and deftly suggesting it was Bush's idea. "Now, how we approach this, this is a matter for discussion," said the prime minister. This is "a situation where [Saddam] continues to be in breach of all the United Nations resolutions, refusing to allow us to assess, as the international community have demanded, whether and how he is developing these weapons of mass destruction. Doing nothing in those circumstances is not an option. . . . The President is right to draw attention to the threat of weapons of mass destruction. That threat is real."

In the months after the Crawford meeting, Blair grew increasingly restive with the drawn-out silence from the White House regarding Blair's conditions for joining the U.S. military operation. Even while he was in Crawford, Israeli forces had invaded several towns in the West Bank in response to a Passover suicide bombing that killed thirty Israelis in the seaside town of Netanya, and laid siege to PLO headquarters in Ramallah. Israeli prime minister Ariel Sharon ignored Bush's call to withdraw his forces from the West Bank. There was little sign that the White House, with its open contempt for PLO Chairman Yasser Arafat, was either willing—or able—to influence the latest Israeli-Palestinian crisis. A presidential trip to Europe in May to sound out European leaders about Iraq served mainly to irritate the United States' increasingly distant European allies.

And on June 1, Bush unveiled the new American military doctrine of "preemption" in a speech to graduating cadets at West Point, declaring that the United States "must be ready for preemptive action when necessary" and "must take the battle to the enemy, disrupt his plans, and confront the worse threats before they emerge." The clear subtext, pundits observed, was the coming war on Iraq.

Unease in Parliament and in Blair's cabinet at the prospect of U.S. military action increased the political pressure on 10 Downing Street to show justification for its support of Washington's war plans. There was no evidence of a U.S. approach to the United Nations to prepare the way for a Security Council resolution that might legally justify the use of military force against Saddam. In short, the Bush White House had done next to nothing to make good on the president's April commitment to Blair to help forge an effective joint American-British military and political partnership.

In mid-July, Blair sent Richard Dearlove, the head of the intelligence service MI6, to Washington for a secret meeting with CIA director George Tenet and other senior U.S. intelligence officials at CIA headquarters in Langley. The daylong session—a post-9/11 version of annual meetings usually held in exotic venues by U.S. and British spymasters—was called at the urgent request of the British, who were apparently under orders to take the measure of American thinking on Iraq and get a "reality check" on war policy from the White House. "I think in hindsight that it is clear that Dearlove was insistent on having the summit because Blair wanted him to find out what was going on," said a former CIA official who attended the meeting.[18]

During the trans-Atlantic summit on Saturday July 20, Dearlove and Tenet, who reportedly had struck up a friendly and candid rapport, slipped out of the meeting for an hour and a half alone together. Exactly what the two intelligence chiefs discussed is unknown. But by then it was clear that CIA analysts concerned with Iraqi WMD had become so inured to the anti-Saddam saber-rattling from the White House and Pentagon that they believed that a war with Iraq was all but inevitable. The former CIA official and others believed analysts were regularly sending reports to policymakers that exaggerated or distorted weak intelligence, but reflected the Bush White House's increasingly obvious pro-war leanings. It had become obvious to CIA insiders that Bush policymakers were not carefully combing through intelligence reports about Iraq's WMD to determine any imminent threat, but rather to justify conclusions the president and vice president had already reached.

Dearlove took this message away from the Langley summit, if not from his tête-à-tête with Tenet. "I doubt that Tenet would have said that Bush was fixing the intelligence," remarked the former CIA official afterward. "But I think Dearlove was a very smart intelligence officer who could figure out what was going on. Plus, the MI6 station chief in Washington was in CIA headquarters all the time, with just about complete access to everything, and I am sure he was talking to lots of people."[19]

As Dearlove returned to London the next day, senior British officials invited to attend a July 23 meeting with Blair at 10 Downing Street received a preparatory briefing from London's Cabinet Office about the lack of American progress on the conditions for joining the United States militarily that Blair had set forth at Crawford. The memo, entitled "Iraq: Conditions for Military Action," made it plain that London still had to "engage the U.S. on the need to set military plans within a realistic political strategy, which included identifying the succession to Saddam Hussein and creating the conditions necessary to justify government military action . . ." Prime Minister Blair, it suggested, planned to call Bush before a scheduled presidential briefing the following week on the Pentagon's war plans. So far, the memo bluntly informed the top British cabinet ministers, U.S. military planning "lacks a political framework" and the White House had given "little thought" to the British preconditions for joining the U.S.-led coalition. The British government urgently needed to reinforce Blair's April message to Bush, or "face the real danger that the US will commit themselves [sic] to a course of action which we would find very difficult to support."[20]

The timing was becoming critical, the memo continued. Unless a decision was made soon, the United Kingdom would not have the necessary lead time to deploy even a single division of British troops, plus supporting naval and air forces, until January 2003. The British legal position also depended on the timing and circumstances of any military campaign, which most legal analysts believed would require UN approval, because the use of force by Britain or the United States was unlikely to be justified by claims of either self-defense or humanitarian intervention, the two other available options. UN Secretary General Kofi Annan already had met with the Iraqis several times and tried to persuade them to accept weapons inspectors, but the UN initiative was stalled. Even so, the memo's authors judged, in the unlikely event Saddam accepted the UNMOVIC inspectors, they would need six months just to reestablish their monitoring and verification systems, much less begin to make any assessments about Iraq's WMD arsenal. "Even if UN inspectors gained access today," the memo said, "by January 2003 they would at best only just be completing setting up."[21]

The British sought a wider international coalition for both military and "political purposes." They foresaw U.S. problems with Saudi Arabia and Turkey, but held out hopes for France, Russia, and even China under the right circumstances.[22] To assemble such a coalition would certainly require UN authorization of hostilities against Iraq—and time.

The meeting at 10 Downing Street on July 23 that produced the eponymous memo included the heavyweights of the British government. Gathered in the prime minister's office were Blair, Foreign Secretary Jack Straw, Defense Secretary Geoffrey Hoon, Attorney General Lord Peter Goldsmith, Joint Intelligence Committee head John Scarlett, Richard Dearlove of MI6, Blair's foreign policy adviser David Manning, and Adm. Sir Michael Boyce, the military chief of the Defense Staff. In addition, Blair's chief of staff Jonathan Powell, his communications chief Alastair Campbell, and Sally Morgan, the director of government relations, were also present. According to notes of the meeting taken by an aide to Manning and later circulated on a "secret and strictly personal—UK eyes only" basis as the Downing Street Memo, Dearlove got right to the point. "Military action was now seen as inevitable," reported the intelligence chief, who was identified as "C" in the memo. "Bush wanted to remove Saddam, through military action, justified by the conjunction of terrorism and WMD. But the intelligence and facts were being fixed around the policy. The NSC had no patience for the UN route, and no enthusiasm for publishing material on the Iraqi regime's record."[23]

This passage from the minutes of the meeting, which came to be known as the "Downing Street Memo" after it was leaked to the *Sunday Times* of London, is cited by some as the "smoking gun" that the White House was distorting intelligence to further its war aims. "The intelligence and facts were being fixed around the policy" certainly suggests just that, and the notation is part of a mosaic of evidence that, taken together, leads inevitably to the conclusion that the White House was guilty of deliberate deception. But more important at the time, Dearlove's report from Washington gave Blair a sense of the accelerating momentum of White House war planning, and directly addressed his immediate concern about how seriously the Americans were taking his offer of British military help. Dearlove in essence confirmed that the Bush administration did not think much of Blair's "UN route" and had done very little, if anything, to encourage it—a message that surely caught the prime minister's attention. Worse, Washington was also dragging its feet on Blair's principal condition that Saddam's human rights record, his track record developing WMD, and his documented use of such weapons should be the center-piece of an Anglo-British public information campaign to force a show-down with Iraq.

The consensus of the meeting was that Blair had to take another run at forging a political strategy with Bush. Straw chimed in that it seemed "Bush had made up his mind" about going to war, although the American case against Saddam was "thin." He recommended that the government redouble its efforts "to work up a plan for an ultimatum to Saddam" on weapons inspectors that "would also help with the legal justification" for war. Attorney General Lord Peter Goldsmith laid out the legal options, noting, as had others, that "regime change was not a legal base for mili-tary action." Adm. Sir Michael Boyce, who was ultimately responsible for deploying British forces, had questions about the U.S. battle plan, in-cluding "the consequences, if Saddam used WMD on day one." Noting that there were already "spikes" of U.S. military activity, Defense Secre-tary Geoffrey Hoon warned that if Blair wanted British military involve-ment, the decision had to be made soon. Hoon "cautioned that many in the U.S. did not think it worth going down the ultimatum route" on weapons inspectors, and reemphasized that it was important for Blair "to set out the political context for Bush."

Blair himself stated his belief that "it would make a big difference po-litically and legally if Saddam refused to allow in the weapons inspectors" and wagered that if the political strategy was right, the British people would support regime change. "The two key issues," the prime minister said, "were whether the military plan worked and whether we had the po-litical strategy to give the military plan the space to work." He assigned Straw to prepare background information on the UN inspectors and "dis-creetly" fine-tune a plan for the ultimatum to Saddam, presumably to take to President Bush. Boyce would fill out the details of the U.S. military campaign and possible British contributions "by the end of the week." Scarlett would provide a full intelligence update. Goldsmith would refine the legal options. The meeting broke up with the understanding that, one way or another, the United Kingdom would take part in any U.S. military action in Iraq—but would keep a range of options open until British offi-cials had "a fuller picture of U.S. planning."

Soon after the meeting, Blair reportedly sent Bush a personal memo-randum via diplomatic pouch restating the importance of U.S. progress with Israel on the Palestinian issue and taking Saddam's transgressions against UN resolutions to the Security Council.[24] He dispatched David

Manning to Washington to meet once more with Rice. During their meeting, Rice was called into the Oval Office, and Manning took the opportunity to press the British case for going to the United Nations with the president. At one point he reportedly warned Bush that Blair's political standing at home might depend upon it. "Manning reiterated the U.N. message very strongly," a senior British official told a reporter for *Vanity Fair*. " 'He said, 'This is very important to us, your main ally.' " Bush seemed to get the message.

Blair's renewed campaign to persuade Bush to go to the United Nations received a timely boost in early August. As far back as February 2002, senior U.S. State Department officials had anticipated the legal problems that potential U.S. coalition partners might have with a unilateral U.S. declaration of war on Iraq.[25] Secretary of State Powell, who with Blair had been a stickler for presenting documented proof of al-Qaeda's responsibility for 9/11 before the Afghanistan campaign, strongly backed forcing regime change in Iraq. But along with other senior State Department officials, Powell also recognized that an ultimatum to Iraq to readmit weapons inspectors would force Saddam to commit himself, either by outright refusal or by obstruction. Either way, the president would have a legal pretext for war and potential coalition members would be mollified.

At about the same time Blair was debriefing Dearlove and his ministers in London, Powell was on a trip to Asia, where he was struck by the rising volume of war talk. On the airplane returning to Washington, the secretary decided the time had come to present his own analysis of the unfolding situation to the president. On the evening of August 5, Powell met with President Bush and Condoleezza Rice for a remarkable conversation that began with dinner at the White House residence and continued into the evening in Bush's office. Uninterrupted by the usual hail of interjections from Cheney or Rumsfeld, Powell invoked his now-famous "Pottery Barn" rule—if you break it, you own it—to dramatize the impact of a U.S. invasion of Iraq and a U.S. occupation that would shatter Saddam's dictatorship and the political status quo for millions of Iraqis.

His major points paralleled many of the same concerns the British had expressed over the past five months. Iraq had no history of democracy. There would be no clear definition of success. The war would dominate Bush's presidency. Lack of American access to bases and facilities in the region and beyond made a unilateral U.S. military effort a nonstarter. A war against Iraq would mean deploying most available U.S. forces and could leave the nation vulnerable in case hostilities should arise elsewhere. The president would have to build an international coalition, Powell said, and internationalize the threat posed by Saddam. To do that, Bush should "make a pitch for a . . . U.N. action to do what needs to be done" to give the war "international cover."[26] Powell even warned Bush renewed UN weapons inspections might solve the problem—and there would be no war. In two hours of conversation, Powell felt he had broken through to the president.

"Colin felt very strongly that the United Nations was the route to go," Bush later told Bob Woodward. But the president also acknowledged that opposition to seeking a UN resolution within the White House, led by Vice President Cheney, was powerful. Cheney believed the United Nations was toothless and could not get the job done. It was not until the night before Bush spoke to the UN General Assembly on September 12 that the president finally told Powell and Rice he would seek a resolution calling for the return of UN inspectors to Iraq. With characteristic bravado, Bush later recalled that "I chose the resolution" route. But, he conceded, "Blair had a lot to do with it."

In truth, Powell had built his case for going to the United Nations with Bush on a foundation erected by Tony Blair. Two weeks later, on August 20, the secretary of state received an urgent request to meet with Jack Straw in the Hamptons on Long Island, where Powell was vacationing. The British foreign minister shared many of Powell's doubts about the president's headlong rush to war, but the central issue for both was building an international consensus that would confer legitimacy on the effort by focusing on Saddam's WMD and reengaging the UN arms inspectors in Iraq. Straw gave the argument another twist. His message to Powell was blunt: Unless the president took the case for military action against Iraq to the United Nations, he might well find himself going to war without the British. Powell knew that Bush had to have Blair with him in Iraq—and saw that the British were ratcheting up the pressure on the president.[27]

In London, Blair faced a growing clamor from Parliament and the press who were questioning his plans for British military involvement, and he concluded that it was past time to provide the public with more information about Saddam's illegal WMD programs. The White House was also under siege by critical elder Republican luminaries such as Henry Kissinger, Brent Scowcroft, and James A. Baker III who were questioning the president's war aims. August was a "miserable month," Bush later remarked.[28] Toward the end of the month, Blair got Bush on the telephone.

They agreed to meet in Camp David in early September to hammer out a political strategy for going to the United Nations to quiet the naysayers and prepare public opinion for the war. "I was increasingly getting messages saying . . . 'Are you about to go to war?'" Blair recalled later. "I remember toward the end of the holiday actually phoning Bush and saying that we have got to put this in the right place straight away . . . we've not decided on military action . . . he was in absolute agreement . . . So we devised the strategy, and this was really the purpose of Camp David . . . where we would go down the UN route."[29]

Blair arrived at Camp David to meet with Bush on Saturday, September 7, and immediately joined the president for a brief press conference. Blair, as usual, got right to the point. "The threat from Saddam Hussein and weapons of mass destruction, chemical, biological, potentially nuclear weapons capability, that threat is real," he said. "The purpose of our discussion today is to work out the right strategy for dealing with this, because deal with it we must." Blair stood by expressionless as Bush mangled a reference to an eleven-year-old IAEA report judging that Iraq was "six months away from developing a weapon," after which he remarked irrelevantly, "I don't know what more evidence we need." The prime minister coolly covered for him. "Absolutely right," Blair said, adding—correctly—that "what has been going on there for a long period of time is not just the chemical, biological weapons capability, but we know that they were trying to develop nuclear weapons capability." Back on message, he added: "This is an issue for the whole of the international community. But the U.N. has got to be the way of dealing with this issue, not the way of avoiding dealing with it."

Blair and Bush were joined by Vice President Cheney in Camp David's main lodge for a three-hour session to work out their political strategy for going to war. Once more, Blair made all the arguments for seeking a resolution to send the arms inspectors back into Iraq that would attract the support of a broad international coalition. And once more, the prime minister repeated his commitment of British troops in the event military force should prove necessary, as all three believed it would. Blair's display of loyalty and backbone apparently impressed the president. "We want you to be part of this," Bush said.[30] The president told Blair—reportedly almost two weeks before informing Powell and Rice—that he had decided to go to the Security Council and that he planned to seek a fresh resolution to send in UNMOVIC weapons inspectors. Bush later told Bob Woodward that he was "probing" and "pushing" Blair during the meeting, as if he had to use all his wiles and persuasive power to bring Blair around. There is no known transcript of the meeting, but more likely it was the other way around. Blair had stuck with his commitment of British troops and, as it would turn out, committed his political legacy to Bush's war effort five months before. The wavering and internal dissension had been all on the White House side.

After the meeting, Woodward reported, Bush met Alistair Campbell, Blair's communications director, in a conference room. "Your man has *cojones*," Bush is said to have told the British prime minister's aide, using the Spanish word for testicles, connoting courage. "And of course these Brits don't know what *cojones* are." Woodward dutifully recorded the president's vow henceforth to call his meeting with Blair "the *cojones* meeting."[30] Thanks to Blair, and the timely intervention of Powell, Saddam's WMD arsenal was now the centerpiece of the White House war effort.

Back on September 3, before he left London for Camp David, Blair once more called on the Joint Intelligence Committee to produce a new public dossier on the case against Saddam that in three weeks' time would be reshaped to include a foreword by the prime minister and a sharper focus on Saddam's weapons programs. Much of the work already had been done. After suspending production of the analysis on Iran, North Korea, and Libya in March, 10 Downing Street had then delayed the JIC project indefinitely, because of Blair's uncertainty about the White House's position. Even so, the Cabinet Office had asked the Foreign Ministry at Whitehall to produce a history of the 1991–98 UNSCOM inspections for eventual use in a political paper. Dr. David Kelly, a British arms specialist whose unexpected suicide would later raise a media outcry over the truthfulness of the dossier, drafted the section on biological weapons. In April and May, the UNSCOM project had grown to include sections describing Iraq's WMD programs and Saddam's human rights violations. A preliminary dossier entitled "British Government Briefing Papers on Iraq" was printed on June 20, 2002, but saw only limited circulation within the government.

The early documents, which included material in the classified government memos that were distributed to senior officials before the July 23 meeting at 10 Downing Street, were important for several reasons. They established that Dr. Kelly was a close collaborator in their production over the spring and summer of 2002 and was privy to the underlying intelligence in the final dossier of September 24. Second, they contained no mention whatsoever of the explosive intelligence that appeared in the final version of the white paper—the now-infamous British claim that Iraqi military units were capable of deploying chemical and biological weapons on the battlefield within forty-five minutes—raising questions about how such a dramatic claim was inserted into the paper.

Lastly, the dossier contained two-year-old intelligence that appeared to confirm CIA assessments that the Iraqi government had approached the government of Niger in 1999 about purchasing yellowcake uranium to manufacture bomb-grade fuel for Saddam's nuclear weapons program. These declarations in the final September 24 version of the British dossier were later used publicly by President Bush, Vice President Cheney, and Prime Minister Blair himself as irrefutable evidence that Saddam possessed an active, reconstituted WMD program.

The early drafts of the published September dossier, which U.S. intelligence would later refer to as the "British white paper," were strikingly more candid than the final version about the weakened state of Saddam's weapons programs after eight years of UN inspections. Senior British officials had acknowledged as much in their pre-Crawford briefings in March 2002. The Blair government's unvarnished position was then that economic sanctions had "effectively frozen Iraq's nuclear programme," Saddam "has been prevented from rebuilding its chemical arsenal to pre–Gulf War levels," "ballistic missile programmes have been severely restricted," and biological and chemical weapons programs "have been hindered."[31] Nonetheless, British intelligence assessed that "Iraq continues to develop weapons of mass destruction" even as it admitted "our intelligence is poor." Evidence for this included ongoing "design work" for missiles, Iraq's capacity to "produce significant quantities" of biological and chemical "agents," and "some indications" of a continuing nuclear program.

The underlying intelligence had not changed. In a March 15 assessment of the status of Saddam's nuclear programs, for example, the JIC declared, "We judge that Iraq does not possess a nuclear weapons capability. . . . Although there is very little intelligence, we continue to judge that Iraq is pursuing a nuclear weapons programme." The JIC conceded that it had "an unclear picture of the current status of Iraq's nuclear programs" and based its judgment on reports that former nuclear scientists had been "recalled" to conduct "research." In the published white paper, that tentative assessment morphed into an authoritative statement that "Iraq continues to work on developing nuclear weapons, in breach of its obligations under the Non-Proliferation Treaty and in breach of UNSCR 687." There was no hint of the thin evidence and uncertainty evident in the original assessment.[32]

The dossier also served as an echo chamber for spurious intelligence. Despite well-documented doubts within MI6 about the Iraqi defector known as Curveball, as late as September 9 the JIC stated that "Iraq has developed for the military, fermentation systems which are capable of being mounted on road-trailers or rail cars"—an assessment strongly reminiscent of information Curveball initially provided that appeared to have been confirmed earlier that year by Mohammad Harith. "These could produce BW [biological warfare] agents," tentatively concluded the JIC. Once more, in the September white paper, the cautious, even uncertain language disappeared. "[Iraq has] developed mobile laboratories for military use, corroborating earlier reports about the mobile production of biological warfare agents," it read.[33]

But most telling were editorial changes that produced a consistent pattern of discrepancies between the JIC's intelligence assessments and the key points of the dossier. The JIC had judged, for example, that Saddam could quickly produce mustard gas, but production of VX within months "would be heavily dependent" on "hidden stocks of precursors." The September 24 white paper simply declared Iraq has "the capability to produce mustard gas . . . and VX capable of producing mass casualties." Senior officials tried hard to explain away the differences in tone and substance between the intelligence assessments and the dossier. They argued that the point of the exercise was to present intelligence on Iraqi WMD in the strongest terms warranted by the underlying intelligence. The "very worthwhile" but "difficult" objective, JIC chairman John Scarlett said later, "was to put into the public domain and to share, as far as it could be done safely, the intelligence assessment on this issue which was being provided to the Prime Minister and the Government."[34] Scarlett insisted that the white paper was not intended to present a case for anything—which to a senior intelligence official would violate the analyst's ethic of telling the truth and letting the chips fall where they may.

Blair, however, had a very clear idea of the case he wanted the dossier to make: namely, to create a vivid public awareness of Saddam's weapons programs that would support a UN resolution to send inspectors to Iraq and, possibly, a decision to go to war. The Blair government was walking a fine (perhaps even nonexistent) line. Intelligence assessment is an evidentiary art that depends for precision on a nuanced command of language and a philosopher's ear for fine distinctions. There was an inherent risk in attempting to simplify or strengthen the gossamer intellectual connective tissue of intelligence for rough public consumption. Although there were changes requested by government officials that the JIC rejected, the inevitable result was at best a distorted and misleading picture of what the spymasters and the intelligence professionals intended for well-educated but untrained Britons to understand.

Nowhere was this clearer than in the forty-five-minute claim. The British had come upon intelligence in late August from an unidentified Iraqi who had been told by a military officer that Iraqi combat units had stocks of chemical and biological weapons that could be fired within forty-five minutes of getting the order. In vetting the intelligence, some British analysts were deeply skeptical. The information was not only from a single source; it was from a secondhand single source. It also did not distinguish between chemical or biological weapons, making the forty-five-minute claim a problem—some chemical agents could be launched in less than twenty minutes, but analysts also knew biological agents behaved in different ways. Worst, there was no corroborating evidence that such weapons even existed.[35]

On that slender thread, the JIC made its assessment that Iraq "has probably" dispersed its "CBW weapons" which "could be with military units and ready for firing within twenty to forty-five minutes." In a memo of September 17, Alastair Campbell, Blair's press secretary, asked Scarlett for approval to strengthen a draft of the dossier that said military units "may" be able to deploy chemical or biological weapons in forty-five minutes. In the final version, which was highlighted in Prime Minister Blair's foreword, the September white paper declared that "Iraq's military forces *are* able to use chemical and biological weapons, with command, control, and logistical arrangements in place. The Iraqi military *are* able to deploy these weapons within forty-five minutes of a decision to do so." (Emphasis added.)[36]

At worst the dossier was a cynical effort by the British spymasters and the prime minister's office to manipulate WMD intelligence to make the case for war. In either case, the British dossier was a radical experiment in publicly deploying the secretive arts of intelligence that went awry.[37] Within a month, the Americans would follow the British lead—and make the same mistakes, if for different reasons—in their hastily produced and widely cited 2002 National Intelligence Estimate on Iraq.

PART IV

WHITE HOUSE SPY GAMES

14

SILENCING THE CRITICS

By the summer of 2002 the palpable sense in the U.S. intelligence community that the United States was headed to war in Iraq had spread to the American public and beyond. The hints were not subtle. Besides the president's "axis of evil" State of the Union Address in January 2002 and his June 1 speech to graduating cadets at West Point, which extolled Bush's new policy of preemptive military action, most Americans were keenly aware of the administration's saber-rattling and anti-Saddam rhetoric. In March, President Bush pulled the elite 5th Group Special Forces out of Afghanistan and secretly redeployed them to Iraq to monitor Saddam's movements. Later that month, *Time* magazine reported, President Bush turned up unexpectedly at a White House meeting between Condoleezza Rice and a bipartisan group of senators. When the subject turned to Iraq, the president shocked the gathering by declaring, "Fuck Saddam. We're taking him out."

Around the same time, Vice President Cheney showed up at a Republican luncheon, informed the attendees that what he was about to say should not leave the room, and told them that the question was not whether the United States was going to attack Baghdad, but when.[1] That squared with what Arnaud de Borchgrave, the right-of-center editor-at-large of *The Washington Times,* had heard from neoconservative officials inside the Bush administration for the first time in April: The war against Iraq was a foregone conclusion. "The Bush administration, they explained, starkly and simply, had decided to redraw the geopolitical map of the Middle East," wrote de Borchgrave. "The Bush Doctrine of preemption had become the vehicle for driving axis-of-evil practitioners out of power."[2]

Tales of Saddam's human rights atrocities and his storehouses of deadly weapons had become the daily grist of special media reports and added immeasurably to the sense of inevitability about the war. Despite all the clamor, though, the White House went to great lengths to keep the actual behind-the-scenes war-planning process out of public view, insisting to both Congress and concerned European allies that no decision had yet been taken to go to war, and that the president had no war plans "on his desk." By June, the pressure created by the administration's obsessive secretiveness—which cloaked significant disagreements between the White House, the State Department, and even within the Pentagon itself about war strategy— began to burst into the open, slowly at first, then in a cascade of leaks to the media.

The first details confirming the Bush White House's secret war planning appeared in *The Washington Post* and the *Los Angeles Times* in late May and June, sketching out various blueprints for a massive invasion of Iraq—one of them already abandoned—involving 200,000 and 250,000 U.S. troops. The leaks from the Pentagon picked up speed—and visibility—in early July, as *The New York Times* reported the first of three front-page Iraq war-planning stories, citing an "American military planning document" that called for a multipronged attack from air, land, and sea that would originate in Saudi Arabia, Turkey, Kuwait, and Qatar. A second *Times* story, five days later, added new information about air and commando raids on Iraq from Jordan from the same leaked document. That provoked a "snowflake," as memos from Secretary of Defense Rumsfeld were wryly nicknamed, to the Pentagon's top brass. "The disclosure of classified information is damaging our country's ability to stop terrorist acts and is putting American lives at risk," groused Rumsfeld. The snowflake reappeared days later in the *Los Angeles Times*.[3]

But it wasn't until the end of July, when *The Washington Post* and *The New York Times* weighed in with back-to-back accounts of discord within the Pentagon over the war plans, that the coverage reached a kind of critical mass. The *Post*'s military correspondent, Thomas Ricks, took the more provocative tack, reporting in some detail the internal dissension among military officers about the Pentagon's planning for Iraq. The front-page story was a devastatingly accurate indictment of the administration's shortsighted military planning—and also put the lie to the contention later voiced by many that virtually "everyone" assumed before the war that Saddam possessed a lethal arsenal of WMD.

Ricks reported bluntly that many senior U.S. military officials believed that "Saddam Hussein poses no immediate threat" and that the United States should continue to follow its eleven-year-old policy of containment. This view was "based . . . on intelligence assessments of the state of Hussein's nuclear, chemical and biological weapons programs and his missile delivery capabilities" and was "shared by senior officials at the State Department and the CIA." Senior military officers believed that the containment policy had kept Saddam from "threatening his neighbors" and "backing terrorist organizations," as well as "updating his military equipment." Ricks reported that the "U.S. intelligence assessment is that [Iraq] has few, if any, operational long-range missiles that could be used to deliver those weapons to attack Israel or other U.S. allies in the region." The joint chiefs of staff had advised the Bush administration about the military's three major concerns about the war plans on the table: namely, Saddam's possible battlefield use of biological weapons; the dangers of close urban fighting in Baghdad and other Iraqi cities; and the costs of a "post-victory occupation" that would have "to keep the peace and support the successor regime" and "prevent Iraq from breaking up."[4]

The *New York Times* story was based on leaked documents that revealed the Pentagon's so-called inside-outside option to strike first at Baghdad and one or two key command centers and weapons depots to decapitate the country's leadership and cause the immediate collapse of Saddam's government—a course that would involve a minimum of U.S. forces. Only then would coalition troops fan out to seize control of the countryside and outlying Iraqi cities and towns. The *Times* report was a partial version of a plan presented in June to Bush by Gen. Tommy Franks designed to avoid getting bogged down in costly street fighting in Baghdad. The story triggered cries within the administration that *The Times* had revealed military secrets to the enemy and breached national security.

Asked about the reports in a cabinet meeting on July 31, the president was dismissive. The incompleteness of the *Times* story gave him plenty of wiggle room. "The stated mission is regime change," said Bush. "But all this talk from level four people . . . [they] are talking about things they know nothing about. There are no war plans on my desk. I believe there is *casus belli* and that the doctrine of preemption applies. We won't do anything militarily unless confident we can succeed. Success is removal of Saddam." Rumsfeld chimed in with a trademark self-serving aphorism. "If it looks untidy in the press, it is," said Rumsfeld. "Preemption is an important discussion to have. Problem is that it gets particularized to Iraq."[5] But both Bush's and Rumsfeld's remarks amounted to classic "non-denial denials," and effectively confirmed that war plans were indeed being drawn up. There was no longer any question that the Bush administration was actively planning to go to war. The broad outlines were plain, even if the details remained unsettled. In the absence of any timetable for military action, the episode signaled that the White House was fast losing control of the public agenda on war planning to media leaks.

Once divisions in the Pentagon over the war plans had surfaced publicly, questions outside the government began to fly hard and fast about Bush's war policy. The first to weigh in was Lt. Gen. Brent Scowcroft, the elder president Bush's trusted national security advisor and friend. Appearing on CBS's *Face the Nation* on August 4, Scowcroft declared that a U.S. invasion of Iraq could destabilize the Middle East and disrupt the war on terror. "There's no question that Saddam is a problem," conceded Scowcroft, who reportedly informed the president's father that he planned to speak out. "He has already launched two wars and spent all the resources he can working on his military. But the president has announced that terrorism is our number one focus. Saddam is a problem, but he's not a problem because of terrorism. I think we could have an explosion in the Middle East. It could turn the whole region into a cauldron and destroy the War on Terror."[6]

Henry Kissinger was next. The Nobel Prize–winning former secretary of state under President Richard M. Nixon published a lengthy op-ed piece in *The Washington Post* the following week urging the Bush White House to exercise caution drafting its war plans. Dr. Kissinger warned against risking diplomatic isolation in the face of determined international opposition.[7] By choosing to fight a preemptive war, Kissinger wrote, the Bush administration would have to counter the skepticism of allies and hostility of enemies through a meticulous diplomatic offensive that would at once prepare the ground for war and assure a stable peace afterward. "Because of the precedent-setting nature of this war, its outcome will determine the way U.S. actions will be viewed far more than the way we entered it," said Kissinger. He warned bluntly, "It is not in the American national interest to establish pre-emption as a universal principle available to every nation," citing the dangers to U.S. interests and international stability if another country such as India decided to imitate the Bush doctrine and attack Pakistan.

The public tutorial from the nation's most venerable—and controversial—practitioner of global realpolitik did not gloss over the difficulty and delicacy of the task at hand. But Kissinger was hardly opposed to military action or regime change in Iraq. Rather, he advised, "The objective of a regime change should be subordinated . . . to the need to eliminate weapons of mass destruction from Iraq as required by the U.N. resolutions. It is necessary to propose a stringent inspection system that achieves substantial transparency of Iraqi institutions. A time limit should be set. The case for military intervention then will have been made in the context of seeking a common approach." Lest the point be misconstrued, by either the White House or its critics, Kissinger declared, "America's special responsibility is to work toward an international system that rests on more than military power—indeed, that strives to translate power into co-operation. Any other attitude will gradually isolate and exhaust America."[8]

It was a prescient variation on the theme the president had heard from Powell only days before and from Blair since as far back as April. Powell invited Kissinger to the State Department the next day to seek his counsel. The White House would later admit that Bush and Cheney had met with Kissinger at regular intervals during the invasion and occupation of Iraq.

Two days after Kissinger's exercise in public influence-peddling, the White House was rocked by a second bombshell from Scowcroft, this time in the form of an essay on the op-ed page of *The Wall Street Journal,* whose headline bluntly warned the administration, "Don't Attack Saddam." This time he sent an advance copy of the op-ed piece to the senior president Bush, who reportedly did not object to it. Noting the regularity with which the Pentagon's war plans leaked to the media and with which the White House denied any decision had been made to attack Iraq, Scowcroft hammered home his argument that fighting in Iraq would be a huge and costly diversion from the war on terror. Yes, Saddam was a "menace" who "terrorizes" and "brutalizes" his own people. And, yes, his strategic objectives to dominate the Persian Gulf and control the flow of oil in the region posed "a real threat to key U.S. interests."

But there was "scant evidence" linking Saddam to terrorist organizations or the 9/11 attacks. "Saddam's goals have little in common with the terrorists who threaten us, and there is little incentive for him to make common cause with them," Scowcroft wrote. "He is unlikely to risk his investment in weapons of mass destruction, much less his country, by handing such weapons to terrorists who would use them for their own purposes and leave Baghdad as the return address. Threatening to use these weapons for blackmail—much less their actual use—would open him and his entire regime to a devastating response by the U.S."

Conceding that the time might one day come to depose Saddam, he got to the point: "Our pre-eminent security priority—underscored repeatedly by the president—is the war on terrorism. An attack on Iraq at this time would seriously jeopardize, if not destroy, the global counterterrorist campaign we have undertaken." Noting the anger that would be touched off in the region if the United States was seen to be "turning our backs on" the Israeli-Palestinian conflict, Scowcroft, like Kissinger, urged the Bush administration to press the UN Security Council "to insist on an effective no-notice inspection regime for Iraq—any time, anywhere, no permission required." If Saddam, contrary to expectations, agreed to such an inspection regime, he would be kept "off balance and under close observation, even if all his weapons of mass destruction capabilities were not uncovered. And if he refused, his rejection could provide the persuasive *casus belli* which many claim we do not now have."[9]

The *Journal* op-ed piece seemed to open the floodgates. "I think Scowcroft has done us all a great favor by his article saying 'don't do it,' " said former Republican secretary of state Lawrence Eagleburger, who had served Bush senior after the Persian Gulf War. "My own personal view is that basically Gen. Scowcroft is correct. Unless the president can make a very compelling case that Saddam Hussein has his finger on a weapon of mass destruction and is about ready to use it, I do not think that now is the time to go to war against Saddam Hussein."[10] James A. Baker III, the elder Bush's political consigliere and secretary of state during the Gulf War, joined the fray in a *Times* opinion piece asserting that "a unilateral preemptive strike would be a detriment" to "our relationships with practically all other Arab countries (and even many of our customary allies in Europe and elsewhere)" and "to our top foreign policy priority, the war on terrorism." Baker would later join former Democratic congressman Lee Hamilton of Indiana in spearheading the Iraq Study Group, a 2006 presidential commission that proposed a gradual withdrawal of U.S. troops from Iraq (and efforts at regional diplomacy)—recommendations that the White House noted but opted not to pursue.

Like Kissinger and Scowcroft, Baker concluded that the "United States should advocate the adoption by the United Nations Security Council of a simple and straightforward resolution requiring that Iraq submit to

intrusive inspections anytime, anywhere, with no exceptions, and author-
izing all necessary means to enforce it. . . . Seeking new authorization
now is necessary, politically and practically, and will help build international support."[11] Senator Chuck Hagel of Nebraska, a Republican and
Vietnam combat veteran, said that the United States had "absolutely no
evidence" that Saddam would have nuclear weapons anytime soon and
was wary about a policy of preemptive strikes. "You can take the country
into a war pretty fast," said Hagel. "But you can't get out as quickly, and
the public needs to know what the risks are."[12]

The firestorm ignited by Kissinger and Scowcroft was read by many as
a break with the Bush administration. Even Fox News, normally a warm
supporter of the president, was moved to ask in a terse headline, "GOP
Backing Out of Iraq Offensive?" *The New York Times* created a fit of
pique at the control-conscious White House by suggesting that the ten-
day burst of criticism by the Republican foreign policy establishment "appeared to be a loosely coordinated effort," suggesting a breakdown of
Republican discipline that brought a chorus of denials from the president's supporters. Among the earliest to leap to the president's defense
was Michael Ledeen, the neoconservative operative associated with Cheney and Under Secretary of Defense Douglas Feith. Ledeen declared that
"Scowcroft has managed to get one thing right, even though he misde-
scribes it"—a reference to Scowcroft's prediction on *Face the Nation* of
"an explosion" in the Middle East. "If we wage the war effectively, we
will bring down the terror regimes in Iraq, Iran, and Syria, and either
bring down the Saudi monarchy or force it to abandon its global assembly
line to indoctrinate young terrorists," said Ledeen. "That's our mission in
the war against terror."[13] Richard Perle, the head of Rumsfeld's Defense
Policy Board and a strong supporter of military action in Iraq, argued that
criticism from the likes of Scowcroft would itself undermine the war on
terror—and President Bush's credibility. "I think Brent just got it wrong,"
Perle said. "The failure to take on Saddam after what the president said
would produce such a collapse of confidence in the president that it would
set back the war on terrorism." Senator Hagel, a former rifleman in the
Vietnam War, quipped to *The New York Times*: "Maybe Mr. Perle would
like to be in the first wave of those who go into Baghdad."[14]

In fact, Ledeen and Perle represented an increasingly embattled faction in the Bush administration debates about how to frame the war
publicly. For its part, the White House tried to play down the barrage of
criticism from the GOP elders. Scowcroft's views "came as no surprise
to top officials in the administration, who have been well aware of his

concerns," said an unnamed White House official. "Scowcroft didn't want to overthrow Saddam Hussein in the first Persian Gulf war. He felt from the beginning that a successor might be worse. His position just reflects the same view he had back then." Other Republicans rushed to President Bush's defense. Senator Fred Thompson of Tennessee said he believed the president was "in the process" of making the case against the Iraqis, and that a new agreement on weapons inspectors would only give Saddam time to develop his nuclear program. "Do we sit back and hope that we can negotiate our way out of that situation with Saddam?" asked Thompson, then a member of the Senate Intelligence Committee. "I don't think so."[15]

Bush, vacationing at his Texas ranch, personally responded to the barrage of criticism on August 16, several days before Cheney, Rumsfeld, and Joint Chiefs Chairman Richard Meyers arrived at Crawford to discuss Pentagon strategy. "I am aware there are some very intelligent people expressing their opinions about Saddam Hussein and Iraq. I listen carefully to what they have to say," said the president. "There should be no doubt in anyone's mind that that man is thumbing his nose at the world, that he has gassed his own people, that he is trouble in his neighborhood, that he desires weapons of mass destruction. I will use all the latest intelligence to make informed decisions about how best to keep the world at peace, how best to defend freedom for the long run." He added: "Listen, it's a healthy debate for people to express their opinion. People should be allowed to express their opinion, but Americans need to know I'll be making up my mind based on the latest intelligence and how best to protect our own country and our friends and allies."[16]

The same day in Washington, Rumsfeld lit into the administration's critics, arguing that it would be suicidal for the United States to wait to mount a preemptive strike against Saddam. "Waiting to be attacked by someone who has been developing and has used weapons of mass destruction where you're looking at risking not several thousands of people but potentially several tens of thousands of people or hundreds of thousands of people is quite a different thing," he said. "What evidence do we want? What do we need to think through as a people? And those are hard calls and I don't suggest they're easy at all." Invoking the forces of appeasement before World War II, the secretary drew a rhetorical analogy between Saddam and Hitler. "Think of the prelude to World War II, think of all the countries that said, 'Well, we don't have enough evidence.' I mean *Mein Kampf* had been written, Hitler indicated what he had intended to do," said Rumsfeld. "Maybe he won't attack, maybe he won't do this or that.

Well, there were millions of people dead because of the miscalculations had he been stopped early as he might have been at minimal cost, minimal cost in lives, but no, that wasn't done."[17]

With the president's comparatively measured response to the onslaught of criticism and Rumsfeld's aggressive flaying of the war critics, the White House counterattack against the Republican old guard was under way. But there was a deeper political reality. The U.S. government may have been united on the need to unseat Saddam—despite the withering objections of its critics—but the Bush administration was still sharply divided, not only about how to achieve that goal, but also how to justify a war strategy to the public. The issue was a sensitive one and it dominated the White House agenda. By mid- to late August, Bush and Blair were already talking about the conditions that would allow Britain to join the war effort as an ally, which would involve putting the spotlight on Saddam's WMD and going to the United Nations to send in weapons inspectors. But no decisions had been made, and the White House had to maintain its open-ended public posture about going to war to keep its options open. Vice President Cheney deeply distrusted the United Nations and was concerned the U.S. war effort would get bogged down in endless diplomatic haggling at the United Nations.

Cheney reportedly felt the ground slipping out from under him as news cycle after news cycle was dominated by the Republican Iraq war critics. At about this time, Bob Woodward reported, the vice president "decided that everyone was offering an opinion except the administration. There was no stated administration position and he wanted to put one out. . . . He was not going to cede the field to Scowcroft, Baker, a misinterpreted Kissinger—or Powell. He spoke privately with the president, who gave his okay without reviewing the details of what Cheney might say."[18]

Precisely what was said during this conversation between Bush and Cheney, or where it took place, is unknown. There is no hard evidence that the subject was discussed at the August 21 military powwow in Crawford, though the president and other senior officials almost certainly considered how to silence administration war critics and concentrate on getting their own message out. But whatever private understanding Bush and Cheney arrived at marked a dramatic turning point in the administration's conduct of war planning and an escalation in Vice President Cheney's already heated rhetoric about U.S. war aims and the dangers of Saddam's WMD.

The White House war effort had plenty to work with on the public relations front. Americans were still shell-shocked by the 9/11 terrorist attacks. Chalabi and his INC defectors had seeded the press with widely circulated anti-Saddam horror stories. According to a CNN/USA Today Gallup poll, 86 percent of those surveyed believed groups supported by Saddam had "plans to attack the United States" and 53 percent thought Saddam was "personally involved in the September 11 attacks."[19] But the president faced another critical challenge. As former Carter administration secretary of defense Zbigniew Brzezinski put it in August, "The president himself has to make, in a speech addressed to the nation, a careful, reasoned case, without sloganeering, on the specifics of the threat. Detailed evidence needs to be presented that the threat is both grave and imminent."[20]

Prime Minister Blair had identified virtually the same weakness in the American war juggernaut months before—that the White House effort lacked a thought-out political framework and a credible rationale for war against Iraq to sell to the public. After taking punches from the elders of the Republican foreign policy establishment for several weeks, the president and his advisers were keenly aware of the problem. But the solution—much like the eventual resolution of Blair's complaint—was built upon another shaky premise and both the British and Americans knew it. The Blair government, despite its six-month campaign to persuade the United States to use Iraq's illegal WMD arsenal to establish a legal foundation for the war, knew full well how unimpressive the WMD case against Saddam really was, as the UN weapons inspectors had reported and various Blair advisers had made clear in secret memoranda going back to March. In late July, after all, Blair had been informed by his spymasters that the Americans were so hell-bent on war in Iraq that they were busy fixing the intelligence on WMD and terrorism around their war policy to make it happen.

Like the British, senior officials of the Bush administration understood from the outset that the evidence against Saddam was perilously thin. A senior Bush policymaker told The Washington Post that the administration greatly exaggerated the immediate threat of Saddam's nuclear weapons program. "I never cared about the 'imminent threat,'" the anonymous U.S. official said. "The threat was there in [Hussein's] presence in office. To me, just knowing what it takes to have a nuclear weapons program, he needed a lot of equipment. You can stare at the yellowcake all you want. You need to convert it to gas and enrich it. That does not constitute an imminent threat, and the people who were saying that, I think, did not fully appreciate the difficulties and effort involved in producing the nuclear material and the physics package."[21]

The president's closest aides—Condoleezza Rice, Karl Rove, Scooter Libby, Karen Hughes—had firsthand knowledge that the WMD evidence was scanty. All were members of the White House Iraq Group (WHIG), a public relations and "marketing" task force set up late in the summer by Chief of Staff Andrew Card to oversee the public rollout of the Iraq war policy in September. Early on, WHIG commissioned a white paper entitled "A Grave and Gathering Danger: Saddam Hussein's Quest for Nuclear Weapons." But making a credible case out of the existing intelligence proved difficult. Drafts of the document—written at about the same time as the summary that would later emerge as the declassified 2002 National Intelligence Estimate—employed an already familiar presidential sleight of hand to make the case for the nuclear threat. One version, for example, stated without qualification that the IAEA had reported, "Since the beginning of the nineties, Saddam has launched a crash program to divert nuclear reactor fuel for . . . nuclear weapons." Bush tried out a similar formulation in his September 7 Camp David press conference with Blair. Like the president, WHIG's draft white paper failed to mention that the Iraqi crash program started in late 1990 and was forced to shut down when the Gulf War began in 1991.

The WHIG group shared a desire with their counterparts at 10 Downing Street to use the white paper to convey dramatic and unambiguous evidence of Iraq's nuclear threat to the public, without the nuances, hedging, and qualifications of the intelligence professionals. But it would not come together. National Security Advisor Condoleezza Rice and the NSC's nonproliferation chief, Robert Joseph, finally decided the nuclear white paper "was not strong enough" and killed it. "There were disagreements over details in almost every aspect of the administration's case against Iraq," said a senior intelligence official familiar with the drafting of both the white paper and the unclassified intelligence estimate. The White House, said the official, did not want "a lot of footnotes and disclaimers."[22]

USA Today, a politically moderate daily with the largest daily circulation in the nation, presciently reported that the White House was in a jam. "U.S. intelligence cannot say conclusively that Saddam Hussein has weapons of mass destruction, an information gap that is complicating White House efforts to build support for an attack on Saddam's Iraqi regime," the paper reported in August 2002. "The CIA has advised top administration officials to assume that Iraq has some weapons of mass destruction. But the agency has not given President Bush a 'smoking gun,' according to US intelligence and administration officials. The most recent unclassified CIA report on the subject goes no further than saying it is 'likely' that Iraq has used the four years since United Nations inspectors left the country to rebuild chemical and biological weapons programs."

Indeed, the most up-to-date official accounting of Saddam's nuclear capability at the time, the 2000 U.S. National Intelligence Estimate, supposed that Iraq was eight to ten years away from building a nuclear weapon—and then only if Saddam possessed weapons-grade uranium or plutonium and a reconstituted nuclear weapons program. He had neither, as the Iraq Survey Group would later independently confirm. In reality, Saddam's nuclear infrastructure was a shambles, in terms of both research facilities in Iraq and the dispirited and cynical morale of Iraqi scientists—those who had not emigrated.

Vice President Cheney was undeterred. Between the beginning and the end of August, the vice president's statements on the Iraqi nuclear threat were transformed from mild-mannered musings about the future development of Iraq's nuclear weapons arsenal to pumped-up declarations that Saddam not only now possessed nuclear weapons, but was willing to use them against Americans. In a speech on Iraq in San Francisco on August 7, for example, Cheney mentioned almost as an aside that "it's the judgment of many of us that in the not-too-distant future, he will acquire nuclear weapons." Nineteen days later—by now Powell had met with the president at the White House and Bush and Cheney had had their mysterious tête-à-tête about getting a stronger war message out—the vice president's measured warnings about the future prospects of Iraq's nuclear program suddenly and inexplicably gained volcanic intensity.

"We now know that Saddam has resumed his efforts to acquire nuclear weapons," Cheney declared to the assembled Veterans of Foreign Wars in Nashville on August 26. "Simply stated, there is no doubt that Saddam Hussein now has weapons of mass destruction [and] there is no doubt he is amassing them to use against our friends, against our allies and against us." Saddam, he said, was a "mortal threat" to the United States, citing "firsthand testimony from defectors, including Saddam's own son-in-law." The vice president then struck upon a rhetorical formula that would become a familiar mantra of administration policy in the months leading up to the war. These weapons in the hands of a "murderous dictator," said Cheney, would be "as great a threat as can be imagined. The risks of inaction are far greater than the risk of action." Two days later, in San Antonio, he asserted without qualification that Saddam had "an aggressive nuclear weapons program." Before Cheney's August 26 speech, not even President Bush had gone further than to suggest that Saddam "desired" nuclear weapons. Now Cheney was leading the charge.

Knowledgeable observers were stunned. Neither the CIA nor any other U.S. or foreign intelligence agency had reported any such reassessment of Saddam's nuclear program. The information allegedly provided by "Saddam's own son-in-law"—a reference to Hussein Kamel—was seven years old. Kamel himself had been dead since February 1996, making the vice president's "firsthand testimony" claim a blatant falsehood. Although the papers allegedly stored on Kamel's farm provided evidence of a stepped-up Iraqi nuclear program, Kamel himself had in fact told weapons inspectors that the program ended in 1991. Bush officials had known about most of the WMD information supplied by various Iraqi defectors—Gen. Khidhir Hamza, Adnan Ihsan Saeed al-Haideri, Curveball, and Mohammad Harith—for between six months and a year. The vice president's office and the CIA also had known about the disputed Niger uranium allegations and the aluminum tubes claims for much of the previous year.

Interestingly enough, the speech may have marked a parting of the ways between Cheney and other senior neoconservatives such as Wolfowitz and Feith, who privately wanted to downplay the WMD threat. They had lost their bitter internal battle against a new resolution at the United Nations and a new round of weapons inspections. What had changed? Edward N. Luttwak, a prominent neoconservative scholar and friend of the White House, believed that Cheney and other senior Bush officials feared that the American people would not go along with deposing Saddam and so simply lied about WMD intelligence to provide a rationale for going to war that would satisfy the United Nations. "Cheney was forced into this fake posture of worrying about weapons of mass destruction," said Luttwak.[23]

In the annals of political make-believe, Cheney's version of the threat posed by Saddam's nuclear program was a stunningly blinkered attempt to dominate the debate based on deceptively selective information, carefully parsed phrasing, and suggestive juxtaposition of language that implied a connection where there was none. Nonetheless, by September 2002, a formidable and frightening alternate reality of Saddam Hussein's weapons of mass destruction had lodged itself in the public imagination, thanks largely to Chalabi's defectors and a compliant press. Now Cheney attempted to defuse the mounting criticism of the White House war plans by publicly aligning himself with the agitprop of the Iraqi opposition, thus stamping it with the imprimatur of the White House to drown out the wave of dissension from senior Republicans. Until the vice president's Nashville speech, the job of painting a bull's-eye on the back of Saddam and the Iraqis had fallen to Chalabi and his minders at the Pentagon. Cheney had found the secret to silencing the administration's critics—and it was firmly under the control of the White House and the Pentagon.

Despite the vice president's outspoken support for U.S. refinancing of Chalabi's intelligence operation, the Iraqi opposition leader and his lieutenants suddenly seemed to drop out of sight in September, as Rumsfeld's Pentagon assumed formal control of the INC brief from the State Department. The exile group's financial backing—restored to the tune of $340,000 a month—was shifted to a secret Pentagon account. The INC's explicit mission from the Pentagon was to collect fresh information about Saddam's WMD, as well as evidence of links between the Iraqi regime and terrorist groups. Under new operating rules established in its secret agreement with the Defense Department, INC intelligence was not to be shared with the press or other U.S. intelligence agencies without Pentagon permission. Rumsfeld had, in effect, fitted Chalabi with a muzzle, and assured that the INC's raw intelligence would continue to be funneled directly to the Office of the Vice President and other top national security officials through a shadowy new agency within the Pentagon called the Office of Special Plans.

Almost simultaneously, the Pentagon's Policy Counter Terrorism Evaluation Group, which was started up just after 9/11 by Rumsfeld and was overseen by Undersecretary of Defense for Policy Douglas Feith, was closed down without explanation. The unit regularly passed anti-Saddam intelligence to the vice president's office, and in August had briefed the CIA and the White House on the alleged meeting between Mohamed Atta and an Iraqi spy in Prague. Originally the brainchild of Rumsfeld and Wolfowitz—almost certainly with Cheney's knowledge and support—the four-person office had been set up by Feith just after 9/11 to sift through raw U.S. intelligence looking for fresh evidence of Iraq's hostility to the West and its ties with terrorist organizations overlooked by U.S. spy agencies. An early version of the new Office of Special Plans, the counterterrorism evaluation unit was a reprise of the Reagan administration's Team B, the alternative intelligence unit created by the CIA to reassess the Soviet military threat. Team B wound up grossly exaggerating Soviet power, but became the foundation of Reagan's anti-Soviet foreign policy. Feith's group would do the same for Saddam's threat.

Feith put two hardline neoconservatives, David Wurmser and Michael

Maloof, in charge of the Pentagon team. They were charged with filtering raw intelligence for nuggets of overlooked information that would make the strongest case Iraq was a grave threat to the region and U.S. interests. Wurmser, a close ally of Richard Perle and a Middle East researcher at the American Enterprise Institute, was a longtime advocate of regime change in Iraq. He and his Israeli wife were associated with a 1996 policy paper for Israeli prime minister Benyamin Netanyahu ("A Clean Break: A New Strategy for Securing the Realm") that strongly advocated transforming the balance of power in the region, in part by deposing Saddam. Wurmser was later transferred to Vice President Cheney's office. Maloof was a former aide to Perle and a veteran Pentagon security technology expert who proposed a system to track terrorists down using existing classified intelligence that would link them to al-Qaeda or state sponsors. He soon received a call from Feith's office.

"I went to these two guys and said, 'Read the intelligence so you can tell me what I need to know about, so I can develop a strategy and policies for dealing with terror networks,'" Feith explained.[24] The idea was to find patterns of activity that would provide links between worldwide terrorism and al-Qaeda as well as state sponsors of terrorism, including Iraq. Such an analysis, or "finished intelligence," would undermine the CIA's cooler and more nuanced assessment of the strategic threats posed by both the terrorists and Saddam. Members of the special intelligence unit, explained Wolfowitz, "are helping us sift through enormous amounts of incredibly valuable data that our many intelligence resources have vacuumed up. They are not making independent intelligence assessments." In intelligence work, he said, "people who are pursuing a certain hypothesis will see certain facts that others won't, and not see other facts that others will. The lens through which you're looking for facts affects what you look for."[25]

By mid-2002, it was apparent that the Counter Terrorism Evaluation Group had become a source of serious friction between the Defense Department and the intelligence community, including the Pentagon's own DIA. "Wolfowitz and company disbelieve any analysis that doesn't support their own preconceived conclusions. The C.I.A. is enemy territory, as far are they're concerned," said one defense official at the time.[26] "They were doing intelligence analysis," said former White House counterterrorism expert Richard Clarke of the Pentagon unit. "But they weren't legally an intelligence analytical office. And they had already decided on the conclusion, and what they were doing was trying to find the evidence to support it."[27] The potential legal problem, combined with their growing public profile, may have proven lethal. A small office deep inside the Pentagon, the counterterrorism group was not subject to congressional oversight— to date, neither the Senate nor House intelligence committees have investigated its inner workings. But after the bitter fight between the State Department and Chalabi over funding for the INC and its Information Collection Program, the obscure Pentagon information-crunchers had attracted enough high-level attention on Capitol Hill to have become a political liability.

For senior defense officials, the various intelligence and policy shops in Feith's domain at the Pentagon that came and went before the war were a movable feast whose outlines are still shadowy and confusing to outsiders. Feith placed neoconservative Harold Rhode, a multilingual foreign affairs specialist, in the Office of Net Assessment, a tiny but vital department under the leadership of then eighty-one-year-old Pentagon legend Andrew Marshall, who specialized in "forward-leaning" (i.e., aggressive) analysis of national security threats from the Soviet Union to North Korea and Iraq. Rhode filled the twelve-person office with like-minded ideologues.

For its eleven months of existence, the tiny Counter Terrorism Evaluation Group seemed to blur into the Near East South Asia office, or NESA, a well-established group of regional experts who were also swept out by neoconservative replacements during Bush's first year in office. In the spring and summer of 2002 the NESA Iraq desk officer, air force colonel William Bruner, a former military aide to former House Speaker Newt Gingrich, was reportedly Chalabi's handler. Bruner often dressed in civilian clothes because he had to travel across the Potomac for frequent meetings in downtown Washington. On several occasions during the summer of 2002, he was seen escorting Chalabi into meetings in the NESA offices on the Pentagon's fourth floor, between the seventh and eighth corridors of D Ring, a floor above the offices of Richard Perle's Defense Advisory Board.[28]

Like the counterterrorism unit, NESA specialized in developing alternative intelligence. "It wasn't intelligence—it was propaganda," recalled air force lieutenant colonel Karen Kwiatkowski, a former speechwriter for the director of the National Security Agency who was transferred to NESA in May 2002. "They'd take a little bit of intelligence, cherry-pick it, make it sound much more exciting, usually by taking it out of context, often by juxtaposition of two pieces of information that don't belong together."[29] NESA was run by William J. Luti with the assistance of Abraham Shulsky, an intelligence specialist and another neoconservative crony of Perle and Wolfowitz. Kwiatkowski saw firsthand the changes in NESA engineered by the Bush people. "Expertise on Middle East policy was not only being removed," she later wrote, "but was also being exchanged for that from various agenda-bearing think tanks, including the Middle East Media Research Institute, the Washington Institute for Near East Policy, and the Jewish Institute for National Security Affairs"—all right-wing, pro-Israeli organizations. Soon after she arrived, Kwiatkowski said, she was advised by a NESA colleague that "if I wanted to be successful here, I'd better remember not to say anything positive about the Palestinians."[30]

Feith also tried and failed to breathe new life into the short-lived Office of Strategic Influence (OSI), a Pentagon shop that was launched in November 2001 to support aggressive military public relations campaigns abroad, plant false news items, and spread strategic disinformation through the foreign media, on the Internet, and in covert operations. An outgrowth of the Coalition Information Center that coordinated public military information with the British and Pakistanis during the early Afghanistan operation, OSI would expand throughout Asia, the Middle East, and Western Europe. Its work would involve army "psyops," or psychological operations, that ranged from "black" disinformation campaigns to harmless, "white" public affairs releases. The Rendon Group, a CIA-backed company that advised Chalabi in the early 1990s, was under contract with the Pentagon for $100,000 per month to develop the proposed office. But soon after OSI's existence was exposed in early February 2002, the White House strongly objected and effectively killed the idea.

Rumsfeld denied outright that OSI would spread disinformation, lie to the press, or compromise the Bush administration. "The Pentagon does not lie to the American people," Rumsfeld told NBC. "It does not lie to foreign audiences." He insisted that he had not even heard of the unit, which reportedly had a proposed price tag of $100 million, until its existence became public. During a chat with reporters during a flight to Chile the following November, Rumsfeld did not try to hide his unhappiness with the decision. "And then there was the Office of Strategic Influence. You may recall that," Rumsfeld said during a scathing and sarcastic commentary on public overreaction to some Pentagon policy initiatives. "And 'oh my goodness gracious isn't that terrible, Henny Penny, the sky is going to fall.' I went down that next day and said fine, if you want to savage this thing, fine, I'll give you the corpse. There's the name. You can have the name, but I'm gonna keep doing every single thing that needs to be done and I have."[31] By this time, of course, Chalabi's covert intelligence operation was under Rumsfeld's control—and the INC was already providing many of the same services planners had proposed for OSI.

The Office of Special Plans rose out of the ashes of the Wurmser-Maloof counterterrorism evaluation unit, with some of the same players and with a similar core intelligence mission. OSP was the jewel in Undersecretary Feith's crown. Essentially, it was an expanded Iraq desk that worked closely with NESA. Its stated mission was to draw up plans for the postwar reconstruction of Iraq, get its oil industry and its economy up to speed, train a new police force, organize war crimes trials, and lay the groundwork for a democratic Iraqi government. OSP's bland, James Bond–style name, Feith later explained, was designed to obscure its official mission, since the White House wanted to pursue, for public consumption at least, a diplomatic solution to the Iraqi crisis at the United Nations on a parallel track with its war plans.[32] The OSP offices opened late in the summer of 2002 on the fifth floor of the Pentagon's D ring, just above NESA's fourth floor suite, with a full-time staff of about ten that grew at one point to include as many as one hundred part-time contractors and consultants.[33]

Feith, a graduate of Harvard and Georgetown Law School, who had served on the National Security Council and as a top aide to assistant defense secretary Richard Perle during the Reagan administration, oversaw the new operation. A youthful-looking forty-eight-year-old with an unlined face and a mop of graying hair, Feith wore thick glasses that gave him the owlish look of an intellectual, though Gen. Tommy Franks once called him "the fucking stupidest guy on the face of the earth." Feith quickly gained a reputation as an inept manager. He "was a case study in how not to run a large organization," said Lieutenant Colonel Kwiatkowski, who recalled Feith's "first all-hands policy meeting at which he discussed for over 15 minutes how many bullets and sub-bullets should be in papers for Secretary Donald Rumsfeld." Feith's half-serious reaction was to call a press conference to deny the charge, though he never did. Still, he was recognized by his superiors as a smart and uncompromising neoconservative. Rumsfeld regarded him as "one of the brightest people you or I will ever come across. He's diligent, very well read, and insightful."

Growing up in the Philadelphia suburbs during the Vietnam years, Feith was sympathetic to his generation of anti–Vietnam War protesters, but he couldn't swallow their general antiwar philosophy. Two of his grandparents, three uncles, and four aunts had disappeared in Nazi concentration camps during World War II. Feith could not abide any policy that smacked of appeasement. "I had done a lot of reading, relative for a kid, about World War Two, and I thought about Chamberlain a lot," Feith told a reporter. "Chamberlain wasn't popular in my house." If war was not the answer, as his antiwar peers insisted, Feith asked, "What's the answer to Pearl Harbor? What's the answer to the Holocaust?" He added: "The surprising thing is not that there are so many Jews who are neocons but that there are so many who are not."[34]

Feith named Abraham Shulsky the director of the new office. From the beginning, Shulsky and William Luti ran OSP and NESA with a firm hand, enforcing strict adherence to the neoconservative line among staffers and expelling those who wavered ideologically. "It was organized like a machine," recalled Kwiatkowski. "The people working on the neocon agenda had a narrow, well-defined political agenda. They had a sense of mission."[35] She was shocked by the lack of respect new members of the neoconservative OSP/NESA group showed to certain high administration officials and ranking military officers who disagreed with them on Iraq. David Schenker, who had been brought in to head NESA's Israel, Lebanon, and Syria desk, confided to Kwiatkowski that "the best service Powell could offer would be to quit right now." In one staff meeting, Luti branded Gen. Anthony Zinni, who ran the U.S. Central Command in the 1990s, a "traitor" because he had expressed doubts about the Bush administration's rush to war.[36]

Luti, a tall, thin, status-conscious former officer who had not attained flag rank in the navy, was known to treat his staff at times with open disdain, and readily compared his stature within the Pentagon to three- and four-star generals. Though he was nominally Shulsky's superior as an assistant deputy secretary, the feeling was that the quieter, more deferential Shulsky reported directly to either Feith or another higher-up, possibly Wolfowitz. Although Feith insisted that OSP did not seek to develop its own intelligence capability, Kwiatkowski and others remember both offices turning out propaganda-style intelligence for Luti and Shulsky.

Luti's special assistant, navy lieutenant commander Youssef Aboul-Enein, for example, was responsible for reviewing "the Arabic-language media to find articles that would incriminate Saddam Hussein about terrorism." Aboul-Enein would translate his findings, which would normally be subjected to tracking, verification, and checking by experienced intelligence analysts before being passed along to policymakers. But unprocessed information from OSP and NESA became the foundation for speeches by the president, the vice president, and other administration officials. Intelligence from the spy agencies was often scorned. OSP officials and their allies behaved arrogantly toward lower-ranking intelligence officers at the CIA or State Department, informing them that their "products" were not what they were looking for.

"It was pretty blatant," said Melvin Goodman, a former CIA official and intelligence specialist at the National War College.[37] State Department intelligence analyst Greg Thielmann said, "The Al Qaeda connection and nuclear weapons issue were the only two ways that you could link Iraq to an imminent security threat to the U.S. And the administration was grossly distorting the intelligence on both things."[38] Thielmann's work for the Bureau of Intelligence and Research had been attacked by John Bolton, an outspoken neoconservative advocate of the war and deputy secretary of state for nonproliferation, who would eventually serve a brief tenure as U.S. ambassador to the United Nations. On the other hand, OSP/NESA-generated intelligence mysteriously bypassed outside intelligence analysts such as Thielmann. The OSP people "were a pretty shadowy presence," he recalled. "Normally when you compile an intelligence document, all the agencies get together to discuss it. The OSP was never present at any of the meetings I attended."[39]

"That office was charged with collecting, vetting and disseminating intelligence completely outside of the normal intelligence apparatus," said Rep. David Obey, a Wisconsin Democrat, who called for an investigation of the OSP in 2003. "In fact, it appears that information collected by this office was in some instances not even shared with established intelligence agencies and in numerous instances was passed on to the National Security Council and the president without having been vetted with anyone other than political appointees."[40] The bid by minority Democrats to initiate a probe of the secret Pentagon intelligence unit was dropped.

Luti and Shulsky, said Kwiatkowski and others, took uncorroborated intelligence that suggested Saddam had links with al-Qaeda, or that Iraq had restarted its WMD programs, and converted it into talking points. Shulsky constantly updated these documents, relying on the secret intelligence unit that had been absorbed into the OSP/NESA operation. "They surveyed data and picked out what they liked," said Thielmann. "The whole thing was bizarre. The secretary of defense had this huge Defense Intelligence Agency, and he went around it."[41] But OSP's intelligence was not limited to gleaning supportive data from existing U.S. work reports and analyses. Chalabi's INC operatives would sometimes route information from their renewed intelligence operation directly to OSP/NESA, and sometimes to the DIA through the Defense Human Intelligence Service, which debriefed their Iraqi defector sources. Earlier, even Michael Maloof at the Counter Terrorism Evaluation Group had turned to Chalabi and the INC when he thought he was "being stonewalled" by U.S. intelligence agencies. "They were quite helpful," he said.[42] But as OSP got up and running in August 2002, Colonel Bruner reportedly released a new stream of phony intelligence that had been fed into the Pentagon by Chalabi and his minions. The INC intelligence was "unreliable," said former CIA counterterrorism chief Vincent Cannistraro. "Much of it is propaganda. Much of it is telling the Defense Department what they want to hear," he said, and much was "cooked information that goes right into presidential and vice presidential speeches."[43]

Kwiatkowski found, to her dismay, that Cheney had a direct, if highly unorthodox, pipeline through Luti into OSP/NESA. As Shulsky refined his talking points based on OSP intelligence, he circulated them directly to Pentagon officials, who included Luti, Feith, Wolfowitz, Undersecretary of Defense for Intelligence Stephen Cambone, and Rumsfeld. But the real shock was that Vice President Cheney and his chief of staff, Lewis Libby, also regularly received the OSP's intelligence products. "Of course, we never thought they'd go directly to the White House," said Kwiatkowski later, after she heard Luti announce at a staff meeting that he had to rush a certain report over to "Scooter." In all her years at the Pentagon, she declared, "never, ever, ever would a deputy undersecretary of Defense work directly on a project for the vice president."

Cheney was not the only senior official whose public statements began to bear the stamp of Feith's operation. In early October 2002, Kwiatkowski was taken aback by the president's speech on Iraq in Cincinnati, where he invoked weapons developed by Saddam's "nuclear mujihadeen," and a "smoking gun—that could come in the form of a mushroom cloud."[44] Soon afterward, she buttonholed DIA intelligence analyst John Trigilio, then Luti's intelligence adviser at NESA, in a Pentagon hallway. Bush's wild rhetoric about Iraq's nuclear capabilities was not supported by any underlying intelligence she'd seen over the years, she said. Where was this "bull" coming from? Unfazed, Trigilio replied that the intelligence was not exaggerated, but refused to comment further. "Karen, we have sources that you don't have access to," he explained.

Kwiatkowski took this to mean the president's speech was based on intelligence generated by the "chummy relationship" between OSP/NESA and Chalabi's Iraqi defectors.[45]

15

SQUEEZING THE CIA

The creation of the Office of Special Plans as an unmonitored, independent intelligence agency within the Pentagon, tasked with gathering damning information on Saddam's ties to terrorists and his WMD programs, amounted to an out-and-out declaration of war by Defense and the White House on the CIA. "This was not 'alternative intelligence assessment,'" OSP head Douglas Feith said later. "It was from the start a criticism of the consensus of the intelligence community."[1] Feith's efforts were directed, in short, at undermining official U.S. intelligence community assessments by excavating and reassessing highly focused information on terror links and WMD. The clearer it became to CIA analysts that White House officials were using Pentagon-generated intelligence to support their case against Saddam, the greater the pressure became to trim their own reports to the prevailing political winds from the White House. Tenet was among the first to get the message—but he did not anticipate the beating the CIA was about to take. "The Pentagon has banded together to dominate the government's foreign policy, and they've pulled it off," said Patrick Lang, a former DIA Middle East intelligence officer, a few months later. "They're running Chalabi. The D.I.A. has been intimidated and beaten to a pulp. And there's no guts at all in the C.I.A."[2]

A streetwise man of rough charm from Queens in New York City, Tenet had worked hard to cultivate a close, amiable relationship with the president. Like Bush, he was an avid sports fan, often did his thinking out loud, and was inclined to instinctive, spur-of-the-moment decisions. In 1999, on Tenet's watch, CIA headquarters was renamed the George Bush Center for Intelligence, after the president's father. Months later, Tenet arranged a CIA-sponsored conference at the George Bush Presidential Library in Houston. He made a point of personally delivering the Presidential Daily Briefing, or PDB, to the new president each morning, a regimen Bill Clinton had abandoned in favor of a close reading and note-taking.

Many CIA officers, like other senior officials in the Bush administration, knew that the evidence that Saddam was rebuilding his WMD arsenal was thin, and that the case against Iraq would be difficult to make. CIA personnel, from analysts to senior managers, privately expressed strong misgivings to Tenet that rushing into another war in Iraq would drain resources from the war against al-Qaeda in Afghanistan. Deputy Director of Operations James Pavitt and others warned that Iraq on top of Afghanistan would badly stretch CIA resources. Tenet was mindful of the danger signals within the agency, but nonetheless brought the message back to the CIA from the Oval Office and the Pentagon that the war against Iraq was inevitable. The time for doubt and equivocation was past. "A lot of people went to George to tell him that Iraq would hurt the war on terrorism," said a former aide. "But I never heard him express an opinion about war in Iraq. He would just come back from the White House and say they are going to do it."[3]

Tenet seemed to understand that he personally was also now under the gun. A rare holdover from the Clinton administration, he was highly suspect to the conservatives around Bush. But he had been backed for the job by the president's father, who believed in the value of continuity and a certain nonpolitical, nonideological aura around the CIA director. After 9/11, Tenet owed his job to his strong personal relationship with the president. Bush allowed him to stay on and protected him in the face of biting criticism that the CIA had failed to see the terror attacks coming. In fact, Tenet had been keenly aware of the threat bin Laden presented in late August and early September of 2001, but, like other Clinton holdovers such as Richard Clarke, he had not been able to impress his warnings on Clinton-averse White House officials. After 9/11, he was among the few senior administration officials of any stature who were familiar with Osama bin Laden and al-Qaeda.

Bush was obviously comfortable with Tenet. Vice President Cheney and Secretary of Defense Rumsfeld, however, kept the CIA director at arm's length. Tenet seemed to have crossed Cheney, whose office the CIA director recognized had become a nerve center for national security matters soon after the terrorist attacks. Cheney had asked Tenet for more information on a report, passed along by one of his OVP aides, that hijacker Mohamed Atta had met with an Iraqi official in Prague. Tenet went back to the CIA and gave the assignment the highest priority. At the next morning's PDB, on September 21, with Cheney listening in via a secure video monitor, the DCI explained to President Bush that the CIA's Prague office was skeptical that such a meeting had taken place. Among other things, credit card and telephone records placed Atta in northern Virginia at the time. Cheney said nothing, but just shook his head.[4]

Tenet also felt increasing pressure from Rumsfeld. The secretary seemed to have sized up the CIA director during their monthly lunches—Tenet would often avoid the talking points prepared by his staff and regale the older man with war stories—as a garrulous and charming pushover. Shortly after 9/11, as part of his military transformation plan, Rumsfeld sent his top intelligence aide, Rich Haver, to ask Tenet if he would sign on to a plan to reorganize the Defense Department's sprawling intelligence divisions by consolidating them under the control of Rumsfeld's office—an unvarnished bid to steal virtually the entire U.S. intelligence community out from under the DCI. Tenet refused, responding mildly that "it looks as if you are trying to do my job," Haver recalled.[5] Rumsfeld soon came back with a scaled-back reorganization plan that Tenet accepted, over the protests of his senior staff. The decision was rendered moot by the postwar intelligence reforms, but it contributed to Tenet's growing reputation among insiders for weakness and inconsistency that became more and more pronounced during the intelligence controversies to come. "George Tenet liked to talk about how he was a tough Greek from Queens, but in reality, he was a pussy. He just wanted people to like him," said one disgruntled former CIA official.[6]

But that was only part of the story. Tenet readily grasped Cheney's view that WMD falling into the hands of terrorists had to be stopped at all costs, and made it the agency's top priority. He moved quickly to assign a top agent to track the movement of nuclear, biological, and chemical weapons and components around the world. Tenet selected Rolf Mowatt-Larssen, a sixteen-year CIA veteran, former army paratrooper, and two-time Moscow station chief, for the job. "You're gonna be wrong sometimes, okay?" Tenet reportedly lectured him when Mowatt-Larssen accepted the job. "You've got to be. You've got to be so far out in front on this WMD issue, calling the shots, spotting potential threats, that you're the one that's wrong—not me, not anybody. . . . Listen, if you're too far out front, and you get picked off when things don't pan out, well, that's the price you have to pay." With the 9/11 disaster obviously on his mind, Tenet added, "You see, all our failures are because we failed to anticipate. Intelligence failures follow a failure of anticipation. They come from only following the information you know and not worrying about what you don't know."[7]

Tenet's forward-leaning, action-oriented instincts sent a strong signal to agency operatives and analysts that war with Iraq was coming—and, perhaps inadvertently, that the office-bound analysts at Langley would have to take a backseat this time to the agency's operational branches and the White House. CIA case officers stationed in Europe were summoned to a conference in Rome in April 2002 that was dominated by the CIA's Iraq Operations Group (IOG), once a bureaucratic backwater that had become a hotbed of pro-war advocates within the agency. Their presentation involved the standard rhetoric about the evils of Saddam that was, as one participant described it, a "pep rally" to build support within the agency for the war. "They said Bush was committed to a change of leadership in Iraq, and that it would start with kinetic energy—meaning bombs. Meaning war," said one officer.[8] Six months later, another meeting was held at the U.S. embassy in London for the CIA's Middle East station chiefs to get the message to holdouts and skeptics that war was coming within months.

It was time to move ahead. The mantra was that the debate was over. Tenet and top management at Langley had read and internalized the signals from the White House. But IOG officials charged that too many regional CIA field officers "were steeped in past practices, unimaginative, uninspiring, and risk-averse" and were unwilling to undertake aggressive covert action and foreign intelligence-gathering on Iraq. Before the meeting was over, talk of sabotage operations to undermine the Iraqi regime—one idea was to blow up a ferry packed with civilians and commercial goods between Dubai and the Iraqi port of Um Qasr—exacerbated a bitter split between Iraq Operations Group and Near East Division officials. Said one former IOG official later, "We kept saying that the President has decided we are going to war, and if you don't like it, quit."[9]

Cheney's August speech in Nashville set off alarms within the CIA. Unlike most vice presidential speeches, it had not been sent to the agency for vetting beforehand, and it was clear that the vice president's office had cut the agency out of a top-level intelligence role. Part of the CIA's problem was that it had few agents on the ground in Iraq. In 2002 the agency had one undercover case officer in country, working as a diplomat in a foreign embassy, but he had no WMD sources. Exile leader Iyad Allawi, who had close ties to Britain's MI6 and would later briefly serve as Iraq's prime minister, was a conduit for Iraqi military sources, but had no direct knowledge of WMD programs. Charlie Allen, a respected veteran in the Directorate of Operations, the covert side of the agency, realized that the current state of Iraqi WMD represented a serious intelligence gap.[10] The Iraq division analysts within the Directorate of Intelligence, keenly aware that there was little hard evidence that Saddam still possessed active WMD programs, much less a reconstituted nuclear weapons program, tended to blame the lack of CIA resources on the ground. Listening to Cheney's speech, Jamie Miscik, then the deputy director of the intelligence directorate, was struck by the vice president's tone of certainty. "He said that Saddam was building his nuclear program," Miscik said later. "Our reaction was, 'Where is he getting that stuff from? Does he have a source of information that we don't know about?' "[11]

The answer was that, in fact, the CIA knew about Cheney's sources—the late Hussein Kamel, Saddam's son-in-law, and other defectors—but the agency had either correctly discounted them as probable fabricators or concluded that their stories did not add up to legitimate evidence that Saddam had restarted his nuclear program.

Inevitably, as the administration's pressure on Tenet and the CIA mounted, analysts and their managers responded by scurrying to revise their assessments of critical intelligence issues. In the winter and spring of 2002, for example, the CIA was initially skeptical of the alleged Iraqi deal to purchase yellowcake uranium from Niger, only to become increasingly supportive of it after Vice President Cheney showed a personal interest. Tenet, however, refused a White House request to include a reference to the Niger sale in the president's October speech in Cincinnati. But he later fell silent on the CIA's handling of the forged Niger documents, and allowed the fraudulent underlying intelligence to appear in the president's State of the Union speech. Yet Tenet was not afraid to give Bush the straight truth. He had reported to the president himself that the CIA doubted Mohamed Atta had met with an Iraqi agent in Prague, and consistently debunked the notion that there were operational ties between Saddam and al-Qaeda. Unlike Feith's intelligence shops, the CIA looked doubtfully upon fresh information from defectors that Saddam had restarted his biological weapons and nuclear programs. Meanwhile, still other CIA analysts issued aggressive assessments to accommodate the public statements of senior officials such as Rice, Cheney, and Bush on Saddam's interest in purchasing aluminum tubes for Iraq's nuclear weapons program and building mobile bioweapons labs.

Not only was the CIA often wildly inconsistent, but it was also usually on the wrong side of almost every issue that Cheney and the White House felt they needed to prosecute a war against Iraq. By September the vice president, often accompanied by Scooter Libby, had made multiple trips to Langley to grill intelligence analysts himself, probing for weaknesses in their arguments. Along with Feith and Wolfowitz, "they were the brow-beaters," said a former defense intelligence official. "In interagency meetings, Wolfowitz treated the analysts' work with contempt."[12] Cheney hammered them with the same questions over and over, often bringing to bear new and unverified information he had received from Feith's Office of Special Plans.

Most analysts took the vice presidential visits in stride. Even so, said a senior CIA official, Cheney and Libby "sent signals, intended or otherwise, that a certain output was desired from here."[13] The vice president did not hesitate to meddle on the operational side either. Besides prodding the CIA to reassess the Niger intelligence reports, Cheney also intervened in a case involving a CIA effort to recruit an Iraqi agent in the Netherlands. Since the Dutch popular opinion was opposed to U.S. plans for war against Iraq, the Dutch intelligence service refused to allow the CIA to recruit on Dutch soil. Cheney took it upon himself to exert his influence with Holland's prime minister—and was rebuffed.[14] Cheney and the OVP also were responsible for pressuring the CIA to breathe new life into year-old reports that Saddam had purchased tens of thousands of high-strength aluminum tubes for use in centrifuges for his nuclear weapons program.

As early as the fall of 2002, the presence of senior White House officials at Langley cross-examining CIA analysts, along with the constant pressure from Feith's operation at the Pentagon, raised concerns within the intelligence community that policymakers were directing analysts to preordained conclusions to bolster the president's war policy. CIA officers briefing Pentagon officials were often sent back to Langley with lists of complaints and demands for new analysis. "There is a lot of unhappiness with the analysis," admitted an intelligence official. "Analysts feel more politicized and more pushed than many of them can ever remember. The guys at the Pentagon shriek on issues such as the link between Iraq and

Al Qaeda. There has been a lot of pressure to write on this constantly, and to not let it drop."[15]

Even soft intelligence queries about whether or not the 9/11 attacks had been greeted with street celebrations in Baghdad were pursued relentlessly. "What became apparent," said Jamie Miscik, "is that some questions kept getting asked over and over and over again . . . as if, somehow, the answer would change, even without any good reason for it to change—like any new information coming in."[16] The constant repetition of the same questions by senior policymakers made it obvious to many analysts what their official interrogators were interested in—mostly WMD programs and links to al-Qaeda that required fresh hard evidence.

Senator Dianne Feinstein of California, a liberal Democratic member of the Senate Intelligence Committee, complained that the Bush administration seemed selective in the intelligence it cited publicly and often overstated its findings. Classified information on Iraq provided to her by the CIA, she noted, "does not track some of the public statements made by senior administration officials. . . . I am concerned about the politicization of intelligence." Others shared her concern. "The intelligence officials are responding to the political leadership, not the other way around, which is how it should be," said Joseph Cirincione, a WMD nonproliferation specialist at the Carnegie Endowment for International Peace. "The politics are driving our intelligence assessments at this point."[17] Tenet, for his part, issued a ringing defense of his boss. "The President of the United States would never tolerate anything other than our most honest judgment," declared Tenet. "Our credibility and integrity are our most precious commodities. We will not let anyone tell us what conclusions to reach."

He defended the right of government officials to ask the CIA hard questions, but categorically denied that agency analysts were caving in to political pressure. "Policymakers, members of Congress and others are free to push us to challenge our assertions and to ask tough, probing questions," said Tenet. "This is healthy. But the notion that we would shape our assessments to please any one of our customers is abhorrent to the ethic by which we work and is simply untrue."[18] But Tenet's efforts to appease his two major constituencies, the White House and Congress, only illustrated the powerful crosscurrents he was attempting to negotiate. At the request of senators Bob Graham and Carl Levin, Tenet sent a letter to the Senate Intelligence Committee in early October declassifying testimony by deputy CIA director John McLaughlin that Saddam was not likely to use WMD against the United States or join forces with terrorists unless he was attacked. Only days afterward, Bush declared on October 7 that the danger posed by Iraq "is already significant, and only grows worse with time."

Tenet added that the CIA's "understanding of the relationship between Iraq and al Qaeda is evolving and is based on sources of varying reliability." There had been reporting, the letter said, that Saddam had trained foreign Arab terrorists in bombmaking and the use of toxic chemical gases at Salman Pak—a reference to al-Libi's charges that were under serious debate in the intelligence community. But in the Cincinnati speech, President Bush stated unambiguously that "We've learned that Iraq has trained Al Qaeda members in bomb making and poisons and deadly gases."[19] Tenet responded to ensuing protests from legislators about the discrepancy by weakly insisting that there was no "inconsistency" between the White House and CIA positions. Stating the obvious, a congressional aide remarked that the CIA director was "in a bad position. He's under fire from the [Senate and House] committees. Then he's under fire from the White House."[20]

That left CIA analysts exposed to the crossfire. "George knows he's being beaten up. And his analysts are terrified," said a former agency official later. "George used to protect his people, but he's been forced to do things *their* way." Now that the analysts are on the defensive, the official went on, "they write reports justifying their intelligence rather than saying what's going on. The Defense Department and the Office of the Vice President write their own pieces, based on their own ideology. We collect so much stuff that you can find anything you want."[21] Another former CIA veteran just shook his head at the arrogance of Feith and his OSP staff. "They see themselves as outsiders," he said. "There's a high degree of paranoia. They've convinced themselves that they're on the side of angels, and everybody else in the government is a fool."[22] By then, Tenet realized that the intelligence game had shifted. What mattered was no longer whether the intelligence on the Niger uranium deal or the aluminum tubes was true or false. The only question was whether there was any intelligence out there that could embarrass senior Bush officials by disproving their public statements.

On August 1 the CIA had published a new intelligence report, entitled *Iraq: Expanding WMD Facilities Pose Growing Threat,* defending in detail its old assessment that Saddam Hussein had purchased high-strength aluminum tubes from the Chinese to enrich uranium for his reconstituted nuclear weapons program. This may have been the trigger for Bush's decision in mid-August for Cheney to go public with charges that Saddam's nuclear program was up and running. In September the Pentagon also weighed in when the DIA produced its own report, *Iraq's Reemerging Nuclear Weapons Program,* concluding that the specifications of the aluminum tubes "are consistent with late-1980s Iraqi gas centrifuge designs." Within weeks, the same analysts at the CIA's Center for Weapons Intelligence, Nonproliferation, and Arms Control, who had already produced fourteen assessments of the tubes, produced "an even more extensive analysis," called *Iraq's Hunt for Aluminum Tubes: Evidence of a Renewed Uranium Enrichment Program,* which discussed Iraqi attempts to hide its procurement efforts and reported that "the tubes 'matched' known centrifuge rotor dimensions." The new CIA report also included a sidebar, summarizing the conclusion of the army's authoritative National Ground Intelligence Center, that the tubes were probably not intended for a conventional rocket program.[23]

These reports, though timely, were hardly new. The new August and September CIA assessments were in fact the fourteenth and fifteenth analyses produced by WINPAC and were based on raw intelligence almost eighteen months old. Cheney himself had first read earlier versions of the same CIA reports about the aluminum tubes six months earlier. The CIA assessments came into his hands as a result of meetings he held during the winter of 2002 with intelligence analysts. Cheney and his aides probed for fresh information on Saddam's WMD and Iraqi links to terror organizations in an effort to smoke out useful intelligence they heard from unnamed analysts about classified reports that Saddam recently had purchased thousands of high-strength aluminum tubes for use in enriching weapons-grade uranium.[24] For Cheney, this was the mother lode: proof that Saddam had restarted his nuclear weapons program.

After repeated requests from the OVP for copies of the classified material, the CIA sent two earlier classified WINPAC assessments on the aluminum tubes to the vice president on March 12, when Cheney was on his swing through the Middle East. Neither report mentioned that the original April 2001 assessment had been strongly disputed by the Department of Energy, or that the clash of views had kicked up a raging, year-long controversy within the intelligence community.[25] Since then, the multiple classified CIA assessments of the aluminum tubes shipments, all based on the same underlying intelligence, had been routed directly to senior policymakers, including the president. Most were not circulated to analysts at other intelligence agencies, and none included mention of any disagreement with DOE about the uses of the tubes.[26]

Even with the barrage of "new" intelligence, senior administration officials—among them Deputy Secretary of Defense Wolfowitz, an architect of the secret Pentagon intelligence operations—were well aware of the potentially crippling dispute about the tubes within the intelligence community. An unnamed senior Bush official who received a half-dozen briefings from WINPAC on the aluminum tubes later said he had known about the debate over their use since late 2001. CIA officials confirmed that WINPAC had briefed senior NSC officials about the internal intelligence battle as early as October 2001, and a DOE spokesperson said the agency "strongly conveyed its viewpoint to senior policy makers."

Ranking senior officials, however, professed ignorance of any problem. Tenet insisted that he first heard about the tubes controversy in September 2002. A spokesman for Cheney claimed the vice president didn't know about the internal debate within the intelligence community until the 2002 National Intelligence Estimate was published on October 1. President Bush was reportedly also unaware of the dispute until after the NIE. The notion that Cheney, a meticulous and aggressive investigator, could have been in the dark about the DOE's view that the tubes were intended for battlefield rockets strains credulity. By July 2002 the infighting over the aluminum tubes was widely known even among foreign intelligence officials. The Australian government knew during the summer that "U.S. agencies differ on whether aluminum tubes, a dual-use item sought by Iraq, were meant for gas centrifuges."[27]

In early September, Wolfowitz reportedly summoned Francis Brooke, Chalabi's right-hand man in Washington, and the Iraqi defector and nuclear scientist, Khidir Hamza, to a secret meeting at the Pentagon. Wolfowitz wanted to pin down once and for all the veracity of CIA assessments that Iraq's bulk purchases of aluminum tubes in early 2001 were intended for Saddam's nuclear centrifuge program.[28] Hamza's book, *Saddam's Bombmaker*, published in 2000, was enjoying a sudden surge of U.S. sales. Brooke and the INC were busily promoting the book. Hamza, who had for a time headed up Iraqi efforts to build a nuclear device, had chosen the moment to deliver warnings about Saddam's nuclear program. On August 30, he testified before the Senate Foreign Relations Committee that Iraq had "more than 10 tons of uranium and one ton of slightly enriched uranium . . . in its possession," which would be "enough to generate the needed bomb-grade uranium for three nuclear weapons by 2005."[29] By then Hamza had been declared an unreliable source by the

IAEA, and discredited by his former colleague and coauthor David Albright, the director of Washington's Institute for Science and International Security, where Hamza worked between 1997 and 1999. "Hamza had some good information about Iraqi nuclear programs until his departure from Iraq, but that's it," said Albright. "He went off the edge. He started saying irresponsible things."[30]

Hamza was still influential among the neoconservative network within the Bush administration, however. His book was taken by many as dramatic evidence of Saddam's nuclear intentions. Iraqi scientists had experimented with electromagnetic isotope separation and gas diffusion centrifuges during Saddam's crash program in 1990 and 1991, and built perhaps a dozen prototypes. All but one flew apart when their rotors snapped under the stress of high-speed tests. None produced enriched uranium. Dr. Mahdi Obeidi, who ran the program, wrote a book describing how he buried centrifuge blueprints and prototype parts under a rosebush in his Baghdad garden when the program was shut down. Hamza had no background in centrifuge technology and was not involved in Obeidi's program. He nonetheless assured Wolfowitz that Saddam was actively pursuing a centrifuge enrichment program and that the aluminum tubes could be adapted for use as centrifuge rotors. Wolfowitz circulated the news promptly to his political allies at the NSC and the White House.[31]

Days later, the explosive September 8 scoop by Judith Miller and Michael Gordon appeared on the front page of the Sunday *New York Times*, detailing for the first time the story of Saddam's aluminum tubes and his restarted Iraqi nuclear weapons program. The story did not mention the sharp dissension of DOE or State Department analysts over the tubes.

Far from being the "indisputable evidence" Cheney would claim, the aluminum tubes intelligence was badly distorted by WINPAC analysts, who were well aware that their bosses and White House policymakers wanted them to produce information that would be useful in selling the war. Tenet himself may have encouraged the young WINPAC analyst who took the lead in pressing the view that the tubes were meant for centrifuge rotors. During a meeting of analysts chaired by Tenet in September 2002,[32] the CIA's deputy director, John McLaughlin, reportedly told the gathering that he'd heard that DOE analysts did not think the aluminum tubes could be used for Saddam's nuclear program. "And this young analyst from WINPAC, who didn't look older than twenty-five, says, no, that's bullshit, there is only one use for them. And Tenet says, 'Yeah? Great,'" recalled a former agency official who was present. "So you had people sprinkled throughout the organization who felt like they could go right to the top, and no one was there to contradict them."[33]

The young WINPAC analyst in the meeting with Tenet was at first identified only as "Joe" or "Joe T." Unlike most post–Cold War analysts, he could claim hands-on experience with modern gas diffusion uranium enrichment centrifuges. Joe Turner received his bachelor's degree from the University of Kentucky in mechanical engineering in the late 1970s and went to work for the Goodyear Atomic Corporation. Goodyear assigned him to the federal research complex at Oak Ridge, Tennessee, where he worked until 1985 learning to test and operate a variety of uranium enrichment centrifuges, then spent a decade analyzing the hazards of nuclear reactors, gaseous diffusion plants, and oil refineries. In 1997 he was transferred to Oak Ridge's Y-12 national security complex and joined the WINPAC in 1999.[34] Turner authored the original CIA report, five months before the 9/11 terrorist attacks, that Saddam had purchased sixty thousand high-strength aluminum tubes from the Chinese and declared that they were designed for centrifuges that "have little use other than for a uranium enrichment program."

Turner and his WINPAC colleagues immediately recognized that the Chinese tubes were constructed out of 7075-T6 aluminum, a very hard alloy able to withstand the tremendous speeds required of rotors in uranium enrichment centrifuges, and was therefore off-limits to Iraq in certain sizes under international nonproliferation rules. The CIA analysts correctly recognized that the tubes might be a proscribed product, and therefore intended for uranium centrifuges. The problem was that the sixty thousand tubes were each 990 millimeters in length, had a diameter of 81 millimeters and walls 3.3 millimeters thick. DOE countered that not only were the tubes too heavy, too narrow, and too long for use as rotors, but also that they perfectly matched high-strength aluminum tubes that Iraq had used for years to make combustion chambers for its Nasser 81 tactical rockets. The Nasser was a reverse-engineered copy of the Italian Medusa ground-launched rocket fired from pod launchers. DOE noted that in 1996 IAEA inspectors examined similar tubes at Baghdad's Nasser fabrication plant where the rockets were built. The high-strength rocket tubes were precisely the same size as those in the new shipment to Iraq.

The WINPAC analysts objected to the DOE assessment by arguing that using tubes for rockets engineered to such fine tolerances made little sense. They declared that the dimensions of the tubes were "similar" to Iraq's prewar Beams gas centrifuge design and "nearly matched" those in a centrifuge designed in the 1950s by German scientist Gernot Zippe, a design publicly available to the Iraqis in scientific journals. Iraq had pursued the Beam centrifuge before the Gulf War, they said, and the design called for aluminum rotors with a wall thickness in excess of 3 millimeters. Based on unclassified documents, they said that the Zippe design could use rotors with wall thickness of between 1 millimeter and 2.8 millimeters. The new tubes might not be ideal, the CIA analysts concluded, but Iraq had successfully built centrifuges before from the old designs using aluminum rotors and could build them again.

Joe Turner and his group, however, left one critical stone unturned. They did not make the effort to contact Dr. Zippe himself about the details of his design. DOE analysts did manage to track down the eighty-four-year old Zippe, who told them that the wall thickness of the aluminum rotors in his centrifuge was a maximum of 1.1 millimeters—far from the 3.3 millimeters of the Iraqi tubes in question. They also pointed out that Beams himself had never been able to successfully enrich uranium with his centrifuge design beyond the pilot plant stage, so any design similarities were irrelevant.

Both the 2004 Senate Intelligence Committee and the 2005 Robb-Silberman WMD Commission reports concluded that the DOE had the stronger argument on the intended use of Saddam's high-strength aluminum tubes—and concluded they were indeed purchased to build conventional battlefield rockets. The DOE case was confirmed in December 2002 by UNMOVIC arms inspectors three months before the war started. They found no traces of a secret nuclear centrifuge program. But in a visit to the Nasser metal fabrication factory in Baghdad, the inspectors found thirteen thousand finished rockets made from 7075-T6 aluminum tubes and were told by Iraqi engineers that they were seeking more since supplies were low. Iraqi plant officials explained that the finer tolerances of the tubes provided the rockets greater reliability and accuracy. How was it, then, that in the final WINPAC report and successive DIA assessments of the army's National Ground Intelligence Center (NGIC) in Virginia, the authoritative Pentagon voice on foreign tactical arms, unaccountably concluded that the aluminum tubes were not for rocket casings? NGIC analysts consistently assessed that the wall thickness of the Iraqi tubes and their length were "excessive for rocket motor bodies and rocket launch tubes" and were "highly unlikely" to be used for rockets.[35]

Two NGIC rocket analysts later told Senate Intelligence Committee investigators they did not know the dimensions of Iraq's Nasser 81 rockets at the time, and did not have access to DOE reports or the 1996 IAEA information on Iraqi rockets. CIA analysts, for their part, explained to committee staff that they had failed to gather the data on Iraqi rockets because they assumed the information was unnecessary—since the CIA had already judged the tubes were intended for use in centrifuges. This astonishing explanation was "a textbook example of an agency prematurely closing off an avenue of investigation because of its confidence in its conclusions," declared the WMD commission report.[36] The Senate Intelligence Committee and the Robb-Silberman commission slapped the NGIC on the wrist for a "serious lapse in tradecraft." But both probes left it there, and looked no further for accountability. Neither the Senate committee nor the presidential commission considered it within their purview to determine whether such serious and obvious lapses of intelligence were a result of pressure or manipulation by senior administration officials in the Pentagon, the CIA, or the White House.

After all the alarming rhetoric from Cheney in August about Saddam's nuclear threat, Senator Bob Graham of Florida, then the veteran Democratic chairman of the Senate Intelligence Committee, asked Tenet during a closed hearing on September 5 for the CIA director's formal, comprehensive intelligence estimate on Iraq. Tenet and the other intelligence officials present looked back at him with blank stares, Graham recalled. The White House had not asked for a formal estimate, Tenet informed the committee, and none had been prepared.[37] Graham and other committee members were stunned. Known in the spy trade and among national security professionals as National Intelligence Estimates, or NIEs, the laboriously produced documents, often running to hundreds of pages, represented the best collaborative judgment of the sixteen-agency U.S. intelligence community on serious questions of foreign policy. They are considered "the most authoritative written means by which the director of Central Intelligence conveys to the President and other senior leaders the judgments of the entire Intelligence Community regarding national security issues."[38] The process had been honed over the three decades since the intelligence reforms of the 1970s, and could take as long as several months to prepare. The documents were designed to provide policymakers in both the legislative and executive branches of government with the "best, unvarnished and unbiased information—regardless of whether analytic judgments conform to U.S. policy."

Yet the Bush White House had not asked for an NIE on Iraq, a pressing issue of war and peace. "I could not believe that the administration was about to take us to war without the best information by which to judge that war's necessity," Graham wrote later. "It seemed clear to me that the President and his national security advisors . . . had made up their minds to go to war and didn't want to take the chance that additional acts might show that decision to be flawed, raise questions about the credibility of their claims or otherwise put their agenda in doubt."[39] Tenet told the nonplussed committee members at the hearing—who included Democrats Carl Levin of Michigan and Richard Durbin of Illinois—that the intelligence community was too busy to produce a full NIE that assessed Iraqi military capabilities, the strategic consequences of attacking Iraq, and the conditions of a post-invasion occupation. It could, however, prepare one on the narrower subject of Iraq's WMD, the administration's primary rationale for going to war. Bob Graham and other committee members, frustrated by Tenet's "dismissive attitude," objected that the narrower focus "was not what we thought was needed." Tenet stood his ground, confident that he had the backing of the White House. The Senate panel members quickly understood that Tenet's offer was all they were going to get.

It was almost three weeks before Tenet responded to the senators' request—and a tumultuous time for the White House. The president was poised to meet with Tony Blair about war policy and was closeted with senior advisers preparing for his major address on Iraq at the UN General Assembly scheduled for the following week. War talk was in the air. On Sunday, September 8, the aluminum tubes story by Judith Miller and Michael Gordon broke on the front page of *The New York Times*. Well-prepared senior Bush officials fanned out to Washington's Sunday morning political talk shows, squeezing valuable mileage out of the anti-Saddam PR bonanza. On NBC's *Meet the Press*, after noting the *Times* story, Cheney declared flatly, "Increasingly, we believe the United States will become the target" of an Iraqi nuclear weapon. "There will always be some uncertainty about how quickly he can acquire nuclear weapons," Condoleezza Rice said ominously on *CNN Late Edition*, "but we don't want the smoking gun to be a mushroom cloud." Secretary of Defense Rumsfeld, appearing on CBS's *Face the Nation*, took the highest marks for vivid imagery. "Imagine a September 11th with weapons of mass destruction," he intoned, that would kill "tens of thousands of innocent men, women and children."

On Monday, Senator Durbin fired off a letter to Tenet formally requesting that the DCI order up an NIE on Iraq's WMD programs, and suggesting that he also produce an unclassified version of the document so that "the American public can better understand this important issue." Durbin's request, intended or not, effectively put Congress on record supporting a CIA effort to produce a declassified version of the NIE for political purposes, thus playing into the hands of those senior officials now focused on making the case for war. In the following days, however, Tenet did not respond to Durbin's request.

Senator Graham had reason to believe the White House wasn't interested in an NIE on Iraq. Back on July 22, he had sent his first request for an NIE on U.S. covert action in Iraq—which risked exposing the CIA's clandestine prewar operations in the country—that would include an assessment of Iraq's WMD programs. The Senate committee was informed verbally by the CIA at the time that covert activity was not an appropriate subject for an NIE, and that none would be forthcoming.[40] As Graham suspected, Cheney and other top White House officials were so concerned about the quality of U.S. intelligence on Saddam's WMD that they wanted to avoid an NIE on Iraq altogether. The president's advisers, said a senior intelligence official, knew "there were disagreements over details in almost every aspect of the administration's case against Iraq" and did not want an NIE with "a lot of footnotes and disclaimers."[41]

On September 10, Graham sent a second letter asking Tenet for an NIE on Iraq's WMD, attempting again to broaden its scope to include "the status of Iraqi military forces . . . ; the effects a U.S.-led attack would have on its neighbors; and Saddam Hussein's likely response to a U.S. military campaign designed to effect regime change in Iraq." Three days later, Senator Dianne Feinstein added her voice to Durbin's and Graham's calls for a new NIE on Iraq, noting that "such an estimate is vital to Congressional decision making, and most specifically, any resolution that may come before the Senate."[42] The reference was to a joint congressional resolution the White House had requested only weeks before that would allow the president to use armed force against Iraq. The usual lengthy production of an NIE could only forestall the vote for a war resolution.

Finally, on September 17, Senator Levin, then chairman of the Senate Armed Services Committee as well as a member of the intelligence committee, wrote a fourth letter to Tenet saying that an NIE on Iraq was "imperative." Almost two weeks had passed since Senator Graham had sent his second request for an updated NIE. In hearings of the Senate Intelligence Committee the same day, Republican Richard Lugar of Indiana remarked to Tenet that no NIE had been produced on Iraq and that President Bush therefore did not have the benefit of the intelligence community's work. The DCI replied defensively that the intelligence community had prepared several NIEs on the international ballistic missile threat—one of them authored in 1979 by Donald Rumsfeld, a detail that went unmentioned—and all had included accounts of Iraq's WMD programs. The CIA director added tersely that he kept President Bush up to date on a daily basis. "I see the President every morning, six days a week," huffed Tenet. "He gets the intelligence I provide."[43] Tenet made no mention that a new NIE might be in the works.

Tenet not only was getting squeezed hard by the Pentagon neoconservatives led by Douglas Feith, but he was now also being forced into a corner by increasingly irritated and skeptical Democratic congressional leaders. When Tenet actually gave the order to prepare the NIE on Iraq is in dispute. The DCI did not formally reply to Graham and the intelligence committee until September 25, when he reiterated his position ruling out covert actions and added that he had "directed the preparation of a new NIE on Iraq's weapons of mass destruction" in response to Senator Durbin's letter of September 9.[44] But on October 2, the day after it was published, a top intelligence official said he had been directed by Tenet to get started on September 11, the day after Tenet received Graham's letter. The successive letters from Feinstein and Levin, and Tenet's testimony in response to Lugar's questioning, however, suggested it wasn't until at least a week later. The October 1 deadline, according to the Republican-controlled 2004 Senate Intelligence Committee report, was negotiated by the CIA and the Senate committee, presumably to accommodate a timely congressional vote on a joint war resolution—though neither side could produce any documentation to prove it. Either way, the 2002 NIE was produced with lightning speed in two to three weeks, and became the shifting, unsteady foundation of virtually every critical decision the Bush administration made between October and the beginning of the war the next March.

Publication of the NIE marked a point of no return for Tenet. Too many powerful players, Cheney and the president foremost among them, had made clear their interest in the analysis and distribution of U.S. intelligence on Iraq's WMD capabilities—and they were whipsawing Tenet and the CIA in several different directions. He had boxed himself in. Tenet could neither reveal the unvarnished truth about what little the CIA knew about WMD without threatening his own standing at the White House, nor could he entirely falsify it, with a restive agency and Graham and the Senate Intelligence Committee breathing down his neck.

16

FIXING THE FACTS AROUND THE POLICY

The 2002 NIE distinguished itself by being wrong, unfounded, or exaggerated in virtually all of its major findings, a testament not only to the haste with which it was produced, but also to the mounting political pressure on the CIA and other spy agencies from the White House and the Pentagon. *The New York Times* called the ninety-three-page report one of the "most flawed documents in the history of American intelligence." The magnitude of the intelligence failure represented by the NIE on Iraqi WMD was too far-reaching to be explained by a sudden lapse in analytical tradecraft. Nor was it simply that mounting political pressure opened up fundamental weaknesses in the foundations of the spy business that created wholesale distortions of ethical and analytical standards—and resulted in intelligence that did not even come close to matching the reality on the ground. In fact, some of the major spy agencies delivered accurate intelligence throughout the prewar period, while others swung back and forth wildly between the extremes of reliable judgment and politically expedient misinformation. Still others quietly fell into a troubled lockstep with the White House and the Pentagon.

Congressional oversight and presidential commission reports have provided repeated assurances that Bush policymakers did not interfere with or politicize intelligence analysis that went into the NIE. By formal definition, that would have meant demonstrating that White House officials had physically coerced, bribed, or browbeat intelligence analysts into changing their judgments against their will. Such draconian tactics, though near impossible to prove, were hardly necessary. The real question was how intelligence was gathered, analyzed, and used by the Bush administration to further its war aims—a subject that remains officially unexamined.

"It has become clear," wrote Paul Pillar, who oversaw all the CIA's intelligence reporting on Iraq between 2000 and 2005, "that official intelligence analysis was not relied on in making even the most significant national security decisions, that intelligence was misused publicly to justify decisions already made . . . and that the intelligence community's own work was politicized."[1] In Pillar's view, the Bush administration turned the normal standard that guided the intelligence community on its head. Instead of using professional intelligence analysis as the foundation of sound policy, the president's war policy relied upon renegade intelligence-gathering—quite literally in the case of Chalabi's INC reporting and Feith's Pentagon domain. Otherwise, the White House and Pentagon seemed to use only precooked or selective intelligence from the CIA and other agencies to justify the war effort.

This was no abstraction. The intelligence community in general and the CIA in particular, Pillar felt, were constantly "pulled over the line" by the administration into a conspicuous role making the public case for war. There were some overt examples of politicization. The most obvious was Colin Powell's famous speech before the UN Security Council on February 5, 2003, when Tenet, seated behind Powell and representing the intelligence community, was a constant presence in the televised effort to sell the Iraq War to the United Nations and the American people. Another lower-profile but equally compromising example was the white paper on WMD that Pillar himself prepared at the request of the White House and later became the unclassified October NIE. Finally, the attempts by Doug Feith and his Pentagon lieutenants at the Office of Special Plans to lobby Tenet and the CIA in August of 2002 with their findings on Mohamed Atta's activities in Prague were unambiguous efforts by policymakers to muscle the intelligence community.

Other instances of political pressure were less visible. Even the still-unexamined charge that the Bush White House bullied the CIA and other agencies does not fully explain some of the distorted and unfounded assessments contained in the October NIE. It was as if a culture of petty deception and ultra-partisan disregard for facts had taken over the process. Time after time, key judgments contradicted readily available information that eventually would discredit or discount them, as in the case of the army's mystifying insistence that the aluminum tubes could not be used for artillery rockets, when the evidence was clear that that was precisely how they were used. These were not the result of garden-variety deceits and distortions involved in tactics like "layering," in which serious caveats and nuances mysteriously disappeared from successively simplified intelligence reports—though these techniques were used. Nor were the distortions attributable merely to interagency rivalry, in which contrary evidence or sources were ignored in favor of in-house alternatives; or to substandard tradecraft, in which intelligence was based on gossamer shreds of probability that defied both credulity and common sense, as in the CIA's assessment of the alleged Niger yellowcake deal.

What made the NIE one of the "most flawed documents in the history of American intelligence" was part of a larger, more troubling pattern that spread like a virus though the intelligence community during the autumn of 2002. This involved the conscious acts of officials—unexplained bureaucratic manipulation, mysteriously misplaced documents, and forgotten facts as well as outright deception. Such tactics were used either to create an aura of legitimacy around Iraqi WMD intelligence where none existed, or to undermine and discredit intelligence that was legitimate. DOE analysts, for example, strongly dissented from the CIA and DIA position that the aluminum tubes were purchased for an Iraqi centrifuge program to enrich weapons-grade uranium. Yet in hurried NIE review meetings, DOE management inexplicably contradicted its own analysts' position to support and legitimize the administration's arguments by declaring that Baghdad was reconstituting its nuclear weapons program. Similarly, despite forceful arguments from U.S. Air Force analysts that Iraq did not have the technology to develop sophisticated unmanned aerial vehicles (UAVs), the CIA unilaterally asserted that Baghdad was capable of operating pilotless aircraft capable of delivering biological weapons to targets in the United States. The CIA assessment undercut the air force argument and was prominently adopted in the NIE.

In an even more neck-wrenching bait-and-switch operation, the ill-fated white paper on WMD that the White House had ordered the CIA to produce in May was rewritten and recycled in October by the DCI's office as the declassified version of the NIE. On October 2, Senator Bob Graham had requested a declassified version of the full NIE, which was made available only to select leaders of House and Senate intelligence and armed services committees the day before. To Graham's amazement, a polished, twenty-eight-page unclassified summary of the NIE, slickly produced with sophisticated graphics—including satellite images of missile test sites, maps showing targeting distances and 550 Iraqi weapons facilities—appeared two days later. In almost every instance its key judgments for public consumption—the only elements lifted from the NIE and grafted onto the declassified version—were stronger than the actual findings and text of the classified document and appeared to be tailored to the priorities of the Bush White House. "It was, in short, a vivid and terrifying case for war," Graham later wrote. "The problem was that it did not accurately represent the classified NIE we had received just days earlier."[2]

Both versions of the NIE—one classified, the other for public consumption—echoed, virtually point by point, a litany of terrors consistent with Cheney's public statements on Saddam's WMD in August. "Iraq has continued its weapons of mass destruction (WMD) programs in defiance of UN resolutions and restriction," the NIE began, introducing the administration's primary theme. The documents further asserted that "since inspections ended in 1998, Iraq has maintained its chemical weapons effort, energized its missile program, and invested more heavily in chemical weapons," all of which eventually proved false. Then came the nub of the argument. "Most analysts assess Iraq is reconstituting its nuclear weapons program. If Baghdad acquires sufficient weapons-grade fissile material from abroad, it could make a nuclear weapon within a year."[3] None of this bore any relation to observable reality. Even the fearsome, if highly speculative, prospect that Baghdad might have a nuclear weapon in a year depended on an array of unspoken and far-fetched assumptions—that the nuclear program was in fact up and running, that Iraqi scientists could miniaturize a crude nuclear device to fit a missile warhead or could buy uranium or plutonium on world markets, despite eleven years of economic sanctions.

In theory, a crude Iraqi nuke was a possibility. But the odds were strongly against it. The truth was, as Pillar suggested, it probably didn't matter. What did matter was the information in the deceptively simple sentence, "Most analysts assess Iraq is reconstituting its weapons program." Yet even as a marker of U.S. intelligence community thinking, the sentence was not true. Despite the pressure-cooker political atmosphere, intelligence analysts at the major agencies were divided about reconstitution.

Both State Department and DOE analysts rejected the view that Saddam had a centrifuge program or had restarted Iraq's nuclear weapons program, and were not afraid to say so. That meant two critical agencies would offset the more hawkish CIA and the DIA on the question of Iraq's nuclear capabilities. The National Intelligence Council, which was responsible for producing the NIE and reported directly to George Tenet, had a serious problem. The split was a formula for an ambivalent and watered-down final estimate on the critical issue of Saddam's nuclear arsenal—just what the White House had previously rejected.

Tenet's NIE was, in essence, an exercise in building and dispensing evidence that would make the strongest possible rationale for war. The task before the Intelligence Council was to coordinate the analysis of multiple government agencies, each subject to the same kind of bureaucratic infighting, strong-arm tactics, and manipulation at which senior members of the Bush administration excelled. In this bureaucratic arena, the simplest way to redress the split over reconstitution was by sleight of hand. Days after the classified NIE text was made available to Congress—which reportedly few legislators read—a strongly worded "alternative view" by State Department analysts disputing the prevailing assessment was quietly and unaccountably dropped from the unclassified (i.e., public) version. "Lacking persuasive evidence that Baghdad has launched a coherent effort to reconstitute its nuclear weapons program," it had read, "INR is unwilling to speculate that such an effort began soon after the departure of UN inspectors or to project a timeline for the completion of activities it does not now see happening. As a result, INR is unable to predict when Iraq could acquire a nuclear device or weapon."[4] The two sentences were gone.

From Tenet's perspective, State was a lost cause anyway. The real problem was with the Department of Energy analysts, the nuclear experts who had firmly rejected the prospect that Saddam was building a cascade of thousands of centrifuges to enrich weapons-grade uranium. DOE, effectively the swing vote on the issue, unaccountably fell into line with the majority on the reconstitution of Iraq's nuclear weapons program during a late September meeting of the National Intelligence Council, which reviewed all the analysis that went into the NIE. Tenet chaired the meeting, the proceedings of which were classified. There has been no official investigation into precisely what happened in the rushed, marathon coordinating session. But during the meeting, the acting director of DOE's Office of Intelligence, Thomas S. Ryder, reportedly declared that although the Energy

Department dissented on the aluminum tubes question and the existence of an Iraqi centrifuge program, it supported other intelligence agencies that concluded that Iraq was actively rebuilding its nuclear arsenal. A DOE analyst who attended the meeting later explained, "DOE didn't want to come out before the war and say [Iraq] wasn't reconstituting."[5]

The contradictory DOE position was reportedly the handiwork of Ryder, a human resources manager with little intelligence experience and close ties to energy secretary Spencer Abraham. Ryder had been acting chief of intelligence for five months. "Ryder is not an intelligence guy by any stretch of the imagination," an unnamed DOE source later told a reporter. "He had no intel background whatsoever. He worked on all the personnel stuff—paperwork for promotions, hiring contractors, stuff like that."[6] Senior DOE scientists and lab officials who did not believe that Saddam had restarted his nuclear program were stunned by Ryder's position. Some blamed the rushed NIE process and Ryder's inexperience. One senior official described Ryder as "a heck of a nice guy but not savvy on technical issues."[7] Others felt he was not up to arguing the technical merits of the case made by DOE's nuclear-weapons researchers against the administration's position. "Time comes for the Iraq NIE, and instead of being hard-charging and proactive and pulling everybody together, he just didn't know what to do," said one critic. "He wasn't a strong advocate. He just didn't have the background."[8]

The DOE position carved out by Ryder "made sense politically but not substantively," a former senior intelligence officer commented later.[9] Ryder's assessment leaned heavily on factually mistaken reports that pre–Gulf War technical personnel now worked in a Baghdad magnet production facility for centrifuges, and that a certain Iraqi front company was trying to procure balancing machines for a centrifuge program. DOE analysts admitted that there was no evidence the magnets were intended for a nuclear program, nor that Iraq had actually received the balancing machines.[10] Ryder also drew on earlier DOE intelligence assessments, including one from July 2002 entitled *Nuclear Reconstitution Efforts Underway?*, a recycled report about Iraqi attempts to buy yellowcake from Niger—another alleged deal that was detailed in the NIE. Armed with the shaky Niger evidence, Ryder made his case that Saddam was reconstituting a nuclear weapons program—despite the absence of a centrifuge program that would have been the only conceivable justification for an Iraqi purchase of Nigerien yellowcake.

DOE thus joined the CIA and DIA on the issue, enabling the drafters of the NIE to note parenthetically, "DOE agrees that reconstitution of the nuclear program is under way, but assesses that the tubes probably are not part of the program."[11] That in turn allowed the NIE drafters to write, "*Most agencies* [emphasis added] assess that Baghdad started reconstituting its nuclear program about the time that UNSCOM inspectors departed—December 1998." The reaction to DOE's new posture among experts inside and outside of government was disbelief. "It surprised me that they would agree to a statement that there's a nuclear weapons program being reconstituted, and then undercut the aluminum tube allegation," said David Albright, the former weapons inspector and head of Washington's Institute for Science and International Security. Albright spoke with senior researchers at DOE's nuclear weapons labs, who had been barred from talking to the press in mid-September by the department. "When I talked to some of the scientists at the labs, there was just this reaction of: 'We just don't believe there's a nuclear weapons program,'" said Albright.

"I thought . . . there must be some other tubes that people were talking about," said Houston Wood, a former DOE consultant and expert on centrifuge enrichment, who had concluded in 2001 that the tubes were too thick and heavy to work. "I just was flabbergasted that people were still pushing that those might be centrifuges. Science was not pushing this forward. Scientists had made their determination, their evaluation, and now we didn't know what was happening."[12]

Without naming Ryder, the Robb-Silberman Commission report (released March 29, 2005) concluded that DOE's position on Iraqi nuclear reconstitution was doubtful on its face, pointing out that the "gossamer nature of the evidence relied upon . . . combined with the later-recalled reporting regarding uranium from Africa . . . had led senior officials in other agencies to question the substantive coherence of DOE's position."

While the commission professed to find "no evidence of 'politicization'" in the production of the NIE, it conceded that "there is no doubt that analysts operated in an environment shaped by intense policymaker interest in Iraq."[13] On Energy's reconstitution flip-flop, the commission reported that "DOE analysts who participated in the NIE coordination meeting stated that there was no political pressure on DOE, direct or indirect, to agree with the NIE's conclusion that Iraq was 'reconstituting' its nuclear program." The report confirmed that senior Energy Department officials felt it could not do otherwise before the war. At the very least that seemed to establish that senior intelligence officials were pushing for a "conclusion" before the NIE was written—and that Ryder and his DOE bosses knew it. The commission failed to consider that the DOE position Ryder awkwardly cobbled together was just what Tenet and the White House needed.

On October 7, 2002, six days after copies of the finished NIE became available for members of Congress at the offices of the House and Senate intelligence committees, President Bush stood at the rostrum at Cincinnati Museum Center and described another chilling threat that Baghdad was preparing to mount against the United States. After cataloguing Saddam's stores of deadly anthrax, poison VX gas, and newly rebuilt weapons production facilities, the president gravely pronounced, "We've also discovered through intelligence that Iraq has a growing fleet of manned and unmanned aerial vehicles that could be used to disperse chemical or biological weapons across broad areas." Bush told the hushed crowd that his administration was now "concerned that Iraq is exploring ways of using these UAVs for missions targeting the United States." That nugget of classified intelligence, although based on a highly speculative reading of threadbare and unconfirmed information, nonetheless allowed President Bush to make an explosive and unprecedented connection: Saddam's deadly reach, like al-Qaeda's on 9/11, might well extend to the American homeland itself.

The information was lifted directly from the NIE. Besides Saddam's nuclear weapons program, the most threatening single finding of the NIE for Americans and Britons—even to those otherwise skeptical about linkage between Iraq and al-Qaeda—was that Saddam was developing pilotless aerial drones, or UAVs, "probably intended to deliver biological warfare agent" that could be programmed to reach targets in Western Europe and the United States. "Baghdad's UAVs could threaten Iraq's neighbors, U.S. forces in the Persian Gulf, and if brought close to, or into, the United States, the United States Homeland," declared the NIE. The Iraqis, the document explained, have "attempted to procure commercially available route planning software and an associated topographic database that would be able to support targeting of the United States."

Upon scrutiny, however, there was less to the Iraqi UAV threat than met the eye. Like most of the overblown intelligence produced at the prodding of policymakers by Tenet's gung ho WINPAC group, the CIA assessment was based on a real pre–Gulf War Iraqi program to convert French-made F-1 Mirage fighters and Soviet MiG-21 jet aircraft into manned and unmanned drones to deliver chemical and biological weapons.[14] But the early UAV program, which had experimented with agricultural spraying systems to disperse the bioweapons, was shut down after the 1991 war. UNSCOM inspectors later created a stir when they found eleven small UAVs at the Salman Pak facility. In the mid-1990s, the Iraqis began testing a modified 1960s-vintage Czech L-29 jet trainer for use as a UAV, but insisted these and other smaller drones were intended only for surveillance and use as airborne targets. In part because of elaborate Iraqi efforts to hide the pre-1991 program, analysts assumed that the new generation of smaller UAVs were also intended to carry deadly payloads.[15]

The U.S. Air Force forcefully disagreed. Analysts at the air force's National Air Intelligence Center at the Wright-Patterson Air Force Base in Ohio, the most authoritative government source on foreign aerospace intelligence, did not believe the intelligence reporting demonstrated any link between Saddam's smaller UAVs and and bioweapons missions. "Iraq is developing UAVs primarily for reconnaissance rather than delivery platforms for CBW [chemical and biological weapons] agents," said the USAF assessment. "The capabilities and missions of Iraq's new UAV remains undetermined, but in this view its small size strongly suggests a primary role of reconnaissance. CBW delivery is an inherent capability of UAVs but probably is not the impetus for Iraq's recent UAV programs."[16]

The air force dissent was presented clearly in the key judgments section of the classified NIE. Yet unlike the wrongheaded assessment of the army's battlefield weapons specialists on the aluminum tubes, which carried great weight with WINPAC analysts, the air force's clear-eyed—and ultimately accurate—view of the Iraqi UAV program was given a backseat by WINPAC, Tenet, and senior CIA nuclear weapons expert Robert Walpole, who headed the National Intelligence Council.

The air force position, it turned out, won the support of intelligence analysts at the State Department and the DIA, although their support was nowhere evident in the October NIE. DIA analysts agreed that the UAVs had missions other than weapons delivery and were primarily for reconnaissance, but hadn't felt it necessary to lodge a dissent. Analysts from State's Bureau of Intelligence and Research (INR) later told Senate investigators that they agreed with the air force that Iraq's UAVs were not intended to deliver biological or chemical weapons. An INR analyst weakly explained that the failure to back the air force was "probably an example of the speed of the [NIE] process. . . . And [the Air Force] had footnoted it. So it was out there."[17]

Even as Tenet and Walpole worked around the clock to pull together the NIE, CIA analysts began backing away from their headline-grabbing position that the Iraqi UAVs presented a threat to the United States. The "special intelligence" that the Iraqi drones were intended to attack the United States came from a single Iraqi source, a "procurement agent" who was believed to have attempted to buy U.S. mapping software in late 2000 or 2001 at the request of an Iraqi general involved in the UAV program. The software, declared an August CIA report, would "provide precise guidance, tracking, and targeting in the United States." But the day Tenet and senior intelligence officials were reviewing the draft NIE, fresh interviews with the original procurement agent persuaded some CIA analysts that although the programming software for UAV autopilots did include U.S. mapping software, the latter may have been purchased inadvertently as part of the package.[18] This new reading injected a deadly air of uncertainty and ambiguity that threatened to dampen the dramatic prospect of an Iraqi attack on the United States with chemical or biological weapons.

The updated analysis never made it into the NIE. At least one analyst got word to Walpole's office that the passage about the UAV threat to the United States should be toned down before the NIE was approved. The language that the president's speechwriters picked up from the NIE for Bush's Cincinnati speech—that the evidence "strongly suggests that Iraq is investigating the use of these UAVs for missions targeting the U.S."—stayed in. Walpole later told Senate Intelligence Committee staff that he raised the issue with Tenet, who decided not to change the finding.[19] Hardliners at the Defense Department were incredulous at the new CIA analysis downplaying the mapping software. Declared Deputy Secretary Wolfowitz, a prime mover of the Office of Special Plans intelligence operation: "The idea that we shouldn't be too worried about a covert Iraqi UAV program that produces aircraft that are small enough to put in a shipping container and big enough to drop a quart of anthrax over Washington, D.C., because he may not really have wanted the map?"[20]

But within the intelligence community, the uncertainty clung to the UAV assessments like a bad odor. In November, a second NIE on the UAV question attempted to deal with the problem by couching the assessment in terms of capability, rather than intent. Iraqi UAVs, it read, "*could* strike the U.S. homeland if transported to within a few hundred kilometers"; route planning software "*could* support [the] programming of a UAV autopilot for operation in the United States." (Emphasis added.) This time, the air force, the DIA, and the army were having none of it. All responded to this watered-down view with a strong collective dissent, stressing that the goal of the Iraqi software acquisition was to obtain generic mapping capability and was "not necessarily indicative of an intent to target the U.S. homeland."[21]

Another critical piece of intelligence was crumbling. In early March 2003, only weeks before the U.S. invasion, the CIA finally pulled back its heart-stopping speculation about Iraqi UAVs targeting the United States. The CIA advised senior Bush administration policymakers, in the words of a classified memo to the chairman of the House Intelligence Committee, Porter Goss, that the agency had "no definite indications that Baghdad [was] planning to use WMD-armed UAVs against the U.S. mainland. . . . [Although] we cannot exclude the possibility that the purchase [of mapping software] was directed by Baghdad, information acquired in October suggests that it may have been inadvertent."[22] Indeed, after U.S. combat operations ended, CIA weapons inspectors dispatched to Iraq confirmed the air force view—and the Iraqis' own contention—that Baghdad's UAV program was limited to developing smaller, pilotless drones for reconnaissance and airborne electronic warfare missions. They found no evidence the Iraqi UAVs were meant to carry chemical or biological weapons. A WINPAC analyst later explained, rather lamely, that the only reason the agency focused on biological weapons, rather than on other possible uses of the UAVs, was because WINPAC's "focus [in] the NIE was WMD delivery systems and not the Iraqi UAV program as a whole."[23]

If the classified October NIE consistently strayed into the realms of exaggeration and distortion to make the case for war, the CIA white paper-cum-declassified version, entitled *Iraq's Weapons of Mass Destruction Programs,* brazenly dropped all pretense of restraint and balance. In virtually every instance, statements about Iraqi weapons capabilities that were speculative or couched as judgments in the NIE were stated in the unclassified document as fact, conveying an unwarranted but politically useful sense of certainty. These garden-variety distortions were explained away later by intelligence analysts and their managers as "stylistic" changes to obscure authorship, or standard practice in declassified documents to avoid airing interagency disagreements that could be exploited as propaganda by the enemy.

That, however, did not explain the bureaucratic maneuvering, illogic, and subterfuge that went into the inclusion of DOE in the trumped-up NIE consensus on Baghdad's "reconstituted nuclear weapons program." This time around, the case for reconstitution appeared even stronger, since DOE's authoritative dissent on the aluminum tubes was nowhere to be found in the key judgments—or anywhere else in the document. The powerfully worded dissent on reconstitution by State Department intelligence that had been pushed back into the text of the classified NIE, where few readers would see it, disappeared altogether. Instead, color maps thick with black-and-yellow international radiation warning symbols illustrating the locations of Iraq's declared nuclear facilities and color photos of Iraqi chemical munitions and an L-29 trainer jet with Czech markings were prominently displayed. Still other graphics showed the locations of storage or production sites for biological and chemical weapons.

The rationalizations of analysts did not explain why the unclassified white paper, produced for the consumption of the U.S. press and public, dropped all mention that air force intelligence did not believe Iraqi UAVs carried biological or chemical weapons any more than it thought Baghdad was capable of mounting UAV attacks on the United States. The key judgments of the unclassified version only asserted that Iraqi missile forces included "a UAV that most analysts believe probably is intended to deliver biological warfare agents" and "could threaten Iraq's neighbors, U.S. forces in the Persian Gulf, and the United States . . ." Along with the "most analysts" mirage, that much matched the classified assessment. But the powerful air force dissent and the paragraph from the classified October NIE about "route planning software" and a U.S. "topographic database" were gone.

As far as the press or public could tell from the unclassified document, the Bush administration had secret intelligence that Saddam was capable of attacking Europe and the territorial United States with anthrax- or VX-laden payloads aboard pilotless drones. The information in the public version of the NIE neatly doubled as both source and confirmation for the president's statements of October 7 in Cincinnati. "It was as if the unclassified version selectively put forward all the arguments in favor of invading Iraq," said Senator Bob Graham when he saw the new document. "In fact, what we were looking at wasn't an unclassified version versus a classified version: it was two different messages, directed at two different audiences. I was outraged. One thing I cannot tolerate is the politicization of intelligence," Graham declared. "Intelligence information must exist free from politics. It cannot be sought to validate positions or opinions. . . . Dictatorships use intelligence to validate opinions. Democracies do not."[24]

The Senate Intelligence Committee chairman had good reason to be angry. He had been outmaneuvered by Tenet, who through his control of the National Intelligence Council and his proximity to the president had found a way to turn Graham's request for a public version of the NIE to the administration's purposes by tacking on a key judgments section to a revised version of the CIA's own white paper and republishing it. Graham's surprise at its bellicose tone and sophisticated production values suggested he had no idea of the document's provenance. Graham and other members of the Senate committee simply had requested a declassified version of the NIE from Tenet. Instead, they unwittingly provided the DCI with the opportunity to substitute an unclassified intelligence product ordered up by the White House to educate the public on Saddam's WMD and the case for war against Iraq. That met Graham's own definition of politicized intelligence—and also made him in some measure responsible for it.

The document pressed into service as the unclassified NIE was originally requested the previous May by the National Security Council Deputies Committee at the White House, which later evolved into the White House Iraq Group, or WHIG. The committee then included, among others, Lewis Libby, Douglas Feith, and John McLaughlin, the deputy director of the CIA. On May 8, an aide to McLaughlin e-mailed Pillar, then the national intelligence officer for the Near East and South Asia desk, to explain that McLaughlin had recently attended a meeting at the White House and wanted Pillar to prepare a white paper on Iraqi WMD programs as a "follow-up to the meeting discussions."[25] Pillar directed an Iraq military analyst in his shop to prepare the paper, which was in draft form later that month. Pillar and his staff believed the leadoff summary of the draft was "somewhat weak" and the analyst continued work on it on and off for several more months until the NIE was under way in mid-September.

The Washington Post later reported that another white paper on Iraqi WMD, *A Grave and Gathering Danger: Saddam Hussein's Quest for Nuclear Weapons,* was commissioned at about the same time by the White House Iraq Group's communications task force. White House deputy director of communications for planning James R. Wilkinson collected a trove of intelligence reports and press clippings on WMD and consulted with members of the NSC and Vice President Cheney's office about the project. As Cheney's deputy for national security, Libby sat on both the NSC deputies committee and the WHIG task force. Two aides to then NSC counterproliferation director Robert Joseph, Will Tobey and Susan Cook, reportedly checked facts, made revisions, and circulated drafts under standard NSC review procedures. At some point, WHIG officials decided the WMD white paper lacked sufficiently dramatic images and gripping stories. A White House spokesman told *The Post* that the president's NSC adviser, Condoleezza Rice, decided against publishing the paper after she and Joseph decided it "was not strong enough."[26]

A draft of the white paper, which leaked to *The Post,* also marked the first time the Bush administration had attempted to use the discredited Niger intelligence. Iraq, it read, had "sought uranium oxide, an essential ingredient in the enrichment process, from Africa."[27] The NSC white paper also treated the 1991 IAEA description of Baghdad's defunct pre–Gulf War nuclear program as if it accurately described the program in 2002, much as the president did in his September 7 Camp David press conference with Blair. The draft also claimed that UN inspectors declared that satellite photos showed "many signs of the reconstruction and acceleration of the Iraqi nuclear program," when inspectors said no such thing and the satellite photos showed only meaningless rooftops. A "senior intelligence official" noticed that "some of the white paper's most emotive and misleading assertions" found their way into talking points and speeches by President Bush and other top officials. The official attributed the similarities to White House speechwriters who "took literary license with intelligence."

Both the CIA and the NSC efforts to produce white papers, drawing on versions of WMD intelligence from either the Pentagon's counterterrorism group or the CIA, and both ordered by the White House, illustrated how steeped in political maneuvering the Bush efforts to justify the war had become in the fall of 2002. In retrospect, Pillar, who shepherded the CIA white paper through the drafting process, was embarrassed at his own involvement in producing it. He later described the exercise as straight policy advocacy that could not be justified as legitimate intelligence analysis. "In retrospect, we shouldn't have done that white paper at all," said Pillar. "One of the biggest regreats of my career is, I didn't find a way to say no. If I had to do it again, I would say, 'Hell, no, I'm not going to do that.'"[28]

The impact of Tenet's hastily produced NIE and the month-long White House public relations blitz on the threat of Saddam's WMD had been overwhelming. By a vote of 296–133, the House authorized President Bush "to use the Armed Forces of the United States as he deems necessary and appropriate" to "defend the national security of the United States against the continuing threat posed by Iraq" and "enforce all relevant United Nations Security Council resolutions regarding Iraq." On Friday morning, after a desultory stab at debate in a near-empty chamber the night before, the Senate approved the identical resolution 77–23.

"America speaks with one voice," declared President Bush. "The Congress has spoken clearly to the international community and the United Nations Security Council. Saddam Hussein and his outlaw regime pose a grave threat to the region, the world, and the United States. Inaction is not an option, disarmament is a must."[29] Not since Lyndon Johnson rammed the Gulf of Tonkin resolution through Congress in 1964 had an American president been given such wide latitude to wage such an undefined military operation on the basis of such doubtful evidence.

The publication of the exaggerated and hyped intelligence in Pillar's unclassified NIE only seemed to whet Tenet's appetite for trying to have it both ways. Graham asked Tenet on October 4 to declassify recent closed-hearings testimony by deputy CIA director McLaughlin that Saddam was unlikely to initiate an attack with WMD unless he was attacked first, an observation that didn't quite contradict the message of the NIE, but certainly softened it. Three days later, Graham wrote, he received a three-page letter from the CIA that "looked as if someone had hastily photocopied it at Kinko's." It conceded that Baghdad "now appears to be drawing a line short of conducting terrorist attacks . . . against the United States" and speculated that Saddam "might decide" to assist "Islamic terrorists in conducting a WMD attack against the United States" only if it were "his last chance to exact vengeance."[30]

After all the dire warnings from the White House and the president himself about Saddam's WMD arsenal, Tenet's newly declassified CIA statement downplaying the Iraqi threat was a political embarrassment. With only days left before the congressional vote on President Bush's war resolution, Graham leaked the CIA letter to *The New York Times*. The paper ran a front-page story by military analyst Michael Gordon entitled " U.S. Aides Split on Assessment of Iraq's Plans," stressing the disparity between the

CIA and White House views of Saddam's military intentions toward the United States.[31] Tenet promptly issued a statement declaring that "there is no inconsistency between our view of Saddam's growing threat and the view expressed by the President." Senator Carl Levin was furious. "That's a fabrication and bullshit," he told a reporter. "It was wrong and totally inappropriate for him to say that. That was important testimony and they were lying about it . . . a lot of countries have WMD. The question is, are they a threat to you?"[32]

The behind-the-scenes machinations surrounding the production of the October NIE were only the beginning of the deceptions and strong-arm tactics the Bush administration deployed to make its case about the lethal threat of Saddam's WMD. Right up to and even after the invasion, senior officials continued to count on the connivance of the Pentagon's Office of Special Plans, the CIA, and other pro-war elements within the spy community to keep intelligence on message. As once dramatic weapons assessments inevitably began to unravel, new intelligence came in from the field that further suggested the extent of the president's vulnerability on the WMD issue. The pressures exerted on the CIA by Vice President Cheney, Deputy Secretary Wolfowitz, and their lieutenants gave way to outright intimidation of dissenters and active suppression of their reports.

Two WINPAC analysts, for example, were asked to leave in 2003 after having second thoughts about the credibility of Curveball, the defector whose revelations had been the foundation of much of the CIA's bioweapons reports. In the aftermath of U.S. combat operations, the two analysts made a strong case that the young Iraqi who now lived in Germany was a fabricator and that WINPAC should reassess his reporting. On a trip to Iraq, the two found that Curveball had lied about the purpose of trailers found by coalition forces, which contained no evidence of germ warfare equipment. Records showed that Curveball was not in Iraq at the time of the Djerf al Nadaf industrial disaster in 1998, which he said he witnessed. He had even lied about the government job that he claimed had given him access to the bioweapons program. WINPAC managers, however, were not interested in a fresh assessment of information provided by Curveball, arguing that some analysts still believed he was credible[33]—and knowing that the CIA's case for the mobile bioweapons would collapse without him.

After the two presented their case, one analyst said he was "read the riot act" by his WINPAC boss and accused of "making waves" and being "biased." Rather than being rewarded for their enterprise, the two were asked to leave WINPAC. Months later, travel records confirmed that Curveball had not been in Iraq to witness the Djerf al Nadaf disaster and was unable to explain discrepancies between his descriptions of the facility and satellite photos of the building where the trucks were allegedly hidden. In March of 2004, after arranging a meeting with Curveball in Germany, CIA officers found him unable to explain discrepancies between his descriptions of the facility and satellite photos of the walled building where the trucks were allegedly hidden. That clinched it for most analysts. The CIA formally recalled the information provided by the Iraqi defector in May, after waiting several months to inform policymakers, charged one of the analysts, for fear of how such a major retreat would look to the "Seventh floor" and to "downtown," meaning top Bush administration officials across the Potomac in Washington.[34] By then, the full-scale Sunni insurgency in Iraq had rendered a mop-up assessment of Iraq's rudimentary biological weapons program moot.

There were other, similar cases. Another WINPAC analyst was told to leave after pushing for a reassessment of Iraq's chemical weapons program, contributing to a mounting atmosphere that actively discouraged debate.[35] But bureaucratic bullying within the CIA and other intelligence agencies was overshadowed by dramatic evidence that the White House and senior administration officials knowingly shut out intelligence that confirmed Saddam had long since abandoned his WMD programs. One of the most extreme examples was the reaction of senior CIA officials to WMD intelligence gathered in a "rogue" operation run by Charlie Allen, the CIA's assistant director for collection. The initiative began in the spring of 2002 as a last-ditch agency effort to make up for the intelligence gap about the current state of Saddam's WMD. A respected and independent-minded CIA veteran, Allen set about correcting an intelligence deficit that even senior U.S. policymakers and CIA officials privately recognized: Washington had virtually no real-time intelligence about Baghdad's WMD programs from assets on the ground in Iraq, and what they did have from after 1998 was paper-thin. Allen's concept was simple. His agents in the Directorate of Operations would approach family members of Iraqi scientists known to be involved with WMD programs and persuade them to act as intermediaries to find out about their relatives' ongoing scientific work in Iraq.[36]

Since most top Iraqi scientists involved in Iraq's weapons programs were known to UNSCOM inspectors, Allen had a ready list of targeted sources. Among them was a senior scientist believed to work in Saddam's clandestine nuclear program named Saad Tawfiq, a British-trained electrical engineer who lived in Baghdad with his wife and three children. The CIA believed that Tawfiq, a Shiite, was in a position to know the most sensitive secrets of Iraqi weapons programs—and might be willing to talk about them. The agency also knew Tawfiq had a sister, Dr. Sawsan Alhaddad, a well-to-do anesthesiologist who had left Baghdad in 1978 and lived in the Cleveland suburb of Moreland Hills with her husband and young daughter. After a CIA agent identifying himself as Chris called and asked to meet with Dr. Alhaddad in May, she gradually overcame her fears of being dragged back into the paranoid, violent world of Iraqi politics and in August finally agreed to meet Chris at a Cleveland Starbucks.[37]

Chris told Dr. Alhaddad that she had an unusual opportunity to assist President Bush in the war on terror. The CIA knew her brother, he said, and wanted her to go to Baghdad to find out if he was willing to defect to the Kurdish zone and then to the West. If so, the CIA would help find a new home for his family. If not, they would supply her with questions to ask him about Baghdad's WMD programs. Alhaddad had not seen her brother since before the Gulf War, but she guessed he might be willing to help. She met with CIA technicians who tried to teach her the basics of espionage, such as secret writing with invisible ink on paper that burned quickly, so she would be able to write down the CIA's questions for Tawfiq, then destroy her notes afterward. A woman of considerable resources, Alhaddad waved off the spy techniques as too cumbersome, and decided instead to memorize the questions.

After a coded telephone conversation with Tawfiq, set up by a go-between traveling to Baghdad, Alhaddad confirmed that her brother was willing to talk to the CIA and departed for Baghdad in early September. His present life in Iraq was largely a mystery to her. As a young Iraqi electrical engineer, he had become a protégé of Jafar Dhia Jafar, a Shiite senior nuclear scientist who for a time was held under house arrest by Saddam. In the early 1980s Jafar regained his freedom by proposing to direct a new program to develop an EMIS, or electromagnetic isotope separation, uranium-enrichment process for Saddam modeled on the American Manhattan Project during World War II. In 1987, Jafar's program was under the control of Saddam's son-in-law, Hussein Kamel, who headed Iraq's powerful Military Industrial Commission. On the eve of the Gulf War in 1990, the EMIS program—under its cover name, Petro-Chemical 3—had built a string of clandestine support facilities and eight uranium separators.

Jafar's strategies to hide the program were no match for American bombs. During the 1991 war, American B-52s carpet-bombed the Iraqi nuclear enrichment facility at Tarmiya north of Baghdad, wiping out the bulk of Saddam's nuclear program, including the uranium-enrichment facilities. After the war, Tawfiq and other members of Jafar's EMIS team packed up equipment that survived the bombing, including the huge magnets for the separators, on 150 tractor-trailer trucks that were eventually buried in the western desert. By September of 2002, when Alhaddad's plane touched down in Baghdad, Saddam's nuclear program had been closed down for eleven years. Tawfiq still worked at the Military Industrial Commission developing nitric acid-producing plants for agricultural fertilizer, and moonlighted teaching classes at Baghdad's University of Technology.[38]

Tawfiq was nervous about the visit of his sister from America at a time of increasing tensions between Baghdad and Washington. On Alhaddad's second night in Baghdad, according to *New York Times* reporter James Risen's exclusive account of her visit, they took a walk in the Mansour district where he lived to avoid being overheard. Tawfiq quickly dismissed the suggestion that he defect to the West as too dangerous, and gave her a look of disbelief when she rattled off the CIA's questions for him about the Iraqi nuclear program.

How close were the Iraqis to having a nuclear warhead? How much weapons-grade fuel did Iraq already have? How advanced is the centrifuge program? What process are you using for isotope separation? Where are the weapons factories? Can you identify the scientists involved in the weapons programs?[39]

Tawfiq told her that there was nothing left of Iraq's nuclear weapons program—and hadn't been for more than a decade. The nuclear program had been abandoned after the Gulf War. There was no effort under way to rebuild it, and it could not have been restarted anyway without attracting notice. He was sorry he couldn't answer her specific questions, but the nuclear program simply no longer existed. He expressed surprise that the American CIA was asking such questions, since Iraq no longer even had enough spare parts for its conventional military weapons and had a hard time just shooting down airplanes. "He just kept saying there is nothing," Alhaddad later recalled.

During a final late-night meeting before her return to the United States, Tawfiq unplugged the telephones in his house, turned up the volume on the television, and insisted that they speak in whispers. Alhaddad asked her brother about a certain Iraqi scientist who had defected to the United States and was spreading the word that Saddam still had WMD. Tawfiq dismissed the defector as a know-nothing who would say anything to get paid. He also reconfirmed that he did not think it made sense to risk defecting, when all he could tell the Americans was that the Iraqis had no WMD programs. He did concede that the weapons programs might be restarted if the economic sanctions levied against Iraq by the United Nations were lifted.

Alhaddad returned to Cleveland in mid-September, at about the time senior CIA officials were preoccupied with drafting the 2002 National Intelligence Estimate. The CIA flew her to Washington and dispatched four officers to debrief her for two hours in a suburban Virginia hotel room. She told them in as much detail as she could what her brother had told her. They asked her at one point what Tawfiq knew about an Iraqi purchase of uranium from overseas—the CIA had included a question for Tawfiq about Iraqi interest in purchasing uranium from Niger. Tawfiq told her there was no need to buy uranium abroad. Jafar oversaw the building of a uranium purification plant in the early 1980s near Mosul that was supplied by indigenous uranium mined in Iraq's Akashat region. When Tawfiq heard about the supposed Iraqi purchases from Niger, he said the "information did not come from anyone in Iraq who knew anything."[40] Dr. Alhaddad told her debriefers that Tawfiq wondered where the CIA got such crazy questions.

Chris, the CIA agent who originally contacted her, later told Alhaddad's husband that CIA officials believed Tawfiq had lied to his sister. The CIA report of the debriefing was filed with those of at least thirty other family members of Iraqi weapons scientists who had all told the same story: Saddam's active biological, chemical, and nuclear WMD programs had been abandoned for years. Charlie Allen had gathered an astonishing body of intelligence that had provided the CIA and the Bush administration with an accurate assessment of Iraq's weapons programs long before the invasion. The raw intelligence from family members of Iraqi scientists was not distributed to intelligence analysts outside the CIA, or to the White House. The CIA's Directorate of Operations reportedly shut down Allen's program. Directorate of Intelligence analysts never included their findings in their reports on WMD.[41] In short, top CIA management, faced with compelling evidence that there were virtually no WMD assets inside Iraq, ignored its own accounts from the Iraqi scientists and refused to pass the information along to senior policymakers six months before the war.

There is no evidence that George Tenet knew about Allen's intelligence-gathering program or approved the CIA's decision to bottle up its findings. But the CIA director was involved in another intelligence breakthrough at about the same time—that the White House summarily rejected. Charlie Allen wasn't the only CIA official in August and September of 2002 who was trying to recruit sources to go into Iraq and report from the inside. The CIA's European and Middle Eastern station chiefs, busy gathering intelligence on Iraq, were also looking for reliable assets inside the country. In September, the efforts paid off. At the opening of the UN General Assembly in New York, French intelligence arranged for a secret meeting between the CIA and an anonymous third party representing Iraq's foreign minister, Naji Sabri. The meetings with the intermediary, or "cut-out" in spy parlance, took place in a New York hotel room and reportedly cost the CIA a considerable sum in "good faith money."[42] Sabri, who was representing Saddam at the United Nations and would soon set about negotiating the return of the UN weapons inspectors to Iraq, relayed remarkably candid information through the cut-out on the status of Iraq's weapons programs.

The Iraqi foreign minister declared that Saddam had no biological weapons program to speak of, and retained only rudimentary chemical weapons that were under the control of regional Iraqi tribal leaders, whom Saddam trusted more than his own military leaders. Saddam was very interested in nuclear weapons, said Sabri, and according to a later CIA account, said that "he was aggressively and covertly developing such a weapon."[43] But Sabri also told them that Iraq had no fissile material and was eighteen months to two years away from building a nuclear weapon—once it secured the necessary enriched uranium or plutonium. That meant only one thing: Contrary to inflamed press reports, Saddam did not have a nuclear weapon and had no prospects of building one in the foreseeable future.[44]

The CIA's director of covert operations for Europe, Tyler Drumheller, who ran the operation, confirmed the report and validated that Sabri was the source. "This was a very high inner circle of Saddam Hussein. Someone who would know what he was talking about," Drumheller said. "We continued to validate him the whole way through."[45] Sabri's revelations, though he indicated Iraq retained limited chemical and no biological weapons, had serious implications for Bush's war policy. Saddam's vaunted WMD programs, contrary to public declarations by the president and vice president, did not appear to have advanced much since the Gulf War. Drumheller was among those CIA officials already skeptical of the reporting on the alleged Niger yellowcake deal, and he had growing doubts about the gradually fraying intelligence on Iraq's bioweapons program from Curveball, a source he was tracking with concern. The Sabri material was consistent with these doubts. "There was no immediate threat to U.S troops," Drumheller said. "Here for the first time we had information that really confirmed, in a lot of ways, what the [UN] inspectors were saying."[46]

Sabri's WMD reporting was formally written up in a limited-distribution CIA assessment that Tenet himself delivered to the White House in a high-level meeting attended by President Bush, Vice President Cheney, and National Security Advisor Condoleezza Rice. The CIA had penetrated Saddam's inner circle and finally had a source who was knowledgeable about Iraq's WMD programs. A Tenet aide told Drumheller afterward that "they were very well received" at the meeting and that the White House was "very excited to have a source inside, because we hadn't had a good source like this inside."[47] Drumheller expected senior administration officials to come back with further queries for the Iraqi foreign minister, who had told his European intermediary he was interested in defecting. Instead there was silence. James Pavitt, Drumheller's boss and the head of the Directorate of Operations, held a meeting in late September at Langley and ordered agents to try to set up a face-to-face meeting with Sabri.[48]

"We waited about three weeks," said Drumheller, "and we got word that there was not interest in the intel anymore, that what they wanted now was for him [Sabri] to defect as a propaganda ploy." In late November, the case officer responsible for the Sabri portfolio, Bill Murray, a top CIA Middle Eastern officer who was Paris station chief at the time, was told by the agency's paramilitary Iraqi Operations Group that they were no longer interested in Sabri's revelations. They didn't have time to read his reports because they were so busy briefing the president. "Aren't they interested in this?" he asked a senior CIA colleague in the Iraqi operations group, noting that Pavitt had ordered them to arrange a meeting with Sabri. "You don't understand," the colleague replied. "This isn't about intelligence. It's about regime change."[49] Once the White House learned what

Sabri had to say about Saddam's weapons, Drumheller said, "they stopped being interested in the intelligence."[50] Said one of two former senior CIA officials who later confirmed Drumheller's account, "The fact is there was nothing there, no threat. But Bush wanted to hear what he wanted to hear."[51]

By December, the CIA was still pursuing the matter. Murray was in contact with the intermediary, reportedly a Lebanese journalist, who shuttled between Murray and the Iraqi foreign minister, confirming details about Saddam's weapons programs. "I know the President heard about this," Drumheller wrote later. Murray filed another assessment, based on the intermediary's reporting, that immediately ran into problems with the CIA's Iraq Operations Group, delaying its distribution. The report finally received wide distribution, going not only to the Iraqi operations group, but also to the White House.[52] Besides high-level interest in getting Sabri to defect, the White House had no further response, beyond the familiar refrain that "Saddam Hussein's possession of WMD was based on the collective judgment of the intelligence community at that time" and that bipartisan investigations "found no evidence of political pressure to influence the pre-war intelligence assessments."[53] Condoleezza Rice later suggested that since the Iraqi foreign minister was only one source, his information was suspect.

Drumheller didn't buy it. "They certainly took information that came from single sources on uranium, on the yellowcake story and on several other stories with no corroboration . . . on many issues they only listened to one source," he said. The twenty-six-year CIA veteran concluded the Bush administration had no interest in what the CIA or anyone else had to say about Iraqi weapons. "It just sticks in my craw every time I hear them say it's an intelligence failure. . . . This was a policy failure," Drumheller said. "The idea of going after Iraq was U.S. policy. It was going to happen one way or the other." He added, "The policy was set. The war in Iraq was coming. And they were looking for intelligence to fit into the policy, to justify the policy."[54]

After the occupation of Iraq, U.S. forces did not arrest Sabri or include him among the Iraqi leaders on the infamous deck of cards. He found his way to an undisclosed location in the Middle East, where he now lives for security reasons.[55] Neither of the two major official probes into the pre-war WMD intelligence fiasco included any mention of Drumheller's revelations. The Republican-controlled Senate Intelligence Committee only spoke to him after publication of its 2004 report. He was interviewed by the Robb-Silberman Commission on WMD on three occasions, yet the

Sabri intelligence wasn't mentioned—not even in the cramped language used in such documents to protect classified information.[56]

Sabri, however, without being named, was cited in a brief addendum to the September 2006 Senate Intelligence Committee report on Iraqi–al-Qaeda connections and the use of INC intelligence. The note by Republican committee chairman Pat Roberts of Kansas and two Republican colleagues dismissed the CIA reports of a "source who had direct access to Saddam Hussein and his inner circle" as beyond the scope of the inquiry. But after checking back with the CIA, the chairman disputed that Sabri ever said Saddam had "no WMD programs" and quoted supporting testimony from George Tenet in July 2006. The former CIA director declared simply that Drumheller, his former European operations chief, "mischaracterized [the source's] information."[57]

The White House kept up the pressure on Tenet and the CIA. By the beginning of 2003, tempers were badly frayed. On Friday afternoon, January 10, the chief of the CIA's Directorate of Intelligence, Jamie Miscik, received a call from Deputy National Security Advisor Stephen Hadley at Lewis Libby's office in the White House. Hadley wanted to remind Miscik that Libby expected her in his office at five o'clock for a meeting about the latest CIA draft report on Saddam's connections with al-Qaeda.[58]

Miscik knew that the vice president's office and the Pentagon had developed their own intelligence sources and wanted the CIA to validate their information. She was fed up with the routine. Miscik and her analysts would knock down a favored bit of intelligence and it would be cut out of the text, only to pop up later in another document, or in a slightly different form from another source. Like Tenet, she knew Libby and the others were more intent on building a defensible position for the administration's war policies than seeking fresh intelligence to aid in shaping one. Earlier in the week, she had delivered a final draft report to Libby and Hadley on Mohamed Atta's alleged trip to Prague to meet with an Iraqi agent. She knew it wasn't what they wanted to hear. But this time she told them this was it, there would be no more reports, period. Once more, they read that the CIA had discredited or withdrawn a favored piece of their intelligence. And once more they wanted to try to put a phrase, or a paragraph, past her like third-rate lawyers working up a real estate contract.

Miscik walked into Tenet's office, reportedly so angry she was almost in tears. "I'm not going back there, again, George," she told him. "If I have to go back to hear their crap and rewrite this goddam report . . . I'm resigning right now." Tenet, too, had had it with the vice president's office. Furious, he called Hadley and killed the meeting. The report in question was apparently not rewritten.[59] But Tenet and the CIA would continue to try play both sides in the escalating White House shell game for another eighteen months—before the hammer came down on both the man and the institution.

17

TOO LITTLE, TOO LATE

The White House decision to make Saddam's WMD arsenal the center-piece of its political strategy for selling the war carried with it a number of liabilities for the Bush administration. For one thing, it was predicated on the enforcement of international law, in the form of the 1991 UN Resolution 687, and that not only meant that Washington would have to cooperate with the United Nations, a prospect that was ideological anathema to many conservatives around the president, but would also mean maintaining the appearance of respecting international legal norms that many held in contempt. But even worse for the unilateralist-minded Bush White House, as Tony Blair had made clear to the president, the path to war would almost certainly have to involve another serious round of UN weapons inspections in Iraq if the United States wanted Blair to bring Britain into any military coalition against Saddam.

For Vice President Cheney, the return of UN arms inspectors to Baghdad was bad policy, bad politics, and bad for him personally. A new round of inspections ran the risk that firsthand information from Iraq might discredit the overheated accounts of Saddam's nuclear weapons program that he and other White House officials had trumpeted publicly. As Colin Powell had warned in August, if the Bush administration backed new arms inspections, it had to live with the possibility that not only would Saddam allow the inspectors back in, but also they would find no WMD—and the drive to war could suffer long delays or even founder. But after his August evening with Powell and Rice, Bush already had in mind the rough shape of a strategy that involved inspections and would provide both Blair and the American people a political framework for going to war against Iraq.

Sending the inspectors back to Iraq also would risk embarrassing the vice president. Bush, after all, had only recently given Cheney the go-ahead to get out front in a major public relations offensive showcasing Saddam's WMD. Yet now, on the question of the inspectors, the president waved off the counsel of his handpicked political mentor in deference to Powell and Blair. Cheney lost the battle of the inspectors before it even began. The vice president may even have felt a bit blindsided by the inexperienced president, who himself reportedly once asked Cheney privately not to contradict him during staff meetings. Bush's awkward declaration of executive independence also set a course that could easily undercut the vice president's credibility and prestige. For the first time, there was daylight between Cheney and the president along an ideological fault line— the political usefulness of the United Nations—that only exacerbated the existing split between the president and the neoconservatives over war strategy. Rumsfeld, Wolfowitz, Feith, and others fell into line behind Cheney, all leery of relying too heavily on the threat of Iraq's WMD arsenal and dead set against dealing with the United Nations and the inspectors. In the meantime, White House loyalists—Chief of Staff Andy Card, communications adviser Karen Hughes, political adviser Karl Rove, and Secretary of State Powell—closed ranks behind the president.

Cheney's public opposition to a new round of inspections was relentless. At San Francisco's Commonwealth Club on August 7, he railed against UN inspectors. "Many of us, I think, are skeptical that simply returning the inspectors will solve the problem," he said. "A debate with Saddam over inspectors simply, I think, would be an effort by him to obfuscate, delay and avoid having to live up to the accords that he signed up to at the end of the Gulf war." Even after the president signaled he was moving in Blair's direction by deciding to address the UN General Assembly on September 12, Cheney did not let up. In a meeting of NSC principals the morning of the Blair summit at Camp David, the vice president argued that because there were now no Americans in the ranks of UN inspectors, they would not be adequately skeptical of Iraqi authorities and might produce an inconclusive report that would make it difficult to justify an attack on Saddam.[1]

Cheney and his allies were not impressed with the past performance of the UN Special Commission, UNSCOM, or the leader of the new inspection team, Swedish diplomat Hans Blix. As head of the IAEA nuclear monitoring effort in Iraq before the Gulf War, Blix had failed, along with the CIA and other foreign intelligence agencies, to recognize Saddam's clandestine network of nuclear weapons facilities. Back in January, while negotiations were under way with Saddam to admit the UNMOVIC team to Iraq for the first time, Deputy Secretary of Defense Wolfowitz ordered a CIA investigation of Blix, apparently in hopes of discrediting the new UN Monitoring, Verification and Inspection Commission chief. Wolfowitz and other neoconservatives reportedly feared that if Saddam allowed Blix and his inspectors into Iraq it would delay and perhaps derail their plans for the war. The CIA probe concluded, however, that between 1981 and 1997, Blix carried out inspections of Iraqi nuclear facilities "fully within the parameters he could operate" as chairman of the IAEA. "The hawks' nightmare is that inspectors will be admitted, will not be terribly vigorous and not find anything," explained a former U.S. official at the time. "Economic sanctions would be eased, and the U.S. will be unable to act."[2]

Watching Cheney inveigh against new arms inspections, Powell thought that the vice president seemed terrified that taking the diplomatic path through the United Nations might actually work. Cheney no doubt understood the risk to his own credibility—and to the Bush administration's war policy—if the UN weapons inspectors proved him wrong about Saddam's WMD. The vice president retreated somewhat, and took a hard line against seeking a UN resolution to approve U.S. military action in the Security Council, arguing that President Bush would suffer needless humiliation and the war effort would be in limbo if a formal U.S. proposal was denied. Again, he pitted himself against the president. Cheney worried that if Saddam used his WMD, the United States would never outlive its failure to act rather than indulge in diplomatic semantics at the United Nations. In the vice president's view, the White House had all the proof against Saddam it needed.[3]

When Powell told a reporter that sending UN inspectors to Iraq was a good "first step" toward neutralizing Saddam, the remark was widely interpreted as a sign of disarray within the Bush administration. Although the press characterized the problem as a rift between Powell and Cheney, Powell's position was actually closer to the president's, for political purposes at least. "Iraq has been in violation of these many UN resolutions for most of the last 11 or so years," said Powell. "So as a first step, let's see what the inspectors find, send them back in, why are they being kept out." The secretary confirmed that Washington's allies—i.e., the British—needed to know the rationale for going to war. "The world has to be presented with the information, with the intelligence that is available. A debate is needed within the international community so that everybody can make a judgment about this," said Powell.[4] The White House moved quickly to paper over the public appearance of internal divisions among the president's top advisers. "There is no difference in position between Cheney, Powell, and President Bush," Fleischer told reporters. "It's much ado about no difference."[5]

Nothing could have been further from the truth. At least one experienced Washington observer suspected that it was Bush and Cheney who were most seriously at odds. "We do not understand the morass we will be walking into, unless the threat is so immediate that we must act," remarked former secretary of state Lawrence Eagleburger. "And Vice President Cheney keeps saying it is immediate, and then we hear immediately thereafter that the president hasn't made up his mind yet," he said. "I think there's a disconnect here, and I don't understand it."[6]

President Bush's speech before the UN General Assembly on September 12, marking the first anniversary of the terrorist attacks, was well received. "The conduct of the Iraqi regime is a threat to the authority of the United Nations, and a threat to peace," Bush declared before an attentive sea of delegates. "Iraq has answered a decade of U.N. demands with a decade of defiance." He challenged the United Nations to enforce the resolutions that the Security Council had imposed on Iraq after the Gulf War and that Saddam had flouted for the past eleven years. Then, as occurred with surprising frequency to official documents during the next several months, Bush noticed that a key line was inexplicably missing from the version of the speech on the teleprompter—the hotly disputed sentence that the United States intended to seek a UN resolution that would open the way for UNMOVIC arms inspectors to return to Iraq. "If Iraq's regime defies us again, the world must move deliberately, decisively to hold Iraq to account . . ." Bush read, hesitating a moment to recall the missing sentence, then smoothly ad-libbed, "We will work with the UN Security Council for the necessary resolutions." The president wrapped up by warning sternly that "the purposes of the United States should not be doubted" and the resolutions "will be enforced—or action will be unavoidable."[7]

The UN speech, Bush later boasted, laid out with "clarity" the path that his administration wanted to travel on Iraq.[8] It also sent the Bush White House down a political path that was fundamentally flawed, riddled

with half-truths and lies, and contested by ideological clashes between senior officials.

Four days after Bush's speech—and marathon meetings with top officials
in his cabinet and Revolutionary Command Council in Baghdad—
Saddam Hussein countered by doing precisely the opposite of what Tony
Blair and George W. Bush had hoped he would do. The Iraqi dictator welcomed the UN weapons inspectors to Baghdad. In a letter delivered by
Foreign Minister Naji Sabri, Saddam assured UN Secretary General Kofi
Annan that Iraq would allow UN inspectors "unconditional" access to
Iraq's weapons sites. His government was prepared to begin talks immediately to discuss terms. "The government of the republic of Iraq," said
the letter, "has based its decision concerning the return of inspectors on
its desire to complete the implementation of relevant Security Council resolutions and to remove any doubts that Iraq still possesses weapons of
mass destruction."[9] In case anyone had missed the point, Iraq's Deputy
Prime Minister Tariq Aziz declared that the decision to readmit weapons
inspectors had removed any justification for U.S. aggression. "All the reasons for an attack have been eliminated," crowed Aziz.[10]

Saddam's lightning counterstroke put the United States and Britain in
a difficult position. After the president's speech before the General Assembly had created momentum for a tough new resolution against Iraq,
the Iraqi leader effectively slowed the U.S. propaganda blitz against him
and momentarily blunted the surge of anti-Iraqi sentiment around the
world. Washington came out swinging. "We've made it very clear that we
are not in the business of negotiating with Saddam Hussein. . . ." declared Bush communications director Dan Bartlett. "Unfortunately, more
than a decade of experience shows you can put very little into his words or
deeds."[11] The White House, followed by 10 Downing Street, rejected the
Iraqi offer outright. "This is a tactical step by Iraq in hopes of avoiding
strong U.N. Security Council action," said deputy White House
spokesman Scott McClellan. "As such, it is a tactic that will fail."[12] Declared British foreign secretary Jack Straw, striving mightily for an upbeat
note: "We shall continue to work with our international partners for an
effective resolution before the Security Council."[13]

Saddam's embrace of the UNMOVIC inspectors was just the kind of
play for international sympathy that Cheney had feared. The vice president immediately reversed field and turned to lobbying for a strong war
resolution. Saddam's move, for the moment at least, effectively rendered

meaningless the president's vow to seek a stronger new resolution against Iraq, especially in the eyes of France and Russia, two members of the Security Council with their own vested economic interests in Iraq—and veto power in the Council. Neither shared the Bush White House's impatience to topple Saddam. The reaction of the Putin government, which had encouraged Iraq to accept the inspectors, was especially disturbing to Washington. "Thanks to our joint efforts, we managed to avert the threat of a war scenario and go back to political means of solving the Iraqi problem," said Russian foreign minister Ivan Ivanov. "It is essential in the coming days to resolve the issue of the inspectors' return. For this, no new [Security Council] resolutions are needed."[14]

This was just the scenario the Bush White House wanted to avoid. If allowed to stand, such sentiments would cut off the possibility of a fresh resolution—and UN approval of action by the American military. This was fine with Paris and other wary U.S. European allies. France's debonair and theatrical foreign minister, Dominique de Villepin, circulated a proposal for an alternative two-stage strategy. De Villepin wanted to separate a first resolution, establishing unfettered UNMOVIC inspections and postponing immediate hostilities, from a second that would approve the use of force if warranted. The United States preferred to accomplish both goals in a single resolution, in part to allow a decent interval for inspections while assuring that military action could begin in January or February to take advantage of the cool Iraqi winter. Indeed, in the next two months, two divisions of U.S. combat troops and their battle gear would begin to arrive in the region.

The American negotiating position reinforced the suspicion among other Security Council members that Washington was interested only in using the inspections as a fig leaf for its determination to go to war, inspections or no inspections. "We built in some time for Saddam to play around with the U.N.," conceded a senior Bush official. "But not much time, and we have to convince the rest of the Security Council that the old timelines—60 days for the inspectors to 'assess' what needs to be done—won't work." Others, who had studied Saddam, argued against a new round of inspections for just this reason. "We've really got our work cut out for us," said Kenneth Pollack, an Iraq expert and former CIA analyst, whose 2002 book, *The Threatening Storm,* was an influential argument for taking the war to Iraq. "At the end of the day, you are betting that Saddam won't give in, and his past record always indicated he would give in," said Pollack. "What's so interesting now is that he's given in at the ideal moment: really early, when it messes us up."[15]

The next step involved talks between UNMOVIC and Baghdad about logistics and procedures for the inspections, prior to the departure of the UN arms experts for Iraq. Blix decided to ignore the unresolved status of President Bush's request for a new UN resolution and move ahead. "We are ready to discuss practical measures, such as helicopters, hotels, the installation of monitoring equipment and so on, which need to be put in place," said UNMOVIC spokesman Ewen Buchanan, a Scot and a veteran of UNSCOM. "We will not be dragging our feet. We have been ready to talk to them for some time."[16]

The Bush administration was at cross-purposes with Hans Blix from the start. Not only was the seventy-four-year-old, professional Swede held in low regard by U.S. conservatives; he was not even the Clinton administration's first choice for UNMOVIC executive chairman. They preferred the more aggressive former UNSCOM chairman Rolf Ekeus, whose reputation for toughness with the Iraqis apparently ensured his rejection by France and Russia in the Security Council. Blix's views on Iraq's proscribed weapons were scoffed at by Washington neoconservatives. From the moment he took the job, he expressed skepticism that the Iraqis had reconstituted their WMD arsenal since 1998. Did he believe the Iraqis were rearming? "No, I don't think you can say that," Blix told an interviewer in the summer of 2000. He noted that there had been reports of suspicious procurement efforts, but nothing had been proven.[17] Besides his alleged softness on the Iraqis, he had another problem that played into his impassive, live-and-let-live reputation.

The document that was adopted in 1999 to create UNMOVIC, Security Council Resolution 1284, stipulated a number of conditions that Blix was obligated to observe that made U.S. observers uneasy. In setting up a monitoring and verification system to replace UNSCOM, the architects of UNMOVIC insisted that the inspection teams would be truly international. No longer would Americans automatically occupy the number two slot or dominate the inspection teams. UNMOVIC was effectively barred from including intelligence agents of member nations on inspection teams. "We are not in the intelligence-trading business," said Blix. "We are not an intelligence organization. We are not giving anything to suppliers in return."[18] As far as demanding access to sensitive Iraqi weapons sites was concerned, Blix's public strategy was to be "correct" and cooperative. "We do not intend to provoke, to harass, or to humiliate Iraq with our inspections," he declared, a statement with a decidedly namby-pamby ring to conservative ears that seemed to guarantee Iraqi prevarication and obstruction.

Despite the pressure from Washington and disarray within the Security Council, Blix wasted no time preparing meet to with the Iraqis to work out the practical details, or "modalities," of the inspection process. As he set about his work, chaos seemed to break loose on several fronts. On September 24, Prime Minister Blair's white paper on Iraq's WMD was made public, triggering an immediate offer by Baghdad for British journalists to inspect purported dual-use weapons sites including the al-Qa'qa chemical complex south of Baghdad and the Amariyah Sera biological research facility. Nothing came of the Iraqi sideshow but distraction.

Four days later, the United States and Britain circulated a first draft of a proposed new resolution that was so transparently self-serving and jingoistic that it could only be considered an opening position for negotiations. The draft allowed the permanent members of the Security Council—the United States, Britain, France, Russia, and China—to place their own nationals on inspection teams, establish bases for inspectors guarded by UN forces around Iraq, allow the landing of aircraft, including unmanned spy planes, anywhere inside Iraq and gave inspectors the right to spirit any Iraqi outside of the country for interrogation. France, Russia, and China issued strong objections to the proposal. The Iraqis condemned it as "a declaration of war."

Meantime, Blix and his top lieutenants, mindful that they were still operating under the authority of Resolution 1284, and not a prospective British-American resolution, traveled to Vienna on October 1 for talks with the Iraqis at IAEA headquarters. In two days of meetings, Blix and Mohamed ElBaradei, the Egyptian-born IAEA director, whose organization was in charge of inspecting Iraq's nuclear facilities, hammered out an agreement with the Iraqis that assured wider access to sensitive Iraqi sites, setting aside the issue of the presidential palaces that was covered by a separate UN agreement. The Iraqis, for their part, handed over computerized records of changes made since 1998 to plants and equipment with dual civilian and military uses.

Prodded by the threat of war, Blix noted that the Iraqis' cooperation was exemplary. "There is a willingness to accept inspections that has not existed before," he said. "The Iraqi representatives declared that Iraq accepts all rights of inspection provided for in all the relevant Security Council resolutions . . . all sites are subject to immediate, unconditional and unrestricted access."[19] UNMOVIC announced plans to send its first teams to Baghdad as early as October 19.

The UN pronouncement did not sit well with Washington. Bush officials feared that the inspectors, if allowed to go forward unchecked, would encourage the belief that there was no need for a new resolution. Colin Powell warned that the United States would take measures to thwart UNMOVIC inspections unless and until there was a new resolution that carried the threat of U.S. military force. "Let there be no doubt in anyone's mind," said Powell, "that the United States will continue to pursue a new U.N. resolution with the Security Council. We do not believe that [the inspections teams] should go back in . . . until they have new instructions in the form of a new resolution."[20] UNMOVIC, he added, needed "the strongest possible authority," which "will only come from a new resolution that keeps the pressure up on Iraq and that has linked to it consequences, so that we can get to the bottom of this once and for all."[21]

Blix, in fact, had come to much the same conclusion. He favored a fresh, unencumbered resolution—uncompromised, for example, by the side agreement between Iraq and UN Secretary General Kofi Annan placing conditions on inspections of the presidential palaces—that would "prevent a repetition of Iraq's cat-and-mouse play." The UNMOVIC chief made this clear at an October 3 State Department meeting of senior U.S. officials chaired by Powell. Blix had witnessed a dramatic change in Iraqi behavior under the threat of U.S. force. He also strongly advocated making the Iraqis draw up a detailed declaration accounting for its WMD programs since the Gulf War, a critical disarmament device he likened to an individual's declaration of annual income taxes and tax deductions. That would foster a dynamic, he wrote, in which "they declare, we verify," instead of "they open doors, we search."[22] The same day, the Security Council informed Washington that the UNMOVIC inspectors would delay their arrival in Baghdad until the Council finished the new resolution. "We hope it wouldn't be a long delay and we are ready to go at the earliest practical opportunity," said Blix.[23]

As the U.S. resolution went through successive drafts, many of its more excessive provisions began to melt away. Blix played a pivotal advisory role in assessing the potential effectiveness of new provisions for Security Council members. On October 28, along with ElBaradei, Blix briefed the Council on the latest draft, approving its tough new language that put Saddam's presidential palaces on the same basis as other sites and its call for a detailed declaration from Baghdad accounting for its WMD programs. Days later, Colin Powell invited Blix to the White House to meet President Bush. He met with the vice president first. Cheney informed him that inspections could not go on forever without results. The

United States, the vice president said bluntly, was "ready to discredit inspections in favor of disarmament." Blix understood this as a warning that if his inspectors found no WMD, the Bush administration "would be ready to say that the inspectors were useless and embark on disarmament by other means."[24]

His meeting with President Bush, whom he described as making "a boyish impression," was friendlier. Bush began by assuring Blix that "he was no wild, gung-ho Texan bent on dragging the U.S. into war." But the president also made it clear he had limited patience for a drawn-out resolution drafting process. He expected the Security Council to move quickly. Blix came away from 1600 Pennsylvania Avenue with the impression that, despite the incessant UN bashing from Cheney and others in the administration, the White House "at least for the time being, was . . . sincerely trying to advance in step with the UN."[25]

On November 6, UN ambassadors John Negroponte of the United States and Sir Jeremy Greenstock of Britain supplied the Security Council with the revisions for a third and final draft of the resolution, the end product of painstaking negotiations for the past six weeks that *The New York Times* called "an intricate work of diplomatic filigree." In other words, the final draft resolution was a masterpiece of linguistic subterfuge that enabled the principal adversaries on the Council—the United States and France—to interpret its provisions as they wished. Yet the French still refused to sign off on it. The sticking point was a sentence in the fourth paragraph of the final draft, which stated "that false statements or omissions in the declarations submitted by Iraq . . . shall constitute a further material breach" of the resolution.[26] The Americans wanted it to read "or," meaning only one of the two conditions would have to be met to trigger "serious consequences," the agreed-upon euphemism for military action. The French insisted that it read "and," thus requiring both "false statements" and "omissions" to constitute a material breach.

Sometime that evening or early the next morning, Powell placed a telephone call to de Villepin, who was aboard a flight with French president Jacques Chirac. Powell offered to drop the "or" and replace it with "and," but only if the French agreed to end the standoff and approve the resolution. The compromise was virtually meaningless in light of the larger conflict between Washington and Paris over the use of military force. The bottom line for the White House was that the resolution would not tie the president's hands if Iraq was found in material breach.

In the American view, Bush had the right to order military action without further consulting the Security Council. The French, on the other

hand, could point to other passages in the resolution that required the Security Council to approve any military action and left open the possibility
of a second resolution to approve the use of force. With Powell on hold,
de Villepin quickly sought and received the go-ahead from Chirac. The
French appeared willing, with classic Hollywood-style Gallic cynicism, to
give the United States and Britain the legal cover to take out Saddam
militarily—as long as they weren't seen as responsible. The Russians went
along, and China followed. The next day, the full Security Council unanimously adopted Resolution 1441 by a vote of 15–0.

On Monday, November 25, a seventeen-member advance team of UN
arms inspectors arrived at Baghdad International Airport aboard a white
C-130 transport emblazoned with UN in large black letters on the fuselage. They carried with them dossiers listing hundreds of suspected
weapons sites and a cargo hold full of computers, high-tech sensors, and
other equipment. Six of the inspectors were nuclear specialists working
for the IAEA. Eleven were weapons experts with UNMOVIC. Two days
later, Dimitri Perricos, a Greek chemist with twenty years of arms-
monitoring experience, led a team without warning to the Al Sajud presidential palace on the Tigris River. After some hesitation by the Iraqis, the
inspectors were allowed into the luxurious presidential guesthouse and
took photographs and samples of soil and dust for later analysis. They
found no archives, documents, or weapons stores. But they did find, as
Blix later noted, refrigerators full of marmalade.[27]

UNMOVIC was not required to report to the Security Council until
sixty days after the inspections began, but Blix was determined to get off
to a fast start. His operation included some three hundred UNMOVIC bi-
ologists, chemists, missile and other weapons specialists, along with several dozen nuclear engineers and physicists who worked for ElBaradei.
About one hundred UNMOVIC and IAEA personnel would eventually be
working in Iraq at any one time, equipped with a fleet of jeeps, German
helicopters, and fixed-wing aircraft based in Larnaca, Cyprus. Blix himself had arrived in Baghdad the previous week, allowing time for meetings
with the director of Iraq's National Monitoring Directorate, Hossam Mohammed Amin, and his deputy, Dr. Amir al-Saadi, who respectively held
the honorific military ranks of general and lieutenant general.

Not-so-subtle pressure on Blix from Washington and London continued even after the adoption of Resolution 1441. His repeated assurances
that he did not intend to repeat UNSCOM's mistakes struck even some

sympathetic observers as too soft. "Blix may go too far down this line," said David Albright, the former inspector and head of Washington's Institute for Science and International Studies. "If you are too weak, the Iraqis will read you in a second and take advantage of it."[28] Respected military analyst Anthony Cordesman of London's International Institute of Strategic Studies also warned, "If he doesn't go to core inspection areas quickly, he understands he will be in a quiet confrontation with the United States."[29]

Blix hoped not to make that mistake. The Al Sajud palace inspection was a pointed signal to his U.S. critics that the United Nations was off to an aggressive start. Although the Americans ostensibly supported the UN inspections, their ambivalence was plain—and Blix got the brunt of it. Friendly U.S. advice always seemed to conceal hidden shortcuts and traps. When administration officials first suggested that his inspectors go after high-level sites, like Iraqi government ministries, Blix at first dismissed the idea as naïve—the Iraqis had long since learned that high government offices were the worst place to hide weapons documents. He quickly "drew the conclusion that the U.S. did not itself know where things were." Blix then began to suspect that the advice was simply a ruse to get the UN inspectors to provoke the Iraqis into denying them access—and allow the United States to declare Baghdad in material breach.

The list of half-baked, devious, or unworkable ideas from the Bush administration flowed unabated. Although Washington had given up trying to place Americans on inspection teams in the horse trading over 1441, U.S. officials still wanted to position U.S. personnel with security clearances high in the UNMOVIC organization to handle requests for U.S. intelligence. The proposal was a recipe for a replay of the UNSCOM disaster, with excellent prospects for blowing up the entire inspection process. The UN inspectors had been thrown out of Iraq in 1998 after the Iraqis became suspicious that UNSCOM was a front for the CIA and other Western intelligence agencies. Blix had already assigned a widely known and respected Canadian intelligence professional, Jim Corcoran, to the post. Blix was sure Corcoran could explain to the Americans everything they needed to know about the intelligence UNMOVIC required. In a similar vein, he was forced to resist suggestions for information sharing and joint operations with U.S. intelligence agencies, another barely concealed bid for using UNMOVIC to generate badly needed intelligence inside Iraq.[30]

The U.S. pressure to force Iraqi scientists to leave the country for interrogations was one of UNMOVIC's most discussed and intractable problems. Blix suspected some U.S. officials wanted to use UNMOVIC as cover for Iraqi defections, and raised the prospect that such tactics could result in "accidents" to Iraqis under escort out of the country at the hands of Saddam's men. A U.S. expert shrugged off the possibility, noting that "these guys [have] devoted themselves to production of weapons of mass destruction, anyway." The comment did not encourage Blix.[31]

Blix's most immediate problem, however, was the thirty-day timetable for Iraq to declare its eleven-year history of prohibited weapons. He strongly supported such a declaration in principle, and believed it might give the Iraqis a fresh start if they used it during inspections to distance themselves from their past behavior and to actively cooperate with UNMOVIC inspectors. But Blix also felt that such a tight deadline would set up any country for failure if its petroleum industry, for example, were required to provide a full declaration of its peaceful chemical programs in thirty days. "A declaration requiring extensive information and giving Iraq little time to prepare it," Blix predicted, "might serve as a tripwire leading to visible violations that justified 'serious consequences.'"[32] Both he and ElBaradei realized that if the Iraqis, as they claimed, had destroyed most of their biological and chemical weapons in the summer of 1991 without UNSCOM inspectors present as required, they had an exceedingly difficult problem of documentation on their hands.

The Americans had set up the short deadline for the Iraqi weapons declaration as a trap for Saddam. Vice President Cheney reportedly had a prominent role in deciding on the thirty-day timetable.[33] Saddam would either declare he had no WMD, which would be contradicted by U.S. intelligence—which would point to reports on the aluminum tubes, the Niger uranium, or the mobile bioweapons labs, among other things—or admit to having some WMD, which would also trigger a condemnation of the Baghdad regime and open the way to war. Unfortunately, Saddam's supposed lies had to be exposed by U.S. intelligence before they were publicly discredited after the invasion of Iraq.

The Iraqis filed their report a day early, on December 7. It consisted of twelve CD-ROMs and forty-three spiral-bound volumes totaling 11,807 pages. "We declared that Iraq is empty of weapons of mass destruction," said General Amin of the Iraqi monitoring office. "I reiterate Iraq has no weapons of mass destruction. The declaration has some activities that are dual-use and they are declared fully, completely and accurately."[34] His deputy, Dr. al-Saadi, added that although the pre-1991 Iraqi nuclear weapons program may have been close to building a bomb, Baghdad did not currently have a continuing program.[35] Blix and his UN team in New York took almost two weeks to complete their initial assessment of the documents, which had to be checked against million of pages of previously collected Iraqi procurement records, blueprints, satellite photos, and intelligence cables from the past decade.

A UN decision to censor sensitive WMD "cookbook" information in the voluminous disclosure of documents, vehemently protested by Bush officials fearful of getting redacted versions of the declaration, only complicated their task. In the end, the five permanent Security Council nations promptly received uncensored copies, while the ten nonpermanent Council members, including Mexico, Syria, and Venezuela, were provided copies after almost two weeks with heavily redacted passages.

On December 19 Blix briefed the Security Council on his preliminary findings. There was very little new information, he said. The presentation was disorganized, and some texts had been repeated in as many as five different places, in an apparent Iraqi effort to demonstrate their good faith effort despite the time constraints. Blix and his team found some useful information on missile programs and peaceful uses of biological research between 1998 and 2002.[36] In a second briefing on January 9, the IAEA's ElBaradei revealed for the first time that his inspectors had concluded that the aluminum tubes sought by Iraq had not been intended for uranium enrichment, but were for battlefield rockets, as the Iraqis claimed. "While it would be possible to modify such tubes for the manufacture of centrifuges, they are not directly suitable for it," ElBaradei said.[37] Earlier in the month, IAEA specialists had visited Baghdad's Nasser metal fabrication plant, where they found thirteen thousand finished rockets manufactured from 7075-T6 aluminum tubes.

There was little new about chemical and biological weapons. Much of the Iraqi declaration, Blix said, consisted of old, unverified data. No attempt had been made by the Iraqis, as Blix had hoped, to use the declaration as a fresh start or as an opportunity to try a new approach. The declaration on biological weapons was "a reorganized version" of information provided to UNSCOM in 1997, and the chemical section merely updated a 1996 Iraqi declaration. Blix told the assembled Council that although individual governments "stated they had had convincing evidence contradicting the Iraqi declaration," UNMOVIC was not in possession of that evidence and had no way to confirm or disprove the Iraqis' documentation.[38] "We have now been there for some two months and been covering the country in ever wider sweeps," Blix told reporters after the January session, "and we haven't found any smoking guns."[39]

The plain fact was that the inspection teams had so far turned up very little. In December, IAEA inspectors visited the Tuwaitha complex, the sprawling nerve center of the Iraqis' pre–Gulf War nuclear weapons program, and found no evidence of activity or rebuilding—despite White House statements that satellite photographs of Tuwaitha were proof that Saddam "may seek to develop nuclear weapons and may be making progress."[40] That did not square with what the IAEA was finding on the ground. "I think it's difficult for Iraq to hide a complete nuclear-weapons program," ElBaradei told reporters. "They might be hiding some computer studies or R & D on one single centrifuge. These are not enough to make weapons."[41]

U.S. ambassador Negroponte responded to the UN reports by pointedly noting that the Iraqis had failed to declare their mobile biological weapons labs, and hadn't acknowledged their procurement of uranium abroad—both subjects of considerable interest to Vice President Cheney and U.S. intelligence sources. Negroponte also noted that the Iraqis had denied that the unmanned aerial vehicles, or UAVs, had anything to do with dispersing biological agents. That too, contradicted intelligence reports the president was receiving. Iraq, the Americans had all but concluded, was in breach of Resolution 1441. The French, for their part, saw little new in the declaration and noted the inspections were just beginning. Moscow registered the U.S. position, but pointed out that Washington had not offered any evidence to support it. Other Council representatives saw no definitive evidence one way or another.[42]

As Blix's remarks before the Security Council on December 19 suggested, the possibility of a breakthrough depended on Washington or London providing the UN inspectors with as yet undisclosed intelligence about Saddam's WMD and reconstituted weapons programs. Blix had first requested help with intelligence in early December. Still irritated by the constant sniping at him from Washington, Blix began to show his impatience. "If the UK and the US are convinced and they say they have evidence, then one would expect they would be able to tell us where is this stuff," Blix told reporters.[43] He conceded that some intelligence had been forthcoming, but he still felt in early January that cooperation from the United States and Britain was inadequate. "We don't get all we need," he declared. French Foreign Minister de Villepin underscored Blix's request by reminding Security Council member nations of their obligation under 1441 to provide whatever information they possessed on Iraq's prohibited weapons programs.

The United States was playing a confidence game with the inspectors. Colin Powell confirmed that the United States had provided Blix's team with "significant" intelligence, reportedly from spy satellites, to help locate chemical weapons stockpiles. But before opening up their intelligence files, Powell said, the United States wanted to see whether the inspectors "are able to handle it and exploit it. It is not a matter of opening up every door that we have."[44] The Bush strategy was to provide the UN inspectors with low-grade intelligence at first, and gradually to step up the quality of information. "Based on our historical experience with UNSCOM," explained a senior U.S. official, "they had a very difficult time keeping information from falling into Iraqi hands."

Pentagon officials were concerned about giving away the locations of WMD sites targeted for bombing.[45] It was hardly a policy designed to enhance the success of the inspections. If doling out information piecemeal was a gratuitous insult, it became apparent to the inspectors that the quality of U.S. intelligence was even worse. As late as February, one inspector described the U.S. intelligence as consistently unreliable. He characterized the information they received as "garbage after garbage after garbage."[46]

By January, U.S. attitudes toward the inspections were hardening. The buildup of U.S. troops in the region was expected to reach one hundred thousand by the end of the month—and the expectation that the troops would soon see action was growing. On the home front, Republican strategists led by Karl Rove had engineered a historic victory in the November midterm elections, and for the first time in recent memory a Republican president enjoyed rubber-stamp majorities in both the House and Senate. "If you look at the polling numbers, they're very clear," a Republican party aide said. "The American people are quite happy to go along with the President for war at the moment, but are also getting sick of this thing dragging out."[47]

As the pressures for war mounted, a controversy broke out about the timing of future reporting from the UN inspectors—largely because Resolution 1441 failed to anticipate how to proceed if they did not find any

WMD. Blix and ElBaradei were required to report their findings to the Security Council sixty days after inspections began, a date that was set for January 27. But what happened after that was uncertain. Washington assumed that after the January deadline, the White House was free to make a decision to go to war. Blix, however, proposed that the inspectors should drop 1441 and readopt the original Resolution 1284, which called for an additional report in late March that would lay out the remaining requirements for Iraq to disarm. The United States strenuously objected, afraid that Blix's approach might force a delay in U.S. military action. "How can you talk about suspending sanctions or outlining key remaining disarmament tasks when the Iraqis have not complied," complained an unnamed Washington official. "They have to first comply. We don't want to reward Iraq."[48]

Blix, who was headed back to Baghdad for a final visit before the January 27 deadline, hoped the Iraqis would be more forthcoming. "There is still time, I think, for the Iraqis to get themselves out of a very dangerous situation," he said. "They have provided prompt access, been very cooperative in terms of logistics. But they need to do a good deal more to provide evidence if we are to avoid any worse development."[49] France, Russia, and Syria, seeing a way to delay U.S. war plans, supported Blix against the United States and Britain. China called on the Security Council to find middle ground. Within days, the debate within the Security Council metamorphosed into a heated rift.

At a foreign ministers meeting on January 19, Powell ran into stiff resistance from the Europeans, who backed Blix's extension and argued that the inspections were working. "We think that military intervention would be the worst possible solution," said France's de Villepin. Russian foreign minister Igor Ivanov backed a political solution. "Terrorism is far from being crushed," Ivanov warned. "We must be careful not to take unilateral steps that might threaten the unity of the entire [anti-]terrorism coalition." Germany's Joschka Fischer, a member of the radical leftist Red Brigades in the 1960s, declared the inspectors should have all the time they needed to disarm the Iraqis. "Iraq has complied fully with all relevant resolutions and cooperated very closely with the UN team on the ground," Fischer said. "We think things are moving in the right direction . . ."[50]

In fact, the inspections were providing modest grounds for U.S. optimism. Only days earlier, UNMOVIC inspectors discovered that the Iraqis had violated UN sanctions by illegally smuggling rocket engines into the country, evidence that they had been testing missiles with a range beyond the proscribed limit of 150 kilometers, or about 93 miles. Then, during an inspection of the Ukhaider Ammunition Storage Area south of Baghdad, they found a crate of twelve warheads apparently configured for sarin gas, but without any trace of chemical agents.[51] The warheads were intended for an older 122-millimeter missile with a maximum range of 20 miles, well within allowable limits, but nonetheless designed to carry chemical weapons.

Almost simultaneously, inspectors searching the private home of an Iraqi nuclear scientist named Faleh Hassam found three thousand research documents on the use of laser isotopic separation technology to enrich uranium, as well as old reports on laser-guided missile guidance systems. Hassam, who had worked on the pre-1991 Iraqi nuclear program, was interviewed at length by ElBaradei's inspectors in a Baghdad hotel room. Hassam's documents failed to provide significant new information for the IAEA, and the missile discoveries were not technically weapons violations. But the fact that weapons hardware and documents were still coming to light suggested to the weapons inspectors that there might be more. Blix, normally not given to idle speculation, later admitted that his "gut feelings, which I kept to myself, suggested to me that Iraq still engaged in prohibited activities . . . and it had the documents to prove it."[52]

The European outpouring of opposition to U.S. war aims and support of the inspectors, on top of the dispute about the timing of Blix's final report, seemed to rattle the White House. Bush himself hauled out the familiar grab bag of anti-Saddam verbal artillery. "He's playing hide-and-seek with inspectors . . ." snapped the president. "It's clear to me now that he is not disarming. And, surely, our friends have learned lessons from the past. Surely we have learned how this man deceives and delays. . . . This business about more time—how much time do we need to see clearly that he's not disarming? As I said, this looks like a rerun of a bad movie and I'm not interested in watching it." Any goodwill between Washington and its European allies was strained to the breaking point. French president Chirac and German chancellor Gerhard Schroeder pushed back hard against Bush, announcing that they would jointly oppose the White House war plans. In Washington, Secretary of Defense Rumsfeld then alienated European leaders with a stunning example of his trademark sophistry when a reporter asked him whether the United States had lost the support of Europe.

"Now, you're thinking of Europe as Germany and France," replied Rumsfeld. "I don't. I think that's old Europe. If you look at the entire

NATO Europe today, the center of gravity is shifting to the east. . . .
Germany has been a problem, and France has been a problem. . . . But
you look at vast numbers of other countries in Europe. They're not with
France and Germany on this, they're with the United States."[53] The comment sent relations between the United States and its long-standing Western European allies into a free fall. The same day Rumsfeld made his "old
Europe" remarks, NATO deferred an American request to deploy NATO
surveillance aircraft and Patriot missiles to protect Turkey and NATO
ships in the eastern Mediterranean and the Persian Gulf for a possible
Iraqi conflict. France and Germany successfully blocked the U.S. request,
said anonymous NATO officials, because they did not want to appear to
endorse U.S. military action in Iraq prematurely.[54]

Politically, both sides in the debate over the effectiveness of the
weapons inspections were grasping at straws. The effort to find reconstituted WMD programs and locate stockpiles of prohibited weapons had
so far confounded American and British expectations. The inspectors had
found virtually nothing that showed Saddam was in possession of nuclear
weapons, or chemical or biological arsenals—or anything that would
warrant an attack on Iraq. Since September, the Iraqis had complained
and railed against the UN "spies," but they had not engaged in the brazen
obstructionist and deceptive practices of the past. The Iraqis had cooperated adequately on matters of process, particularly access to sensitive sites
like the presidential palaces, and even set up their own commissions to
look into the missile warheads and the nuclear documents, which heart-
ened the French and Russians. But they had not seized the moment to
clarify questions of substance that, in Blix's mind at least, would have
helped smooth the way to full disarmament and complicated, if not
stopped, the U.S. military push to topple Saddam.

By the time Blix and ElBaradei entered the Security Council chamber on
January 27 to deliver their sixty-day reports to the fifteen-member
Council—mostly foreign ministers—sitting around the horseshoe-shaped
table amid the television cameras and microphones, neither side was
even close to achieving their aims. Blix took a surprisingly hard line,
telling the Council that it was still too early to determine whether Iraq
possessed or was developing weapons of mass destruction, but he also declared that the Iraqis had failed to answer important questions about
weapons that remained unaccounted for. He said UNMOVIC teams had

carried out 300 inspections at 260 sites, 20 of them previously uninspected. He complained that the Iraqi government had provided UNMOVIC with only 400 of the 3,500 names of Iraqi scientists who played a role in Saddam's weapons programs, and resisted producing them for private interviews. He also took Baghdad to task for harassing inspectors, and for refusing to guarantee the safety of U-2 surveillance planes unless "certain conditions" were met, including an end to attacks by U.S. and British fighters in the no-fly zones. "Iraq appears not to have come to a genuine acceptance—not even today—of the disarmament, which was demanded of it and which it needs to carry out to win the confidence of the world and to live in peace," said Blix.[55]

Although the weapons inspectors had no firm evidence that Iraq possessed WMD, Blix made it clear that they had serious questions about some prohibited weapons systems that required clarification—or "unresolved disarmament issues." The list was substantial. There was evidence Iraqi scientists had worked on weaponizing VX gas, contrary to official declarations. The Iraqis failed to document their claims that small stores of VX were destroyed after the Gulf War. A serious discrepancy existed between Iraqi Air Force claims that it had dropped 13,000 chemical bombs during the Iran-Iraq War and government records that 19,500 were used. What had happened to the other 6,500 chemical weapons, representing about 1,000 tons of missing chemical agent? The prohibited chemical warheads for 122 mm. missiles, found in a relatively new storage facility, probably had been recently moved and shouldn't have been in Iraqi possession at all. Could the Iraqis have hidden thousands of similar warheads and rockets that Baghdad previously had listed as missing? On the biological side, Iraq said it produced 8,500 liters of anthrax, which it claimed to have destroyed in 1991. But the Baghdad government had not yet provided convincing evidence of either the production or destruction of its anthrax stores.

Perhaps Blix's most serious questions involved the liquid-fueled al-Samoud 2 and solid-propellant al-Fatah missiles. The two ballistic missiles, said Blix, "might well represent *prima facie* cases of proscribed systems." Iraqi test records showed the al-Samoud had a range of 183 kilometers and the al-Fatah 161 kilometers, both exceeding the 150 kilometers limit. The Iraqis insisted that once guidance systems and other systems were installed, the ranges would fall under the limit. The inspectors found that Iraq had refurbished its missile production programs, which was perfectly legal as long as sanctions on range limits and warheads were observed. But the Iraqis had also reconstituted casting chambers, previously destroyed by UNSCOM, that were capable of producing engines for missiles with a far greater range than allowed. Why had such missile infrastructure been rebuilt? As late as December 2002, the Iraqis had also purchased 380 rocket engines that could be used for the al-Samoud that were prohibited for use in ballistic missiles.

ElBaradei, for his part, reported that the IAEA had seen no sign that Iraq had reconstituted its development of nuclear weapons. "We have to date found no evidence that Iraq has revived its nuclear weapon program since the elimination of the program in the 1990's," said ElBaradei. "No prohibited nuclear activities have been identified during these inspections."[56] He also indicated that his team was close to finishing its work. "We should be able within the next few months to provide credible assurance that Iraq has no nuclear weapons program," he said, reminding the Council that the continued presence of inspectors was perhaps the best deterrent to the resumption of secret weapons programs. ElBaradei repeated his findings that the controversial aluminum tubes bought by Iraq were used for rocket tubes "and, unless modified, would not be suitable for manufacturing centrifuges."

The reaction was predictable, deepening the already serious divisions over Iraq in the Security Council. Colin Powell chose not to respond to ElBaradei's assessment of Saddam's nuclear reconstitution efforts, but instead focused on Iraqi intransigence. "Iraq's time for choosing peaceful disarmament is fast coming to an end," Powell said. "The issue is not how much more time the inspectors need to search in the dark. It is how much more time Iraq should be given to turn on the lights and to come clean. And the answer is not much more time."[57] In Berlin, the politically opportunistic Gerhard Schroeder, who just had ridden his anti-U.S., antiwar rhetoric to reelection, spoke for the Europeans. "We are of the opinion . . . that the inspectors will get more time for their work," said the German chancellor. The message from Iraq's neighbors in the Middle East was more of the same. "War is a very serious and dangerous proposition," said Amr Moussa, the secretary general of the twenty-two-nation League of Arab States. "You have to avoid it by all means. . . . So if they need more time, they should be given more time. Why should we be in a hurry to wage war?"

Only London sided firmly with the United States. Even so, British UN envoy Jeremy Greenstock said the Blair government, too, welcomed a delay, a transparent bid for a second UN resolution that might approve British-American military action. "We wish to hear further how the inspectors are getting on," he said. Iraqi foreign minister Naji Sabri officially fired off a letter complaining about Blix's report to Kofi Annan. But several days later Blix received a message from Dr. al-Saadi inviting UNMOVIC leaders back to Baghdad for talks. It was potentially a hopeful sign. But Blix knew it was now up to the Iraqis. "I feared," Blix wrote later, "that the Iraqis might, again, do too little too late."[58]

PART V

FREE RIDE TO BAGHDAD

18

ENDGAME FOR POWELL

Powell's relationship with Blix and his handling of the diplomatic intricacies of the new round of UN inspections demonstrated that the former army general and chairman of the joint chiefs of staff possessed considerable skill and influence as the nation's chief diplomat. Throughout, Powell forthrightly hewed to the fundamental rationale of Blair-Bush policy, not only artfully negotiating Resolution 1441 with the French and other skeptical members of the Security Council, but also enforcing its provisions once it was adopted and the UN inspectors were in Iraq. The achievement was all the more impressive since the secretary of state—who had long favored UN inspections as a last chance to avert war, a position strenuously opposed by Cheney and Rumfeld—kept his own personal views in check. Soon after 1441 was adopted, the president, who had been preoccupied with the midterm elections as well the Security Council negotiations, had nothing but praise for Colin Powell's performance. "In the end," Bush said, "we got a great resolution, to Colin's credit."[1]

All that would soon begin to change. Only days before Blix and ElBaradei delivered their January 27 report to the Security Council, Powell received another assignment from the president that would test the limits of his talents as a diplomat and policymaker. From the White House perspective, the outcome of the UN inspections had turned into just the inconclusive muddle Cheney had feared. The inspectors were finding no WMD and the Iraqis were civil, but unhelpful and sullen. To make matters worse, in late December CIA deputy director John McLaughlin had briefed the president on the CIA's case for Iraq's WMD and the presentation had fallen flat with Bush, just as the same information six months earlier had failed to impress Rice and the National Security Council deputies. The only memorable product of the session was George Tenet's infamous assurance to the president: "Don't worry, it's a slam dunk." On January 24, Rice's NSC sent the last of three requests to the CIA for the definitive intelligence Tenet had promised on Saddam's nuclear, biological, and chemical weapons. Robert Walpole, the agency's chief of nuclear programs responsible for producing the October National Intelligence Estimate, confirmed later that "the NSC believed the nuclear case was weak."

The next day, Lewis Libby, Cheney's top aide, delivered a dramatic presentation to a collection of senior policymakers in the White House Situation Room. His account of Iraqi deception and concealment of WMD effectively overshadowed the bad news that Blix and ElBaradei presented on the twenty-seventh. Libby's hour-long classified briefing electrified most of the officials present, including Paul Wolfowitz, Condoleezza Rice, Stephen Hadley, former Bush adviser Karen Hughes, and Karl Rove.[2] Libby and Hadley had been assigned to use information from the fresh CIA reports on WMD ordered up after the December meeting. The rest came from the briefing Libby and others, including Tenet, had received from Doug Feith and his aides back in August on the alleged ties between Saddam and al-Qaeda. Powell's deputy Richard Armitage, who was also present, rolled his eyes at Libby's presentation and found it somewhat alarming. But Rove and others around the table thought he had made a gripping case. Rove, wrote Bob Woodward,

> was particularly struck by the evidence that Saddam had hundreds of millions of dollars, probably several billion, from illicit oil revenue that could be used to buy WMD. For Rove, it was a potent, deadly combination—a history with WMD, a desire for more, scientists with the know-how, a closed police state and a bunch of money.[3]

Karen Hughes suggested that a Joe Friday–style, "Just the facts, ma'am," public presentation of the Libby material might be very effective. Rove saw that laying out Libby's "facts" and letting people draw their own conclusions could have a powerful political impact. Rove, the political wizard of the Bush administration who rarely distinguished between politics and policy, was actively stage-managing what would become the single most effective bid to use classified intelligence to win over public opinion for the president's war policy.

The existing accounts of what happened next are murky and almost certainly incomplete. Woodward reported that Rice's office came up with the idea of using the material in Libby's briefing to fashion a case on Saddam's WMD and the United Nations as a public forum, much as Adlai Stevenson did during the 1962 Cuban Missile Crisis when he dramatically presented evidence that Soviet missiles in Cuba were poised to strike the United States. According to Woodward's sources, Rice and Hadley recommended that Powell, as the nation's top diplomat, should deliver the presentation. With his reputation as a reluctant warrior ("everyone knew that Powell was soft on Iraq," wrote Woodward), the secretary of state's credibility would be unquestioned. Since the material presented at the White House on January 25 was the work of Libby and John Hannah, there was a strong suggestion that the vice president's office, too, had played a role. Whatever its origins, Bush liked the idea and asked Powell to present the U.S. case before a special, televised session of the Security Council. "I want you to do it," the president reportedly told Powell. "You have the credibility."[4] For the U.S. drive to war in Iraq—and for Powell personally—the endgame was now in sight.

Powell had taken a harder line at the United Nations than his political enemies acknowledged. His public comments in response to the January 27 Security Council report on the status of the UN inspections was of a piece with the president's rhetoric on WMD in his State of the Union Address the next evening. Both were predictably dismissive of the UN briefings—except for Blix's condemnation of the Iraqis' lack of cooperation—and bullish about more dramatic intelligence against Saddam that was either ginned up for Cheney or produced independently by Feith's Pentagon operation. Powell, like the president, ignored the substance of the Blix and ElBaradei reports. He also raised the specter of Iraqi VX and anthrax stores, mobile biological weapons labs, and illegal, sanctions-busting ballistic missiles. The Iraqis, Powell charged, had "moved or hidden items at sites just prior to inspection visits. That's what the inspectors say, not what Americans say . . . this is information from the inspectors."[5] Such a description might have accurately portrayed UN inspections a decade before; Blix flatly denied that the UNMOVIC inspectors had reported any such thing.[6]

Michael Gerson, the president's chief speechwriter, wrote the same allegation into Bush's address. "The Iraqi dictator is not disarming . . . he is deceiving," declared the president, citing "intelligence sources" who reported that "thousands of Iraqi security personnel are at work hiding documents and materials from the U.N. inspectors, sanitizing inspection sites and monitoring the inspectors themselves."[7] The charge apparently was based on a U.S. satellite photo showing Iraqi cleanup crews at a suspected chemical weapons site two days after U.S. intelligence had provided its location to UNMOVIC. Bush administration officials voiced suspicions that UNMOVIC had been penetrated by Iraqi spies, and that Iraqi workmen were carting away illegal weapons materials. Some even intimated that UNMOVIC inspectors were secretly cooperating with the Iraqis to ensure no WMD would be found. In fact, the inspectors had concluded that the site was an old ammunition dump. They had turned up no evidence that the site had anything to do with proscribed weapons activities. Blix vigorously denied U.S. suggestions that UNMOVIC had been infiltrated by Iraqi spies, or that any sensitive U.S. intelligence information had leaked to the Iraqis.[8]

Both the secretary of state and the president ignored ElBaradei's report that the Iraqi purchases of aluminum tubes were for rockets, not centrifuges, and that inspections of Iraq's Tuwaitha nuclear site provided no evidence that Saddam was rebuilding his nuclear weapons program. By late January, both issues were the subject of heated disputes within the U.S. intelligence community. The White House—and some evidence suggests the president himself—knew full well that at least one high-ranking CIA source, Iraqi foreign minister Naji Sabri, had declared months before that there was no reconstituted nuclear weapons program. Most nuclear experts without an ax to grind and who were knowledgeable about Iraq knew that Saddam's nuclear program had been exposed and destroyed by the mid-1990s, and that rebuilding it without detection was virtually impossible. The mounting evidence, together with the reported absence of evidence from the weapons inspectors' efforts, threatened to undermine White House claims about the nuclear threat presented by Saddam.

President Bush was reduced to repeating the familiar and disputed allegations—and forced to hedge them with obvious provisos. Indeed, the famous sixteen-word sentence alleging Iraqi interest in "uranium from Africa" was lifted from the September 24 British white paper because by then Tenet had discredited the underlying U.S. intelligence reports. But that was only one of several elusive assertions in a passage that mentioned Iraq's nuclear program in the past tense, and stopped well short of anything approaching the certainty Cheney had mustered six months before. Declared Bush,

> The International Atomic Energy Agency confirmed *in the 1990s* that Saddam Hussein *had* an advanced nuclear weapons development program, *had a design* for a nuclear weapon and *was working* on five different methods of enriching uranium for a bomb. The British government has learned that Saddam Hussein recently sought significant quantities of uranium from Africa. . . . Our intelligence sources tell us that he has attempted to purchase high-strength aluminum tubes suitable for nuclear weapons production. Saddam Hussein has not credibly explained these activities. He clearly has much to hide. [Emphasis added.][9]

The administration's evidence for the case against Saddam was breaking down, and the president's speech reflected it. Only once did he even suggest that Saddam might have nuclear weapons—and even then he fudged it. "The gravest danger in the war on terror," Bush had said moments earlier, "the gravest danger facing America and the world, is outlaw regimes that seek and possess nuclear, chemical, and biological weapons."[10] There was no mention of Iraq, and Bush left unspoken which outlaw regime might possess nuclear weapons, but he clearly meant Iraq. The president's knack for creating political illusions by omission and innuendo went back to his days running for governor in Texas.

There were other signs that official confidence in the WMD intelligence was deteriorating. Senior intelligence officials had known since at least October that German intelligence had serious questions about the reliability of Curveball, the primary source of information about the Iraqi mobile biological weapons labs, which seemed to embody both Saddam's deceitfulness and his lethal ruthlessness. The day before the State of the Union speech, the CIA's Berlin station chief was asked by Langley to update the status of Curveball with the Germans. He reported back that German intelligence still considered Curveball "problematical" and recommended that the CIA give "serious consideration" to using information that might prove unverifiable.[11]

Three months before, in early October, Tyler Drumheller, the CIA's chief of European operations, had met with a German intelligence official at a Georgetown restaurant to try to set up a meeting with Curveball. The

German said it wasn't going to happen. "First off, the guy hates Americans," he said, as Drumheller recalled the conversation. "Well just between us, and I'll deny it if it ever comes out," continued the German, "we have a lot of doubts about this guy. He's a very erratic character. We've had to move him a couple of times. And it's a single-source whose reporting can't be validated, and I personally think he could be a fabricator."[12] Drumheller relayed this stunning information to Langley, triggering what he described as "the most contentious meetings I have ever seen" at the CIA. Curveball's defenders at WINPAC insisted his story was too detailed to be wrong.

This time, on the eve of Bush's State of the Union Address, the report from Berlin about Curveball went directly to Tenet's office.[13] Other sensitive material was also unraveling. By January 2003, the air force intelligence's dissent on the Iraqi UAVs became public, undermining the claim in the October NIE that drones carrying chemical and biological weapons might be used to target the United States. None of this seemed to faze senior Bush officials. In the face of serious doubts about critical intelligence and unproductive weapons inspections, the response at the White House officials was to push back against the entropy that began to besiege them. Scooter Libby and Vice President Cheney's office had prepared the secret weapon, and Colin Powell had agreed to deliver it.

The plan came together quickly. On January 28, in the State of the Union speech, Bush announced that Powell would present the U.S. account of "Iraq's ongoing defiance of the world" before a special session of the Security Council on February 5. "Secretary of State Powell," said President Bush, "will present information and intelligence about Iraqi's legal— Iraq's illegal weapons programs, its attempt to hide those weapons from inspectors, and its links to terrorist groups." He added, to thunderous applause, "If Saddam Hussein does not fully disarm, for the safety of our people and for the peace of the world, we will lead a coalition to disarm him."[14]

As the president spoke those words, Colin Powell remarked, "I just got my orders." Earlier in the day he had received the forty-eight-page, single-spaced copy of the "script" prepared for him by John Hannah and Lewis Libby. Cheney reportedly told him, "We've done some work. This is what you can work from."[15] The remark suggested that, along with Rove, the vice president's office had a proprietary interest in the UN presentation by Powell. It quickly became apparent that the draft was going to be a problem. Powell was spooked by the Libby-Hannah draft, which was packaged ready-to-deliver, full of drama, rhetorical devices, and allegations without supporting evidence. He immediately placed a call to Condoleezza Rice, asking her to buy more time with the White House for him to pull his own presentation together. Rice reported back minutes later that advance word on the February 5 date had already gone out to the press. The date was set.

The next morning at ten o'clock, Powell appeared at the inner door between his seventh floor State Department office and that of his chief of staff, army colonel Lawrence Wilkerson, and dropped Libby's draft on Wilkerson's desk. "Here you go," said Powell.[16] "Go out to CIA." The plan was to relocate a half-dozen State Department staffers to CIA headquarters for as long as it took to transform Libby's literary work into a hard-hitting Powell presentation. The team included a Powell speechwriter who once worked for Tenet at the CIA, a former CIA officer on Powell's policy planning staff, and Wilkerson, who would direct the drafting of the presentation. They would be joined at Langley by John Hannah, William Tobey, the NSC counterproliferation director who had helped draft Rice's ill-fated NSC white paper in 2002, and others.

Wilkerson and his State Department team settled into the conference room down the hall from Tenet's office at CIA headquarters on January 29. Wilkerson had spent the better part of the past thirteen years as a top aide to Powell, going back as his days as chairman of the joint chiefs. His job now was to assemble the most convincing, evidence-packed, air-tight case possible against Saddam. Wilkerson recognized that Powell's command of intelligence on Iraq had become somewhat slipshod at the United Nations, where Powell often cited in his public comments the increasingly disputed administration cases for the aluminum tubes, Iraqi interest in importing uranium ore from Africa, and the purported linkages between Iraq and al-Qaeda. His boss had read the October NIE and kept abreast of daily intelligence reports, but he did not have detailed knowledge of the underlying intelligence in the controversial cases that made up the foundation of the White House case for war.[17] Wilkerson knew that the information they presented had to be based on unassailably solid evidence and backed up by two or three credible sources. Yet he also knew he had to protect Powell's back from the powerful forces in the Cheney and Rumsfeld camps who were poised to undercut the secretary at any time. Cheney approached Powell and counseled him not to worry. "Your poll numbers are in the 70s," Cheney said. "You can afford to lose some poll points."[18]

Hannah brought a stack of backup documents into the Langley conference room. "John came amply papered in order to support that document," said a senior official, referring to Libby's script, "but what he was amply papered with was not a professional intelligence trail, it was a trail to a newspaper article, it was a trail to an INC defector, it was a trail to someone else's speech that was as unsupportable as that."[19] Powell's team pored over the OVP draft and began to unearth overwhelming problems. "We went through that for about six hours—item by item, page by page," said the senior official, "and about halfway through the day I realized, this is idiocy, we cannot possibly do this, because it was all bullshit—it was unsourced, a lot of it was just out of newspapers, it was—and I look back in retrospect—it was a Feith product, it was a Scooter Libby product, it was a Vice President's office product . . . and it had no way of standing up. It was nuts."[20]

It was also taking forever to sift through the OVP draft. Tenet, McLaughlin, Walpole, and others came in as new problems were identified and busied themselves dispatching aides to find critical documentation. "This is not going to meet your time schedule," Tenet finally said to Wilkerson. "We've got to move faster than this." Wilkerson agreed. At Tenet's suggestion, the State Department team decided to toss out the Cheney draft altogether and replace it with the October NIE, exchanging one headache for another seriously flawed, hastily thrown-together set of intelligence. But at least the NIE was a finished product with traceable sources and a paper trail. "I don't understand why we weren't doing that from the start," said Tenet, turning to Hannah. "You've wasted a lot of our time."[21]

The command decision to scrap the White House speech brought both Libby and Stephen Hadley to Langley on Thursday morning. Cheney telephoned Powell to ask him to "take a good look at Scooter's stuff." Wilkerson took calls from Wolfowitz's and Feith's offices and assumed the White House crew was "covering for them." In the afternoon Colin Powell joined them at the conference table and got down to work. With a growing number of bodies in the room, the operation was shifted to the nearby offices of the National Intelligence Council, where the NIE was produced. They often went back to Tenet's conference room for late afternoon drafting sessions.

By the weekend, tempers had become short. On Saturday, Libby brought in a new twenty-five-page document the Office of the Vice President had prepared on Iraqi links to terrorists, and asked Powell to reconsider material from the tossed-out draft.[22] Much of the tension between

Powell and the White House officials, who now included Condoleezza Rice, was over the purported linkage between Saddam and the 9/11 attacks and Mohamed Atta's alleged meeting in Prague. "On a number of occasions," said the senior official involved, Powell "simply said, 'I'm not using that, that is not good enough. That's not something I can support.' "[23] In virtually every case, Rice, Libby, or Hadley, occasionally joined by McLaughlin and Tenet, fought hard to keep in what one participant called "the garbage on terrorism." Powell wasn't buying it. Even so, said the official, they "wanted that stuff back in there. And one occasion the secretary actually threw the paper down on the table and said, 'I'm not saying that.' "[24] Rice showed insufficient deference to Powell, Wilkerson thought, and was often dismissive of his views. "I was taken aback by the way Dr. Rice talked to him," he said. "She would just say, 'Oh, come, you know that ought to be there.' "[25]

Powell and Tenet eventually retired into the CIA director's office to sort out what they really knew about Saddam's ties to al-Qaeda. Tenet had never been impressed with the evidence behind the Prague story, and had politely rebuffed Feith's team when they briefed him on the evidence in August. The Iraqis certainly had tolerated some terrorist groups. They had winked at the presence of the Kurdish separatist group Ansar al-Islam in their northern Iraqi camps, and had for a time allowed the Jordanian-born terrorist Abu Musab al-Zarqawi safe haven in Iraq to recover from wounds sustained in Afghanistan. (Later, during the U.S. occupation, al-Zarqawi would become the ruthless leader of al-Qaeda in Iraq and was eventually killed by U.S. commandos.) It was also true that during the last Palestinian intifada, Saddam had promised sizable cash rewards to the families of suicide bombers. But there was no evidence of a sustained relationship between the Baghdad government and either Ansar al-Islam, al-Zarqawi, or any other terrorist group, much less instances of cooperation or planning for terrorist acts.

Powell threw out the Atta material and decided to refer to the overall relationship between Iraq and the terrorists as an "association."[26] At one point, a passage on Atta that Powell had crossed out mysteriously reappeared in a new draft of the text. "We cut it and somehow it got back in," recalled the senior official. "And the Secretary said, 'I thought I cut this?' And Hadley looked around and said, 'My fault, Mr. Secretary, I put it back in.' 'Well, cut it, permanently!' yelled Powell."[27]

However, the transcript of the interrogation of "a captured bin Laden aide" caught Powell's eye. According to the document, the terrorist lieutenant, Ibn al-Shaykh al-Libi, had informed his captors that Iraq had provided training to al-Qaeda members in the use of biological and chemical weapons. Powell decided to use al-Libi's dramatic testimony about Iraqi weapons training to replace the Prague information as evidence of Iraqi terrorist links.[28] It was a mistake. Al-Libi was already damaged goods. After his capture in Afghanistan, he was sent in early 2002 to an Egyptian prison for intensive questioning as part of the CIA's controversial rendition program. Powell, a strong advocate of the sanctions against torture in the Geneva Conventions, apparently failed to realize—or perhaps Tenet neglected to inform him, or didn't know himself—that the al-Qaeda prisoner had told the story under threat of torture by his Egyptian interrogators. In February 2002, a month after the interrogation, the Defense Intelligence Agency issued a classified report that questioned al-Libi's information and his credibility as a source. Not long after the U.S. invasion of Iraq, al-Libi recanted the story altogether. The CIA eventually withdrew the discredited intelligence that Iraq provided weapons training for al-Qaeda in March 2004.[29]

Powell ordered the team to throw out any WMD intelligence from Chalabi or the Iraqi National Congress. Oddly, the White House contingent did not push to include the reports about Iraqi efforts to buy African uranium, despite its prominent mention in the president's State of the Union Address days before, perhaps because Hadley and others knew Tenet had questioned the sourcing of the Niger story several months earlier and nixed it for Bush's Cincinnati speech. But the proposition that the Iraqis had purchased aluminum tubes for centrifuges sparked hours of debate. McLaughlin was a strong advocate of the underlying intelligence on the tubes. The CIA, Powell later recalled, "pulled in their experts and swore on a stack of Bibles that they'd done every analysis imaginable, and [the tubes] simply were not for rockets, but for centrifuges."[30] Despite the by then well-known dissent of analysts at the State and Energy departments, the aluminum tubes were treated by Powell as powerful evidence of Saddam's nuclear weapons program, though he noted the sharply differing opinions about their uses.

Secretary Powell was assured by Tenet and the CIA that the intelligence for the Iraqi mobile biological weapons labs was "totally reliable information" backed up by three sources besides Curveball—al-Haideri, Harith, and possibly Abu Zeinab al-Qurairy, the Mukharabat officer. Tenet and his aides apparently skipped over the fact that at least two of those sources—all of whom were subjects of U.S. intelligence reports then at least a year old—had demonstrable connections with Chalabi. Instead, the CIA presented drawings of the laboratories built into railroad cars and trailer trucks, presumably based on sketches done by Curveball. "It was all cartoon," said the senior official.[31] Powell reportedly was bothered that there were no photographs of the mobile labs, but let it pass.

Arguments also ensued over what to make of intercepted communications about prohibited weapons, including a recent one eavesdropping on two Iraqi military officers as they discussed taking "nerve agents" out of an Iraqi battlefield communications manual. The dialogue between a "Captain Ibrahim" and a fellow Republican Guard commander, which had a dramatic immediacy and vividness that appealed to Powell, suggested that the two officers were talking about scrubbing references to battlefield nerve agents in the field manual so that weapons inspectors wouldn't find them. But the dialogue easily could have been interpreted in another way—and everybody knew it. "Well, suppose he's being told to take nerve agents out of the instructions because there aren't any nerve agents?" Wilkerson said later. "There were a number of things like that, where we said there were at least two, opposite interpretations."[32]

Satellite imagery purporting to show evidence of illegal activities on the ground posed another set of challenges. One overhead photo of an Iraqi unmanned aerial vehicle (UAV) site near Basra, for example, was so grainy and indistinct it was next to impossible to identify it. Powell replaced it with a generic photo of an old Iraqi UAV to give visual punch to his account of the allegedly deadly UAV weapon systems. Yet another salient fact escaped Powell's attention. More than two months before, in response to an intelligence estimate reassessing the UAVs, the U.S. Air Force, Army, and Defense intelligence agencies dismissed the view that the pilotless drones threatened the Gulf region and the territorial United States, or that they were intended for anything other than reconnaissance.

Similarly, it was impossible to identify satellite pictures of trucks and industrial storage facilities as production sites for chemical weapons. "Don't you have a picture of chemical weapons canisters being moved around?" a frustrated State Department public affairs official asked Tenet, who replied that the Iraqis just didn't leave such things lying around. Presented with a shot of Iraqis moving an illegal vehicle away from an alleged chemical storage site, Wilkerson, too, had his doubts. "It could be because [the Iraqis] wanted to hide it. Or maybe a general was telling them to move it out because he was supposed to have gotten rid of it six months ago. We were beginning to get leery of our own presentation."[33]

Powell had been placed in an excruciating position, caught between his duty to the president and his own instincts of caution and thoroughness. By the weekend, tensions also had grown between senior CIA officials and the White House personnel, particularly Hadley, who continued to insist on including material from the original White House draft. In the face of all the lawyerly haggling, the focus for the State Department team inevitably shifted away from vetting the intelligence toward putting out the strongest possible indictment of Saddam. "What we were all involved in," Wilkerson admitted later, wasn't "groupthink," but "it was a process of putting data to points in the speech rather than challenging the data itself."[34] Powell knew the stakes were high, but was still concerned about the quality of the intelligence and he let Tenet know it. "George, you're going to be there with me at the UN, you're going to be sitting behind me," said the secretary. "You have got to put your imprimatur on it—this is your presentation as much as it is mine." The CIA chief replied that he would. "Mr. Secretary," he told Powell, "I've got to go defend it on the Hill after you say it. And that's going to be a much tougher audience."[35]

Powell had made his choices, and the early reviews were encouraging. On Monday he and Rice and McLaughlin attended a lunch held by Rumsfeld at the Pentagon to brief a group of former national security officials who would be sought out by the media after his UN presentation. In his remarks at the lunch, Powell did not review the WMD evidence, but he made it clear that his UN presentation would be based on real knowledge, not hypotheses or loose talk. Zbigniew Brzezinski, the former national secretary advisor in the Carter administration and a critic of the Bush rush to war, was favorably impressed. "Your doubts, honestly, tend to shrink when three people who you respect, whom you trust, whom you have known for years, tell you they *know*," he later commented.[36]

On Tuesday night, while aides made last-minute changes in the text, Powell joined Tenet and McLaughlin at the U.S. Mission in New York for a dress rehearsal. Wilkerson thought Powell was unusually nervous. But his seventy-five-minute run-through of his remarks in a room that had been made over to resemble the Security Council chamber went smoothly and the secretary seemed to relax afterward. As he left for his hotel, Powell buttonholed Tenet. "You're going to be there with me tomorrow," he reminded the CIA chief. Powell clearly did not want any slipups as far as Tenet was concerned. He had asked aides to collar Tenet the next morning and have him waiting outside the Security Council chamber when he arrived. Back at his room at the Waldorf, he changed his mind and telephoned

Tenet to say that he would swing by Tenet's hotel himself to pick him up on the way to the United Nations the next morning.[37] Wilkerson was up most of the night, fielding worries from Tenet's staff that too much had been taken out of the speech on Iraq's ties to terrorism. The White House had complained to the CIA, and Libby had called Powell's staff asking why deletions had been made. Wilkerson dispatched the final text changes to Tenet's hotel room in a briefcase handcuffed to the wrist of a government courier.[38]

Tenet spent a harried night as well. Just before midnight, he placed a call to the Vienna, Virginia, home of Tyler Drumheller, his chief of European operations, looking for the telephone number of Richard Dearlove, the head of MI6 in London. Drumheller rummaged through his basement office, but couldn't find the number. He called Tenet back on his secure line and offered him the number of the Secret Service representative at the British embassy, which would likely have Dearlove's number. The sound of jocular voices in the background at the other end of the line aroused Drumheller's curiosity. "How are you doing?" he recalled asking Tenet. "It sounds like you're having a party."[39]

"We've been up seventy-two hours and we're a little goofy," replied Tenet.

Curveball had been on Drumheller's mind since the State of the Union Address, when an early draft of Powell's speech crossed his desk. Two officers in his division had pointed out questionable language in the text about the mobile bioweapons labs, and Drumheller agreed they should recommend editing them out. Concerned about the doubtful intelligence, he went straight to McLaughlin's office and sat down with the deputy director and an aide and reiterated his concerns that Curveball might be a fabricator and his doubts about the reliability of the mobile labs intelligence. "Oh my! I hope that's not true," said McLaughlin, who seemed surprised to hear that there was a problem. He noted that Curveball was "the only tangible source" for the information about the mobile labs. Drumheller guessed that Curveball was a critical source in the White House's case for war. He later asked a WINPAC officer if the CIA had any backup sources. "This is it," he was told. "This is the smoking gun."[40]

Drumheller's message to McLaughlin obviously sank in. The day before Drumheller's call to Tenet, the deputy director's assistant had sent Drumheller a memo asking him once more about Curveball's status and whereabouts. "We want to take every precaution against unwelcome surprises that might emerge concerning the intel case," it said. "Clearly, public statements by this émigré, press accounts of his reporting or credibility, or even direct press access to him would cause a number of potential concerns."[41] Powell's speech was scheduled for ten thirty the next morning, and with Tenet still on the phone, Drumheller decided that it wouldn't hurt to warn the boss directly about Curveball's shaky status as a source and the questionable mobile weapons labs intelligence. "Look, as long as I've got you," Drumheller said, "and I'm sorry to sort of spring this on you, but make sure you look at the final version of the speech because, you know, there are some problems with the German reporting."

"Yeah, yeah, yeah, don't worry about it," answered Tenet, leaving Drumheller with the impression that he had registered the warning. "We are exhausted. I have to go."[42]

Unknown to Drumheller, the one CIA officer who had actually met Curveball, the doctor who had traveled to Germany to examine him in 2000, also reviewed a copy of Powell's speech. When he had finished, he e-mailed the agency's Joint Task Force on Iraq flagging his "concern with the validity of the information based on Curve Ball." The doctor, identified only as Les, wrote that the questions surrounding Curveball "warrant further inquiry before we use the information as the backbone of one of our major findings of the existence of a continuing Iraqi BW program!"[43] The deputy head of the CIA Iraq task force met with the doctor that evening, and e-mailed him the next morning. "As I said last night, let's keep in mind the fact that this war's going to happen regardless of what Curve Ball said or didn't say, and that the Powers that Be probably aren't terribly interested in whether Curve Ball knows what he's talking about . . ."

As Drumheller waited in his Langley office for Powell's speech to begin on the morning of February 5, he checked with his assistant to make sure she'd passed along his suggested cuts in the text to Powell's staff. She assured him she had, with the material on the mobile biological labs highlighted for deletion. Wilkerson went straight to the Security Council chamber, assuring himself that the various audiovisual materials and tapes for his boss's presentation were ready to go. Informed that he had a call from the vice president's office, he passed it off to another State Department official. Libby, Wilkerson later learned, had called in a last-minute attempt to get the Prague allegation and other deleted parts of his draft back in the speech.[44]

Powell's remarks before the special session of the Security Council were televised worldwide and, as planned, the television cameras framed the secretary at a table, with Tenet seated behind him over his right shoulder, and U.S. ambassador to the United Nations John Negroponte over his left. From the beginning, Powell hammered away at the folly of the weapons inspections, using Blix's phrase about the Iraqis' failure to "come to a genuine acceptance" of disarmament to indict the Iraqis for stalling, obstruction, spying, prevarication, and worse. "I cannot tell you everything that we know," Powell said, looking into the camera. "But what I can share with you, when combined with what all of us have learned over the years, is deeply troubling."[45] He introduced a U.S. electronic intercept of two Republican Guard officers discussing "forbidden ammo" by recalling that inspectors had recently found twelve empty chemical warheads and the Iraqis had promised to search for more—which was all true. Implicit, however, was that the officers were discussing getting rid of more "forbidden ammo," or chemical warheads, before the inspectors showed up. Without the overlay of Powell's interpretation, the officers' dialogue could have been about any ammunition dump.

Powell followed his tape of the intercepted dialogue between the two officers with a stirring declaration of his methods. "My colleagues," he intoned with straight-backed military authority, "every statement I make today is backed up by sources, solid sources. These are not assertions. What we're giving you are facts and conclusions based on solid intelligence. I will cite some examples, and these are from human sources."[46] Moments later, discussing how "Iraqi government officials, members of the ruling Baath Party and scientists have hidden prohibited items in their homes," Powell noted that recently when the weapons inspectors "searched the home of an Iraqi nuclear scientist, they uncovered roughly 2,000 pages of documents." That, too, was true enough. But Powell failed to reveal that inspectors found the papers outdated and about a well-known laser nuclear enrichment technology that the Iraqis had experimented with briefly in the late 1980s and abandoned.

He wrapped up the long, exaggerated opening section of the presentation on Iraqi duplicity with a ringing rhetorical flourish. "The issue before us is not how much time we are willing to give the inspectors to be frustrated by Iraqi obstruction," declared Powell, "but how much longer are we willing to put up with Iraq's noncompliance before we, as a council, we, as the United Nations, say: 'Enough. Enough.'"

The section on biological weapons was equally full of imaginative drama. Describing the "vast" quantities of Saddam's bioweapons, Powell held up a vial of harmless white powder and stated matter-of-factly that less "than a teaspoon of dry anthrax, a little bit—about this amount. This is just about the amount of a teaspoon. Less than a teaspoonful of dry anthrax in an envelope shut down the United States Senate in the fall of 2001. This forced several hundred people to undergo emergency medical treatment and . . . killed two postal workers just from an amount just about this quantity that was inside of an envelope."

Describing the "the thick intelligence file we have on Iraq's biological weapons"—in fact, most of it was either a decade old or from a source whose credibility was already in serious doubt—he invited listeners to hear more. "Let me take you inside that intelligence file and share with you what we know from eyewitness accounts. We have firsthand descriptions of biological weapons factories on wheels and on rails." Powell assured his international audience that these vehicles "are designed to evade detection by inspectors" and "can produce a quantity of biological poison equal to the entire amount that Iraq claimed to have produced in the years prior to the Gulf War." Piling detail on detail that had not been made public before, he said that the mobile production system began in the mid-1990s and its existence was confirmed in 2000.

"The source was an eyewitness, an Iraqi chemical engineer who supervised one of these facilities," said Powell. "He actually was present during biological agent production runs. He was also at the site when an accident occurred in 1998. Twelve technicians died from exposure to biological agents." How Powell—or the United States—knew how the workers died in a five-year-old industrial accident was not revealed. After describing the numbers of trucks and rail cars deployed as biological weapons production centers, Powell segued back to the problems this posed for the UN inspectors. "Just imagine trying to find 18 trucks among the thousands and thousands of trucks that travel the roads of Iraq every day."

This section of Powell's remarks, taken from Curveball's account, was just what Tyler Drumheller did not want to hear. For the third time—in October, January, and now, after raising questions about the intelligence reporting with Tenet directly—his warnings about Curveball had gone unheeded. "My worst fears were confirmed," Drumheller wrote later. "Powell . . . was standing up sharing the insights of a man who was suspected of having a drinking problem by the only member of the U.S. intelligence community who had ever met him. It was only one small section of the speech, but it was crucial, because it hinted not only at intent, but also at actual capability."[47] The next day Drumheller talked to his boss, Jim Pavitt, who was also surprised at how prominently Powell had played the crumbling mobile labs intelligence. Drumheller also mentioned the setback to CIA Paris station chief Bill Murray, who had been the case officer for Sabri and his Lebanese go-between. "We fed them a load of shit," Murray said, referring to WINPAC's reports on Curveball. "It's worse than you know," Drumheller replied. "I talked to Tenet the night before and told him there were problems with the reporting, but he obviously didn't take it seriously."[48]

It would get even worse. Tenet later claimed he did not recall talking to Drumheller about Curveball. The DCI insisted that he didn't know about the problems with Curveball's credibility at the time and said that it was "simply wrong" for anyone to say otherwise. "Nobody came forward to say there is a serious problem with Curveball or that we have been told by the foreign representative of the service handling him that there are worries that he is a 'fabricator,'" declared Tenet.[49]

In testimony before the Robb-Silberman Commission, McLaughlin backed up Tenet, claiming that he did not remember having a conversation with Drumheller about Curveball in his office. "If someone had made these doubts clear to me, I would not have permitted the reporting to be used in Secretary Powell's speech," he later told the commission.[50] Wilkerson, for his part, recalled that "Powell and I were both suspicious because there were no pictures of the mobile labs," but said he didn't recall hearing anything about Curveball before the speech. "No one mentioned Drumheller, or Curveball," he said. "I didn't know the name Curveball until months afterward."[51]

Powell's impressively detailed rundown of other key evidence in the case against Saddam—the aluminum tubes, the UAVs with a supposed range of 310 miles, the ballistic missiles capable of 745-mile flights, as well as the purported links between Baghdad and al-Qaeda—was equally dramatic and, on the surface at least, persuasive to most Americans. Careful or skeptical viewers, however, easily detected the conditional nature of Powell's argument that Iraq was colluding with the terrorists. Tenet himself doubted that Saddam's contacts with terrorists had evolved into any operational linkages. Powell found his way back from there to the White House's hard line by acknowledging that "some claim these contacts don't amount to much," then simply said that the thought did not comfort him. "Ambition and hatred," Powell declared, "are enough to bring Iraq and Al Qaida together, enough so Al Qaida *could learn* how to build more sophisticated bombs and learn how to forge documents, and enough so that Al Qaida *could turn* to Iraq for help in acquiring expertise on weapons of mass destruction" [emphasis added]. For most TV viewers, the detailed story that followed about al-Libi and Iraq's weapons training for al-Qaeda fighters left an indelible impression that Baghdad already was sharing WMD with bin Laden.

It was strong stuff. Few noticed the glaring misstatements and plain misinformation that peppered Powell's presentation. In January 2003, the Jordanian terrorist Abu Musab al-Zarqawi was not an associate or collaborator of bin Laden and al-Qaeda, as Powell claimed. A troubled, long-distance alliance was not negotiated by al-Qaeda's leadership and al-Zarqawi until 2005, long after the Iraqi insurgency began and a year before al-Zarqawi was killed. Powell's mention of a purported training camp allegedly set up by al-Zarqawi for training in the use of poisons and explosives at Khurmal, in Kurdish-dominated northern Iraq, left Kurdish officials scratching their heads. Powell's advisers at the OVP apparently had confused a moderate group, Komal Islami Kurdistan, which controls Khurmal, with Ansar al-Islam. "I don't know anything about this compound," said one senior Kurdish official. "All of it is not true," said another.[52]

On the nuclear side, Powell's statement that "we have more than a decade of proof that [Saddam] remains determined to acquire nuclear weapons" inexplicably glossed over the widely recognized fact that U.S. intelligence had no idea about the status of Iraq's nuclear program after the first round of UN inspectors were forced out in 1998, other than that the extensive prewar program had been fully exposed by the mid-1990s and destroyed in the 1991 Gulf War. But perhaps this misinformation was related to another glaring error, when Powell asserted that "after his invasion of Kuwait, Saddam Hussein had initiated a crash program to build a crude nuclear weapon." The crash program was ordered a year before the invasion of Kuwait and ended in 1991. Powell made it sound like the program had been up and running for eleven years.

He ended with a variation on the theme he struck in his opening remarks: The time was fast approaching that Iraq's failure to take the inspections seriously would have serious consequences. "Leaving Saddam Hussein in possession of weapons of mass destruction for a few more months or years is not an option, not in a post-September 11th world . . ." Powell declared. "Today Iraq still poses a threat and Iraq still remains in material breach. Indeed, by its failure to seize on its one last opportunity to come clean and disarm, Iraq has put itself in deeper material breach and closer to the day when it will face serious consequences for its continued defiance of this council. . . .

"We must not shrink from whatever is ahead of us," he concluded, addressing the Security Council and its president, Kofi Annan. "We must not fail in our duty and our responsibility to the citizens of the countries that are represented by this body."

As Powell finished his speech, Larry Wilkerson looked over at the Iraqi delegation to gauge its impact on them. They seemed unimpressed, as if they had just witnessed a predictable American exercise in intimidation they knew to be wide of the mark. Wilkerson was depressed and deflated. Although Powell was satisfied with his performance, Wilkerson thought his boss's remarks should have been stronger and was skeptical of the intelligence Powell had just staked his reputation on. He later told reporters that Powell's speech was "the lowest point in my professional life . . . I never would have gone to war on that intelligence."[53]

Most members of the Security Council had a similar response. France, Russia, and China promptly called for more intensive inspections and rejected Colin Powell's suggestion that military action was imminent. France's foreign minister, Dominique de Villepin, was unambiguous. "Let us double, let us triple the number of inspectors," he said. "Let us open more regional offices. Let us go further than this."[54] War was only a last resort, said de Villepin. "Given the choice between military intervention and an inspections regime that is inadequate because of a failure to cooperate on Iraq's part, we must choose the decisive reinforcement of the means of inspections." He added, "France is convinced that we can succeed on this demanding path if we maintain our unity."[55] Igor Ivanov, Russia's foreign minister, emphasized that Iraq's cooperation was imperative, and firmly backed a political solution. "Iraq should be the first to be concerned about providing final clarity about the question of weapons of mass destruction and their delivery systems," he declared. "That is the only way to a political settlement."[56] China, too, believed the weapons inspectors should be allowed to complete their task. "China remains in the belief that this problem should be worked out through political means," said Chinese foreign minister Tang Jiaxuan.[57] Dr. Amir al-Saadi, the head of Iraq's inspection monitoring agency and reportedly a crony of Saddam's, dismissed the speech as a "typical American show complete with stunts and special effects."[58]

Britain's foreign minister, Jack Straw, was the first to come to Powell's defense and defend the U.S. view of the inspections and Iraqi obstructionism. "Saddam is defying every one of us," said Straw, whose government had its own interest in extending the inspections. "He questions our resolve and is gambling we will lose nerve rather than enforce our will." Powell backtracked slightly during the lunch for foreign ministers that followed the presentation, reportedly telling de Villepin that the United States was not prepared to go to war immediately and that the United States was interested in hearing France's proposals for strengthening the inspections.

In Washington and London, however, Powell's reviews were more positive, if not unanimously uncritical. Senator Joe Biden, the Delaware liberal and senior Democrat on the Senate Committee on Foreign Relations, called the secretary's address "powerful and irrefutable." The *Washington Post*'s pro-war editorial page thundered, "After Secretary of State Colin L. Powell's presentation to the United Nations Security Council yesterday, it is hard to imagine how anyone could doubt that Iraq possesses weapons of mass destruction." *The Post* lauded Powell's "powerful new case that Saddam Hussein's regime is cooperating with a branch of the al Qaeda organization that is trying to acquire chemical weapons and stage attacks in Europe." *The New York Times* called the speech "the most powerful case to date" against Saddam, but doubted that Iraq posed an "immediate danger" to the United States. Even venerable *Washington Post* columnist Mary McGrory declared that Powell "persuaded me, and I was as tough as France to convince." Won over in part by his "strong and unwavering" manner, McGrory concluded, "I'm not ready for war yet. But Colin Powell has convinced me that it might be the only way to stop a fiend . . ."[59]

The British were more muted in their praise. The conservative *Times* of London called the UN address "the strongest piece of political advocacy that the United States has yet mustered in the cause of war." Powell's case was abetted by "the passion of someone entirely convinced of his case, all the more striking for his previously dovish stance within the administration."[60] Although the paper's diplomatic analyst conceded that Powell was "quite convincing," he noted that the U.S. secretary of state was unable to "produce the killer fact" that "is going to swing world opinion. Depending on where you stand, you can pick lots of holes in the case." Even if the inspections continue, he wrote, there was already "a detectable shift in opinion around the war towards the US. Most . . . realize there's going to be a war and they have to take a side."[61] Sir Christopher Meyer, Britain's ambassador in Washington, like many other Europeans who privately believed Powell was being manipulated by the White House, was unimpressed by his presentation. "I remember saying, 'I do hope he's got something really strong to say,' " recalled Meyer. "And, of course, he didn't."[62]

Britain's ambassador to the United Nations, Sir Jeremy Greenstock, appearing on PBS's *NewsHour with Jim Lehrer*, provided some insight into the ambivalent British response—and set the stage for the endgame that would play out in the next six weeks. Like Powell, Greenstock expressed no great confidence in the inspection process. But he declared it was nonetheless critical to the British, even if there was no "other recourse except military action [and] enforcement of the U.N.'s resolutions." Britain, he said, was already working on the wording of a second resolution for "enforcement with military force" if Iraq was found in breach of UN resolutions. The aim, he said, was winning a "high degree of consensus" in the Security Council. The problem for the Blair government was a political one. "In the U.K.," explained Greenstock, "there is a much clearer acceptance of the unhappy necessity of going to war if the U.N. is behind it." He conceded, however, that after Powell's speech, the "majority of the Security Council is extremely uncomfortable about the thought of the use of force."[63]

19

THE RUSH TO WAR

Within little more than a year, Powell's star turn before the Security Council was transformed into a blunder that would forever tarnish his reputation and fuel speculation that a supremely confident and deeply experienced soldier-statesman had become the willing dupe of an administration that had no other leader, including the president, who could touch his political stature or popularity. Powell, astonishingly, had early intimations that Saddam's supposed WMD might be trouble. "I wonder what we'll do," Powell once mused idly to Wilkerson, "when we put half a million troops on the ground in Iraq and search it from one end to the other—and find nothing." Powell, the reluctant warrior, did not react well to the notion that his pivotal speech, like much else about the Bush White House's handling of the war, contained almost no accurate information, yet very effectively cleared the way for war.

"What I said was what they told me to say," said an embittered Powell later. "I'm not an intelligence officer. I was secretary of state. Whatever was in that speech was what they [the CIA] told me. I kept asking them, 'Are you sure of this? Are you confident of that?'" He was told the mobile bioweapons lab intelligence "was multisourced. I had no way of knowing it all went back to one guy," he said.[1] But Powell made no effort to shift the burden from the shoulders of the messenger. "It's a blot," he told ABC's Barbara Walters in a *20/20* interview several years later. "I'm the one who presented it on behalf of the United States to the world, and [(it)] will always be part of my record. It was painful. It's painful now."[2]

For the record at least, he refused to blame George Tenet or complain that Tenet had misled him. "No, George Tenet did not sit there for five days with me, misleading me," he said. "He believed what he was giving to me was accurate . . ." But Powell knew that there were plenty of people who were aware how unreliable some of the intelligence was and who nevertheless failed to warn him. "There were some people in the intelligence community who knew at that time that some of these sources were not good, and shouldn't be relied upon, and they didn't speak up," Powell acknowledged. "That devastated me." Tenet was almost certainly among them. Caught between his loyalties to the White House and the task before the secretary of state, Tenet had no real choice. A CIA director reports to the president. Tenet almost certainly knew more—and certainly should have known more—than he let on about the shaky intelligence he pushed forward for Powell's use.

Powell himself was hardly faultless. He failed to listen to a number of prominent voices in his own intelligence divisions who tried to let him know that much of the intelligence on Iraqi WMD was outdated or highly suspect. Greg Thielmann, a veteran foreign service officer and acting director of the State Department office responsible for analyzing Iraqi WMD, alerted Powell's office that the aluminum tubes were not intended for a nuclear program a year before the CIA resurrected interest in the cause.[3] The State Department's Bureau of Intelligence and Research (INR) had accurately reported on the reconstitution of Iraq's nuclear program, a key assessment that Powell seemed to ignore. While Powell and Tenet were vetting intelligence at the CIA on January 31, the INR sent Powell a memo warning him that fully thirty-eight allegations in the draft speech were questionable, citing objections the weapons inspectors had raised, such as the likelihood that the "decontamination" trucks seen in the surveillance photos were probably just water trucks, and that the site might contain conventional explosives rather than prohibited chemical weapons.[4] INR analysts also objected, once more, that the aluminum tubes evidence was "weak." Although Powell threw out many of these objectionable items, he ignored the State Department's own experts on the more dramatic issues.

At the time of Powell's address, Thielmann believed, Iraq posed no threat to the United States. "I think it didn't even constitute an imminent threat to its neighbors at the time we went to war." He believed Powell carried out his assignment out of loyalty to the president and to make the strongest case for using military force. The UN speech was "probably one

of the low points in his long, distinguished service to the nation," Thielmann concluded.[5]

Yet the real status of Saddam's weapons arsenal was increasingly in plain
sight and accessible to U.S. officials, including Tenet and Powell—through
the UN inspectors, even if few swept up in the White House war fever
were paying any attention to their reports. Most of the weapons production or storage sites mentioned in Powell's speech had been made available to Blix's inspectors by U.S. and foreign intelligence agencies. None of
them had turned up any illegal weapons. "This shocked me," Blix later
wrote. "If this was the best, what was the rest?" He also found it strange
that in Washington there seemed to be "100 percent certainty about the
existence of weapons of mass destruction," yet "zero percent knowledge
about their location."[6] UNMOVIC and IAEA inspections of three sites in
particular put the mild and deferential Blix in a unique position to rebut
some of Powell's most dramatic conclusions. "We had inspected most of
the sites he described," said Blix. "In no case had we found convincing evidence of any prohibited activity."[7]
    Speaking before a special session of foreign ministers in the Security
Council on February 14, Blix quietly mounted a counterattack on Powell.
He began by putting Powell's guilty-as-charged view of Iraq in perspective
by emphasizing that in four hundred inspections conducted at three hundred different sites, the inspectors had found no WMD. "So far," he
said, "UNMOVIC has not found any such weapons, only a small number
of empty chemical munitions, which should have been declared and destroyed." Blix acknowledged that the most troubling weapons the Iraqis
had not accounted for—notably, undeclared stores of anthrax, the nerve
agent VX, and long-range missiles—still presented a problem. He was
careful to say that that did not mean Iraq still possessed these weapons—
or, for that matter, that they did not still possess them—but that their status was yet undetermined.
    Further undermining Powell's case, Blix denied outright, as he had in
January, that the Iraqis had eavesdropped or spied on inspectors to determine the time and places of inspections. "In no case have we seen convincing evidence that the Iraqi side knew in advance that the inspectors
were coming," he said. Blix then questioned the secretary of state's interpretation of U.S.-supplied satellite photos of the al-Musayyib chemical
weapons production site. Powell had alleged that two photos taken weeks

apart showed that munitions had been removed from the site before inspectors arrived. The inspectors noted that Powell's "decontamination" trucks, whose presence purportedly signified a chemical weapons site, were indistinguishable from water trucks they had seen on the site. Moreover, the same trucks could have been photographed there at any time, not just before the arrival of inspectors.

"The reported movement of munitions at the site could just as easily have been a routine activity, as a movement of proscribed munitions in anticipation of an imminent inspection," said Blix, noting drily that although governments might have their own sources of information, his staff had to "base their reports only on evidence which they can themselves examine . . ."[8]

Blix dismissed Powell's analysis of an Iraqi missile testing stand whose proportions allegedly showed it was "clearly intended for long-range missiles with a range of 1200 kilometers" or some 745 miles. Not so, he said. The testing stand had a longer exhaust facility because it was set up horizontally, not vertically like the smaller stand in the U.S. reconnaissance photo Powell displayed.[9] Inspectors had visited the site four times since November because it was the facility where the al-Samoud 2 missiles were assembled. At that point, there was no conclusive evidence that missiles tested on the site contained outlawed components or exceeded illegal flight limits. "So far, the test stand has not been associated with proscribed activity," Blix said.[10] Powell's case suffered yet another blow when the IAEA's Mohamed ElBaradei revealed that nothing in the two thousand pages inspectors had taken from the house of Iraqi scientist Faleh Hassam had altered "the conclusions previously drawn by the IAEA concerning the extent of Iraq's laser enrichment program."

Blix's damaging assault on Powell's credibility emboldened Dominique de Villepin to attack the United States for stooping to build a case for war on distortions and misinformation. "War is always the sanction of failure," de Villepin declared when Blix had finished. "This message comes to you today from an *old country*, France, from a continent like mine, Europe, that has known wars, occupation, and barbarity."[11] The slap at Rumsfeld's characterization in January of uncooperative France and Germany as "old Europe" drew a rare burst of applause in the normally staid Security Council chamber. Powell listened without expression, pushing away with disgust a paper he had been reading. The next day, Saturday, February 15, according to the BBC, some six to ten million demonstrators in up to sixty countries around the world marched against the coming

American war in Iraq. In London alone, the number of demonstrators was estimated at between 750,000 and two million people. An estimated 100,000 took part in the New York City demonstration. The largest turnout of all was in Rome, where an estimated three million marched against the war.

But the game was no longer really about WMD. The White House was already intent on containing any damage to the president's war plans, and finding a justification for war that would replace the unraveling UN strategy Bush and Tony Blair had cobbled together at Camp David six months before to give the war legal and political legitimacy. On Friday, January 31, while Powell and his lieutenants struggled to pull together a coherent intelligence brief against Saddam at CIA headquarters in suburban Virginia, Blair met with Bush at the White House and found the president already preoccupied with preparations for war. Five days before Colin Powell's UN address, according to a five-page confidential memo written after the meeting by Blair's top foreign policy adviser, David Manning, the White House already had decided to order the invasion without a second resolution seeking Security Council approval, whether or not the inspectors turned up any banned Iraqi weapons programs. "The start date for the military campaign was now penciled in for 10 March," wrote Manning. "This was when the bombing would begin." He was nine days early.[12]

Both leaders candidly acknowledged that the inspectors had found no WMD in Iraq, and that the prospect of turning up any prohibited munitions in the time remaining was unlikely. Bush spent much of the two-hour meeting going over military strategy with Blair, indicating that there were probably three weeks before military commanders had to begin preparing an invasion. "The air campaign would probably last four days, during which some 1,500 targets would be hit," said the memo, paraphrasing Bush. "Great care would be taken to avoid hitting innocent civilians. Bush thought the impact of the air onslaught would ensure the early collapse of Saddam's regime. Given this military timetable, we needed to go for a second resolution as soon as possible. This probably meant after Blix's next report to the Security Council in mid-February."[13]

Bush said he thought the planned air campaign "would destroy Saddam's command and control quickly." The president reportedly expected Iraq's army to "fold very quickly" and that the Republican Guard would be "decimated by the bombing."

Blair wanted to ensure that a second resolution would provide Saddam one last chance. "We had been very patient. Now we should be saying that the crisis must be resolved in weeks, not months," Blair said.

"Bush agreed," the memo continued. "He commented that he was not itching to go to war, but we could not allow Saddam to go on playing with us. At some point, probably when we had passed the second resolutions—assuming we did—we should warn Saddam that he had a week to leave. We should notify the media too. We would then have a clear field if Saddam refused to go."[14]

Tensions surfaced when Bush brought up several alternative casus belli that might be acceptable to other countries. "The U.S. was thinking of flying U2 reconnaissance aircraft with fighter cover over Iraq, painted in U.N. colours," the memo noted. The idea was a variation on a similar plan suggested by Defense Secretary Rumsfeld just after 9/11 to provoke the Iraqis into firing on U.S. fighters in the no-fly zones. "If Saddam fired on them, he would be in breach." Bush also proposed that "the U.S. might be able to bring out a defector who could give a public presentation about Saddam's WMD." Lastly, Bush mentioned the possibility of assassinating Saddam. The memo was silent on Blair's response.

Bush had left the door ajar for a last-minute diplomatic solution. Blair said he felt it was important for both the United States and Britain to press for a second resolution "as an insurance policy against the unexpected," said the memo. "If anything went wrong with the military campaign, or if Saddam increased the stakes by burning the oil wells, killing children or fomenting internal divisions within Iraq, a second resolution would give us international cover, especially with the Arabs." Bush said he would go along with Blair on a second resolution, promising that the "U.S. would put its full weight behind efforts to get another resolution and would twist arms and even threaten." Yet the president made it clear, wrote Manning, "that if we ultimately failed, military action would follow anyway."[15]

President Bush had all but backed out of his September 7 Camp David agreement with Blair, and the timing of White House war plans, along with the progress of the inspections, virtually closed off all possibility that the Security Council would approve military action. Blair was now in a political jam—and Manning knew it. "This makes the timing very tight," his memo concluded. "We therefore need to stay closely alongside Blix, do all we can to help the inspectors make a significant find, and work hard on the other members of the Security Council to accept the noncooperation case so that we can secure the minimum nine votes when we need them, probably the end of February."

On February 22, Bush met with Spanish president José María Aznar at his Crawford ranch to map out the final effort to get a second Security

Council resolution. Bush likened the negotiations to "Chinese water torture" and declared, "We've got to put an end to it." According to a transcript by Spain's ambassador to the United States, Javier Ruperez, who attended the meeting, Bush made it clear that if the UN initiative failed, he expected U.S. troops to "be in Baghdad by the end of March." After Aznar asked Bush to "show a little more patience," the president railed against the Europeans, especially Chirac, who "thinks he's Mr. Arab." He then informed Aznar that Saddam was open to a deal in which he would agree to leave Iraq and go into exile to avert war. "The Egyptians have been talking to Saddam Hussein," said Bush. "He seems to have indicated he would be open to exile if they would let him take one billion dollars and all the information he wants on weapons of mass destruction." But later in the conversation, the president made it clear that there would be "no guarantee" for Saddam. "He's a thief, a terrorist and a war criminal," said Bush.[16]

Nothing came of Saddam's overture. U.S. and British officials were already at work on the second UN resolution. On February 24 the United States and Britain, with the backing of Spain, submitted a draft resolution to the Security Council that declared Saddam had taken "the final opportunity afforded him by Resolution 1441." In response to the U.S.-British draft, the French and Germans prepared an alternative version that called for five more months of UN inspections. The competing draft resolutions set off a late-starting round of lobbying and arm-twisting directed at the six undecided countries elected to temporary membership on the sixteen-member Security Council: Pakistan, Chile, Mexico, Cameroon, Guinea, and Angola. The European faction led by France had four votes: itself, Russia, China, and Germany, the most recently elected temporary member. The United States, with Britain, Spain, and Bulgaria, also had four. Both sides needed at least five of the undecided countries to reach a majority of nine—which had to be finessed without triggering a veto among the permanent members.

The politicking quickly became fierce. The sudden surge of global power politics overwhelmed the smaller nations, many of whom felt they were placed in a no-win situation between competing world powers. Because the five permanent Security Council members, plus Germany, were deadlocked, each of the so-called U-6 nations risked painful economic or political repercussions for their vote. State Department officials were dispatched to Africa with promises of aid to Angola, Cameroon, and Guinea. Former secretary of state Henry Kissinger traveled to Mexico City to secure the vote of President Vincente Fox's government. He warned Washington would be "very unhappy" with a vote against the war.[17] Like other U.S. envoys, he encountered stiff resistance. So did Prime Minister Aznar, who made a special trip to win over the Mexicans. If the powerful nations with veto power can't agree, complained Adolfo Aguilar Zinser, Mexico's UN ambassador, "why do you transfer this responsibility to us, the little guys?" To many smaller nations, strong-arm political tactics by the powerful were offensive. Said the Pakistani ambassador, "We are poor, but we are important. Pakistan doesn't respond very well to pressure."[18] Mexico in particular, with strong public sentiment against the war and its special relationship to the United States, did not want to risk being singled out by voting against Washington. In the end, Mexico and Chile made a pact to abstain from any vote on a second resolution.

U.S. intimidation tactics featured prominently in the haphazard and last-minute American effort. In an apparent attempt to publicly embarrass Blix, a senior State Department official slammed U.S. surveillance photos on Blix's desk in his New York office and demanded to know why the inspectors had not found the pictured munitions, which turned out to be a mix of scrap metal and legal weapons. The official refused to tell Blix where the photos were taken. On March 2, a classified internal e-mail from the National Security Agency, apparently leaked to London's *Observer,* revealed that the NSA had ordered electronic surveillance of the homes and offices of UN delegates from the U-6 countries to learn how they would vote on a resolution submitted to the Security Council by the United States and Britain.

"The Agency is mounting a surge particularly directed at the U.N. Security Council members (minus US and GBR of course) for insights as to how membership is reacting to the ongoing debate," it read. The memo instructed NSA operatives to collect "the whole gamut of information that could give U.S. policymakers an edge in obtaining results favorable to U.S. goals or to head off surprises."[19] The paper reported that the operation had been ordered by National Security Advisor Condoleezza Rice. Although some officials of the nations affected were reportedly angered by the U.S. action, most UN delegates shrugged off the report of U.S. spying as business as usual.

A week earlier, on February 26, President Bush seemed to settle on a new rationale for war against Iraq in a speech before the right-wing American Enterprise Institute at the Washington Hilton. Adopting the long-held views of senior neoconservatives within his administration who bitterly opposed seeking UN approval for the war, the president set out a new vision of peace and democracy in the Middle East. "A liberated Iraq can show the power of freedom to transform that vital region, by bringing hope and progress into the lives of millions," said the president.[20] Recalling the victories of World War II, Bush invoked the U.S.-administered reconstruction of postwar Japan and Germany. "After defeating enemies, we did not leave behind occupying armies, we left constitutions and parliaments," Bush declared. "We established an atmosphere of safety, in which responsible, reform-minded local leaders could build lasting institutions of freedom. In societies that once bred fascism and militarism, liberty found a permanent home."[21]

If the president had alighted on a positively Reaganesque vision of war with Iraq, it immediately ran into heavy flak. The very same day, a State Department intelligence analyst and Middle East specialist named Wayne White published a classified report that expressed deep skepticism that regime change in Baghdad would advance the spread of democracy in the region—the so-called democratic domino theory long espoused by Paul Wolfowitz and other leading neoconservatives. "Liberal democracy would be difficult to achieve," White's report asserted. "Electoral democracy, were it to emerge, could well be subject to exploitation by anti-American elements." Said an intelligence official familiar with the report, "This idea that you're going to transform the Middle East and fundamentally alter its trajectory is not credible."[22]

While Bush was rolling out his kinder, gentler war rhetoric, Tony Blair suffered a stunning blow at the hands of his own Labour Party. On February 26, a motion in Parliament to back the prime minister's policy seeking Iraqi disarmament at the United Nations had narrowly passed, but 122 Labour MPs voted against Blair, one of the worst rebellions against a sitting prime minister in British history. Soon afterward, Bush called for a vote on the second resolution in the Security Council, as if this would give Blair a fighting chance for political cover. But then he vowed, "We will act, and we really do not need the United Nations approval to do so"— badly undermining Blair's tenuous political position at home.[23]

By then, however, evidence was mounting that not even Blair believed in his own rhetoric anymore. On March 5, amid the fight to get a second resolution before the Security Council, Blair met with the leader of the House of Commons and former foreign secretary Robin Cook, a Labour stalwart who came away from the meeting with the strong impression that the prime minister, while he continued to press his policy, no longer believed Saddam possessed significant WMD programs, or put much stock in the UN weapons inspections.

Cook had suspected that something was amiss two weeks earlier after a briefing by John Scarlett, the chief of Britain's Joint Intelligence Committee, who had played a key role in putting together the September 24 British white paper on Saddam's banned unconventional weapons. "The presentation was impressive in its integrity and shorn of the political slant with which No 10 encumbers any intelligence assessment," Cook later wrote in his diary of the session with Scarlett. "My conclusion at the end of an hour is that Saddam probably does not have weapons of mass destruction in the sense of weapons that could be used against large-scale civilian targets."[24]

In his meeting with Blair, wrote Cook, "the most revealing exchange came when we talked about Saddam's arsenal. I told him, 'It's clear from the private briefing I have had that Saddam has no weapons of mass destruction in a sense of weapons that could strike at strategic cities. But he probably does have several thousand battlefield chemical munitions. Do you never worry that he might use them against British troops?'" Blair responded, "'Yes, but all the effort he has had to put into concealment makes it difficult for him to assemble them quickly for use.'"[25] Cook was struck by what Blair had *not* said in the exchange. "The timetable to war was plainly not driven by the progress of the UN weapons inspections," wrote Cook. "Tony made no attempt to pretend that what Hans Blix might report would make any difference to the countdown to invasion." The second and more troubling element "was that Tony did not try to argue me out of the view that Saddam did not have real weapons of mass destruction that were designed for strategic use against city populations and capable of being delivered with reliability over long distances."[26]

In Cook's reading, both Scarlett and Blair had now "assented" to the view that Saddam had no WMD. Even if Saddam had retained a stock of battlefield chemical weapons, he wrote, they hardly amounted to "a clear and present danger" to Britain, and would only threaten British soldiers if they were deployed on a battlefield within range of Iraqi guns. Even if Blair had believed the previous September that Saddam really had weapons ready for firing with forty-five minutes, as the famous dossier stated, "what was clear from this conversation was that he did not believe it himself in March." For Cook, that raised "the gravest of political questions." Government ministers, he wrote, were required by the rules of the House of Commons to correct the record if they become aware they may have misled Parliament. If this was the case, "should they not have told Parliament before asking the Commons to vote for war on a false prospectus?"[27]

On March 7, Blix and ElBaradei gave what would be their last reports to the Security Council before the war. As Bush and Blair had anticipated, there was almost no good news for the United States and Britain. The inspectors had unearthed next to nothing to support U.S. and British claims that Iraq had weapons of mass destruction or active programs to develop them. Blix announced that thirty-four al-Samoud 2 missiles and certain missile components were destroyed after inspectors confirmed their range exceeded the 150-kilometer limit. Blix did his best to play up the significance of UNMOVIC's action. "We are not watching the breaking of toothpicks," he said. "Lethal weapons are being destroyed."[28] He went on to say that several inspections of mobile production facilities had taken place, but no banned activities were discovered. Despite reports of underground weapons sites, Blix said, inspections of both declared and undeclared sites with ground-penetrating radar found no evidence of underground facilities for chemical or biological production or storage. He concluded that UNMOVIC needed more time "to verify sites and items, analyze documents, interview relevant persons and draw conclusions. It will not take years, nor weeks, but months."

ElBaradei, for his part, quietly reported a finding that would become a political time bomb for the White House. In February, the IAEA had finally received copies of the documents from the United States that were the basis of reports that the Iraqis had an interest in buying uranium from Niger. ElBaradei reported that IAEA inspectors had examined the papers and found that they "are in fact not authentic. We have therefore concluded that these specific allegations are unfounded." Foreshadowing the postwar reporting of U.S. weapons hunter David Kay, ElBaradei also noted that Iraq's "industrial capacity has deteriorated substantially," due to the departure of the foreign industrial support since the late 1980s, the exodus of many skilled Iraqi personnel in the past decade, and Iraq's lack of maintenance of sophisticated equipment. "This overall deterioration," said ElBaradei, "is naturally of direct relevance to Iraq's capacity for resuming a nuclear weapons program."[29]

French foreign minister de Villepin, as usual, seized the opportunity to declare that the reports "testify to the progress" of the UN weapons inspections and vowed that France would not support another resolution because "we cannot accept any ultimatum, any automatic use of force."

Playing his strongest remaining card, Secretary of State Powell described Iraq's behavior as "a catalogue of non-cooperation" and asserted that Saddam's regime "continues to possess and conceal some of the most lethal weapons ever devised." Declared Powell: "We must not find ourselves here this coming November with the pressure removed and with Iraq once again marching down the merry path to weapons of mass destruction, threatening the region, threatening the world."

The pace of events quickened in the next ten days. Sir Jeremy Greenstock, Britain's UN ambassador, set to work on a compromise draft proposal for a second resolution. The proposal was organized around six tests Saddam would have to pass, based in part on a televised confession about Baghdad's WMD and a list of unresolved weapons issues from Blix that had to be met. On March 11, French president Jacques Chirac all but cut off the possibility of Security Council approval of the war by going on television and promising to veto any second resolution. "My position is that, regardless of the circumstances, France will vote 'no,'" said Chirac.[30] That gave Bush the justification he needed to withdraw the second resolution, and on March 16 he flew to the Azores for a meeting with Blair and Spain's Aznar and informed them of his plan to pull out of the Security Council and issue a final warning to Saddam in a speech on March 17. War would follow within forty-eight hours. The White House had wanted to meet in London, but 10 Downing Street opposed the idea, since the final vote on British military participation in Parliament was scheduled for the eighteenth. Blair was afraid Bush's presence in London would spark antiwar demonstrations.

On Monday morning, March 17, Bush told Gen. Tommy Franks to be ready to go into action within seventy-two hours. He spoke with Blair about heading off the possibility of a counter-resolution in the Security Council that might undermine the slender legal authorization for war U.S. and British lawyers now claimed was provided by Resolution 1441. Blair reportedly expressed confidence that he would win the vote in Parliament the next day, but was concerned about the size of the Labour vote. At 8:55 A.M. Powell briefed the president and the NSC on diplomatic activity at the United Nations, and assured him there had been no changes. Presidential spokesman Ari Fleischer met with the press and announced at 9:45 that "the United Nations has failed to enforce its own demands that Iraq immediately disarm. As a result, the diplomatic window has now been closed."

In London, Robin Cook resigned from Blair's cabinet. "I can't accept collective responsibility for the decision to commit Britain now to military action in Iraq without international agreement or domestic support," said Cook, a former foreign secretary who was the first of several senior Blair officials to quit in protest over the war.[31] The next evening at 10:15 P.M., the House of Commons voted to approve British participation in the invasion of Iraq by a margin of 396–217. The number of Labour MPs voting against Blair's war policy rose from 122 in February to 139 on the eve of war, or about a third of the prime minister's party.

But the seven-month diplomatic ordeal was finally over. Bush had turned public opinion against the Iraqi dictator and won a valuable coalition partner in his war effort. Blair had gained an influential role with Washington and received the blessing of Parliament. Both had waged a legitimate battle to force the United Nations to stand behind its ideals and principles. But their world-class political victories had come at a cost that would only become evident as the credibility of their tortured and misconceived rationale for going to war on Iraq came under increasing attack, crumbled, and finally disintegrated in the months and years ahead. Bush called Blair on the morning of March 20, after the attack on Saddam had begun. An expansive Blair told the president, "I kind of think that the decisions taken in the next few weeks will determine the rest of the world for years to come. . . . As primary players, we have a chance to shape the issues that are discussed. Both of us will have enormous capital and a lot of people will be with us."[32] Neither the prime minister nor the president could guess at that moment that it was the decisions they already had made that would change the course of events in the world for years into the future—and how few people would be with them.

The war began overnight on March 19 with a thundering surprise attack by U.S. cruise missiles and F-117 fighter-bombers on Saddam and his two sons at Dora Farms, a complex of buildings southeast of Baghdad. The Iraqi dictator was apparently badly shaken, but the invasion was under way at last. For more than a year, the American public had been saturated with warnings from senior White House officials about Baghdad's deadly WMD arsenal. Americans were persuaded in overwhelming numbers that the president was taking the war on terror to Iraq in order to strip Saddam of his weapons. A CBS News poll taken a few weeks into the war showed that 81 percent of Americans surveyed believed that Saddam probably had WMD and 60 percent believed the Iraqi threat required a military response—a measure of the success of the relentless White House campaign to shape public opinion.

Even after the war began, the White House continued to hammer away at Saddam's weapons of mass destruction. During a press conference on the second day of the war, White House spokesman Ari Fleischer insisted that the weapons justified the invasion of Iraq, and declared that coalition forces would find prohibited weapons in Iraq. "There is no question that we have evidence and information that Iraq has weapons of mass destruction, biological and chemical particularly," said Fleischer. "This was the reason that the President felt so strongly that we needed to take military action to disarm Saddam Hussein, since he would not do it himself." Asked if he expected these weapons to be found in Iraq, Fleischer was unequivocal. "There's no question," he said. "We have said that Saddam Hussein possesses biological and chemical weapons, and all this will be made clear in the course of the operation, for whatever duration it takes."[33] Fleischer carefully skirted any mention of Saddam's reconstituted nuclear Iraqi program.

The next day, President Bush, in his regular Saturday radio address to the nation, reaffirmed the reasons for the war. "Our mission is clear, to disarm Iraq of weapons of mass destruction, to end Saddam Hussein's support for terrorism, and to free the Iraqi people."[34] From his command headquarters in the tiny Persian Gulf emirate of Qatar, Gen. Tommy Franks said that locating and destroying Iraq's WMD was one of the U.S. military's primary objectives in Iraq. "There is no doubt that the regime of Saddam Hussein possesses weapons of mass destruction," said Franks. "As this operation continues, those weapons will be identified, found, along with the people who have produced them and who guard them." He conceded that none had been found in the early going. In Washington, unnamed U.S. officials helpfully cautioned that the illegal munitions could be scattered in small batches throughout the Iraqi desert and might be difficult to find.[35]

It fell to army major general James Marks, who had been assigned the top intelligence slot for the U.S.-led invasion forces the previous September, to oversee the search for Saddam's WMD in Iraq. From his first meetings at the Pentagon with DIA intelligence analysts, who had compiled a master list of 946 locations in Iraq identified as WMD storage sites or weapons production facilities, Marks was struck by the vagueness of the information. He was amazed at how little the analysts seemed to know about the locations, the relative importance of each, or how troops in the field should prioritize and treat them. Many sites on the list were from five-year-old satellite photos, intercepts, or other imagery that struck Marks as having questionable value for an invasion in early

2003. "I was shocked at the lack of detail," said Marks, who found himself unable to say with any certainty that a single location supplied by U.S. intelligence actually had WMD—the same problem Hans Blix would complain about.[36]

Marks also wondered why the DIA and his staff were the only ones on the WMD search-and-destroy detail. After all, Saddam's weapons were touted by the CIA and other U.S. intelligence agencies as the primary rationale for going into Iraq. In December, just as the Iraqis submitted their declaration on prohibited weapons, Marks told his commanding officer, Lt. Gen. David McKiernan, that he could not confirm what was inside buildings at any of the sites on the Pentagon's master list, despite an abundance of U.S. overhead satellite surveillance photos. Marks found an artillery brigade at Fort Sill, Oklahoma, that could be repurposed to handle the search for WMD on the ground in Iraq. It was renamed the 75th Exploitation Task Force, or XTF. By January, Marks had moved into Kuwait with tens of thousands of other U.S. troops as part of the buildup for the war. After a candid conversation with General Franks's deputy, Lt. Gen. John Abizaid, a Middle East expert whom Marks had known since they both had attended West Point, Marks realized he would have to plan as if the sites had WMD, whether or not the intelligence actually showed it.[37]

By early March, the intelligence picture had not improved. Marks was still trying to prioritize 946 suspected WMD sites—whether to search individual locations, post guards, and bypass them or just note them and move on. He tried unsuccessfully to reach up the chain of command for more information. When the 75th XTF weapons-hunting brigade was deployed, it was immediately cut back to four teams that would accompany the lead combat forces and, as Judith Miller of *The New York Times* reported, two mobile exploitation teams, or MET units, with the expertise to do intensive searches of the WMD sites. After more than a month of combat operations, the MET units had found little but looted warehouses and laboratories, and Marks blamed General Tommy Franks's Central Command for not supplying them with better information. "They are completely asleep at the switch," Marks wrote in his diary about the Centcom command. "How idiotic are these guys! Incredible!"[38]

In late May, during a swing through Europe and the Middle East, President Bush created a stir by declaring to a Polish TV reporter, "We found the weapons of mass destruction." He said U.S. forces had found two mobile biological laboratories, and reminded viewers of Colin Powell's presentation in February and that such weapons programs violated UN resolutions. "For those who say we haven't found the banned manufacturing devices or banned weapons," said the president, "they're wrong. We found them." But Bush had spoken without confirmation from the army. After tests were conducted, weapons experts decided that the labs were probably intended to manufacture hydrogen for weather balloons. When the president arrived in Qatar in early June, he sat down with Defense Secretary Rumsfeld and Paul Bremer, the new U.S. administrator for the Iraqi provisional government, and asked point-blank who was in charge of searching for WMD. Like a latter-day Laurel and Hardy, Rumsfeld and Bremer each pointed to the other. The president reportedly almost exploded, and said the job should go to someone else. He decided to hand the task over to the CIA, which had proved its mettle ensuring the rout of the Taliban in Afghanistan and consistently had advised the White House that Saddam possessed WMD.[39]

By then, the news had spread to the United States and around the world that U.S. troops had found no evidence of Saddam's weapons or production facilities in Iraq. Senior officials from the president down insisted that finding them was just a matter of time. Despite this disturbing twist of events, virtually every political poll showed President Bush with approval ratings of more than 70 percent. Assurances by senior U.S. officials that the missing WMD would soon turn up were bolstered by the credibility bestowed upon a successful wartime president who was embraced by most Americans. In the eighteen months since 9/11, the White House had earned a reputation for aggressive handling of the press and disciplined message control, especially after the astonishing success of the 2002 midterm elections restored Republican control of both houses of Congress. Along the way, Bush officials had also gained a darker reputation for equating opposition to their policies with disloyalty to the nation and regularly charged Democrats and critics with being unpatriotic and soft on terrorism.

The aura of strength and determination around the White House was only enhanced as the Executive Office of the President, fashioned to the purposes of war by the powerful vice president and his staff, methodically wrested the levers of privilege and power from a compliant Republican Congress. With troops still in harm's way in Afghanistan and now in Iraq, the Bush White House, determined to claim executive privileges well beyond its Supreme Court–driven electoral mandate, began to take on the trappings of an imperial presidency. Few could imagine in the months following the end of combat in Iraq that within two years the Bush presidency would be pulled apart and isolated at home and abroad by the forces it had set in motion. Although many Americans believed there might be good reasons the WMD had not been found, few imagined that the Bush administration, operating behind its carefully constructed walls of secrecy, might have consciously exaggerated and distorted the intelligence on Iraq's weapons in its rush to war in Iraq.

20

THE WHITE HOUSE UNDER SIEGE

On the morning of Sunday, July 6, 2003, former ambassador Joseph Wilson awoke at his home in the Palisades neighborhood of northwest Washington, a few short blocks west of Foxhall Road. Late the night before, Wilson had received a telephone call from a reporter asking for comment on an opinion piece he had written for *The New York Times* that had just popped up on the *Times* Web site, and would appear in the paper Sunday morning. Soon after he hung up, the phone rang again. This time it was a producer from NBC's *Meet the Press* who asked if Wilson would appear on the show the next morning to discuss his article with Senator John Warner, the senior Republican from Virginia, and the liberal Democrat Senator Carl Levin of Michigan. Both legislators had just returned from Iraq, where U.S. military units were still struggling to turn up evidence of Saddam's formidable arsenal of weapons.

Wilson, of course, quickly agreed. In a serendipitous, if calculated, bit of timing, his Sunday *Times* op-ed piece would appear simultaneously with a profile in the *Washington Post*'s style section of Wilson and his wife Valerie Plame Wilson, a vivacious and successful energy consultant—as far as anyone knew at the time—and their four-year-old twins, Samantha and Trevor. But the profile was overwhelmed by the news Wilson's *Times* op-ed article generated. It was riveting reading—and would set off an explosive chain of events that within months triggered a grand jury investigation of senior White House officials, exposed the weakness and deception of the president's case for war, and concluded almost four years later with a criminal verdict against the vice president's top aide, Lewis Libby. Wilson began the piece by asking, "Did the Bush administration manipulate intelligence about Saddam Hussein's weapons programs to justify an invasion of Iraq?" He answered bluntly in the second sentence that there was little doubt "some of the intelligence related to Iraq's nuclear weapons program was twisted to exaggerate the Iraqi threat."

Knowing he would come under political attack, the former ambassador was careful to set forth his bona fides. He was a government insider who had served both Republican and Democratic presidents for more than twenty years. He was a senior adviser to the National Security Council on Africa policy during the Clinton administration, chargé d'affaires at the U.S. embassy in Baghdad during the Gulf War in 1991, and ambassador to Gabon and São Tomé and Príncipe under presidents George H. W. Bush and Ronald Reagan. Although he did not mention it in his *Times* piece, Wilson was the ranking embassy official in Baghdad in late 1990, when more than one hundred U.S. diplomatic personnel were refused travel documents and forced by the Iraqis to hole up in the U.S. embassy compound, where they were effectively held hostage by the Baghdad regime in the months before Operation Desert Storm. Wilson took it upon himself to organize their sustenance and work to ensure their release before bombs started dropping. Upon his return to the United States, President Bush hailed him as a hero.

Wilson's *Times* story was straightforward. Uncorroborated intelligence emerged in the months after 9/11 that Iraq was interested in illegally purchasing processed uranium ore, or yellowcake, from the tiny former French African colony of Niger. Given his background in African affairs, Wilson was asked by the CIA to travel to the country's capital, Niamey, to make discreet inquiries. His CIA briefers told him that Vice President Cheney had expressed interest in a particular report on the purchase and asked the CIA for more information. Wilson wrote, "While I never saw the report, I was told that it referred to a memorandum of agreement that documented the sale of uranium yellowcake. . . ." He recounted in some detail how he met with U.S. embassy officials, including Ambassador Barbro Owens-Kirkpatrick, who had heard such allegations before and had debunked them in cables to Washington. Nonetheless, Wilson wrote, he and Owens-Kirkpatrick, along with a U.S. military attaché for the region, set about meeting with current and former Nigerien government officials, businessmen, and people associated with the uranium trade, but they turned up virtually nothing.

After more than a week in Niamey, Wilson wrote, he concluded that "it was highly doubtful any such transaction had ever taken place." No one he spoke with recalled such a deal. Niger's two mines were run by a consortium that included French, Spanish, Japanese, and German interests, which would have known about the removal of any uranium ore, which in turn was strictly monitored by the IAEA. There was "simply too much oversight over too small an industry for a sale to have transpired," he wrote. Wilson described checking his conclusion with Owens-Kirkpatrick and embassy staffers, who submitted their own separate reports in agreement. When Wilson returned to Washington in mid-February 2002, he was debriefed by a CIA official and that was the end of it—for the moment.

Then in September 2002, the British white paper on Iraq's WMD reached Washington reporting the assessment of British intelligence that Iraq's prohibited weapons presented an immediate danger. The British dossier specifically cited Iraq's interest in buying uranium from an unnamed African country as evidence that Saddam was rebuilding his nuclear weapons program. Subsequently the president, wrote Wilson, repeated the charge in his January 2003 State of the Union message, attributing the information to the British report. Wilson at first accepted a State Department colleague's explanation that the president must have meant another uranium-producing African country, like Gabon or Namibia. But further evidence persuaded him that the British report was a recycled version of the Niger story. If his information about the Niger uranium sale proved inaccurate, Wilson wrote, he would understand—though he very much would like to know why.

"If, however, the information was ignored because it didn't fit certain prescriptions about Iraq," he declared, "then a legitimate argument can be made that we went to war under false pretenses." Wilson knew firsthand the dangers that would be posed if Saddam had weapons of mass destruction. He concluded the fifteen-hundred-word article by declaring that "America's foreign policy depends on the sanctity of its information. For this reason, questioning the selective use of intelligence to justify the war in Iraq is neither sniping nor 'revisionist history,' as Mr. Bush has suggested. The act of war is the last option of a democracy, taken when there is a grave threat to our security. More than 200 American lives have been lost in Iraq already. We have a duty to ensure that their sacrifice came for the right reason."[1]

When the Sunday *Times* hit the newsstands, Wilson's position against the war was well known. He had authored other opinion pieces since the president had uttered the sixteen-word sentence about uranium from Africa in his State of the Union message six months before. But none of his previous writings so much as hinted at his own personal involvement in the Niger affair, or criticized how the administration was using intelligence. In a February 6, 2003, op-ed piece for *The Los Angeles Times,* Wilson had cautioned against sending "American troops to fight a war of 'liberation' that can be waged only by the Iraqis themselves." Like many others, Wilson assumed that Saddam possessed weapons of mass destruction and worried that he would have "no incentive . . . to comply with weapons inspectors and to refrain from using" them if the United States attacked. "And he will use them," wrote Wilson, who had personally bargained with Hussein over the fate of 150 American "human shields" whom Iraqi forces threatened to use as protection during the first Gulf War. In early March, weeks before the 2003 U.S. invasion, Wilson had warned in a *New Republic* article that any neoconservative-inspired attempt to implant governments in the Middle East that "ape our worldview" was a "breathtakingly ambitious undertaking" and involved "a huge risk of overreach" that might turn out to be "a bitter lesson" for Americans.

Wilson was keeping his powder dry on the Niger story. But on March 7, Mohamed ElBaradei, the head of the Vienna-based International Atomic Energy Agency, declared that documents that had been circulating in the intelligence community about the alleged sale of uranium to Iraq from Niger were transparent forgeries. Wilson was stunned to hear a State Department spokesman remark to the media, "We fell for it." During an appearance on CNN several days later,[2] Wilson voiced skepticism for the first time about the administration's profession of ignorance. He knew from his Niger experience that the State Department had on file multiple internal reports more than a year old that debunked the uranium story. Wilson told David Ensor, the cable network's national security reporter, that either the State Department's profession of ignorance and surprise was a ruse to deceive the public or the spokesman had been deceived by his superiors. Wilson did not reveal to Ensor how he knew, but told him the Bush administration reaction convinced him something was awry.

Ensor was one of several Washington reporters Wilson subsequently talked to on background about his role in the Niger trip. Another was Nicholas Kristof of *The New York Times,* who wrote two columns, one on May 6 and another on June 13, sketching out Wilson's story in some detail, but did not use his name, referring instead to "a person involved in the Niger caper." Wilson also told Walter Pincus of *The Washington Post* about the trip and his concern about the administration's ignorance of the record. Between ElBaradei's dismissal of the Niger documents as forgeries in early March and the publication of his July 6 op-ed account in *The Times,* Wilson tried repeatedly, in his words, "to get the White House to come clean" on the Niger intelligence. By his account, he spoke with contacts with close ties to White House officials, senior State Department officials, and staff at the Senate and House intelligence committees.

Senior White House officials had known about Wilson's role in the Niger business well before his article appeared in *The Times.* Wilson heard from "a respected reporter" that soon after his CNN appearance in March, the vice president's office held a meeting to do a "workup" for a political strategy to discredit him. Wilson was told that senior members of the OVP staff attended, along with senior Republicans, including Newt Gingrich.[3] The meeting would have taken place two months before the earliest documented date that Lewis Libby and the vice president's office began to focus on Wilson. Whatever the earlier machinations, on May 29 Lewis Libby requested a State Department report on Wilson's trip to Niger from then undersecretary of state Marc Grossman. Grossman asked Carl Ford, the chief of the State Department's Bureau of Intelligence and Research (INR), to produce a classified memorandum on Wilson's mission and the circumstances surrounding it. The report the INR produced was stamped SECRET. Key paragraphs, including one that mentioned Valerie Wilson, were marked "S/NF," for "Secret/No Foreign," meaning the classified information was not for the consumption of foreigners. The INR forwarded copies to Grossman, Secretary Powell, and Deputy Secretary Richard Armitage.[4] Grossman briefed Libby on the memo and mentioned that Wilson's wife had selected her husband for the Niger trip.

From the beginning, Vice President Cheney appears to have personally orchestrated the White House effort to discredit Wilson's charge that the Bush administration had used flawed intelligence to rationalize going to war in Iraq. Contrary to the administration's reputation for tight discipline, senior officials were in a state of disarray. The military's failure to locate WMD in Iraq was fast eroding the president's justification for invading Iraq. Between late June and early July—it is not clear exactly when—the president authorized the declassification of two CIA documents, a section of the October 2002 National Intelligence Estimate and a March 2002 summary of Wilson's visit to Niger—to rebut the former ambassador's claims.[5] Through the vice president, President Bush reportedly authorized Libby to inform the press that "a key judgment of the NIE held that Iraq was 'vigorously trying to procure' uranium."[6] A British parliamentary inquiry had just issued a scathing denunciation of claims by British intelligence that Britain had fresh evidence of an Iraqi deal to purchase African uranium ore. The report concluded that the information was recycled from the same forged reports about a purported sale of Niger yellowcake that had been discredited in March.

Meanwhile, as the president and vice president dispatched Libby to leak classified information to selected members of the Washington press corps to shore up their political position, other officials at the White House, including Deputy National Security Advisor Stephen Hadley, were kept in the dark about what would be declassified and made public and what wouldn't. Libby, it seemed, "consciously decided not to make Mr. Hadley aware of the fact that [he] himself had already been disseminating the N.I.E. by leaking it to reporters while Mr. Hadley sought to get it formally declassified," according to later court filings.[7] On June 27, Libby met with Bob Woodward and told him that the classified October NIE described "vigorous" Iraqi efforts to obtain processed uranium ore in Africa.

During a meeting in Cheney's office on July 7, the day after Wilson's article appeared, the vice president also instructed press aide Catherine Martin to inform the news media that the 2002 NIE left no doubt about Iraqi efforts to buy uranium in Niger. She took down the information Cheney wanted conveyed to reporters on lined notebook paper. "As late as last October," her notes read, "the considered judgment of the intel community was that SH [Saddam Hussein] had indeed undertaken a vigorous effort to acquire uranium from Africa, according to NIE [the National Intelligence Estimate]." At one point, Libby also asked her to find out from the CIA which reporters were asking about Wilson's trip to Niger, then telephoned one of them himself in an attempt to influence a news broadcast.[8] Also in early July, Martin recalled being with Libby one day when he telephoned a CIA official to ask about the Wilson trip. He handed the phone to her to speak with CIA spokesman Bill Harlow, who confirmed that Wilson had made the trip and and informed her that his wife worked for the agency. In a meeting later that day, Martin reported back to Cheney and Libby that Harlow told her Wilson's wife worked for the CIA.[9]

It was not the first time either Libby or the vice president had heard about Wilson's wife or her involvement with the Niger trip. Each had made separate inquiries to the CIA about Wilson a month earlier. Libby had placed a call to CIA associate deputy director Robert Grenier on June 11 requesting background on Wilson's trip to Niger. Later that afternoon, Libby called back, forcing Grenier to interrupt a meeting with Tenet to take the call. Grenier confirmed that Wilson had made the Niger trip to check on reports Iraq had tried to buy uranium from the Niamey government for nuclear weapons, and had concluded that the reports were unfounded. Grenier then told Libby that Wilson's wife was a CIA officer, and apparently had suggested her husband for the trip. He later recalled that Libby seemed intent on finding out whether the CIA would deflect attention from the vice president's presumed role in triggering Wilson's trip with a statement to the media that State and Defense were also interested. "I think they were trying to avoid blame for not providing [the truth] about whether or not Iraq had attempted to buy uranium," Grenier said later.[10]

In fact, back in September 2002, before the October intelligence estimate had been completed, both Tenet and his top nuclear analyst, Robert Walpole, had expressed strong doubts about the Niger intelligence and relegated it to minor status on page twenty-four of the NIE. The information was judged too uncertain to appear in the "key judgments" section of the estimate. The classified document assessed that "we do not know the status" of the alleged sale of unrefined yellowcake to the Iraqis and "cannot confirm whether Iraq succeeded in acquiring" it. Despite repeated efforts of the White House Iraq Group to pitch the Niger story for speeches of senior administration officials, the National Intelligence Council drafted an authoritative memo in January 2003 concluding that the Niger intelligence was baseless. The memo was distributed to the White House just as the president's speechwriters were preparing the infamous sixteen words for his State of the Union message.[11]

Cheney queried the CIA separately about Valerie Plame Wilson's role in the Niger mission at about the same time. Libby later testified that Cheney had learned about Wilson's wife in a conversation with George Tenet, although the DCI's office would not confirm that such a conversation had taken place. But classified CIA reports about Wilson's assignment were sent "to the personal attention of Libby and another person in the Office of the Vice President" on June 9 and may have been in response to inquiries from either Libby or Cheney. In any case, three days later, apparently during an Air Force Two flight on Saturday, June 12, from the Norfolk, Virginia, naval station to Washington, the vice president told Libby "that Wilson's wife worked . . . in the Counterproliferation Division" of the CIA[12]—a strong suggestion to knowledgeable consumers of intelligence, such as Cheney, that she was employed by the Directorate of Operations, the CIA's clandestine branch, and was probably a covert agent.

Libby began to drop hints that he knew about Wilson's wife. In his daily CIA briefing two days later, Libby complained that agency officials were trying to blame the vice president's office for initiating the Niger trip—and mentioned Valerie Plame Wilson by name. Libby's briefer, Craig Schmall, later confirmed that Libby was annoyed by Wilson's Niger trip.[13] Schmall also reported that both he and Libby were excited about the actor Tom Cruise's recent visit to the White House with actress Pené-lope Cruz. The two had complained about the treatment of Scientologists in Germany.

In a matter of days, members of the Washington press began hearing about Wilson's wife's CIA employment from senior administration officials—fully a month before her name appeared publicly in Robert Novak's column. On June 13, *Washington Post* assistant managing editor Bob Woodward, whose book *Bush at War* had come out the previous year, met with Deputy Secretary of State Richard Armitage at his office in the course of doing research for a new book. Woodward's ground rules were well known to senior government officials: Any revelations, however newsworthy, would await the book's publication, and under no circumstance would they appear in the next day's, or the next Sunday's, *Washington Post*. During the background interview, Armitage, who had seen Grossman's memo, apparently wanted to make it clear to Woodward that the State Department had nothing to do with the president's remarks on uranium from Africa in the State of the Union Address—or with former ambassador Wilson's trip to Niger, which its analysts had actively discouraged.

In the course of explaining that the State Department was "clean as a [expletive deleted] whistle" on the dubious Niger intelligence, Armitage, who had a well-known penchant for Washington gossip, couldn't resist slipping in the fact that Wilson's "wife works in the agency." Woodward immediately got the point. "Why doesn't that come out?" he asked. "Why does . . . that have to be a big secret?" Armitage described Wilson's frustration after the trip "because he was designated as a low-level guy," and returned to Wilson's wife, declaring, "It . . . it's perfect. This is what she does, she is a WMD analyst out there." Woodward pressed Armitage on whether Wilson's wife had gone to Niger with her husband. Armitage was not sure. "I don't know whether she was out there or not. But his wife is in the agency and is a WMD analyst. How about that [expletive deleted]!"[14] Woodward later dismissed Armitage's remarks about Wilson's wife as having been "mentioned in passing," and maintained that he didn't see Wilson's wife or the brewing controversy over her role inside the White House as news. Woodward spoke to Libby two weeks later about the legitimacy of the Niger story. When *Plan of Attack* was published the next year, it contained a single sentence about Wilson's trip to Niger—and no mention at all of Valerie Plame Wilson.[15]

Woodward wasn't the only veteran Washington reporter who learned about Wilson's wife well before the rest of the Washington press. Ten days later, on June 23, *New York Times* reporter Judith Miller met with Lewis Libby at his office in the Old Executive Office Building. Miller had just returned from Iraq and was working on a story about what happened to the missing WMD. She knew Libby was an avid consumer of prewar intelligence and had talked to him before about Iraq's WMD. He was, as she put it, "a good-faith source who was usually straight with me."[16]

Libby, however, was more interested in talking about Joe Wilson and his trip to Niger. He was annoyed that the CIA was engaging in "selective leaking" of information that made it appear Langley had sent a certain former diplomat to Africa "at the behest" of Cheney, as Nicholas Kristof reported on June 13. To Libby, the Kristof column and a story in *The Post* by Walter Pincus the day before seemed to represent an escalation of CIA hostilities toward the vice president. To Miller, Libby appeared angry that the president might have made inaccurate statements because the CIA wouldn't step up and admit that it had doubts about the intelligence—though he must have known Tenet himself had blown the whistle on the Niger story for Bush's Cincinnati speech. "No briefer came in and said, 'You got it wrong, Mr. President,'" Libby insisted. Toward the end of the interview, recalled Miller, Libby mentioned that Wilson's wife possibly worked for the CIA. She entered a question in her notebook, "(Wife works in Bureau?)," but gave no indication that Libby suggested Wilson's wife might have had a role in sending her husband to Niger. It was the first time that Miller had heard of Wilson's wife.[17]

By the morning of Sunday, July 6, the basic outlines of the Niger story and the allegations in Wilson's *New York Times* op-ed piece were known to Washington insiders. The only real mystery was the role Joe Wilson himself had played, and that was about to change. As his wife, Valerie, straightened his tie before he left for NBC's television studio in Washington, she told him that an appearance on *Meet the Press* was not only stepping up to the major leagues, "it was the World Series," Wilson recalled. "I needed to be at the top of my game," he said.[18]

The day before, the president took a much-needed break from his official duties. Bush played a relaxed round of golf with old friends in the muggy summer heat at Andrews Air Force Base, and Saturday evening attended a party the first lady threw for him to celebrate his fifty-seventh birthday. Events in Iraq were not going the president's way, as evidenced by the Sunday papers and TV reports, and he needed a rest before taking off on Air Force One Monday for a weeklong diplomatic tour of African countries from South Africa to Nigeria. Only ten weeks had passed since the president, wearing an aviator's flight suit, had flown out to the aircraft carrier USS *Abraham Lincoln* off San Diego on May 2 and declared "major combat operations in Iraq have ended." Behind him, an oversize banner, which would later become a looming symbol to his critics of presidential arrogance and impatience, ruffled in the breeze on the ship's superstructure, proclaiming MISSION ACCOMPLISHED.

Optimistic White House predictions that U.S. forces would be welcomed as liberators by grateful Iraqis had not materialized. Sunni backers of Saddam, ex–Iraqi military personnel, and Revolutionary Guard cadres, along with growing numbers of al-Qaeda and Islamist revolutionaries from Syria, Iran, and other Arab countries, had joined together in a growing insurgency. Shootings, car bombings, and even suicide bombers targeting civil authorities were on the rise daily. The bloodshed and disorder were a direct threat to the ill-planned, slow-moving American efforts to rebuild the country's infrastructure and establish a democratic government in Baghdad. Worse, with each passing day, the administration's prewar intelligence became increasingly suspect, as U.S. forces failed to find the anticipated arsenals of weapons of mass destruction in Iraq. In Washington the CIA and the White House staff already had begun a low-level war of leaks, each trying to place blame the other for what was shaping up as a drastic U.S. intelligence failure. The internecine war within the U.S. government would soon escalate.

The Sunday morning media blitz by former ambassador Wilson caught senior White House officials off guard. Coming all at once in *The Times*, *The Washington Post*, and on *Meet the Press*, it was as if Wilson had thrown down his gauntlet at the president's feet. The tightly wound, secretive Bush administration was not used to such treatment, to put it mildly. Wilson himself did not anticipate the extent to which senior Bush officials considered his attack on the president's misuse of the Niger intelligence a veiled assault on the White House by the CIA, which key officials in the Office of the Vice President and Pentagon regarded with open contempt. Libby's first mention of Wilson to the *Times'* Judith Miller on June 23 was about the "clandestine guy" the CIA sent to Niger.

Libby apparently blamed the CIA for spreading the word that the president's State of the Union remarks about uranium from Africa were false[19] and had been disavowed by weapons experts at the IAEA and by many intelligence analysts.

Evidence later emerged that suggested just how closely the vice president's office had been following the Niger affair. In the margins of his copy of Wilson's *Times* story, Cheney himself had scribbled a set of queries, "Have they done this sort of thing before? Send an Amb. to answer a question? Do we ordinarily send people out pro bono to work for us? Or did his wife send him on a junket?"[20] However much Cheney and Libby may have learned about Wilson and his wife up to that point, the Bush administration's response was immediate—if strangely confused and bullheaded.

The White House public counteroffensive began at 9:30 A.M. Monday, July 7. Presidential spokesman Ari Fleischer met with reporters and insisted that the administration stood by the president's remarks on Africa in his January 28 speech. "There is zero, nada, nothing new here," Fleischer said. But as reporters questioned him, Fleischer seemed to grow more uncertain, suggesting that there had been a problem with the president's account of Saddam's interest in buying African uranium after all. "Specifically on the yellowcake, the yellowcake for Niger," Fleischer later said, "we've acknowledged that that information did turn out to be a forgery."[21]

Before he and other top White House aides departed on Air Force One for Africa later that day, Fleischer met for lunch with Libby at the vice presidential aide's invitation. It was the first time Libby and Fleischer had socialized together, and at least nominally the occasion was to celebrate Fleischer's imminent departure from the administration. The two men exchanged small talk about their mutual admiration for the Miami Dolphins before Libby turned the conversation to the controversy about the president's use of intelligence on African uranium in the State of the Union speech. "Ambassador Wilson was sent by his wife," Libby told Fleischer. "His wife works for the CIA." Libby added that this "was hush-hush, on the Q.T., and that most people didn't know it."[22]

Libby, who by now had learned of Wilson's wife's identity from four separate government sources—State's Marc Grossman, CIA's Robert Grenier, OVP press aide Catherine Martin, and Cheney himself—later told FBI agents that he heard about Valerie Plame for the first time in a conversation with NBC's Washington bureau chief Tim Russert on July 10, three days after Libby told Fleischer about Plame.

During the lunch, Libby reportedly never invoked White House protocol designed to warn the president's spokesman when classified information was in play that could not be shared with reporters. Even on the plane, when Fleischer heard presidential adviser Dan Bartlett ventilate about news stories that said Vice President Cheney was behind sending Wilson to Niger, he later claimed there was no warning that classified information about Wilson's wife might be involved. "His wife sent him," Bartlett said. "She works at the C.I.A."[23] Fleischer said that he didn't give a thought to the possibility there might be a problem disclosing Valerie Plame Wilson's identity to reporters. Indeed, during the president's stopover in Uganda on July 11, Fleischer decided to let NBC's David Gregory and Time's John Dickerson in on the secret. "If you want to know who sent the ambassador to Niger," Fleischer told them, "it was his wife; she works there."[24] The way the president's top White House spokesman remembered it, there was no reaction. "They didn't take out their notebook," said Fleischer. "They didn't ask any follow-up questions. It was a great big 'So what.'"

It was only later, at the end of September, when the CIA asked the Justice Department to investigate charges that White House officials might have illegally leaked Valerie Wilson's identity as a covert CIA agent, that Fleischer said he woke up to what he might have done. "I thought, 'Oh, my God. Did I play a role in somehow outing a CIA officer?'" he recalled later. "'Did I just do something that I could be in big trouble for?'" He claimed that he "never in my wildest dreams thought this information would be classified."[25]

There were, however, indications that Scooter Libby, the veteran Washington lawyer, may have known very well what he was getting into. He hinted at one point later in the week that he suspected Valerie Plame may have worked undercover for the CIA and that identifying her might be illegal. When one of Libby's deputies asked if information about Wilson's trip could be shared with the press, Libby replied that "there would be complications at the CIA in disclosing that information publicly," strongly suggesting that Libby was aware of Plame's covert status.[26] Libby also seemed concerned about the legality of President Bush's unilateral and secretive declassification of material from the 2002 NIE. In a private conversation with OVP counsel David Addington, who had previously served as a CIA lawyer, sometime between July 6 and July 12 Libby asked about the declassification of government secrets and whether the CIA would have kept records documenting its work. Addington recalled that as he replied, Libby held out his hands in front of him, palms down, as if

reminding him that this was sensitive material. "He said, 'Keep it down,'"
Addington said.[27]

By the evening of Monday, July 7, after the president's party had boarded
Air Force One in Washington for the flight to Senegal, Fleischer changed
the official narrative. Officials on the plane began placing calls to *The
Times* and *Post* saying that they no longer could confirm the legitimacy of
the president's remarks about an Iraqi uranium purchase. The White
House authorized a statement to *The Washington Post* from "a senior administration official" admitting that the intelligence supporting the president's statement was questionable. "Knowing all that we know now, the
reference to Iraq's attempt to acquire uranium from Africa should not
have been included in the State of the Union speech," said the statement.
Phone logs reportedly indicated that about this time Fleischer placed a call
from Air Force One to the well-connected conservative columnist Robert
Novak, whose syndicated columns appeared regularly in *The Washington
Post*.[28] During the night flight over the Atlantic, the State Department
memo that had been authored by Undersecretary of State Marc Grossman
was requested by Secretary of State Colin Powell and faxed to Air Force
One. The memo officially identified Wilson's wife by name as a CIA official in a passage marked "S" for secret, indicating her likely status as an
undercover agent, and outlined her role in the decision to send her husband to Niger.

The next afternoon, an acquaintance of Joseph Wilson ran into
Robert Novak on Pennsylvania Avenue in Washington. They were headed
in the same direction and struck up a conversation. Wilson's friend asked
about the African uranium story. Novak responded that the White House
should have dealt with it weeks ago. He then asked what Novak thought
of Wilson. "He's an asshole," said Novak. "The CIA sent him. His wife,
Valerie, works for the CIA. She's a weapons of mass destruction specialist. She sent him."[29] Taken aback, the fellow headed for Wilson's office
and told him about the run-in with Novak. Wilson called Eason Jordan,
then the head of the news division at CNN, and asked him to have Novak
call him. Novak called on Wednesday, but didn't make contact until the
next day. Novak listened politely to Wilson's account of his friend's story
and apologized. He then told Wilson he had heard from a CIA source that
his wife worked for the CIA and asked Wilson if he would confirm it. Wilson refused. After some discussion of Wilson's role in the 1990 evacuation

of Americans from Baghdad, Novak apologized again for mentioning his wife to a stranger and hung up.

At the White House, both Karl Rove, the president's top political strategist, and Libby, the vice president's chief of staff, along with Deputy National Security Advisor Stephen Hadley, stayed behind to figure out how to smother the political firestorm Wilson had started. It was a busy week for Libby. Messages from Air Force One on Monday night intimated that the president's sixteen words about Iraq's interest in African uranium may have been in error. Yet the right hand didn't seem to know what the left hand was doing. On Tuesday morning, at Cheney's urging, Libby mounted a strong defense of U.S. intelligence on Saddam's nuclear program with *Times* reporter Judith Miller during his second meeting with her, a two-hour breakfast at Washington's St. Regis Hotel. The choice of venue, beyond the reach of office logs and witnesses, was standard practice for Washington national security reporters meeting with official sources.

Miller asked Libby about Wilson's radioactive op-ed piece two days before. Visibly agitated, Libby dismissed the article as "inaccurate." But before the conversation went much further, he abruptly decided to change the ground rules. Anything he said about Wilson, Libby said, had to be attributed to a "former Hill staffer," not to a "senior administration official" as they had agreed. Miller acquiesced, at least for the moment, knowing that Libby had once worked as an aide on Capitol Hill. (The agreement, however, was moot. Miller never published an article about the Wilsons.) She assumed Libby did not want it to appear that the White House was attacking Wilson.[30]

Libby then launched into a detailed chronology of "credible" evidence that Iraq had been in the market for Niger's uranium ore, and criticized the CIA for backing away from intelligence after the war began. Miller later recalled that Libby alluded to two reports, the first from 1999 indicating that Baghdad was interested in a trade pact with Niger and that Nigerien officials read that as a signal that the Iraqis were interested in their uranium. The second report, she recalled, was in February 2002. On the basis of the two documents, Libby said, the vice president's office had asked for more details on Iraq's dealing with Niger and the CIA had sent Wilson. Libby told Miller that Wilson's report on his mission to Niger was so inconsequential that it "barely made it out of the CIA," according to Miller's notes of the conversation.

Apparently in an effort to further undermine Wilson, Libby added that CIA director George Tenet had never heard of the former ambassador. Libby also mentioned the classified October 2002 National Intelligence Estimate on Iraq, which said that Iraq was seeking uranium from Niger. Miller knew the NIE had been distributed in an unclassified version for public consumption soon after its publication in the fall of 2002, and pushed Libby for more detail. He was not forthcoming, but assured her that that classified version of the document expressed even greater certainty than the unclassified version. Libby told her that the uranium intelligence was a "key judgment" of the NIE.[31] In fact, neither version of the estimate included the Niger material in the all-important "key judgments," an introductory section listing brief summaries of the estimate's most important findings.

Libby brought the conversation back to Saddam's nuclear weapons. He insisted that administration claims about the Niger uranium deal and that Saddam was developing a nuclear capability were credible, despite Wilson's attack. There was reason for concern about Iraq's nuclear program, he said, based on the regime's past history, its use of chemical weapons, and "fresh intelligence reports"—apparently a reference to the operations of Feith's Counter Terrorism Evaluation Group and Office of Special Plans units at the Pentagon. Although Miller had first heard about Wilson's wife in her June interview with Libby, he now told Miller that she worked with a group at the CIA known as WINPAC, an acronym for the agency's office of Center for Weapons Intelligence, Nonproliferation, and Arms Control, which specializes in analysis of unconventional weapons. Although Miller couldn't have been aware of it, this contradicted the information Libby had received a month before from the vice president that Wilson's wife worked for the CIA's Counterproliferation Division.[32]

Was Libby just confused, or was he engaging in a bit of disinformation? Many WINPAC officers were analysts, not undercover agents, as Miller understood, and could be identified publicly without legal consequences. Or was Miller's recollection simply mistaken? Miller concedes that she wrote down the name "Valerie Flame" in her notebook at some point. Elsewhere, she had written down the name "Victoria Wilson" and drawn a box around it, though she explained this could have been from another interview. Both, of course, are incorrect variations of Wilson's wife's name, Valerie Plame Wilson. Libby insists he never actually knew or revealed her name at the St. Regis meeting and Miller could not recall whether Libby said that Wilson's wife sent her husband to Niger.

Robert Novak was also busy reporting a column on the political hornet's nest Wilson had stirred up at the White House. After two years of trying unsuccessfully to land an interview with Richard Armitage, Colin Powell's deputy at the State Department, Novak said Armitage's office abruptly called him at the end of June and made an appointment for a background chat on Tuesday afternoon, July 8. Less than a month had passed since Armitage spoke with Woodward, and two days since the White House was thrown into chaos by Wilson's allegations that senior Bush officials had "twisted" prewar intelligence. "The only people in the room were Secretary Armitage and me," Novak later recalled. "No aides, no tape recorders on either side. I did not take notes. It was by tacit agreement on background, [so I] assumed I could write what was said, [but] couldn't be able to quote him or identify him."[33]

Armitage had agreed to see Novak informally, as a favor to Ken Duberstein, a friend and former Reagan chief of staff. He also may have wanted to get out the word that the State Department had nothing to do with Wilson's trip. Novak wanted to know why the CIA would choose Wilson to send to Niger. Novak had met Wilson once while waiting for a TV interview and found him unpleasant. He believed Wilson was a "questionable choice" to review the Niger case.[34] Novak recalled asking Armitage, "Why in the world would they name Ambassador Wilson when he had been a staffer in [the] Carter administration, critical of Bush, no experience in nuclear policy . . . had not been to Niger since he was a very junior foreign service official?" Armitage replied that the trip had been suggested by Wilson's wife, Valerie Plame, who worked in the Counterproliferation Division at the CIA.[35]

The next day, Wednesday, July 9, at a press conference in Johannesburg, President Bush was asked by a reporter if he regretted that the uranium reference had appeared in his State of the Union message. Irritated, Bush ducked the question, refusing to admit outright there had been a mistake. "Look, I am confident that Saddam Hussein had a weapons of mass destruction program," he said. Given the U.S. failure to find actual unconventional weapons in Iraq, Bush's public statements had now shifted to the softer emphasis on weapons programs.

In Washington, Libby and Rove were still busy gathering chapter and verse on Wilson. On June 9, the CIA faxed classified accounts of how Wilson had gotten the Niger assignment to Libby and another unnamed person in the Office of the Vice President. The same day, Karl Rove spoke with Robert Novak on the telephone. He later reported that the columnist had told him Wilson's wife worked for the CIA and had a hand in setting up her husband's trip to Niger. Rove responded that he'd heard the same thing, thus confirming for Novak what he had learned the day before from Armitage. Novak told the same story. During their conversation, said Novak, he asked Rove about Wilson's mission to Niger. "I commented that I heard she was a—I had been told she was an employee of the Counterproliferation Division of the CIA. He said, 'Oh, you know about that, too.' I took that as a clear affirmation."[36]

Novak later called Libby, but got nothing out of him. "What I'm confident of," Novak said later, "is that I got no help and no confirmation of it from Mr. Libby. . . . I kind of discard unhelpful conversations about it, so I am sure he gave me no information about it."[37] But Libby apparently knew about Novak's conversation with Rove. He later said that Rove "was animated that Novak was animated about this" and "thought it was a good thing that somebody was writing about" Wilson and his wife.[38]

By week's end, Libby was debriefed for a second time by the State Department's Marc Grossman, who reconfirmed in light of Wilson's *Times* op-ed that the former ambassador's wife, Valerie Plame Wilson, worked at the CIA and had been involved in planning the African trip. This time, some who worked closely with Libby noticed that the conversation with Grossman seemed to rattle him. "I think this just hit a nerve," said a senior official. "The blind, deaf and dumb had to be aware that something was wrong in Iraq," given reports coming in of army weapons hunters coming up empty-handed. The Wilson controversy over the Niger uranium deal, he said, was "the beginning of the unraveling of the big story . . . calling attention to a huge mistake he was part of. So it's no wonder he took this personally."[39]

By Friday, July 11, the administration's two-pronged strategy for dealing with Wilson was becoming apparent. Administration officials were intent on distancing President Bush from any responsibility for the sixteen words about African uranium in his State of the Union Address—and placing the blame squarely on the CIA. In Uganda, with the president's party, Condoleezza Rice repeatedly emphasized to reporters that the inclusion of the controversial passage in the State of the Union speech had been cleared, if not by the CIA, then "by. the intelligence services," as Bush put it when asked whether he should hold anyone accountable for the mistake. She added, "If the CIA, the director of central intelligence, had said, 'Take this out of the speech,' it would have been gone, without question." On the home front, Libby, Rove, and Hadley were putting the finishing touches on a statement by CIA director George Tenet, who was preparing to announce that the responsibility was his for overlooking the flawed intelligence in the president's speech. The DCI later explained that he had left the vetting of the speech to aides, and had gone home the evening of the president's address and fallen asleep, "exhausted from fifteen months of nonstop work and worry since the tragedy of 9/11."[40]

Tenet's statement was released by CIA headquarters at Langley on Friday night. In what he later called his "*mea* somewhat *culpa*,"[41] Tenet declared that reviewing the text of the State of the Union Address was his responsibility and that CIA officials had in fact cleared the president's speech, despite the questionable Niger intelligence, on the strength of its attribution to the British white paper on African uranium. But he had also instructed his press spokesman, Bill Harlow, that the statement "needed to be a roadmap and to convey the clear impression that we never believed the Niger story," Tenet later wrote.[42] "Legitimate questions have arisen about how remarks on how alleged Iraqi attempts to obtain uranium in Africa made it into the President's State of the Union speech," Tenet began. "Let me be clear about several things. First, CIA approved the President's State of the Union address before it was delivered. Second, I am responsible for the approval process in my agency. And third, the President has every reason to believe the text presented to him was sound. These sixteen words should never have been included in the test written for the President. This did not rise to the level of certainty which should be required for Presidential speeches, and CIA should have ensured that it was removed."[43]

Tenet never said he actually approved the sixteen words, but there was no mistaking the seriousness of his statement. For once, regardless of who was at fault, the White House had made a serious political miscalculation. In his carefully worded statement, Tenet declared that the CIA "should have" taken responsibility for the president's statement. Despite news reports to the contrary, Tenet stopped well short of assigning the blame for the sixteen words to either himself or the CIA, though his words certainly left that impression. After he had finalized the statement, he privately raised the question of his personal intervention in the president's Cincinnati speech—when Tenet had scrubbed all mention of the Niger deal—during a last-minute conference call with Condoleezza Rice aboard Air Force One. "What are you going to do about Cincinnati?" Tenet asked her. He reported "dead silence on the line" and that the "conversation ended uncomfortably."[44]

The second part of the White House offensive was a more aggressive plan to neutralize Joseph Wilson, now that the weakness of the Niger intelligence had been effectively conceded. Politically speaking, if anyone was to blame beyond the CIA, it was Wilson, who was now squarely in the sights of Rove and Libby and others in the vice president's office. By this time, Libby had met twice with Judith Miller of *The Times* about Wilson and the Niger intelligence, and Rove had confirmed for Novak that Wilson's wife had sent him to Niger, presumably on a nepotistic boondoggle. On Friday, the day Tenet's statement hit the headlines, Rove was busy discrediting the CIA by passing the word to newly minted *Time* magazine White House correspondent Matthew Cooper that Wilson's wife was a CIA agent and had a role in sending him to Niger.[45]

On the morning of Saturday, July 12, Vice President Cheney, whose query about the intelligence from Niger in late 2001 and early 2002 had triggered the entire affair, flew to the Norfolk naval base, the home part of the U.S. Atlantic fleet, for christening ceremonies of the new aircraft carrier, the USS *Ronald Reagan*. With him aboard Air Force Two were Libby and his press aide, Catherine Martin. On the flight back to Washington, Cheney took charge of micromanaging the White House attack on Wilson. The vice president reportedly "discussed with other officials aboard the plane" the administration's response to "pending media inquiries" about Joe Wilson.[46] Cheney specifically instructed Libby to respond to *Time* magazine's Matthew Cooper, who had e-mailed Martin a query about whether the faulty African intelligence had been a basis of the decision to go to war. Libby came back to Martin's seat in the rear of the plane with a handwritten card from Cheney with instructions on what to say to Cooper. Libby told her that the vice president had authorized him to give Cooper an on-the-record quote in his—Libby's—name.[47] Cheney and Libby were so concerned that reporters were not getting out their side of the story about Wilson and his criticisms that they directed Martin and her staff to monitor TV reports on the Niger trip and provide them with daily transcripts.

Cheney was also apparently preoccupied with coordinating the Wilson strategy with Air Force One. As his entourage flew back to Washington from Norfolk, "the vice-president instructed Libby to alert reporters of an attack launched hours before on Wilson's credibility by Fleischer."[48] At a press briefing in Abuja, Nigeria, that morning, Fleischer had responded to a question about the president's reaction to the Tenet statement by telling the traveling press corps that a "greater truth" was being lost in the Niger uranium controversy. "The greater truth is that nobody, but nobody, denies that Saddam Hussein was seeking nuclear weapons," said Fleischer. "He was pursuing numerous ways to obtain nuclear weapons."

Fleischer went on to describe what became an administration talking point on Wilson and the Niger intelligence. He told the press aboard Air Force One, correctly, that Wilson had reported back to the CIA that a former Nigerian official had told him he had been approached by an Iraqi delegation in 1999 about bilateral trade pact talks with Niger. The official had told Wilson that he'd assumed at the time that Baghdad might be interested in Nigerien yellowcake, since Iraq had bought supplies from Niger in the 1980s. But Fleischer conveniently failed to mention that the official also told Wilson that the overture never came up again, and that no such meeting ever took place. In Fleischer's version, Wilson reported back to the CIA "that officials in Niger said that Iraq was seeking to contact officials in Niger about sales." It was an outright falsehood.

After Air Force Two touched down Saturday afternoon after the flight from Norfolk, Libby got on the phone with both Matt Cooper of *Time* and the *New York Times'* Miller. He confirmed for Cooper what the *Time* correspondent had learned from Rove the day before, that Wilson's wife, Valerie Plame, worked at the CIA. Libby talked to Miller at her home in Sag Harbor on Long Island. She later recalled that the Saturday conversation was possibly the first time Libby used Valerie Plame Wilson's name with her unprompted. "In my notebook I had written the words 'Victoria Wilson' with a box around it, another apparent reference to Ms. Plame," Miller later wrote. "I was not sure whether Mr. Libby had used this name or whether I just made a mistake . . ."[49] Libby was still interested in criticizing Wilson's report on the Niger deal, she said. But he also wanted to explain that the "disputed uranium allegation" had gotten into the president's State of the Union Address as the result of "a simple miscommunication between the White House and the CIA." She recalled Libby telling her that "it was unclear whether Wilson had spoken with any Niger officials who had dealt with Iraq's trade representatives." Miller did not hint that by raising the "disputed uranium allegation," Libby undercut his own confident defense of the Niger intelligence four days before—and thus considerably softened the White House line, presumably to shift the blame to Tenet and the CIA. Libby seemed to be correcting the record, but the *New York Times'* national security reporter either didn't notice the inconsistency, or chose to let it pass.

The same afternoon, veteran *Washington Post* investigative reporter

Walter Pincus was in the office working on a story about Wilson's mission to Niger when an administration official returned an earlier telephone call. The official revealed to Pincus for the first time that Joe Wilson was married to CIA undercover agent Valerie Plame. For four years Pincus refused to reveal the identity of the caller: Finally, in 2007, he reported it was former White House spokesman Ari Fleischer, who had learned about Wilson's wife from Libby five days before. Only after Pincus had testified before a Washington grand jury probe and received a waiver from Fleischer, who by then had worked out an immunity deal with the prosecutor, did Pincus finally name him. As he later recalled the conversation, "The person I was calling suddenly swerved off and said . . . 'Don't you know, in effect, his wife works at the CIA, is an analyst on weapons of mass destruction?' " said Pincus.[50] Fleischer told him that "people aren't paying attention" to Wilson's view that the Niger intelligence was unfounded because the trip was a "boondoggle" set up by his wife. Soon afterward, Pincus called Wilson with a cryptic message: "They are coming after you," he said.

On Monday, July 14, the news that Valerie Plame Wilson worked for the CIA and had sent her husband to Niger, with its suggestions of shady nepotism and political connivance, was the talk of Washington. Robert Novak, who only days before had been in contact with Fleischer, Rove, Libby, and Richard Armitage (who would remain an anonymous senior administration official until the trial of Lewis Libby in 2007), wrote the story that had been bubbling inside the White House for weeks. Novak's column was an oddly eclectic, meandering account of the Niger trip that seemed intent on little more than establishing that CIA director Tenet had nothing to do with either choosing Wilson as envoy or reading his Niger report. There was a strong suggestion that Wilson may have overplayed his hand. If the column had any point, it appeared to be that the CIA should declassify its report of Wilson's post-Niger briefing so that the public could determine whether the White House "deliberately ignored" Wilson's advice. Although Novak treated Wilson respectfully, the clear subtext was that the CIA would do the White House a favor by making Wilson's report available, which would show that the CIA discounted his judgment—and in fact was treated by CIA analysts as evidence that Iraq might have been interested in a uranium sale after all.

None of this caused the slightest ripple. The live ammunition was buried in the sixth paragraph of a ten-paragraph column. "Wilson never worked for the CIA, but his wife, Valerie Plame, is an Agency operative on weapons of mass destruction," Novak wrote. "Two senior administration officials told me Wilson's wife suggested sending him to Niger to investigate the Italian report. The CIA says its counterproliferation officials selected Wilson and asked his wife to contact him. 'I will not answer questions about my wife,' Wilson told me."[51]

Wilson and his wife had married five years before, and Valerie Wilson seldom used her maiden name, so it was strange Novak had used "Plame" to identify her. Valerie Wilson was stunned. She was in the bedroom Monday morning when her husband came in and threw a copy of *The Post* with Novak's column on the bed. "He did it," Wilson told her, referring to her exposure as a CIA agent. "I felt like I had been hit in the gut," she said.[52] Though she was now based in Washington and had two small children, Valerie Wilson was still a clandestine agent, having made several secret missions to gather intelligence on Iraq's presumed WMD program just before the war. She recognized immediately that her undercover career was over. Reporters quickly seized on the word "operative," and a number of publications confirmed that Valerie Wilson had been a longtime covert agent for the CIA's Counterproliferation Division. Her undercover status was later reconfirmed by Special Counsel Patrick Fitzgerald in 2005.[53]

"My name and identity were carelessly and recklessly abused by senior government officials in both the White House and the State Department," she said later in testimony before the House Oversight and Government Reform Committee on March 16, 2007.[54] Wilson testified that the resulting security breach may have "jeopardized and even destroyed entire networks of foreign agents, who in turn risk their own lives and those of their families to provide the United States with needed intelligence. Lives are literally at stake. We in the CIA always know we might be exposed by foreign enemies. It was a terrible irony that administration officials were the ones who destroyed my cover."[55]

While she scrambled to minimize the damage to agency projects she was involved in, she was forced to maintain a public silence under the same secrecy rules that had governed her behavior as a CIA employee in classified positions during her twenty-year career. Neighbors acquainted with the Wilsons and even close friends confirmed they had no idea that Valerie worked for the CIA, but believed she was an energy consultant. With her glamorous, schoolgirl good looks and an outspoken husband, Valerie Wilson struggled to maintain her career at Langley. When she and the gregarious Wilson appeared in a photo spread in *Vanity Fair* magazine in January 2004, the tension between public notoriety and professional requirements of secretiveness created a new discomfort with her at CIA headquarters—and gave her an outsize celebrity profile somewhere between Mata Hari and Greta Garbo. "Having lived most of my life very much under the radar, my learning curve was steep," she later conceded wryly.[56] But what was left of her professional life became unsustainable. On December 9, 2005, she tendered her resignation at the CIA.

Novak was just the messenger. It seemed to administration critics that the real miscreants who sabotaged her career were the "two senior administration officials"—identified much later as Rove and Armitage—who provided Novak with Valerie Wilson's name and her status as a CIA operative. The tactic struck many observers, including her husband, as just the kind of hardball, underhanded stunt Karl Rove would pull to discredit a political enemy, much as he had smeared fellow Republican Senator John McCain during the 2000 South Carolina primary. Valerie Wilson's colleagues at the CIA at strongly rallied to her support. "She was still undercover and there was concern that political people were being very cavalier with a serious issue," said a former senior covert officer. "It was not just a legal, statutory thing; it was that politicians for their own purposes could throw out all aspects of cover" to punish her husband.[57]

But by blowing Valerie Plame Wilson's cover as a CIA agent, the as yet unnamed Bush officials had plunged into much deeper waters. If they had security clearances that gave them access to classified information—such as Valerie Wilson's identity as a covert agent—and knowingly identified her, they were subject to criminal prosecution under the Intelligence Identities Protection Act of 1982. The statute was passed by Congress to outlaw the public identification of undercover agents after rogue CIA agent Philip Agee named a number of agents in Europe and the Middle East in the late 1970s. Two senior CIA officials wound up murdered as a result. The president's own father, President George H. W. Bush, a former head of the CIA, once described those who exposed undercover agents as "the most insidious of traitors."

A week after Novak's column appeared, Wilson received a telephone call from Chris Matthews of MSNBC's *Hardball*. "I just got off the phone with Karl Rove," Matthews told him. "He says, and I quote, 'Wilson's wife is fair game.' I will confirm that if asked." Wilson was livid. What Rove was doing "was tantamount to declaring war on two U.S. citizens, both of them with years of government service."[58] Weeks later, at an August 21 town meeting in Seattle on the subject of the administration's use of prewar intelligence sponsored by Washington Democrat Jay Inslee, Wilson provoked enthusiastic catcalls and whistles by asking, "Wouldn't it be fun to see Karl Rove frog-marched out of the White House in handcuffs?" On his return to Washington, D.C., his wife was not pleased. Valerie let him know she had heard about the remark from office colleagues and asked him to please tone down the rhetoric.[59]

PART VI

CASUALTIES OF THE INFORMATION WAR

21

PROBING THE PRESIDENT'S MEN

Virtually none of the behind-the-scenes maneuvering that took place inside the Bush administration between the publication of Wilson's jolting op-ed story and Novak's column outing Valerie Plame Wilson even began to emerge publicly for another two years. But thanks to the leak controversy, by mid-July 2003 the reputation of the Bush White House for strict internal discipline and staying on message was in tatters. At every turn, the White House seemed able to draw only more attention to its blunders. The scandal that began with a lone critic questioning the president's war policies on the *Times*' op-ed page was now sharply focused on whether senior administration officials had criminally exposed the identity of a covert CIA agent. Bush officials couldn't seem to get their story straight about the disputed African intelligence at the heart of both the leak case and their rationale for going to war, and/or about why discredited intelligence had appeared in the State of the Union Address in the first place. "These stories get legs when they're mishandled and this story has been badly mishandled," one senior administration official explained ruefully. Said Mary Matalin, a former White House adviser, "It's impossible to have a consistent message when the facts keep changing."[1]

While tensions simmered at the White House over Tenet's barbed statement about the president's use of the flawed African intelligence, Bush was compelled by events on the ground in Iraq to assign a fourteen-hundred-member special CIA-led team of military and scientific experts, called the Iraq Survey Group, under former weapons inspector David Kay, to scour that war-torn country for the WMD that U.S. Army weapons-hunting troops had failed to turn up.

On July 17, 2003, three days after Novak's column appeared, Bush made a joint appearance in Washington with British prime minister Tony Blair, who had just addressed a session of Congress to assure continued British support for the Iraq campaign. Despite the barrage of questions emerging about the reliability of prewar U.S. intelligence, the two leaders insisted that the decision to go to war was sound. "I take responsibility for putting our troops into action," Bush said. "I take responsibility for making the decision, the tough decision, to put together a coalition to remove Saddam Hussein. Because the intelligence—not only our intelligence, but the intelligence of this great country—made a clear and compelling case that Saddam Hussein was a threat to security and peace." The president expressed confidence that Saddam's weapons would be found in Iraq. "We will bring the information forward on the weapons when they find them," he said. "And that will end up—end all this speculation."[2]

Blair, too, Bush's lone ally in Iraq among the major European powers, was being buffeted by an angry chorus of critics at home. In Parliament, the House of Commons began a series of formal probes into Blair's decision to go to war. One committee began to examine the origins of the British white paper of September 2002 that contributed to the African intelligence dispute. Another investigated the claims of British intelligence on Iraq's arsenal of weapons of mass destruction, including the assertion that Iraq possessed chemical munitions that could be deployed on the battlefield within forty-five minutes. Like Bush, Blair still strongly defended the decision to go to war, and denied charges that he or his staff had tampered with intelligence. "The whole debate, for weeks," Blair said, "revolved around a claim that either I or a member of my staff had effectively inserted intelligence into the dossier we put before the British people against the wishes of the intelligence services. Now, that is a serious charge. It never was true."[3]

The next day, as Blair was en route to Japan, the BBC reported that David Kelly, fifty-nine, a veteran weapons expert with Britain's Ministry of Defence, was found dead near his home in Oxfordshire, an apparent suicide. His death followed a BBC report that the prime minister's office at 10 Downing Street had "sexed up" the 2002 intelligence dossier about Iraq's weapons of mass destruction. Earlier in the week, Kelly had testified before the House of Commons foreign affairs committee that he had spoken to the BBC reporter who filed the report, but was not his main source.[4] Kelly's death became the subject of a judicial inquiry by Lord Brian Hutton that eventually absolved the Blair government of responsibility for Kelly's death, but turned British public opinion increasingly against the prime minister and the war.

With disputed African intelligence at the center of the leak controversy, hostilities between the White House and the CIA soon broke into the open. George Tenet had for the past twenty months not only enjoyed a close personal relationship with President Bush but also unhesitatingly protected the White House by taking personal responsibility for the famous sixteen words in the State of the Union Address. Tenet's action triggered a fierce bureaucratic counterattack by the CIA that forced the White House to repeatedly revise its story of how the intelligence made it into the president's speech and provided a more nuanced—and damning—picture of the White House role in the controversy. At the prodding of the CIA, National Security Council deputy director Stephen Hadley and White House communications chief Dan Bartlett, for example, produced memos that showed Tenet had insisted on dropping any mention of the Niger intelligence in the draft of an October 7, 2002, presidential speech in Cincinnati. Hadley also revealed that White House speechwriters tried to finesse the discredited U.S. information by using references to British intelligence reports on the African yellowcake deal in the unclassified 2002 U.S. intelligence estimate.

Why would the DCI have personally intervened to remove mention of the Niger material from one presidential speech, but not from another, more important address? And why hadn't Hadley remembered Tenet's earlier memos while vetting of the State of the Union Address? Alan Foley, the former head of the CIA's Center for Weapons, Intelligence, Nonproliferation, and Arms Control, or WINPAC, made matters worse for the White House by testifying before the Senate Select Committee on Intelligence that he had warned NSC nonproliferation expert Robert Joseph, a Hadley subordinate, not to use the Niger intelligence in the State of the Union speech. Despite the fact that Tenet had taken the fall for the president, the CIA had deftly placed the mistake squarely on the doorstep of the White House. Deeply embarrassed, Hadley offered to resign. President Bush refused his request.[5]

A week later, the CIA quietly launched another round at the White House. On July 24, a CIA attorney telephoned the counterespionage chief of the Justice Department and left a message reporting a possible criminal violation in the disclosure that Valerie Plame Wilson was a covert agent.

The CIA requested a Justice Department investigation. The legal basis of the CIA request was the Intelligence Identities Protection Act of 1982, which made it a felony for a government official to knowingly disclose the identity of an undercover agent. The message, sent with Tenet's full knowledge, was followed by letters on July 30 and August 5 informing the Justice Department's criminal division that the CIA's inspector general was investigating the possible criminal violation. The CIA informed the attorney general on September 16 that the CIA's investigation was complete, enclosed a memorandum summarizing its results, and requested that the FBI launch a criminal investigation of the White House leak.

The counterespionage section at Justice formally responded on Monday, September 29, that it had asked the FBI investigate the matter. But the CIA's two-week-old criminal referral to Justice had leaked to the Washington press over the weekend. As the news that the Justice Department planned to investigate the White House leak case exploded across the nation, evidence of deeper internal divisions suddenly emerged at the White House. On Sunday, September 28, an unnamed senior administration official told *The Washington Post* that two top Bush officials had talked to no fewer than six journalists before the Novak column appeared. The administration leaks, the official said, were "wrong and a huge miscalculation, because they were irrelevant and did nothing to diminish Wilson's credibility."

The next day, Novak telephoned Rove, whom he had known since 1992, when Rove was fired from the elder Bush's reelection campaign on suspicion of leaking information to Novak. The columnist assured Rove that he would not get burned in the new Plame investigation. Rove later confirmed the call had taken place, but called it a "curious conversation." He said he took Novak to mean he would not name him as a source for the Valerie Plame column.[6] Meanwhile, the White House scrambled to present a unified, cooperative public response to the investigation. White House counsel Alberto Gonzales sent around a memo on September 30 ordering staff cooperation. "If there is a leak out of my administration I want to know who it is," declared President Bush. "And if the person has violated the law, the person will be taken care of."

Bush's tone hardened a week later when he fielded questions about the possible impact of the leak investigation. "I want to know the truth," he said. Then again, the president pointed out, how many reporters were likely to expose sources they had promised not to identify? "Probably none," he answered. "This is a large administration and there are a lot of senior officials . . . I have no idea whether we'll find out who the leaker is, partially because, in all due respect to your profession, you do a very good job of protecting the leakers." Shortly thereafter, White House spokesman Scott McClellan gave his personal assurances that none of the prime suspects whose names were floated in the press—Rove, Libby, NSC staffer Elliot Abrams—were involved in the Valerie Wilson leak.

"At a time like this, there are a lot of rumors and innuendo," said Mc-Clellan. "There are unsubstantiated accusations that are made. And that's exactly what happened in the case of these three individuals. They're good individuals, they're important members of our White House team, and that's why I spoke with them, so that I could come back to you and say that they were not involved. I had no doubt of that in the beginning, but I like to check my information to make sure it's accurate before I report back to you, and that's exactly what I did."[7]

From the beginning, the Justice Department investigation was beset with questions. Attorney General John Ashcroft immediately ruled out appointing a special counsel in the case, effectively giving himself subpoena power over the probe. Several days after putting the White House on notice, he appointed John Dion, a thirty-year veteran who headed the Justice Department's counterintelligence unit, to take the lead in the case. Critics charged that the initial lag in getting the probe under way gave administration officials, including employees at the White House, the State Department, and the Department of Defense, ample opportunity to destroy incriminating documents, e-mails, notes, phone records, diaries, and calendars that might have a bearing on the case. Gonzalez reportedly held on to records submitted by White House employees for weeks deciding which to send along to prosecutors. "I am very troubled by the fact that the White House counsel seems to be a gatekeeper," said Senator Charles Schumer of New York. "I want to know what precautions [the Justice Department] is taking to ensure that it gets all relevant information from the administration."

Dion and four staff prosecutors began interviewing administration officials between October and December 2003, assisted by a dozen FBI agents. Their boss, the special agent in charge of the FBI's Washington field office, was reportedly cut out of the loop by Ashcroft. Polls showed that 70 percent of Americans wanted to see a special prosecutor assigned to get to the bottom of the leak. The spectacle of the Bush administration investigating itself rankled administration critics. Ashcroft himself reportedly received FBI briefings on the investigation several times a week, giving rise to charges that the probe was not aggressive enough and that the attorney general must recuse himself. "This investigation is all blue smoke and mirrors," said Melanie Sloan, a former federal prosecutor and executive director of the watchdog group Citizens for Responsibility and Ethics in Washington. "It has the appearance of looking like an investigation without really doing enough to get to the bottom of this." Even so, White House officials still privately expected heads to roll. "Somebody will have to go before it's over," an administration official told New York's *Daily News.* "The only question is whether it's a low-level person following orders or somebody higher up."

Among the first White House officials the FBI interviewed was Karl Rove. In the 1980s and 1990s he had worked for Ashcroft as a political adviser in three campaigns in Missouri, for which Rove's company received a total of $764,000. Rove also had been a powerful administration advocate for Ashcroft's appointment as attorney general. The intertwined histories of the two men worried several of the career Justice Department prosecutors on the case, who were acutely aware of Ashcroft's potential conflicts of interest. They were not the only ones. When James B. Comey, a former U.S. attorney for New York's southern district, was appointed as Ashcroft's deputy attorney general that fall, Senator Schumer of New York noted during Comey's confirmation hearings that Ashcroft's close relations with Rove and others were likely to be questioned during the leak probe. "How could there not be an appearance of a conflict given the close nexus of relationships?" asked Schumer. Comey replied, "I agree with you that it's an extremely important matter."[8]

When he was confirmed in early December, several prosecutors took their reservations about Ashcroft straight to Comey and suggested that the attorney general recuse himself. Investigators also reportedly had another concern. Murray Waas, an independent investigative reporter in Washington, later learned that federal investigators had evidence that Rove had misled them during his early interviews. Rove had insisted, for example, that he had not talked to *Time* correspondent Matt Cooper and that he had first heard about Wilson's wife from a journalist, whose name he couldn't remember.[9]

When prosecutors on the case learned that Ashcroft had been briefed on at least one FBI interview with Rove, the game was over. Representative

John Conyers of Michigan, the ranking Democrat on the House Judiciary Committee, issued a terse statement on "the appearance of impropriety" created by Ashcroft's involvement in the briefing. Wrote Conyers, "The new information, that Ashcroft had not only refused to recuse himself over a period of months, but also was insisting on being personally briefed about a matter implicating his friend, Karl Rove, represents a stunning ethical breach that cries out for an immediate investigation by the Department's Office of Professional Responsibility and Inspector General."[10]

Three weeks after Comey's appointment, Ashcroft abruptly recused himself from the leak case. He left his new deputy as acting attorney general in charge. Comey moved quickly to extend Ashcroft's recusal to include the attorney general's senior staff, which included two officials active in Republican party affairs who had worked closely with Rove in the past. Comey then appointed Patrick Fitzgerald, a former colleague and thirteen-year veteran of the southern district of New York, who had a reputation as a relentless, unsparing prosecutor of unquestioned toughness and probity, as special counsel in the White House leak case. Fitzgerald, who was then U.S. attorney for the northern district of Illinois in Chicago, prosecuted the terror cell responsible for the 1993 World Trade Center bombing. The son of an Irish doorman in New York City, Fitzgerald also had indicted the former governor of Illinois and the mayor of Chicago on corruption charges. Comey took care to transfer subpoena power, normally wielded by the acting attorney general, directly to Fitzgerald to assure the new special counsel unrestricted access to witnesses.[11]

Fitzgerald picked up where John Dion had left off. He moved quickly in January 2004 to convene a grand jury, dividing his time between his duties in Chicago and Washington's Judiciary Square, where the grand jury was convened. Fitzgerald and his team soon found themselves competing with the upcoming November presidential elections for the attention of a White House preoccupied with reelection and the deteriorating U.S. occupation of Iraq. Even so, by the end of June, Fitzgerald had met with both President Bush and Vice President Cheney, under the stipulation that their testimony was not under oath. Bush and Cheney, who met with the special counsel together, were accompanied by the president's personal lawyer, James Sharp. Fitzgerald also reportedly met with both Rove and the vice president's chief of staff, Lewis Libby.

Besides the president, vice president, and their top advisers, Fitzgerald reportedly met with other top Bush officials, including then national security advisor Condoleezza Rice, Secretary of State Colin Powell, National Security Council staffer and veteran GOP infighter Elliot Abrams, and White House Counsel Alberto Gonzales, along with a half-dozen prominent Washington reporters. At least five journalists received subpoenas from Fitzgerald. Besides Matt Cooper and Judith Miller, Tim Russert of NBC, the *Washington Post*'s Walter Pincus, and his *Post* colleague Glenn Kessler met with Fitzgerald and answered the prosecutor's questions. Several first negotiated ground rules about what they would and would not discuss. *The Columbia Journalism Review* later reported that *The Washington Post* attempted to demonstrate flexibility in their response to the subpoenas, while drawing the line at testifying about confidential information. Pincus, for example, reportedly agreed to confirm the time, date, and length of his conversation with a source other than Libby who had waived his right of confidentiality, but would not reveal his identity. Cooper, too, agreed to talk about his contact with Libby, who had waived his pledge of confidentiality.

The sixth and most controversial journalist involved in the case was of course Robert Novak. Novak did not reveal until 2007 that he was subpoenaed by Fitzgerald and testified before the grand jury. Because he had direct contact with the officials who leaked Plame's identity, the presumption in Washington was that he was subpoenaed and talked to Fitzgerald. Lucy Dalglish, the director of the Washington-based Reporters Committee for Freedom of the Press, believed that Novak may have cut a deal that allowed him to identify lower-ranking personnel involved in the leak, but who did not meet the stringent standards of the Intelligence Identities Protection Act, without naming the "senior administration officials" mentioned in his 2003 column. Such speculation lent credence to reports that Fitzgerald had subpoenaed records of every contact White House or other administration personnel had had with reporters during the period in question, and was engaged in a meticulous search to match such times and dates with records of meetings and telephone calls between reporters and Bush officials. But by the fall of 2004, no senior officials, including Rove and Libby, had been officially identified by Fitzgerald's staff as targets of the investigation.

Fitzgerald's apparent concentration on the press led some to speculate that he had been frustrated in identifying leakers indictable under the Intelligence Identities Protection Act. Others believed that he may have identified lower-level administration officials who spoke to the press about Valerie Wilson, but was still sifting through the evidence to identify higher officials who might have given them orders. But Fitzgerald's leak-proof operation made the White House look like a sieve. There also may have been a less-well understood reason the special counsel was not naming targets of his investigation. As Comey told reporters after he appointed Fitzgerald, "We also don't want people that we might be interested in to know we're interested in them." The truth was, no one knew what Patrick Fitzgerald was thinking.[12]

Nor did they seem to care that much after Bush was swept back into office in November 2004. Once it had become clear during the fall that Iraq harbored no arsenal of the much-heralded weapons of mass destruction or even production facilities that posed a threat to the United States, the Bush administration managed to persuade American voters that going to war had been justified by the bloody record of Saddam's regime and that Washington's real motive all along had been to engage the terrorists in Iraq, export a democratic system of government to Baghdad, and make the Middle East safe for democracy. Iraq, it seemed, had not been in serious breach of UN Resolutions 687 and 1441, since there was no evidence that Iraq still possessed WMD. The careful legal basis for the war constructed by Prime Minister Blair and President Bush had crumbled. Yet once Saddam was deposed and free elections were held in Iraq, even those many Americans who bitterly opposed the president's reelection found it difficult not to hope that the Bush administration's occupation of Iraq, despite the cost in blood and treasure, would be successful.

In this postelection atmosphere, Americans were hardly clamoring to find out who in the Bush administration had blown the cover of an obscure CIA operative. At least half of the American electorate seemed willing to give the "wartime president" a free pass, even if the truth about Iraq's WMD was ignored and laws were broken in the rush to invade Iraq and protect the United States from domestic terrorist attacks. As historians such as Arthur M. Schlesinger, Jr., have written, Americans have a deeply protective instinct about the presidency and always have been uneasy about criticizing a sitting president during U.S. overseas military operations. In Bush's case, the public instinct to refrain from further undercutting the president's already vulnerable authority and battered credibility, especially in the face of terrorist threats abroad, was palpable. In the early months of 2005, as half of the country bitterly absorbed the defeat of John Kerry and the other half happily applauded George W. Bush's reelection, many Americans quickly forgot that the White House was still the subject of a criminal investigation—and had been since well before the election. Bush critics with longer memories recalled that the public was not tuned in to the early stages of the Watergate investigation or the Iran-Contra scandal either.

With public interest at a low ebb, the Fitzgerald investigation all but dropped off the public's radar screen—and none too soon for the forces in league with the president's ambitious second-term plans for Social Security at home and democratic elections in Iraq. In early 2005, the *Wall Street Journal's* conservative editorial page drew a bead on Fitzgerald, seizing on the president's surging fortunes and bluntly calling on Fitzgerald to close down the grand jury investigation. Arguing that Wilson's "wife's role was bound to become public," the *Journal* editorial declared, "A wiser prosecutor than Mr. Fitzgerald might well have come to this same conclusion and shut down the probe. But like so many 'special' counsels who have only one case to prosecute, Mr. Fitzgerald seems to believe he'll be a failure if he doesn't charge someone with something. Thus his overzealous pursuit of reporters and their sources."

At issue, in part, was the paper's interpretation of the 1982 Intelligence Identities Protection Act. Victoria Toensing and Bruce W. Sanford, veterans of the Washington legal community who helped draft the law, wrote an influential op-ed piece for *The Washington Post* in January 2005 arguing that a very high standard of evidence was built into the statute to avoid prosecuting people such as reporters or government employees who might unintentionally or carelessly identify covert agents.[13] The agent's covert status must be classified, the law says, and the agent must either be currently assigned to undercover assignments outside the country or have been assigned such duty within the past five years. The disclosure also must be made intentionally, with knowledge that the government has taken "affirmative measures to conceal [the agent's] relationship" to the United States.

A guilty verdict under the 1982 law would have to show that the leaker either had security clearance and access to the agent's classified status, or had received inside knowledge from someone who did, and intended to compromise the agent's covert identity. For many conservatives, this interpretation of the 1982 law raised the possibility that no crime had been committed. Why investigate the White House if there was no crime? Toensing and Sanford made no secret of their doubts that Plame's work with the CIA met the required legal standard. "It's time for a timeout on a misguided and mechanical investigation in which there is serious doubt that a crime was even committed."[14]

Washington observers pointed out, however, that the CIA would not have referred a criminal case to the Justice Department unless it believed there was reason to believe the law had been broken. And the Justice Department was under no obligation to take on a case involving leaks to the press, which are notoriously difficult to prosecute. Justice's decision to undertake a grand jury proceeding certainly indicated that a crime or crimes might have taken place, though it hardly guaranteed that anyone under investigation would be indicted.

The CIA referral effectively put Plame's status as an undercover operative beyond question. Nonetheless, Tim Phelps of *Newsday* confirmed on the record that Plame had been a covert operative with the CIA. James Gordon Meek and Kenneth Bazinet of the New York *Daily News* quoted a former CIA counterterrorism official who said that Plame "ran intelligence operations overseas" for the agency "recruiting agents, sending them to areas where they could access information about proliferation matters, weapons of mass destruction." That did not stop *Wall Street Journal* editorial writers and other conservatives from putting out the word that Plame had a suburban desk job at the CIA and had not been a covert agent for years. The germ of truth in the charge was that Valerie Wilson, who had been based in Brussels for the Counterproliferation Division of the Directorate of Operations, the agency's clandestine branch, before her twins were born in 1999, had since transferred to CIA headquarters at Langley. It was a convenient political talking point that subtly evaded the truth, yet no one that mattered doubted Wilson met the standard established by the law. No law enforcement agency or legal authority ever seriously questioned her status.

Even so, the prospect of getting an indictment under the Intelligence Identities Protection Act was daunting. Journalists involved were no more likely to talk to prosecutors about Valerie Plame Wilson than their confidential sources were, thanks to widespread assumptions about first amendment protections for both parties. Without documentary evidence or witness testimony, it would be hard to implicate even lower-level administration aides without security clearances—who may have passed the word to reporters about Plame's CIA identity, but could credibly claim they had no personal knowledge of her status themselves. Applying a narrow legal definition, their cases would not meet the high evidentiary standards of the 1982 statute. There was speculation in Washington that the White House legal strategy was predicated on the Toensing-Sanford interpretation of the law and Valerie Wilson's job status. Other legal experts believed the leakers could still be indicted under other statutes that made it a crime to release classified material, commit perjury, or obstruct justice. Fitzgerald had made a career in both New York and Chicago of sending up indictments for obstruction of justice and perjury.

There was little question by January 2005 that the grand jury investigation had ground to a halt. Washington reporters theorized that the investigation had reached a climax the previous June, and that Fitzgerald believed the leak had come from a high-level official, since he had taken an hour to question the president. Newly minted attorney general Alberto Gonzales, the former White House counsel, recused himself from the case as soon he was confirmed in January. Further progress in the case was hostage to Fitzgerald's campaign to force Judith Miller of *The New York Times* and Matt Cooper of *Time* to testify before the grand jury. Both had refused the previous fall, citing their duty to protect their sources. The two were found in contempt in October 2004 by U.S. District Court Judge Thomas Hogan and threatened with jail for the duration of the grand jury if they did not reveal the identities of their sources and what they were told about Valerie Plame Wilson. Both Cooper and Miller vowed to go to jail rather than expose their sources. Their lawyers promptly appealed Hogan's decision.

On February 15, 2005, a three-judge panel of the U.S. Court of Appeals in Washington upheld the special counsel's right to compel the reporters to talk or go to jail, brushing aside the journalists' contention that they enjoyed a privilege in this case under the first amendment to protect the confidentiality of news sources and therefore should not have to testify. Many journalists and legal experts considered the case against the two reporters the most serious challenge to the freedom of the press in a generation. Although the circumstances differed that put Cooper and Miller at the mercy of Fitzgerald and the courts, both reporters and their news organizations took a strong stand that they were protected by the first amendment against being forced by the government to testify about their confidential sources. A journalist's privilege, in this view, is much like confidentiality privileges enjoyed by doctors and patients, lawyers and clients, or priests and confessors—a premise that has never sat well with jurists, or the general public for that matter.

After the two were found in contempt by Judge Hogan, *The New York Times* and *Time* combined forces and brought in Floyd Abrams, one of the nation's foremost experts in first amendment law. Abrams knew that the 1972 Supreme Court decision *Branzburg v. Hayes* established that reporters who witnessed confidential sources in the commission of a crime could be compelled to reveal their identities if the public interest in justice outweighed the news value that resulted. But ever since, reporters had enjoyed an informal agreement with government prosecutors based on Justice Department guidelines that allowed them to protect their confidential sources in most circumstances.

Abrams saw an opening for a better deal. Like other first amendment lawyers, he believed that the late Justice Lewis Powell, in his concurrence to *Branzburg,* offered the promise that future legal developments might bring about a codification of the reporter's privilege in common law. For years after the decision, reporters were subpoenaed left and right. But the tacit agreement between reporters and the government had held up. As Justice Powell predicted, thirty-one states now have shield laws on the books, and eighteen others have recognized some limited reporter-source privilege. Abrams asked the appeals panel in December to recognize an unqualified confidentiality privilege for reporters. The case came before the Washington courts at a time when public esteem for the press was at the lowest ebb in memory. Press privileges were—and still are—under challenge by courts around the country and have been threatened by Bush administration lawyers at an unprecedented clip.

The disappointing result for Abrams was the unanimous February appeals panel ruling against Cooper and Miller. Judge David B. Sentelle declared that the high court's "transparent and forceful" reasoning in *Branzburg,* a case which in part focused on Louisville *Courier-Journal* reporter Paul Branzburg's interviews with two Kentucky drug dealers about selling hashish in 1969, applied as well in the White House leak case. "In language as relevant to the alleged illegal disclosure of the identity of covert agents as it was to the alleged illegal processing of hashish, the Court stated it could not 'seriously entertain the notion that the First Amendment protects the newsman's agreement to conceal the criminal conduct of his source, or evidence thereof, on the theory that it is better to write about a crime than to do something about it,' " Sentelle wrote.[15]

All three judges, including Judge David S. Tatel, a Clinton appointee, agreed that Fitzgerald had demonstrated that the grand jury's need for the reporters' testimony about the leaks overcame any protection due the reporters and their sources. Eight pages of the decision, presenting the special counsel's case that testimony from the reporters was unavailable from other sources, were blacked out of the court record to preserve the secrecy of the grand jury proceedings. Tatel wrote that a common law privilege based on qualified protections available in forty-nine states was an appropriate way for federal courts to balance the interests of the press and the grand jury. However, in this case, the judge argued that protecting those who disclosed Valerie Wilson's identity harmed national security while adding nothing of real news value, so that the reporters would have lost anyway.

Arthur Sulzberger, Jr., the publisher of *The New York Times,* warned that if Miller went to jail, "it would create a dangerous precedent that would erode the freedom of the press." He promised that the newspaper would challenge the decision before the full court of appeals. "The protection of confidential sources was critically important to many groundbreaking stories, such as Watergate, the health-threatening practices of the tobacco industry and police corruption," said Sulzberger. He vowed that his newspaper would continue "to fight for the ability of journalists to provide the people of this nation with the essential information they need to evaluate issues affecting our country and the world." *The Times* declared it would aggressively seek a federal shield law for reporters. Two bills have been introduced in Congress, and though they have strong support in the journalistic community, few believe they have much chance for passage with a Republican-controlled Congress.[16]

After the February federal appeals panel decision, as Sulzberger promised, Abrams declared he would seek another appeal of the Cooper-Miller case before the full U.S. Court of Appeals. Fitzgerald, vilified on one side by supporters of the president for bird-dogging White House officials who may not have committed crimes, and excoriated by supporters of a free press for hounding journalists to surrender their constitutional privileges on the other, appeared confident and serene. "We look forward to resuming our progress in this investigation and bringing it to a prompt conclusion," he said in a rare public statement.

Two months later, in April 2005, the full U.S. Court of Appeals in Washington delivered another blow to Cooper and Miller by refusing to hear the case, putting news organizations and first amendment advocates on notice that their clash with the special counsel and the courts was escalating. That left Abrams no recourse but to petition the Supreme Court to put the case on its docket. Judge Hogan, it happens, told an audience in Montana that he expected the Supreme Court to hear the Miller-Cooper case. The nine high court justices, however, were often reluctant to take on first amendment cases, preferring instead to allow lower courts to decide press privileges on a case-by-case basis, a course that avoided establishing hard-and-fast precedents in law.

For the two reporters involved, the prospect of jail suddenly looked less like an honorable grand gesture and more like a bleak and unpleasant inevitability. "What is the alternative?" Miller told an interviewer. "To go in and talk? I'm not going to do that. There's not much choice. If it comes to prison, I'm going to have to do it. I don't want to do it. My family doesn't want it. But what choice do I have?" Cooper was more circumspect. "Journalists, we believe, have the privilege and the duty to protect their confidential sources," he said. "This is not an exotic privilege. It's one that is the law in 31 states and we believe it's there in federal law as well."[17]

On June 27, 2005, without comment, the U.S. Supreme Court declined to hear the Miller-Cooper case. Fitzgerald admitted that the grand jury's "factual investigation—other than the testimony from these reporters and any further investigation that might result—was for all practical purposes completed" in October 2004. He promised that the eighteen-month-old probe was nearly over. "Now that the legal obligations of the reporters are settled and all appeals exhausted," Fitzgerald said, "we look forward to resuming our progress in this investigation and bringing it to a prompt conclusion."[18]

Like his codefendant, Judith Miller, on the morning of July 6 the affable and portly Matt Cooper was steeling himself for a long stay in jail. Like Miller, he had stuck with his refusal to name a key source in the White House leak case. Cooper arrived at Washington's E. Barrett Prettyman federal courthouse with his wife, Mandy Grunwald, a prominent political consultant and the daughter of the late Time Inc. editor-in-chief and ambassador to Austria, Henry Grunwald. He had already said his good-byes to his six-year-old son, Benjamin. In a new agreement between their two news organizations, Miller and Cooper no longer shared the services of Floyd Abrams as their joint counsel. Cooper's bosses at *Time* had grown wary of the joint defense arrangement and, on the eve of his likely imprisonment, had provided Cooper with his own lawyer, the personable Richard Sauber.

The reasons for the split had become apparent the week before. Days after the Supreme Court ruling, Time Inc. editor-in-chief Norman Pearlstine ordered Cooper to hand over all his e-mails and computerized notes of his conversations with his unnamed White House source to Fitzgerald, arguing that the venerable newsmagazine was not above the law. "If presidents are not above the law, how is it that journalists are?" asked Pearlstine. Behind his principled stand, however, was a colder calculation.

Unlike *The Times*, where Miller's notes were legally her property, Time Inc. legally owned Cooper's work product, right down to his unpublished electronic notes. Pearlstine was plainly worried that the corporation itself could be charged by Fitzgerald with obstruction of justice if *Time* took an absolutist position on Cooper's first amendment rights and stonewalled the federal prosecutor, as Sulzberger and *The Times* had vowed to do.

Pearlstine's concern seemed to be that bucking the civil contempt charge against Cooper could damage Time-Warner's considerable corporate interests, most notably its cable television operations, which depended on good regulatory standing with the federal government. Still, *Time* magazine's top editor was careful to respect Cooper's right to protect his sources. Pearlstine promised Cooper that *Time* would support him if he was forced to go to jail to defend the presumptive first amendment guarantees to the press.

Any thought that the decision to force Cooper to hand over his notes would allow him to escape jail was short-lived. On July 5, the day before he and Miller were scheduled for sentencing, Fitzgerald issued a filing directing that, although Cooper had handed over his notes, the *Time* correspondent would still have to testify and answer questions before the grand jury—or go to jail. After reluctantly going along with his bosses and giving up the name of one confidential source, Cooper was still looking at a lengthy jail term. Like Miller, he understood that he could be held until the grand jury was disbanded at the end of October. Cooper's only request was that he be sent to the relatively comfortable federal penitentiary in Cumberland, Maryland. Fitzgerald turned him down cold.

The next day, Judge Hogan tightened the screws by backing Fitzgerald and rejecting any last-minute notion that Pearlstine's action would excuse Cooper from testifying. Hogan pointedly warned that Cooper's continued failure to cooperate "could be seen to be obstruction of justice," a criminal offense. Cooper then asked to read a statement to the court. He explained that *Time*'s intervention had not absolved him of his promise of confidentiality to his source and that an earlier general waiver from the source had not influenced him. Both Cooper and Miller believed that such waivers, forced upon administration staff by prosecutors, were coerced and therefore illegitimate. Then he shocked the court by explaining that a resolution had been found. "A short time ago, in somewhat dramatic fashion," he read, "I received an express, personal release from my source. It's with a bit of surprise and no small amount of relief that I will comply with this subpoena."[19] Hogan promptly released Cooper.

In a flurry of last-minute negotiations that morning, lawyers for Cooper and Rove had hammered out a waiver that applied personally to Cooper. It was explicitly limited to one conversation with "one source"— Rove was not to be revealed as the source until Cooper testified a week later—and released Cooper from his promise of confidentiality, thus allowing him to stay out of jail and testify.[20] Cooper was off the hook, but it didn't quite work out as neatly as the lawyers intended. Within days of Rove's decision to reconfirm his waiver, copies of Cooper's internal e-mails about Rove written to his *Time* editors leaked to *Newsweek*. On Monday, July 11, two days before Cooper was scheduled to testify before the grand jury, the first big break in the Valerie Plame Wilson leak case hit the newsstands. The rival newsmagazine published an explosive account that identified deputy White House chief of staff Karl Rove as the source of Cooper's July 11, 2003, online posting on *Time*'s Web site that identified Wilson's wife as a CIA employee.

The *Newsweek* story was the first public indication that Fitzgerald's probe might reach to the highest levels of the White House. Cooper's original web story had appeared five days after Joseph Wilson's stinging op-ed in *The Times* accusing the Bush White House of "twisting" intelligence to suit its war aims, and three days before Robert Novak's column in *The Post* outing Valerie Wilson. Rove's lawyer, Robert Luskin, cautioned *Newsweek* that Rove, Bush's master of shadowy political maneuvering, "never knowingly disclosed classified information" and "did not tell any reporter that Valerie Plame worked for the CIA." By that he meant Rove had not used her name or given it to Cooper.[21] "This was not an effort to encourage *Time* to disclose her identity," said Luskin. "What he was doing was discouraging *Time* from perpetuating some statements that had been made publicly and weren't true."[22]

If Cooper's last-minute reprieve was the stuff of TV courtroom drama, the account he wrote for *Time* about his August 13 appearance before Fitzgerald's grand jury read like a real-life political thriller. Deputy White House chief of staff Karl Rove, Cooper wrote, had supplied him with information for the first time that Wilson's wife worked at the CIA, where she worked on weapons of mass destruction, and had played a role in sending him to Niger. "Was it through my conversation with Rove," wrote Cooper, "that I learned for the first time that Wilson's wife worked at the C.I.A. and may have been responsible for sending him? Yes. Did Rove say that she worked at the 'agency' on 'W.M.D.'? Yes."[23]

Cooper's July 11, 2003, telephone conversation with Rove was on "deep background." A sometime stand-up comic, Cooper explained that he e-mailed his editors that it was on "double super secret background," an allusion to the film *Animal House* when the character played by John Belushi was placed on "double secret probation." According to his notes, Rove told him "material was going to be declassified in the coming days that would cast doubt on Wilson's mission [to Niger] and his findings." He confirmed that Rove never identified Wilson's wife by name. Cooper couldn't remember whether he'd seen her name for the first time in Novak's column, or later Googled it himself.[24]

But Cooper was crystal clear that Rove had identified Wilson's wife as a CIA employee—and that he had not known about her until Rove told him. "Rove did, however, clearly indicate that she worked at the 'agency'—by that, I told the grand jury, I inferred he obviously meant the CIA and not, say, the Environmental Protection Agency," wrote Cooper. "Rove added that that she worked on WMD (the abbreviation for weapons of mass destruction) issues and that she was responsible for sending Wilson. This was the first time I had heard anything about Wilson's wife."

The revelation of Rove's leak to Cooper galvanized Washington, leading to speculation that Bush's top political operative was at the center of the administration attacks on Joe Wilson and his wife—and may have been part of a White House campaign to deflect charges that the president had used doubtful intelligence to sell the Iraq war. Confirmation that one prominent reporter had first learned about Valerie Wilson from a senior White House official also starkly contradicted assurances offered back in 2003 by hapless White House spokesman Scott McClellan that neither Rove nor Libby had anything to do with the leak. Cooper's testimony offered a tantalizing piece of the puzzle. But it fell well short of the Holy Grail for White House critics. Cooper offered no evidence that suggested Rove had crossed the line into criminality. He had not, by Cooper's account, said anything about Valerie Wilson's status as a covert agent.

Cooper had talked to the other senior official suspected in the leak, Lewis Libby, on June 12, the day after his chat with Rove. He had gotten nowhere. Libby earlier had released Cooper from his pledge of confidentiality, so Cooper agreed to speak to Fitzgerald about their brief contact on the condition Rove would remain off-limits. Cooper recounted that he had asked Libby if he knew the rumors about Wilson's wife, and Libby had replied, "Yeah, I heard that too."[25] Despite the prior agreement, Fitzgerald turned around and subpoenaed Cooper to talk about Rove. The subject was a sore point between Cooper and Fitzgerald. The move did not inspire either Cooper or Judith Miller with confidence in Fitzgerald. Yet within months, after steadfastly refusing to testify and suffering the consequences, Miller would reconsider the trustworthiness of the special counsel.

22

VERDICT OF THE WEAPONS HUNTERS

On Thursday, June 5, 2003, David Kay was ushered into George Tenet's office after just returning from Iraq as a consultant for NBC News. The CIA director posed a simple question to Kay: "What do you think? Why aren't they finding anything?" For Kay, who led the UN-SCOM weapons inspection team in the early 1990s and first exposed Saddam's extensive pre–Gulf War nuclear weapons program, the answer was simple. Kay knew that the CIA had staked its case with the White House on Saddam's possession of biological and chemical super-weapons and a robust nuclear weapons development program. He also knew that the army's 75th Exploitation Task Force was not finding any such weapons in the aftermath of the initial ground invasion in Iraq. Kay felt that the military never had a real interest in Saddam's WMD, beyond the threat of chemical weapons in the early phase of combat—and that hadn't materialized. "You're not going to get there with the military leading it because the military has shown a massive lack of interest," he told Tenet. "They were interested in deterring their use, and they didn't view finding WMD as a military task."[1]

The worst way to proceed was to use the Pentagon's master site list, Kay continued, as army intelligence chief Maj. Gen. James "Spider" Marks had done. "You simply cannot find weapons of mass destruction using a list," said Kay. A decade earlier he had personally visited many of the same sites that were still on that list. "You have to treat this like an

intelligence operation. You go after people. You don't go after physical assets. You don't have enough people in the country. It's too big . . . So you
treat it by going after the expertise, the security guards that would have
been there, the movers, the generals that would have seen it, the Special
Republican Guard."[2]

Kay's experience had led him to believe years before that the only way
to disarm Iraq was to take out Saddam, and he had little doubt that Iraq
harbored WMD—the reports of Blix, ElBaradei, and company to the contrary notwithstanding. He was confident about the likelihood of finding
Saddam's weapons. After his brief stint in Iraq as chief UNSCOM
weapons inspector ended in 1992, Kay joined the California-based Science Applications International Corporation, a major defense contractor,
where he was a vice president until 2002. In 1999, a year after the UN-
SCOM inspectors left Iraq, he told a PBS interviewer that what stood between the Iraqis and a nuclear weapon was "not scientific talent. They
don't lack the secrets and technology. They've solved all those problems.
What they lack is time and access to nuclear materials. If the Iraqis were
able to import, for example, from a Soviet program . . . plutonium or
high-enriched uranium, it would take them only a matter of months to
fabricate a crude weapon." Like the neoconservatives in the Bush administration, Kay believed that Baghdad without Saddam could become a
model of stability in the region. "I think we should have crafted a package that said, 'Look, with Saddam's replacement, Iraq will be reintegrated
into the world,'" said Kay. "'The debts and all will be forgiven. We view
you as a major rock of stability in the Middle East . . .'"[3]

Tenet apparently liked what he heard. The following weekend, the
CIA asked Kay to undertake the hunt for Saddam's proscribed weapons
ordered by the president. He would be a special adviser to Tenet and the
chief weapons inspector for the Iraq Survey Group (ISG). Kay, after ex-
tracting a promise from Tenet to provide him with all the resources and
independence he would need to get the job done, agreed to head the outfit. The group had been formed by Rumsfeld's top intelligence aide, Steve
Cambone, and Maj. Gen. Keith Dayton of the Defense Intelligence
Agency in late April. The Iraq Survey Group already had set up a base of
operations in Doha, Qatar, that would house more than nine hundred
support staff. Their job over the next two years would be to collect and
translate more than 36 million pages of Iraqi documents and scan them
into a main ISG database. The operation would be fed by some two hundred forward staff in Baghdad, many of them Arab speakers, who were
responsible for locating and identifying important documents. Special

teams were assigned to track down and interview "high-value" former Iraqi government and military officials and knowledgeable members of Baghdad's scientific establishment.[4]

Besides support staff to handle logistics, communications, housing, computers, and food, the ISG set up two laboratories to analyze suspected WMD materiel, from nerve agent rounds to lethal chemical substances. The survey group set up its own bomb-removal team and a security force to provide transportation and armed protection for the weapons hunters. Representatives of the National Security Agency and the National Geospatial-Intelligence Agency were on hand to advise ISG in the collection and interpretation of satellite imagery and electronic intercept data. Lastly, the analytic staff was responsible for pulling all this information together into a coherent picture of Iraq's WMD program. They would also plan and direct further interviews, document collection activities, and inspections. The analysts were mostly U.S. weapons experts from American intelligence agencies, including the CIA, DIA, DOE, the State and Defense departments, as well as experts from the British and Australian intelligence services. Some had served previously as UN weapons inspectors. All in all, Kay presided over a weapons-hunting force that might number as many as fourteen hundred people at any one time.

If anything, the search for Saddam's weapons in the midst of the occupation and the mounting Baathist insurgency proved more limited and difficult than Kay's experiences a decade before had led him to expect. Iraq was a more dangerous and chaotic place. Many sites had been looted, and there was some evidence pro-Saddam saboteurs were responsible. The army's MET units had not helped, often leaving presumed weapons sites unguarded and vulnerable to more looting. Iraqi witnesses knowledgeable about WMD were often afraid to speak to ISG investigators, caught between their fear of retribution from Baathist thugs and imprisonment by coalition forces. Just moving around the countryside had become a dangerous business.

In the early 1990s, Kay's UNSCOM inspectors had been shot at by Iraqi soldiers and survived potentially deadly confrontations with Iraqi security forces. But this was different. By November 2003, the threat of the insurgency to ISG inspectors in Baghdad and the Sunni triangle to the west was enough to require armored vehicles and constant protection by U.S. military units. Even so, ISG armored jeeps were regularly destroyed by gunfire or IEDs, the improvised explosive devices that would become familiar to American TV viewers. As many as four soldiers attached to the ISG were killed by hostile fire during weapons-inspection operations. At one point, the ISG uncovered an insurgent group employing former Iraqi government experts to develop chemical weapons, including ricin, for use against the American and British occupation forces. The threat was reportedly neutralized in a raid by counterterrorism personnel.[5]

The deteriorating security situation discouraged many ISG personnel from spending more than a few months in Iraq, creating awkward inefficiencies as detainees were interviewed several times by different interviewers, and staff regularly departed with the expertise they had gained during their time in Iraq.[6] On the plus side, there were fifteen to twenty ISG weapons hunters—including Kay—who had been in Iraq as UN inspectors before and were acquainted with some of their Iraqi interlocutors, which made it more difficult for the Iraqis to lie.

Kay had been out of the intelligence loop on Iraqi WMD since 1992. But he was unimpressed by a weeklong immersion in the CIA's classified WMD files after he accepted the job. The intelligence, predating the forced departure in 1998 of the UN inspectors from Baghdad, seemed to him reasonable and solid, but Kay was struck that much of the intelligence from after 1998 seemed to depend too heavily on foreign intelligence services or Iraqi defectors, or both. He was most surprised at the sloppiness of the CIA's case on Iraq's biological weapons, for which Curveball appeared to be the lone source. Kay learned to his consternation that neither the CIA nor any other U.S. intelligence agency had independently interviewed the Iraqi defector, but instead relied on secondhand information from more than one hundred interrogations reported by the Germans—who he understood had begun to question Curveball's credibility. "The more you look at it, the less is there," Kay later said of the CIA's WMD dossier. "It was an eye-opening experience."[7] He nonetheless remained confident that under his leadership, the ISG would find Saddam's weapons arsenals, once the emphasis was taken off the site searches and ISG inspectors sought out the accounts and documents that knowledgeable Iraqis could provide.

Once he settled into his Baghdad quarters in the Green Zone in mid-June—his lodgings consisted of a shipping container converted into a living space—Kay lost no time sending out ISG inspectors to find the evidence underlying the major intelligence cases supporting Washington's case for war. Much of the spadework already had been done by Blix's UNMOVIC inspectors before the invasion, but Kay insisted that the ISG teams, billeted in quarters outside the city near Baghdad International

Airport, reach their own independent conclusions. The summer and early fall of 2003 proved a taunting reprise of his first impressions of the CIA assessments. The harder the weapons hunters looked for WMD, the more they came up empty.

Kay's confidence was unflagging. He told NBC anchor Tom Brokaw in mid-July that he'd "already seen enough to convince me" that Saddam had WMD, and predicted that his weapons hunters would have enough evidence to convince "everyone" in six months. But by the end of the month, Kay was saying in his private e-mail messages to John McLaughlin and George Tenet that the ISG was more likely to find evidence of dual-use facilities, such as chemical plants capable of switching from civilian products to the production of weaponized agents on short order, than actual stockpiles of WMD. In the lingo of weapons experts, Kay called it "surge production capacity."[8]

An early focus of ISG inspectors were the mobile biological weapons labs that President Bush had declared had been found in Iraq six weeks earlier. The president had based his remarks on a white paper that the CIA and DIA had produced and rushed to the White House after the discovery. DIA had provided photos of the trailer trucks to Curveball in Germany, who confirmed that the equipment pictured looked like components he had once worked on at the Djerf al Nadaf factory near Baghdad. The CIA and DIA white paper dismissed as a "cover story" the theory that the truck probably produced hydrogen for weather balloons. Yet in the classified DIA review of the evidence that followed, fourteen out of fifteen bioweapons experts determined that the trucks could not possibly have been used for manufacturing biological agents for weapons. In July, a former British army officer and bioweapons expert named Hamish Killip flew into Baghdad to inspect the trailers as part of Kay's team, and quickly agreed with the DIA assessment. Killip and his investigators found the idea laughable that anyone thought the trailer-trucks could be used to make biological weapons. "The equipment was singularly inappropriate," said Killip. "We were in hysterics over this. You'd have better luck putting a couple of dust bins on the back of the truck and brewing it in there." He concluded that the trucks were intended to generate hydrogen.[9]

The lone holdout in the DIA review was a WINPAC intelligence analyst, who has been identified only as Jerry, and who continued to insist that the trucks were transportable weapons production facilities. Jerry had helped draft the original white paper on the mobile labs for the White House in 2001, and had become one of the CIA's chief advocates for the mobile weapons labs theory. In the two-year-old white paper, Jerry and his WINPAC colleagues reported that seven such labs working around the clock for six months could produce 30,000 liters of germ warfare agents.[10] The seat-of-the-pants calculation was pure speculation, but it became received wisdom in the pressure-cooker atmosphere of the U.S. intelligence community after the September 11 attacks.

Like the German intelligence officials and some CIA officers on the clandestine operations side, Jerry eventually began to have his doubts about Curveball. He traveled to Baghdad to lead a painstaking ISG investigation into the Iraqi defector's background. Kay's ISG investigators fanned out to the Djerf al Nadaf plant and other sites identified by Curveball, following the trail of the UN inspectors from the previous February. While searching a personnel file in an Iraqi government storeroom, they came across powerful evidence that Curveball was not who he said he was. He had claimed he graduated first in his engineering class at Baghdad University. Jerry's team now discovered that in fact he had graduated last. Nor was he an engineering project or site manager, as he had claimed, but an entry-level trainee. In 1995, at a time he told interrogators that he had been working on the bioweapons trailers, he had already been fired from his job. Worse, he had been thrown in jail for a sex crime and wound up driving a taxi.

The investigators interviewed some sixty friends, family, and coworkers of Curveball. The reports came back with a remarkable consistency. His former bosses knew nothing about mobile germ-producing weapons trucks and dismissed the idea as a product of "water cooler gossip" and "corridor conversations." His childhood friends called him a "great liar," a "con artist," and "a real operator." People "kept saying what a rat Curveball was," the team reported. They found it hard to believe the CIA had fallen for Curveball's story. "The Iraqis were all laughing," a member of ISG said later. "They were saying, 'This guy? You've got to be kidding.'"[11] Curveball's parents were Sunni Muslims who lived in a middle-class neighborhood in Baghdad. His mother looked shocked when one investigator said he understood their son didn't like Americans. "She said, 'No, no! He loves Americans,'" recounted Kay. "And she took him into [her son's] bedroom and it was filled with posters of American rock stars. It was like any other teenage room. She said one of his goals was to go to America."[12]

Jerry appeared crestfallen. He departed Baghdad abruptly with a CIA colleague and returned to Washington aboard a military flight. "They had been true believers in Curveball," Kay said. "They absolutely believed in him. They knew every detail in his file. But it was total hokum. There was no truth in it. They said they had to go home to explain how all this was all so wrong. They wanted to fight the battle at the CIA."[13] Back at a Langley, Jerry was "read the riot act" and accused of "making waves" for challenging the accepted line at WINPAC.[14] "Jerry had become kind of a nonperson," recalled Michael Scheuer, the head of the bin Laden division, who himself had been sidelined for criticizing CIA counterterror tactics in Afghanistan. "There was a tremendous amount of pressure on him not to say anything. Just to sit there and shut up." The agency, said Kay, was "very, very vindictive."[15]

Kay returned to Washington in late July to brief closed sessions of the Senate intelligence and armed services committees. Tenet invited him to attend the president's morning intelligence briefing on July 29, two days before the hearings. To his surprise, Kay found himself doing the briefing to an Oval Office audience that included Cheney, Rumsfeld, and Wolfowitz, among others, with the notable exception of Powell. Kay softpedaled the ISG's progress up to then, highlighting the difficulties the postwar looting had caused, the tense security situation, the snags the ISG ran into locating Iraqi scientists and getting them to talk. Besides some evidence of a surge production capacity for chemical weapons, said Kay, there were no smoking guns, and his investigators had ruled out the possibility that the trailer-mounted labs were designed for producing biological weapons. Bush, Kay noticed, had no particular reaction one way or another to his gentle but disturbing message. The other senior officials in the room calmly deferred to the president. The passive reaction was striking, especially from President Bush, and it puzzled Kay.

"I came out of the Oval Office uncertain as to how to read the President," said Kay later. "Here was an individual who was oblivious to the problems created by the failure to find the WMDs. Or was this an individual who was completely at peace with himself on the decision to go to war, who didn't question that, and who was totally focused on the here and now and what was to come?"[16]

Later in the day, however, Cheney grilled Kay with specific questions at a meeting in the vice president's office, with Libby present. The vice president wanted to know whether Kay was relying on CIA intelligence, or developed his own independent information. Kay took the question as a measure of Cheney's deep distrust of the CIA. He described Tenet's assurances that he would be able to run the hunt for weapons with complete independence and assured Cheney that his teams developed their own sources and data. The vice president then wanted to know whether Kay had seen satellite photos and signal intercepts of trucks moving from Iraq across the border into Syria, and how he intended to find out whether Saddam had spirited weapons over the border before the war. The vice president knew that Kay's investigators had been bargaining with arms dealers in Damascus, offering to sell documents about Iraqi weapons deals. "This was a Vice President who was well read in the intelligence and knew the details of the WMD issue," Kay said later.[17]

But this was also the senior official closest to the president who several weeks before had sent Kay an urgent message in the middle of the night about new WMD-related intelligence he'd seen. Aides had provided Cheney with a raw National Security Agency signals intercept that they believed contained the coordinates of a WMD storage site in Iraq. Cheney wanted the ISG to investigate. Kay's analysts ran down the coordinates, which pinpointed a site in Lebanon's Bekaa Valley. Kay suspected that the vice president's aides and his allies at the Pentagon were sifting through highly classified, unanalyzed intelligence hoping for a breakthrough that the CIA and the rest of the intelligence community had missed.[18]

Some of the vice president's spycraft produced outright scorn at ISG headquarters. Cheney's office alerted Kay to satellite photos apparently showing the opening of a tunnel in a hillside in Iraq, which the vice president's people believed might be a hiding place for WMD. After analyzing the photo, Kay's weapons hunters reportedly laughed out loud. The object of the high-tech surveillance was a trench dug in the side of a hillside to collect water for cows, a common practice among Iraqi farmers. Kay saw a pattern in the vice president's constant focus on obscure details. "He kept remembering little facts that he thought proved big conclusions," Kay said later. "The problem with intelligence is that little facts often don't prove anything, let along something big. They're just pieces of puzzles—sometimes just pieces that don't even make a puzzle."[19]

Still, Kay remained upbeat with the Washington press, emphasizing during a brief encounter with reporters between Senate hearings on July 31 that his inspectors had found some evidence regarding WMD. "We are making solid progress," he said. "It's very likely that we will discover remarkable surprises in this enterprise."[20] He added: "The American people should not be surprised by surprises. We are determined to take this apart and every day, I must say, we're surprised by new advances that we're making."[21]

The nature of those surprises would not become public for another several months—but it was not good news for the White House, which was reeling from the Valerie Wilson controversy and new tensions with Tenet and the CIA. Shortly after Kay returned to Baghdad, it became clear that he was on a collision course with both the White House and the CIA. His weekly e-mail reports to Tenet and McLaughlin were a steady diet of bad news for the agency. Besides debunking Curveball and the mobile bioweapons labs, Kay's inspectors had sifted through records that might indicate the locations of chemical weapons storehouses, and had talked to Iraqis who directed them to places where they said chemical weapons were hidden. Time and time again, they turned up nothing. The weapons hunters carefully examined Iraqi pilotless drones—the unmanned aerial vehicles (UAVs) that Bush officials believed were capable of projecting payloads of chemical and biological weapons to Europe and the United States. "We knew the range, navigation, and payload capability," Kay said. "There was no way this was a threat to anyone."[22]

Tenet stopped responding to Kay's private, unvarnished weekly secure e-mail reports, and began passing up the weekly interagency videoconference sessions on the ISG's progress. McLaughlin, for his part, seemed to have difficulty accepting the ISG's findings. In one e-mail, Kay explained that if the Iraqis had maintained surge production capacity, it would probably mean there would be no stockpiles of weapons. McLaughlin was unsettled by this. "Don't tell anyone this," the deputy director e-mailed Kay. "This could be very upsetting. Be very careful. We can't let this out until we're sure."[23] Kay took a lesson from McLaughlin's responses. "John and George had believed the WMDs were there," Kay recalled afterward. "I think they understood how weak the available evidence was. They understood the holes. But . . . they were confident the WMDs would be there . . . I became the turd on the table."[24]

It would only get worse. The centerpiece of the White House case for war, Kay knew, was the charge voiced repeatedly before the war by Cheney and the president that Saddam was rebuilding his nuclear weapons program. Kay knew that the CIA's assessment of Iraq's nuclear capabilities depended on a blizzard of intelligence that Iraqi purchases of high-strength aluminum tubes were meant for uranium enrichment centrifuges—and that Baghdad had tried to buy raw uranium from Niger. Kay was skeptical, and the alleged Iraqi nuclear program was low on his list of priorities. Several months passed before the weapons hunters visited the Nasser fabrication plant, which was only thirty miles northeast of Baghdad, where the Iraqis manufactured 81 mm. Nasser conventional artillery rockets. When they did make the trip, ISG investigators, like the UNMOVIC inspectors before them, found an inventory of twenty thousand high-strength

7074-T6 aluminum tubes, which the CIA said were engineered to fine tolerances for use as centrifuge rotors—but were precisely the length, thickness, and diameter of Nasser 81 rocket housings.

Two members of the ISG—Department of Energy intelligence analyst William Domke, who was in charge of the ISG centrifuge team, and Jeffrey Bedell, an analyst with DOE's Lawrence Livermore National Laboratory—had inspected the Nasser facility the previous December and January and had taken samples of the tubes while on temporary loan to ElBaradei's IAEA.[25] Domke and Bedell, who were the authors of the critical DOE dissent in the 2002 NIE, confirmed their prewar conclusion that the Iraqis intended the tubes for rockets.

But the investigators did not stop there. New evidence that the tubes were a poor substitute for any restarted Iraqi centrifuge program was provided by former Iraqi nuclear scientist Mahdi Obeidi, who had directed Saddam's pre-1991 centrifuge program. After the fall of Baghdad, Obeidi turned himself in to U.S. forces. The next day—after U.S. troops mistakenly raided his house and arrested him—the Iraqi scientist led them to a cache of 200 centrifuge blueprints, 180 documents on centrifuge operation, and samples of critical parts that he had buried under his rosebushes in 1991 to hide them from UNSCOM inspectors. Obeidi's secret stash of documents, besides assuring him U.S. protection, was proof positive that Iraqi scientists acted to preserve their scientific and technical knowledge base. But it showed more than that. Obeidi's earliest designs for a gas centrifuge used rotors, or tubes, fabricated from maraging steel, not aluminum. In 1990 Obeidi's shop succeeded in building a more sophisticated prototype centrifuge using carbon fiber rotors that produced an isotope of uranium from uranium hexafluoride gas—a significant technical milestone, but well short of the thousand-centrifuge cascade need to produce weapons-grade uranium.

The aluminum tube theory unraveled from there. High-strength aluminum rotors, unlike rotors made up of maraging steel or carbon fiber, the inspectors concluded, wouldn't stand up to the physical stresses of high-speed centrifuge operation. Obeidi's successful prototype design called for rotors 145 millimeters in diameter. The Iraqi's aluminum tubes were only 81 millimeters. Beyond that, a working cascade of gas centrifuges to enrich uranium would require a fluorine plant for converting uranium ore, or yellowcake, to gaseous form, as well as a technically sophisticated system of magnets and other parts to connect the array. Kay's investigators found no evidence of a fluorine plant or fabrication of other specialized parts.[26] ISG inspectors also searched the huge Tuwaitha nuclear facility outside Baghdad, which had been bombed by the Americans in 1991, and found only rusted and outdated equipment that had been sitting unused for more than a decade. Inspections of once active smaller sites in the pre-1991 nuclear weapons system also failed to turn up any evidence of a reconstituted program. Obeidi, along with other Iraqi scientists, insisted that Saddam's nuclear program was discontinued after the Gulf War in 1991.

Australian brigadier general Stephen D. Meekin, who commanded the five-hundred-strong Joint Captured Enemy Materiel Exploitation Center, the largest of the half-dozen ISG units that reported to Kay, put the aluminum tubes controversy to rest with Aussie bluntness. "They were rockets," he said. "The tubes were used for rockets." Meekin conceded he did not know what happened to the twenty thousand tubes after the ISG investigation was concluded, but assumed they had been stolen. "They weren't our highest priority," he said. They "could be in arms plants, scattered around . . . perhaps in scrap metal yards." Or perhaps looters could have "sold them as drain pipe."[27]

Kay returned to Washington again in mid-September to prepare an interim report on the ISG's progress to the Senate and House intelligence committees. Working at an office at CIA headquarters, he was immediately plunged into disputes with Tenet and McLaughlin, who resisted the conclusions of the ISG teams on the aluminum tubes and the mobile bioweapons labs—adding to the din of complaints coming from advocates for both at WINPAC. Tenet apparently found it hard to believe there were no chemical weapons stockpiles in Iraq. McLaughlin, already uneasy with preliminary reports from Kay, counseled him to try not to be too definitive in his testimony about not finding any weapons. Kay later claimed he pushed back hard. "I went there to find WMDs, and if I went up on the Hill and didn't say I found any, all dialogue would be over," he recalled later. "I knew the agency was going to be unhappy and disturbed by these conclusions. But if anyone was disturbed, I was disturbed. I had thought there were WMDs. I was not just discomforting the CIA. I was discomforting myself."[28]

That may have accurately described Kay's feelings, but in his statement to the Senate and House committees on October 2 he seemed to heed McLaughlin's advice. "Kay's interim testimony," Tenet later wrote, "was a damning portrait of deception and dissembling" by the Iraqis, and he claimed Kay was frustrated that little of what the ISG had found made headlines in the media.[29] Tenet had a legitimate point, though he may have been a bit churlish about the press's treatment of Kay's remarks. While Kay did not hide the fact that in three months of investigation the ISG had come up empty-handed, he strongly emphasized the weapons hunters' most provocative, if very preliminary, findings and signaled that the search for WMD was far from over. "It is far too early to reach any definitive conclusions," he testified. "We have not yet found stocks of weapons, but we are not yet at the point where we can say definitively either that such weapons stocks do not exist or that they existed before the war and our only task is to find where they have gone." Kay later told interviewers that the ISG would need another six to nine months to finish its work.

His most powerful point was that the weapons hunters had discovered "dozens of WMD-related program activities and significant amounts of equipment that Iraq concealed from the United Nations during the inspections that began in late 2002." The most eye-catching was the unearthing of "plans and advanced design work for new long-range missiles with ranges up to 1000 km" and secret Iraqi attempts to obtain North Korean technology for longer-range missiles and antiship cruise missiles. Kay also described "a clandestine network of laboratories and safe houses" run by the Iraqi intelligence service, the Mukhabarat, that had not been declared to the United Nations and contained equipment for chemical and biological weapons. The ISG found Iraqi labs working on undeclared "new research" into bioweapons-applicable agents such as brucellosis and Congo-Crimean hemorrhagic fever as well as ricin and aflatoxin. Investigators had discovered seventy-nine vials containing strains of biological organisms hidden in one scientist's refrigerator since the Gulf War. They had found Obeidi's hidden documents and equipment "that would have been useful in resuming uranium enrichment by centrifuge and electromagnetic isotope separation."

Hans Blix, who had overseen the prewar UNMOVIC inspections, disputed Kay's contention that the UN operation had missed these weapons-related activities—and that some of them involved proscribed weapons at all. But Kay was parsing his case finely, and his point was that these were areas that would require further investigation. He had not overstated his findings. After all, the ISG had not physically found long-range missiles or warheads full of hemorrhagic fever germs, but rather "plans . . . and design work" and "new research."

Likewise, Kay cautiously talked around the ISG's view of Saddam's purportedly reconstituted nuclear program, the mainstay of the CIA's and the White House's case for war. He declared that his staff had evidence and testimony that Saddam "remained firmly committed to acquiring nuclear weapons," and that "working groups [of scientists] were preserved in order to allow a reconstitution of the nuclear weapons program" that had ended in 1991.[30] But Kay's bottom line was clear. "Despite evidence of Saddam's continued ambition to acquire nuclear weapons, to date we have not uncovered evidence that Iraq undertook significant post-1998 steps to actually build nuclear weapons or produce fissile material." The best the weapons hunters could come up with was an aging nuclear scientist who "some . . . former colleagues" from Saddam's pre-1991 nuclear program suspected might be "considering a restart of the centrifuge program."[31] There was not a word about the aluminum tubes. It was as close as Kay could have come to saying there was no reconstituted Iraqi nuclear weapons program without actually coming out and saying it.

When the hearings were over, unnamed White House officials reportedly called the top CIA brass and asked them why Kay had to emphasize that the ISG had not found stocks of weapons. Tenet and McLaughlin then apparently passed the word to Kay that the White House was displeased and wondered why he didn't play down the missing stockpiles.[32] Powell, too, called Tenet, angry that the administration hadn't put a more effective spin on Kay's report. The next day, in an apparent effort to compensate, Bush said, accurately enough, that Kay said "Saddam Hussein's regime had a clandestine network of biological laboratories. They had a live strain of deadly agent called botulinum. And he had sophisticated concealment efforts. In other words, he's hiding his program. He had advanced design work on prohibited longer-range missiles."[33]

All of Kay's technical weapons-speak, tortured phrasing, and skills at circumlocution could not conceal the fact that the ISG was not finding any evidence of WMD. Later that October, after Kay had returned to Baghdad, BBC reporter Jane Corbin, a veteran of Iraqi arms inspection missions, asked Kay point-blank if he was still convinced he'd find WMD. "No," Kay said. "I'm convinced we will find the truth about WMD." But the prospect that there was nothing, no substance, to something he had personally believed for more than a decade was obviously weighing on him. Kay came back to the subject later in the interview. "If we get to the end of the day and we find nothing," he said, "we will all be able to say this is the evidence that leads us to the conclusion that there was nothing there or there was something there. It's probably because of the background and training, but you always have to be prepared to examine your hypotheses and for them to be proved wrong. That's how you make progress, and that's why we put in this process here that will do that."[34]

Vice President Cheney's intrusive directives about promising WMD intelligence did not end once Kay was back in Iraq. Now they began coming through the CIA. When Kay received a cable from Langley informing him that the vice president wanted him to send ISG officials to Switzerland to meet with former Iranian arms dealer Manucher Ghorbanifar about WMD, Kay drew the line. He knew Ghorbanifar was involved in the Iran-Contra scandal during the Reagan era and was a CIA asset. He also knew that the agency had put a "burn notice" out on Ghorbanifar in the early 1980s for fabricating information. Cheney's Pentagon intelligence network apparently had heard that Ghorbanifar had an Iranian source who was asking $2 million to reveal what he knew about Iraqi nuclear weapons, but would only talk to the United States through Ghorbanifar.[35]

Kay found out that the deal also involved Michael Ledeen, the militant right-wing American Enterprise Institute scholar and former NSC staffer. Ledeen had longstanding ties to Cheney and Wolfowitz. He was the go-between with Italian intelligence who helped Ghorbanifar set up the shadowy December 2001 meeting in Rome between officials from Feith's Pentagon unit and Iranian dissidents. Kay reportedly took one look at the CIA cable and dismissed it. "I recognize this one," he said. "This one I'm not going to do."[36] Kay sent a cable back to the CIA refusing to "have any member of the ISG talk to this guy" who was "a known fabricator-peddler" unless he was under direct instructions from Tenet. That was the end of it.[37]

A meddlesome vice president, who seemed intent on undercutting his operational independence, wasn't Kay's only problem. The security situation in Iraq—and Baghdad in particular—was deteriorating badly. An Iraqi suicide bomber drove into a crowd of policemen in Baghdad on October 9, killing nine and injuring scores. Brutal coordinated suicide attacks on three other police stations and an Islamic Red Crescent emergency medical clinic killed forty-three and wounded more than two hundred. Sixteen U.S. troops were killed and twenty-one wounded when their Chinook helicopter was shot down by insurgents.[38]

Threats and attempts to intimidate ISG personnel were also on the rise. In September alone, an ISG base in Arbil was bombed, injuring four staff members, two of them seriously. Two investigators escaped gunmen at a roadblock by opening fire at their attackers through their own windshield.

ISG headquarters in Baghdad was attacked by mortar rounds. [39] "Today, I go around—I'm armed today," said Kay in October. "Almost every one of our inspectors and personnel is armed, and it's not because we're Rambo-like. It's because we are under constant threat as we move around. This building has been hit with mortars just a week ago. It's an environment that in fact makes it difficult to rapidly move around the country freely."[40]

Besides the effect of the increased violence on the morale of Kay's investigators, U.S. soldiers were being killed in numbers unseen since combat operations ended five months earlier. Senior U.S. military officials, already badly undermanned for counterinsurgency warfare, were desperate for new resources, especially when it came to intelligence. In late November, Gen. John Abizaid, the U.S. commander in the Iraq theater, summoned Kay to his headquarters. Abizaid told Kay he was badly in need of good intelligence to fight the insurgency, and that Kay's organization was the best intelligence network around. "I need these resources," Abizaid said. "You've got translators. You've got analysts."

Kay demurred. "I have analysts who are experts on WMD," he objected. "They're not going to help anyone on counterinsurgency." Kay protested that if he lost his two operational officers who were fluent in Arabic, the ISG's ability to debrief Iraqis would be sharply compromised. Abizaid said he'd be happy with a dozen of Kay's sixty-odd analysts, then whittled the number down to six or seven. Kay was still adamant. "No, I can't do it because I got assigned this mission," he told Abizaid. "I have absolutely no problem if you go back to Washington and Washington decides at this point in time that counterinsurgency is more important than WMD . . . I understand. But it's not my decision."[41] But Abizaid did not want to ask Washington; he wanted to do a deal then and there with Kay. Kay refused.

Tenet, whose shining moment post-9/11 had been the CIA paramilitary operations in Afghanistan, was furious that Kay had essentially turned down an invitation for the CIA to play a pivotal military role in Iraq from a four-star general. What happened next was unclear. According to Bob Woodward, Tenet informed Kay that "he had lost his tug of war with the military" and his "Iraq Survey Group would have to take on other missions besides WMD." Kay then flew back to Washington to remind Tenet personally that he had taken the job to focus on WMD, and that maybe it was "time to go." Tenet, worried about what Kay might say publicly about not finding Iraqi weapons, suggested he might be planning to write a book about it. "I don't do that," snapped Kay. "I've never done that. I didn't do it after the first Gulf War." Tenet reportedly decided it was best to try to keep Kay on the reservation and suggested that he stay on the CIA payroll as a consultant. Kay agreed.[42]

Tenet told a slightly different story. In his book *At the Center of the Storm* he wrote that his deputy John McLaughlin found U.S. intelligence personnel who "could be sent to Iraq to replace anyone diverted from the ISG staff," but that Kay nonetheless "became obstreperous, claiming that he was not getting the support he needed to do his job," and said he wouldn't "stake his reputation" on the WMD mission unless he got full support. "Had he been a regular CIA officer," Tenet later wrote, "I would have relieved Kay of his command and ordered him home."[43] Tenet claimed that on November 19 he heard rumors that Kay intended to quit and called Kay, who confirmed that he intended to step down, and "expressed a general unhappiness that anyone in the ISG might be asked to help control the increasingly deadly insurgency." Realizing that Kay's resignation might come just as President Bush was arriving in London for a state visit with Tony Blair, Tenet claimed, he responded that quitting now was unacceptable. "No, I won't allow you to embarrass the president in that way," Tenet said he told Kay.[44]

Tenet later said that he then suggested that Kay return to Washington for the Christmas holidays. "Look, David," Tenet recalled saying, "why don't you come home for the holidays, take some time off to think about continuing the job?" Kay remembered a different sequence of events. He said that when he flew back to Washington in December to talk to Tenet, he told him that he thought Curveball was a liar and that he now believed Iraq possessed no mobile bioweapons labs or any other illegal weapons—an exchange that was confirmed by other CIA officials.[45] The CIA then assigned Kay to an office without windows or a working telephone. At the end of December, Kay said he was going to resign. Tenet contended that he asked Kay to stay on until he could find a replacement, but reportedly was really interested in getting Kay to hold off on announcing his resignation until after President's Bush's January 20 State of the Union Address.[46]

This time around, after Kay's embarrassing performance in the October congressional hearings, the administration apparently wanted more disciplined message control about Iraq's WMD. In his address, the president picked up Kay's October formulation verbatim, hailing Kay and the ISG for finding "weapons of mass destruction–related program activities . . . Had we failed to act, the dictator's weapons of mass destruction program would continue to this day." Kay was not opposed to another Bush exercise in obfuscatory political sleight of hand, and privately met with several GOP legislators to urge them to retreat from the Iraqi WMD issue as well. "Be really careful, because you're not going to find that," he told them.[47]

Three days later, on January 23, 2004, a Friday, Kay announced his resignation, along with a statement coordinated with the CIA press office declaring that there were many unresolved issues left for the ISG to resolve. Then, no longer constrained by his ties to the government, Kay opened up to the press. He told reporters that, in fact, few issues were left unresolved, and that "there were no Iraqi stockpiles to be found." In an expansive *New York Times* interview published the following Monday, Kay foreshadowed the themes that emerged almost a year later in the ISG's final report.

Iraq's WMD programs were in disarray under Saddam's increasingly erratic leadership, he said. Although there appeared to be some interest in restarting a nuclear program, it was at best rudimentary. Iraq hadn't produced stockpiles of chemical or biological weapons since the end of the Gulf War in 1991. He described Baghdad as "a vortex of corruption," where Iraqi scientists and government officials presented fanciful programs to an increasingly isolated and delusional Saddam for funding, then proceeded to spend the money for other projects. "The whole thing shifted from directed programs to a corrupted process," explained Kay. "The regime was no longer in control; it was like a death spiral. Saddam was self-directing projects that were not vetted by anyone else. The scientists were able to fake programs."[48]

Based on interviews with scientists, reviews of documents, and examinations of Iraqi facilities, Kay said, he had concluded that the Bush administration had been wrong that Saddam maintained significant arsenals of unconventional weapons. "I'm personally convinced that there were not large stockpiles of newly produced weapons of mass destruction," he said. "We don't find the people, the documents or the physical plants that you would expect to find if the production was going on." He conceded that there was probably "an irreducible level of ambiguity" because of severe looting and the loss of documents and other materials, but estimated that "around 85 percent of the significant things" left behind had been found.

The Baghdad regime had been more worried about UN weapons inspections than the Bush administration realized, Kay said. "The Iraqis say that they believe that UNSCOM was more effective, and they didn't want to get caught." Despite the Bush administration's interest in Iraqi reports of cargo being moved across the border into Syria, Kay said there was no evidence that proved they involved banned weapons or that Iraq had moved unconventional weapons to Syria.

He declared that the consensus within the U.S. intelligence community was now that the mobile bioweapons trailers were designed to make hydrogen for weather balloons or rocket fuel. Kay was critical of U.S. intelligence for its unquestioning certainty before the war that Iraq still had illicit weapons. "Alarm bells should have gone off when everyone believes the same thing," he said. "No one stood up and said, 'Let's examine the footings for these conclusions.' I think you ought to have a place for contrarian views in the system." He confirmed that he had resigned as head of the ISG because the administration's November decision to shift intelligence resources from the weapons hunt to military counterinsurgency efforts was contrary to written assurances he had received from CIA director George Tenet. Kay said that the weapons hunt had been hampered as a result.[49]

If Kay's message to the press was plainspoken and candid, he was far more restrained two days later when he appeared in his new unofficial capacity before the Senate Armed Services Committee on January 28. "We were almost all wrong, and I certainly include myself here," said Kay. But it was not the venue for him to air his conclusions about the weapons hunt. Instead, Kay fell back on his view that "the Ali Baba looting" back in April 2003 and the wholesale destruction of documents and material would leave an "unresolved ambiguity here" about "the negatives and some of the positive conclusions that we're going to come to." He also underscored that as ISG chief, he did not believe prewar intelligence mistakes were due to undue pressure, or "inappropriate command influence" on intelligence analysts to change their judgments to fit a political agenda. Kay praised Tenet and his successor, Charles Duelfer, a former weapons inspector and Washington think-tank scholar, for having the courage and independence "to understand why reality turned out to be different than expectations and estimates."

Despite the tribute, Kay had been an unmanageable thorn in Tenet's side. Reviewing Kay's upbeat testimony, the CIA chief was unforgiving. "I can only say that I regret the manner of Kay's departure," he wrote.

Tenet later complained that Kay had offered Congress and the president his personal opinion, but had failed "to make the case persuasively and in a definitive way that would put the issue to rest."[50] It was no wonder. The CIA chief seemed to forget that at virtually every turn, he and McLaughlin had pressed Kay to limit himself to politically palatable bromides and pull up short of any definitive explanation of why the ISG had found no WMD. Tenet, who suddenly became an advocate of embracing the whole truth about the missing Iraqi weapons once Kay had made his detailed statements to the press, declared that "to close this chapter of history in a responsible way, we needed hard data . . . organized and presented in a manner that would give future policy makers and historians confidence that we had gone about this thoroughly and professionally."[51] He later proclaimed that Duelfer, whom he had described as having a "reputation for being iron-willed" and "a strong independent streak," delivered the goods from the beginning.

Tenet recalled that upon arriving in Baghdad, Duelfer took up residence in the investigators' airport headquarters, eschewing the comparative safety of the Green Zone where Kay had stayed. Tenet, who made a trip to Iraq at about the time Duelfer set up shop, denied that he had ended a meeting with ISG investigators to introduce their new leader at the Baghdad airport by exclaiming, "Now, go out there and find WMD." He described how Duelfer had set up an elaborate time line between 1980 and 2003, tracing everything about Iraq's WMD on a wall at ISG headquarters, and insisted on personally mastering all the underlying information his investigators had collected and analyzed under Kay. The time line, claimed Tenet, gave Duelfer the ability to track the "relationship between funding and WMD activity"—a staple of Iraqi weapons inspections going back to Rolf Ekeus in the 1990s, Blix's prewar probes, and Kay's ISG operation.

Tenet's after-action efforts to bolster Duelfer's reputation—and downgrade Kay's—included a harrowing story about a carefully planned ISG search that Duelfer ordered in Baghdad for people and material suspected in chemical weapons production. The team, wearing full body armor, was accompanied by military escorts in armored vehicles with .50 caliber machine guns and a U.S. surveillance drone overhead. The Tenet-style paramilitary operation ended with an unexplained explosion at a chemical storage installation that killed two ISG military escorts and badly burned five more. There was no indication whether Duelfer was present. But Tenet's handpicked ISG chief was caught in an IED bombing on the notoriously dangerous road between Baghdad and the city's airport in early November. Duelfer's car was badly damaged in the blast when his convoy was hit. He was unhurt, but two soldiers were killed. Tenet noted that Duelfer later visited the families of the two slain U.S. servicemen. The point of the stories seemed to be that under Duelfer, "the ISG worked heroically to find the truth."[52]

After Kay, there were certainly important loose ends to tie up. Duelfer too, concluded in September 2004, in Tenet's words, "that Saddam did not possess stockpiles of biological, chemical, and nuclear weapons at the time of the U.S. invasion of Iraq."[53] Duelfer put the chance of finding "a significant stockpile" at "less than five percent." Whether the CIA in truth had overseen "a process that independently and unflinchingly drew un-flattering conclusions about our work," as the DCI claimed, was open to serious question.

Tenet had resigned from his post at the CIA on June 3, 2004, in a tear-ful ceremony at Langley headquarters, three months before Duelfer com-pleted his report. He had been out of government for a month by the time the Senate Intelligence Committee published its compromising report on prewar CIA activities in July. Eleven days after his resignation the devas-tating 9/11 commission study of the events leading up to the terrorist at-tacks was published.

Duelfer still had one critical question left to answer. If there were no WMD, what was Saddam thinking? What were his intentions? Kay had provided a solid foundation for understanding Saddam's inexplicable be-havior before and during the invasion, but Duelfer delivered his own analysis that squared with a major study by three U.S. Army officers pub-lished two years later. ISG investigators pieced together what went on during the final months of Saddam's regime through extensive interviews with former military government officials, military officers, and scientists. Duelfer himself spoke with Saddam during his imprisonment after he was captured by U.S. forces in December 2003. The picture of Saddam that emerged was of an isolated and increasingly remote figure with an idio-syncratic grasp of international affairs, moving from one presidential palace to another at regular intervals for fear of being assassinated by in-ternal political enemies.

His son Uday had been badly wounded during an assassination attempt in 1996, and the failure of his security services to avert the attack on his son was believed to have shaken Saddam. He was said to have become preoccupied with personal priorities, such as his family's security, novel writing, and Iraq's grand strategic position in the region. Gone was the in-tense micromanager who was known by his ministers for rigorously testing and screening their advice. Former officials told investigators that Saddam's subordinates were forced to become more attuned, out of fear and ambi-tion, to what Saddam wanted to hear than the reality at hand, whether it involved industrial programs or military calculations. The phenomenon went a long way toward explaining Iraq's pathetic lack of military preparation before the coalition invasion.[54]

This Iraqi "culture of lies," as Duelfer's ISG report described it, resulted in significant confusion about the status of Iraq's WMD, even among Saddam's top aides. In the late 1990s, Saddam began spending on selected conventional weapons programs. Revenues from the United Nations' Oil for Food program under international sanctions, abetted by administrative corruption, increased from $4.2 billion in 1997 to a peak of $17.87 billion in 2000, providing Saddam with increasing revenues for weapons expenditures and redeveloping Iraq's scientific capabilities. By 2000, the president was said to believe that sanctions were no long effective and would inevitably be suspended. Nonetheless, except for using some of the oil revenues to provide jobs for former scientists involved in WMD programs in the 1980s, Saddam appeared to hold back on new development of WMD, despite deep concerns among his military and civilian lieutenants about the possibility of a U.S. invasion after Bush named Iraq as a member of the "axis of evil" in his January 2002 State of the Union Address.

In the view of some of his own ministers, Saddam had missed an opportunity to placate the Bush administration after 9/11 by rejecting their advice to publicly condemn the terrorist attacks and offer condolences to the American people. Saddam refused on the grounds that the Iraqi people were suffering under the American-backed sanctions. His advisers, reported Duelfer, feared Iraq would suffer by being associated with al-Qaeda—an impression exacerbated by Iraq's media, which openly praised the terrorist attacks. Despite "extensive, yet fragmentary and circumstantial evidence" that Saddam wanted to maintain his capacity to produce WMD when sanctions were lifted, he had "no formal written strategy or plan for the revival of WMD," reported the ISG. Even this knowledge was based largely on the testimony of his political aides about Saddam's "infrequent, but firm verbal comments and directions."

The rest was based either on ISG assessments of old information about Saddam's actions before 1991, or on the evidence of "plans and designs" and "infrastructure improvements" investigators found—as distinguished from production of actual weapons, such as VX nerve gas, which ISG investigators did not find. Duelfer concluded that "Iraq unilaterally destroyed its undeclared chemical weapons stockpile in 1991," in spite of claims about the decades-old chemical munitions found scattered around Iraq. The ISG report even conceded that the undeclared chemical laboratories run by the Iraqi Intelligence Service were not intended for WMD, but to "test various chemicals and poisons, primarily for intelligence operations."

Saddam personally dominated the ebb and flow of information about Iraq's WMD as well as Baghdad's often skewed strategic decision-making. The ISG reported that Saddam's long rumored WMD were critical to maintaining Iraq's strategic position in the Middle East, especially given the potential threats from Israel and Iran, and speculated, based on circumstantial evidence and past behavior, that Saddam intended at some point (after sanctions were lifted) to restore the glory days of Iraqi WMD development that had existed before the Persian Gulf War. But not even his closest aides could fathom the dictator's thoughts at any given point. The former head of the Military Industrial Commission, Abd-al-Tawab al-Mullah Huwaysh, for example, told investigators that he was approached by Saddam in 1999 and asked how long it would take to develop a production line of agents for chemical weapons. He answered that it would probably take six months for simple mustard gas, and substantially longer for the more complicated sarin and VX. Saddam never followed up.

Again in 2001, Saddam stopped Huwaysh after a meeting and asked, "Do you have any programs going on that I don't know about?" This time he assumed Saddam was probing to find out whether his ministry had any chemical programs prohibited by the United Nations, and answered with a firm no. At the time, ministers reportedly had a clear understanding that they were not to initiate or operate weapons projects that might violate UN prohibitions without explicit permission from Saddam. Again, Saddam seemed satisfied with the answer, and again there was no follow-up.[55]

As the 2003 war drew closer, Saddam's mixed messages to his top advisers effectively kept them in the dark about the status of Iraq's WMD. After 1998, Iraq's WMD aspirations were not discussed openly by the Iraqi leadership, except perhaps as part of Iraq's overall scientific and engineering development. Saddam gave his top officials the impression that Iraq could resist a U.S. ground attack with WMD. But after President Bush's "axis of evil" speech in January 2002, Saddam made a puzzling statement to his lieutenants that strongly implied Iraq had no unconventional weapons. "What can they discover, when we have nothing?" Saddam declared. Huwaysh and other officials were confused at the sudden change.

After Bush's September 2002 speech at the United Nations, which all but declared war on Baghdad unless the Iraqis could show they no longer had WMD, senior Iraqi officials were alarmed at the seriousness of the developing international consensus. Although Saddam at first objected to Resolution 1441, which called for Baghdad to declare its WMD on pain of U.S.-led military action, he reportedly began to think that the risk of invasion—and the possibility that sanctions might be lifted if Iraq cooperated—warranted allowing the intrusive new inspections. In December 2002, for the first time, the Iraqi president began to tell groups of senior military officers and Baathist government officials explicitly that Iraq had no WMD. Iraqi military leaders reportedly were instructed to "cooperate completely" with the inspectors. Saddam informed Iraqi generals that they would have to fight the Americans without WMD—which had a devastating effect on military morale. Saddam, however, was careful to intimate that he still had something "in his hand." That led some senior officials, once more, to believe that Saddam had squirreled away a secret weapon, even if they themselves had no knowledge of it.

In March 2003, Saddam repeatedly told the final gathering of top ministers as the war began to resist the Americans for a week, "and after that I will take over." Many present took him to mean that he possessed some kind of hidden superweapon. But what Saddam may have had in mind, the ISG suggested, was triggering an insurgency—releasing the Fedayeen Saddam and other paramilitary security forces that he and his sons had built up to protect the regime against the Americans. Still, at the end, Saddam did not reveal his real intentions. Even his top advisers were confused and in disarray about whether or not he was about to unleash WMD against coalition forces.

The Duelfer report was not the only analysis of Saddam's erratic handling of the WMD question after American forces had occupied Baghdad. After the combat phase of operations was completed, the U.S. Joint Forces Command commissioned a study of the inner workings of Saddam's regime, based on interviews with officials and captured documents, which was partially declassified in early 2006.[56] The military study also concluded that Saddam tried to have it both ways on WMD, attempting "to convince one audience that they were gone while simultaneously convincing another that Iraq still had them." Saddam, the authors concluded, "found it impossible to abandon the illusion of having WMD, especially since it played so well in the Arab world."

Among Saddam's ministers, Ali Hassan al-Majid, nicknamed by the Western press "Chemical Ali" for having killed thousands of Kurds with chemical weapons in the Iraqi attack on the village of Halabja in 1988, seemed to grasp what Saddam was doing. He was personally convinced that Iraq no longer possessed WMD, but understood that many close to Saddam continued to believe they existed. Majid told military interviewers that he recalled a Revolutionary Command Council meeting in late 2002 when Saddam flatly rejected a suggestion that Iraq publicly declare it had no WMD, explaining that doing so would only encourage Israel to attack. If Chemical Ali's account was accurate—and it did have an inexorably pragmatic logic—why did so many senior Iraqi officials still believe Saddam might still possess hidden caches of WMD? In part, the authors concluded, they had been taken by a system that had once possessed WMD and in which secret, compartmentalized programs were highly plausible.

But more tellingly, the study suggested, faced with Saddam's deceptions about weapons of mass destruction, they did not so much base their belief on anything in particular he said, but rather "on the fact that so many Western governments believed such programs existed." When the plugged-in director of Iraq's Military Industrial Commission recalled Saddam's denial that Iraq had WMD after the Bush "axis of evil" speech, he told ISG interviewers that he began to wonder why "Bush believed that we had these weapons." Why would the United States challenge Iraq in such harsh and threatening terms, reasoned Huwaysh, unless it had irrefutable information?[57] If for no other reason, even members of Saddam's inner circle believed the misinformation about Iraq's WMD because the world's most powerful democracy, the United States, seemed so convinced of it.

23

A REPORTER NAMES HER SOURCE

When it was all over, Judith Miller smiled weakly, stood up and unclipped the delicate gold necklace with the ruby pendant she was wearing, and handed it to her husband, Jason Epstein. Bill Keller, the executive editor of *The New York Times,* who was sitting near Miller and her husband in the courtroom, later told a reporter that her wordless gesture seemed to say, " 'I'm not going to need this for a while.' " As he and others watched, Miller was escorted through a side door by two U.S. marshals to a holding cell near a rear exit of the Washington, D.C., courthouse.

The veteran fifty-seven-year-old *Times* correspondent had been found in contempt of court by Chief U.S. District Court Judge Thomas F. Hogan the previous October 2004. Her offense was in refusing to name her source in the high-profile grand jury probe of unnamed senior Bush administration officials, who were believed to have leaked the identity of a covert CIA operative, to the press, a possible felony. Now, following months of legal wrangling, Judge Hogan had made it clear during the sentencing hearing that he considered Miller's "a case in which the information she was given and her potential use of it was a crime . . . This is very different than a whistle-blower outing government misconduct." Hogan declared he was going to pack Miller off to "a suitable jail" in the Washington metropolitan area until either such time as she changed her mind about testifying, or for four months until the grand jury disbanded, whichever came first. "I have a person in front of me," insisted Hogan, "who is defying the law."

Miller's lawyer, Robert Bennett, promptly called the decision an "absolute tragedy."

Judge Hogan was having none of it. "I don't understand how this is a tragedy. It is her choice. She has the keys to release herself," the judge said. "She has a waiver she chooses not to recognize." Bill Keller, with a forthrightness he later may have come to regret, praised her willingness to go to jail as heroic. "The law presented Judy with the choice between betraying a trust to a confidential source or going to jail," he said outside the courthouse. "The choice she made is a brave and principled choice, and it reflects a valuing of individual conscience that has been part of this country's tradition since its founding."[1]

Judith Miller's deepening legal travails meant different things to different people. Those who, like Keller, wished her well were legion. A rash of editorials would appear in *The Times* and other newspapers trumpeting Miller's principled defense of a reporter's constitutional duty to protect the identity of sources who provided them with secret or hard-to-come-by information in exchange for promises of anonymity. A full-column *Times* editorial the next day, July 7, 2005, put Miller in the exalted company of the nation's founders. " 'Among those principles deemed sacred in America, among those sacred rights considered as forming the bulwark of their liberty, which the government contemplates with awful reverence and would approach only with the most cautious circumspection, there is no one of which the importance is more deeply impressed on the public mind than the liberty of the press,' " the editorial declared, quoting James Madison.

However principled and correct, that sentiment did not ring true for many Americans in the summer of 2005. Nor did it have much currency within the administration of President George W. Bush. *The Times* itself was a big part of the problem. The paper had suffered unprecedented public criticism two years earlier when it was revealed that a young reporter named Jayson Blair had fabricated multiple news stories in its pages. Worse, *Times* editors had been forced to admit that much of its reporting on weapons of mass destruction before the Iraq war was wrong—and much of it was written by Judy Miller. Even so, many of Miller's colleagues in the press and her wide circle of acquaintances in government treated her jailing as a cause célèbre. They applauded her as a stalwart defender of press freedom who had bravely chosen jail over capitulation to an overzealous federal prosecutor.

Yet, among experienced Washington reporters, fully aware of their own symbiotic relations with officialdom and its secrets, there were skeptics. Many were uneasy with Miller's and *The Times*' insistence, against the evidence of a succession of federal court decisions, that the law absolutely guaranteed journalists in Miller's circumstances immunity from prosecution for protecting their sources, especially in a criminal case. There was also growing discomfort with the inescapable fact, noted by Judge Hogan at the sentencing, that Miller was protecting government officials suspected of using dirty tricks and of perhaps even breaking an obscure espionage law to smear a political opponent and his wife. These observers saw Miller's ordeal as an unfortunate test case for any privileges the Constitution might have bestowed upon the press. "This is not the Pentagon Papers," Bob Woodward of *The Washington Post* told the *Columbia Journalism Review*. "It's not a case I'd choose to make law on." The skeptics tended to view Miller as a self-obsessed diva who had used anonymous administration sources before—to press the now-discredited case before the Iraq war that Saddam possessed weapons of mass destruction—and was now making a melodramatic bid to save her reputation and her job at *The Times*.

Then there were her detractors. Miller had written or cowritten five of the six stories about Iraq's weapons of mass destruction that *The Times* had repudiated in its famous May 2004 editor's note, the paper's mea culpa for publishing erroneous and misleading information about Saddam's prohibited weapons programs. Hard-core editorial writers, bloggers, and left-wingers could not forgive Miller for her WMD coverage. They believed, cynically, that Miller was grandstanding and that imprisonment was exactly what she deserved for serving as the Bush administration's chief propagandist on Iraq's alleged weapons of mass destruction. "Miller's no fool," wrote journalist Rosa Brooks. "She understood the lesson of the Martha Stewart case: When you find yourself covered with mud, there's nothing like a brief stint in a minimum-security prison to restore your old luster." (Stewart, the doyenne of American entertaining, had spent a year in jail after her conviction for obstruction of justice in a 2004 insider trading case. On her release, she basked in such public sympathy that she emerged with a tighter grip on her business empire—and a new television show.)

Yet for President George W. Bush and his top aides at the White House, the incarceration of Judith Miller meant something altogether different.

Gloat as they might about the crosscurrents of public criticism that buffeted *The New York Times* and the rest of the media, Miller's jailing was a cold signal that special counsel Patrick Fitzgerald was deadly serious about identifying the two "senior administration officials" who had surreptitiously passed CIA agent Valerie Plame Wilson's identity to syndicated columnist Robert Novak, even if it meant naming the president's men.

Once more in the on-again, off-again leak controversy, which began in earnest in late December 2003 when Fitzgerald was appointed special counsel by the Bush Justice Department, Washington was riveted by White House dissembling and official tap dancing about who had said (or not said) what to whom and when. Americans were also reminded of the underlying cause of all the fuss in the first place: the secret information campaign that appeared to have been orchestrated by the Bush White House and reached deep into U.S. intelligence agencies and gathered wildly exaggerated claims about Iraq's weapons of mass destruction. The high-level efforts to fashion a rationale for taking down Iraqi dictator Saddam Hussein—which the vice president's office had spearheaded—would turn out to be wrong in almost every detail. Worse, the White House had seen fit to hold no one in the administration accountable for the weapons debacle or even to admit there had been a problem—a lapse of judgment that only increased the appearance of its own culpability.

That Patrick Fitzgerald had unblinkingly carried out his threat to send Miller to jail was a powerful sign that this might soon change—and of coming political turmoil. Before the month was out, *The Wall Street Journal* published a long analysis declaring, for the first time, that the "CIA Leak Probe May Cause Bush Long-Term Worry." And in an editorial without a trace of irony—or acknowledgment of the newspaper's own role in the WMD mess—*The Times* became the first major newspaper to call for a congressional investigation of the intelligence fiasco that President Bush and top administration officials had used to sell the war to Congress and the American people.[2]

When Judith Miller arrived at the Alexandria Detention Center, a well-camouflaged, hard-to-find complex of brick buildings several miles south of the Capital Beltway across the Potomac from Washington, she was assigned inmate number 45570083 and handed a dark green jumpsuit with the word PRISONER emblazoned across the back. The short drive from the Washington courthouse to the jail was disorienting for the stylish and well-to-do Miller, who kept a vacation hideaway in Sag Harbor on the fashionable east end of Long Island. "They put shackles on my hands and my feet," she said. "They put you in the back of this car. I passed the Capitol and all the office buildings I used to cover. And I thought, 'My God, how did it come to this?' "[3]

Her first hours in prison were daunting. Her jail cell, which she at first had to share with another inmate, was an eighty-square-foot concrete slab cubicle with a thin foam mattress for a bed and two slits for windows, out of which Miller could see trees in the distance. It was equipped with a sink and a toilet. She later denied a report that she was not allowed a hair-brush (inmates had been known to fashion weapons from them) and brushed her hair with her toothbrush. Prison food took some getting used to—it was hardly the Manhattan gourmet fare Miller was accustomed to, and she would later complain of stomach problems. But she made do with institutional standards like ham and beans and pressed turkey. She worked as a floor monitor, charged with duties such as cleaning up trays after meals. By all accounts, she was treated like the other inmates and staff, and she treated them, said chief deputy sheriff Veronica Mitchell, in a "very unassuming" and modest manner.

The only hint of any difference in her standing from other inmates was that, from the beginning, she received far more mail than they did—and got many more visitors. As with Matt Cooper, Miller's attorneys had re-quested that their client be sent to a prison outside of the District of Co-lumbia. Although D.C. officials insisted they had not received any "instruction from the court to provide any special treatment" for Miller, her attorney Robert Bennett made it clear that the aging District of Co-lumbia facility, with a reputation as "an inhumane, nightmarish, over-crowded mess," in the words of one prisoners' rights advocate, was not an option. At the D.C. jail, Bennett pointedly warned Judge Hogan, "Ms. Miller's safety, I believe, would be in serious jeopardy."

Despite Hogan's tough posturing, the message apparently got through. The Alexandria jail, with its aquamarine and off-white dormitory-style appointments, was a well-established "New Generation" facility built in 1987, a time when enlightened jail officials emphasized contact between inmates and staff, effectively managed tensions between inmates, and kept noise levels down with the aid of cells constructed with solid con-crete walls and doors, instead of clanging bars. Alexandria had a reputa-tion as a reasonable place for women, and its staff was unfazed by the presence of many high-profile federal prisoners.

The detention center was the first stop in the United States for John Walker Lindh, the so-called American Taliban from California who was captured by U.S. paramilitary forces in Afghanistan and brought home to face treason charges. Aldrich Ames, the CIA spy who traded U.S. secrets with the Soviets, was also held in the jail, as were United Way chief William Aramony after his embezzling conviction and right-wing maverick Lyndon LaRouche. Some 440 inmates were incarcerated at the exurban Virginia detention center when Miller arrived, about 150 of them federal prisoners. Zacarias Moussaoui, the French-Algerian terrorist convicted in the 9/11 terror attacks, reportedly occupied a cell one floor above Miller's. The word was that Robert Hanssen, the convicted FBI spy, was hustled out of his cell to accommodate Moussaoui, who complained bitterly about the conditions.

By August, Miller, who spent most of her time reading one- or two-day-old newspapers and trying to answer her reams of mail, was described by jail officials as adjusting well. "Let's face it, jail is not fun. But she is not having any unusual difficulty adjusting to the environment," said Alexandria sheriff James H. Dunning. Miller's only real beef, said one visitor, Lucy Dalglish, the head of the Reporters Committee for Freedom of the Press, who visited Miller on several occasions, was that she did not have access to the Internet. She complained of developing cramps trying to answer all her mail by hand. She was also frustrated, said Dalglish, because she could not follow developments in her case or fight back against allegations she heard about from her steady flow of visitors.

Often enough, however, her A-list messengers brought good news. Paul Steiger, the managing editor of The Wall Street Journal, and Tom Brokaw, the recently retired anchor of NBC News, brought tidings of support for Miller from the Committee to Protect Journalists, which was protesting her imprisonment and calling for her immediate release. "The U.S. government is not only undermining the ability of a free press to function in this country," declared the statement from the CPJ board, "but also sending a signal to other governments that such a course is acceptable when dealing with journalists of whose actions they do not approve." The Paris-based group Reporters Without Borders sent a petition supporting Miller signed by such luminaries as Spanish filmmaker Pedro Almodóvar, German novelist Günter Grass, and French philosopher and writer Bernard-Henri Lévy.

Miller's visitors' list was astonishing for both its numbers and celebrities, who spoke with her via telephone handsets through a Plexiglas partition. Although visits were limited to thirty minutes, which usually meant seeing no more than three people a day, The Washington Post reported that during the month of August she saw nearly one hundred prominent colleagues and celebrities from the world of media and government.[4] One old friend who visited Miller just after she was jailed was unable to get back on the visitors' list after that. "She's very popular," said Ellen Chesler, the author of a biography of Margaret Sanger and director of a women's policy institute at Manhattan's Hunter College. "It's kind of hard to get on the schedule. She has to turn people away." Other visitors included former senator Robert Dole, John R. Bolton, Bush's controversial ambassador to the United Nations, and, on several occasions, *Times* publisher Arthur Sulzberger, Jr., and executive editor Bill Keller. Others who stopped by Alexandria included Mort Zuckerman, the billionaire publisher of *U.S. News & World Report,* book editor Alice Mayhew, who was rumored to be discussing a million-dollar book deal with Miller, Senator Arlen Specter of Pennsylvania, film director Irwin Winkler and his actress wife, Margo, and Richard Clarke, the former counterterrorism adviser to presidents Clinton and Bush. Even constitutionally low-key prison employees were impressed. "Well, she's not the *most* famous person we have here," said one. "But she does have some visitors." Declared a court official familiar with her visitors' schedule, "She's running an office down there."[5]

However heartening it was to see fresh faces from the outside every day, Miller was still left with plenty of that bane of prison life: time. Besides consulting with legal aides, who screened her visitors' list, she took a part-time job in the prison laundry, cleaning the ubiquitous green jumpsuits along with inmates' sheets and blankets, and worked on the card catalog at the the prison library.

Yet as she passed the four-week mark in jail, Miller's unease became more pronounced. Disturbing reports filtered back to her that her imprisonment was taking its toll in the *Times* newsroom on Manhattan's West Forty-third Street. There were just too many unanswered questions about her WMD reporting and her role in the leak affair for hyper-curious reporters. Speculation surfaced inside *The Times* that Miller was standing on principle to protect a source in order to distract people from her discredited Iraq WMD reporting. In early August, veteran Washington investigative reporter Murray Waas published a disturbing—and credibly detailed—report the source she was protecting was Lewis Libby, the vice president's chief of staff. Waas wrote that Miller had met with Libby on July 8, 2003, just after she had returned from Iraq.[6] Was it possible that Libby had leaked Plame's identity and her status as an undercover operative to Miller? Was Libby involved in some Bush administration campaign to smear Joe Wilson? If so, why hadn't Miller written about it?

As news of the July 8 meeting circulated, *Times* staff members began playing out other, more fevered and imaginative scenarios of Miller's involvement. She was known to be close to a number of senior officials, such as Libby, who made up a network of neoconservatives at the White House, the Pentagon, and the State Department. Some openly speculated that Special Counsel Fitzgerald might have the direction of the leak between Libby and Miller backward. Had Miller somehow found out that Valerie Plame Wilson was a covert CIA operative and then taken it upon herself to provide the information to Libby, not the other way around? It was unadulterated, baseless rumor, but it took on a certain cachet as it was quickly amplified in the blogosphere by Arianna Huffington,[7] among others, and passed into general circulation on the Washington–New York gossip circuit.

Behind the rumblings at *The Times* over Miller was the charge from some staffers that the newspaper's management had been less than forthright with them about what Miller knew, and what editors knew about her sources. Bill Keller dismissed such criticism. "I think the prevailing sense in the newsroom—regardless of what feelings individual reporters have about Judy and her past work—is that they are glad the paper is standing up for her and defending the principle of reporters' need to protect their sources."[8]

Such sentiments suggested to many that *Times* management was tying itself in knots over Miller and backing away from unpleasant realities at the newspaper. Yet even as the *Times* editorial page declared on August 15 that "Ms. Miller is not going to change her mind" and "appears unwavering in her mission to safeguard the freedom of the press," Miller was thinking about giving the go-ahead to her lawyer to approach Libby about securing a waiver that would release her from jail—and would allow her to testify before the grand jury about their conversations. Miller's new course, however, flew in the face of her outspoken opposition to the "coercive" waivers that President Bush and Patrick Fitzgerald had required administration officials to sign if they had entered into confidential agreements with reporters. Fitzgerald believed that such waivers would ensure reporters' cooperation with the investigation. With the strong backing of Keller, Miller denigrated these blanket waivers as illegitimate because they were obtained under the threat of losing jobs.

The issue had driven a wedge between Miller and Matt Cooper. He, unlike Miller, had accepted Libby's waiver early on and met with the grand jury. He only balked when Fitzgerald then subpoenaed him to reveal his confidential conversations with Karl Rove. Cooper's experience made Miller even more leery, since there was no guarantee Fitzgerald wouldn't declare open season on all her confidential sources. Miller showed a snappish edge when Cooper received a direct waiver from Rove the day they were both supposed to be sentenced. At the time—barely a month before—Miller pointedly told the court that she had not received similar permission from her sources. "Your Honor, in this case I cannot break my word just to stay out of jail," she said. "The right of civil disobedience based on personal conscience is fundamental to our system and honored throughout our history."[9]

Now she was stewing in jail and thinking about using the tactic herself. As early as mid-August, Miller began to think about getting "a personal, voluntary waiver" from Libby, according to a special *Times* report written several weeks after her release to explain her about-face. "The longer I was there," Miller told the *Times* reporting team, referring to jail, "the more chance I had to think about it." At least three other reporters subpoenaed by Fitzgerald, including Cooper of *Time* magazine and Glenn Kessler and Walter Pincus, both of *The Washington Post*, had received waivers with the personal assurances of their sources and proceeded to negotiate limited terms for their testimony, which Fitzgerald honored. Miller's attorney Robert Bennett wanted to make a pitch for a new waiver to Libby's lawyer, Joseph Tate. Miller was uncomfortable with the idea, objecting that if Libby wanted to release her to testify, he would have said so by now. "I interpreted the silence as, 'Don't testify,'" Miller said later.

Both sides had secretly gone around on this before. Floyd Abrams had begun talks with Tate about a waiver in the late summer of 2004, after Miller was first subpoenaed. According to the *Times* account, Tate took the position that Miller was free to testify, since Libby had signed a waiver. But he also revealed that Libby had told the grand jury that he did not tell Miller Wilson's wife's name, nor discuss her covert status. Miller immediately worried that this was an indirect message that Libby hoped her testimony would be consistent with his—in other words, Tate was either very close to suborning perjury, or, thought Miller, he was signaling that Libby really didn't want her to testify. Miller knew she had written several misspelled variants of Valerie Plame—"Valerie Flame" and "Victoria Plame"—in her notes from the conversation, which would contradict Libby.

Abrams had refused repeated entreaties by Libby's lawyer the year before to preview Miller's testimony, effectively declining to give him any assurances that Miller would exonerate Libby. The Miller camp was uneasy, and Libby never stepped forward to volunteer a personal waiver for her. Believing that that in itself was a negative signal, Miller decided to break off negotiations. "Judy believed Libby was afraid of her testimony," Keller said later. "She thought Libby had reason to be afraid of her testimony." At that point, Keller later confessed with apparent chagrin, he had not read Miller's notes or pressed her about the substance of her interviews with Libby.

Now, in periodic meetings with her lawyers in the prison library, Miller listened as the arguments flew back and forth. She felt Libby would have been in touch if he was interested in a genuine waiver. Bennett argued that she should try again. Abrams was concerned that if she received an acceptable waiver, then was released from jail and testified, both Miller and *The Times* would be seen as unprincipled. Richard Freeman, the *Times*' lawyer, urged caution, counseling Miller to wait out the October 28 deadline, when she would be automatically released. Bennett countered that that would only spur the special counsel to call a new grand jury and could mean as many as eighteen months more in jail. That pushed Miller, according to the *Times* report, over the edge. "At that point I realized if and when he did that, objectively things would change, and at that point I might really be locked in."[10]

Bennett placed a call to Tate on August 31. Tate heard him out, and responded promptly that Libby had released Miller to testify a year before. "Bob, my client was given a waiver," Tate declared, according to Bennett. Tate professed to be nonplussed and insisted the 2004 waiver was authentic. "We told her lawyers it was not coerced," he said. "We are surprised to learn we had anything to do with her incarceration." Abrams was pulled into the fray to vouch for Miller's earlier understanding and insisted that Tate had explicitly waved Miller off the idea the year before. Tate heatedly responded that he never said any such thing. Fitzgerald calmed matters with a letter to Tate on September 12 expressing his concern that Miller's jailing had been based on a misunderstanding. Three days later, Libby, the sometime novelist, wrote an oddly lyrical two-page letter to Miller noting, among other things, that the aspens out West were now "turning in clusters, because their roots connect them," and insisting that "testimony by all will benefit all." He also wrote that "every other reporter's testimony makes clear that they did not discuss Ms. Plame's name or identity with me." Miller and her lawyers had heard that before.

Miller wanted to get the message from Libby personally. In a ten-minute telephone call on September 19, with three lawyers listening in, Miller listened to what Libby had to say. According to the *Times* report:

Ms. Miller said she was persuaded. "I mean, it's like the tone of the voice," she said. "When he talked to me about how unhappy he was that I was in jail, that he hadn't fully understood that I might have been going to jail just to protect him. He had thought there were other people whom I had been protecting. And there was kind of like an expression of genuine concern and sorrow."

Ms. Miller said she then "cross-examined" Mr. Libby. "When I pushed him hard, I said: 'Do you really want me to testify? Are you sure you really want me to testify?' He said something like: 'Absolutely. Believe it. I mean it.' "[11]

After another week of deliberations, Miller and her lawyers met in the jail library and decided that Libby's waiver was the genuine article. On September 27, Bennett called Fitzgerald and asked him to meet a second, critical condition: that Miller's testimony must be limited to her conversations with Libby about Plame. Abrams had sounded out Fitzgerald about limiting testimony a year before. Fitzgerald flatly refused. That Fitzgerald had double-crossed Cooper on just such a promise didn't seem to enter the equation now. This time, Bennett assured the prosecutor that Miller's interview notes indicated that Libby was her only "meaningful source," as *The Times* phrased it. Miller reportedly talked to other sources about Plame and Wilson.

But Miller may have had larger strategic aims in mind. Some of her earlier and most controversial stories on Iraqi weapons of mass destruction—a special area of expertise for Vice President Cheney, Libby, and other top aides in the Office of the Vice President—were based on interviews with unnamed officials in the Bush administration who were still unidentified. *The Times* later confirmed that Miller's July interviews with Libby were nominally for a front-page story that appeared on July 20, 2003, about what had happened to Saddam's prohibited weapons of mass destruction, which American troops had been unable to find after the March 2003 invasion. Miller had only returned weeks before from Iraq, where she was embedded with a weapons-hunting outfit attached to the 108th Airborne. Her insistence on limited testimony would quietly blanket any administration sources who might have leaked classified information to her in 2002 about Iraqi WMD and effectively discourage wider investigation of the underlying causes of the CIA leak.

This time, Fitzgerald agreed to limit Miller's testimony. Two days later, he visited the Alexandria jail to confer with Miller in more detail about her upcoming testimony. At about four o'clock on Friday afternoon, September 29, after eighty-five days in jail—reportedly the longest term ever served by an American journalist defending a constitutional principle—Judith Miller walked out of the Alexandria Detention Center. "It's good to be free," Miller said in a written statement. "I went to jail to preserve the time-honored principle that a journalist must respect a promise not to reveal the identity of a confidential source. I am leaving jail today because my source has now voluntarily and personally released me from my promise of confidentiality . . ." Her first stop after gaining her freedom was the Ritz-Carlton across the river in Georgetown, where she reportedly was treated to a massage and a manicure, followed by "a martini and a steak dinner" with *Times* publisher Arthur Sulzberger.

Before the day was out, newspapers confirmed that Miller's source was Vice President Cheney's chief of staff and national security advisor, Lewis "Scooter" Libby. Leaks from within Libby's camp made it clear that Miller had met with Libby on at least two occasions when Plame was discussed, July 8 and July 12. She had asked him about why Wilson had been selected to go on the Niger trip for the CIA. *The Washington Post* reported that Libby told her the White House was asking the CIA the same thing, but that he had heard Wilson's wife had something to do with it. *The Post*'s source, most likely Libby's lawyer, Joseph Tate, said Libby did not know Valerie Wilson, who she was, or where she worked. In a Saturday telephone call four days later, Libby told her that he had learned that Wilson's wife had played a role in sending him on the trip and that she worked for the CIA. But, *The Post* reported, Libby did not know her name, or that she was a covert operative.[12]

Miller would testify before the grand jury the next day for four hours, and was recalled days later for more testimony when Fitzgerald discovered that there had been an earlier meeting with Libby on June 23. But the broad outlines of the case against the White House were now emerging, and with each new detail it became increasingly clear that the Bush administration had a serious problem that was linked directly to its deceptive handling of information that was central to its rationale for going to war in Iraq. President Bush's polls, which had been sliding ever since the president's reelection—and after the disastrous federal response to Hurricane Katrina on August 29, 2005—plummeted further.

From the beginning, the Bush administration had waged a sophisticated information war to achieve its diplomatic, military, and domestic political aims. With the gathering grand jury probe of the CIA leak scandal apparently about to yield its first indictment of high administration officials, the political dynamic of the information war suddenly and subtly shifted to new and unfamiliar terrain. After a yearlong battle in the courts, the imprisonment of a prominent journalist and the near imprisonment of another had not changed the combatants appreciably, but it had confirmed and sharpened the focus on the role of the witnesses. Besides other White House officials, whose interests would not parallel those of Libby or Rove much longer, Judith Miller and Matt Cooper, long inured to professional lives as observers of the Washington scene, had become active witness-participants in the indictments and possible trials of powerful presidential aides. Like common citizens, they would be called upon to testify against officials they formerly depended on for information, thus becoming permanently part of the tapestry of the political narrative, rather than those who stitched it together. Miller was the first victim of the Bush wars of deception and misinformation that animated the shooting war in Iraq and sought to silence Joseph Wilson. She would not be the last.

Miller's release in late September brought headlines and public attention flooding back to the White House leak case. But her testimony before the grand jury was the beginning of the end. Throughout the summer and fall of 2005, media coverage of the leak case was sustained and aggressive. Enterprising news reports digging into previously unknown meetings held by Rove, Libby, and other Bush officials began to appear through the summer with disturbing frequency for the White House.

Once more, the Bush administration seemed uncharacteristically paralyzed when it came to mounting defenses against the fast-breaking flow of new and often damning information. The president's game-faced chief political strategist, Karl Rove, kept his head down, despite the occasional video clip of him chatting with the president on the White House lawn, demonstrating that he was still in the loop. "The Rove thing has gotten to be enormously distracting," said one observer with ties to the White House. "Knowing the way the White House works, being under subpoena like this, your mind is not on your work, it's on that." This observer added, "My sense is Karl knows he has spent a lot of political capital with the president on this CIA leak case. No matter how close Karl is to the president, there is a limit of how much capital you can spend even with a close, close friend."[13]

Miller's testimony focused exclusively on her conversations with

Libby. In her initial grand jury session on September 30, the day after she was released from jail, she described her two meetings with Libby back in July 2003, as well as the telephone conversation between them. But Miller failed to bring up her meeting with Libby at the Old Executive Office Building on June 23, with either Fitzgerald or the grand jury. When Secret Service logs were shown to Miller indicating the time and place of the meeting, she said she still did not remember it.[14] Her memory was finally jogged when she found references to the meeting in notes she had misplaced. In a second round of testimony before the grand jury on October 12, she recalled that during the June meeting Libby talked for the first time about Joe Wilson's CIA-sponsored trip to Niger, and mentioned that his wife worked for the CIA.

The fact that Miller had to be called back to testify a second time only contributed to mounting suspicions within *The Times* that Miller was being less than forthright with her colleagues and raised new doubts about whose interests she was protecting, hers or the *Times'*. As days and weeks passed after she left jail, the major stories Keller publicly promised to publish in *The Times* about Miller's role in the leak case failed to materialize. Besides a first-person account by Miller herself, Keller had assigned a team of *Times* reporters to write a long quasi-investigative account of Miller's odyssey. The reporters' frustration with Miller was spreading through the newsroom. Keller fired off a memo to the *Times* staff urging patience, reiterating that the paper still intended "to write the most thorough story we can of her entanglement with the White House leak investigation . . ." Miller had already talked to the reporters, he explained, but "the story is incomplete until we know as much as we can about the substance of her evidence, and she is under legal advice not to discuss that until her testimony is completed."[15]

As the end of the grand jury's term approached on October 28, press coverage homed in on Rove and Libby as the prime candidates for indictments. It turned out that Rove, like Miller, had failed to mention a key conversation, in this case his July 2003 telephone chat with Matt Cooper, in several earlier interviews with FBI agents and appearances before the grand jury. Fitzgerald also called Rove back to testify. In an eleventh-hour revelation, Rove seemed to turn on Libby, as sources privy to his testimony declared that Rove had testified to the grand jury that he first heard that Valerie Wilson worked for the CIA during a conversation with Libby in the weeks before publication of the Novak column. Last-minute maneuvering between Fitzgerald and Rove's attorney appeared inconclusive.

At the least, that also confirmed that the two White House insiders had discussed Wilson before his wife's identity became public. At worst, it also made it sound like the White House heavyweights were beginning to eat their own.[16]

After a twenty-two-month investigation, Fitzgerald held a thirty-minute televised press conference on Friday, October 28, to announce that the grand jury had indicted Lewis Libby, Vice President Cheney's chief of staff, on one count of obstruction of justice, two counts of perjury, and two counts of making false statements. Rove was not mentioned, and there was no mention of the criminal charges that had spurred the leak probe. Fitzgerald had not been able to prove to his satisfaction that government officials with security clearances had knowingly betrayed a U.S. secret agent. But the indictment made it clear that Libby, who was privy to top-secret classified information, had reached out to the administration's national security network to help discredit former ambassador Joseph Wilson. Despite earlier White House assurances that he had not been involved in leaking information, the facts set forth in the twenty-two-page indictment told a starkly different story.

A month before Joseph Wilson's op-ed piece appeared, Libby had confirmed through the State Department and the CIA that Valerie Wilson worked at the CIA and that some believed she helped arranged her husband's trip to Niger. Soon afterward, the indictment charged, Libby heard from Vice President Cheney himself that Valerie Wilson worked at the CIA for the Division of Counterproliferation, part of the agency's clandestine arm, the Directorate of Operations. The indictment was silent on whether Libby knew Valerie Wilson's job was classified, but he had to know his information about her was extremely sensitive. When asked by an aide whether they could use the information about her, Libby waved him off, saying he could not discuss the issue on a "non-secure telephone line." Days later, on June 23, he leaked information about Valerie Wilson to Judith Miller in their meeting at the Old Executive Office Building.

Libby, the indictment showed, also spread around what he knew about Joe Wilson's wife to others at the White House, including press secretary Ari Fleischer and Karl Rove.[17] Fitzgerald noted that Libby had spoken about Valerie Wilson with at least seven different administration officials and several members of the press before July 12, the day Libby told the grand jury that he first spoke with Cooper and Miller, but professed to be largely ignorant about Wilson's wife except for what he had heard from reporters. If convicted, Libby faced up to thirty years in prison and $1.25 million in fines. On crutches because of a touch football injury, Libby seemed unfazed. "I am confident that at the end of this process I will be completely and totally exonerated," he said in a statement to the press.

Fitzgerald gave no quarter to those who would play down the significance of the perjury and obstruction charges against the vice president's chief of staff. He launched into an elaborate, homespun baseball metaphor that gave viewers a revealing glimpse into the mind of the special counsel and how he viewed his work and its limitations. "What we have when someone charges obstruction of justice, the umpire gets sand thrown in his eyes," Fitzgerald said. "He's trying to figure what happened and somebody blocked [his] view . . . The harm in an obstruction investigation is it prevents us from making the fine judgments we want to make." He continued: "This is a very serious matter and compromising national security information is a very serious matter. But the need to get to the bottom of what happened and whether national security was compromised by inadvertence, by recklessness, by maliciousness is extremely important. We need to know the truth. And anyone who would go into a grand jury and lie, obstruct and impede the investigation has committed a serious crime."

Fitzgerald's carefully phrased explanation of perjury and obstruction of justice had to resonate unpleasantly with Rove's lawyer, Robert Luskin. Without hesitation Luskin confirmed that his client was still under investigation, but strongly insisted on his innocence. "The Special Counsel has advised Mr. Rove that he has made no decision about whether or not to bring charges," Luskin said. "We are confident that when the Special Counsel finishes his work, he will conclude that Mr. Rove has done nothing wrong." Rove was in the clear for the moment, but Fitzgerald had planted signposts of his own. The indictment mentioned a senior White House official, referred to only as "Official A," who had talked to Robert Novak about Valerie Wilson before Novak's column was published. "Official A" was understood to be prosecutor-speak for Rove. A reporter asked Fitzgerald to explain why Official A had not been charged. "I'll explain this," Fitzgerald shot back. "I know that people want to know whatever it is that we know, and they're probably sitting at home with the TV thinking, 'I want to jump through the TV, grab him by his collar and tell him to tell us everything they figured out over the last two years.' We just can't do that." He added: "We can't talk about information not contained in the four corners of the indictment."

Another reporter tried the direct approach. "Is Karl Rove off the hook?" Fitzgerald refused to answer yes or no. "What I can say is the same answer I gave before: I'm not going to comment on anyone named, because we either charged someone or we don't talk about them." Fitzgerald made it clear he would continue to hew closely to the law as special counsel—and that another grand jury would make the decision whether to indict Rove.[18] Overnight, the special counsel became a celebrity of sorts, receiving favorable reviews in the press for his blunt candor and refreshing honesty.

As news of the indictment sank in, the president and the White House were hammered by both Republicans and Democrats on the Hill. Fed-up Republican congressional leaders, forced to weather the disorganized White House response to Hurricane Katrina and the embarrassing Supreme Court nomination and subsequent withdrawal of Harriet Miers, were downright curt. Thomas Davis III, a loyal Virginia Republican and chairman of the House Committee on Oversight and Government Reform, declared he was "very disappointed in Libby, and the White House and the vice president and the president." Davis told *The Washington Post,* "They should have taken care of this a long time ago. They're going to get very little sympathy on Capitol Hill, at least from me. . . . They brought this on themselves."[19] Oklahoma Republican Representative Mickey Edwards was more direct. "The president got a pretty good wake-up call," said Edwards. "He needs to stop thinking about his grand legacy and being the all-time hero of the Republicans and concentrate on doing the job he was elected to do. He really has to get a grip on his administration."[20] Citing the president's two-year-old vow to fire anyone involved in the leak case, Democratic House Minority Leader Harry Reid of Nevada called for Rove's dismissal. "The president said anyone involved would be gone," Reid said. "And we now know that Official A is Karl Rove. He's still around. He should be let go."[21] Bush quickly declared that "anyone in his administration who committed a crime would be fired," thus raising the bar for White House dismissals and putting Rove out of harm's way for the time being.

Christopher Shays, a GOP moderate from Connecticut, articulated the dismay felt by many disaffected supporters of the president at evidence of White House dishonesty and the loss of its ethical compass. "They wanted the president to restore honor and integrity to the White House," Shays said. "Whatever agenda the president wants to pursue, if he hasn't reestablished a strong ethical standard, he's going to fail . . . Americans don't like to be lied to."[22] A *Washington Post*–ABC News poll, taken just after the indictment was announced, found that 46 percent of Americans now thought that the level of ethics and honesty had declined during Bush's presidency. Fully 55 percent believed that the Libby case indicated wider problems with "ethical wrongdoing" in the Bush administration, while 41 percent believed the indictment was an isolated incident.[23]

Despite some Republican commentary to the contrary, 70 percent of Americans thought that the charges against Libby were serious. The president's job approval rating dropped to 39 percent, a record low for the *Post*–ABC surveys. However dramatic their short-term impact, such polls are always dependent on immediate political circumstances. Few believed that Rove and the White House political operation wouldn't quickly begin to devise strategies for improving those numbers, despite their habit of publicly dismissing negative poll results.

The fallout from Fitzgerald's leak investigation and the Libby indictment was not limited to the White House. On November 9, Judith Miller was forced to resign after twenty-eight years at *The New York Times*. Her resignation came after weeks of tension within *The Times*, triggered by her lack of forthrightness with her colleagues and *Times* management about her dealings with Libby, her abrupt and seemingly self-serving decision to testify before the grand jury after spending eighty-five days in jail, and, lastly, the persistent taint of her discredited reporting on weapons of mass destruction before the war. At best, Miller's determination not to reveal her sources, though praised and supported by the paper's hierarchy, "constrained" the *Times'* coverage of the leak probe, said Managing Editor Jill Abramson. *Times* reporters knew Libby was Miller's confidential source well before she got out of jail, but had not been allowed to print it even though other papers had done so. While *The Times* publicly championed Miller's privilege to protect her sources, said Abramson, it would have been "unconscionable then to out her source in the pages of the paper."[24]

Keller and Sulzberger were sharply criticized for misjudgments that in retrospect consistently seemed to put Miller's personal interests above those of *The Times*. Keller conceded that he knew Libby was Miller's source early on, but did not tell reporters who were working to identify him. Beyond that, Keller and Sulzberger knew little about Miller's conversations with Libby and had not bothered to review Miller's notes. Both men learned about the "Valerie Flame" notebook entry not long before Miller testified about it. "I didn't interrogate her about the details of the interview," admitted Keller. "I didn't ask to see her notes. And I really didn't feel the need to do that." Both publisher and editor said they felt that major decisions in the case should be left up to Miller. "This car had her hand on the wheel because she was the one at risk," Sulzberger famously explained.[25] In a special letter to the editor in *The Times* that Miller negotiated as her final farewell, she acknowledged that many of her colleagues disagreed with her decision to testify, but said doing otherwise would seem "a deliberate effort to obstruct the prosecutor's inquiry into serious crimes." In the end, she said, "I have chosen to resign because over the last few months, I have become the news, something a *New York Times* reporter never wants to be."[26]

24

THE RENEWED FUROR OVER WMD

Fitzgerald's conduct of the leak investigation had put tremendous pressures on news organizations, and *The Times* at times seemed close to buckling under the strain. But there was a larger and potentially more serious problem at the heart of the special counsel's grand jury investigation. The probe was about "serious crimes," as Judith Miller belatedly recognized in her farewell letter to the editor. Fitzgerald carefully explained in his press conference that, unlike Congress or past independent counsels, he was forbidden by law to report his findings in the case unless they were contained in a criminal indictment. While he possessed all the legal power of an independent prosecutor, thanks to James Comey's foresight, he had no political mandate or responsibility to report his findings about official wrongdoing that fell short of crimes. As Fitzgerald pointed out, this meant that the privacy of both the guilty and innocent—people whose misdeeds fell short of criminal behavior—would be protected. "My job is to investigate whether or not a crime was committed, can be proved and should be charged," Fitzgerald said. "I'm not going to comment on what to make beyond that. It's not my jurisdiction, not my job, not my judgment."[1]

Even former members of the Clinton administration, who endured independent counsel Kenneth Starr's 445-page exegesis of presidential sexual peccadilloes with Monica Lewinsky, believed that Fitzgerald brought needed discipline to the investigative process. "Mr. Fitzgerald has proven that we are all better off without an independent counsel law," said Lanny

J. Davis, a former Clinton counsel. "We should not use the criminal justice system to make findings of fact that are not in a courtroom. That is
why we have due process."[2]

Perhaps. But Davis overlooked a long tradition of congressional oversight of the executive branch of government that, for all its flaws, had
been instrumental in holding deceitful, corrupt, or unethical public officials accountable for their actions, whether laws were broken or not.
With the Bush White House openly clamoring for greater executive powers, and both houses of Congress controlled by Republicans actively discouraged from pushing too hard against White House policies—especially
in matters involving national security—the normal process of congressional monitoring that so often had served as a check on the executive
was short-circuited. In the case of the White House leak probe, in which
an independent investigation was properly initiated by the CIA and the
Justice Department, there was no political will for Congress to play an investigative role or to serve as a check or balance on any excessive, corrupt,
or illegal exercise of executive powers. Congress's original rationale for
the 1979 Independent Counsel Act was that an aggressive executive branch
could not be trusted to investigate itself in cases involving corruption or
lawbreaking. But after the excesses and expense of the Iran-Contra investigation during the Reagan presidency and the Whitewater investigation
under Clinton, Republicans and Democrats agreed in 1999 that the law
had become a license to conduct budget-busting political witch hunts—
and declined to renew it.

That may have been short-sighted. Fitzgerald made it clear that the
grand jury probe into the White House leaks, for all his disciplined
investigative work, would not provide Congress or the public with answers to legitimate questions about the conduct of the Bush White
House—unless perhaps there were more indictments. Basic questions
remained after Libby was indicted: Who was the second unnamed "senior administration official" besides Rove who leaked Valerie Wilson's
identity and covert status to Robert Novak? Did Karl Rove perjure himself or obstruct the course of the investigation since October 2003? Did
Libby or Rove violate the Intelligence Identities Protection Act? What
did Vice President Cheney know about the campaign to discredit the
Wilsons?

Even more fundamentally, the Libby indictment and the ongoing Fitzgerald investigation reignited larger questions about the WMD fiasco and the

Bush administration's rationale for going to war against Iraq. During the course of the leak probe, the CIA-sponsored Iraq Survey Group sent by President Bush to scour Iraq for weapons of mass destruction came home empty-handed. Within a year, a Gallup poll taken in April 2005 found that 50 percent of respondents believed that the Bush administration "deliberately misled the American public" about Iraq's WMD. This was despite successive official reports on the prewar intelligence failures commissioned by either the White House or the Republican-controlled Congress. In every instance, the reports blamed the intelligence agencies, most notably the CIA, for flawed intelligence reports and exonerated the White House of everything but well-meaning zealotry. The Robb-Silberman Commission "found no evidence of political pressure to influence the Intelligence Community's prewar assessments of Iraq's weapons programs," blaming instead a "paucity of intelligence and poor analytical tradecraft."[3]

A *Times* editorial in July 2005 went straight to the heart of the matter. Washington "has consistently shied away from the more delicate issue of how political leaders used those reports. The intelligence failures on Iraq will not be fully understood until Congress insists on a thorough investigation of what happened after those faulty reports left the analysts' offices and went to the policy makers." It was true, as the president's supporters argued, that the subject was mentioned in the 2004 report of the Senate Select Committee on Intelligence. But Fitzgerald's probe was instrumental in forcing the press and the public to recognize the web of connections between the White House leak of Valerie Wilson's undercover status and the near-complete collapse of U.S. intelligence before the war, particularly on the alleged Niger uranium deal. Despite the hopes of those on both sides of the partisan divide who wanted to see Fitzgerald take on the role of an independent counsel or work with Congress to conduct a wider probe into the White House role in the WMD fiasco, it wasn't going to happen.

The leak investigation left the press and the president's Democratic critics hungry for more details about White House manipulation of prewar WMD intelligence. The shifting explanations of how discredited intelligence about African uranium got into the president's State of the Union Address—and the extreme measures the White House officials used to defend it—only raised more questions about the Niger intelligence and how it was picked up by the White House. The president's critics also wanted to know why the administration had failed to marshal accurate intelligence about the enemy's arsenal of nuclear, biological, and chemical weapons.

New questions emerged about the second phase of the July 2004 Senate Intelligence Committee report, promised by the Republican-controlled leadership the previous February. The probe into the possible political manipulation of WMD intelligence by the administration failed to materialize after Bush's reelection.

Fitzgerald's investigation into the disclosure of a covert CIA officer's identity was the opening round in a renewed battle over the Bush White House's justification for going to war. That battle had preoccupied the White House on and off since the end of combat operations in Iraq in the spring of 2003 and had contributed to the steady erosion of President Bush's credibility and political stature. Once more, with the Libby indictment, attention was riveted on Vice President Dick Cheney and the central role his office played in gathering and analyzing intelligence about Iraq's weapons programs in the eighteen months between 9/11 and the invasion of Iraq.

In the days after Libby was forced to resign on October 28, 2005, emboldened Democratic leaders opened a second front in the prewar intelligence battle. Frustrated by the passivity of their Republican counterparts and stung by criticism that they had failed to adequately monitor the White House role in the intelligence debacle, Senate Democrats, led by Minority Leader Harry Reid of Nevada, invoked a little-used rule to close the Senate chamber to force a showdown on the second phase of the 2004 Senate Intelligence Committee report. After two hours in closed session, the Republicans agreed to review progress on the stalled investigation into how the White House used the faulty WMD intelligence. Behind all the maneuvering was the question that for three years had preoccupied the president's Democratic critics—especially those who cast their votes in favor of the war: Had the Bush White House exaggerated Saddam's weapons arsenal and links to al-Qaeda, then fended off potentially damaging probes into their own intelligence failures? Reid held up Libby's indictment as proof that "this administration engaged in actions that both harmed our national security and are morally repugnant."[4]

It was a rare, fleeting moment of satisfaction for the Democrats, and it infuriated the Republican leadership. Senate Intelligence Committee chairman Pat Roberts of Kansas, who had resisted the original Senate Intelligence Committee probe for months during the summer of 2003, denied he had held up phase two of the report, which he declared was nearly complete. The Senate action, he said, was meaningless. "We have agreed to do what we already agreed to do, and that is to complete as best we can phase two of the Intelligence Committee's review of prewar intelligence in reference to Iraq," said Roberts, who insisted that there was no political manipulation of intelligence. A year earlier, Roberts told CBS's *Face the Nation* that Senate Intelligence Committee staff had "interviewed over 250 analysts and we specifically asked them: 'Was there any political manipulation or pressure?' Answer: 'No.'"

The Democratic counterattack in the Senate only escalated tensions. Senator John D. Rockefeller of West Virginia, the Democratic vice chairman of the intelligence committee, noted that "an iron curtain comes down" every time the committee questioned White House handling of the intelligence. "I have to say in all honesty that I am troubled by what I see as a concerted effort by this administration to use its influence to limit, delay, to frustrate, to deny the intelligence committee's oversight work into the intelligence reporting and activities leading up to the invasion of Iraq," he said.[5] Chimed in New York senator Chuck Schumer: "We have seen over and over again that this administration does not want to hear information they don't like. Instead of . . . meeting the arguments, they simply choose to belittle the arguer." Rockefeller came close to openly accusing the White House of ordering Republican committee members not to cooperate with the probe. "Any time the intelligence committee pursued a line of inquiry that brought us close to the role of the White House in all of this in the use of intelligence prior to the war, our efforts have been thwarted time and time again," said Rockefeller. "The very independence of the United States Congress as a separate and coequal branch of the government has been called into question."[6]

"We see the lengths they've gone to," said Senator Richard J. Durbin of Illinois, speaking of the White House's handling of the leak case. "And now the question is, will this Senate meet its responsibility under the Constitution to hold this administration, as every administration should be held, accountable?"[7]

Vice Chairman Rockefeller's early suspicions about the administration's role in manipulating the WMD intelligence were aroused by revelations just before the war that documents used by the White House to claim that Iraq had sought to purchase uranium from Niger were forged. At the time, he wrote to FBI director Robert Mueller requesting that the FBI investigate the origins of the forgeries. "There is a possibility that the fabrication of these documents may be part of a larger deception campaign aimed at manipulating public opinion and foreign policy regarding Iraq," wrote Rockefeller. The FBI began a desultory two-year investigation that ended in the summer of 2005, although it was not made public until the eve of Libby's indictment. The FBI probe absolved the Italian

government of conservative prime minister Silvio Berlusconi of any responsibility for producing or circulating the forgeries. This was, of
course, the mysterious intelligence that first attracted the attention of Vice
President Cheney in late 2001; that triggered Joe Wilson's trip to Niger in
early 2002; that the president used in the 2003 State of the Union; and
that, for reasons that were still murky, was at the heart of the White
House leak case that Libby had lied about repeatedly.

As Senate Democrats began their push to complete phase two of the
intelligence study, the FBI abruptly reopened its investigation into the
Niger forgeries. New information had been published in the Italian magazine *La Reppublica* that suggested the forgeries may have been the work
of the Italian government in concert with Americans who favored war
against Iraq, or by members of the Iraqi National Congress, the exile
group led by Ahmed Chalabi. The FBI reversal also followed reports that
its agents had failed to interview a key player in distributing the Niger
documents, the former Italian military intelligence operative Rocco Martino, who the FBI believed had operated purely for his own personal
profit. A bureau source told the *Los Angeles Times* that the FBI didn't expect the new probe to come up with much new.[8]

Rockefeller and other Democratic members of the intelligence committee welcomed news of the restarted FBI probe. But they did not hesitate to up the ante on the White House when major newspapers reported
that the Bush administration had ignored intelligence warnings in 2002
that a captured al-Qaeda official, Ibn al-Shaykh al-Libi, was a suspected
fabricator. Al-Libi was the source of U.S. intelligence reports that al-
Qaeda members had received Iraqi training in chemical and biological
weapons. Rockefeller's reaction was swift and unambiguous. "Once
again, we have another important example of where the administration
was warned that information was questionable, yet they turned around
and presented it as fact to the American people," said Rockefeller. "This
most recent example underscores just how important it is that the Senate
Intelligence Committee get to the bottom of whether this administration
knowingly misrepresented intelligence in making their case for war."[9]

Rockefeller's use of the word "knowingly" was a red flag for Republicans. But the next day the West Virginia Democrat stepped up his attack,
explicitly rejecting intelligence committee chairman Roberts's stated preference that the second phase of the Senate report, like the first, would
compare public statements by administration officials with the best intelligence available at the time. Instead, Rockefeller pushed for formal
interviews with Bush administration officials if that proved necessary to

determine whether intelligence on Iraqi weapons had been distorted or misused. "Comparing public statements with what the intelligence community published does not alone tell the story," Rockefeller said. "If necessary, we may need to conduct interviews and request supporting documents. If the committee is denied testimony or documentation, we must be prepared to issue subpoenas."[10]

The White House counteroffensive was not long in coming. President Bush's normally reserved national security advisor, Stephen Hadley, who had taken the brunt of the blame for allowing the sixteen words about African uranium in the 2003 State of the Union message, was dispatched in November 2005 to debunk "the notion that somehow the administration manipulated prewar intelligence about Iraq." Hadley attacked those critics who not only believed Saddam had weapons of mass destruction and had voted to authorize the use of force, but also believed Saddam was a threat. "For those critics to ignore their own past statements exposes the hollowness of their current attacks," he declared.

The next day, speaking before a Veteran's Day gathering at the Toby-hanna Army Depot in Pennsylvania, President Bush issued the harshest condemnation of his critics to date. He questioned their patriotism and integrity for making "baseless attacks" that "send the wrong signal to our troops and to an enemy that is questioning America's will," and cited findings of the Senate Intelligence Committee report that there was no misuse of intelligence. "While it is perfectly legitimate to criticize my decision or the conduct of the war, it is deeply irresponsible to rewrite the history of how that war began," Bush continued, dusting off the old theme of "historical revisionism" he used to batter critics before the war. "Some Democrats and antiwar critics are now claiming we manipulated the intelligence and misled the American people about why we went to war. These critics are fully aware that a bipartisan Senate investigation found no evidence of political pressure to change the intelligence community's judgments related to Iraq's weapons programs."[11] He failed to mention, of course, that the Senate investigation hadn't been completed.

Vice President Cheney followed up the president's aggressive defense of his administration's handling of prewar intelligence on November 21 before the conservative American Enterprise Institute in Washington. "The flaws in the intelligence are plain enough in hindsight," Cheney admitted, "but any suggestion that the prewar information was distorted, hyped, fabricated by the leader of the nation is utterly false." Acknowledging that the war was a legitimate subject of debate, he said, "What is not legitimate, and what I will again say is dishonest and reprehensible, is the suggestion by some U.S. senators that the president or any member of his administration purposely misled the American people on prewar intelligence." Picking up on the president's themes, Cheney called this "revisionism of the most corrupt and shameless variety. It has no place anywhere in American politics, much less in the United States Senate." He then added, "One might also argue that untruthful charges against the Commander-in-Chief have an insidious effect on the war effort."[12]

With Bush's approval ratings at record lows, the White House campaign to silence critics of the prewar intelligence mess was blunted by the transparency of their in-your-face partisan rhetoric. Cheney's credibility with the public had especially suffered. He was closely associated with the WMD controversy. A *Newsweek* poll found that only 29 percent of Americans regarded Cheney as honest and ethical—and a stunning one in four Republicans agreed with the assessment.[13] Americans had seen it all before in the White House's treatment of Joe Wilson, and whatever they thought of Wilson, they didn't like it. Worse for the president, in November 2005 Representative John Murtha of Pennsylvania, a conservative Democrat and veteran of the Marine Corps with close ties to the Pentagon, suddenly turned against American involvement in Iraq and called for the troops to come home. For the moment at least, President Bush and his political advisers had lost the ability to move the poll numbers more than a point or two by attacking their Democratic critics—revealing an apparent political vulnerability that sparked hopeful talk of a Democratic resurgence in the 2006 midterm elections.

Thanks in part to the publicity that attended Murtha's defection on the war, the White House launched a new effort to sharpen the president's message on U.S. military engagement in Iraq. Over the next several weeks, President Bush gave a series of major addresses on the progress of the war. At the Naval Academy on November 30, he discussed how the U.S. forces had changed their approach to training Iraqi security forces, a linchpin of Bush war policy that would eventually dictate the size and timing of any U.S. withdrawal. At the Council on Foreign Relations in New York, the president analyzed the Iraqi insurgency, acknowledging for the first time publicly the role of the various factions, from disgruntled Saddamists to foreign terrorists sympathetic to al-Qaeda. At the Philadelphia World Affairs Council, he outlined the political steps Iraqis were taking toward a working democracy, noting that continued progress was increasingly the responsibility of Iraqis, not their American advisers.

In mid-December, President Bush delivered the final of these addresses at Washington's Woodrow Wilson International Center, outlining his plans for ultimate victory. He described Iraq as the "central front" in the war on terror and a "a crucial part of our strategy to defeat the terrorists, because only democracy can bring freedom and reconciliation to Iraq, and peace to this troubled part of the world." The president gave his clearest account to date of the reasons he took the nation to war, playing down the importance of the massive U.S. failure of weapons intelligence with carefully chosen words.

> We removed Saddam from power because he was a threat to our security. He had pursued and used weapons of mass destruction. He sponsored terrorists. He ordered his military to shoot at American and British pilots patrolling the no-fly zones. He invaded his neighbors. He fought a war against the United States and a broad coalition. He had declared that the United States of America was his enemy.[14]

There was, of course, nothing new in this laundry list. And it was no truer in December 2005 than it had been in December of 2002. As he had before, the president went on to admit that U.S. intelligence on Iraq's weapons of mass destruction was mistaken, but blamed "what went wrong"—as the Senate Intelligence Committee and his own presidential commission had before him—on U.S. intelligence agencies.

> When we made the decision to go into Iraq, many intelligence agencies around the world judged that Saddam possessed weapons of mass destruction. This judgment was shared by the intelligence agencies of governments who did not support my decision to remove Saddam. And it is true that much of the intelligence turned out to be wrong. As President, I'm responsible for the decision to go into Iraq—and I'm also responsible for fixing what went wrong by reforming our intelligence capabilities. And we're doing just that.[15]

This became an increasingly familiar White House refrain in Bush's troubled second term: The administration broadly conceded responsibility for past mistakes, but drew the line at revealing further details that would explain them or hold anyone accountable. Once more, the president failed to explain how Iraq had represented a deadly threat to American security without possessing weapons of mass destruction. Nor did he explain how shuffling the organizational charts of the U.S. intelligence community would prevent similar intelligence failure in the future—or acknowledge that literally dozens of key intelligence veterans had left the CIA, the Defense Intelligence Agency, and other agencies since the White House had instituted his reforms. But, most important, he failed to explain or take any responsibility for how his administration had made among the gravest and fundamental policy blunders in recent American history by leading the nation to war in Iraq under false pretenses.

By the time of the Wilson Center speech, the bitter debate about prewar intelligence was overtaken by two news stories that embroiled the Bush presidency in new controversies over secret and legally questionable intelligence operations—and quickly drew the national press even deeper into White House political calculations. In early November, Dana Priest, a top *Washington Post* national security reporter, published a lengthy investigation that revealed a network of secret U.S. "black prisons" abroad where enemy combatants and others detained in the war on terror were spirited off for interrogation and warehousing. Priest based her reporting on leaks from government sources. The CIA, which ran the secret rendition operation, was now headed by former Republican Florida congressman and CIA agent Porter Goss, a Bush ally. Agency lawyers reflexively filed a complaint with the Department of Justice seeking a criminal investigation into the identity of Priest's sources for illegally revealing classified information.

Without elaborating or providing supportive detail, Goss later told a Senate Intelligence Committee panel that the damage done by revelations of the secret CIA detention sites abroad "has been very severe to our capabilities to carry out our mission." The CIA director said he hoped "that we will witness a grand jury investigation with reporters present being asked to reveal who is leaking this information. I believe the safety of this nation and the people of this country deserves nothing less." Senator Rockefeller, the ranking Democrat present, wondered aloud "whether the very independence of the U.S. intelligence community has been co-opted . . . by the strong, controlling hand of the White House."[16]

There was more to come. In mid-December, James Risen and Eric

Lichtblau, Washington-based reporters for *The New York Times*, broke another story revealing that soon after 9/11 President Bush secretly authorized the National Security Agency, a sprawling eleven-thousand-employee operation responsible for sophisticated electronic and satellite surveillance overseas, to eavesdrop without special court-approved warrants on American citizens believed to be in telephone or e-mail communication with terrorists. In doing so, President Bush had assumed powers outlawed by the 1978 Foreign Intelligence Surveillance Act (FISA), which established an elaborate secret court to monitor requests by executive branch agencies to spy on American citizens without their knowledge. Ever since FISA became law—shortly after the Senate Church Committee revealed that President Nixon had ordered the FBI to spy on anti–Vietnam War dissidents—the FISA courts and a half-dozen specially appointed FISA judges had approved some fourteen thousand such domestic surveillance requests and turned down less than a dozen.

Not only had the Bush administration ordered warrantless domestic wiretapping without the approval of the FISA court, but the program had become the focus of bitter administration infighting. In early March 2004, Bush's own Justice Department ruled that the surveillance program was illegal. In an attempt to reverse the ruling, the White House dispatched chief of staff Andy Card and counsel Alberto Gonzales to persuade Attorney General John Ashcroft, who was then in the hospital suffering from acute gallstone pancreatitis, to overrule his deputy James Comey, who had signed off on the decision. Alerted by Ashcroft's chief of staff, Comey rushed to the hospital to find Card and Gonzales trying to persuade a groggy Ashcroft to sign papers certifying a forty-five-day reauthorization of the law. In a dramatic scene, Ashcroft refused, deferring to Comey. "He lifted his head off the pillow and in very strong terms expressed his view of the matter, rich in both substance and fact, which stunned me," Comey later said. The White House approved the executive order without a signature. Along with Ashcroft, Comey and FBI Director Robert Mueller, who was also summoned to Ashcroft's bedside, threatened to resign unless the White House agreed to put the law on legal footing. Faced with mass Justice Department resignations, Bush relented.[17]

Now, only weeks after the *Times* story first revealed the secret eavesdropping, NSA officials set in motion the machinery to request a Justice Department probe to find out who leaked information on the classified surveillance program to the newspaper. News organizations had already absorbed a body blow to their self-confidence during the White House leak investigation, when Judith Miller, Matt Cooper, and others had been forced to testify about their sources. News executives and reporters were hardly sanguine now that the tables were turned again. Now the Bush administration, with its long antipathy toward the media, was positioned once more to use the full investigative powers of the federal government to haul reporters into court and compel them to reveal their confidential sources. Both Priest and Risen made it clear they had no interest in cooperating with any such investigation.

In early 2006, Lewis Libby's defense team further cranked up the pressure on the Washington press corps by filing papers enjoining Fitzgerald to produce the notes and depositions of journalists questioned during the White House leak case. If successful, that meant Libby's lawyers could reveal the names of confidential sources whom news organizations and reporters had expended considerable legal and financial resources to keep out of the public eye—and seemed to assure another round of expensive, possibly career-breaking first amendment battles over whether courts could compel journalists to provide details about their sources.

"Sounds to me like deja vu all over again," Charles Tobin, a veteran media lawyer, told *The Washington Post*. "We just finished with one fishing expedition, and we're about to launch into another one. When is this going to stop? At some point, the court needs to let the reporters get back to their work, and the lawyers need to focus on the facts in their case."[18]

The Justice Department publicly announced its investigation into who leaked the domestic eavesdropping story in late December 2005, two weeks after the story was first published—by contrast, the White House leaks probe began three months after the Novak column and Fitzgerald wasn't appointed special counsel for five months. The new case was framed by some as a constitutional clash between the government's right to seek sanctions against officials who leaked classified information and the right of the news media to protect confidential sources and report on national security issues. But while every administration discourages leakers, few have relied on running roughshod over press freedoms to find or punish them. Investigators began by gathering information to find out which government officials had been in contact with reporters and who had been authorized to know about the eavesdropping program. That did not stop the conservative *Commentary* magazine from reporting, "What *The New York Times* has done is nothing less than to compromise the centerpiece of our defensive efforts in the war on terrorism."

At issue are provisions of the 1917 Espionage Act that forbid the disclosure, dissemination, or publication of classified national security information. *The Times*, for its part, whose editors met at the White House with

Bush officials before the warrantless eavesdropping story was published, did not believe it compromised the country's counterterrorism efforts. "We were not convinced then, and have not been convinced since, that our reporting compromised national security," said *Times* executive editor Bill Keller. "What our reporting has done is set off an intense national debate about the proper balance between security and liberty—a debate that many government officials of both parties, and in all three branches of government, seem to regard as in the national interest."[19] Keller's point was a key one, since a reporter's common-law privilege to protect confidential sources depends to a large degree on demonstrating that the information published was strongly in the public interest, in this case attested to by the widely covered Senate Judiciary Committee hearings in early February on the domestic spying controversy chaired by Pennsylvania Republican senator Arlen Specter.

How strongly government prosecutors pursued the domestic eavesdropping case would depend on whether they could show that the disclosure damaged national security. "If the program is as sensitive and critical as it has been described, and leaking its existence could put the lives of innocent American people in jeopardy, that surely would have an effect," said George J. Terwilliger III, a former deputy attorney general in the administration of President Bush's father.[20] There was another legal twist that put news organizations on notice. In a recent national security case concerning U.S. defense secrets passed to Israel, a Virginia court indicted not only the source of classified information, but also those who passed along the information. Federal District Court Judge T. S. Ellis III declared that private citizens and government employees must obey laws against illegally disseminating classified information. "Persons who have unauthorized possession, who come into unauthorized possession of classified information, must abide by the law," said Judge Ellis. "That applies to academics, lawyers, journalists, professors, whatever."[21]

Arguably there hasn't been such a potentially far-reaching assault on the press since the Nixon administration tried to quash publication of the *Pentagon Papers* in 1971. For all its troubles, the Bush administration had operated with a compliant, Republican-dominated Congress that for the most part rubber-stamped its most controversial decisions—and dutifully accepted official explanations that a majority of Americans refused to believe. That led Walter Isaacson of the Aspen Institute, a former managing editor of *Time* magazine and editorial director of CNN, to observe that "in an administration that has little appreciation for Congressional authority" and "controls all branches of government," healthy and aggressive news media "have become a de facto fourth branch that provide some small check on executive power." If Isaacson was right, a disproportionate and uncomfortable burden was now placed on the press. It suggested not only why disgruntled and concerned government officials sought out reporters, but also how additional constraints on the ability of news organizations to challenge White House policies threatened to leave a functional vacuum in the place of even small checks and balances on the president. So far the rewards of the White House leak case had proved limited and costly. "An outgrowth of the Fitzgerald investigation is that the gloves are off in leak cases," said former deputy attorney general Terwilliger. "New rules apply."[22]

The news media was now deeply and uncomfortably involved in the judicial process that eventually would decide whether the Bush White House had exceeded its lawful powers in all three major national security cases. The foremost, of course, was the trial of Lewis Libby for perjury and obstruction of justice. There were also critical outstanding questions about Karl Rove's role in the White House leak case. Prosecutors suspected that Rove lied to the grand jury about his July 11 conversation about Wilson's wife with *Time*'s Matt Cooper. They also believed that Rove might have obstructed justice by contriving a cover story with Robert Novak during their September 29, 2003, telephone call to hide the truth about whether he had provided information about Valerie Wilson to the columnist. Just as in the Libby case, the role of reporters was critical in resolving both questions. Soon after Libby's indictment, Fitzgerald convened a new grand jury, whose only business was apparently to examine Rove's actions. Unlike Libby, however, Rove was able to slip through the web of half-truths he spun during five appearances before the grand jury and avoided an indictment.

On Monday afternoon of June 12, 2006, at about four o'clock, Rove was aboard a Southwest Airline flight on his way to make a campaign speech in New Hampshire when he received a call from his lawyer, Robert Luskin. Luskin had waged a fierce behind-the-scenes battle with Fitzgerald for much of the past eight months to vindicate his client in the leak case, and he had just received formal notification that the special counsel did "not anticipate seeking charges" against Rove. For many who knew Rove's impressive history of squirming out of tight, self-inflicted legal jams, Fitzgerald's decision was not a surprise.

The investigation of Rove had been a major distraction for the White

House. Besides having to prepare his testimony on five separate occasions, Rove met regularly with Luskin's legal team to plot his complicated
defense and was constantly called away from his political duties as the
president's deputy chief of staff. He was criticized for his inattention to
pressing political matters, from Social Security reform to the disastrous
Supreme Court nomination of White House Counsel Harriet Miers. Rove,
who once assured Press Secretary Scott McClellan that he had nothing to
do with outing Valerie Wilson, also lost credibility within the White
House, especially with the press operation. The threat of indictment was
ever-present. "You cannot have that kind of thing swirling around you
without an enormous amount of anxiety," said Republican lobbyist Vin
Weber, a former Minnesota congressman and Rove ally. "I can tell you
this: It demoralized the whole White House, not because they thought the
guy in their midst was crooked but . . . because he is very well liked in the
White House."[23]

Many Republicans blamed a preoccupied Rove for the high-profile
Miers nomination fiasco, a defining moment in Bush's plummeting popularity among conservatives. "That really damaged Bush," said William
Kristol, editor of the conservative *Weekly Standard* magazine. "It was not
an accident that it happened . . . when Rove was at his weakest."[24] Despite
the damage, administration insiders from the president on down were
hugely relieved at the news that Rove received a clean bill of health just in
time for the 2006 elections. A criminal charge against Rove would have
been a devastating blow to the White House, severing the campaign genius
and political partner who had engineered Bush's rise to the presidency.
Bush himself heard the news aboard Air Force One returning from a trip
to Baghdad. "It's a chapter that has ended," said the president. "Fitzgerald is a very thorough person. I think he's conducted his investigation in a
dignified way. And he's ended his investigation."[25]

Because there was no indictment against Rove, it was impossible to
know exactly what Fitzgerald had been after. But Rove was the only Bush
official still in the special counsel's sights, after the Libby indictment, and
accounts of witnesses and legal counsel familiar with the prosecution's
line of questioning provided a reasonably clear picture. When the grand
jury indicted Libby, Fitzgerald had known for some time that Rove had
been a source for both Cooper and Novak on stories about Valerie Wilson. But Rove had neglected to tell both FBI investigators and the grand
jury that he had ever talked to Cooper. Then he abruptly changed his
story. Rove testified in October 2004 that he had simply forgotten about
his talk with Cooper in the summer of 2003, claiming that his memory

had been jogged by a forgotten e-mail his lawyers turned up. Now Fitzgerald wanted to know whether Rove had purposely hidden the fact during earlier testimony in February 2004 that he had spoken to Cooper the previous July.

Was Rove telling the truth, or had he tried to cover up his leak to Cooper? Fitzgerald appeared skeptical. At issue, in part, was the timing of Luskin's discovery of the e-mail. Luskin had searched for and found the electronic message only after *Time* Washington correspondent Viveca Novak (no relation to Robert Novak) told him in early 2004 over drinks at Washington's Deluxe Café that she had heard Rove was the source for Cooper's July 2003 *Time* item. Novak testified that her meeting with Luskin took place in March or May 2004, or perhaps as early as January. She recalled that Luskin seemed surprised and visibly unsettled at her remark about Rove's conversation with Cooper. "There's nothing in the phone logs," he commented. As Luskin walked Viveca Novak back to her car, she recalled him saying, "Thank you. This is important."

Months later, Luskin told her that her remark about Rove had led him "to do an intensive search for evidence that Rove and Matt had talked," and that he found the e-mail from Rove to Stephen Hadley at the NSC confirming the conversation had taken place.[26] Rove reportedly told Hadley in the e-mail that he had waved Cooper off Wilson's claim the administration had misused intelligence on Iraq.[27] Luskin told Viveca Novak that he sent a copy of the e-mail to Fitzgerald "when he found it" in October 2004, just prior to Rove's third session before the grand jury.[28] In his discussions with Fitzgerald, Luskin, who realized he had overlooked a critical piece of evidence, insisted that his meeting with Viveca Novak took place in October 2003.[29] Novak was interviewed at length twice by Fitzgerald in late 2005 and testified that her meeting with Luskin had not taken place in October 2003, but between January and March or May 2004, undercutting Luskin's case.

Rove's story never quite added up anyway. Even if Novak's meeting with Luskin was as late as May, why did it take Luskin's team until October to find the Hadley e-mail and contact Fitzgerald about Rove's possible false testimony? All the legal maneuvering in the fall of 2004 also recast Rove's last-minute offer to waive Cooper's pledge of confidentiality just before Cooper was about to be sentenced a year later as a self-interested ploy by Rove to reposition himself legally. After Rove had neglected to mention his July 2003 conversation with Cooper to investigators for more than a year, in July 2005 he was ready to broadcast it for all to hear through his magnanimous gesture to save the *Time* correspondent from jail—which also served to establish very publicly that the telephone call had taken place. Luskin's campaign to prove Rove's innocence hinged on Rove's stepping forward in light of new evidence and openly admitting his memory had failed him. In that context, the discovery of the Hadley e-mail—evidence that he had in fact talked to Cooper—also proved to Fitzgerald that Rove had concrete justification for changing his story and setting the record straight. Without the e-mail, Rove's truthfulness would have remained in doubt. Whether prosecutors actually believed Rove or not, he had come forward to set the record straight, thereby making it difficult for Fitzgerald to prove beyond a reasonable doubt that Rove had purposely lied, and had not simply forgotten about talking to Cooper. In the end, the grand jury had little choice but to give Rove, a critical senior official in the Bush administration, the benefit of the doubt. It was a classic Rove escape act, creating appearances out of thin air and uncertainty.

There was also some evidence that Fitzgerald was looking at more than just the possibility that Rove lied about his conversation with Cooper. Rove's September 29 conversation with Robert Novak occurred three days after the Bush Justice Department announced its investigation of the Valerie Plame leak case. Early in the probe, Rove, who was suspected of involvement, and Novak, whose column had first named Plame, were questioned by FBI officials, who quickly homed in on their suspicious conversation and the possibility they had obstructed justice by coordinating their stories. The agents were concerned enough to take the issue to then attorney general John Ashcroft, who himself had a political relationship with Rove going back years. The FBI briefing led to Ashcroft's recusal from the leak case.

It didn't help that Robert Novak appeared to have changed his story about the circumstances of his July 9 phone call with Rove. Novak told *Newsday* on July 22 that administration officials initiated the Valerie Plame leak. "I didn't dig it out, it was given to me," Novak was quoted as saying. "They thought it was significant. They gave me the name, and I used it." But on September 29, the very same day Novak assured Rove that he would not "get burned" in the leak investigation, Novak changed his story. "Nobody in the Bush administration called me to leak this," declared Novak on CNN's now defunct *Crossfire* show. Novak later claimed he was "badly misquoted" by *Newsday*. Tim Phelps, then the newspaper's Washington bureau chief, confirmed the accuracy of Novak's quote.[30]

Aside from the well-established pattern of leaks to members of the press by Libby and Rove—Novak had first privately confirmed Rove was a source for the July 14 column during a meeting with Fitzgerald on January 14, 2004, at his attorney's office in Washington—investigators were also struck by the similarity in the respective testimony Rove and Novak later gave to the grand jury about their July 9 conversation. Both testified that Novak, not Rove, had raised the subject of Wilson's wife, her CIA job, and her husband's trip to Niger. Rove testified that he simply told Novak he had heard the same things, which he said could have been unsubstantiated rumor as far as he knew. Investigators were suspicious, doubting that Novak would have been content to treat such an offhand remark as confirmation that Wilson's wife worked for the CIA.

But, once again, on the central question of whether Rove and Novak agreed to a cover story on September 29, no one could prove beyond a reasonable doubt that the two had engaged in a cover-up or obstructed justice—except for Rove and Novak themselves. "As long as neither [Novak nor Rove] breaks, and there is no reason for them to, no matter how much evidence there is," said an anonymous friend of both. "These are two people who go way back, and they are going to look out for each other."[31]

On July 12, 2006, a month after Fitzgerald finally informed Rove he would not bring criminal charges, Novak broke three years of silence about his actions during the grand jury probe by revealing that on October 7, 2003, he had met with FBI investigators about the Valerie Plame Wilson leak, without revealing his sources. On January 14 he met with Fitzgerald, who held waivers from Richard Armitage, Rove, and CIA spokesman Bill Harlow. Novak answered Fitzgerald's questions, using the names of all three. He had a second meeting with Fitzgerald on February 5, 2004, then received a subpoena to appear before the grand jury on February 25. Novak claimed that he "revealed Rove's name because his attorney has divulged the substance of our conversation." He insisted that every time he disclosed confidential sources, "the special prosecutor knew their identities and did not learn them from me."[32] Novak did not say whether he talked to Fitzgerald about his relationship with Rove after the Libby indictment.

As the trial of Lewis Libby opened in U.S. District Court at Washington's Prettyman Courthouse on January 16, 2007, the defendant received an outpouring of support from political allies and friends in the Bush administration. "This is incomprehensible to me," declared Dennis Ross, the former State Department Middle East envoy and a friend of Libby. "He's a lawyer who's as professional and competent as anyone I know. He's a friend, and when he says he's innocent, I believe him. I just can't account for this case." Mary Matalin, the political consultant and former communications adviser to Cheney, aired a view of the Libby prosecution articulated by *The Wall Street Journal* and widely shared by conservatives. "He's going to be the poster boy for the criminalization of politics, and he's not even political," said Matalin.[33] But Libby's most noteworthy pretrial admirer—and one expected to play a historic role in the trial—was his boss, Vice President Cheney.

The taciturn Cheney, not known for public garrulousness or displays of emotion, seemed to make an exception as he praised his top aide and expressed his personal support before the trial. Libby was "one of the finest individuals I've ever known," said Cheney. "I believe he's one of the more honest men I know. He's a good man. And I obviously appreciate very much his service on my staff over the years and have very high regard for him and his family." Cheney admitted that he had strong views on the Fitzgerald investigation, and he went out of his way to confirm pretrial suggestions from the Libby camp that he would testify at the trial. "I am likely to be a witness in this trial," he said. "It would be inappropriate for me, at this point, shortly before the trial begins, to enter into a public dialogue . . . about my views on this issue."[34] Nonetheless, the vice president made clear, "I have indicated from the very beginning my wholehearted cooperation with the investigation and with whatever legal proceedings emerge out of that. And this will all unfold here in the very near future."

Cheney's appearance on the witness stand seemed to be part of an aggressive defense strategy by Libby's lawyer, Theodore V. Wells. In his opening statement, Wells made the case that Libby was scapegoated by the White House during the grand jury investigation. The defense contended that Libby had been sacrificed in order to save Karl Rove, who was also under scrutiny for his role in trying to discredit former ambassador Wilson and protect Cheney from charges that the White House had exaggerated prewar intelligence. Wells's legal team had sought pretrial motions before Judge Reggie B. Walton seeking classified information for Libby's defense, a prospect that could not have pleased the White House. Now Wells appeared to ratchet up the pressure by charging that unnamed White House officials had tried to set up Libby to take the fall. He revealed that Libby had realized something was amiss in October 2003 when press spokesman Scott McClellan, who had disparaged reports that Karl Rove was involved in the leak case as "ridiculous," said nothing to defend Libby.

Libby, Wells told the jurors, had complained directly to Cheney. "They're trying to set me up. They want me to be the sacrificial lamb," Wells said Libby told Cheney. "I will not be sacrificed so Karl Rove can be protected." Wells entered a note the vice president had later penned as evidence. "Not going to protect one staffer + sacrifice the guy who was asked to stick his neck in the meat grinder because of the incompetence of others." However, Rove was Bush's longtime political adviser and "the man most responsible for making sure the Republican Party stayed in office," Wells told jurors. "He had to be protected. Libby was an important staffer. But Karl Rove was the lifeblood of the Republican Party."[35] Wells even presented talking points that Libby drafted for McClellan to use with the press to redress the offense. "People have made too much of the difference in how I described Karl and Libby," McClellan was directed to say. "I've talked to Libby. I said it was ridiculous about Karl, and it is ridiculous about Libby."[36]

The fact was that Libby had been singled out by the vice president, with President Bush's knowledge, to talk to reporters about the intelligence Bush had cited on African uranium. But reporters found very little evidence of a White House conspiracy against Libby to save Rove for the critical 2004 midterm elections, although it was a clever gambit on Wells's part—and gave greater credence to the promise that Vice President Cheney would testify on Libby's behalf. Perhaps as an unintended consequence, it also stirred up renewed interest among the press in Cheney's involvement in the underlying intelligence controversy, and in his increasingly evident participation and interest in discrediting Joe Wilson and his wife. Wells drummed home his theme that Libby had often simply forgotten details of meetings and conversation during those hectic days of controversy in July 2003. But he never made it quite clear how the scapegoat strategy would exonerate Libby on the five felony charges against him, which included lying to the grand jury, making false statements to investigators, and obstructing the investigation.

Wells's opening statement succeeded in creating a buzz during the first few days of the trial. Fitzgerald's opening for the prosecution, by contrast, stuck narrowly to the evidence in the indictment. "How could we reach a point where the chief of staff for the vice president was repeatedly lying to federal investigators?" Fitzgerald asked the jury. "That's what this case is all about." The special counsel spent an hour walking the jurors through the events of early July after Wilson's op-ed was published and the ensuing "firestorm" in the White House over the charge that the Bush administration may have "twisted" intelligence about Iraq's weapons.

Fitzgerald focused on Libby's contention that he first heard that Valerie Plame was married to Wilson from Tim Russert at NBC, but several days earlier told Ari Fleischer about Plame over lunch and the next day talked to a reporter, Judith Miller, and also mentioned her. Libby's claim that he had forgotten what he knew, declared Fitzgerald, was simply not plausible. "You can't learn something startling on Thursday that you're giving out Monday and Tuesday of the same week," Fitzgerald said.[37]

The Libby trial promised to lay bare the secret workings of the White House, particularly the vice president's office, in formulating strategies to tailor intelligence to the Bush administration's aims before going to war in Iraq. It would also put on display how the White House dealt with war critics and increasingly hostile Washington reporters, whose livelihood depended on maintaining and exploiting their relationships with senior government officials. The prospect of a sitting vice president testifying at a criminal trial was unprecedented, especially since the defendant was privy to White House decisions about a war whose origins were in question. Not incidentally, the trial also would be a proving ground for the special counsel, appointed by the Justice Department and given subpoena powers to conduct criminal probes of senior government officials, the first such instance since the independent special prosecutor statute was allowed to lapse in 1999.

Conservatives already had protested that Fitzgerald's protracted investigation and Libby's trial would accomplish little except to criminalize politics. The argument became the basis for a widespread conviction among Republicans since Libby's indictment that President Bush should pardon Libby in the event he was convicted—if not before Libby served any time in prison, then certainly before the president left office. After all, Gerald Ford had pardoned Richard Nixon for far more serious offenses after the Watergate crisis in 1974. The president's father granted Christmas Eve pardons just before he left office in 1993 to six officials indicted in the Reagan-era Iran-Contra scandal. Bill Clinton pardoned political friends convicted of crimes, most notoriously the fugitive financier Marc Rich, the husband of a prominent Clinton campaign contributor. Rich had been convicted in absentia in 1983 of tax evasion and illegal trading during Iran-Contra. By the eve of the trial, a presidential pardon for Libby had become a widely accepted subtext of the proceedings. Even so, no one knew exactly what political liabilities a Libby pardon would involve after the White House had been weakened by losing control of the House and Senate in the 2006 midterm elections.

From the beginning, a parade of witnesses for the prosecution presented new evidence that was devastating for Libby and Wells's planned foggy-memory defense. The CIA's Robert Grenier detailed Libby's calls to Langley seeking information about Plame. Craig Schmall, another CIA officer and Libby's briefer, recalled Libby being angry about Wilson and mentioning Wilson's wife by name. Marc Grossman, then a deputy undersecretary of state, testified that Libby had contacted him seeking confirmation of Wilson's trip to Niger and the details of Valerie Wilson's CIA employment. Ari Fleischer, the former White House press secretary, recalled that he and Libby had lunch the day after Wilson's article appeared and Libby had given Fleischer the inside story on how Wilson's wife had sent her husband on an agency mission to Niger. Perhaps most damaging—because she had worked in the vice president's office under Libby—Cheney press aide Cathie Martin testified that Libby had placed her in charge of talking to a CIA official about Valerie Wilson and she had personally debriefed both Libby and Cheney later that day about Valerie Wilson's employment at the CIA and her role in the Niger trip.

Martin's testimony, like the others, established that Libby, along with Cheney, knew about Valerie Wilson long before Joe Wilson wrote his op-ed piece in *The Times,* or Bob Novak published his column reporting that two "senior administration officials" had identified Wilson's wife as a CIA "operative." But most important, the new evidence established beyond any doubt that Libby lied in his own grand jury testimony that he had not known about Valerie Plame Wilson until July 10 or 11, when, he claimed, NBC's Washington bureau chief and *Meet the Press* host Tim Russert mentioned her to him in a telephone conversation. Russert appeared before the grand jury and confirmed that he had spoken with Libby, but consistently denied that he knew Valerie Plame's name before he read it in Novak's column.

In a surprise maneuver to keep Libby off the witness stand, Wells responded by playing the jurors two hours of tapes from Libby's May 2004 grand jury testimony that presented a stark contrast to the accounts of the prosecution witnesses. Under questioning from Fitzgerald, Libby's disembodied voice declared he had no recollection of asking the State Department's Grossman about Wilson's trip to Niger. He said he could not recall the details of any doubts expressed in the 2002 National Intelligence Estimate about the Niger trip. Had he spoken to Ari Fleischer, asked Fitzgerald. "Not that I recall," said Libby. His testimony amounted to an outright denial of accounts jurors had heard from Grenier and Schmall at the CIA and Cheney aide Cathie Martin, among others. Wells filed a motion asking Judge Walton about the consequences of keeping Libby off the witness stand. Walton had firmly asserted earlier that a "faulty memory" defense would require his client take the stand to testify about his overwhelming schedule.[38]

In the tapes, Libby also took the offensive against the White House and Cheney. He described the vice president as "upset" and "disturbed" by Wilson's allegations about the administration's use of intelligence, adding that he was told by an "animated" Karl Rove that conservative columnist Robert Novak was preparing a column about Wilson and told him Novak "had a bad taste in his mouth" about the former ambassador.[39] Libby testified on tape that his July 8 meeting with Judith Miller was approved by the vice president. Cheney, Libby said, had asked Bush to declassify the National Intelligence Estimate in order to counter Wilson's claim that there had been no Iraqi bid to buy uranium from Niger. "The vice president instructed me to go and talk to Judith Miller and lay this out for her," said Libby, who claimed he had not mentioned Wilson's wife during the meeting.[40] In response to a question about his conversation with Russert, Libby told the grand jury "it seemed to me as if I was learning it for the first time" when Russert told him about Plame. It was only later, he added, after consulting his calendar and notes, that he remembered he had heard about Plame for the first time in June from Cheney.

Russert appeared in court on February 6, 2007, on crutches from a broken ankle, the last in a parade of reporters that included Judith Miller, Matt Cooper, Robert Novak, and Bob Woodward. Earlier in the day the jury had heard taped testimony from Libby praising Russert as "in my view . . . one of the best of the newsmen, the most substantive." Libby's description of his conversation with Russert was similarly admiring. "It struck me that not only did he know this, and I didn't know it," said Libby, referring to Valerie Wilson's employment at the CIA, "but he also thought it was important."[41] Fitzgerald argued that Libby had fabricated the story about learning of Wilson's wife from Russert to protect himself from criminal charges under the 1982 Intelligence Identities Protection Act. Passing along gossip from Russert to other reporters would not meet the stringent conditions of the statute, but exposing Valerie Wilson's classified status after learning about it from Cheney could have opened him up to criminal charges.[42]

Fitzgerald took nine minutes to extract Russert's denial that the subject of Valerie Wilson had ever come up during his telephone conversation with Libby. Russert said Libby had called him "agitated" that Chris Matthews, the host of MSNBC's news show *Hardball,* had twice mentioned that Cheney was responsible for the Niger trip and had made critical remarks about Libby. "What the hell is going on with 'Hardball'?" Libby demanded, according to Russert. "Damn it. I'm tired of hearing my name over and over again. What is being said is not true." Russert testified that Valerie Wilson or Valerie Plame was never mentioned—and that it "would be impossible" for him to have told Libby about her, "because I didn't know who that person was until I read the Bob Novak column" on July 14. When he did, Russert said, he thought, "Wow, this is really big."

The *Meet the Press* host's normally confident on-air demeanor was shaken at times during his two court appearances. At one point Wells forced an embarrassed Russert to admit that, in an effort to avoid testifying about his sources, he had withheld information from the court about his conversation with Libby that he had disclosed to the FBI. Wells had posted copies of Russert's statement on video screens in the courtroom, mocking Russert's signature tactic of flashing past quotes from his *Meet the Press* guests on TV.[43] Despite his often cautious, subdued responses under Wells's rapid-fire cross examination, Russert's testimony was devastating for the normally ebullient Libby, who looked on from the defense table while nervously fiddling with a pencil.

With Russert's testimony, Fitzgerald rested his case. Wells, observers at the trial noted, refrained from signaling that either Libby or Cheney would be called as a witness by the defense. It soon became apparent why. On February 13, Libby's defense team abruptly announced that they would rest their case without calling either Libby or Vice President Cheney to the stand. In one sweep, Wells wiped out Libby's bad-memory defense as well as the argument that Libby had been made a sacrificial lamb by a White House and a vice president who seemed to have been deeply engaged in the smear campaign to discredit Joe Wilson. Although there was half-hearted speculation that Wells's team believed that they had presented a strong case that Libby had no recollection of talking to reporters, the truth was, as Carl Tobias, a University of Richmond law professor, commented, "It's a pretty tepid defense that's been mounted, and I wouldn't even say mounted . . ."[44]

The defense simply seemed to have collapsed under the onslaught of evidence by Fitzgerald, and Libby's defense team appeared to have concluded that the risks of putting Libby on the stand, where he would have to endure Fitzgerald's civil but relentless cross-examination, far outweighed the benefits. Wells also may have calculated that subjecting Cheney to similar treatment would have driven a wedge between Libby and the White House—and put the possibility of an eventual pardon in jeopardy. It was conceivable that the White House, displeased by how much already had been revealed about its internal operations during the investigation and trial, simply decided to pull the plug on any testimony by Cheney. With the exception of one or two witnesses like John Hannah from the vice president's office, who testified that under his crushing schedule "on certain things, Scooter just had an awful memory," the vaunted defense of Scooter Libby ended on a whimpering note.

Grasping at straws in his summation, Wells reminded the jury that Russert had initially told the FBI, according to an agent's notes, that he couldn't rule out discussing Wilson's wife with Libby since he talks to so many people. "That's reasonable doubt right there," claimed Wells. "If you say, 'I believe Mr. Russert beyond a reasonable doubt,' my client's life would be destroyed. His reputation would be destroyed."[45] Wells insisted that Libby was so preoccupied with questions about the U.S. failure to find weapons of mass destruction in Iraq, he had no time to pay attention to Ambassador Wilson's wife. "The wheels are falling off the Bush administration," said Wells. "Thousands of young kids are on the ground there. It's a crazy period." He added, "If it turned out that what he said was wrong that doesn't mean he is a liar. It means he may have misrecollected what happened."

"This is a man with a wife and two children; he is a good person," Wells concluded emotionally. "He's been under my protection for the last month. I give him to you. Give him back to me." At that, the veteran defense attorney teared up, sobbed out loud, and sat down.[46]

Fitzgerald was all business in his closing remarks. He and another prosecutor, Peter Zeidenberg, emphasized that witness after witness had demolished Libby's contention that he had a bad memory and had forgotten where he learned about Valerie Plame Wilson. Zeidenberg noted that Libby "claims he forgot nine conversations with eight people over a four-week period" and had testified that they all were wrong because he learned Plame's identity from Tim Russert. As for Wells's attempts to undercut Russert's credibility, Fitzgerald was contemptuous. "If Tim Russert were run over by a bus and had gone to the great news desk in the sky," he cracked, "you can still find plenty of evidence that the defendant lied."[47]

Fitzgerald's team emphasized that Libby had learned about Wilson and her employment at the CIA from other administration officials, including Vice President Cheney, and had subsequently talked to reporters about Valerie Wilson to discredit her husband's allegations that the Bush administration had distorted intelligence about Iraq seeking uranium in Niger. "Mr. Libby had a motive to lie and the motive matches up exactly with the lie he told," Fitzgerald said. "He made up a story and stuck to it." The disclosure of Valerie Wilson's identity, declared Fitzgerald, had "left a cloud over the White House over what happened" and over Vice President Cheney, who was behind the effort to counter Joseph Wilson's charges. He made it clear that Libby was not charged with illegally disclosing Valerie Plame's identity, but with misleading investigators and the grand jury. "Don't you think the American people are entitled to a straight answer?" Fitzgerald asked the jurors. "A critic points fingers at the White House and as a result his wife gets dragged into the newspapers," Fitzgerald concluded. Libby "made a gamble, he threw sand in the eyes of the grand jury."[48]

After eleven days of deliberation, the jury returned a guilty verdict against Libby, much as American voters the previous November had returned a verdict on the Bush administration's disingenuous and deceptive campaign to go to war in Iraq—and on the U.S. military and political quagmire that was its legacy. "This has been a huge cloud over the White House," said Republican lobbyist Ed Rogers, echoing Fitzgerald's summation. "It caused a lot of intellectual, emotional and political energy to be expended when it should have been expended on the agenda. They're never going to fully recover from this. If you're looking at legacy, this episode gets prominently mentioned in every recap of the Bush administration, much like Iran-contra and Monica Lewinsky."[49] Other Libby sympathizers leapt to Libby's defense. "Scooter didn't do anything," Mary Matalin insisted. "And his personal record and service are impeccable. How do you make sense of a system where . . . a guy who is rebutting a demonstrable partisan liar is going through this madness?"[50]

Besides Libby, the biggest loser in the trial was probably the vice president. Cheney's approval ratings hovered at a rock-bottom 17 percent in an NBC poll. "The trial has been death by 1,000 cuts for Cheney," said Scott Reed, a Republican strategist. "It's hurt him inside the administration. It's hurt him with the Congress, and it's hurt his stature around the world because it has shown a lot of the inner workings of the White House. It peeled the bark right off the way they operate."[51] Even old friends of the vice president who knew how painful the trial was for him felt Cheney needed to explain his actions. "I don't think he has to do a long apologia," said Vin Weber after the trial. "But I think he should say something, just to pierce the boil a little bit." Instead, Cheney limited his comments to boilerplate. He was "very disappointed with the verdict" and "saddened for Scooter and his family." Much as he had said before the trial, he added blandly, "Scooter has served our nation tirelessly and with great distinction through many years of public service."[52] The vice president, it seemed, had nothing further to say.

EPILOGUE

On July 2, 2007, only hours after Federal District Judge Reggie B. Walton ruled that Lewis Libby would have to begin serving his thirty-month prison term, President Bush commuted Libby's sentence, wiping out any jail time for the vice president's chief of staff, but leaving the underlying conviction for perjury and obstruction of justice intact. Bush noted carefully that he "respected the jury's verdict" but had "concluded that the prison sentence given to Mr. Libby is excessive." The president explained that Libby had received punishment enough. "My decision to commute his prison sentence leaves in place a harsh punishment for Mr. Libby," he said. "The reputation he gained through his years of public service and professional work in the legal community is forever damaged. . . . The consequences of his felony conviction on his former life as a lawyer, public servant, and private citizen will be long-lasting."[1]

The next day, following a visit to Walter Reed Army Medical Center, Bush elaborated on his reasons for the decision. "I felt like some of the punishments that the judge determined were adequate should stand," he said. "But I felt like the thirty-month sentencing was severe." He then raised the possibility of an eventual pardon for Libby, which probably would not come until the end of his term in 2008. "As for the future," he said pointedly, "I rule nothing in or nothing out."[2]

The commutation ignited a heated controversy in Washington. Republicans praised the president for his compassion toward Libby and his shrewd political balancing act, mollifying conservatives while keeping the hard right in line with the promise of a possible pardon. Mitt Romney, the former Republican governor of Massachusetts, campaigning in Council Bluffs, Iowa, backed Bush and dragged out a favorite GOP canard about Libby's innocence that would appeal to conservative caucus voters. "I believe that the circumstances of this case, where the prosecutor knew that there had not been a crime committed, created a setting where a decision of this nature was reasonable," said Romney. The premise, of course, was that Libby was not the first to leak Valerie Wilson's identity as a CIA operative—Richard Armitage was—therefore Libby had committed no real crime. That conveniently ignored the fact that the only reason Armitage knew about Wilson was because he read it in a State Department report commissioned by Libby—and that Libby had repeatedly lied to investigators about how he came upon that information during the grand-jury probe. Even after his conviction, few on either side of the aisle grasped that without Libby, there would have been no Armitage leak.

Democrats were incensed at the president's decision to provide special treatment for a senior White House official–turned-convicted-felon, which once more offered conclusive proof that the Bush White House had no moral compass and held itself above the law. Senator Joseph R. Biden, Jr., of Delaware, a Democratic presidential contender, heard about the commutation of Libby's sentence at a backyard campaign event in Iowa City. "These guys think they are above the law," he said. "That translates around the world." Special counsel Patrick Fitzgerald, for his part, sharply disputed Bush's characterization of Libby's sentence as unduly harsh. Fitzgerald noted that "an experienced federal judge . . . imposed a sentence consistent with the applicable law" and declared that it "is fundamental to the rule of law that all citizens stand before the bar of justice as equals."[3]

Fitzgerald broke his silence on national-security investigations in October 2007 by publicly inveighing against a federal shield law to protect journalists from ambitious prosecutors making its way through Congress. Without critical provisos, he argued in *The Washington Post,* a shield law "would have the unintended but profound effect of handcuffing investigations" of classified information leaked to the press. Once more, Fitzgerald homed in on the difficult balancing act between competing public interest in effective law enforcement, especially in national-security matters, and in the free flow of information to the media. But he drew up short of any discussion about strengthening the special counsel's role to counterbalance weakened congressional oversight and the public's right to know about White House wrongdoing.[4]

Is there a need to expand the special counsel's role—or to re-create a truly independent special prosecutor outside the Justice Department—to investigate not only possible criminal offenses, but also official corruption and serious breaches of public trust? Since Libby's conviction, there has been virtually no discussion of the issue, despite widespread criticism of both the national press and the congressional oversight process. Yet during extensive hearings conducted before the expiration of the Independent Counsel Act in 1999, prominent voices in the Washington legal community spoke strongly in favor of renewing a modified and strengthened statute, arguing in essence that removing the appearance of conflict of interest from any Justice Department investigation of high-ranking federal officials was critical to public confidence.

Indeed, a bipartisan group of senators—including Republicans Arlen Specter of Pennsylvania and Susan Collins of Maine and Democrats Joseph Lieberman and Carl Levin of Michigan—sponsored legislation in 1999 that would have strengthened an independent-counsel law and might be a starting point for reconsideration of new legislation a decade later, now that the foreign challenges faced by the United States have changed dramatically. Among other things, any new independent-counsel law, following the 1999 proposal, might apply only to the president, the vice president, their top staff and cabinet members, raise the threshold for triggering an investigation, and make the independent counsel's office permanent.[5]

As it stands, the unresolved issues that remain after the four-year Fitzgerald probe are not just the possible illegality of efforts by Karl Rove and others to leak Valerie Wilson's status as a CIA employee and cover up their attacks on Wilson and her husband. We still do not have a full picture of the role the highest-ranking Bush officials played in creating and manipulating classified intelligence to abet the march to war in Iraq, an abuse of power and the public trust of the highest magnitude. That, too, would have been the business of any special independent counsel—and the American public.

The dangerous legacy of Congress's failure to adequately monitor and check the abuses of power and illegal activities of senior Bush administration officials is a tarnished national U.S. intelligence community, with sharply reduced independence and credibility. After the Iraq fiasco, U.S. intelligence assessments of Iran's nuclear program are skeptically viewed as serving the Bush administration's hard line against the Tehran government, whose regional fortunes it has done so much to advance with the occupation of Iraq. Washington and the International Atomic Energy Agency are once more at loggerheads over the Iranian nuclear program, though they share a concern about Tehran's secrecy. Despite the IAEA's track record on Saddam's nuclear program, neither the United States nor Israel informed the UN agency about a Syrian reactor allegedly under construction that the Israelis subsequently destroyed in a September 2007 airstrike. U.S. satellite surveillance reportedly had not picked up the Syrian reactor site, but Bush and Cheney nonetheless supported the Israeli action as a warning to Iran.[6]

The sense of déjà vu is palpable. And it is likely to continue until the misuse and manipulation of intelligence by policymakers are curbed through reforms that assure the independence of the National Director of Intelligence and the ability of operatives and analysts to produce objective and unvarnished information without regard for the expectations of policymakers or fear of political retaliation. Given the trauma and upheaval within the U.S. intelligence community after Iraq, the prospect is exhausting in the short term and probably unlikely anytime soon. Nonetheless, the first priority is to strengthen congressional oversight. Former CIA analyst Paul Pillar and others have proposed that monitoring the separation of intelligence and policy should fall to a nonpartisan office modeled on the General Accounting Office that would undertake inquiries at the request of members of Congress, without duplicating the work of the House and Senate oversight committees.

Most important, Pillar advocates repositioning the office of the Director of National Intelligence within the executive branch, much like the Federal Reserve, with greater independence from the White House and an ability to communicate directly with Congress and the public, within the bounds of national security. No reform is likely to eradicate the politicization of intelligence altogether, since independent judgment without some closeness to senior policymakers is unlikely to have much influence. Even so, Pillar believes this would provide public accountability that would in turn force those making foreign policy decisions to pay greater attention to the independent judgments of the intelligence community.[7] Any legitimate intelligence reform, he warns, will be a difficult and complex undertaking for Congress. But the stakes are high in an age of terrorist threats: Without a politically independent and rigorous U.S. intelligence community working in concert with international law-enforcement agencies, future debacles like the intelligence failures that led America into Iraq are probably just a matter of time.

ACKNOWLEDGMENTS

As usual, there are many people without whose encouragement, good judgment, and forbearance this book would not have been written. The first who comes to mind is Schuyler Chapin, who encouraged me to pursue my idea of a writing a book about why the United States went to war in Iraq. Sometime later, the eighty-something former World War II pilot and New York City arts commissioner, an author in his own right, kindly consented to review my first effort at a book proposal—and, sharp as ever, summarily dismissed it as utterly inadequate. I slunk away, tore up the offending proposal, and went back to work. I have been in Schuyler's debt ever since for both his generous encouragement—and his unsparing good judgment.

In researching and writing *Going to War*, however, my greatest debt is to the reporters and correspondents who lay claim to key parts of this story and from whose daily labors this book was drawn. Many of them, and the publications for which they work, endured painful charges that they allowed themselves to be rolled by the Bush administration during the run-up to the Iraq war. But more remarkably, this handful of industrious, persistent, and independent-minded reporters, who clearly understood what was going on before the war began—if for a time they failed to get their stories in the face of government calumny and secrecy, as well as editorial queasiness—only redoubled their efforts after the war to tell critical elements of the story with consummate skill.

Among them are Barton Gellman of *The Washington Post,* who has been reporting the circumstances that led to the Iraq war as well as its aftermath for fully a decade now. Seymour Hersh's dispatches for *The New Yorker* defined the outlines of the intelligence fiasco with impressive accuracy, as did Jane Mayer's reporting on Ahmed Chalabi and the later intelligence controversies. Bob Drogin and John Goetz of the *Los Angeles Times* were the first to dig into the story of the Iraqi defector Curveball and the CIA's handling of his case. Thomas Ricks, Walter Pincus, and Joby Warrick at *The Washington Post* turned in first-rate, prescient work before the invasion and after. In *Plan of Attack,* their colleague Bob Woodward put together with great accuracy the definitive chronology of Bush White House actions during the eighteen months before the war. At Knight Ridder (now McClatchy Newspapers), Washington bureau chief John Walcott and correspondents Warren Strobel and Jonathan Landay were out in front of the pack on the Bush administration's war plans. At the much-maligned *New York Times,* the work of James Risen, Douglas Jehl, David Sanger, Michael Gordon, David Barstow, and others gave readers important glimpses into critical aspects of what was going on inside the government and intelligence agencies.

Washington-based investigative reporter Murray Waas broke story after story that shed light on the prewar period, especially after the outing of Valerie Plame Wilson. Michael Isikoff, his *Newsweek* reporting partner Mark Hosenball, and Isikoff's *Hubris* coauthor, David Corn of the *Nation,* also broke important pieces of the story and added salient details. Ron Suskind's access to insiders at the White House and the CIA paid off in important stories. Bryan Burrough and his coauthors at *Vanity Fair* put together a stunningly comprehensive early account of the prewar period in 2004, although they were not privy to later revelations forthcoming from the CIA leak case and the Libby trial. Even Judith Miller's reporting, however flawed, was in retrospect a rare and revealing window into how the Bush administration operated before the war.

There were others, especially during Fitzgerald's grand-jury probe, the incarceration of Miller, and the indictment and trial of I. Lewis "Scooter" Libby, whose work is detailed in the endnotes of this book. My former colleagues at the New York *Daily News* Washington bureau, Tom DeFrank, Ken Bazinet, and James Gordon Meek, deserve special thanks for their generous guidance as I began my research and reporting in Washington. In London, Gordon Brown biographer Tom Bower introduced me to key British journalists and others deeply involved in covering Tony Blair's march to Iraq with George W. Bush. These included Mick Smith of *The*

Times of London, who broke the Downing Street Memo story, Richard Norton-Taylor of the *Guardian*, Andrew Gilligan of the *Evening Standard*, and the incomparably tough-minded and personable lawyer-author Philippe Sands, whose book *Lawless World* is a must-read for anyone interested in understanding Blair's role in Iraq. I want to thank all of them for the engaging hours they spent with me providing British perspectives on the American-led military misadventure. None on either side of the Atlantic, however, is responsible for any mistakes or misrepresentations I may have made in the book.

In New York, I want to thank my friend George Gibson, who provided timely support and guidance, and my agent, Michael Carlisle, who came up with the title of the book and encouraged me to write the full-blown, cinemascope treatment of the White House's march to war after 9/11. Michael pushed me to follow the WMD, despite all the half-hidden moving parts and dangers of mind-numbing complexity. Ditto to Thomas Dunne, editor and publisher of the eponymous imprint at St. Martin's Press, who saw something in the concept or the spirit in which it was offered that persuaded him to back the project. Ever since, Tom has been unwaveringly supportive, offered impeccable judgments about the manuscript, and skillfully packaged the book for the marketplace. Along the way, senior editors Sean Desmond, Mark LaFlaur, John Parsley, and Joel Ariaratnam of Thomas Dunne Books have helped move the book along with timely insights and support. Thanks also to editorial assistants Lorrie McCann and Katie Gilligan for their help and patience at critical junctures. Thomas Dunne Books publicity director, Joe Rinaldi, deserves special mention for his keen attention to the book in the commercial trenches, as does production editor Edward Allen.

Closer to home, I also owe a debt of gratitude to my friend George Conk, a New York City law professor, sailor, and fellow Labrador retriever owner who endured my endless rehashing of the book for three years worth of late-night walks in Washington Heights; and also to Dick Brainerd, my good conservative friend and sounding board, who was forced to suffer my endless fulminating during hours of dinners and walks in the Connecticut hills. Thanks to Jeff Spiegel and Katie Gardner for their good advice and encouragement. Special thanks also to my mother, Jinny Hoyle, to whom with my late father, a marine who fought two wars and died too soon, this book is dedicated, for her great faith, high spirits, generosity, and support.

And finally, my heartfelt thanks to my wife, Ellen, who somehow managed to thrive in her own increasingly demanding and responsible professional life in New York, for her constant support while enduring the absence of her husband, whom she would joke had "disappeared into his bubble again." Our son, Henry, a college senior, may have had the last word when he presented me with a hand-drawn cartoon that put his preoccupied father squarely in his place. The first panel shows a man (yours truly) working intently at the computer, the dog curled up at his feet. In the second, the man leans back, hands clasped behind his head, holding forth on some weighty issue. The third panel depicts the suddenly animated dog sitting up, a blank dialogue bubble over its head. In the last panel, the man turns to the dog and exclaims, "You know what, I wouldn't have thought of that, but you're dead on. God, that's good."

What can I say to that? Thank you, Ellen and Henry, for your marathon patience and good humor.

Prologue: Last Mission to Al Muhawish

1. Judith Miller, "Illicit Arms Kept till Eve of War, an Iraqi Scientist Is Said to Assert," *New York Times*, April 21, 2003.

2. Franklin Foer, "The Source of the Trouble," *New York*, June 7, 2004.

3. Ibid.

4. Howard Kurtz, "Embedded Reporter's Role in Army Unit's Actions Questioned by Military," *Washington Post*, June 25, 2003.

5. Foer, "The Source of the Trouble," June 7, 2004.

6. Miller, "Illicit Arms Kept till Eve of War," April 21, 2003.

7. Ibid.

8. Judith Miller, interview by Ray Suarez, *NewsHour with Jim Lehrer*, PBS, April 21, 2003.

9. Foer, "The Source of the Trouble," June 7, 2003.

10. Judith Miller, "A Chronicle of Confusion in the Hunt for Hussein's Weapons," *New York Times*, July 20, 2003.

11. Douglas McCollum, "The List," *Columbia Journalism Review*, July/August 2004.

12. Jane Mayer, "The Manipulator," *New Yorker*, June 7, 2004.

13. Foer, "The Source of the Trouble," June 7, 2004.

14. Kurtz, "Embedded Reporter's Role in Army Unit's Actions Questioned by Military," June 25, 2003.

15. Ibid.

16. Howard Kurtz, "Intra-Times Battle over Iraqi Weapons," *Washington Post*, May 26, 2003.

17. Ibid.

18.   Kurtz, "Embedded Reporter's Role in Army Unit's Actions Questioned by Military," June 25, 2003.

19.   William Broad and Judith Miller, "Some Analysts of Iraq Trailers Reject Germ Use," *New York Times,* June 7, 2003.

20.   Douglas Jehl, "Agency Disputes CIA View of Trailers as Iraqi Weapons Labs," *New York Times,* June 26, 2003.

21.   Barton Gellman, "Frustrated, U.S. Arms Team to Leave Iraq," *Washington Post,* May 11, 2003.

22.   Miller, "A Chronicle of Confusion in the Hunt for Hussein's Weapons," July 20, 2003.

23.   Barton Gellman, "Covert Unit Hunted for Iraqi Arms," *Washington Post,* June 13, 2003.

24.   Ibid.

25.   Judith Miller, interview in "Newswar," *Frontline,* PBS, February 13, 2007; Judith Miller e-mail to author, September 5, 2007.

26.   Murray Waas, "The Meeting," *The American Prospect,* August 6, 2005; U.S. Department of Justice, affadavit by Judith Miller.

1. Another Shot at Saddam

1.   Although there is some dispute about Rumsfeld's whereabouts between 9:39 A.M. when Flight 77 hit the Pentagon, and about 10:10 A.M., when he entered the National Military Control Center, multiple accounts and direct quotations from Rumsfeld make it reasonably clear that the secretary had gone to the scene of the crash and lent aid to some of the victims. See *Parade* magazine, November 12, 2001, ABC News, October 11, 2001, *Larry King Live,* January 5, 2002, and Andrew Cockburn, *Rumsfeld: His Rise, Fall, and Catastrophic Legacy* (New York: Scribner, 2007), 1–7. The total death toll in the 9/11 attacks was compiled by CNN.

2.   For the early NSC meetings, I have relied on Ron Suskind, *The Price of Loyalty: George W. Bush, the White House, and the Education of Paul O'Neill* (New York: Simon & Schuster, 2004), 72–75.

3.   Paul Wolfowitz, "Rising Up," *New Republic,* December 7, 1998.

4.   Suskind, *The Price of Loyalty,* 85.

5.   Ibid., 86.

6.   Bob Woodward and Dan Balz, "We Will Rally the World," *Washington Post,* January 28, 2002.

7.   Richard Clarke, *Against All Enemies* (New York: Free Press/Simon & Schuster, 2004), 32.

8.   *9/11 Commission Report: Final Report of the National Commission on Terrorist Attacks Upon the United States* (New York: W.W. Norton & Co., 2004), 334.

9.   Clarke, *Against All Enemies,* 33.

10.   Suskind, *The Price of Loyalty,* 26.

11.   Ibid., 26.

12. For information on the 2000 Bush presidential bid, the campaign, and background on key officials, I have relied largely on James Mann, *The Rise of the Vulcans: The History of Bush's War Cabinet* (New York: Penguin, 2004).

13. Federal News Service, Bush-Cheney press conference, July 25, 2000.

14. Cockburn, *Rumsfeld: His Rise, Fall, and Catastrophic Legacy,* 67.

15. Condoleezza Rice, "Campaign 2000: Promoting the National Interest," *Foreign Affairs,* January/February 2000.

16. Mann, *The Rise of the Vulcans,* 190.

17. Paul Wolfowitz and Zalmay Khalilizad, "Overthrow Him," *Weekly Standard,* December 1, 1997.

18. Bryan Burroughs, et al., "The Path to War," *Vanity Fair,* June 2004, 234.

19. Michael R. Gordon and Gen. Bernard E. Trainor, *Cobra II: The Inside Story of the Invasion and Occupation of Iraq* (New York: Random House, 2006), 10; *9/11 Commission Report,* 559–560, footnote on DOD memo from Feith to Rumsfeld, September 20, 2001.

20. Mark Danner, *The Secret Way to War: The Downing Street Memo and the Iraq War's Buried History* (New York: New York Review Books, 2006), 77. Also see *Cobra II,* 18–19.

21. Danner, *The Secret Way to War,* text of Ricketts memo, 140.

22. Ibid., 145–146.

2. Cheney Goes Over to the Dark Side

1. David J. Rothkopf, *Running the World: The Inside Story of the National Security Council and the Architects of American Power* (New York: Perseus, 2004), 422.

2. Jane Mayer, "The Hidden Power: The Legal Mind Behind the White House's War on Terror," *New Yorker,* July 3, 2006.

3. Michael Duffy, "Cheney in Twilight," *Time,* March 19, 2007.

4. Rothkopf, *Running the World,* 426.

5. Scott Shane, "As Trial Begins, Cheney's Ex-Aide Is Still a Puzzle," *New York Times,* January 17, 2002.

6. Rothkopf, *Running the World,* 421–422.

7. Bob Woodward, *Plan of Attack* (New York: Simon & Schuster, 2004), 29.

8. Mann, *The Rise of the Vulcans,* 61.

9. Ibid., 169.

10. Kenneth T. Walsh, "The Cheney Factor: How the Scars of Public Life Shaped the Vice President's Unyielding Views of Executive Power," *U.S. News & World Report,* January 23, 2006.

11. Mann, *The Rise of the Vulcans,* 144. For Mann's account of Cheney's role in the Reagan era continuity of government exercises, see pages 139–145.

12. Ibid.

13. Barton Gellman and Susan Schmidt, "Shadow Government at Work in Secret," *Washington Post,* March 1, 2002.

14.   Woodward, *Plan of Attack,* 29; Dick Cheney, interview by Tim Russert, *Meet the Press,* NBC, September 16, 2001.

15.   Gellman and Schmidt, "Shadow Government at Work in Secret," January 20, 2002.

16.   Sam Tanenhaus, "The Hard Liner," *The Boston Globe,* November 3, 2003.

17.   Mayer, "The Manipulator," June 7, 2004.

18.   Thomas Powers, *Intelligence Wars* (New York: *New York Review Books,* 2004), xiii–xv.

19.   Woodward, *Plan of Attack,* 29–30.

20.   Ron Suskind, *The One Percent Doctrine* (New York: Simon & Schuster, 2006), 61–62.

21.   White House, Presidential Executive Order 1392, March 25, 2003. See whitehouse.gov.

22.   Shane, "As Trial Begins, Cheney's Ex-Aide Is Still a Puzzle," January 17, 2007.

23.   Mark Leibovich, "In the Spotlight and on the Spot," *Washington Post,* October 23, 2005; CNN, February 23, 2002.

24.   For Libby biographical detail, see Daniela Deane, "Cheney's Right Hand Man Never Sought Limelight," *Washington Post,* October 28, 2005.

25.   Shane, "As Trial Begins, Cheney's Ex-Aide Is Still a Puzzle," January 17, 2007.

26.   Mann, *Rise of the Vulcans,* 187.

27.   Ibid., 211.

28.   Ibid., 213.

29.   Lewis Libby, interview by Larry King, *Larry King Live,* CNN, February 16, 2002.

30.   Judith Miller, "My Four Hours Testifying in the Federal Grand Jury Room," *New York Times,* October 16, 2005.

3. Masters of the Universe

1.   James Moore and Wayne Slater, *Bush's Brain* (Hoboken, N.J.: John Wiley & Sons, 2003), 4.

2.   Leibovich, "In the Spotlight and on the Spot," October 23, 2005.

3.   Robert Dreyfuss, "Vice Squad," *American Prospect,* May 8, 2006.

4.   Ibid.

5.   Barton Gellman and Jo Becker, "A Different Understanding with the President," *Washington Post,* June 24, 2007.

6.   Rothkopf, *Running the World,* 408.

7.   Duffy, "Cheney in Twilight," March 19, 2007.

8.   Robert Dreyfuss, "Vice Squad," May 8, 2006.

9.   David Ignatius, "Cheney's Cheney," *Washington Post,* January 6, 2006.

10.   Robert Dreyfuss, "Vice Squad," May 8, 2006.

11.   Rothkopf, *Running the World,* 409.

12. Ibid., 426.

13. Ibid., 406.

14. Ibid., 406, 429.

15. Ibid., 412.

16. Speculation that Rumsfeld acted as the prime mover of U.S. war policies in a chain of command that went from Rumsfeld to Cheney to the president, as Gen. Wesley Clark has suggested, almost certainly underestimated the power that Cheney consolidated in the OVP—as well as the formidable center of gravity that Cheney and Rumsfeld together provided for the Iraq war effort.

17. Interview with Lt. Gen. Mike DeLong, "The Dark Side," *Frontline*, PBS, June 20, 2006.

18. Ibid.

19. Rothkopf, *Running the World*, 414.

20. Ibid., 418.

21. Ibid., 419.

22. Rothkopf, *Running the World*, 436. Armitage later moderated his criticism of Rice.

23. Col. Lawrence B. Wilkerson, speech before the New America Foundation, Washington, D.C., October 19, 2005.

24. Lawrence B. Wilkerson, "The White House Cabal," *Los Angeles Times*, October 23, 2005.

25. Gellman and Becker, "A Different Understanding with the President," June 29, 2007.

26. Jane Mayer, "The Hidden Power," *New Yorker*, July 3, 2006.

27. Richard L. Berke, "Bush Adviser Suggests War as Campaign Theme," *New York Times*, January 19, 2002.

28. Moore and Slater, *Bush's Brain*, 291.

29. Nichola Lemann, "The Controller," *New Yorker*, May 12, 2003.

30. I have relied on Moore and Slater, *Bush's Brain*, for much of the biographical material on Karl Rove.

31. Moore and Slater, *Bush's Brain*, 119.

32. Ibid., 127.

33. Ibid.

34. Ibid., 130.

35. Ibid., 145.

36. Ibid., 257.

37. James Bamford, *A Pretext for War: 9/11, Iraq, and the Abuse of America's Intelligence Agencies* (New York: Random House, 2004), 324–325.

38. Woodward, *Plan of Attack*, 290; Peter Wallsten and Tom Hamburger, "Rove's Security Clearance Widely Questioned," *Los Angeles Times*, November 6, 2005.

39. James Carney and John F. Dickerson, "W. and the 'Boy Genius,'" *Time*, November 9, 2002.

4. War Fever on the Potomac

1. William Langewiesche, *American Ground: Unbuilding the World Trade Center* (New York: North Point Press, 2002), 2.
2. Ibid.
3. James Fallows, "Councils of War," *Atlantic Monthly*, December 2001.
4. Thomas DeFrank, in an interview with the author July 2006.
5. Faye Fiore, "Schools Shy Away from Washington Field Trips," *Los Angeles Times*, February 11, 2002.
6. "Operation Noble Eagle," Armed Forces Institute of Pathology, November 16, 2001.
7. Eric Lichtblau, "Bias Against Arabs Taking Subtler Forms," *Los Angeles Times*, February 10, 2002.
8. Warren P. Strobel, "Former CIA Director Looks for Evidence That Iraq Had a Role in Attacks," Knight-Ridder (now McClatchy), October 11, 2001.
9. Ibid.
10. Toby Harnden, "Building the Case Against Iraq," *Telegraph* (London), October 26, 2001.
11. Julian Borger, "Interview: Richard Clarke," *The Guardian* (London), March 23, 2004.
12. Bamford, *A Pretext for War*, 256–257.
13. Seymour Hersh, "A Case Not Closed," *New Yorker*, November 1, 1993.
14. Murray Waas, "Key Bush Intelligence Briefing Kept from Hill Panel," *National Journal*, November 22, 2005.

5. A Preemptive Fog of War

1. Lesley Stahl, "The Man Who Got Away: The Yasin Interview," *60 Minutes*, CBS News, June 2, 2002.
2. Dick Cheney, interview by Tim Russert, *Meet the Press*, NBC News, September 4, 2003.
3. Michael Hirsch, John Berry, and Daniel Klaidman, "A Tortured Debate," *Newsweek*, June 21, 2004.
4. Walter Pincus, "Newly Released Data Undercut Pre-War Claims," *Washington Post*, November 6, 2005; Douglas Jehl, "Report Warned Bush Team About Intelligence Doubts," *New York Times*, November 6, 2005; Michael Isikoff and Mark Hosenball, "Al-Libi's Tall Tales," *Newsweek*, November 10, 2005.
5. Douglas Jehl, "High Qaeda Aide Retracted Claim of Link with Iraq," *New York Times*, July 31, 2004.
6. BIS is the Czech acronym for *Bezpcnostni Informacni Sluzba*, the Czech intelligence service
7. Associated Press, September 18, 2001.
8. Patrick E. Tyler with John Tagliabue, "Czechs Confirm Iraqi Agent Met with Terror Ringleader," *New York Times*, October 27, 2001.

9. Ibid.
10. BBC News, "Hijacker 'Did Not Meet Iraqi Agent,'" May 1, 2002.
11. Martin Walker, "Czechs Retract Terror Link," United Press International, October 20, 2002.
12. Romesh Ratnesar, "Iraq and al Qaeda: Is There a Link?" *Time*, September 2, 2002.
13. Michael Isikoff, "The Dots Never Existed," *Newsweek*, July 19, 2004.
14. Testimony of George Tenet, Senate Armed Services Committee, March 9, 2004.
15. John Crewdson, "In Prague, a Tale of Two Attas," *Chicago Tribune*, August 29, 2004.
16. McCollum, "The List: How Chalabi Played the Press," July/August 2004.

6. The Vice President and the Niger Deal

1. SISMI is the Italian acronym for *Servizio per le Informazioni e la Sicurezza Militare.*
2. Senate Intelligence Committee report, July 9, 2004, 38.
3. Ibid., 42.
4. Tom Hamburger, Peter Wallsten, and Bob Drogin, "French Told CIA of Bogus Intelligence," *Los Angeles Times*, December 11, 2005.
5. Senate Intelligence Committee report, July 7, 2004, 43.
6. Ibid., 46.
7. *Washington Post*, October 2, 2005.

7. How Joseph Wilson Got to Africa and What He Found There

1. Joseph Wilson, *The Politics of Truth* (New York: Carroll & Graf, 2004), 7–8.
2. Senate Intelligence Committee report, July 2004, 39.
3. Ibid., 39.
4. Wilson, *The Politics of Truth*, lv.
5. Timothy M. Phelps and Knut Royce, "Columnist Blows CIA Agent's Cover," *Newsday*, July 22, 2003.
6. Report on the U.S. Intelligence Community's Prewar Intelligence Assessments on Iraq, Select Committee on Intelligence, U.S. Senate, July 7, 2004, 41. Referred to below as the Senate Intelligence Committee report.
7. The account of the Niger trip relies on Wilson, *The Politics of Truth*, and the Senate Intelligence Committee report of July 7, 2004.
8. Senate Intelligence Committee report, July 7, 2004, 41.
9. Wilson, *The Politics of Truth*, 21.
10. Ibid., 28.
11. Senate Intelligence Committee report, July 7, 2004, 44.

12.   Wilson, *The Politics of Truth*, 28.
13.   Senate Intelligence Committee report, July 7, 2004, 44.
14.   Ibid., 44; Senate Intelligence Committee report, "Additional Views," July 7, 2004, 444.
15.   Paul Pillar, "Intelligence, Policy, and the War in Iraq," *Foreign Affairs*, March/April 2006.
16.   Senate Intelligence Committee report, "Additional Views," July 7, 2004, 144, 146.

8. An Onslaught of Bad Intelligence

1.   Senate Intelligence Committee report, July 2004, 47. Redactions in the report obscure the duration of the alleged deal.
2.   Ibid., 47.
3.   Franklin Foer and Spencer Ackerman, "The Radical," *New Republic*, December 1, 2003.
4.   Hamburger, Wallsten, and Drogin, "French Told CIA of Bogus Intelligence," December 11, 2005.
5.   DGSE is the French acronym for *Direction Generale de la Securite Exterieure*.
6.   Hamburger, Wallsten, and Drogin, "French Told CIA of Bogus Intelligence," December 11, 2005.
7.   Michael Gordon and Judith Miller, "U.S. Says Hussein Intensified Quest for A-Bomb Parts," *New York Times*, September 8, 2002.
8.   As is well known, administration officials fanned out to appear as guests on Washington's influential Sunday morning political talk shows to tout the revelations in *The Times*. On ABC's *Issues and Answers,* Condoleezza Rice even used a phrase first deployed in the article when she declared, "We want to make sure the first sign of a smoking gun isn't a mushroom cloud"—a memorable formulation that would be used repeatedly by Cheney and the president in the months ahead.
9.   Senate Intelligence Committee report, July 7, 2004, 88.
10.   Charles Duelfer and the Iraq Survey Group, "Comprehensive Report of the Special Advisor to the DCI on Iraq's WMD," Nuclear section, 7–8, 21–30, September 2004.
11.   Senate Intelligence Committee report, July 7, 2004, 49.
12.   Ibid., 52.
13.   Ibid., "Additional Views," 450.
14.   Senate Intelligence Committee report, July 7, 2004, 53–54.
15.   Ibid., 51.
16.   Ibid., 54.
17.   Ibid., 56.
18.   Ibid., 58.
19.   Woodward, *Plan of Attack*, 222.

20.   Senate Intelligence Committee report, July 7, 2004, 62.

21.   Ibid., 67.

22.   Murray Waas, "Iraq, Niger, and the CIA," *National Journal,* February 2, 2006.

23.   Dick Cheney, interview by Tim Russert, *Meet the Press,* NBC, September 14, 2003.

9. The Mystery of the Forged Documents

1.   Sen. John D. Rockefeller, "Additional Views," Senate Intelligence Committee report, July 7, 2004, 450.

2.   Seymour Hersh, "Who Lied to Whom," *New Yorker,* March 31, 2003.

3.   Senate Intelligence Committee report, July 7, 2004, 69.

4.   Carlo Bonini and Giuseppi d'Avanzo, "Berlusconi's Men 'Doctor' Niger Uranium Dossier," *La Repubblica* (Rome), November 13, 2005. Chékou's telex, dated February 1, 1999 (ref. N° 003/99/ABNI/Rome), read: "I have the honor to inform you that the Iraqi Embassy to the Holy See in the person of His Excellency Wissam Al Zahawi, Iraq Ambassador to the Holy See, will set out on an official mission to our country as the representative of Saddam Hussein, President of the Republic of Iraq. His Excellency will arrive in Niamey on Friday February 5, 1999 at approximately 18:25 aboard Air France Flight 730 originating in Paris." Senate Intelligence Committee report, July 7, 2004, 29.

5.   Carlo Bonino and Giuseppi d'Avanzo, "Berlusconi Behind Fake Yellow-cake Dossier," *La Repubblica* (Rome), October 24, 2005; Carolo Bonini and Giuseppi d'Avanzo, *Collusion: International Espionage and the War on Terror* (Hoboken, NJ: Melville House, 2007).

6.   Ibid.

7.   According to a former CIA official, the agency was offered the Italian documents in 2001 and quickly rejected them as forgeries. It is not clear exactly when the CIA received them. But according to former CIA and DGSE officials, the CIA contacted French intelligence in the summer of 2001, before the 9/11 attacks, and asked them to check on the security of uranium in Niger and elsewhere (Hamburger, Wallsten, and Drogin, "French Told CIA of Bogus Intelligence," December 11, 2005). Had the phony documents raised enough questions to trigger the U.S. query to the French? Or had the forged papers appeared later, perhaps during Pollari's trip? In any case, the CIA appears to have been well aware of the forged Niger documents long before January 16, 2003, when it has acknowledged receiving copies.

8.   Bonini and d'Avanzo, "Berlusconi's Men 'Doctor' Niger Uranium Dossier," November 13, 2005.

9.   Bonini and d'Avanzo, "Nigergate: The Nuclear Centrifuge Scam," *La Repubblica* (Rome), October 26, 2005.

10.   Ibid.

11.   Bonino and d'Avanzo, "SISMI's War in Iraq, Part I: From Chalabi to Iranian Agents," *La Repubblica* (Rome), October 31, 2005.

12.   James Risen, "How a Shady Iranian Dealmaker Kept the Ear of the Pentagon," *New York Times,* December 7, 2003.

13.   Ibid.

14.   Knut Royce and Timothy Phelps, "Arms Dealer in Talks with U.S. Officials About Iran," *Newsday,* August 9, 2003.

15.   Bonino and d'Avanzo, "Nigergate: The Nuclear Centrifuge Scam," October 26, 2005.

16.   Elaine Sciolino and Elisabetta Povoledo, "Italy's Top Spy Names Freelance Agent as Source of Forged Niger-Iraq Uranium Documents," *New York Times,* November 4, 2005.

17.   Ibid.

18.   Peter Wallsten, Tom Hamburger, and Josh Meyer, "FBI Is Taking Another Look at Forged Prewar Intelligence," *Los Angeles Times,* December 3, 2005.

19.   Ibid.

20.   Ibid.

10. Primed for Disinformation

1.   David Kay, interview by Stephen Talbott, "Spying on Saddam," *Frontline,* PBS, April 27, 1999.

2.   Ibid. Many of David Kay's exploits with UNSCOM rely on Talbott's April 1999 interview with David Kay.

3.   Barton Gellman, interview by Stephen Talbott, "Spying on Saddam," *Frontline,* PBS, April 27, 1999.

4.   Scott Ritter, interview by Stephen Talbott, "Spying on Saddam," *Frontline,* PBS, April 27, 1999.

5.   Kay, "Spying on Saddam," April 27, 1999.

6.   Gellman, "Spying on Saddam," April 27, 1999.

7.   Ibid.

8.   Ibid.

9.   Ritter, "Spying on Saddam," April 27, 1999.

10. Ibid.; also see Scott Ritter, *Iraq Confidential: The Untold Story of America's Intelligence Conspiracy* (London: I.B. Taurus & Co. Ltd., 2005), and Scott Ritter, "Spying on Saddam," April 27, 1999.

11. Gellman, "Spying on Saddam," April 27, 1999.

12. Richard Butler, interview by Stephen Talbott, "Spying on Saddam," *Frontline,* PBS, April 27, 1999.

13. Scott Ritter, "What, If Anything, Does Iraq Have to Hide?" *Newsday,* July 30, 2002.

14. Ibid.

15. UN Security Council, *The Amorim Report,* March 1999, paragraph 25.

16. Ibid., paragraphs 16–18.

NOTES **487**

17. Ibid., paragraphs 19–20.
18. Ibid., paragraphs 22–27.
19. Ibid., paragraphs 14–15.
20. Interview with Rolf Ekeus, "Leaving Behind the UNSCOM Legacy," *Arms Control Today,* vol. 27, No. 4, June/July 1997.
21. David Albright and Khidhir Hamza, "Iraq's Reconstitution of Its Nuclear Weapons Program," *Arms Control Today,* vol. 28, No. 7, October 1998.
22. Kay "Spying on Saddam," April 27, 1999.
23. Hans Blix interview, "UNMOVIC Readies Itself for Iraq," *Arms Control Today,* vol. 30, No. 6, July/August 2000.
24. Albright and Hamza, "Iraq's Reconstitution of Its Nuclear Weapons Program," October 1998.
25. Richard Butler interview, "The Lessons and Legacy of UNSCOM," *Arms Control Today,* vol. 29, No. 4, June 1999.
26. Kay, "Spying on Saddam," April 27, 1999.

11. Who Is Ahmed Chalabi?

1. For opening section of chapter, see Khidhir Hamza, *Saddam's Bombmaker: The Terrifying Inside Story of the Iraqi Nuclear and Biological Weapons Agenda* (New York: Scribner, 2000), 32–34, 271–282.
2. Jack Fairweather and Anton La Guardia, "Chalabi Stands by Faulty Intelligence That Toppled Saddam's Regime," *Telegraph* (London), February 19, 2004.
3. Mayer, "The Manipulator," June 7, 2004.
4. McCollum, "The List," July/August 2004.
5. For background on Chalabi and his family, see Mayer, "The Manipulator," June 7, 2004.
6. Ibid.
7. Robert Dreyfuss, "Tinker, Tailor, Neocon, Spy," *American Prospect,* November 18, 2002.
8. Mayer, "The Manipulator," June 7, 2004.
9. Ibid.
10. Kenneth M. Pollack, *The Threatening Storm, the United States and Iraq: The Crisis, the Strategy, and the Prospects after Saddam* (New York: Random House, 2002), 72–73.
11. Ibid., 82–84.
12. Mayer, "The Manipulator," June 7, 2004.
13. Ibid.
14. Ibid.
15. Ibid.
16. Julian Borger, "Washington Fetes Its Enemy's Enemy," *Guardian* (London), February 22, 2002.
17. Thomas E. Ricks, *Fiasco: The American Miliary Adventure in Iraq* (New York: Penguin, 2006), 23.

18. Daniel Byman, Kenneth Pollack, and Gideon Rose, "The Rollback Fantasy," *Foreign Affairs*, January/February 1999.

19. Bob Woodward, *State of Denial: Bush at War, Part III* (New York: Simon & Schuster, 2006), 157.

20. Jonathan S. Landay and Warren P. Strobel, "Pentagon Civilians' Lack of Planning Contributed to Chaos in Iraq," Knight-Ridder, July 12, 2003.

21. Ricks, *Fiasco*, 124.

22. Mayer, "The Manipulator," June 7, 2004.

23. Ibid.

24. Burroughs, et al., "The Path to War," May 2, 2004.

25. Mayer, "The Manipulator," June 7, 2004.

26. Burroughs, et al., "The Path to War," May 2, 2004.

27. Joby Warrick, "In Assessing Iraq's Arsenal, the 'Reality Is Uncertainty,' " *Washington Post*, July 31, 2002.

12. Chalabi's Rogue Intelligence Operation

1. Jonathan Landay and Warren P. Strobel, "Former CIA Director Used Pentagon Ties to Introduce Iraqi Defector," Knight-Ridder, July 16, 2004.

2. Bob Drogin, "U.S. Suspects It Received False Iraq Arms Tips," *Los Angeles Times*, August 28, 2003.

3. Senate Intelligence Committee report, July 7, 2004.

4. U.S. State Department audit, May 2002.

5. McCollum, "The List," July/August 2004.

6. Douglas Jehl, "Report Warned Bush Team About Intelligence Doubts," *New York Times*, November 6, 2005.

7. David Rose, "Inside Saddam's Deadly Arsenal," *Vanity Fair*, May 2002, 120.

8. Ibid.

9. Ibid.

10. Bob Drogin and John Goetz, " 'How the U.S. Fell Under the Spell of 'Curveball,' " *Los Angeles Times*, November 20, 2005.

11. Robb-Silberman Commission report, March 31, 2005, 82.

12. Senate Intelligence Committee report, July 7, 2004, 150.

13. Evan Thomas and Roy Gutman, "Iraq in the Balance," *Newsweek*, March 19, 2002.

14. Josh Tyrangiel, "What Saddam's Got," *Time*, May 13, 2002.

15. Christopher Hitchens, "Does Blair Know What He's Getting Into?" *Guardian* (London), March 20, 2003.

16. McCollum, "The List," June/July 2004.

17. Mark Bowden, "Tales of the Tyrant," *Atlantic Monthly*, June 2002.

18. McCollum, "The List," July/August 2004.

19. Ibid.

20. Karen DeYoung and Walter Pincus, "Rhetoric Fails to Budge Policy on Iraq," *Washington Post,* January 25, 2002.

21. Mark Hosenball and Michael Hirsh, "A Questionable Use of Funding," *Newsweek,* April 5, 2004.

22. McCollum, "The List," July/August 2004.

23. General Accounting Office report, number 04-559, May 20, 2004.

24. Michael Isikoff and Mark Hosenball, "Exclusive: Cheney and the 'Raw Intelligence,'" *Newsweek,* December 15, 2003.

25. Franklin Foer and Spencer Ackerman, "The Radical," *New Republic,* December 1, 2003.

26. Michael Isikoff and Mark Hosenball, "Rethinking the Chalabi Connection," Newsweek.com, May 20, 2004.

27. Ibid.

13. Blair Raises the Stakes on WMD

1. Danner, *The Secret Way to War,* 131.

2. David Rose, "Bush and Blair Made Secret Pact for Iraq War," *Observer,* April 4, 2004; Burrough, et al., "The Path to War," May 2004, 238.

3. Danner, *The Secret Way to War,* 94–149. These seven leaked briefing papers were published along with the more famous Downing Street Memo, which was taken from notes made during MI6 director Richard Dearlove's July 23, 2002, account to Prime Minister Blair of a meeting that month with CIA director George Tenet and other senior intelligence officials in Washington. Like the Downing Street Memo, the related memoranda were made public by Michael Smith of London's *Sunday Times.*

4. Clarke, *Against All Enemies,* 24.

5. Colin Powell, interview by Tim Russert, *Meet the Press,* NBC, September 23, 2001.

6. White House, press release, www.whitehouse.gov, September 24, 2001.

7. Eric Lichtblau and Josh Meyer, "Proof Against bin Laden Cited," *Los Angeles Times,* October 5, 2001.

8. Burroughs, et al., "The Path to War," May 2004, 283.

9. Ibid.

10. Danner, *The Secret Way to War,* 135.

11. Burroughs, et al., "The Path to War," May 2004, 283.

12. Danner, *The Secret Way to War,* 140.

13. Ibid.

14. Ibid., 141.

15. Ibid., 147.

16. Michael Smith, "Blair Hit by New Leak of Secret War Plan," *Sunday Times* (London), May 1, 2005.

17. White House, press release, www.whitehouse.gov, April 6, 2002.

18. James Risen, *State of War* (New York: Free Press, 2006), 114.

19. Ibid., 114.

20.   Danner, *The Secret Way to War,* 153.
21.   Ibid., 158.
22.   Ibid., 159.
23.   Ibid., Downing Street Memo, July 23, 2002, 88–89.
24.   Burroughs, et al., "The Path to War," May 2004, 283.
25.   Warren P. Strobel and John Walcott, "Bush Has Decided to Overthrow Hussein," Knight-Ridder, February 13, 2002.
26.   Woodward, *Plan of Attack,* 150–153.
27.   Lord Butler of Brockwell, Review of Intelligence on Weapons of Mass Destruction, Report of a Council of Privy Counselors, House of Commons, July 14, 2004, 71 (referred to below as the Butler Report); Woodward, *Plan of Attack,* 161–162.
28.   Ibid., 165.
29.   Butler Report, July 14, 2004, 72.
30.   Woodward, *Plan of Attack,* 178.
31.   Butler Report, July 14, 2004, 261.65–66.
32.   Ibid., 86.
33.   Ibid., 84.
34.   Ibid.
35.   Ibid., 85–86.
36.   Lord Hutton, Report of the Inquiry into the Circumstances Surrounding the Death of Dr. David Kelly C.M.G., the-hutton-inquiry.org.uk, January 28, 2004, sections 161–214.
37.   Butler Report, July 14, 2004, 78.

14. Silencing the Critics

1.   Daniel Eisenberg, "We're Taking Him Out," *Time,* May 5, 2002.
2.   Arnaud de Borchgrave, "Iraq and the Gulf of Tonkin," *Washington Times,* February 10, 2004.
3.   Jack Shafer, "Newspaper War," *Salon,* July 30, 2002.
4.   Thomas Ricks, "Some Top Military Brass Prefer Status Quo in Iraq," *Washington Post,* July 28, 2002.
5.   Woodward, *Plan of Attack*, 137–138.
6.   Interview with Brent Scowcroft, *Face the Nation,* CBS, August 4, 2002.
7.   Henry Kissinger op-ed, *Washington Post,* August 12, 2002.
8.   Andrew Gumbel, "Kissinger Joins Protests at Bush Plan to Attack Iraq," *Independent* (London), August 17, 2002.
9.   Brent Scowcroft, "Don't Attack Saddam," *Wall Street Journal,* August 14, 2002.
10.   Fox News, "GOP Backing Out of Iraq Offensive?" August 16, 2002.
11.   James A. Baker III. "The Right Way to Change a Regime," *New York Times,* August 25, 2002.
12.   Todd S. Purdum and Patrick E. Tyler, "Top Republicans Break with Bush on Iraq Strategy," *New York Times,* August 16, 2002.

13.   Michael Ledeen, "Scowcroft Strikes Out," *National Review*, August 6, 2002.

14.   Purdum and Tyler, "Top Republicans Break with Bush on Iraq Strategy," August 16, 2002.

15.   Roland Watson, "Bush Risks Isolating U.S., Cautions Kissinger," *Times* (London), August 13, 2002.

16.   Remarks by the president on Iraq, Crawford, Texas, White House, www.whitehouse.gov, August 16, 2002.

17.   Bret Baier, "Rumsfeld: Attack Can't Wait," Fox News, August 20, 2002.

18.   Woodward, *Plan of Attack*, 163.

19.   Gallup News Service, CNN/*USA Today* poll, August 23, 2002.

20.   Zbigniew Brzezinski, "If We Must Fight . . . ," *The Washington Post*, August 18, 2002.

21.   Barton Gellman and Walter Pincus, "Depiction of Threat Outgrew Evidence," *Washington Post*, August 10, 2003.

22.   Ibid.

23.   Robert Dreyfuss and Jason Vest, "The Lie Factory," *Mother Jones*, January/February 2004.

24.   Jeffrey Goldberg, "A Little Learning," *The New Yorker*, May 9, 2005.

25.   Eric Schmitt and Thom Shanker, "Pentagon Sets Up Intelligence Unit," *New York Times*, October 24, 2002.

26.   Ibid.

27.   Interview with Richard Clarke, "The Dark Side," *Frontline*, PBS, June 20, 2006.

28.   Karen Kwiatkowski, "The New Pentagon Papers," *Salon*, March 10, 2004.

29.   Dreyfuss and Vest, "The Lie Factory," January/February 2004.

30.   Kwiatkowski, "The New Pentagon Papers," March 10, 2004.

31.   Department of Defense, press release, www.defenselink.mil/releases, November 18, 2002.

32.   Goldberg, "A Little Learning," May 9, 2005.

33.   Julian Borger, "The Spies That Pushed for War," *Guardian* (London), July 17, 2003.

34.   Goldberg, "A Little Learning," May 9, 2005.

35.   Dreyfuss and Vest, "The Lie Factory," *Mother Jones*, January/February 2004.

36.   Kwiatkowski, "The New Pentagon Papers," March 10, 2004.

37.   Dreyfuss and Vest, "The Lie Factory," January/February 2004.

38.   Ibid.

39.   Borger, "The Spies That Pushed for War," July 17, 2003.

40.   Ibid.

41.   Ibid.

42.   "On the Dark Side," *Frontline*, PBS, June 20, 2006.

43.   Dreyfuss and Vest, "The Lie Machine," January/February 2004.

44.   White House, transcript, www.whitehouse.gov, October 7, 2002.

45.   Kwiatkowski, "The New Pentagon Papers," March 10, 2004.

15. Squeezing the CIA

1.   Walter Pincus and R. Jeffrey Smith, "Official's Key Report on Iraq Is Faulted," *Washington Post*, February 9, 2007.
2.   Seymour Hersh, "Selective Intelligence," *New Yorker*, May 12, 2003.
3.   Risen, *State of War*, 76.
4.   Suskind, *The One Percent Doctrine*, 23–24.
5.   Risen, *State of War*, 68.
6.   Ibid., 66.
7.   Suskind, *The One Percent Doctrine*, 51.
8.   Risen, *State of War*, 77.
9.   Ibid., 79–80.
10. Ibid., 89.
11. Suskind, *The One Percent Doctrine*, 168–169.
12. Walter Pincus and Dana Priest, "Some Iraq Analysts Felt Pressured by Cheney Visits," *Washington Post*, June 5, 2003.
13. Ibid.
14. Risen, *State of War*, 78.
15. Greg Miller and Bob Drogin, "CIA Feels Heat on Iraq Data," *Los Angeles Times*, October 11, 2002.
16. Suskind, *The One Percent Doctrine*, 124.
17. Miller and Drogin, "CIA Feels Heat on Iraq Data," October 11, 2002.
18. Ibid.
19. Ibid; also, White House, transcript, October 7, 2002.
20. Miller and Drogin, "CIA Feels Heat on Iraq Data," October 11, 2002.
21. Ibid.
22. Hersh, "Selective Intelligence," May 12, 2003.
23. Senate Intelligence Committee report, July 7, 2004, 93.
24. David Barstow, William J. Broad, and Jeff Gerth, "How the White House Embraced Disputed Arms Intelligence," *New York Times*, October 3, 2004.
25. Ibid.
26. Senate Intelligence Committee report, July 7, 2004, 93.
27. Barstow, Broad, and Gerth, "How the White House Embraced Disputed Arms Intelligence," October 3, 2004.
28. Burroughs, et al., "The Path to War," May 2, 2004, 281.
29. CNN, "Defector: Iraq Could Have Nukes by 2005," August 1, 2002.
30. Robert Collier, "Bush's Evidence of Threat Disputed," *San Francisco Chronicle*, October 12, 2002.
31. Burroughs, et al., "The Path to War," May 2, 2004, 281.
32. Senate Intelligence Committee report, July 7, 2004, 94.
33. Risen, *State of War*, 112.
34. Barstow, Broad, and Gerth, "How the White House Embraced Disputed Arms Intelligence," October 3, 2004.
35. Senate Intelligence Committee report, July 7, 2004, 94.

36. *The Commission on the Intelligence Capabilities of the United States Regarding Weapons of Mass Destruction: Report to the President of the United States*, Laurence H. Silberman and Charles S. Robb, Co-Chairmen, March 31, 2005 (referred to as Robb-Silberman Commission report hereafter).

37. Bob Graham, *Intelligence Matters* (New York: Random House, 2004), 179–180.

38. Senate Intelligence Committee report, July 7, 2004, 9–10.

39. Graham, *Intelligence Matters*, 180.

40. Robb-Silberman Commission report, March 2005, 185.

41. Barton Gellman and Walter Pincus, "Depiction of Threat Outgrew Supporting Evidence," *Washington Post*, August 10, 2003.

42. Senate Intelligence Committee report, July 7, 2004, 298.

43. Ibid.

44. Robb-Silberman Commission report, March 2005, 185.

16. Fixing the Facts Around the Policy

1. Paul R. Pillar, "Intelligence, Policy and the War in Iraq," *Foreign Affairs*, March/April 2006.

2. Graham, *Intelligence Matters*, 183.

3. White House, background briefing and release of declassified 2002 NIE key judgments, July 18, 2003; see Federation of American Scientists, Intelligence Resource Program, www.fas.org.

4. Ibid.

5. Robb-Silberman Commission report, October 31, 2005, 75.

6. Paul Sperry, "Energy Rep at Iraq Meeting Lacked Intelligence Savvy," WorldNetDaily.com, August 6, 2003.

7. *The New York Times*, October 3, 2004.

8. Sperry, "Energy Rep at Iraq Meeting Lacked Intelligence Savvy," August 6, 2003.

9. Robb-Silberman Commission report, October 31, 2005, 7.

10. Ibid., 75.

11. White House, declassified NIE key judgments, July 18, 2003.

12. Scott Pelley, "The Man Who Knew," *60 Minutes II*, CBS, February 4, 2004.

13. Robb-Silberman Commission report, October 31, 2005, 188–189.

14. Senate Intelligence Committee report, July 7, 2004, 221.

15. Robb-Silberman Commission report, October 31, 2005, 134.

16. Senate Intelligence Committee report, July 7, 2004, 225.

17. Ibid., 226.

18. Ibid., 229; Robb-Silberman Commission report, October 31, 2005, 138–139.

19. Senate Intelligence Committee report, July 7, 2004, 229–230.

20. Woodward, *Plan of Attack,* 247.
21. Robb-Silberman Commission report, October 31, 2005, 140.
22. Ibid., 140. See footnote, 618–619.
23. Ibid., 137, 145.
24. Graham, *Intelligence Matters,* 183.
25. Senate Intelligence Committee report, July 7, 2004, 287.
26. Gellman and Pincus, "Depiction of Threat Outgrew Supporting Evidence," August 10, 2003.
27. Ibid.
28. Michael Isikoff and David Corn, *Hubris* (New York: Crown, 2006), 139.
29. President's remarks, White House transcript, October 10, 2002.
30. Graham, *Intelligence Matters,* 187.
31. Michael Gordon, "U.S. Aides Split on Assessment of Iraq's Plans," *New York Times,* October 10, 2002.
32. Isikoff and Corn, *Hubris,* 142.
33. Robb-Silberman Commission report, October 31, 2005, 193.
34. Ibid., 193.
35. Ibid., 194.
36. Risen, *State of War,* 90.
37. The account of Sawsan Alhaddad and Allen's successful but discredited prewar CIA effort to contact Iraqi scientists draws heavily on exclusive reporting by James Risen in *State of War.*
38. Ibid., 94–102.
39. Ibid., 103.
40. Ibid., 99.
41. Ibid., 106.
42. Aram Roston, Lisa Myers, and the NBC Investigative Unit, "Iraq Diplomat Gave U.S. Pre-War WMD Details," MSNBC, March 21, 2006.
43. *Report of the Senate Select Committee on Intelligence on Postwar Findings About Iraq's WMD Programs and Links to Terrorism and How They Compare with Prewar Assessments,* September 8, 2006, 144.
44. Tyler Drumheller, interview by David Gregory, *Hardball with Chris Matthews,* MSNBC, April 25, 2006.
45. David Gelber and Joel Bach, "A Spy Speaks Out," *60 Minutes,* CBS News, April 23, 2006.
46. Interview with Tyler Drumheller, *Hardball with Chris Matthews,* April 25, 2006.
47. Ibid.
48. Tyler Drumheller, *On the Brink* (New York: Carroll & Graf, 2006), 95.
49. MSNBC, April 25, 2006.
50. Gelber and Bach, "A Spy Speaks Out," April 23, 2006.
51. Sidney Blumenthal, "Bush Knew Saddam Had No Weapons of Mass Destruction," *Salon,* September 6, 2007.
52. Drumheller, *On the Brink,* 96.

53.   Gelber and Bach, "A Spy Speaks Out," April 23, 2006.

54.   Ibid.

55.   Roston, et. al., "Iraq Diplomat Gave U.S. Pre-War WMD Details," March 21, 2006.

56.   Josh Marshall, TalkingPointsMemo.com, April 23, 2006.

57.   Senate Intelligence Committee report, September 2006, 141–144.

58.   Suskind, *The One Percent Doctrine*, 190.

59.   Ibid., 190–191.

17. Too Little, Too Late

1.   Woodward, *Plan of Attack*, 176.

2.   Walter Pincus and Colum Lynch, "Wolfowitz Had CIA Probe Diplomat in Charge," *Washington Post*, April 15, 2002.

3.   Woodward, *Plan of Attack*, 182.

4.   Andrew Gumbel and Marie Wolff, "U.S. in Disarray over Iraq As Powell Backs Call for Weapons Inspectors," *Independent* (London), September 2, 2002.

5.   CNN, "WH: No Administration Conflict on Iraq," September 3, 2002.

6.   Ibid.

7.   President Bush's address to the UN General Assembly, White House, www.whitehouse.gov, September 12, 2002.

8.   Woodward, *Plan of Attack*, 184.

9.   Kim Sengupta and Andrew Buncombe, "Iraq Offers Unconditional Return of Arms Inspectors," *Independent* (London), September 17, 2002.

10.   "UN Divided over Inspections Offer," BBC News, September 17, 2002.

11.   Sengupta and Buncombe, "Iraq Offers Unconditional Return of Arms Inspectors," *Independent* (London), September 17, 2002.

12.   Julia Preston and Todd S. Purdum, "UN Inspectors Can Return Unconditionally, Iraq Says," *New York Times*, September 17, 2002.

13.   "UN Divided Over Inspections Offer," BBC News, September 17, 2002.

14.   Ibid.

15.   Todd S. Purdum, "Bush Left Scrambling to Press Case on Iraq," *New York Times*, September 18, 2002.

16.   "UN Divided over Inspections Offer," BBC News, September 17, 2002.

17.   Interview with Hans Blix, *Arms Control Today*, vol. 30, No. 6, July/Aug. 2000.

18.   Ibid.

19.   Wire reports, "Iraq, UN Reach a Deal," *Baltimore Sun*, October 2, 2002; Nicholas Kralev and Betsy Pisik, "U.S. to 'Thwart' UN Team Headed to Iraq," *Washington Times*, October 2, 2002.

20.   Wire reports, "Iraq, UN Reach a Deal," October 2, 2002.

21.   Kralev and Pisik, "U.S. to 'Thwart' UN Team Headed to Iraq," October 2, 2002.

22. Hans Blix, *Disarming Iraq* (New York: Pantheon Books, 2004), 81–82.

23. Evelyn Leopold and Randall Mikkelsen, "Bush Threatens End Run Around Recalcitrant UN," Reuters, October 3, 2002.

24. Blix, *Disarming Iraq,* 86.

25. Ibid., 87.

26. "Resolution 1441 (2002)," United Nations Security Council, un.org, November 8, 2002.

27. Blix, *Disarming Iraq,* 95–96.

28. Colum Lynch, "U.S., UN Differ on Arms Hunt," *Washington Post,* November 17, 2002.

29. James Dao, "Arms Inspectors Set to Begin," *New York Times,* November 25, 2002.

30. Blix, *Disarming Iraq,* 91–92.

31. Ibid., 93.

32. Ibid., 101.

33. Woodward, *Plan of Attack,* 222.

34. Peter Beaumont, David Rose, Ed Vulliamy, and Rory McCarthy, "U.S. Seeks One Excuse for War in 12,000 Pages of Denial," *Observer* (London), December 8, 2002.

35. Associated Press, "U.S. Gains Early Access to Iraq Arms Declaration," *Baltimore Sun,* December 10, 2002.

36. Blix, *Disarming Iraq,* 107.

37. Oliver Burkeman, "Allies in a Spin over Lack of Evidence," *Guardian* (London), January 10, 2003.

38. Blix, *Disarming Iraq,* 108.

39. Burkeman, "Allies in a Spin over Lack of Evidence," January 10, 2003.

40. Beaumont, Rose, Vulliamy, and McCarthy, "U.S. Seeks One Excuse for War in 12,000 Pages of Denial," December 8, 2002.

41. Marge Michaels, "Q and A with the Top Sleuth," *Time,* December 12, 2002.

42. Blix, *Disarming Iraq,* 108–109.

43. Rupert Cornwall and Andrew Grice, "UN Weapons Inspectors Turn Fire on Britain and U.S.," *Independent* (London), December 21, 2002.

44. Burkeman, "Allies in a Spin over Lack of Evidence," January 10, 2003.

45. David Sanger and Julia Preston, "U.S. to Release Spy Data on Iraq to Aid Inspectors," *New York Times,* December 21, 2002.

46. Mark Phillips, "Inspectors Call U.S. Tips 'Garbage,'" CBS News, February 20, 2003.

47. Beaumont, Rose, Vulliamy, and McCarthy, "U.S. Seeks One Excuse for War in 12,000 Pages of Denial," December 8, 2002.

48. Colum Lynch, "U.S. Fights Late Report on U.S. Arms," *Washington Post,* January 16, 2003.

49. Ibid.

50. Glenn Kessler and Colum Lynch, "France Vows to Block Resolution on Iraq War," *Washington Post,* January 21, 2003.

51. Blix, *Disarming Iraq,* 117.

52. Ibid., 112.
53. BBC News, "Outrage at 'Old Europe' Remarks," January 23, 2003.
54. Brian Knowlton, "NATO Wavering on War with Iraq," *International Herald Tribune,* January 23, 2003.
55. Hans Blix, "An Update on Inspection," United Nations Security Council, January 27, 2003.
56. Mohamed ElBaradei, "The Status of Nuclear Inspections in Iraq," United Nations Security Council, January 27, 2003.
57. Ian MacKenzie, "U.S. More Isolated in Iraq After Arms Expert Reports," Reuters, January 28, 2003.
58. Blix, *Disarming Iraq,* 142.

18. Endgame for Powell

1. Woodward, *Plan of Attack,* 227.
2. Ibid., 289.
3. Ibid., 290.
4. Ibid., 291.
5. Transcript of UN Security Council meeting, Associated Press, January 27, 2003.
6. Judith Miller and Julia Preston, "Blix Says He Saw Nothing to Prompt a War," *New York Times,* January 31, 2003.
7. The President's State of the Union Address, White House transcript, www.whitehouse.gov, January 27, 2003.
8. Miller and Preston, "Blix Says He Saw Nothing to Prompt a War," January 31, 2003.
9. State of the Union Address, January 27, 2003.
10. Ibid.
11. Walter Pincus, "Pre-War Findings Worried Analysts," *Washington Post,* May 22, 2005.
12. Drumheller, *On the Brink,* 79–80.
13. Joby Warrick, "Warnings on WMD 'Fabricator' Were Ignored, Ex-CIA Aide Says," *Washington Post,* June 25, 2006.
14. State of the Union Address, January 27, 2003.
15. Isikoff and Corn, *Hubris,* 176.
16. Karen DeYoung, *Soldier: The Life of Colin Powell* (New York: Knopf, 2006), 439–440.
17. Ibid., 441.
18. Burroughs, et al., "The Path to War," May 2004.
19. Bamford, *A Pretext for War,* 369.
20. Ibid., 368–369.
21. Isikoff and Corn, *Hubris,* 178.
22. DeYoung, *Soldier,* 442.
23. Bamford, *A Pretext for War,* 370.
24. Ibid., 370.

25.   Isikoff and Corn, *Hubris,* 181.
26.   DeYoung, *Soldier,* 445.
27.   Bamford, *A Pretext for War,* 370.
28.   DeYoung, *Soldier,* 441.
29.   Douglas Jehl, "Qaeda-Iraq Link U.S. Cited Is Linked to Coercion Claim," *New York Times,* December 9, 2005.
30.   DeYoung, *Soldier,* 444.
31.   Bamford, *A Pretext for War,* 371.
32.   DeYoung, *Soldier,* 443.
33.   Ibid., 444.
34.   Ibid., 445.
35.   Bamford, *A Pretext for War,* 371–372.
36.   DeYoung, *Soldier,* 446.
37.   Ibid., 447.
38.   Ibid.
39.   Drumheller, *On the Brink,* 100.
40.   Ibid., 83.
41.   Robb-Silberman Commission report, March 2005, 104; Isikoff and Corn, *Hubris,* 183.
42.   Drumheller, *On the Brink,* 99–100.
43.   Senate Intelligence Committee report, July 7, 2004, 248.
44.   Isikoff and Corn, *Hubris,* 185.
45.   Secretary Colin Powell, "Remarks to the United Nations Security Council," Department of State, www.state.gov, February 5, 2003.
46.   Ibid.
47.   Drumheller, *On the Brink,* 102.
48.   Ibid., 104.
49.   Warrick, "Warnings on WMD 'Fabricator' Were Ignored, Ex-CIA Aide Says," June 25, 2006.
50.   Robb-Silberman Commission report, March 2005, 102–105.
51.   Warrick, "Warnings on WMD 'Fabricator' Were Ignored, Ex-CIA Aide Says," June 25, 2006.
52.   C. J. Chivers, "Kurds Puzzled by Report of Terror Camp," *New York Times,* February 6, 2003.
53.   Isikoff and Corn, *Hubris,* 190.
54.   Glenn Kessler and Colum Lynch, "Powell Lays Case Out Against Iraq," *Washington Post,* February 6, 2003.
55.   "Nations Take Sides After Powell Speech," CNN News, February 6, 2003.
56.   Ibid.
57.   Ibid.
58.   Ibid.
59.   Mary McGrory, "I'm Persuaded," *Washington Post,* February 6, 2003.
60.   Bronwen Maddox, "Foreign Editor's Briefing," *Times* (London), February 6, 2003.
61.   Richard Beeston, "Analysis: Colin Powell Speech to the UN," *Times* (London), February 6, 2003.

62.   Burroughs, et al., "The Path to War," May 2004, 290.

63.   Jeremy Greenstock, "Britain's View of Iraq," interview by Jim Lehrer, *NewsHour with Jim Lehrer*, PBS, February 6, 2003.

19. The Rush to War

1.   De Young, *Soldier*, 424.

2.   Barbara Walters, "Colin Powell on Iraq, Race, and Hurricane Relief," *20/20*, ABC News, September 8, 2005.

3.   Scott Pelley, "The Man Who Knew," *60 Minutes II*, CBS News, February 4, 2004.

4.   Isikoff and Corn, *Hubris*, 179.

5.   Pelley, "The Man Who Knew," February 4, 2004.

6.   Blix, *Disarming Iraq*, 156.

7.   Ibid., 154–155.

8.   Hans Blix, Brief of the Security Council, United Nations, www.un.org, February 14, 2003.

9.   Dan Plesch and Richard Norton-Taylor, "U.S. Claims on Iraq Called into Question," *Guardian* (London), February 15, 2003.

10.   Blix, Brief of the Security Council, February 14, 2003.

11.   Burrough, et al., "Path to War," May 2004, 290.

12.   Don Van Natta, "Bush Was Set on Path to War, British Memo Says," *New York Times*, March 27, 2006.

13.   Ibid.

14.   Ibid.

15.   Ibid.

16.   Karen De Young and Michael Abramowitz, "Report Says Hussein Was Open to Exile Before 2003 Invasion," *Washington Post*, September 27, 2007.

17.   Kevin Sullivan, "War Resolution Puts Mexico in Bind," *Washington Post*, March 1, 2003.

18.   Burroughs, et al., "The Path to War," May 2004, 292.

19.   Martin Bright, Ed Vulliamy, and Peter Beaumont, "Revealed: U.S. Dirty Tricks to Win Votes on Iraq War," *Observer* (London), March 2, 2003; Scott Shane and Ariel Sabar, "Alleged NSA Memo Details U.S. Eavesdropping at UN," *Baltimore Sun*, March 4, 2003.

20.   White House, transcript of president's remarks at AEI, www.whitehouse .gov, February 26, 2003.

21.   Ibid.

22.   Greg Miller, "Democracy in Iraq Doubtful, State Dept. Report Says," *Los Angeles Times*, March 14, 2003.

23.   Burroughs, et al., "The Path to War," May 2004, 291.

24.   David Cracknell, "Blair 'Knew Iraq Had No WMD,'" *Sunday Times* (London), October 5, 2003.

25.   Ibid.

26.   Ibid.

27.   Ibid.

28.   CNN, "Transcript of Blix's UN Presentation," www.cnn.com, March 7, 2003.

29.   CNN, "Transcript of ElBaradei's UN Presentation," www.cnn.com, March 7, 2003.

30.   Burroughs, et al., "The Path to War," May 2004, 292.

31.   BBC News, "Cook Quits over Iraq Crisis," March 17, 2003.

32.   Woodward, *Plan of Attack*, 399.

33.   White House, press release, www.whitehouse.gov, March 21, 2003.

34.   Mike Allen and Dana Milbank, "Question of the Day Dogs Administration Officials," *Washington Post*, March 23, 2003.

35.   Ibid.

36.   Bob Woodward, *State of Denial* (New York: Simon & Schuster, 2006), 96.

37.   Ibid., 115.

38.   Ibid., 185.

39.   Ibid., 213.

20. The White House Under Siege

1.   Joseph Wilson, "What I Didn't Find in Africa," *New York Times*, July 6, 2003.

2.   Ibid.

3.   Wilson, *The Politics of Truth*, 326.

4.   Isikoff and Corn, *Hubris*, 236.

5.   Barton Gellman and Dafna Linzer, "A 'Concerted Effort' to Discredit Bush Critic," *Washington Post*, April 9, 2006.

6.   Carol P. Leonnig and Amy Goldstein, "Ex-Aide Says Cheney Led Rebuttal Effort," *Washington Post*, January 26, 2007.

7.   David Sanger and David Barstow, "Iraq Findings Leaked by Cheney's Aide Were Disputed," *Washington Post*, April 19, 2006.

8.   Leonnig and Goldstein, "Ex-Aide Says Cheney Led Rebuttal Effort," January 26, 2007.

9.   Neil A. Lewis, "Ex-Aide Contradicts Libby," *New York Times*, January 26, 2007; see also Carol P. Leonnig and Amy Goldstein, "Ex-CIA Official Testifies About Libby's Calls," *Washington Post*, January 25, 2007.

10.   Gellman and Linzer, "A 'Concerted Effort' to Discredit Bush Critic," April 9, 2006.

11.   U.S. Department of Justice, Libby indictment, "United States of America vs. I. Lewis Libby," www.usdoj.gov, October 28, 2005; "Full Text: U.S. v. Libby indictment," *Washington Post*, October 28, 2005.

12.   Isikoff and Corn, *Hubris*, 2.

13.   Lewis, "Ex-Aide Contradicts Libby," January 25, 2007.

14.   Max Frankel, "The Washington Back Channel," *New York Times*, March

25, 2007; U.S. District Court for the District of Columbia, transcripts of Libby trial, February 11 and February 12, 2007.

15. Woodward, *Plan of Attack*, 202.

16. Don Van Natta Jr., Adam Liptak, and Clifford Levy, "The Miller Case: A Notebook, a Cause, a Jail Cell and a Deal," *New York Times*, October 16, 2005.

17. Judith Miller, "My Four Hours Testifying in the Federal Grand Jury Room," October 16, 2005.

18. Wilson, *The Politics of Truth*, 334.

19. Van Natta, Liptak, and Levy, "The Miller Case: A Notebook, a Cause, a Jail Cell and a Deal," October 16, 2005.

20. Michael Isikoff, "A Fresh Focus on Cheney," *Newsweek*, May 13, 2006.

21. John Prados, *Hoodwinked: The Documents That Reveal How Bush Sold Us a War* (New York: New Press, 2004), 332; White House, press release, July 7, 2003.

22. Neil A. Lewis, "Ex-Bush Aide, in Testimony, Disputes Libby," *New York Times*, January 30, 2007.

23. Ibid.

24. Amy Goldstein and Carol P. Leonnig, "Former Press Secretary Says Libby Told Him About Plame," *Washington Post*, January 30, 2007.

25. Lewis, "Ex-Bush Aide, in Testimony, Disputes Libby," January 30, 2007.

26. U.S. Department of Justice, Libby indictment, October 28, 2005.

27. Lewis, "Ex-Bush Aide, in Testimony, Disputes Libby," January 30, 2007.

28. Scott Shane, "Ex-Diplomat's Surprise Volley on Iraq Drove White House into Political Warfare Mode," *New York Times*, July 24, 2005.

29. Wilson, *The Politics of Truth*, 343.

30. Miller, "My Four Hours Testifying in the Federal Grand Jury Room," October 16, 2005.

31. Gellman and Linzer, "A 'Concerted Effort' to Discredit Bush Critic," April 9, 2006.

32. Miller, "My Four Hours Testifying in the Federal Grand Jury Room," October 16, 2005.

33. CNN News, "Columnist Testifies Rove Confirmed Plame Was CIA," www.cnn.com, February 14, 2007.

34. Carol P. Leonnig and Amy Goldstein, "Journalists Testify That Libby Never Mentioned CIA Officer," *Washington Post*, February 13, 2007.

35. CNN News, "Columnist Testifies Rove Confirmed Plame Was CIA," February 14, 2007.

36. Ibid.

37. Ibid.

38. Ibid.

39. Barton Gellman, "A Leak, Then a Deluge," *Washington Post*, October 30, 2005.

40. George Tenet with Bill Harlow, *At the Center of the Storm: My Years at the CIA* (New York: HarperCollins, 2007), 452.

41. Ibid., 461.
42. Ibid., 460.
43. CIA, Tenet press release, www.cia.gov, July 11, 2003.
44. Tenet, *At the Center of the Storm,* 466.
45. See Chapter 21 for details of Rove-Cooper conversation.
46. U.S. Department of Justice Libby indictment, October 28, 2005.
47. Leonnig and Goldstein, "Ex-Aide Says Cheney Led Rebuttal Effort," January 26, 2007.
48. Gellman and Linzer, "A 'Concerted Effort' to Discredit Bush Critic," April 9, 2006.
49. Miller, "My Four Hours Testifying in the Federal Grand Jury Room," October 16, 2005.
50. Leonnig and Goldstein, "Journalists Testify That Libby Never Mentioned CIA Officer," February 13, 2007.
51. Robert Novak, "Mission to Niger," *Washington Post,* July 14, 2003.
52. Greg Miller, "Bush Administration 'Recklessly' Blew Her Cover," *Los Angeles Times,* March 16, 2007.
53. U.S. Department of Justice, Libby indictment, October 28, 2005.
54. U.S. House of Representatives, transcript, Oversight and Government Reform Committee, March 16, 2007.
55. Mark Leibovich and Neil A. Lewis, "Purely Political Motives in Outing, Ex-Agent Says," *New York Times,* March 17, 2007.
56. Amy Goldstein, "Plame Says White House 'Recklessly' Revealed Her," *Washington Post,* March 17, 2007.
57. Richard Leiby and Walter Pincus, "Valerie Plame, the Spy Who's Ready to Speak for Herself," *Washington Post,* March 16, 2007.
58. Wilson, *The Politics of Truth,* 1.
59. Ibid., 372.

21. Probing the President's Men

1. Dan Balz and Walter Pincus, "Why the Commander in Chief Is Losing the Battle of the 16 Words," *Washington Post,* September 28, 2003.
2. President's remarks, White House press release, www.whitehouse.gov, July 17, 2003.
3. Ibid.
4. "Missing Iraq Expert—Body Found," BBC News, July 18, 2003.
5. White House, special press conference by "senior official," July 18, 2003; David Sanger and Judith Miller, "National Security Aide Says He's to Blame for Speech Error," *New York Times,* July 23, 2003; Dana Milbank and Walter Pincus, "Bush Aides Disclose Warnings from CIA," *Washington Post,* July 23, 2003.
6. Murray Waas, "Rove-Novak Call Was Concern to Leak Investigators," *National Journal,* May 25, 2006.
7. White House, press briefing by Scott McClellan, www.whitehouse.gov, October 7, 2003.

8. Murray Waas, "What Now Karl?" *Village Voice*, August 13, 2005.

9. Ibid.

10. Ibid.

11. Walter Pincus, "Letter Shows Authority to Expand CIA Leak Probe Was Given in '04," *Washington Post*, October 23, 2005.

12. Waas, "What Now Karl?" August 13, 2005.

13. Victoria Toensing and Bruce W. Sanford, "The Plame Game: Was It a Crime?" *Washington Post*, January 12, 2005.

14. Ibid.

15. Adam Liptak, "Appeals Court Says Reporters Must Testify or Go to Jail," *New York Times*, February 15, 2005; also see U.S. Department of Justice, "In re: grand jury subpoena, Judith Miller, consolidated," United States Court of Appeals, usdoj.gov.usap, February 15, 2005.

16. Ibid.

17. Matt Cooper and Judith Miller, interview with mediabistro.com, February 17, 2005.

18. Adam Liptak, "Court Declines to Rule on Case of Reporters' Refusal to Testify," *New York Times*, June 28, 2005; also see U.S. Department of Justice, "Judith Miller v. United States of America/Matthew Cooper and Time, Inc. v. United States of America," Supreme Court of the United States, usdoj.gov.usao, June 26, 2005.

19. Adam Liptak, "For Time Inc. Reporter, a Frenzied Decision," *New York Times*, July 11, 2005.

20. Adam Liptak, "New York Times Reporter Jailed for Keeping Source Secret," *New York Times*, June 7, 2005; also see Adam Liptak, "Court Declines to Rule on Case of Reporters' Refusal to Testify," *New York Times*, June 28, 2005.

21. Michael Isikoff, "Matt Cooper's Source: What Rove Told Time Inc. Reporter," *Newsweek*, June 18, 2005.

22. Josh White, "Rove Told Reporter of Plame's Role but Didn't Name Her, Says Attorney," *Washington Post*, July 11, 2005.

23. Matthew Cooper, "What I Told the Grand Jury," *Time*, July 25, 2005.

24. Ibid.

25. Ibid.; also see Lorne Manly and David Johnston, "Reporter Says He First Learned of CIA Operative from Rove," *New York Times*, July 18, 2005.

22. Verdict of the Weapons Hunters

1. Woodward, *State of Denial*, 214.

2. Ibid.

3. David Kay, interview by Stephen Talbot, *Frontline*, PBS, October 1999.

4. Charles Duelfer, "Comprehensive Report of the Special Advisor to the DCI on Iraq's WMD," Iraq Survey Group, September 30, 2004, Scope Note, 1–2. Referred to below as Iraq Survey Group report.

5. Ibid., 5.

6. Ibid., 3.

7.   Woodward, *State of Denial,* 217.

8.   Isikoff and Corn, *Hubris,* 306.

9.   Drogin and Goetz, "How the U.S. Fell Under the Spell of 'Curveball,'" November 20, 2005.

10.   Senate Intelligence Committee report, July 7, 2004, 150; Robb-Silberman Commission report, 82.

11.   Drogin and Goetz, "How the U.S. Fell Under the Spell of 'Curveball,'" November 20, 2005.

12.   Ibid.

13.   Ibid.

14.   Robb-Silberman Commission report, October 31, 2005, 193.

15.   Drogin and Goetz, "How the U.S. Fell Under the Spell of 'Curveball,'" November 20, 2005.

16.   Isikoff and Corn, *Hubris,* 311.

17.   Ibid.

18.   Woodward, *State of Denial,* 237–238.

19.   Isikoff and Corn, *Hubris,* 311.

20.   Ibid.

21.   Woodward, *State of Denial,* 239.

22.   Isikoff and Corn, *Hubris,* 309.

23.   Woodward, *State of Denial,* 235.

24.   Isikoff and Corn, *Hubris,* 312.

25.   Barton Gellman, "Search in Iraq Fails to Find Nuclear Threat," *Washington Post,* October 26, 2003.

26.   Ibid.

27.   Ibid.

28.   Isikoff and Corn, *Hubris,* 328.

29.   Tenet, *At the Center of the Storm,* 403.

30.   David Kay, Statement on the Interim Progress Report on the Activities of the Iraq Survey Group Before the House Permanent Select Committee on Intelligence, the House Committee on Appropriations, Subcommittee on Defense, and the Senate Select Committee on Intelligence, CIA, www.cia.gov., October 2, 2003. Referred to below as Kay Interim report.

31.   Ibid.

32.   Isikoff and Corn, *Hubris,* 328–329.

33.   White House, press release, www.whitehouse.gov, October 3, 2003.

34.   David Kay, interview by Jane Corbin, *Frontline,* PBS, October 2003.

35.   Woodward, *State of Denial,* 239.

36.   Ibid.

37.   Ibid.

38.   Tenet, *At the Center of the Storm,* 405.

39.   Kay Interim report, October 2, 2003.

40.   David Kay, interview by Jane Corbin, October 2003.

41.   Woodward, *State of Denial,* 272.

42.   Ibid., 272.

43.   Tenet, *At the Center of the Storm,* 406.

44. Ibid., 407.
45. Drogin and Goetz, "How the U.S. Fell Under the Spell of 'Curveball,'" November 20, 2005.
46. Woodward, *State of Denial*, 277.
47. Ibid.
48. James Risen, "Ex-Inspector Says CIA Missed Disarray in Iraqi Arms Program," *New York Times*, January 26, 2004.
49. Ibid.
50. Tenet, *At the Center of the Storm*, 410.
51. Ibid., 410.
52. Ibid., 313.
53. Ibid., 315.
54. Iraq Survey Group report, September 30, 2004, 58.
55. Ibid., 59.
56. Kevin Woods, James Lacey, and Williamson Murray, "Saddam's Delusions: The View from the Inside," *Foreign Affairs,* vol. 85, No. 3, May/June 2006. Adapted from Iraqi Perspectives Project, "A View of Operation Freedom from Saddam's Senior Leadership," Kevin M. Woods with Michael R. Pease, Mark E. Stout, Williamson Murrary, and James G. Lacey, U.S. Joint Forces Command, March 24, 2006.
57. Iraq Survey Group report, September 30, 2004, 62.

23. A Reporter Names Her Source

1. Lorne Manly, "A Difficult Moment, Long Anticipated," *The New York Times*, July 7, 2005; Adam Liptak, "Reporter Jailed After Refusing to Name Source," *The New York Times*, July 7, 2005; Carol P. Leonnig, "New York Times Reporter Jailed," *Washington Post*, July 7, 2005.
2. Editorial, "Judith Miller Goes to Jail," *The New York Times*, July 7, 2005; Douglas McCollum, "Attack at the Source," *Columbia Journalism Review,* March/April 2005; Rosa Brooks, "The Judy Miller Hug Fest," *Los Angeles Times,* July 6, 2005; "CIA Leak Probe May Cause Bush Long-Term Worry," *Wall Street Journal,* July 7, 2005.
3. Liptak, "Reporter Jailed After Refusing to Name Source," July 7, 2005. The account of Judith Miller's eighty-five days in jail is drawn from reports by Paul Schwartzman, Carol Leonnig, and Jerry Markon of *The Washington Post* (July 7, 2005, August 4, 2005, September 17, 2005), Joe Strupp for *Salon* (August 17, 2005), Arianna Huffington of *The Huffington Post* (July 27, 2005, September 8, 2005), the Committee to Protect Journalists (July 28, 2005), James T. Madore of *Newsday* (August 12, 2005), Adam Entous of Reuters (September 9, 2005), Don Van Natta, Jr., Adam Liptak, and Clifford Levy of *The New York Times* (October 16, 2005), and the Alexandria Detention Center Web site.
4. Jerry Markon, "N. Va. Jail's 'Unassuming' Celebrity," *Washington Post,* August 4, 2005.

5. Ibid.
6. Murray Waas, "Scooter Libby and Judy Miller Met on July 8, 2003 . . . and Patrick Fitzgerald Is Very Interested," *The American Prospect*, August 6, 2005.
7. Arianna Huffington, "Judy Miller: Do We Want to Know Everything or Don't We?" *Huffington Post*, July 27, 2005.
8. Joe Strupp, "Cracks in the Fortress?" *Salon*, August 17, 2005.
9. Liptak, "Reporter Jailed After Refusing to Name Source," July 7, 2005.
10. Van Natta, Liptak, and Levy, "The Miller Case: A Notebook, a Cause, a Jail Cell and a Deal," October 16, 2005.
11. Ibid.
12. Susan Schmidt and Jim VandeHei, "New York Times Reporter Released from Jail," *Washington Post*, September 30, 2005.
13. Jim VandeHei and Peter Baker, "Scandals Take Toll on Bush's Second Term," *Washington Post*, October 14, 2005.
14. Murray Waas, "Secret Service Records Prompted Key Miller Testimony," *National Journal*, October 20, 2005.
15. Howard Kurtz, "The NYT Pinata," *Washington Post*, October 12, 2005.
16. Jim VandeHei and Carol D. Leonnig, "Rove Told Jury Libby May Have Been His Source in Leak Case," *Washington Post*, October 20, 2005.
17. U.S. Department of Justice, Libby indictment, October 28, 2005.
18. Patrick Fitzgerald, "Transcript of Special Counsel Fitzgerald's Press Conference," *Washington Post*, October 28, 2005.
19. Jim VandeHei and Carol D. Leonnig, "Cheney Aide Libby Is Indicted," *Washington Post*, October 29, 2005.
20. Dan Balz and Juliet Eilperin, "A New Moment of Truth for a White House in Crisis," *Washington Post*, October 29, 2005.
21. Dana Milbank and Carol D. Leonnig, "Democrats Demand Rove's Firing," *Washington Post*, October 31, 2005.
22. Balz and Eilstein, "A New Moment of Truth for a White House in Crisis," October 29, 2005.
23. *Washington Post*, "White House Ethics, Honesty Questioned," *Washington Post*-ABC News poll, October 30, 2005.
24. Van Natta, Liptak, and Levy, "The Miller Case: A Notebook, a Cause, a Jail Cell and a Deal," *New York Times*, October 16, 2005.
25. Ibid.
26. Judith Miller, "Judith Miller's Farewell," Letters to the editor, *New York Times*, November 10, 2005.

24. The Renewed Furor over WMD

1. Fitzgerald press conference, *Washington Post*, October 28, 2005.
2. Richard B. Schmitt, "Who Talked? It Wasn't the Prosecutor," *Los Angeles Times*, October 30, 2005.

3. Robb-Silberman Commission report, March 31, 2005, 50–51.

4. Carl Hulse and David D. Kirkpatrick, "Partisan Quarrel Forces Senators to Bar the Doors," *New York Times*, November 2, 2005.

5. Ibid.

6. Charles Babington and Dafna Linzer, "GOP Angered by Closed Senate Session," *Washington Post*, November 2, 2005.

7. Hulse and Kirkpatrick, "Partisan Quarrel Forces Senators to Bar the Doors," November 2, 2005.

8. Peter Wallsten, Tom Hamburger, and Josh Meyer, "FBI Is Taking Another Look at Forged Prewar Intelligence," *Los Angeles Times*, December 3, 2005.

9. Eric Lichtblau, "No Evidence of Pressure on Iraq Data, Senator Says," *New York Times*, November 7, 2005.

10. Walter Pincus, "Wider Scope in Prewar Probe Sought," *Washington Post*, November 8, 2005.

11. Presidential remarks at Tobyhanna Army Base, White House transcript, www.whitehouse.gov, November 11, 2005; Richard W. Stevenson, "Bush Contends Partisan Critics Hurt War Effort," *New York Times*, November 12, 2005.

12. Cheney remarks at the American Enterprise Institute, White House transcript, www.whitehouse.gov, November 21, 2005.

13. Princeton Survey Research Associates International, "Newsweek Poll: President's Approval Rating Drops to All-time Low," *Newsweek*, November 21, 2005.

14. Presidential remarks at the Woodrow Wilson International Center, White House transcript, www.whitehouse.gov, December 14, 2005.

15. Ibid.

16. Spencer S. Hsu and Walter Pincus, "Goss Says Leaks Have Hurt CIA's Work, Urges Probe," *Washington Post*, February 3, 2006.

17. Dan Eggen and Paul Kane, "Gonzales Hospital Episode Detailed," *Washington Post*, May 16, 2007.

18. Carol D. Leonnig, "Libby Team to Subpoena Media," *Washington Post*, January 21, 2006.

19. David Johnston, "Inquiry into Wiretapping Articles Widens," February 12, 2006.

20. Ibid.

21. Ibid.

22. Ibid.

23. Jim VandeHei and Dan Balz, "Fall Elections Are Rove's Next Test," *Washington Post*, June 17, 2006.

24. Ibid.

25. David Johnston and Jim Rutenberg, "No Rove Charges over Testimony on CIA Leak," *New York Times*, June 14, 2006.

26. Viveca Novak, "What Viveca Novak Told Fitzgerald," *Time*, December 11, 2005.

27. Jim VandeHei, "Rove's Time in Limbo near End in CIA Leak Case," *Washington Post*, May 8, 2006.

28.   Novak, "What Viveca Novak Told Fitzgerald," December 11, 2005.
29.   Ibid.
30.   Waas, "Rove-Novak Call Was Concern to Leak Investigators," May 25, 2006.
31.   Ibid.
32.   Robert Novak, "My Leak Case Testimony," July 14, 2006.
33.   Shane, "As Trial Begins, Cheney's Ex-Aide Is Still a Puzzle," January 17, 2007.
34.   "Cheney Calls Ex-Aide Libby 'Honest,'" Associated Press, January 14, 2007.
35.   Michael J. Sniffen, "Lawyers Paint Libby As Sacrificial Lamb," Associated Press, January 23, 2007.
36.   David Johnston and Jim Rutenberg, "At the Libby Trial, Hints of Intrigue and Betrayal," *New York Times,* January 25, 2007.
37.   Amy Goldstein and Carol D. Leonnig, "Defense Portrays Libby as Scapegoat," *Washington Post,* January 24, 2007.
38.   Neil A. Lewis, "Libby Speaks on Tape, but May Not in Court," *New York Times,* February 7, 2007.
39.   Amy Goldstein and Carol D. Leonnig, "Court Hears Libby Describe Cheney as 'Upset' at Critic," *Washington Post,* February 7, 2005.
40.   Lewis, "Libby Speaks on Tape, but May Not in Court," February 7, 2007.
41.   Amy Goldstein and Carol D. Leonnig, "Russert Says He Didn't Tell Libby About CIA Officer," *Washington Post,* February 8, 2007.
42.   Ibid.
43.   Neil A. Lewis, "NBC's Russert Wraps Up Prosecution Case at Libby Trial," *New York Times,* February 9, 2007.
44.   Amy Goldstein and Carol D. Leonnig, "Libby Defense to Rest Without Testimony by Him or Cheney," *Washington Post,* February 14, 2007.
45.   Amy Goldstein and Carol D. Leonnig, "Libby 'Told a Dumb Lie,' Prosecutor Says in Closing Argument," *Washington Post,* February 21, 2007.
46.   Neil A. Lewis, "In Closing Pleas, Clashing Views on Libby's Role," *New York Times,* February 21, 2007.
47.   Ibid.
48.   Ibid.
49.   Peter Baker, "For an Opaque White House, a Reflection of New Scrutiny," *Washington Post,* March 7, 2007.
50.   Ibid.
51.   Sheryl Gay Stolberg, "A Judgment on Cheney Is Still to Come," *New York Times,* March 7, 2007.
52.   Amy Goldstein and Carol D. Leonnig, "Libby Found Guilty in CIA Leak Case," *Washington Post,* March 7, 2007.

Epilogue

1.   Remarks by President Bush, White House, www.whitehouse.gov, July 2, 2007.

2. Sheryl Gay Stolberg and Jim Rutenberg, "Bush Is Said to Have Held Long Debate on Decision," *New York Times,* July 4, 2007.

3. Scott Shane and Neil A. Lewis, "Bush Spares Libby from Jail Term," *New York Times,* July 3, 2007.

4. Patrick J. Fitzgerald, "Shield Law Perils . . . ," *Washington Post,* October 4, 2007.

5. Press release "New Independent Counsel Law Proposed," Senate Government Affairs Committee, U.S. Senate, www.senate.gov, June 29, 1999.

6. Robin Wright and Joby Warrick, "Syrians Disassembling Ruins at Site Bombed by Israel, Officials Say," *Washington Post,* October 19, 2007.

7. Pillar, "Intelligence, Policy, and the War in Iraq," *Foreign Affairs,* March/April 2006.